31970263

Women, Feminism, and Social Change

in Argentina, Chile, and Uruguay,

1890–1940

Engendering Latin America
Volume 3

EDITORS:

Donna J. Guy
University of Arizona

Mary Karasch
Oakland University

Asunción Lavrin
Howard University

Women, Feminism, and Social Change

in Argentina, Chile, and Uruguay,

1890–1940

Asunción Lavrin

University of Nebraska Press
Lincoln and London

Publication of this book was assisted by a grant from The Andrew W. Mellon Foundation.

⊛ The paper in this book meets the minimum requirements of American National Standard for Information Sciences— Permanence of Paper for Printed Library Materials, ANSI Z39.48-1984.

Library of Congress Cataloging-in-Publication Data
Lavrin, Asunción.
    Women, feminism, and social change in Argentina, Chile, and Uruguay, 1890–1940 / Asunción Lavrin.
        p.   cm. – (Engendering Latin America; v. 3)
    Includes bibliographical references and index.
    ISBN 0-8032-2897-x (alk. paper)
        1. Women–Argentina.   2. Women–Chile.   3. Women–Uruguay.
    4. Feminism–Argentina.   5. Feminism–Chile.   6. Feminism–Uruguay.
    7. Social change–Argentina.   8. Social change–Chile.   9. Social change–Uruguay.   I. Title.   II. Series.
    HQ1532.L38   1996
    305.4'0982–dc20   95-2729
                                                                            CIP

CONTENTS

PLATES, TABLES, AND FIGURES

PLATES, following page 180

TABLES

FIGURES

ACKNOWLEDGMENTS

In researching and writing this book I have become indebted to many people in several countries. Personal friends, scholars, librarians and archivists have generously given time, hospitality and advice. In Chile, my long-time friend and colleague Prof. Cristián Guerrero and his wife Victoria Lira welcomed me in their home in two different visits to Santiago and introduced me to other scholars and friends. To the young historian Cristián Guerrero Lira, who has followed the steps of his father, I am indebted for assistance in my research. Three dedicated feminists, Felícitas Klimpel, Blanca Poblete, and Elena Caffarena, shared their wonderful memories with me in personal interviews. Klimpel spiced up her recollections with food and the company of other friends in an idyllic rural retreat. Poblete and Caffarena were gracious and courageous, since our meeting took place in a period of political uncertainty. I must also thank Profs. Armando de Ramón and Sergio Vergara Quirós for intellectual support.

In Argentina I am grateful to Dr. Alicia Vidaurreta for guiding me through libraries and archives. Profs. María del Carmen Feijóo and Gwen Kirkpatrick, and Lea Fletcher, Hebe Clemente, María Cristina Arévalo and Norma Sepeg, gave support and encouragement. They helped me establish contacts with the various libraries in the city, with other scholars, and with women such as Raquel Forner and the late Alicia Moreau de Justo. Although her advanced years and failing health prevented me from meeting Moreau de Justo personally, I will always remember her voice over the phone. The special attention received from the staff at the Biblioteca Justo and the Biblioteca Nacional deserves mentioning.

In Uruguay I am particularly indebted to the members of the *Grupo de Estudios Sobre la Condición de la Mujer* (GRECMU), especially historians Silvia Rodríguez Villamil, Graciela Sapriza, and the late Suzana Prates, who welcomed me at the Center and offered their critique and advice. The

Jardí family—descendants of María Abella de Ramírez—opened their home and their treasure trove of memories to me and gave me the opportunity of meeting Abella's two surviving daughters. Although their memories were very frail, the emotional linkage established by that meeting was precious. I was also fortunate to meet Sofía Alvarez Vignoli de Demichelli, one of the notable feminists of the 1930s, as well as Ofelia Machado Bonet, who has dedicated much of her life to sustain women's causes in her country and abroad. Margarita Cardozo, at the National Library, María Julia Ardao, and the late Dinora Echani de Wonsever, offered their warm friendship.

Among the many colleagues in the United States whose advice I want to acknowledge is Prof. Donna Guy, whose critical comments were very useful to me. Profs. Sandra McGee Deutsch and Lynn Stoner had no direct input into this book, but their commitment to the study of women has been a source of inspiration to me. My friends Profs. Edith Couturier and Dauril Alden have continued to supply moral support beyond expectations, for which I will always be thankful. Friendship and research assistance were always available from the staff of the Hispanic Division of the Library of Congress and the Handbook of Latin American Studies. Special thanks are due to Dr. Georgette Dorn, present head of the Hispanic Division; Dolores Martin, editor of *The Handbook of Latin American Studies;* Susan Mundel; and David Dressing. Several foundations and institutions have provided funds for travel, research, and writing, for which I am deeply grateful. They are, the Organization of American States for travel funds and the Social Science Research Council, the National Endowment for the Humanities, and the Wilson Center for International Studies for fellowships for research and writing. To my daughter Cecilia and her husband Christopher Hauge, and my son Andrew go my thanks for their love. To my husband David, my companion through many years of marriage, many research trips, and many pages of proof reading, go my love and hope for many happy returns.

——————— Feminism has not been an alien concept for twentieth-century Latin American women.[1] It has grown steadily, sometimes under adversity, and in this century's closing years it continues to be a matter of faith for some and a topic of debate or scorn for others. The roots of feminism in the last quarter of the nineteenth century, when women's writing for the public media intersected with their industrial work to undermine the confident assumption that the restrictions imposed on the female sex by law and custom were needed to maintain the integrity of family and society. Educated urban women began publishing poetry, novels, and other prose, mostly in newspapers and magazines, in the first sustained expression of their own minds.[2] Even though many made no particular statements on the condition of women, their work was an eloquent expression of their readiness to be admitted into the most sacrosanct area of men's domain, the intellectual.

Yet women's world was not all writing and education. There was a growing demand for their physical labor beyond the home and its domestic chores. Industrial development, even the most meager, called for cheap labor, and women were a marketable commodity as wage earners. They were trustworthy, inexpensive, and docile. Urban growth and the development of manufacturing brought uncomfortable fluctuations in the value of money and the cost of living. To make ends meet, the young of both sexes were recruited, and women stepped out of the home to work in sweatshops and factories. The odd combination of education and labor, disparate as the two may seem, brought women into the light of public debate. Their merits as mothers and wives were added to their legal rights under the law and their role as objects and subjects of public policies. The meaning of womanhood gained an important dimension when mixed with affairs of state. And when working women published their first newspapers after 1895, they signaled that the gates of self-expression were wide open to all.

The search for answers to problems raised by recognition of the new social, economic, and political dimensions of womanhood was aided by a new ideology taking shape in Europe by 1880: feminism. Its origins and meaning were not altogether clear when it first came to the attention of alert minds in some of the fastest-growing urban areas of Latin America. The capitals of Argentina, Uruguay, and Chile, the "Southern Cone" nations of South America, were the scene of a remarkable development of feminist ideas. Historical memory has shortchanged the women and men who wrote and spoke for the recognition of women's coming of age. The women rarely left personal papers, let alone organized archives, that could have helped preserve the memory of their work. Only a few among the many dedicated female labor leaders, journalists, educators, physicians, writers, and lawyers have been given any notice in national histories. Some of the men have earned a place in history for other reasons, but rarely for their commitment to women's causes.

The persistent selectivity of historical memory creates many difficulties in reconstructing the early work of male and female feminists. To write their history demands tracing and collecting materials as diverse and ephemeral as pamphlets defending bills before Congress, books written with enthusiasm but neglected by scholars, fiery but long-forgotten speeches in the legislature, and hundreds of essays in newspapers and magazines. In the end, however, we are rewarded by a new and refreshing view of society and gender relations, new angles in the interpretation of social history, and a more equitable view of women's role in early twentieth-century society.

Argentina, Chile, and Uruguay shared several key political and economic characteristics in addition to their geographical proximity. In the late 1870s a generation of statesmen nurtured in liberal and positivist thought attempted to bring their countries into the mainstream of European and North American "progress." Their plans for social and economic reform called for industrial growth and urban development as catalysts for changing the old order. The educational system was to be reformed to reach the efficiency required to sustain economic growth and to develop a progressive urban class in charge of the national destiny. European immigration would supplement the small labor pool available to carry out such far-reaching plans and help create a new work ethic.

The nature of politics between 1890 and 1920 favored the social and economic transformations under which feminism flourished. Emerging urban professionals challenged the political pattern inherited from the early republican period—not an easy task. Strong personalities and social elites dominated the scene up to the second decade of the twentieth century in Chile and Argentina. Uruguay was plagued by caudillismo up to the election of José Batlle y Ordóñez in 1904. Despite perilous encounters with political disorder, constitutional reforms and an increasingly assertive working class and urban middle class permitted important changes in the representive system between 1912 and 1925. Men committed to social reform and democratization forced some key changes upon traditionalists. The result was a slow but steady opening of political space and social recognition to groups that in the early 1900s were at the edges in nation building. Women were one such group owing to the limitations placed on them by social mores and the legal system.

The decades from 1890 to 1940 proved a receptive time for raising questions about women and about gender relations within the family. The social and political elites of the turn of the century lost ground to more people-oriented, if not populist, regimes in which the needs of workers, peasants, students, and women were voiced, heard, and to some extent heeded. The broadening of the political base was sustained by ideologies that challenged the political exclusion of groups increasingly essential to carrying out the developmental policies formulated by the men of the 1890s. Although turn-of-the-century statesmen recognized the contribution of many, their willingness to endorse radical social changes was limited.

Between 1890 and 1925 political parties from the center and the Left shared one key guideline: the administration of justice, education, legislation, national health, and national defense should be in the hands of the state. The groups in charge of proposing reforms and change in those areas were liberal reformers, specialists in public health [*higienistas*], socialists, and feminists. Liberal reformers endorsed political and socioeconomic changes to break down some traditional structures without social disorder. Socialists were to persuade liberal reformers that the welfare of the working class was essential for the prosperity of the nation. *Higienistas,* the technocrats of public health, attempted to convince the executive and the legislators that health was a key factor in progress and change. Nations could not advance if their population was weakened by sickness or toiled and lived in unhealthful conditions. Feminists endeavored to convince men that women were citizens who contributed with their labor and their minds to the task of building a better nation. They were not to be left out of any scheme for change and progress. The issue was just how to emulate the European models.

The history of feminism is intellectual and social. Tracing it involves examining ideas and activities that constituted a process of social change and not simply a claim for specific rights. Feminism entailed gaining personal consciousness of the meaning of being female and awareness of the idiosyncratic needs of women, since both were essential to determine what policies would promote change in the status of women and in gender relations. At the turn of the twentieth century most changes in the social and political structure were defined and undertaken by men. Feminism was the approach used by women and sympathetic men to make gender relevant to the discussion of the politics affecting the family, the school, and the workplace, the three areas where women had a recognized presence. Such a transformation required leadership, a body of men and women sharing the new concepts of gender relations and gender roles. It also required understanding and willingness to accept changes within the group wielding effective power. Once the debate and the work of persuasion began, the idea of recasting women's status and roles gained credibility and feasibility.

Several fundamental needs were perceived as essential for female participation in social change. They were the recognition of women's new economic role, their full juridical personality within the family, and their participation in the political systems of their countries. Was feminism an ideology capable of persuading men to yield to women the freedom and the rights they needed to help establish the new order envisioned by Southern Cone social reformers? The answer was fluid and unclear at the turn of the century, but lack of certitude about the outcome did not stop many men and women of that period from exploring the grounds of feminism and subscribing to whatever aspect of its capacious prospects appealed to them.

To examine the many issues raised by feminists in times of economic and demographic expansion, political diversification, and social unrest in areas distant from its intellectual sources requires an unembarrassed search for a viewpoint true to women's interests. This perspective reveals an intricate pattern of overlapping issues, intimately connected and revolving around the axis of gender roles and gender relations. There is no single formula to unravel its complexities, because the notion of feminism varied among those who claimed to practice it or to sympathize with it, and it developed some significant nuances over time. Chapter 1 opens the discussion of the meaning of feminism in the knowledge that the territory demands further exploration. Tracing the evolution of the meaning of feminism involves recognizing that feminists went through several stages of reinterpreting the concept and adapting it to the social and political circumstances of the nations under study. There was not one feminism, but a diversity of female-sensitive answers to the problems experienced by women of several social strata.

The two important nuances of feminism, socialist and liberal, developed almost simultaneously in the Southern Cone, albeit with different degrees of intensity and rates of maturity. They made mutual accommodations to soften their differences and to avoid open confrontation. Thus class, the only issue with the potential to open a chasm among feminists of different political orientations, was frequently glossed over. Feminists found common lines for bonding in the redress of legal subordination to men, especially within the family, in the justice of recognizing women's capacity to meet any economic and civic demands imposed on them by life or the state, and in the protection they felt society owed to motherhood. The potentially disruptive note of anarchism in this collective picture of female unity was cut short by the relentless persecution of its practitioners. Another potential source of conflict, the distinction between personal liberation and gender liberation, was avoided by the development of a distinctive brand of feminism. Known as "compensatory feminism," it combined legal equality with men and protection of women based on their gender and its specific functions.

The inequalities that early twentieth-century women feminists underlined in their programs were technical and legal — the impediments depriving them of rights men had within and outside the family. At the same time they did not wish to lose qualities they deemed essential to women or the privileges they entailed. Having been denied intellectual capacity and personal freedom of action for a long time, feminists wanted to assert their right to be considered *as good as men,* but *not the same as men.* They saw no conflict between equality in one area and protection in another. They had been raised in cultures with a long tradition of reverence for motherhood, and knowing that maternity gave women a modicum of authority, they protected their turf as women and mothers. Redefining motherhood as a social function, they "modernized" their role to suit a new political scenario without changing some aspects of its traditional core.

The earliest conceptualizations of feminism were permeated by a strong commitment to social reform as it involved women's needs. That such needs were either neglected or overlooked by the men in power was obvious to working women as well as to the first professionals who pored over the law or visited sweatshops and tenements. Feminist preoccupation with the problems besieging working women and, more specifically, working mothers remained central throughout the period under review. The analysis of how women's increasing participation in the labor market contributed to social change, and how it became relevant to feminists, is developed in chapter 2. Because little has been written on women in the labor force in the early twentieth century, putting together basic information about its extent and nature was imperative. Was women's work important enough to the family and the nation to merit social and legal attention? Were the feminists correct in assuming that work validated women's claims to other rights? Gathering statistics and attempting to reconstruct the urban female labor profile yielded mixed results. There are grounds for comparison before the early 1920s, but the picture is more difficult to follow thereafter, when labor department and national census information rapidly dwindled. Nonetheless, available data show that enough women were engaged in paid work outside and inside the home to substantiate labor and feminist claims that women's work had become economically and politically important enough to receive the attention of the state. The task of reconciling labor to home and motherhood became the common thread binding together the political Left, feminists, and liberal social reformers. Their answer was an array of blueprints for protective legislation and state welfare schemes, some of which became a reality throughout the years. Although such laws were opposed by many interested parties, the discussion of their desirability mandated the inclusion of female labor in the agenda of all ideological groups through the 1940s and beyond.

As wage earners women comprised minors, single women, and mothers, introducing competition for wages, a source of concern for male workers, and a new set of social problems. They also posed a challenge to laws that put their wages under their husbands' control. The reexamination of the legal control of women's earnings triggered a reevaluation of the civil rights of all married women. Women workers also were ready to become members of anarchist, socialist, and Catholic labor organizations. Although women only infrequently assumed leadership in the labor movement, by 1940 they had become an identifiable group with legitimate demands for public policy and legislation. The need to regulate the conditions and hours of work was explored and exploited by several political parties. As family members and as mothers, working women also needed pre- and postnatal health care, which were extended to all women once the health of mothers and children became a national preoccupation.

In the mid-1930s efforts to "sell" women's work were met by calls to restrict it and by the lingering desire of many men, regardless of class, to pull women out of the labor pool after marriage. Ambivalence toward women's working was fed by deeply rooted cultural attitudes that defined the home as the preferred space for women and saw the street and outside labor as signs of lower class. To these we must add new concerns that labor in factories could erode women's morals and health and ultimately threaten the family and the nation by causing a decline in fertility. All together, the emergence of female workers in spaces previously dominated by men created conflicts that demanded a revision not just of legislation, but of behavior and attitudes.

In their search for public support, some middle-class feminists sought to enhance the image of working women as economically independent, capable, industrious, and a pride to the nation as they adapted to modernity. An image of independence was essential to sustain reforms in the Civil Code and to obtain full citizenship for all women. The facts revealed by the labor data in chapter 2 belie this optimistic vision and explain why opinions on women's work remained divided.

Motherhood was another powerful ingredient in building a special ideology of gender. Southern Cone feminists embraced it wholeheartedly as the highest signifier of womanhood. Women's rights as individuals were important, but they never lost sight of the fact that most women became mothers and that motherhood caused some of the most serious problems they faced. The toil and sacrifice of working mothers were only one side of the coin. Motherhood demanded respect as a practical service to the nation. Personal issues gained relevance and meaning when elevated to the plane of national interests. Thus came the introduction of mothering—motherhood guided by education, a conscious effort to go beyond the natural functions of maternity to project women's importance in the task of raising future generations. The reconciliation of education and motherhood came through child care [*puericultura*], the topic of chapter 3.

No study of feminism in its social context can afford to ignore the special attention given to the "mother-child dyad" by early twentieth-century social reformers. Long before suffrage caught their eye, early feminists were attempting to channel their own and other women's energies into improving women's and children's health. If there was a social problem amenable to women's special understanding, it was child care. Frightening rates of child mortality demanded better-designed public policies. The figures culled from contemporary data are essential to understanding the dimensions of the problem and why feminists made child care a part of their mission.

Child-care campaigns aimed at giving all women the tools for a conscientious assumption of their maternal tasks, but their goal was to influence health policies and to give women a share of the responsibility implied in their design and implementation. The 1910 First International Feminine Congress and the several congresses on childhood that took place before 1930 identified women as subjects and objects of health policies. As objects they gained additional services in the capital cities; but women also began administering health care and social care after graduating from the first schools of nursing and social work. The presence of women as physicians, nurses, and social workers speaks of an important social change. New careers broadened the occupational choices for middle-class women and gave working-class women the chance to escape factory work and gain some social mobility. That the professionalizing of child care did not change the image of women as nurturers did not worry Southern Cone feminists. Scientific child care was a way out of the stultifying female stereotypes in the early years of the century. More important, women's caring for women was the highest feminist ideal, and they pursued it relentlessly.

Confronting the problems of working mothers and children led feminists to reexamine gender relations at their base: the sexual mores traditionally handed down by law and custom. From freethinkers and anarchists several of the early feminists borrowed a concern with the double standard for judging the sexual behavior of men and women. The examination of what was natural and what was a social construction in matters of sexuality, and the different consequences for men and women, were subjects that not all self-defined feminists felt comfortable with. In this, as in the discussion of other topics, there was a self-imposed restraint that betrays the mores of the period. Implicit in the discussion of unwed mothers, illegitimacy, high child mortality rates, and prostitution, however, there was an indictment of laws and customs that held women accountable while absolving men of responsibility.

In chapters 4 and 5 I explore several aspects of human sexuality that stirred considerable public debate in the 1920s and 1930s, some of them part of the feminist quest for gender equality. The highest emotional appeal was raised by the double standard of morality, which put the burden of sexual honor on women and punished those who failed by depriving them and their offspring of their rights. The discussion of the double standard led to viewing problems such as illegitimacy as not simply being a personal matter, but carrying important social consequences that challenged the strength of the family and perpetuated unjust ethical values. Under a legal light, illegitimacy raised questions about the rights of single mothers and their children. The laws regulating this situation were deeply sexist, limiting the avenues open to children born out of wedlock and the chances of single mothers to pursue their rights against presumed fathers. Feminists proposed to eradicate legal differences among children. This was a tough bone to chew. In asking for the removal of social stigmas feminists faced a dilemma: any law giving women equality within marriage strengthened their position as mothers and pitted legally married women against unwed women.

Other complex issues related to human sexuality and affecting gender relations came under scrutiny in the 1920s and 1930s. Sex education was brought out into the open. It was considered a medical issue by public health authorities and an ethical question by feminists, who denounced the stress on the biological aspects of sex rather than its social consequences. The discussion of the terms for achieving control over sexual behavior expanded to other topics involving both sexes, going beyond personal experience into legal and health issues, punctuated by religious beliefs. Among the most controversial subjects discussed in the 1930s was the high rate of abortion, a problem that ran parallel to high infant mortality and raised difficult health and moral questions. If motherhood was so important as a personal experience, as a way of gaining authority within the family, and for gaining power in the public arena, how could one explain the medical reality of countless abortions? What reasons moved women to take that step? There was a good dose of ethical ambivalence and social hypocrisy in this situation. The most outspoken feminists saw that poverty could force a woman — married or single — to seek an illegal and dangerous abortion to ease the economic burden of unwanted children. On the other hand, the double standard of morality put women under enormous social pressure. Married women were trapped in their husbands' sexuality and had no escape from unwanted pregnancies. Unwed women resorted to abortion to protect their honor, the alternatives being to remain anonymous when they registered their children or else to assume complete legal and economic responsibility for them. Their choice had nothing to do with maternal feelings; it concerned economics and social shame.

If abortion was widespread despite being illegal, could women be given the option of controlling their reproductive life? This was an issue few were prepared for, including most feminists. The medical and the legal professions carried on an open debate in Chile and Uruguay, a little-known chapter in social and women's history, and they placed their chips on the protection of motherhood and on child care. That outcome meant reaffirming traditional sexual mores. Regardless of how well feminists understood women's dilemma, they also opted for protecting motherhood. This is not surprising but reflects the feminist message on sexual ethics. The feminist script for sexuality had women setting the standards and asking men to upgrade their behavior to match them. This approach put many social ills affecting the nation in the limelight but did not significantly change the sexual behavior of men and women.

Feminism also had a furtive rendezvous with eugenics as a tool for sexual and social reform. Eugenics, as understood and promoted in the Southern

Cone, focused on public health programs to combat diseases that weakened a significant portion of the population. Thus, many feminists of both genders supported eugenics policies because they promised better health for future generations through attention to mothers and children, the elimination of sexually transmitted diseases, and the hope that prenuptial certificates would detect such diseases before marriage. Such an attractive promise was difficult to ignore, and many outstanding female physicians, feminist or not, who advocated state programs for healthy mothers and babies also supported state policies that promised to change male sexual behavior. It was all part of a broad change in gender relations.

The discussion of eugenics as policy did not bring any advantage to feminism, because eugenicists saw men and women as procreators and gender relations mostly as a matter of public health requiring supervision. The debate on compulsory prenuptial certificates affected women insofar as it opened the issue of male social and sexual responsibility for reproduction, a topic that may have satisfied the intellectual aspirations of some early twentieth-century radical feminists and anarchists. But male sexuality was discussed for demographic and health purposes, in strictly medical terms. This approach deprived the discussion of the deep sense of gender respect that feminists had always demanded. Men were made responsible for the tests because their sexuality was recognized as the "active" element in the marital partnership. Women were excused from being tested because their sexuality was passive and had to remain private and within marriage to be acceptable. Thus sex roles did not change.

Gender relations had other aspects linking the private and the public within the family. The discussion of the rights of married women and the reform of the Civil Codes involved the fundamental issue of the hierarchy of the sexes in the family and was a subject privileged by feminists and social reformers. The legal subordination of women as wives and mothers and the indissolubility of marriage offered nineteenth-century liberalism a target for testing its ideas about the equality of the sexes and the need to cut the ties between church and state. The proposals to reform the Civil Codes to return to women the rights they had lost in marriage, and the dissolution of marriage itself, were serious challenges to the authority of the pater familias and his parental monopoly over the children [*patria potestad*]. This important chapter in the history of feminism and social reform is developed in chapter 6.

When these issues were first discussed by liberals, hardly twenty years after the enactment of the Civil Codes, they did not present a frontal attack on family law. They followed what appeared to be a less threatening path by questioning men's authority in the political economy of marriage. Gender equality had to be defined in the exercise of the two roles that were assumed to define a woman's life: wife and mother. But since wives and mothers were becoming wage earners, their economic independence was also at stake. For lawyers who first discussed the equality of married women, this was a neatly defined legal right that served to correct a rapidly outmoded economic situation while weakening the apparently impregnable male control of the home.

At the bottom of long-winded analyses of family law were two issues: whether the home should have an incontestable male head controlling the property and behavior of wife and children, and whether the hypocrisy implied in the social cult of motherhood and the reality of mothers' lacking any jurisdiction over their own children should be allowed to remain unchanged. Socialists and feminists pushed the issue to obtain a share of *patria potestad,* a far more pressing need than political rights. The reforms of the Civil Codes in Argentina in 1926 and in Chile in 1934 represent "evolutionary" steps in social change. Concessions obtained did not deliver complete gender equality within marriage. The issue was debated to the bitter end in Uruguay, where the Civil Code was not reformed until 1946, in recalcitrant disdain toward the proposals of the most notable sponsor of women's civil rights, Baltasar Brum, whose blueprint for reform was among the most sensitive to women's claims in the Southern Cone.

Another challenge to family law, to traditional social mores, and to gender roles was the discussion of divorce. Outwardly this was a political question between church and state, but it also unveiled significant nuances of gender construction in the three nations under review. The impassioned parliamentary debates, legal analyses, and writings of its proponents and opponents provide a rich source for exploring the traditional as well as the reformist scripts of femininity and masculinity. Divorce sought the equality of both genders not in their submission to the indissolubility of marriage, as traditionalists and the church saw it, but in their options to gain personal freedom from an unwanted marital relationship. Traditional conventional wisdom established that the stability of the family guaranteed social order, and the sacrifice of personal freedom saved the institutions that preserved order: church and family. Argentina and Chile never accepted divorce during the period considered here, an indication of the pervasiveness of their conservatism in matters of family law. In Uruguay the reform was imposed from above by the Colorado Party, following its own ideological dictum to give women the freedom that only radical feminists and anarchists supported early in the century. The Uruguayan divorce law gave credibility to the idea of separating church and state in the area of family law. Genderwise it established a new concept: that women should have a choice men would not have. Divorce by the sole will of the woman was a revolutionary idea for its time, possible only in a small state experimenting with new forms of social and political change. As an example, it had few followers. As of today (mid-1990s), Chile has not yet conceded men and women complete freedom of divorce.

Women's participation in politics through suffrage is regarded as the touchstone of feminism and social change. In the Southern Cone suffrage became a topic of debate in the second decade of the century. Male universal suffrage, in effect in the three nations in the early 1920s, began to change the physiognomy of the voting mass and gave male and female feminists the base they needed to argue for the inclusion of women. The political mobilization for suffrage needs to be known in full detail if we are to appreciate the conscious efforts women made to reach a full understanding of their goals and gain the support needed to achieve them. Chapters 8, 9, and 10 survey the diverse political activities undertaken by women in each of the three countries. Although I survey the ideological underpinnings guiding feminists in their entrance into politics in chapter 1, these later chapters offer more specific information on the work of individual women and women's associations, the campaigns to overcome female diffidence, and the internal struggle among different interpretations of feminist political activism.

No single organization spoke for women before or after enfranchisement. Numerous associations emerged in the 1920s and 1930s with a claim to one or another feminist interpretation or social interest, and though the variety of groups confirmed the maturity of their supporters, it also diluted the impact of their efforts. The political reforms fought for by a small group of women did not translate into support of women in politics by the majority of men and women. The rhetoric of political purity and an "apolitical" stance sustained by women's "parties" put off assimilation by traditional male parties. The suffrage campaign yielded mixed results. When women voted, few were elected, and those who did gain access to public posts were mostly centrists or conservative Catholics. The nature of political transactions did not change significantly. Although the initiation of women into political life in the Southern Cone may seem meager in electoral results, it changed women and men in many subtle ways. Women feminists gained self-confidence when they defined themselves as a participating pressure group. Their understanding of the political meaning of social reforms was important for them, as were managing their own organizations and planning campaigns to popularize their message.

In a study of suffrage and social mobilization, the Argentine sociologist Darío Cantón posits that extending the franchise depends on a demonstrated capacity for political participation, generally after long and bitter struggles.[3] Southern Cone women showed such ability through their feminist organizations. They renounced violence or confrontation, however, preferring to use persuasion. The Southern Cone suffragist movement had cultural aspects of its own that do not fit any model based on the need to struggle for political results. Other recent analyses of women's political activities by Elsa Chaney, Evelyn Steven, and Jane Jaquette have delved into cultural values and developed the concepts of *supermadre* and *marianismo* to explain the projection of the home, motherhood, and women's special sensitivity into politics.[4] Although their interpretations are based on more contemporary events, they fit the genesis of women's political activities since the mid-1910s. The extensive use of an ideology of social mission based on gender functions and attributes helped early twentieth-century feminists as they tried to raise themselves by their own bootstraps and make a case for their participating in public life. Women used the appeal of culturally safe images to carve a niche in politics. Some feminists showed an almost religious determination to project the role of women as social redeemers to gain social acceptability. Since gender typing can be a double-edged sword, in politics it reinforced the stereotype of women's biological image that confined them to specific areas in public life.

My main purpose in the pages that follow is to underline the message I found in all women's activities and writings: the rise of women's self-consciousness as actors in the body politic. As a response to changing social and economic circumstances, feminism had a variety of nuances and depths but did not fail to elicit tangible results in the drafting and redrafting of civil legislation, in the construction of new social policies, and in the acceptance of women as political beings. Unquestionably, not all women were actively involved. Like men, a small group led the way. This group, however, cut across class. Beginning with the initial stages of self-consciousness, workers as well as professionals helped elaborate a body of stated aspirations that expressed their faith in their own ability to change their lives. Feminism was not the exclusive province of the middle class, although it was mostly confined to the economic and political centers. It is also important to emphasize that this process involved men as much as women, because it was framed within the family and conceived in terms of complementarity of the sexes. Gender relations were put under rigorous scrutiny for the first time in the history of these nations, and though in practice they did not change much, they were not to remain in unchallenged complacency.

To embrace the history of feminism and social change in three countries in a limited space is a daunting task that I undertook out of admiration and respect for the women and men who first contested the justice of considering women a lesser version of men. Most of them left us more of their thoughts than of personal information about themselves. To do them justice I dwell as much on the elaboration of concepts, the exchange of ideas, the debate between tradition and modernization, the strategies for mobilization, and the meaning of activities as on the actual accomplishments. The analysis of those historical elements brings to life the reality of all those who contributed to make gender relevant to the state, to the law, and to themselves.

CHAPTER 1

Feminism in the Southern Cone:
Definitions and Objectives

When feminism appeared as the topic of a 1901 dissertation at the University of Buenos Aires, the term had already been discussed and analyzed by a small group of intellectuals in that city. For the next three decades feminism stirred the curiosity of some, gained the acid condemnation of others, and became the stimulus for a variety of changes in the juridical status and the economic and social condition of women.[1] Feminism described many situations and reflected the aspirations of several groups at different times, but there was an underlying commonality of feelings and attitudes that bound together the diverse people who expressed their ideas and hopes under that broad umbrella.[2] Identifying commonalities and divergences is not an easy task, but it is necessary to mapping the territory for further exploration.

Southern Cone feminism developed mostly in urban centers. Three capital cities—Buenos Aires, Montevideo, and Santiago, in that order—were the main cradles of feminist ideas and organizations. Legislators and jurists in the three nations shared ideas and arguments and closely watched each other's responses to pressure for legal change. Women's groups communicated with each other frequently. The tie was specially strong between Montevideo and Buenos Aires, on either side of the Río de la Plata estuary, but the Andes did not pose any great obstacle to the movement of ideas. Reprints from Uruguayan women's magazines appeared in Santiago, and the example of women voting in that city's municipal elections in 1935 raised hopes and frustrations among Argentines.

Feminism began to be discussed and defined between 1898 and 1905, and by 1920 it was part of the political vocabulary of socialists, liberal middle-class women, social reformers, national deputies, and even conservative and

Roman Catholic writers.[3] The evolution of feminism in these nations reflects various ideological roots and the subtle nuances of class. Two main feminist interpretations were adopted before 1910. One was socialist oriented, finding its inspiration in the writings of August Bebel. This feminism was conscious of class issues and found a niche in the labor movements of the three nations, especially after 1905, when the plight of women workers was discussed alongside that of their male counterparts.

The other feminism had closer ties to the mid-nineteenth-century liberal feminism of men such as John Stuart Mill. It reflected the aspirations of middle-class women and men who approached gender issues with an emphasis on the natural rights of individuals and the need to establish in law the equality of women and men. There was no sharp cleavage or confrontational antagonism between these two interpretations, even though during the formative period socialism stressed the class message to gain the attention of women workers. Rather than antagonize liberals, socialists struggled with anarchists for the allegiance of the labor force. Anarchists had convincing arguments for workers, male and female, but they rejected feminism as a bourgeois ideology. By the early 1920s anarchist appeal was in decline—partly owing to strong repressive government policies—and socialist feminism was in a position to lend its ideas and support to liberal feminism. In fact, what was distinctive about Southern Cone feminism was its flexibility. By the mid-1920s socialist ideas on the need to protect female and children workers had been assimilated by middle-class feminists, while socialist feminists joined the campaigns for the reform of the Civil Codes and suffrage, essentially liberal feminist objectives.

A social profile of the feminists in the Southern Cone remains to be done. The men and women who followed the intellectual call of gender and social reform were a fascinating mix of working-class and middle-class people of European ethnic origins, combining established groups closely tied to Spanish colonial traditions with recent immigrants from several countries, including Spain. Some of the male feminists reached national stature, mostly as deputies and senators and occasionally even as presidents. Women became labor leaders, writers and publicists, and public officials in chosen government appointments, or simply practiced professions. Any attempt to draw a general feminist profile for the Southern Cone must acknowledge that few of the women had a full sense of their own historicity. Only one feminist, Paulina Luisi, left her work-related papers to public institutions. These policy-oriented women did not consider history as part of their future, though they shaped it in significant ways. There are no institutional archives or available family papers that could help with a historical portrait. For those reasons I have chosen to focus on their writings rather than attempting to create a social profile.

In the fifty years covered by this book, two feminist cohorts can be identified. One was composed of women born between 1875 and 1895, active between 1900 and 1930. The second comprised women born between 1895 and 1915, active in the 1930s and early 1940s. There are some remarkable figures, such as Alicia Moreau, who lived to be one hundred years old, or Uruguayan Paulina Luisi, born in 1875 and active through 1950. Chilean Elena Caffarena and Uruguayan Ofelia Machado Bonet, already active in the 1920s, also stretched their service to feminism through the 1980s. The first cohort gave feminism and social change meaning before 1915. They had to face and fight the closed conservatism of a generation of men and women for whom the terms "women's emancipation" and "feminism" sounded twice alien — in origin and in meaning. Their inspired leadership laid the foundations on which the second cohort would establish their identities as "new women" — no longer oddities, much less vilified, and at times even eulogized.

Ethnic extraction and social class are two important signifiers among feminist women. The abundance of foreign names in the ranks of Argentine and Uruguayan social and political activists — male and female — has caught the attention of social historians. The migratory wave reaching Argentina and Uruguay between 1880 and 1910 made significant changes in these nations' ethnic makeup and in the nature of politics. In Uruguay foreigners made up 17 percent of the total population in 1908; they were concentrated in Montevideo, where they were 30 percent of the urban population. In 1914 in Argentina, over one-third of the population was foreign born, and about 80 percent could trace their parentage to immigrants arriving since 1850. In contrast, the foreign-born proportion of Chile's population was only 4.1 percent in 1907, and a significant number were Bolivians and Peruvians, not Europeans. Among the Europeans, 38 percent came from Spain, Italy, Germany, and France. Only 3.8 percent of Santiago's population was foreign born.[4] Most demographic studies have focused on men, or on "people" with no gender signifier, so the meaning of ethnicity in the history of feminism and women's history in general has not been tackled in depth. Although it is beyond the scope of this book to expand on the topic, a few comments are due. Was the *criolla* or native-born woman less interested either in advocating reform for her sex or in shaping it than the immigrant or the daughter of immigrants? Generalizations for the three countries are risky, but there are no grounds for believing that native-born women were less enthusiastic or less dedicated feminists. Immigration was important because it brought ideological challenges and created a new social milieu, but close ties to Europe did not move either of the two cohorts to imitate "foreign" feminists. In Argentina there was a definite first-generation immigrant presence among female social activists and feminists. Anarchists active in the late 1890s and early 1900s included Spaniards, Italians, and others with names reflecting Eastern European ancestry, such as María Collazo, Juana Rouco Buela, Marta Newelstein, Teresa Caparoletto, and Thomasa Cupayolo. Among the socialists' first leaders were women with such names as Fenia Chertcoff—of Russian Jewish parentage—Carolina Muzilli, daughter of Italian immigrants, and Gabriela Laperrière, French. The same cannot be said for Chile. Early labor-socialist-anarchists developing gender consciousness in that nation had names such as Valdés de Díaz, Cádiz, Jeria, and Quezada. They were extraordinarily competent and versatile and in no way less capable than their counterparts in Buenos Aires.

Among mainstream liberal feminists the picture is also mixed. Argentina shows the larger number of non-Spanish names for the first quarter of the century. Elvira Rawson de Dellepiane epitomized the rapid assimilation taking place in Buenos Aires, having an English family name and a husband of Italian descent. Julieta Lanteri was born in Italy; Cecilia Grierson's parents were Scottish and Irish; Alicia Moreau was of French parentage, and Paulina Luisi was of French-Italian ancestry. They are typical of the first generation of immigrants. As a counterpart we find traditional Spanish surnames, as in María Abella de Ramírez, Ernestina López, and Elvira López, but in a definite minority.[5]

In Uruguay the picture is more evenly divided between Spanish and non-Spanish names. The National Council of Women's roster in Uruguay includes names like Pinto Vidal, Carrió, and Castro, balanced by others such as Horticou, Dufrechou, and Martorelli.[6] Chile had comparatively more Spanish names than Argentina, but the list was sprinkled with foreign names derived from older immigration. Amanda Labarca—born Pinto Sepúlveda—Sofía de Ferrari Rojas, and Ester La Rivera set the first feminist landmarks. Eloísa Díaz and Ernestina Pérez share honors with Cora Mayers as actively engaged in feminist professional activities.[7]

In the 1930s, when the second feminist cohort assumes leadership in a more complex scenario, Argentina is the only country with a persistent cohort of non-Spanish names, such as Gucovski, Horne de Burmeister, and Scheiner, even though immigration had declined sharply. In Uruguay we find Sara Alvarez Rey, Zulma Núñez, and Sofía Alvarez Vignoli joining the feminist ranks, and new women such as Magdalena Antonelli Moreno emerge in the 1940s. In Chile Graciela Mandujano, Elvira Rogat, Felisa Vergara, Marta Vergara, Aurora Argomedo, and Elcira Rojas mixed with blue bloods of the established elite such as Adela Edwards, the industrialist's daughter Elena Caffarena Morice, and the less socially exalted Delia Ducoing. A survey of the Unión Femenina de Chile's steering board or the National Executive Committee of Chilean Women (1933), for example, finds mostly Spanish surnames.[8] But there is another side to the immigration issue. Foreign-born teachers who came to educate women in the three countries exercised a significant influence on the generation coming of age in the 1890s. In Chile Catholic French- and German-speaking secular and religious teachers were very important in elementary and secondary education. In Argentina the North American teachers President Domingo F. Sarmiento brought to change women's education have become legendary. The situation is less clear for Uruguay.[9] We should not forget, however, that in the 1850s and 1860s native-born women had begun to assess their own social role and status, breaking the ground for gender sensitivity. This small group of women left their mark as writers and teachers. The dialogue between older Spanish traditions and newer ideas brought by immigrants or read in European and North American literature gives Southern Cone feminism its specific characteristics. Traditional elements such as the cult of motherhood were not simply a Spanish heritage, however: they were part of the Catholic culture shared by most immigrants. Feminists' repeated disclaimers about copying "Anglo-Saxon models" or behavioral patterns alien to the national culture should be taken seriously as intellectual self-definers: focusing exclusively on names and dismissing the stated objectives of feminist personalities and groups will miss the point.

Class, access to education, and location in urban centers where communication permitted the flow of new ideas from within and from outside were central in the formation of feminism. Class signifiers are fuzzy and contested by practically all writers on the topic, but there were women who made a living in trades and whose leadership emerged in factories and was oriented to the interests of other working women. Argentine Carolina Muzilli, Uruguayan María Collazo, and Chileans Carmela Jeria, Eloísa Zurita, and Esther Valdés de Díaz can easily be defined as working-class feminists and social reformers.

The middle class comprised those who did not have to forfeit an education owing to economic need and who attended secondary schools, normal schools, or professional university schools. A common aspiration of late nineteenth-century women regardless of class, education became a common bond that made feminism and gender reform intelligible to women of diverse social origins. Feminism had a solid urban middle-class base because it appealed to educated women whose legal rights and potential for achievement were curtailed by law and prevailing mores. The education of feminist leaders permitted them, though not necessarily affluent, to understand the gender bond with working women and supported their attempt to reach them and campaign in their favor.

Socialist Feminism

Socialism did not fail to address the issue of women in industrializing and rapidly changing societies, as it had done in Europe since the early 1830s.[10] As socialism spread to South America it carried the concept of gender equality as an integral part of its agenda. The Argentine Socialist Party adopted universal suffrage for both sexes at its 1900 convention without any reference to feminism, though several of the first female socialists in Argentina called themselves feminists.[11] In 1902, still a small party courting emerging workers' organizations, it founded the Socialist Feminine Center and the Feminine Guild Union [Unión Gremial Femenina]. Party congresses of 1903 and 1904 seated women as delegates with full voting rights and adopted a plan subscribed to by the Socialist Feminine Center proposing full civil and political rights for women and protective legislation for female workers.[12] The party began to encourage women followers to participate and urged those who worked in factories to organize, following socialist guidelines. The party's newspaper *La Vanguardia* wrote sympathetically about the activities of English suffragists in 1907.[13]

Yet neither working women's participation nor their organizing within the party amounted to feminism. It was the task of the emergent female leaders and of several sympathetic male leaders in the Socialist Party to define their position in gender politics—partly by airing ideas and opinions in *La Vanguardia*, in the Argentine case, or in *La Reforma*, the mouthpiece of the Democratic Party in Chile. Although anarchists loathed feminists, their sharply focused analysis of women's status in society between 1895 and 1905 raised questions on women's labor that feminists and social reformers could not ignore. By far the most influential source was the writings of women themselves. They were published mostly in women's magazines, many surviving for only a few issues but compensating by the intensity of their message. *La Aurora, La Palanca,* and *La Alborada* are three Chilean examples of early socialist newspapers with an explicit feminist orientation. *La Voz de la Mujer*, published from 1896 to 1897 in Buenos Aires, was anarchist in ideology but helped define gender issues for workers. In Uruguay there was no female socialist press, but the labor press regularly published on women's issues.

A telling example of how feminism was carved out of the general pool of socialist egalitarian principles was the debate between the Uruguayan María Abella de Ramírez, a liberal freethinker and self-defined feminist, and Argentine socialist Justa Burgos Meyer. Their exchange was published in *Nosotras*, a magazine Abella founded in 1902 in La Plata. In 1903 she criticized protective legislation for women proposed by the Argentine Socialist Party. Such restrictions ran against the true spirit of freedom advocated by feminism as she understood it. She also questioned the lack of any socialist plans to change gender relations and women's status within the family.[14] Piqued by the criticism, Burgos Meyer responded in several articles by explaining the Argentine socialist position on women and feminism.

> I consider myself a feminist because I aspire to see woman's intellectual capacity recognized . . . and not excluded from any activity in social life. . . . She should be able to exercise the profession or occupation of her choice, and she should participate in government, designing the laws under which she lives. . . . [We accept] the feminist theory that the dominant sex should not deprive society of the [benefit of] female abilities and condemn woman to stay at home. . . . These ideals, so contrary to male egotism, are the conscious will of women and the source of feminism. We must struggle to form a feminist consciousness. Nothing in the socialist program is incompatible with these ideas.[15]

In this statement three ideas stand out as the pillars of early feminism in the Southern Cone: the acknowledgment of women's intellectual capacity, their right to work in any occupation for which they had the ability, and their right to participate in civic life and politics. Early socialists thus stood on the same grounds as liberal feminists. Their use of the term "feminism" for the social and gender changes proposed is significant. Both groups believed that women would not become full persons and full citizens until men acknowledged them as intellectual equals and allowed them to take a place in the world beyond the home. Socialists' preoccupation with working women's issues did not preclude a meeting of the minds with women who did not share their credo.

Lack of documentation prevents our tracing the internal debate on feminism among socialist leaders or the evolution of the party's policy. Statements of principle in any party's program do not necessarily imply adoption of a policy. Judging from a discussion in the socialist daily *La Vanguardia*, by 1907 the party was ready to accept the connection between feminism and socialism at an economic and political level. An essay on feminism posited that a woman capable of earning her living became the equal of any man. The equalizing power of labor was an argument shared by socialists and liberal feminists, and it gained in strength as time passed, comparing gender equality with class leveling: "The leveling of the sexes is as important as or more important than the leveling of the classes." This rather striking conclusion was tempered by the writer's remark that women had to fear capitalism above all, reaffirming the task of socialism as protecting them from its abuses. Socialism defended women by pursuing the regulation of their wages, their working hours, and their working conditions.[16] Feminism remained open to further revision and definition by socialist leaders and, conversely, socialists remained open to fighting the cause of liberal feminists. The first elected socialist deputy, Alfredo Palacios, endorsed a bill reforming the Civil Code to broaden women's civil rights, acknowledging its intellectual origin in the female wing of the party. He felt obliged to add, however, that the feminism of his bill was not "declamatory and exaggerated." A symmetrical equality between men and women was impossible because the physical and psychological nature of women did not allow it. Nonetheless, socialists wished to see all legal limitations on women's activities removed to achieve a "relative emancipation" in the social and domestic realms.[17] The caution against exaggerated expressions of feminism may have been an oblique reference to English suffragists' tactics, well known in South America, but as socialists penetrated politics they became less averse to women's demonstrations on their behalf. In 1912 they were proud to see female socialist volunteers passing out political propaganda during the elections, calling their behavior "electoral feminism."[18]

Uruguayan workers' newspapers showed less interest in a public debate on feminism. Socialist and anarchist groups in that country made slow progress, being squeezed between the two most powerful parties in that country, the reformist Colorado and the traditionalist Blanco, which left little room for other political groups. After 1905 the Colorado Party undertook a vast program of social, political, and legal reform that preempted many socialist reform ideas, including raising women's legal status, and introduced a series of protective welfare bills similar to those espoused by socialists elsewhere in the Southern Cone. Nonetheless, by 1914 Uruguayan socialists had defined their own reformist position on legal equality, which they carried through into the 1915 debates on the reform of the Constitution and through the parliamentary debates of the 1920s and 1930s on civil and political rights for women. Deputies Emilio Frugoni and Pablo María Minelli gallantly stood for women's suffrage and the abrogation of legal restrictions on their juridical personalities, giving full support to similar proposals by the more powerful Colorado Party.[19]

Chilean labor leaders, despite being less organized and under greater political pressure than their Argentine counterparts, tried to come to grips with feminism early in the century. *La Aurora Feminista*, an early women's newspaper, published a single number in January 1904, defining itself as "a defender of women's rights." It called on all women to escape the silk chains that tied them to a life of vanity and do something constructive for the nation. For this ephemeral publication, feminism meant a break with the past and a willingness to work for a new role and a new freedom for women.[20] A longer-lasting publication was *La Alborada* [The dawn] a needleworkers' newspaper published in Santiago between 1905 and 1907. When it first appeared, *La Alborada* defined itself as a "defender of the proletarian classes," but by the end of its second year it was being addressed as a "feminist publication." It was by definition a socialist paper devoted to the defense of working women, but it also discussed other topics less directly related to labor. In 1907 *La Alborada* discussed the need to reform the Civil Code, claiming a growing consciousness of their own inequality among all women, but especially working women.[21] Yet despite its claims to feminism, there were fewer discussions of what feminism meant in the social arena than of the problems working women encountered in their daily toil, with calls for a female workers' union. Feminism as used in *La Alborada* meant concern for the needs of all women as a gender, regardless of class boundaries, but class struggle overshadowed feminism and remained its main preoccupation. *La Palanca,* appearing from May to September 1908, sought to fill the void left by *La Alborada*'s demise. In July 1908 the newspaper requested communications from other publications of "a feminist character,"[22] but the search for connections had hardly begun when the newspaper caved in. *La Palanca* espoused economic independence for women as its first goal, but social and political liberation for all women was high on its agenda. In its short life it published the translation of an article in which feminism was lauded as a doctrine of equality, freedom, and harmony that applied to both genders. *La Palanca* also discussed women's education as well as birth control to end compulsory motherhood among working women. This concern for problems specific to women suggests a desire to broaden its message beyond class interests, even though the newspaper remained focused on working women. The editors of *La Alborada* and *La Palanca* described as feminism all undertakings by working women organized to overcome their economic exploitation. There was an open desire to find an ideological basis for binding *all* women together. That was also the tenor of other early socialist and leftist organizations of the Southern Cone. Chilean socialist leader Luis Recabarren, writing in *La Reforma* (1906) and *El Despertar de los Trabajadores* (1913–21), conflated women's labor activism and feminism.[23] An essay titled "Feminism" published in *La Reforma* in 1906 praised the working woman who shook off her inertia and joined the social struggle to support socialist men. Women were encouraged to demand just salaries for themselves and to join men in trying to reduce working hours. Women were to aid men in their struggle, while men's duty was to help women fulfill their destiny as wives and mothers.[24] For those Chilean women who read Recabarren, redemption through socialism was still far from advocating more than a militant attitude within labor and support for their men in the fight against capitalism.

After he became more openly socialist and founded *El Despertar de los Trabajadores* in 1912 in the port city of Iquique, Recabarren and his circle of followers published articles on suffrage and continued to encourage female workers to take part in labor politics. To further that goal he helped found a series of women workers' clubs called Centros Belén de Zárraga in honor of a notable contemporary Spanish anarchist. The clubs supported freethinking and anticlerical education and served as nuclei for socialist workers. The tenor of the writings and the programs organized by the clubs show that the message of *El Despertar de los Trabajadores* in time became more anticlerical and class-based than feminist: when the Chilean Socialist Party published its platform on 16 January 1915 no single point addressed the needs of women.[25] *El Despertar de los Trabajadores* was nonetheless, the major forum for essays on women and their social role. In 1913 Salvador Barra Wohl, an important socialist figure and Recabarren's close friend, specifically endorsed English feminism. When he expanded his analysis to the French situation, however, he distinguished between bourgeois feminism and socialist feminism, defining the latter as truly concerned with the problems of working women.[26] Education, engagement in social problems, and hope for a more positive role of working women in society were the themes discussed in *El Despertar de los Trabajadores* through 1917. Socialists' endorsement of women's community work had its political ramifications: the newspaper encouraged women to support the candidacies of socialists Dr. Isidoro Urzúa and Luis Recabarren through the Recabarren-inspired Feminine Centers. After his conversion to communism in the early 1920s, women's issues received much less attention. Exhortations for union among workers and discussions of coeducation and sex education formed the core of the message.[27]

The feminist socialist message in these three countries was above all for women to organize, to seek intellectual emancipation through socialism, and to force the government to grant working women the welfare benefits they should have based on the special functions of their sex. Economic independence and protective legislation for female workers were the centerpiece of socialist plans for social reform. Discussion of gender inequality within the family or in society was much less frequent, but the problem was addressed by several men and women in Argentina and Chile. Socialists (and anarchists) had some difficulty translating the paradigm of equality into equal relationships in the home, and the language they used betrayed an acceptance of secondary roles for women. Uplifting words encouraged them to pursue their rights, but they were often painted as companions ready to follow men, support them, and give them solace in their bitter hours. Some socialists however, openly criticized men who preached equality in the streets and practiced oppression at home. Recabarren's newspaper exposed the problem of gender relations in the 1920s but blamed it on capitalism and bourgeois civil law.[28] The first women's Argentine anarchist newspaper, *La Voz de la Mujer*, recorded male hostility, as *Nuestra Tribuna*, Juana Rouco Buela's publication, did years later.[29]

The assumption that in a utopian future the female worker would find a haven at home, educating her children and being her husband's tender companion, was clearly articulated by the women and men who collaborated for *La Alborada*, and in *El Despertar de los Trabajadores* as late as the early 1920s. It was also expressed by Argentine socialists throughout the first two decades of the century. Socialists and anarchists, like liberal feminists, did not wish to see their sexual roles subverted, and they placed their hopes on a future in which women would climb to meet men's intellectual and political standards. Women, especially in the early 1910s, were regarded as still immature, in need of light to reveal the possibilities that centuries of darkness and oppression had hidden. Awakening, seeing the light, were frequent metaphors in the writings of the Left. Even women's newspapers carried articles portraying women as lagging behind men and needing education to become better companions.[30]

Liberal Feminism

Another search for the meaning of feminism began among the women of the educated urban elite in the last quarter of the nineteenth century. Female university graduates were sensitive to the social prejudices they faced in societies where "decent" women were not encouraged to walk in the streets alone, much less leave home for an education and an independent life. In Argentina, the only country with a body of professional women prepared for such a movement, a National Council of Women was founded in 1900. This institution, a miscellaneous group of charitable and educational organizations, never developed a feminist orientation. It proposed to follow the guidelines of the international councils of women in Europe and North America for the general elevation of womankind, and it never veered from that course. A member of the library committee defined the council's concept of feminism as "judicious and moderate. Its goals are to raise women's intellectual [level,] cultivating their intelligence with study, instruction, and the fine arts to produce the perfect equilibrium between the reasoning brain and the feeling heart."[31] The National Council adopted evolution and education as its policies and rejected any political or ideological commitment or any undertaking that would compromise its aseptic dedication to the improvement of women as individuals. Women's emancipation was not yet within the reach of its members; as time passed it dissociated itself from feminism altogether.

Unhappy about the ideological position assumed by the National Council, a group of university women split off in 1905 and began a process of defining attitudes and gaining publicity for their ideas that laid the foundations of Argentine liberal feminism. Among the most outspoken of that group was a physician, Dra. Elvira Rawson de Dellepiane, who later played a distinguished role in the suffrage campaigns. In 1905 she assessed the problems women faced in her country and encouraged her professional companions along the course they had chosen. Denouncing intrigues meant to keep women under men's thumbs from time immemorial, she also reproved women who maligned those working for the redemption of their own gender.[32]

The Centro Feminista, founded in 1905, was to be a feminist center for women like Elvira Rawson. At its inauguration, Rawson delivered a speech defining its goals, rich in action verbs and the imagery of war and sprinkled with phrases like "preparing our arms for the forthcoming battle." Rather than men waking women from their sleep—a common metaphor in socialist newspapers—she saw women challenging men to share the patrimony they had so far enjoyed as absolute masters.[33] "We are neither a few, nor are we alone," she stated with assurance.

The sweeping definition of their goals was emblematic of the understanding of feminism held by a cadre of educated women: (1) reform of all the laws in the Civil Code that deprived women of their juridical personality and made them dependents of men; (2) a share in decision-making educational posts, not as an exception but as a rule, because women were a key element in education; (3) women's presence in the judiciary (as judges in the Latin American system), particularly in the courts ruling on women's and children's cases; (4) laws to protect maternity and determine paternity; (5) abolition of regulated houses of prostitution (then under municipal control); (6) equal pay for equal work; and (7) full political rights (to vote and to be elected).

This comprehensive plan addressed social, ethical, economic, family, and individual issues where gender was preeminent. The first three points aimed at dismantling the inequalities encoded in law and gaining access to power through two channels that Rawson thought accessible to women. Being accepted on educational councils was a reasonable expectation based on the increasing number of women gaining university degrees and becoming professionals. But her proposal for judgeships was premature when women had not yet earned men's confidence for making any civic or public-oriented decisions and had no civil or political rights. The rest of her plan reflected current aspirations of liberal feminism, with a nod toward the needs of working women as expressed more fully by the Left. Her longed-for participation in institutional decision making had to be dropped from her agenda and did not appear in any other early feminist wish list: women in Argentina did not have enough political clout. Most of the early feminists—male and female—were keenly aware of this and focused on reforming the laws that maintained women's legal subordination.

Another important figure in defining liberal feminism was Uruguayan María Abella de Ramírez, who lived in the Argentine city of La Plata most of her life. Abella de Ramírez, born in 1866, was a housewife and the mother of four daughters. Her search for women's liberation from the legal restrictions and prejudices of her times led her to explore several ideological options between 1900 and 1912. She wrote on a variety of topics, from child care and unwed mothers to the negative influence of clericalism, but women's problems were the central theme of her many essays and the constant preoccupation of her mature life. She was fearless in her choice of feminism as early as 1902. As a freethinker, she attended a congress in 1906, then represented this group at the First International Feminine Congress of Buenos Aires in 1910.[34] She was a convinced advocate of gender equality within and outside the home who could not suffer the assumption of women's subordination to men under any circumstances. Women's first right "is the right to be free," she wrote in 1903.[35] Aware of labor's stirring, she appealed to women in all walks of life with the conviction that feminism was above all a concern for gender issues regardless of class: "For feminists there are no workers or bourgeois women, or marchionesses, or queens, or even prostitutes. There is only one oppressed and mistreated sex, and we want to redeem it whether its oppression comes from monarchs or from workers." [36]

She understood that many women had to work, and in reevaluating their worth to society she knew that women's labor was a key factor in national progress as well as an individual asset. She rejected outright the notion of special protection for working women "as if all women were pregnant or had a home to take care of." Pregnant women should be protected, but not at the cost of losing their means of sustenance.[37] Although she appreciated motherhood, she never admitted that women had to give up any rights when they became mothers. "Women have not been born only to be mothers, as men have not been born to be fathers. Both have the duty to conserve the species, but they also have the right to be free . . . to enjoy life." [38] The family was not the only arena where women should exercise their abilities, while other social duties went begging.

Biological determinism was not part of her intellectual landscape, yet she did not shun motherhood. On the contrary, motherhood was a potential producer of wealth for the nation. Though never stating it in Marxist terms — she was too individualistic in her thought — she asked the state to recognize the reproductive contribution of women. There should be no stigma attached to women who had children out of wedlock. They did not deserve the hardship imposed on them and their children by a state that did nothing to help them and by a society that condoned male seduction. In her ideal society mothers would be protected by the state rather than by a particular man, to prevent their economic and personal subjection. Abella's concept of motherhood as a social function predated Paulina Luisi's understanding of that notion, establishing a solid ideological foundation for those who in the late 1910s would move Uruguay to welfare legislation reflecting those views.[39]

Abella promoted women's groups beginning in 1900, and in 1903 she called for a "feminist center" where freethinking women would have a gathering place to choose those ideas most suitable to their aspirations. In 1906 she presented her "minimum plan of female vindications" at the

Freethinkers' Congress. Her uppermost concerns, judging by the ranking of the proposals, were equal education, equal employment opportunities, and equal salaries, followed by financial equity, freedom of movement, and choice of lifestyle for married women, sharing of rights with the father, absolute divorce, equality of all children before the law, toleration of prostitution but not regulation, and political rights for women.[40] This plan shows a progressive widening of women's horizons, from freeing the mind, to freeing the self from economic dependence and marital subordination, to the ultimate accomplishment of casting a free vote in society.

In 1910 Abella founded the National Feminist League in La Plata, with a "broad plan" and a "narrow plan." The broad plan had four goals: restoration of civil rights to married women; allocation of political rights to all adult women; absolute divorce as opposed to "legal separation," the only form allowed under most civil codes in South America; and protection of children. These fundamental rights supported the narrow plan, focused more sharply on the reforms of the Civil Code essential to grant women greater personal freedom within marriage and equal legal control of their children. Divorce had been approved in Uruguay in 1907 and was then being redefined to give women the option to act first. She kept divorce in her plan for the sake of other women on the continent. Abella de Ramírez and Rawson de Dellepiane were the boldest and earliest self-defined middle-class feminists in the Southern Cone. Although a small core of women, especially in Argentina, was willing to share those objectives with them, most men and women were unsure about the meaning of feminism and very cautious about accepting any ideology that socialists and "freethinkers" endorsed.

The First International Feminine Congress and the Definition of Mainstream Liberal Feminism

The 1910 International Feminine Congress that took place in Buenos Aires marked an important moment in the development of a feminist consciousness in the Southern Cone. Socialist feminists, moderate liberal feminists, and freethinkers mingled and expressed their views on law, social welfare, and women's rights and education. The organizers called the congress "feminine" to accommodate women who were not ready to accept the label of feminism but were willing to work for women's rights and for other social welfare causes relevant to women, the family, and society.[41]

The intellectual pedigree of the keynote speaker, Ernestina López, was nineteenth-century liberal feminism.[42] When she addressed her audience she defined the congress as "feminist," despite its official title, and said it would help those in Argentina who "worked for raising the concept of feminism and achieving its acceptance."[43] She compared the women who had joined the movement for independence a hundred years earlier with the generation of 1910: both had committed themselves to their country and to the future of women's causes. The congress's motto was "Let Us Work." In 1910 "work" meant social involvement beyond the home. To live a comfortable life within the home was a sterile form of egotism, and women should engage in pursuits that elevated the moral and material standards of their sex. The work ethic adopted by the congress suited the middle-class women who formed the bulk of the participants. The female emancipation it upheld was understood not as "the freedom to do all that one wanted, but as the wish to do all that one should."[44] This self-imposed discipline was appropriate for women who were not compelled to work for a living but wanted to use their abilities for a higher social purpose. Sweating over a machine was not what they envisioned; they had in mind the service and leadership that educated women could give to others of lower social status who needed understanding and help.

López identified work and economic freedom as the bases of feminism because they permitted women the dignified development of their personality. The new professionals understood the nature of legal and social subordination and realized that women also needed to free themselves from self-imposed inhibitions born of centuries of social pressure. She argued that women's freedom depended on their own will to take advantage of the natural rights of all individuals to enjoy the freedom to work, the benefits of education, and legislation nurtured by equity.[45] The congress was expected to create a common consciousness of gender among women—irrespective of class—by fostering ties and supporting a common desire for education. It would also dissipate prejudices about women's intellectual ability. It was important that their thoughts be expressed, not just to break the traditional female silence in the public arena, but to prove they had something important to say.

Congress speakers attempted to reconcile two important concepts: feminism and femininity. The feminist component would help to earn recognition for the labor of mothers, artists, professional women, and working women. The congress would also remain feminine, as it expressed the interests of humanity through distinctly female voices.[46] In assuming this task it was attempting to legitimize two cultural values in the formation of women in Latin American societies. The preoccupations, hopes, and plans for the future of these early twentieth-century women were reflected in the decisions this congress reached. Education, health, and social welfare were paramount in the papers and recommendations. It advocated state-supported female education, especially physical, technical, and professional, along with domestic science and child care. The lack of medical and health services for the urban poor was noted, as well as the need for "reform" institutions for homeless girls and young female delinquents.

Speakers in the sociology session addressed a variety of themes affecting women's lives. Socialist Juana María Beguino shunned the concept of charity in dealing with working and poor women and strongly endorsed legislation that would protect them from unhealthful and exploitative working conditions. The double standard of morality and the social fate of unwed or abandoned mothers were intensively debated. The fate of those women and their children deeply concerned congress participants, yet few attempted to link it with sexuality, a topic most women felt was still beyond public debate.[47] The session on law included divorce, feminism, and suffrage, topics already under discussion in the three nations. Paradoxically, in this Feminine Congress, organized by women who were feminists either explicitly or implicitly, only one paper analyzed feminism as an ideology. The author was Peruvian María Jesús Alvarado Rivera, who one year later delivered a lecture on the topic in her native Lima, the first woman ever to address the subject in that country.[48] Alvarado's feminism followed the lines established by its first proponents in South America: juridical equality of the sexes and equality of opportunity in education and work. She did not believe in absolute gender equality, since women had their special maternal mission. She was also unready to support complete equality of civic and political rights, not as a matter of principle but simply as a pragmatic stance. As a Peruvian, she felt Peruvian society was not ready to accept such rights. Alvarado's position on suffrage was not shared by all the participants in the Feminine Congress, but she was probably close to the feelings of most women and men in South America.

Only four papers in the law sessions dealt with suffrage—a very small proportion for the congress as a whole. The congress approved the concept of universal suffrage for *both* sexes, a motion presented by the Argentine Socialist Feminine Center, but voted down the freethinkers' proposal to request abrogation of Argentina's laws denying women the vote. Lacking any debates on that motion, we cannot discern whether the congress opposed the freethinkers or the notion of female suffrage. It is evident that it was prepared to adopt principles but not ready to take practical steps to obtain such goals. Facing the theme that would be the touchstone of future women's endeavors, the Feminine Congress responded with a lukewarm affirmation of the right to suffrage but did not rank it as its most important concern. The diversity of the participants precluded any action other than the statement of principles. Another decade passed before the political arena of the Southern Cone was ready for an intensive female suffrage campaign.

Feminism: Second Phase

The First International Feminine Congress helped establish the general direction of feminist development in the ensuing decade, but the leadership in each country defined its own course of action. Political events in the three countries between 1910 and 1920 favored discussion of the feminist agenda. In Uruguay the Colorado Party, having initiated reforms to change the nation's social and political structure — without women's participation — designed and approved a new constitution in 1917. Debates over women's suffrage led nowhere. Unable to overcome their own doubts on the subject, members of the assembly left the door open for its future approval. In Argentina and Chile the old regimes based on the rule of a small social elite were displaced between 1918 and 1920, when universal male suffrage and the emergence of populist leaders changed the political complexion of both countries. Issues concerning labor, urban affairs, public health, and women were examined by politicians, jurists, and intellectuals who engaged in vigorous discussion over the next two decades.

The ideas of feminists outside South America were inspiring models, since these women had already advanced a great distance toward personal and social liberation. Latin American women's participation in several inter-American and European conferences strengthened their convictions and encouraged them to enlist followers at home.[49] In a speech defending suffrage delivered in the Argentine Chamber of Deputies, Radical Party member Leopoldo Bard performed an intellectual tour de force by citing well-known advocates of women's rights in Europe and North America to support his argument. He mentioned Montesquieu and Condorcet, Alice Zimmer, Louis Marin, Hugh Lush, Gaston Brissier, Gaston Richard, Carolina Schultze, Anna Howard Shaw, and Emmeline Pankhurst. Ellen Key, John Stuart Mill, Theresa Rankin, and Carrie Chapman Catt were the sources of inspiration most frequently cited by male and female feminists of the Southern Cone, who found in their ideas suitable models for the moderate feminism that might be acceptable to South American societies.

Several major themes enable us to explore the main threads running through the debate on feminism in the Southern Cone. These themes are essential to understanding how participants understood gender relations, the role of women in social change, and the nature of feminism itself. They were also central to the strategies adopted by feminist organizations and personalities. The orchestration of these concepts to achieve specific reforms such as the revision of the civil codes and suffrage in each country is discussed in chapters 6, 8, 9, and 10.

Gender Roles: Femininity and Feminism

In femininity, feminism had a challenge from within the Southern Cone. Most of the women and men who examined the meaning and objectives of feminism ended up arguing over whether femininity could stand the challenge of feminism, and vice versa. Femininity was understood as the qualities that constituted the essence of being a woman. Those qualities were socially defined, though they were also connected with the biological functions of womanhood and motherhood: a feminine woman was charming, genteel, delicate, and selfless. Those virtues could be acquired, and women's education took their inculcation very seriously throughout the second half of the nineteenth century.[50] Women should recognize their biological destiny and their true definition in marriage and motherhood, an equation that was not new to Latin American culture but was part of an Iberian and Mediterranean heritage reinforced by Roman Catholicism. Religion stressed the worship of Mary, the mother of Christ, and womanhood was synonymous with motherhood.

Although we cannot trace the roots of this value system here, it was validated by centuries of tradition, and Italian and Spanish immigrants in Uruguay and Argentina, and German Catholics in Chile, reinforced the essential message at the end of the nineteenth century. This cultural heritage influenced opponents as well as supporters of women's liberation, who shared the belief that biological differences determined social and individual abilities and behavior and should be preserved to maintain the balance of the two genders' contributions to the social order. Mainstream feminism and socialist feminism had no quarrel over this point. Both camps rejected antagonism between men and women and pursued gender equivalence and complementarity, though their ultimate objectives differed.[51]

From the outset most feminist discussions also debated femininity, either explicitly or implicitly. Argentine lawyer and jurist Ernesto Quesada, speaking at the closing ceremony of a feminine exposition in November 1898, traced the history of feminist movements and the advancement of women's rights throughout the nineteenth century. He equated feminism with legal equality allowing women the same opportunity as men to exercise any craft or profession as well as equal access to education to guarantee their economic independence. He was dazzled by the "marvelous spectacle" of North American women: their education, their artistic and literary productions, and the equality that social customs had granted them impressed Quesada deeply. What he most admired was how the essential femininity of those women was not hurt. He encouraged Argentine women to unite in associations to teach the public that they could achieve such goals and that "feminism does not intend to masculinize women."[52]

Elvira López, the first woman to write a doctoral dissertation on feminism (1901), described feminism in Europe and the United States as a struggle to obtain the economic and legal equality of women without gender conflict. Uruguayan María Abella de Ramírez knew well how attacks against femininity could hurt feminism. "What is a woman feminist?" she asked. "Rumor has it that she knows nothing about the poetry of the home and lacks feminine charms and grace. She is accused of being useless for love and a ridiculous being from whom man should keep away. The contrary is the truth. The feminist woman is an intelligent woman who wishes to disengage her economic and social standing from that of the male of the family." Feminists did not pretend to the "absurdity" of becoming men; they wished to be men's companions or their capable mothers.[53]

To offset the negative implications of masculinization, the early feminists shone in the task of reconciling personal rights, social justice, and motherhood. Since motherhood was an affirmation of femininity, the mother who performed other social tasks could not be accused of masculinization and was the perfect expression of the potential for social change. The metaphor of motherhood was used persistently by many advocates and sympathizers to explain the goals of feminism. When Ernestina López addressed the First International Feminine Congress in 1910, she saw in women's new pursuits the triumph "of their condition as mothers." Through feminism, women would evolve toward a maternity that would not stop at nurturing their own children but would embrace all humanity.[54] Uruguayan Paulina Luisi, fervent advocate of abolishing the white slave trade, promoter of sex education, organizer of antialcohol campaigns, and indefatigable supporter of suffrage, also linked feminism's search for equality to the eventual fulfillment of motherhood as she defined the goals of the Uruguayan National Council of Women in 1917.[55] Argentine Alicia Moreau, in one of her first writings on feminism, connected the birth of feminism with the new socioeconomic conditions that had sent women into the labor force, yet without depriving them of their qualities as mothers. Working outside the home had changed the scope of women's influence. The narrowness of "home" had been superseded by the new social role of the working woman. "Feminism is not an isolated issue. . . . Even though it signifies the emancipation of woman, it cannot refer to her alone; to elevate the woman is to elevate the child, the man, the family, and humanity." Throughout her long career, she relied on this comprehensive and harmonious blending of home, motherhood, and social justice to advance the tenets of feminism and to counter attacks against the destruction of femininity and the home.[56]

Feminists never totally succeeded in removing the "masculine" label applied to their endeavors, though not necessarily to them as individuals. It was a malicious concept easily resorted to by opponents and a leitmotiv in most writings of the period. Do not emulate men at their worst, advised Argentine journalist Herminia Brumana. She claimed to support the concept of strong, capable women but spurned "feminists."[57] Brumana was a classic example of the women who supported legal and economic reforms for women but nurtured a deep prejudice against the concept of feminism, taking it as an ideology that promoted the masculinization of women and competition with men. More clearly directed against the subversion of gender roles that he saw in feminism was the attack of Uruguayan J. Fernando Carbonell. He regarded suffragist feminism as an "occupation" for only those women who "could not exercise their maternal and wifely functions. . . . The feminist is a hybrid being who does not feel maternity and, even when experiencing it physically, does not fulfill it morally, because she considers her children a burden."[58] *Marimacho,* a female cross between male and female, was a term used against feminists across Spanish America to deny their femininity and portray them as sexually deviant and therefore abhorrent.

There was in feminism, however, a powerful and positive message of service to society that not even its enemies could dismiss. That message could be captured and assimilated by any capable personality or group and put to work on ideologically safer grounds. Catholic and conservative groups needed some time to come to grips with this possibility, but by the mid-1930s they had incorporated some of the early social feminist goals and begun to reap their political fruits. As early as 1907 Catholic groups in Montevideo and Buenos Aires began to react to feminism with their own formulation that, paying lip service to gender equality, rejected any ideology that deprived women of their femininity. The female author of *Feminismo cristiano,* published in Montevideo in 1907, argued that feminism had been introduced by Christianity in that it made men and women equal while respecting their unequal mission. Healthy feminism was not the "warring feminism" that demanded for women all the rights of men. This pamphlet was praised by the bishop of Montevideo as "true feminism, the legitimate feminism that never forgets the true mission of women" and did not "intend to convert woman into another man."[59] While admitting the justice of rebelling against the stricture of unjust laws, an Argentine Catholic hoped that eventually feminism would become the gospel of the home by giving women the opportunity to achieve moral and intellectual independence and liberate themselves from constant male tutelage, and by giving them the freedom of not having to marry for economic reasons. That kind of feminism would succeed when women stopped making imperious demands on legislators and stopped aspiring to exercise functions improper to their sex.[60]

As the suffragist campaign gained momentum in the early 1920s, the Argentine anarchists entered the arena to attack feminist women, accusing them of having abandoned "the sweet mission of their sex to snatch the whip of oppression, forsaking their gracious feminine personality, and assuming a hybrid masculine behavior [hombrunamiento]."[61] Other accusations took the matter one step further. An Argentine detractor equated feminism with sexual anomaly, calling feminists women who reneged on their sex and become caricatures of men. "When women appear in public claiming for themselves a male occupation they undergo a sexual inversion; this is immoral."[62]

Under such attack, those who felt the feminist call were careful to define their position. A preamble defending their femininity was de rigueur in most feminist writings. The founders of the Chilean Partido Cívico Femenino, established in Santiago in 1922, disclaimed following those women who, in Spain and elsewhere in Hispanic America, gave the impression that feminists were "beings without sex." That "grandiose movement, . . . true feminism, does not denature women." Supporters of the party emphatically rejected the "anarchic, libertarian, and materialist feminism that threatens to rob women of their charms, converting them into neutral beings and breaking the harmonious equilibrium established by nature between the two sexes."[63] Southern Cone feminists—and their opponents—refused to disengage from the debate over the biological and psychological differences between the sexes. In fact the acceptance of feminism hinged on its reaffirming the positive contrasts between men and women before accepting their intrinsic equality.

Time did not wear out the argument of the threat to femininity. Writing in the 1930s, Chilean writer Lucía Marticorena de Martín endorsed feminism and extolled suffrage and civil equality, but she thought that "despite all equalities feminine psychology has its peculiarities. Women's activity must adjust to them to yield all its fruits."[64] Her compatriot Esmeralda Zenteno (Vera Zuroff) posited that men and women "will complete each other, as the two sides of a coin, and in that spiritual and material society . . . all responsibilities will be shared always to maintain an equilibrium."[65] Echoing her sentiments in Buenos Aires was editorialist Nelly Merino Carvallo, founder of *Mujeres de América,* who in its second issue (March–April 1933) celebrated women's new rights and new roles, warning, "We must learn how to use independence, freedom, rights, and feminism. And let us be always feminine!"[66] "Let men and women preserve their respective biological and psychological characteristics," Argentine socialist feminist Rosa Scheiner stated in 1934. Her colleague Josefina Marpons acknowledged that feminism's worst enemy was women's fear of becoming masculine if they participated in politics. Women, however, should not become men's imitators; they should use their own distinct voice to state their own truths: "To be a feminist does not mean to stop being feminine. To participate in public life we do not have to neglect our homes; quite the contrary, we will have new means to protect it. . . . There is no struggle between the sexes."[67]

Femininity in the 1930s was also a response to the discussion of "biological" and eugenic jurisprudence that reinforced the association of femininity with motherhood while attacking feminism as a denial of both. Uruguayan Darwin Peluffo Beisso was among the most determined feminist detractors, and a volume of his journalistic pieces appeared while suffrage was under discussion in his country. He hoped that his work would prevent women's gaining the vote. Peluffo Beisso argued that social relations should be based on the biological characteristics and needs of the individual, but he placed social needs above individual needs. Thus the issue was not whether women could have political rights, but whether they should. Was it convenient for society to have women engage in "biologically" male activities? Feminism had "demonstrated" that women could masculinize themselves. This was too great a sacrifice for womanhood and for the nation. If feminists rejected the option of motherhood, they were bound to lose their battle. The maternal function in women was so overwhelming, however, that he believed it would defeat any feminist distortion. The future, he opined, would bring a greater differentiation of the sexes: men would be more masculine and women more feminine, more motherly. He denied any assumption that he considered women mere reproductive machines, for he believed that mothers played a key role in inculcating moral values in the next generation.

Peluffo Beisso recommended that political activity be forbidden to women during the fertile period of their lives lest it hinder their potential maternity. Sterile women, by contrast, would have the "moral duty" of participating in politics to help the collective interests of the nation.[68]

Throughout the years the theme of motherhood became an integral part of feminist discourse as an expression of femininity, as a definer of the female mission in the home and the community, and as a qualifier for social and political action. Motherhood eventually redefined the relationship between women and the state, which would owe women protection for their nurturing of new lives. Motherhood was a key asset in supporting women's claims for empowerment, a fact that was not overlooked by any major feminist leader from María Abella de Ramírez onward. It is not surprising that Southern Cone feminists opted for a feminism that would fit into their social milieu and be acceptable to other women as well as to the men who held the reins of power. Feminism oriented toward motherhood was more than a strategy to win favorable legislation, it was an essential component of their cultural heritage: a tune that feminists not only knew how to play but wished to play.[69]

Compensatory Feminism

As she hailed the first reform of the Civil Code in Chile, Amanda Labarca, a pioneer feminist, reiterated her vision of a world where men and women retained their gender roles and were recognized for their "spiritual equality." In her inspired prose she wrote: "We do not ask for our civil equality in a tragicomic effort to be exactly like you [men]. We know that our functions are different . . . but our spirit is equal, and our ideals for the redemption of humankind are identical. We only wish to reside harmoniously with you at the same level of spiritual equality. We dislike equally the man who feminizes himself and the woman who adopts the deportment of a man."[70]

Absolute equality, if carried to its logical conclusion, could mean the loss of certain privileges that most feminists would prefer women to retain. The solution lay in a "compensatory feminism" that would go beyond mere equality to rationalize special protection. Most of the bills on women approved or debated between 1907 and the end of the 1930s in the Southern Cone were based on an implicit compensatory logic, best explained by Uruguayan essayist and philosopher Carlos Vaz Ferreira, who wrote a lengthy essay on feminism in 1915. His influence on the legislation of his country was stronger than has been assumed. He convinced Colorado Party deputy Domingo Arena to find a "just" formula for the divorce bill under discussion in 1912. He also served as inspiration to socialist deputy Emilio Frugoni's proposed reforms to the Civil Code in 1938.[71]

Vaz Ferreira proposed that the controversy over feminism rested on three issues: equal rights before the law, gender relations, and the roles of the sexes within the family. He identified the last two as the basic issues. Those people who wished to make men and women completely equal he called *hoministas*, and those who wished to maintain differences between men and women, *feministas*. His approach to gender relations and to the construction of a social philosophy of feminism was biological. The physical relationship between men and women was different for them, he posited. For men there were no consequences; women had babies. Antifeminists found this situation acceptable; feminists who only sought equality before the law ignored it. To acknowledge the difference that gender made for women and the injustices it could mean for them, was for him the essence of true feminism and the only ideological stand he would support. He called his formula compensatory feminism. Simply put, one sex had a physiological advantage and therefore society had to provide women redress by suppressing any form of subordination. Vaz Ferreira thought it was unjust to accept the notion that women could assume all the functions of men in addition to those that were intrinsically theirs. This gave them a double burden that men did not have, since they did not share the responsibilities of motherhood.

In Vaz Ferreira's universe the apex of femininity was maternity, and women tended "naturally" to marriage. He expected that, given a choice, most women would choose marriage and maternity over any other occupation. Therefore there was no reason to deny them an opportunity for education. He expounded on the desirability of having educated mothers but resorted to a Darwinian selection that would regulate the flow of women into the professions either by lack of capacity or by marriage and maternity. Some women would survive such tests and shine. Vaz Ferreira's interpretation of feminism preserved femininity and the ideal of home and maternity and gave feminists the right to enjoy more opportunities by removing legal obstacles. His feminism also protected and compensated workers, thus satisfying the socialists, while his defense of motherhood pleased the conservatives. This eclecticism provided a satisfactory answer to how to apply natural rights and justice to women within a safe framework. Compensatory feminism was flexible enough to accommodate changes in the legal and economic status of women without removing cherished differences in gender roles. Compensatory feminism, under that name or another, was possibly the most popular interpretation of feminism in the Southern Cone. Vaz Ferreira expressed what had been and would remain the ideological foundation of a large sector of feminist thought in the Southern Cone as well as in the rest of Latin America at the turn of the century. In the 1930s compensatory feminism was translated into welfare legislation and public health programs that highlighted the "mother-child dyad" to ameliorate high infant mortality and poor prenatal and postnatal care.[72]

Compensatory feminism did not seek genderless "equality" before the law. It created a gendered social space where the woman-mother's "spiritual equality" was recognized and legal reforms repaired previous inequities. Male supporters pressed the argument that the disqualification [incapacidad] of women was imposed by society and that to restore the natural rights of women the law had to undo what the law had created.[73] They were confident that reforms would not challenge gender relations. The achievement of legal equality of women and men within the family strengthened women's faculties as mothers and did not undermine men's authority or rights as head of the family. The compensation of gender-related disadvantages did not challenge men either.[74] There would be no revolution in feminism, only reparation and compensation. Most feminists were happy to go along with that.

Feminism as Political Activity

The details of how women organized to win suffrage in the Southern Cone are given in other chapters, but a general discussion of how feminists conceived of politics and their own participation deserves special attention here. The strategies feminist organizations devised to gain support for their causes hinged on their perception of how they could most effectively project them into the national arena.

Although feminists spent a great deal of energy on social reform schemes and did not begin to focus on political rights until the late 1910s, they became more involved in national politics in the 1920s and 1930s. An inevitable process of maturation led them to understand the mechanisms necessary to obtain the changes they pursued. Before 1920 suffrage was not a priority for feminists and reformers in the Southern Cone because they had a nationality but limited citizenship. By definition nationality was acquired at birth—or by adoption through legal mechanisms. Political citizenship was acquired or confirmed by qualifying for suffrage, and suffrage was limited by several requirements, including literacy, property, or service in the army. The constitutions of these three nations mentioned citizens, but the use of the generic male article el before "citizen" left no doubt in men's minds that women were not included. This point had been much debated by jurists since the late nineteenth century. The ambiguity of the situation allowed some feminists to argue that a literal interpretation of electoral laws or even the constitutions did not explicitly exclude women from suffrage. This was the line argued by María Abella de Ramírez in 1910 and adopted by Dra. Julieta Lanteri in 1911 when she requested a certificate of citizenship.[75] This was simply a strategy to demonstrate the law's lack of logic. Women did not win suffrage by pursuing this point.

The political climate of these nations did not provide a natural setting for women to exercise political rights until the end of the 1910s. In Argentina, after years of regional fragmentation and caudillismo, the nation was finally put together in the early 1870s under a nominal federal constitution dominated by the capital, Buenos Aires, and strong executives. At the turn of the century the political scene was controlled by rural and mercantile oligarchies. Electoral participation was low and plagued by corruption. The many foreign immigrants residing in Buenos Aires and certain rural colonies had to register for the draft as a precondition for citizenship. As a consequence most did not have voting rights. This changed after the enactment of male universal compulsory suffrage effective in 1916, when the populist Radical Party took power. Chile had maintained a stable political system since the 1850s under authoritarian presidents. In 1891 there was a successful challenge to presidential power, with a subsequent shift toward an elitist parliament under the influence of a landed oligarchy and successful entrepreneurs. Although the constitutional rhythm was respected, electoral corruption and minimal voter participation were commonplace at the turn of the century. Urbanization and mining wealth created an urban middle class and a proletariate that lacked a political outlet until the election of Arturo Alessandri in 1920. Throughout and beyond this period, suffrage was limited by a literacy requirement. Uruguay had been torn by caudillos throughout the nineteenth century; in the early years of the twentieth it had finally achieved a political compromise that allowed one "progressive" majority (the Colorado Party) to exercise power for two decades. Universal male suffrage was not yet a reality and was achieved only through reforms drafted between 1912 and 1918 and put into effect from 1916 to 1920.[76]

Cultural traditions of gender roles buttressed male dominance over politics. At the end of the nineteenth century some experts on constitutional law either regarded political activity as incompatible with the natural functions of women at home or wished to see married women excluded from suffrage.[77] Opposition to women's suffrage claimed that politics was a "virile activity" and that women need not participate to be useful to society.[78] Most nonfeminist women's magazines accepted that reasoning. For example, the biweekly *La Mujer,* published in the Chilean town of Curicó in 1898, assumed a conservative line and published articles by men extolling traditional virtues. A celebration of women's work as educators argued that the obligations of motherhood should keep them out of politics.[79] The few men who expressed contrary opinions argued that social reform would be impossible without revising women's political status.[80] If most men were averse to suffrage before 1910, educated middle-class turn-of-the-century women thought that suffrage might be desirable but had serious doubts about its being attainable soon. Hence they focused on other issues, counting on the evolution of attitudes to change the situation. Instead of politics they wrote on education, the great equalizer. Peruvian-born novelist Clorinda Matto de Turner, who lived several years in Buenos Aires and edited *El Búcaro Americano,* wrote genteel pieces praising women's intellect and applauding the men who lent their support to "the grandiose task of women's redemption through work and science, crowned by virtue."[81]

Education, which in the second half of the nineteenth century had been regarded by many women as the only route to intellectual equality, was never considered sufficient qualification for political rights by antisuffragists. Early in the twentieth century the first professional women began to realize that education did not guarantee access to decision making let alone politics. Opponents of women's suffrage argued that women were not well enough educated in "citizenship" and emotional control to vote. The persistence of these arguments caused hesitation among some educated women. Unión y Labor, a Buenos Aires group of professional women engaged in social work, was not enthusiastic about suffrage. The editorial board believed some women wanted to go too fast. Argentine women, they argued, had to be prepared to exercise the vote "consciously and effectively." In 1911, having run several articles on female suffrage, they reiterated that their intention was not to encourage women on the voting issue, but to inform their readers about the progress achieved by other societies. One of the ablest members of the group, Sara Justo, denounced the idea of women's "aping" men. There was an intellectual search for a genuine gender-based definition of political activity that was still elusive and slightly confusing.[82]

The search for meaning continued at the First International Feminine Congress. Peruvian J. María Samamé argued that the law had gone too far in "protecting" women and isolating them from civic life. On the eve of a new era when democracy would be the ruling political ideology, women could not be excluded from participation. Argentine Raquel Messina, representing the Socialist Feminine Center, claimed to speak for the "popular women who work and think" and demanded universal suffrage for *both* sexes, since most men in the country did not enjoy it. Suffrage was particularly relevant for working women, who, deprived of political rights, were reduced to begging men for social reforms. María Josefa González, of the National League of Freethinking Women, accused women of inertia and apathy. Women could ill afford to remain indifferent to their destiny and ignore the fact that only suffrage would give them the power to change the laws that subordinated them. Ana A. de Montalvo followed nineteenth-century liberalism in arguing that women's claims for political rights were based on justice and equity. Since women worked, paid taxes, and were considered equal to men in the enforcement of penal justice, they should vote. If men "paid" with military service for their right to vote, women paid with maternity and with the sacrifice of their children to war. Women were prepared and ready to vote, but without unity their isolated efforts would bear no fruit. These papers blended liberal and socialist arguments for suffrage, placing on women themselves the responsibility for rescuing their rights.[83]

The bridge between feminism and suffrage was not easy to build.[84] Reluctance to accept suffrage as a female right began to diminish in the 1910s. After World War I, suffragist movements in Europe and North America, reinforced by the emergent populism and the democratization of the electoral system in the Southern Cone, made suffrage an attractive issue whose time seemed to have arrived. Beginning in 1917 feminist women and women's organizations in the capitals of the three nations began to reassess their position. It was not a difficult task, given earlier efforts of women such as María Abella de Ramírez, Elvira Rawson de Dellepiane, the socialists' stand on the rights of women, and the drift of electoral reforms in the three nations. One of the best summations was written by Alicia Moreau, an editor of the socialist feminist magazine *Nuestra Causa*, founded in 1919. *Nuestra Causa* welcomed collaborations from feminists of all political orientations, and its message was at the crossroads of Argentine feminism. Suffrage, as Moreau saw it, was a right that belonged to anybody paying taxes. It was a tool for expressing and defending one's basic rights, and it would permit women to elect those who represented their interests, including legislation on education, child care, labor regulation, and alcoholism. The time was ripe, and women were ready. The 800,000 women who earned their living in Argentina offered the most decisive argument on their own behalf.[85]

The preoccupation with measuring productivity and worth in terms of money suggests that the men and women who supported female suffrage knew the effectiveness of an argument the labor movement used to make its way into the politics of power. A feminist socialist like Alicia Moreau was sensitive to the fact that women's work remained undervalued and underpaid. Reiterating its significance was essential so that working women themselves would become aware of their participation in the economy and drive home the message to men within the family and the nation. The state could not ignore and demean women's "admirable effort" on its behalf and should grant them the right to vote.[86]

At the crossroads of involvement in the politics of suffrage, Southern Cone feminists had to face not just fear or apathy among women but active opposition as well. In theory the intellectual opposition to female suffrage declined after World War I, but in practice it remained a powerful factor through the 1930s. Reluctance was often expressed subtly. Suffrage could be accepted in principle as feasible and even desirable, but many men and women argued that it hinged on the *level* of female education and that most women were still not ready for it. Argentine Isabel Salthou, discussing feminism and political militancy, believed that educated women who would know how to vote were a minority. Most women were impressionable and weak and lacked enough education: "Although there are many ignorant men who vote, to add all ignorant women to their ranks would cause a greater problem." Argentine women were demanding suffrage without considering whether they had achieved a complete education or perfected their maternal roles. Political militancy preferably should fall to single women or those who had no aptitude for motherhood.[87] Writing from the Argentine city of San Luis, a man lamented the idea of women's entering the corrupted political struggle and abandoning their noble role in the family. He argued that rural women depended too much on men (they would vote like them) and lacked the civic culture of more advanced nations. Yet most high-class women, he argued, were not interested in suffrage either, "the exception being the feminist, who egotistically enjoys success before the crumbling feminine altar."[88]

To disprove such misconceptions was the task of women's associations and parties. These groups had to create a political culture for women and to make it acceptable to the men who would decide the future of suffrage. At least four types of associations were created from 1919 onward. There were the presuffrage "parties" founded in the 1920s before suffrage was approved anywhere in the Southern Cone, such as the Argentine Partido Feminista Nacional and the Chilean Partido Cívico Femenino. There were associations to promote suffrage as a cause and integrate women into existing political parties, such as the Argentine Asociación Pro-Derechos de la Mujer and the Chilean Unión Femenina de Chile. After Uruguay granted women the right to vote in national elections in December 1932 and Chile extended the municipal vote in March 1933, several women's parties sought to mobilize the female electorate, such as the Uruguayan Partido Independiente Democrático Feminista. Finally, in the mid-1930s there were umbrella organizations that promoted strength through union, seeking to make women visible as an interest group and press for social and economic reforms. Such was the Chilean Movimiento Pro-Emancipación de las Mujeres de Chile (MEMCH), organized in 1935.[89]

Most of these organizations purported to be feminist, and all tried to mobilize women for a more active political role. Yet as they defined their goals, they reflected the prevailing opinion in each country, and their "feminism" had many nuances. Argentine and Uruguayan organizations developed at a time when feminism had strong advocates among men and brilliant leaders among women. Argentina's political climate in the late 1910s was agitated by restless labor and by student movements. Uruguay had embarked on political experimentation with a new constitutional formula. Chilean feminist organizations jelled at a slower pace, but the seeds of change were sowed by the confrontation of the executive and the legislative powers in 1924, which led to rewriting the constitution. Although neither Uruguay nor Chile incorporated female suffrage into its constitution, the political ferment was propitious to the emergence of female constituents.

The first step in redefining women's traditional role in society was the organization of women's "parties" to give women the opportunity to train in politics. Two parties were founded in Buenos Aires in 1920, the Partido Humanista, by Adelia de Carlo, and the Partido Feminista Nacional, the brainchild of Julieta Lanteri. The latter was the first to go beyond the legalistic goals of feminism and address broad economic and social issues affecting not just women, to prove that women were capable of thinking of politics in national terms.[90]

Women-only political parties and female activist organizations had a great appeal to Southern Cone women. The working women who joined socialist parties as well as those who participated in "women's wings" of traditional parties were not free to formulate objectives departing from the party's main ideological stand. Although they had the right to speak for the party, they remained in a woman's niche. Strict behavioral codes about mingling of the sexes in public were beginning to relax in the 1920s, but the women founding and joining these parties or joining women's organizations had been brought up under the old rules. Within the female parties women felt comfortable and free from masculine influence in determining their course of action and their own goals.

A strong sense of solidarity was common. An almost imponderable faith in women's ability to change their nations' future permeated the editorials and articles in their magazines. Images of women helping their sisters to lift the weight of prejudice and exploitation, women's own enlightened spirits rising from the dead body of ignorance, hands breaking their shackles, vessels sailing ahead, and the sun of a new day shining over female heads embellished the covers of these publications. They signified the liberation the editors saw ahead. For women, what mattered most was to discover themselves, argued Adelia de Carlo in 1920.[91]

There was a significant difference between parties as a means to political participation, and the parties that really attempted to gather women as a voting bloc. Before suffrage, women's parties were exercises in organization and mobilization to lobby for political rights and other causes. After municipal suffrage was achieved in Chile and complete suffrage in Uruguay, the exercise had to be carried out in men's terrain, and it was real. The challenge was picked up by several organizations in both countries. One women's party that typifies liberal middle-class feminism was founded by Uruguayan Sara Rey Alvarez, an active feminist and suffragist. Rey Alvarez saw limitless possibilities for women in public service and envisioned nothing short of a total transformation of the social structure. In January 1933 she launched the Partido Independiente Democrático Feminista. Its platform was written entirely by a group of feminists, and it addressed a number of national political issues, discussed in the party's magazine *Ideas y Acción*. But for all its intellectual adroitness, it failed to get any candidate elected in the 1938 national election.[92]

Few of the female parties active in the 1930s became true political organizations capable of having their candidates elected without the support of traditional male parties. This failure does not negate their success in mobilizing unprecedented numbers of women and giving their members political direction in a very confusing decade. Their strength lay in their appeal to women who sought to engage in politics but were reluctant to mingle with men in traditional parties. Yet that strength was also a weakness. Women-only organizations—whether parties or activist institutions—relied on contradictory appeals. They claimed to have political objectives, yet they insisted on calling themselves "apolitical" and engaged in worthy civic causes. Even when their "civic" objectives were political in nature, such as pursuing the reform of the Civil Codes or suffrage, female groups cultivated an image of disinterest, above the sweat and mud of male politics. Perhaps this attitude was admissible at the turn of the century, but in the 1930s refusing to accept politics on the same premises as men perpetuated the idea of female political leaders as oddities and lessened their potential for exerting power in national politics.

In the early 1930s traditional male parties either organized their own "feminine" wings to protect their stake in politics and gain votes or rejected the idea of female parties outright. Socialists in particular had a special ax to grind. The programs of the few women's parties that attempted to act as serious political entities were heavily oriented toward public welfare, and socialists argued that they offered a better tool for social reform. If socialism was not their choice, however, any political party would be better than women-only parties. That was the opinion of Uruguayan socialist senator Pablo María Minelli, who in 1933 advised Argentine and Uruguayan women not to subscribe to exclusively female parties.[93] Other socialists had only bitter criticism for the foundation of the Uruguayan Partido Independiente Democrático Feminista. They claimed that its members were making laughingstocks of themselves, aping "the grotesque type of the famous Mrs. Pankhurst, the caricatured English suffragette."[94] There were nonsocialist critics as well. Uruguayan journalist Zulma Núñez, founder of the feminist magazine *América Nueva,* resorted to old arguments of gender roles to attack women's parties. A woman's party simply mimicked men's parties, creating "an absurd situation of battle between the sexes." Women should join established parties. Clotilde Luisi attacked the idea of a "feminist party in opposition to men's parties, because it opened an absurd and egotistic cleavage, in open struggle with the highest ideals of solidarity, peace, and mutual understanding."[95]

Seeing nothing wrong with an apolitical stand, most Southern Cone feminists remained firm in their belief that "feminism cannot become an increment to the existing political parties. . . . Feminism is not a political party."[96] For them the integrity of female organizations depended on their being anchored in gender and having an overarching ethical purpose. In 1933 Adela Edwards de Salas, a conservative upper-class Chilean leader, called for a consolidation of all female civic and feminist associations, regardless of political ideas, to address national problems. As women, she wrote, we "need to break our dependence on male influences and the ties to political parties and form one block: the feminine."[97] Argentine and Uruguayan feminists shared the Chileans' feeling that men's political parties lost much time creating rhetorical smoke screens and that women would waste their time and energy joining the establishment. To be effective, they had to remain separate from traditional political parties—and attempt a reordering of politics from the pedestal of their own flawless cleanliness.

Most liberal or mainstream feminists believed that within women-only organizations they could formulate and carry out changes that would bear their gender's imprint. Association with men would dilute or even inhibit their effectiveness in solving problems for the benefit of other women and children. The characterization of "apolitical" that feminists preferred to apply to their endeavors did not, in their eyes, signify a rejection of politics, but was a way of creating authority for themselves and earning men's respect.

Feminism as Moral and Social Reform

In the early 1920s, when socialist and mainstream feminists began to de-lineate their role in the public arena, they planned to build a new order in society and in politics, yet one anchored in traditional values. Southern Cone feminists extended women's role at home to society at large and used motherhood as the path to active participation in public life throughout the late 1930s—and beyond. The "innate female qualities"—those ineffable attributes exploited by all sides—were called forward to serve the general cause of social reform and to validate women's presence in politics. Their presumed "higher sensitivity" to others' feelings and their higher sense of moral duty were the bases for their claim to a place in the sun. Women would be the ones to eradicate vice, rectify injustice, and create a more equitable society in the Southern Cone.

Altruism was a word much used in the 1920s to describe women's capacity to give themselves to the causes of others. It was the opposite of egotism—sometimes described as male and ascribed to men in politics—and it was enhanced by motherhood. Women's moral superiority did not depend exclusively on that function, however: it belonged to them as a gender. This belief in the greater ability of women to tackle moral issues was shared by male feminists. When male suffrage supporters introduced their bills in the three nations, they argued that women would inject moral values into politics and strengthen the social order by defending family, motherhood, and childhood.[98] Women's altruism was also the basis of their ability to deal with children and other "weak" or needy social elements. In 1924 Uruguayan feminist Mathea Falco defined feminism in Uruguay as "more than a beautiful hope. It is the beginning of a great work . . . of social improvement, channeled through love to redeem people, and geared toward dignity and the consecration of truly human values. Feminism will triumph because its task is to heal all misery and all social vices. Only a woman's heart is capable of feeling, of sacrificing, and of renunciation."[99] This female sensitivity was a social construct already accepted as the motto for the First International Feminine Congress. The moral ethos was strengthened by a sense of duty and service that women had acquired through many years of education oriented toward serving the family.

Southern Cone socialist and liberal feminists also adopted the cause of world peace since the end of the First World War, and they returned to this issue with vigor in the mid-1930s as the threat of fascism and Nazism began to loom. Male social reformers (socialists and "liberals" from established parties) sided with women against the rise of military dictators and the somber prospect of corporatist societies in Europe. They had plenty of reasons to worry about their own future as conservatism gained the upper hand in politics, eventually leading to military interventions in the early 1930s. Feminist values were contrasted with the inflexible interpretation of gender roles favored by the military, the ultranationalists, and the corporatists. The rejection of militarism became more vocal when Bolivia and Paraguay entered a war for the Chaco region in 1935. Argentina and Brazil were officially nonparticipants but had antagonistic interests in the outcome. After 1936 the Spanish civil war gave Southern Cone feminists the opportunity to express their political rejection of all sorts of oppression and inhumanity generated by men. Alicia Moreau extended the rejection of totalitarian regimes to Hitler and Germany at the close of the decade.[100]

In the early 1930s reform politicians expressed their confidence in women's special ethical mission and their ability to use their maternal interests to lead their nations to a thorough social reform. A socially oriented feminism was used as a rational defense of women's rights by men in the public arena, and it gave women access to the press, to men in the legislative chambers, and to other women. Most women feminists believed they were feminine and embodied the most advanced expression of womanhood, at the service of their families and the nation. Suffrage, the ultimate accolade and the key to gaining a voice in social reform, was almost within reach. Their belief that they could change the contours of political life was infectious. In Argentina, *Mujeres de América* began to publish its feminist message for suffrage by restating that "from a practical viewpoint the vote will place women in an advantageous position and face to face with civic life. Women will contribute part of their bounty of goodness to the political battle. They will smooth more than one rough corner and will contribute to bringing peace to the belligerent spirits [of men] when they lose their self-restraint."[101] This utopian worldview and self-view reached a peak in the 1930s and was enhanced by access to political participation in Chile and Uruguay, while it kept alive Argentine women's hopes of reaching that goal. The message did not fade through the early 1940s, and it still resonated in the political discourse of the women and men who achieved national suffrage in Argentina and Chile in the 1940s.

Feminism meant different things to different people, and any attempt to define that meaning must rely heavily on writings and efforts aimed at proposed goals as well as the changing social, economic, and political features. Early twentieth-century socialists mobilized female workers, and they first regarded feminism as any women's endeavor to organize within their ideological and class parameters. Anarchists did not venture beyond the confines of class, and their main contribution was to enhance the concept of women's personal freedom vis-à-vis society and men. Socialists had a very broad social agenda that in time became flexible enough to accommodate other social views as long as the welfare of the working people was not jeopardized. Their contribution to the pool of ideas on gender relations was significant, but their main role was to inject economic and class consciousness into the male middle-class reformers' dry, legalistic approach to gender equality. By exposing the working conditions of women and children and the inequity of salaries for male and female workers, they shaped and strengthened a sense of social mission among liberal-nurtured feminists.

Mainstream liberal feminists who organized women's associations, published newspapers and essays, paid visits to legislators, and sat in the galleries of Congress during the discussion of legislation on the Civil Codes or divorce or discussed such reforms from the Congress floor, added a valuable dimension. They were legalistic and socially oriented at the same time. Their first target was the legal shackles of the past, such as laws restricting women's rights within marriage and denying them access to certain professions. For them feminism was modernity and freedom. Modernity meant recasting assumptions about women's capabilities in twentieth-century terms. Freedom signified removal of all the legal encumbrances that hampered women as persons. These were moral necessities for a redefinition of a new female self. By demanding the recognition of a woman's personality, Southern Cone feminists, despite their reluctance to radically alter the bases of gender relationships, slowly eroded men's patriarchal grip on the family. We should not exaggerate the depth of such changes, but we cannot deny that the politics of the family and marriage began to change as reform legislation was enforced. Under the influence of left-oriented feminists who joined their struggle, most liberal feminists developed a sensitivity to social problems that better defined their mission — of social reform within or outside a political framework.

A political framework had developed by 1920. The suffrage campaign gave all feminists the opportunity to refine their objectives and project their ideas beyond their own organizations, with the valued support of a dedicated group of men. The campaign brought together women from all walks of life and drew the men and women involved much closer. Since the mid-1910s men who chose to debate or endorse women's interests knew there was a growing public that was willing to listen and a political situation favorable to their pursuits. Political involvement bridged many gaps between the genders and among women themselves, although it did not dispel class distinctions. Most women's organizations were led by middle-class educated women rather than working women, and it was such women who gained access to politics. This class status also applied to most male political parties and to politics in general, except the radical Left. Nonetheless, the intersection of gender and class within feminism did not produce disruptive encounters because the leaders deftly averted confrontation. Middle-class feminists learned much from their exposure to poverty, illegitimacy, and disease. The concept of social service careers was largely a triumph of early feminist analysis over their own class. They did not change the social structure, but they began to do something about it.

Another key element in the earlier definition of feminism, whether among working or professional women, was freedom for their gender. In their many writings they defined that freedom not as Freedom, but as many freedoms parceled out in specific areas of life and relationships. Perhaps the most important was the self-respect they gained as they recognized they could discern, without male aid, what was good for themselves, their marriages, their children, and their future. It was an ability some disputed until the bitter end, but even those who attacked feminism were eventually forced to accept the moral premises of those freedoms. Friends and enemies, however, assimilated the morality of the principles with the moral capacity of women themselves, injecting a grandiose teleological scheme as social redeemers. In that role women were forced to subsume individual freedoms to social service and social reform. The cultivation of the "self" had not been part of their education. They defined freedom in terms of being useful to themselves, to their families, and to society. Armed with that assumption, women claimed personal freedom to help carry out reforms much needed by society.

Social service required the abrogation of laws that limited individual rights, and it liberated women from social and family restrictions. The reconciliation of the individual with the familial and with social interests occurred through the cultivation of gender-specific qualifications, through the icon of motherhood. In the Latin American societies of the 1920s and 1930s, the perception that women had superior aptitude for the stoic and the noble relied on long-accepted social conventions that such qualities belong to women qua women and mothers. Mixing the modernity they pursued with values deeply rooted in the culture of the area was the peculiar imprint of Southern Cone — and Latin American — feminists. Some things were not negotiable; others were simply unnecessary to define the new freedoms and the new women. Public violence was unnecessary; the English and North American models of street demonstrations were not for them. They also opted not to create gender antagonism and to abide by the formula of sex equity and orderly change. They made this choice because the price of family and motherhood was not negotiable. They could see a useful and satisfying social and political role exercising the qualities they believed made them different from men. Although we may not share their conviction that separate spheres of power and authority provide the right answer to women's plight, they drew much strength and considerable success from their beliefs.

CHAPTER 2

Labor and Feminism:
Foundations of Change

Nothing could have been further from the mind of a woman toiling in a sweatshop about 1910 than feminism or social change. The scenario was much the same whether it was Santiago, Buenos Aires, or Montevideo. She had to sit in front of a sewing machine or stand at an industrial textile machine for eight to ten hours, with only a short break for lunch. Lighting and ventilation were poor, and cotton or wool dust made the air heavy. Toilet facilities were limited. Women working in tobacco and cigarette manufacturing plants had to wash the floors and machinery after work and move packages after closing hours.[1] The pay was sometimes less than one peso a day, but low as the wages were, they could make a difference in the family budget, since male workers were increasingly unable to cover their families' living expenses.[2] The only change many women workers had in mind was never to have to return to work.

Women's increasing participation in the labor market at the turn of the century prompted many thoughts on their new economic capacity. Female labor had different meanings for different people. Middle-class observers commented on women's "economic independence" and saw it as the foundation of feminism. Jurists justified the reform of the Civil Codes to give women full juridical recognition based on their labor. For feminists, especially socialist feminists, female urban labor had a different meaning. They saw the inequality of wages between men and women and the lack of consideration for women's safety threatening to them as persons and as the mothers of future generations. The political significance of women's work was quickly understood by socialists, feminists, and social reformers, who argued that women who worked and paid taxes were entitled to full voting rights. As an economic issue male socialists and anarchists had mixed feelings about women's work. There was potential value in their helping to organize resistance groups and unions. On the other hand, women offered "unfair" competition because they worked for less and displaced men from certain occupations. Women empowered by earning wages could threaten the stability of the family and the authority of the husband.[3]

Since the 1870s the intellectual elite of the three countries had debated how educated women could serve society as enlightened mothers, educators, and coworkers. Women who could earn their own living were better protected against poverty should their husbands or fathers die.[4] Seen as an exceptional circumstance rather than a need, this view of women's work did not really fit the starker realities that began to take shape in urban centers of the three nations in the early twentieth century. Nonetheless, women's entrance into the labor market began putting a value on their work, whether fair or not, and whether their work was exploited, restricted, or bolstered by those who discussed it. By 1920 female labor had become an economic and political issue, transcending the boundaries of the home but still heavily charged with the emotions surrounding family issues.

An analysis of the labor force and the demand for women laborers can verify whether claims made for female labor as liberating were appropriate or whether feminists and the Left had an accurate understanding of reality. I focus mostly on blue-collar work because it was the most socially and politically controversial. It was also the target of the gender-oriented legislation that created special rewards for working women, reinforced the cult of motherhood in society, and linked women and children to public health issues. The overview of the labor force also explains why some saw female labor as contradictory to home values, whereas for others it reaffirmed women's best contributions to their nation's future. .

Women as Numbers in the Labor Force

The sight of women hurrying toward work became increasingly familiar in the capital cities of the Southern Cone. These were not middle-class women working in comfortable places; they were working women leaving uncomfortable homes in tenements to work in even less comfortable factories. Men who reached adulthood in the first decade of the century, under nineteenth-century mores, perceived women as mothers, sisters, or daughters in the safe environment of the home. The erosion of that image created an emotional climate that made female industrial labor a political issue.[5]

At the beginning of the twentieth century, women urban workers in the

Southern Cone bore all the characteristics of a labor force catering to incipient industrial development. They were employed in two large sectors: domestic work and urban industries such as textiles, garments, tobacco, matches, shoemaking, and food processing. Temporary labor in agriculture was open to women in Chile and Argentina, where they helped pick fruit. By 1920 department stores, telephone companies, and pharmaceutical companies required women workers, and the governments of the three nations provided some clerical jobs. In all cases, women's chief asset lay in the cheapness of their services and their reliability.

In theory all working women lacked a legal condition for employment during their minority—being under *patria potestad,* their fathers' authority —and after marriage, when that authority passed to their husbands. In the three countries this meant that women technically should have been required to prove the express permission of fathers or husbands when seeking employment. In practice few employers required any proof, and women had few restrictions in nonprofessional jobs. Other regulations applied to female work. Some government jobs required official "citizenship," understood narrowly as the right to vote. Lacking that right, women who had been occupying some skilled positions since the late 1910s were illegally employed, though they were rarely challenged.

Women's and children's earnings became critical in the volatile economic situation that affected the three countries in the 1890s. The financial crisis of 1890–93 pushed wages down for over a decade and forced more women to work.[6] The immigrants providing manual labor in Montevideo and Argentina were mostly male, but enough women arrived to be counted in national statistics and noted for the special trades they engaged in.[7] These foreign women did not significantly alter the structure of the female labor market, which had already been defined by native-born women. The female immigrants who came with their families remained as part of the families' working or settlement patterns. Those who came alone were, often enough, associated with prostitution.[8] Chile had no great influx of foreign workers; its migration was internal, from rural to urban areas and from the central valley to the mines of the north. Although women were not part of the mining labor force, their significance for the development of other industries on the Santiago-Valparaíso axis was much the same as in Argentina and Uruguay. The issue was not one of nationality but of economics and gender.[9]

National and provincial censuses, and those issued by departments—or offices—of labor and industry, furnish data on gender distribution between 1890 and 1920. The information is generally reliable, although not homogeneous. After 1920 the information sags badly and there are only fragmentary data that do not cover all aspects of the labor market. Comparing the three countries is difficult and at times impossible: the classification of occupations varied from country to country and even from one census to another within the same country. Also, although Chile maintained a regular census Argentina and Uruguay did not, creating information gaps impossible to fill and undermining any thorough assessment of labor composition.[10] Despite these problems, there are common threads that let us compare the three nations and enough data to give a general view of the labor market.

The occupational pattern shows a strong gender imprint in the three countries. Homebound women were classified as housewives, and so national censuses characterized them as "without occupation" even though thousands of them contributed significantly to the family's economy by working at home. Labor Department officials realized this and were able to define and investigate the working conditions of industrial piecework at home. Industrial work and teaching were the most readily identifiable and measurable occupations, however, and they are better reflected in the national censuses.

Women's Labor in Argentina: Statistical Profile

Argentina began to employ women and children as soon as the country began to industrialize in the late 1860s. Before then the nation had no large industry, and the weaving and dyeing of cloth and the manufacturing of soap, oil, and candles, to name a few products, were often in the hands of women as cottage industries.[11] In 1873 a wool textile plant near Buenos Aires employed 60–100 workers, reported as "mostly women and children."[12] Another source of employment for women was the garment industry, which began to develop seriously after 1885. In that same year Dell'Acqua, a textile factory, employed about 200 workers, also mostly women and children, who worked eleven hours a day. A manufacturer of handbags, La Primitiva, had one plant in the capital and another in Rosario, employing almost exclusively women at 50 to 80 centavos a day for a ten- to fourteen-hour working day. The match factory Compañía General de Fósforos employed 220 women and 50 men in 1888. Women also worked in sugar refining plants in Rosario.[13]

Two relatively close national censuses in 1895 and 1914 delineated the growth of female labor and its occupational categories, despite the disparity of their classifications. Between 1895 and 1914 women's participation in the industrial and commercial sectors of the economy was striking (see table 1).

TABLE 1   Composition of the Labor Force in Argentina, 1895 and 1914

Occupation	1914		1895	
	Male	Female	Male	Female
Agriculture	488,288	41,578	326,504	67,444
Industries, manual arts	488,238	352,999	185,357	180,730
Commerce	272,429	21,217	133,141	10,222
Transportation	109,156	1,618	62,617	3,389
Service	35,908	182,711	23,630	199,144
Public administration	102,573	6,279	23,686	248
Health professions	10,395	4,368	3,550	1,396
Education	39,544	43,640	11,151	7,207
Arts and sciences	20,287	1,713	4,596	581

Source: Adaptation of the 1895 and 1914 censuses in Elena Gil, *La mujer en el mundo del trabajo* (Buenos Aires: Libera, 1970), 43.

The 1914 census ranked service after industrial labor, but this conclusion is suspicious; no subsequent data agreed with it. The intercensal decline in female rural work reflects a trend that would consolidate throughout the twentieth century. The growth of women in education is significant, since teaching was a favorite choice for middle-class women at the turn of the century. Women also advanced considerably in "public administration"— employment in federal or provincial administrative offices. Under health professions one finds mostly midwives, not physicians, and the expansion here was a sign not of social change, but of concern with public health.

Two labor censuses of the capital in 1904 and 1909 offer data for measuring the changes in the nation's most complex labor market. The number of men and women with an established profession or occupation increased between 1904 and 1909. While the number of men with an occupation rose roughly 50 percent, from 312,718 to 462,352, the number of women doubled from 104,114 to 223,769. The percentage of females who were economically productive grew rapidly, from 25.1 percent of the total in 1904 to 32.6 percent in 1909. This implied a commensurate decline in male workers from 75 to 67.3 percent.[14] Focusing more specifically on the personnel working in manufacturing, the increase of women in the industrial sector was not quite as sharp (see table 2).

The increase of women in the labor force was in nonindustrial areas, as data for 1909 show (table 3). "Manual arts" in the 1909 census is an undefinable category that probably comprised seamstresses working under the

TABLE 2   Industrial Workers in Buenos Aires, 1904 and 1909

Sex	1904	1909	Increase
Male	55,435	76,976	21,541
Female	13,077	16,187	3,110
Total	68,512	93,163	24,651

Source: Buenos Aires, *Censo general de población, edificación, comercio e industrias*, 3 vols. (Buenos Aires: Compañia Sudamericana de Billetes de Banco, 1910), 1:lxxxiv.

TABLE 3   Buenos Aires Labor Statistics, 1909

Occupation	Male	Female	%	Total
Agriculture	6,701	377	5.3	7,078
Industries, manual arts	166,048	51,629	23.7	217,677
Commerce	109,153	12,594	10.3	121,747
Transportation	21,343	544	2.4	21,887
Service	14,101	136,473	90.6	150,574
Government, administration	4,024	1,481	26.9	5,505
Liberal professions	11,156	1,946	14.8	13,102
Education (Including students)	10,137	5,482	35.1	15,619

Source: Argentina, National Department of Labor, no. 16 (March 1911): 24–31; Buenos Aires, *Censo general* 1:li–liii.

putting-out system. The main industrial occupations for working women of all ages were manufacturing shirts, knitwear, corsets, stockings, raffia and leather shoes, chocolates and cookies, printing, and doing dry cleaning. Most other women worked in the service sector, as domestics.[15]

Buenos Aires was the center of all industrial and political organization, and its figures do not reflect the circumstances in smaller cities. The city of Rosario, in the province of Santa Fé, had almost as many women employed in industry and commerce as in domestic service. But in La Plata, the provincial capital of the province of Buenos Aires, the predominance of women in the personal service sector was overwhelming. Other "unclassified" occupations — probably housewives — formed the bulk of the working population. The census gives no clue to the possible occupation of the "unclassified" male population (see table 4).[16]

The national census of 1914 showed an uneven profile of industrial employment in the nation (table 5). In the cities listed above, between 90 and

TABLE 4   La Plata Occupational Profile, 1909

Occupation	Male	Female	%	Total
Industries, manual arts	6,531	1,575	19.4	8,106
Commerce	4,708	310	6.1	5,010
Personal service	532	14,520	96.4	15,052
Administration	4,362	132	2.9	4,494
Professions	985	139	12.3	1,124
Education	700	855	55.1	1,551
Unclassified other	11,586	10,256	46.9	21,842

Source: Argentina, Provincia de Buenos Aires, Censo general de la ciudad de La Plata (La Plata: Popular, 1910), xxxix. Population over fifteen years of age.

TABLE 5   Women Employed in Key Industries, 1914

	Food	Garment/ Toiletries	Chemical	Textiles	Other
Buenos Aires (21,142)	1,409	10,508	577	4,738	3,910
BAP[a] (11,494)	6,148	1,934	1,455	913	1,044
Santa Fe (4,216)	1,935	1,410	34	116	721
Córdoba (6,754)	1,336	951	105	36	110
Mendoza (1,408)	1,055	344	5	—	4

Source: Argentina, Tercer censo nacional (Buenos Aires: Rosso, 1917), 7, passim.
[a]Buenos Aires Province.

93 percent of the women in industrial work were in five occupational categories. The number of industrial employees in this census is well below that of the 1909 occupational census of Buenos Aires, and these figures are questionable. Considerable underrepresentation was confessed by the director of the national census operations.[17] A 1917 industrial labor census of 3,520 factories in the capital showed that women made up 18.2 percent of the industrial labor force. Together with children they constituted 21.2 percent, or close to one-quarter, of industrial workers.[18] Unfortunately we lack labor information for the 1920s and 1930s comparable in quality to that provided by previous national and provincial reports, as was acknowledged by the Labor Department in 1934.[19] A 1939 national industrial census showed that women holding blue- and white-collar jobs in the federal capital and the province of Buenos Aires were over one-third of the labor force. The provinces lagged behind, as they had at the turn of the century. Nationwide, women made up

TABLE 6   Number of Persons Employed
in Industrial Establishments in Argentina, 1939

	Employees (White-Collar)			Workers (Blue-Collar)		
	Male	*Female*	*%*	*Male*	*Female*	*%*
Federal capital	30,644	4,108	11.8	199,715	69,190	25.7
Buenos Aires Province	14,278	904	6.0	141,027	53,286	27.4
Córdoba	2,882	266	8.4	25,501	2,118	7.7
Entre Ríos	1,357	78	5.4	13,063	1,126	7.9
Mendoza	1,634	45	2.7	13,563	748	5.2
Santa Fe	5,922	292	4.7	50,168	5,346	9.6
Tucumán	1,747	50	2.8	11,797	418	3.4
Total	58,464	5,743	8.9	454,834	132,232	22.5

Source: Selected data from Carlos Bernaldo de Quirós, *Problemas demográficos argentinos,*
2 vols. (Buenos Aires, 1942), 2:151.

21.8 percent of the industrial employees, a figure comparable to that of the capital in early 1917 (see table 6).

Female Occupational Profile in Uruguay

Uruguay was predominantly urban by 1860 (40.9 percent of the population), and in 1908 cities contained 45.8 percent of the population.[20] Rural colonization did not achieve much success, and most immigrants settled in Montevideo, which also attracted the rural population displaced by modernization of the cattle industry. Unlike the situation in Argentina, in Uruguay urbanization did not mean industrialization: 90 percent of Uruguayan exports were beef products. Until 1913 the meat packed in Uruguayan plants did not surpass the production of salted beef. Small industrial and artisanal establishments began to appear in the 1890s, and in 1898 the first textile plant was established. The first meatpacking plant was established in 1902; by 1917 there were four important meatpacking companies, including Swift and Armour. Shoe and bag manufacturing and the textile industry were other key users of industrial labor.[21]

The 1892 municipal census for the department and capital city of Montevideo showed there were more foreign workers than native Uruguayans, and that men and women were mostly engaged in artisanal and unskilled jobs, with a smaller number in commerce. For women, domestic employment and sewing were the main occupations, but those who earned wages did so mostly in the shoe industry.[22] The nation suffered a financial crash in 1890 after a period of high urban speculation, which must have had negative effects on the unskilled female labor. The 1908 national census provides an overview of female participation; no other national census was taken until 1963. In 1908 there were 24,074 women economically active compared with 117,603 men, 17 percent of the total working force. Women in the industries and commerce made up 12.8 percent of the total. Between 1889 and 1908 the number of women in the industrial sector declined from 36.5 percent to 31.9 percent. Most working women were single (70 percent) and young: 77 percent were under thirty-five.[23]

In 1908 the National Labor Office reported women working in the leather industry, cigar and paper factories, garment factories, the telephone company, chemical and food industries, and in the service sector as cooks and servants.[24] These are also the occupations registered in the labor newspapers as organized in *gremios* or resistance associations. The Department of Labor's records for labor offer and demand in the 1910s show that the women most in demand were cooks and servants, nursemaids, wet nurses, and nurses.

In 1919 there were 21,892 women and minors of both sexes working in trade and industry in Uruguay. Data for the industrial sector show that the workers were predominantly Uruguayan (87 percent) and under sixteen years of age. The overwhelming majority of these women—85.7 percent— were single. Also significant, in 1919 male minors working in the industrial and commerce sectors surpassed the total number of women. Thus there was strong competition among these demographic components for under-paid jobs.[25]

A 1923 report from the National Labor Office lists the occupations women engaged in. There were eighty-three categories in industry and fifty in commerce. The industrial sector, with 6,624 employees in the capital and the provinces, dominated the labor market. Only 1,579 women were reported to be employed in the fifty commercial categories. Some occupations such as the jerked-beef plants, meatpacking plants, sugar refineries, and wool-washing plants were not beyond reach of the 176 women employed in them. However, most women had more traditional jobs. Ten key industries employed 5,165 women or 70.8 percent of the total female workforce: making canvas and leather shoes, cigarettes, candies and cookies, matches, cards, printing presses, garments, pasta and flour products, male garments, and textiles. By far the most important commercial employers were department stores, with hotels and export-import companies in second and third place.[26] The 1923 report shows some important discrepancies compared with the 1919 statistical yearbook published by the Labor Department. For example, the latter recorded 1,207 women working in meatpacking. The problem of conflicting information may never be solved.

The Chilean Female Labor Profile

The first survey of the Chilean labor force in the twentieth century was part of the 1907 national census. Women worked mostly in the cities, although the census listed female *gañanes,* or unskilled farm workers.[27] It also listed an artisan category that may refer to special and unidentified female trades. Nonetheless, the traditional categories dominated the occupational spectrum (see table 7).

Several surveys of industrial establishments in the next decade and a half offer a more accurate view of female urban employment. In 1913 women made up 21.1 percent of the total labor force: 97 percent of them were blue-collar workers. Minors were a surprisingly large 8 percent, most of them in blue-collar jobs.[28] A 1916 report on the labor force of 2,625 manufacturing plants in the country shows only small variations from 1913. Out of 50,930 workers reported, 65.7 percent were men (33,466), 26.2 percent were women (13,345), and 8 percent were minors (4,119). Women composed 11.5 percent of the workforce in industries manufacturing alcoholic beverages, 15.8 percent in food industries, 61.3 percent in the textile industry, 32.1 percent in the chemical industry, and 78.7 percent in the garment industry. The female chemical workers were mostly in the match and perfume factories.[29]

Between 1917 and 1921 the percentage of women in the total workforce of those industries responding to the government's inquiries varied little, the only exception being pharmaceuticals, where it increased. In 1917 the female workforce was 27.1 percent of the total; in 1919 it was 27.05 percent; and in 1921 it was 27.9 percent.[30] In 1921 the breakdown by industries was as shown in table 8.

The 1925 industrial survey carried out in 1,082 manufacturing plants reported 27,528 workers. Women made up 26.4 percent of that labor force (7,286) and minors 6.5 percent (1,796). The women clustered in four industries: textiles, chemical products, food packing, and leather goods. Women in those four categories constituted 22.7 percent (6,261) of all workers and 85.9 percent of all female industrial workers.[31]

The 1920 census was not published until 1925. It followed the 1907 model

TABLE 7   Labor Profile and Occupational Categories in Chile, 1907

Occupation	Male	Female	% Female	Total
Agriculture	15,921	1,088	5.8	18,687
Artisans	42,097	4,714	10.0	46,810
Commerce	36,290	5,451	13.0	41,741
Employees	40,381	12,188	23.1	52,569
Gañanes[a]	69,235	1,751	2.4	70,966
Midwives		507	100.0	507
Seamstresses		50,398	100.0	50,398
Servants	7,692	29,030	79.0	36,722
Shoemakers	9,019	1,876	17.2	10,895
Telegraph operators	749	236	23.9	985
Teachers	1,335	1,821	57.7	3,156
Tailors	2,425	11	0.4	2,436

Source: Chile, Censo de la República de Chile, 1907. These are select categories and cover only the three leading provinces of Santiago, Concepción, and Valparaíso.
[a]Unskilled farm workers.

TABLE 8   Labor Profile in Chilean Industries, 1921

Industry	Male	Female	% Total	Total
Alcohol	2,379	458	15.2	3,030
Food	8,465	2,204	19.02	11,586
Garment	2,177	6,162	72.7	8,476
Textiles	985	1,757	61.2	2,870
Leather	6,318	1,741	20.5	8,462
Chemicals	1,855	1,110	34.6	3,205

Source: Chile, Anuario estadístico (Santiago: Universo, 1922), 9:24–25.

of classification by occupations, although the concept of occupation—renamed "profession"—expanded greatly and all occupations were grouped by economic sectors such as agriculture, mining, industry, transportation, commerce, liberal professions, and education (see table 9). The occupations of embroiderer, seamstress, washerwoman, and fashion seamstress, as opposed to what one assumes were women who sewed for industrial plants, are included under "industry." Equally important, over half of the women classified as professionals were midwives, but there were only 34 female doctors. Classified as in "various" occupations were employees in department stores,

TABLE 9   Chilean Labor Profile, 1920 Census

Occupation	Male	Female	%	Total
Agriculture	437,800	50,052	10.2	487,852
Industry	176,984	149,240	45.7	326,224
Transportation	62,027	2,609	4.0	64,636
Commerce	96,383	22,629	19.0	119,012
Professions	13,062	3,788	25.5	14,810
Domestic service	30,448	102,475	77.0	132,923
Various	71,153	6,106	7.9	77,259
Total	887,857	336,899	27.5	1,222,716

Source: Chile, Dirección General de Estadística, Censo de población de la República de Chile, 1920 (Santiago: Universo, 1925), 405–8.

TABLE 10   Chilean Labor Profile by Gender, 1930

Occupation	Men	Women	Total	% Female
Mining	76,930	639	77,569	0.8
Agriculture, fishing	401,034	25,307	506,341	6.3
Industry	204,857	91,344	296,201	30.8
Commerce	119,623	28,183	147,806	19.06
Communications	51,072	3,158	54,230	6.1
Administration	40,327	8,506	48,883	17.4
Liberal professions	12,763	14,702	27,465	53.5
Other	28,721	12,324	41,405	29.7

Source: Chile, Décimo censo de la población, 3:viii.

offices, and such. Men still dominated that source of employment. Among those "without profession" were 1.3 million women, mostly housewives.

The 1930 census changed occupational categories enough to make comparisons with 1920 slightly difficult, but some patterns are obvious. Agriculture occupied 40.8 percent of all workers, industry 23.8 percent, commerce 11.9 percent, and mining 6.2 percent.[32] The gender breakdown is shown in table 10. The occupational analysis included all people in a given category, whether business owners, employees, or blue-collar workers. A more concise analysis of some categories discloses that, for example, of the 25,258 women in the agricultural sector, 12,303 were patronas (either administrators or owners). In the industrial sector, textiles employed 8,436 women, the food industry 8,589, and garment making a whopping 70,221 women. In the public service area — artisans, employees of the government and its welfare services — there were 10,381 women. The textile industry included rural weavers, important in the province of Cautín. Most of the women employed in the commercial sector worked in markets, small shops, hotels, and restaurants. Women working in the post office were counted as in commerce. Teaching occupied 12,568 women. A great flaw of this census is that it assimilated domestic servants into their employers' occupations. The occupational breakdown of the active population nonetheless listed 84,313 women and 12,494 men as servants.[33]

Working Conditions

Census figures and statistical data do not convey any information on the working conditions and wages of women and minors. The personal observations of labor inspectors and social reformers provide a much more useful social commentary and give us the key to the meaning of those issues in the first years of the century. Argentina excelled Uruguay and Chile in labor inspection and reports, although its labor conditions were no better than theirs for the effort.[34]

Of all the issues raised by the incorporation of women into the labor force, the least well documented was "economic independence." The wages women earned were far from adequate to sustain more than one person and only sufficient to help ends meet in a family. Mainstream liberal feminists extolled the social value of women's work in rosy tones, seeking to enhance the image of women as partners in the national efforts toward "progress." Socialist feminists, although mostly middle-class women, were less enchanted by economic independence than by the need to enhance the health, safety, and economic rewards of working women.

The earliest official reports on the wages and working conditions of women and children in the Southern Cone were those of Dr. Juan Bialet Massé and Juan Alsina for Argentina. Bialet Massé, a French doctor commissioned to survey the state of the working classes in the provinces, left the most comprehensive description of early industrial Argentina outside the capital. Alsina's work included the capital and was written with an eye to reform of the legislation.[35] Bialet Massé's report is largely narrative, peppered by personal comments and lacking charts or analytical data, but he spared no detail in describing the number, working conditions, wages, health, and quality of life of all workers. It covered all industrial establishments — even the most primitive ones — offering a rare view of the extent of poverty beyond the thriving capital.

Needlework was the main source of income for most working women in the provinces. Unlike those in Buenos Aires, they mostly sewed at home. In the few garment factories (Río Cuarto, for example) literate young women worked under crowded conditions in poorly lit and ventilated rooms for ten hours a day for less than 1 peso. Washing and ironing were mostly done at home, but Bialet Massé reported a few commercial operations. When women learned to iron well, they left to work on their own. Unskilled women ironing in commercial plants in Tucumán earned 40 to 70 centavos, or 1 peso daily for skilled work. They worked from 6:00 or 6:30 A.M. through 7:00 P.M. with two short breaks for a lunch provided by the owner. Although they worked ten hours, they were away from their homes for over twelve. Few married women could stay away so long, and the workers were all between fifteen and twenty years old.

In the western city of Mendoza he found about fifty women typesetters. The city of Rosario had fifty telephone operators, a working elite at the time. Only single women were hired, and they worked seven hours for six and a half days a week. All employers agreed that women never missed work and were submissive and easy to handle. Similar comments were made about women working in the vineyards and in the preparation of raisins, the main agricultural industry in Mendoza and San Juan provinces. Women were reputed to be careful and trusted workers, but good performance did not improve their wages. They were paid 50 centavos daily, whereas men earned 1.20 pesos. Not surprisingly, one winery employed 400 women and 200 men. The women employed in the raisin industry of that province earned 1 peso a day, while men earned between 1.50 and 1.80 pesos.

Alsina's report did not differ much from Bialet Massé's. He also noted the exploitation of minors of both sexes in factories making matches, garments, food, and buttons, among other products. He attributed the low wages to an excess of supply, which created stiff competition for work. Alsina was no social reformer: he suggested that as long as there was a labor surplus, workers could help themselves best by joining mutualist societies to ameliorate their conditions.[36] Workers thought otherwise. At the time Alsina and Bialet Massé were carrying out their inquiries, labor in Buenos Aires, and to some extent in the main riverine and provincial cities, was undergoing rapid mobilization. Socialists and anarchists were engaged in a struggle to control the budding workers' unions, especially in the capital, where the bulk of the industrial workers were. Strikes were on the increase, and the governing elite, uncomfortable about the large number of unruly immigrants, enacted a law in 1902 to oust undesirables. In 1904 sweeping labor legislation proposed by the interior minister, Joaquín V. González, met the opposition of industrialists and workers alike.[37]

In response to workers' pressure and the election in 1904 of the first socialist deputy, Alfredo Palacios, the Argentine government created a Labor Department in 1907. Unquestionably the government's interest in learning more about workers was not idle curiosity. Although the official attitude of President Figueroa Alcorta was not antilabor, there was a sense among the intellectual elite that social reforms were due. A similar feeling prevailed in Chile and Uruguay. In Chile, men such as Catholic conservative Francisco Hunneus, as well as the advanced wing of the Radical Party and the Democratic Party, began to show more sensitivity to the social problems of the working class.[38] In Uruguay the reformist Colorado Party took control in 1904 and, though challenged from several political angles, began a long parliamentary battle for social reform.[39]

In a gesture of goodwill toward the increasing claims of labor in Argentina, the municipality of Buenos Aires appointed Gabriela Laperrière de Coni, French-born socialist and activist married to public health expert Dr. Emilio Coni, as "honorary inspector." There is no indication that she submitted any reports before she died on 8 January 1907.[40] A second female inspector appointed by the Labor Department, Celia La Palma de Emery, was a politically traditional associate of the National Council of Women and charity organizations. La Palma's duty was to report whether the industrial establishments employing women and children were observing the regulations issued by the department. She visited 114 sweatshops and small artisanal shops in four months, only thirty-two of them large enough to be considered "industrial." She also visited thirty-two charity establishments where women and children worked to earn part of their keep. Her first report was issued on 10 December 1908.[41] In La Palma's opinion the working conditions of women and children in state-owned establishments were acceptable, but those that were privately owned had terrible hygiene and safety conditions, especially the garment factories attached to department stores. The wages were minimal and the working day was long. With few exceptions, lack of light, poor ventilation, and total disregard for cleanliness prevailed.

A shorter report on working conditions in the garment factories by a male physician inspector, Dr. Láutaro Durañona, was submitted to the head of the Labor Department on 18 November 1908. Durañona visited twenty-eight establishments with 1,100 workers and reported on the ages and gender of 859. The profile was typical, with 54 percent of the female workers under twenty-two years of age. The general hygiene in such establishments was appalling. Workers had neither washing facilities nor safe water to drink. Damp, cold rooms, low ceilings, poor lighting and ventilation, and crowded conditions were common. Nine-hour days were standard, and most establishments did not observe the reduced working hours for children under sixteen.[42]

Fenia Chertcoff de Repetto, a socialist activist who founded the female workers' society Unión Gremial Femenina in Buenos Aires, also took it upon herself to visit factories in the city to learn about the working conditions, to inform the Labor Department, and to publish her findings in La Vanguardia. She organized a committee to make those visits and demand the enforcement of labor regulations. Between 1910 and 1916 she carried out her work in Buenos Aires on behalf of the Centro Socialista Femenino and with members of many workers' groups who engaged in voluntary inspections.[43] Official inspections brought few immediate changes. Textile factories, already reported in 1907 as one of the main sources of female employment and with ten-hour workdays, were inspected again in 1910. The survey included thirty-four textile plants with 4,028 women workers, 1,054 children of both sexes, and 2,060 men. The tasks performed by men and women were not described. One of the largest manufacturers of canvas shoes employed 728 women (60 percent of the labor force), 202 minors, and 275 men. The factory was well ventilated and spacious, although some areas were unhealthful because of dust and fabric particles floating in the air.[44] Subsequent reports do not change the picture drawn by 1910.[45] Unfortunately we lack such detailed information about Uruguayan and Chilean working conditions, but there is little reason to assume they were better.[46]

Wages and Gender

The significant difference between men's and women's wages was common to the three nations. It was a source of discontent among male workers, who saw cheap female labor as unfair competition. The efforts of anarchist and socialist labor organizers, and the feminist concern over wage disparity, helped to change attitudes and focus the denunciation of exploitation under either capitalism or employers. The economic difference between men's and women's earnings was also an issue among those intellectuals who had advocated women's work as a panacea for the nation. For example, conservative Argentine educator Carlos Octavio Bunge, who supported women's education for a variety of social reasons, was convinced that women's incomes would inevitably remain below men's because fewer women would achieve the education necessary to compete. Women lacked intellectual aptitude because of their intrinsic nature. "Women's wages tend to remain below those of men not so much because of sociological circumstances, but because of the biological laws of human sexuality. The difference between their wages will never disappear, but it will be smaller among women of high social class, with a better preparation for collective life." His ideas reflect the feelings of positivist social scientists at the beginning of the century.[47]

Women's employment followed the law of profit. In 1907 women in Buenos Aires were consistently paid less than men, and sometimes less than male minors. In factories where men were paid between 2.80 and 7 pesos daily, women were paid 2 to 4 pesos for the same job. In other instances women were given less skilled jobs that paid less than the jobs men performed. In the match, paper, and starch factories women were packers or stamped seals on boxes while men provided the more skilled labor. In the knit-garment industries men cut and dyed fabrics, earning 2.50 to 4 pesos daily. The women did the needlework, ironing, and darning for 1.50 to 3.50. The extremes of gender discrimination were experienced in the underwear factories. There male apprentices cutting and pressing patterns earned as much as adult females sewing and pressing, and more than those preparing the fabric for cutting.[48] In that same year La Palma reported that among the 1,194 employees working for 200 managers, skilled workers earned anything from 60 to 120 pesos a month, with few women earning more. The best-paid workers were hatmakers. The most common workday was eight to nine hours.

The most genuine and heartfelt evaluation of the female predicament was that of Carolina Muzilli, a seamstress born into a poor immigrant family, who died of tuberculosis a few years after she wrote her report. A socialist by affiliation, Muzilli carried out a personal inquiry in the sweatshops of Buenos Aires, taking a job in a department store to experience the employees' working conditions. In 1913 she gathered her results in a paper to be delivered at the International Exposition at Ghent.[49] Muzilli's report confirmed previous official accounts. Garment factories kept their employees for nine to ten hours a day, paying between 60 centavos and 2.50 pesos (to very skilled workers). Those in laundries and ironing plants worked eleven and even twelve hours; the best paid earned 2.50 pesos a day. Women in department stores were not permitted to use the elevators or to sit down when not helping customers. They also had to stay after closing to perform menial cleaning jobs and to price and dust merchandise.

For women of low-income families there was no escape from working for low wages. The increasing cost of life and the surplus of labor between 1900 and 1915 forced all members of less-skilled workers' families to work to supplement the men's wages. Such was the conclusion of the official report on the cost of living and family labor in Argentina for 1912. A foundry worker earning 100 pesos a month who had a wife and two children had to spend 124 pesos to cover the family's basic needs. The wages of the male head of the family could not be considered the sole income of the home. The family depended "on the increasing number of women and children who in the city of Buenos Aires work in manufacturing plants, artisanal shops, and commercial establishments. . . . We cannot forget either that outside the shops there is a burgeoning home industry that makes up another source of income."[50]

Between 1913 and 1920 Argentina's economy deteriorated considerably. A depression set in in 1913 and stretched through 1917; the costs of imported manufactured goods and coal increased significantly, and unemployment rose.[51] A 1919 study of 32,583 male and female wage earners in Buenos Aires showed that men's earnings had declined by 3 percent and women's by 5 percent. Inflation aggravated the situation by lowering the workers' purchasing ability. Women's wages remained one-half to two-thirds those of men across all industries.[52]

The economic situation of families in Chile was not much different. The Chilean Labor Office was also concerned about inflation in the prices of staple foods, which it followed meticulously for many years. The economy had suffered a strong setback after 1915. After an inflationary year in 1920, a report observed that working families in the capital suffered "economic discomfort" and that larger families suffered most. In 1925 the median wage for Chilean children was 2.88 pesos a day; for women it was 4.95, and for men 10.80.[53] The scant information available for subsequent years shows no change. In 1934 a Chilean magazine reported seamstresses working at home for the garment sector for 3 to 3.5 pesos a day. A woman employed in a department store earned a maximum of 150 pesos a month, and the man who ran the elevator earned 180–200 pesos. Professional women in the pharmaceutical industry could earn as much as 500–600 pesos a month. Their overseer, always a man, earned over 2,000 pesos.[54] The gap between seamstress and manager was unbridgeable.

Between 1914 and 1920 the Uruguayan economy deteriorated and the cost of living rose by 40 percent, with declining purchasing power and a lower standard of living. Uruguayan female workers had been subject to wage discrimination since the beginning of the century. In 1908 a skilled male cigarette worker earned 1.80 pesos daily while his female counterpart was paid only 1 peso; a male cook's top salary was 100 pesos monthly, but a woman was rarely paid more than 25. In the shoe industry the disparity was less acute: the male top salary was 1.30 pesos a day while the female was 1.20.[55] The efforts of the *batllista* and socialist politicians to redress some of the economic inequalities of working people in Uruguay left much to be desired. In 1912 Deputy Frugoni gave a detailed account of women's low earnings in the textile industry when he introduced a bill to establish a minimum wage. The highest-paid skilled needleworker earned 15–20 pesos monthly, while an unskilled male worker earned 20–35 pesos.[56] A 1923 publication of the Labor Department disclosed that women who worked in factories took work home to supplement their low wages, described as "laughable." The report compared the salaries in a match factory and a small container factory. Men earned two or three times more per day than women in the former, and one and a half times to twice as much in the latter. The best-paid women were store and electric company employees: they earned 60–80 pesos monthly, while men received twice as much. There were 1,579 women working in commercial enterprises and 6,624 in industrial establishments. Telephone operators were categorized as "industrial workers"; the 683 women employed by the telephone company received a maximum of 39 pesos monthly.[57]

A study of the income of 91,436 Uruguayans working in industry and commerce in the second decade of the twentieth century concluded "with justifiable pessimism" that 30,713 persons (nearly 33 percent) could not cover their own minimal needs with their individual wages. Sixty-five percent of the total (60,396 persons) could not establish a family on their earnings: "The worker's home cannot subsist with the sole income of its head; the collaboration of the wife and the children is an imperative and cruel necessity."[58]

Women made up 11.1 percent of the adult Uruguayan industrial and commercial workforce in 1924, little changed since 1913. Grouped by income, 70.3 percent of all working women earned less than 360 pesos yearly, while only 29.2 percent of male workers fell in that category (see table 11). The Ministry of Industries had set 355.65 pesos a year as the minimum to satisfy one person's needs. Among the 30,760 adults who fell below that minimum income there were 6,949 women (22.5), of whom 5,537 worked in industrial (blue-collar) plants and the rest in commerce.

Although it is impossible to establish accurate comparisons across the

TABLE 11   Uruguay: Male and Female Wages, Industry and Commerce, 1924

Pesos per Year	Men	Women	%	Total
Under 240	11,807	3,453	22.6	15,260
241-360	12,140	3,496	22.4	15,636
361-600	27,659	2,024	6.8	29,683
601-1,200	26,481	870	3.1	27,351
1,201-2,400	3,082	36	1.1	3,118
2,401-3,600+	580	1	0.1	581

Source: Uruguay, Ministerio de Industrias, El salario real (1914-20) (Montevideo: Imp. Nacional, 1927), 62-65. Minors are not included in these data.

three nations, given their different statistical data and the periods when they were gathered, the main thread running through the figures is that female workers—whether in commerce or industry—were ill paid and largely unable to live on their income, which remained as a necessary supplement to the domestic unit.

Industrial Home Work

The hidden face of female labor was home work, or *trabajo a domicilio*. Labor at home was divided into two categories: servant chores such as the work of cooks, maids, or nursemaids, and labor performed for a factory, paid by the piece or by the dozen items. The first category was excluded from any kind of regulation. A servant's work was regarded as a private affair between employer and employee, beyond the purview of the state. Only when the home was used as a base for wage labor did it gain juridical recognition. Even then the labor of members of a family supervised by its head was beyond any regulation.

When women's labor became a relevant topic in the early years of the century, it was argued that it was necessary to regulate the labor of the "weak" in the name of health, family, and the progress of the motherland. Women working in traditional industries in the nation's urban centers benefited the most from labor legislation.[59] The ambiguous situation of those working at home raised concern among male social reformers and socialists in the early years of the century, but the issue was not fully debated until the 1910s.

The putting-out system, the backbone of the garment industry by the 1910s, involved thousands of women whose age or family commitments did not permit them to leave home. They ranged in age from adolescence to advanced middle age. Girls began to help their mothers as soon as they could handle sewing work competently, usually at between thirteen and fifteen years of age. Bialet Massé's survey of Argentine workers revealed an impressive homogeneity in the female occupational spectrum and women's scant monetary reward. Home labor was the most common female occupation outside Buenos Aires, and needlework was the most frequent choice. Washing and ironing clothes was the resource of the poorest women; the alternative was to become a domestic or a prostitute. In Tucumán washerwomen earned 1.20 pesos a day; domestic servants earned between 5 and 10 pesos a month. Bialet Massé reported over 2,000 seamstresses working at home in that city. A garment company had 300 women working for it; two others had 130 and 120 home seamstresses. Workers were paid by the dozen pieces; among the most profitable were children's suits, which paid 4.80 to 9 pesos a dozen. The ablest seamstresses earned 1.40 pesos daily, but less proficient ones made less—hardly enough to feed themselves, as Bialet Massé calculated that three women living together at home required 2.64 pesos daily to live decently. In poor areas such as Río Cuarto, south of Córdoba, seamstresses earned 60-70 centavos daily. To succeed, some women provided their own sewing equipment and thread and counted on home assistance from younger and older female members of the family.

The best paid home needlework was men's suits. Women seamstresses had a monopoly on manufacturing men's trousers and vests; tailors made the jackets. Although this was well-paid work, it was irregular, and women made only 36–40 pesos monthly. This being the condition of the "queens" of the trade, most seamstresses were ill fed, lived in unhygienic homes, and many suffered from tuberculosis. Writers, such as Bialet Massé feared that such women were passing their disease to their customers, and increased sensitivity to information on the sources of infectious diseases raised concern among public health authorities. In their zeal to obtain some form of regulation for the work of these women, no other argument seemed more appropriate, since long working hours made no impression on the bureaucrats. Bialet Massé found so many women with tuberculosis sewing in Rosario, a city upstream on the Paraguay River, that he suggested that all products they manufactured should be disinfected before being sold.[60]

Two Labor Department surveys in Buenos Aires in 1913 and 1914 showed that as many women worked in their homes as in factories. There were 13,882 women employees in garment establishments and 13,823 women working *a domicilio*. Together they made up roughly 20 percent of the total population working for all industries in the capital. A more detailed analysis of these workers revealed that in 899 homes there were 915 workers. Of these 113 were minors (12.3 percent) who worked 8⅓ to 10½ hours daily, the same mean time as the adults.[61]

The Argentine military was one of the main employers of *trabajo a domicilio*. In 1913 the Intendencia de Guerra [Ministry of War] employed 4,002 workers, 3,919 (97.8 percent) of them women. The 83 men made footwear, overcoats, suit jackets, and special shirts. They could earn 5.40 to 7 pesos daily. Women were in charge of sleeves, trousers, underwear, headgear, vests, and uniform embroidery. They earned by the piece, and the prices varied from 2.80 for fencing trousers to 4.75 for riding breeches. Embroidering was well paid but demanded so much work that the women who did it earned only about 4 pesos daily. Unlike private industry, work done for the army was under strict regulation. Workers had to be over sixteen years of age and were notified by mail when their services were required. All had to have a bondsman, and all work was recorded in a personal passbook. The amount of work a person could undertake was also regulated: Nobody could take on more than ten overcoats or fewer than five, for example, and all work had to be performed within ten days. All finished pieces were inspected to verify that they met the regulations. Finally, the intendancy was free to withdraw work from any person.[62] No doubt the women who worked for the army were an elite corps. Their income was better, but they worked under exacting conditions and had to be highly skilled to qualify.

In 1917 another home labor survey of 930 persons showed that 731 women and 196 men worked *exclusively* at home. For 447 persons the home was their working and living space. The mean income for those surveyed was 877 pesos a month. Women earned 1.86 pesos daily; minors under sixteen, 1.67 pesos, and young women above that age, 1.22 pesos. Male heads of household earned 3.91 pesos daily, and young men above 16 earned 4.11 pesos. Men working at home were often skilled craftsmen (tailors, shoemakers) who earned more than women in their traditional occupations (needlework by the piece).[63]

Argentine labor reports are the most complete for the Southern Cone, and the data above do not exhaust the possibilities of analysis. However, they establish that *trabajo a domicilio* was one of the most important components of the income for a large number of people — about 60,000 in Buenos Aires alone — who lived on the edge of poverty. Because there were so many women in this group of workers, their income was crucial to the subsistence of poor families. Quoting a French study, socialist deputy Enrique del Valle Iberlucea agreed that though home work appeared to be freer and more dignified than working in a manufacturing plant, the truth was that female home workers were pariahs.[64]

This opinion about the hateful conditions of the home as a workplace was shared by Elena Caffarena, a Chilean in charge of one of two known reports on *trabajo a domicilio* in that nation. Caffarena was a sincere and tireless social reformer who rose to a leading political role in the feminist movement in the 1930s. Early in his first administration (1921–24), President Arturo Alessandri sent a bill to Congress for the approval of a labor code and social welfare legislation. This bill was still unresolved when Caffarena wrote her report. *Trabajo a domicilio* appeared to favor homelife and the protection of children, but the reality disproved that misconception. Neither hygienic nor safe, it simply favored the interests of industrialists who wished to avoid welfare regulations while saving the capital they would have to spend to provide a secure workplace.

Caffarena denounced the low pay, the long workday, the unhealthfulness of the conditions, and above all the assumption that because women performed the jobs their earnings were simply pin money used for extra niceties. To the issue of gender she added the issue of class. The rich condemned uncleanliness in workers' homes and the lack of a saving spirit but refused to acknowledge that no woman working ten hours a day and earning 15–20 centavos an hour would spend the money on a broom or have any time left to clean her home or her children. Using case studies, she gave examples of how much working women earned, how they spent their money, and how many people lived on their income. Her solution was to end the sweatshop system and female exploitation by strong government regulation.[65] Amanda Hermosilla Aedo, another Chilean female lawyer writing in the mid-1930s, corroborated Caffarena's findings, noting how businessmen evaded existing protective legislation while saving money by contracting home work.[66]

Protection and Reform through Legislation

Two apparently disparate groups took a great interest in female industrial labor: public health specialists and activists of the Left. For physicians and public health specialists at the turn of the century, the sight of women and minors working long hours in factories presaged disease and harm to future generations. For anarchists and socialists organizing the first resistance cells or aiming at consolidating themselves as a political force, women workers could become a threat unless they were incorporated into the movement.[67] There was more than mere self-interest among male labor leaders in dealing with women workers: A working-class family needed the contribution of the wife, and sometimes the children, to survive.[68] Most single female industrial workers were the young daughters of a family or single heads of households, who worked out of necessity. Women working at home were often wives attempting to combine homemaking with earning money because the long hours of factory work and their lack of child care gave them no other option. Male workers, as husbands and parents, had a legitimate concern for the work of their female kin.

Regulating women's and children's labor constituted a social reform program that took several decades to evolve. Changes in population growth, immigration patterns, economic crises, and political viability marked the pace of the legislation, which moved inch by inch toward designing more equitable conditions for the laboring classes. The first goal of reformist legislators working on behalf of women and children was to establish a six-day workweek and a maximum eight-hour workday. This had to be followed by improving working conditions within the factories, imposing some order on the industrial home work of minors and women, and eventually establishing some financial security for working mothers and old age pensions for all workers.

Regulating Industrial Work

Labor's goal of restricting working hours was first achieved in Argentina. Although socialist and anarchist organizations had endorsed the principle since the late 1890s, the Socialist Party first had the opportunity to exercise political pressure after Alfredo Palacios was elected a national deputy in 1904. The first law aimed at enforcing Sunday rest in industry and commerce in the capital city was passed in 1905, followed in 1907 by another regulating the hours of all workers and night work of women and children. Both applied *only* to the capital.[69]

The national regulation of female and child labor did not take place until 1924, when Law 11.317 was approved. Children under twelve could not be employed at all, and older minors had to finish primary school first. Working children and women would be removed from the street or public spaces. Applied to women, this law aimed at restricting prostitution. Forty-eight-hour and thirty-six-hour work weeks respectively were prescribed for those over eighteen and for minors under eighteen. Workers should also have a two-hour daily rest at midday. Females and minors were prohibited from working between 8:00 P.M. and 7:00 A.M. They were also removed from unsafe or unhealthful industries.[70]

Early in the century Uruguayan deputies had introduced a bill to limit the workday in the textile industry to ten hours.[71] As a result of his efforts to reform labor conditions, President José Batlle y Ordóñez was able to pass the eight-hour workday during his first administration. Not until after Batlle's second administration were a compulsory weekly rest and the eight-hour day approved in November 1915 (Law 5350, put into effect in 1916). Under this law minors worked three-quarters of adult working hours. In November 1915 Uruguayans copied the 1915 Chilean Ley de la Silla that mandated provision of chairs for department store employees that guaranteed women's right to rest. A pension fund for all workers was established in 1919. In 1920 the administration under Baltasar Brum passed legislation requiring weekly rest times for working women and children, legislation that was redrafted and tightened in the early 1930s. Labor bills established Sunday as a compulsory rest day for women, children, and domestic workers. Uruguay was the only country in the Southern Cone that addressed the issue of rest for domestics workers.[72]

Chile established a minimum wage for private employees in February 1937.[73] Up to the end of the second decade of the century Chile lagged behind Argentina and Uruguay in protective legislation. In 1912 the Congress had passed a bill for the protection of children, but it was more concerned with helping homeless poor children than with child labor, and on 13 January 1917 it approved a bill mandating the provision of child-care rooms in industries employing more than fifty women. Sunday rest was legislated in 1917 and put into effect in 1918.[74]

Regulating Home Work

As early as 1913 Argentine deputies began to discuss a bill regulating work at home, but the interparliamentary commission took five years to present supporting data for the bill. In the meantime the socialists took the initiative. In September 1915 Deputy Enrique del Valle Iberlucea advanced his own bill regulating industrial home work. It followed the examples of England, Australia, and New Zealand, where a minimum wage for home work had been approved without an undue price rise in the merchandise. He also cited the example of the Uruguayan socialist deputy Emilio Frugoni, who had introduced a bill to establish government committees to determine minimum wages in all industries.[75] The Argentine legislation was finally enacted in 1918 (Law 10.505), and its compulsory regulation articles were approved by the executive the same year.[76]

As in previous cases, this law applied only to the federal capital and "national territories." Provincial (state) governments were free to pursue their own policies. The key failure of this law was the exemption of domestics. It also excluded families working under the authority of their head, whether male or female, and applied only to persons working at home for a business or an industry. The amount of work, wages, work to be performed, and fines would be recorded for inspection. Work by persons with infectious diseases (tuberculosis was named) was forbidden, and neighbors and doctors were encouraged to denounce any infectious worker. The national Labor Department was assigned the task of creating "salary commissions" with equal representation from labor and management, to determine a minimum wage or the price of piecework. The commission was to verify that the workers were paid in cash. This measure was not for the benefit of workers only: as one contemporary commentator pointed out, some businesses suffered from the "unfair competition" of industrial home work, especially in the capital, where many were willing to work at home for substandard wages.[77]

Uruguay completed the regulation of *trabajo a domicilio* in 1934, implementing and refining it in 1940 and 1943. It demanded that all employers register their workers and provide each with a personal book to record the amount and nature of work performed and the compensation, which had to meet minimum levels set by the government. Security provisions had to be observed if dangerous machinery was used in the home. Hygiene provisions attempted to ensure that people with contagious diseases would not do putting-out work. Like the Argentine law, Uruguay's proposed a commission to establish fair wages. Since the Uruguayan Civil Code was not yet reformed by 1943, labor regulations had to avoid the legal pitfall posed by the theoretical subordination of the wife to the husband. In case of any litigation over wages, married women could sue without their husbands' permission. This pragmatic solution supported the feminists' contention that a wage-earning woman had to be an independent person and equal to any man before the law.[78]

The Chilean Labor Code

The Treaty of Versailles after World War I and the First and Second International Labor Conferences (Washington, D.C., 1919 and Geneva, 1920) established world standards for labor legislation. The only Southern Cone nation to prepare a thorough labor code soon after 1919 was Chile. In 1921 Argentine president Hipólito Yrigoyen, whose policies against labor had already tarnished his rapport with workers, had proposed a labor code [*código del trabajo*], but his proposal was not carried through and Argentina continued to legislate piecemeal.

The 1919 international guidelines were the bases for the labor code and social welfare bill sent to Congress in 1921 by Chilean president Arturo Alessandri.[79] The bill was intended to incorporate all existing, pending, and newly proposed legislation into one body of modern laws. It claimed to endorse the "legitimate aspirations" of the proletariat and proposed new social welfare legislation to attract immigration and settlement and lessen conflict between labor and capital.

The Chilean bill paid special attention to the wages paid for home work and the enforcement of a minimum wage, particularly for women and minors. The articles regulating home work followed the 1918 Argentine legislation. The definition of equal pay for men and women for the same work was reasserted, but the bill made allowances for discrimination for single workers of any sex, who could be paid 20 percent less than the minimum. Single minors' wages could be 30 percent less than the minimum. Since a considerable number of commercial and industrial workers were single females and minors, the principle of wage equality was undermined by this proposal.

Labor for children under fourteen was forbidden, and those under eighteen had to finish primary school before they could be hired. The eight-hour day was recommended for all adult workers, but especially for women and for minors between sixteen and eighteen. Minors under sixteen could work no more than six hours a day. Night work was forbidden for women and minors except for women working in medical and charitable institutions. Any work deemed beyond women's physical strength or dangerous to the "physical and moral" condition of their sex was prohibited, such as jobs in docks or mines and those involving moving machinery or intense heat.

Pregnant women were forbidden to work for six weeks before giving birth. They would receive six weeks' paid postpartum leave and were entitled to return to their jobs. Any industrial or commercial institution employing over twenty women had to provide a child-care room for children under one year of age. Nursing mothers could take breaks to nurse their children. This blueprint contained the standard aspirations of the social reformers in the three Southern Cone nations. Because of the bad working relationship between Alessandri and his Congress, the bill was not acted on for several years.

The enactment of the key recommendations of the Labor Code was precipitated by a military takeover on 8 September 1924, which forced Congress to take action. The legislation adopted covered welfare issues such as insurance, accident indemnity, and the regulation of female and child labor. Government Decree 442 set the standards of protection for working mothers, mandated the establishment of child-care facilities in industries employing women, and extended the maternity leave prescribed by the 1917 law. The number of female workers that obligated an employer to offer maternity leave and child care remained at twenty, but the law extended the coverage to charity establishments. The period of maternity leave was to be duly registered and the worker's return to her job guaranteed. The maternity leave was for forty days before and twenty days after delivery, with an extension if medically necessary, and the mother would receive 50 percent of her salary. Women would have a total of one hour daily to nurse their children at work. The law prescribed the size, lighting, and ventilation of the child-care room and stipulated that it should shelter no more than twenty-five children. Three cradles for each twenty children were required. The child-care center should be in the charge of a competent attendant, paid by the management. Children had to be healthy or under medical treatment to be admitted.[80] In the ensuing years, several presidential law decrees created institutions to implement and enforce the legislation and extended the breadth of welfare legislation. Eventually a government decree of 13 May 1931 consolidated all social labor legislation into a body that was officially known as Código del Trabajo. This thoughtful piece of legislation was not properly enforced, however.

Protecting Working Mothers

One key item on the agenda of social reformers, socialists, and feminists was prenatal leave for working mothers. Since the turn of the century there had been a growing consensus on protecting women because of their maternal potential. This view was later strengthened by the increasing popularity of eugenics doctrine proposing that the state assume responsibility for the health of future generations. Medical ideas of the time recommended four to six weeks' rest before delivery to allow the baby to gain weight and combat the high neonatal mortality risk. In Uruguay Batlle y Ordóñez proposed pre- and postnatal leave in a 1906 bill, later improved in two Colorado Party bills in 1908 and 1911 and a socialist bill in 1913.[81]

In 1914 Argentine socialist deputy Alfredo Palacios proposed a similar bill. He had to endure criticism and debate with the dean of the Faculty of Medicine, and the bill was mutilated in its content and stalled in the chambers.[82] In September 1915 socialist deputy Enrique Dickmann proposed a bill to establish a subsidy to compensate working mothers after delivery with a minimum sum of 45 pesos. The subject came under discussion again in 1919, the year the First International Labor Conference met in Washington, D.C., and Argentina had to declare in an international forum that it lagged in maternity protection. Law 5291 attempted to remedy this situation by forbidding mothers to work during the period *before* delivery. Concerned legislators knew the law had to be rewritten to expand the rest period to six weeks and compensate for lost wages.[83] The issue was tackled by another bill introduced by Radical Party deputy Leopoldo Bard on 6 August 1924. In spirit Bard followed Dickmann's bill, but he established a higher subsidy of 100 pesos. The goals defined and planned by several legislators to protect pregnant working women came together under the title "Protection to Motherhood," article 13 of Law 11.317, approved on 30 September 1924. This law stated that women "must abandon their jobs" after presenting medical proof of the expected delivery date. Working women were protected from being fired if they became pregnant, were entitled to six weeks of pre- and postnatal leave, and were to return to their jobs after delivery. The employer was required to wait longer if the woman was under medical advice to extend her postpartum rest. All nursing mothers had to have fifteen minutes every three hours to feed their babies if they so desired. All businesses employing fifty or more women would provide child care on the premises.[84] The similarity between the Argentine and the Chilean labor regulations shows that these nations kept a close watch on each other's ideas and that legislators were steering toward adopting what they viewed as "advanced" labor legislation.

By the early 1930s almost all the important objectives of labor legislation on women's and children's working hours and wages had been adopted on paper. What remained was to refine some concepts of social welfare. Eventually, with the enactment of the Código del Niño in 1934, Uruguay unified its protective legislation for mothers and children. Argentina advanced its own legislation on maternity protection with the approval of Laws 11.932 and 11.933, based on a bill introduced by Socialist senator Alfredo Palacios.[85] Law 11.932 established that all working and nursing mothers would be given two periods of half an hour each to nurse their babies. Law 11.933 forbade women to work thirty days before and forty-five days after childbirth. Their right to return to their jobs was guaranteed. The additional benefit established by this law was a subsidy no higher than 200 pesos that could not be impounded or ceded to anybody else. Women had the right to the services of a physician or a midwife for delivery. The funds for these benefits were to be accrued by a compulsory trimester contribution equivalent to one day's work from every female worker between fifteen and forty-five years of age. By government decree 80.229, given on 15 April 1935, the rules governing

Law 11.933 were put in place. Benefits for state employees were regulated by Law 12.111, issued on 30 November 1934, which guaranteed six weeks' leave after birth. Women were entitled to return to their jobs and would receive full compensation during their leave.[86]

The ideological base of the legislation enacted in the mid-1930s was in tune with the interest generated by scientific approaches to motherhood and child care in that decade. The primacy of biological destiny for women was explicit in the wording of the Argentine law. "The legislation relative to female work is generally oriented to take care of the subjects' vital forces, preserving them for the specific function of their sex: maternity. Society's interest is at stake."[87] In the same spirit, Chilean economist Francisco Walker Linares argued for the protection of working women and of women in general. "One of the main duties of society in regulating labor is that of protecting women; this is not just a moral task of justice and tutorship, but also a duty for the self-preservation of society. Women will be the mothers of future generations, and by protecting them we protect the home and the family, society's foundations."[88] These sentiments were similar to those uttered by conservatives and reformers alike in the early years of the century.

The ultimate "refinement" of maternity protection led the state into direct intervention in the "mothering" of babies. The 1931 Chilean Sanitary Code contained an article stipulating that "maternal milk is the exclusive property of the children, and consequently mothers are obliged to nurse their children until the age of five months, barring impediments by sickness."[89] The legislators sponsoring this law meant to eradicate professional wet-nursing. Nursing for "mercenary" purposes was regarded as leading to the neglect of those children whose legitimate source of food—their own mothers—was used for other babies. The Chilean model was copied by Argentina, which in 1936 created the Dirección de Maternidad e Infancia and enacted a law that, among other things, established the duty of all mothers to nurse their own children and forbade any nursing mother to "sell" her milk before her own baby was five months old.[90]

Although these "protective" laws covered all mothers, it was clear that the 1920s and 1930s legislation was intended to serve the needs of working women who were unable to provide for their own and their children's health. The protection of mothers and children had been one of the most important objectives of the first generation of social reformers and socialist feminists, and the legislation adopted throughout these years fulfilled many of their dreams. The "engendering" of the law had led, in some instances, however, to an inflexible predetermination of maternal duties. The bills forbidding the sale of mothers' natural milk amounted to depriving women of their individual judgment and obliging them to adopt criteria defined by the state for the sake of society's interests. The politics of authoritarianism of the 1930s imposed "social benefit" over personal discernment.

Protective Legislation: The Problem of Compliance

Legislative effectiveness can be measured by enforcement. Southern Cone nations lacked the economic resources for labor inspectors in industrial and commercial centers to supervise compliance with labor regulation. Sources indicate that the array of regulatory laws did not prevent abuses. Women continued to receive lower wages than men, and health ordinances were not observed. Rooms for child care were installed in only a few factories. In the 1920s, lack of executive orders to implement the laws precluded the enforcement of pre- and postnatal leave. Few workers took advantage of the existing facilities.[91] In Argentina several bills sponsored by socialists and the Radical Party to fine evaders of labor rest days met stiff opposition from conservative senators. Procedures to punish infractions were eventually approved in 1919.[92] As for domestic labor, a perusal of the want ads in the Buenos Aires *La Prensa* in the 1920s shows people requesting the services of *muchachas* (servants) between twelve and sixteen years of age for house help or as baby-sitters.[93] Domestic work remained unregulated and child labor abuse continued.

In the 1930s Chilean employers paid recently delivered mothers the six weeks' subsidy they were entitled to but fired them immediately afterward to avoid installing child-care facilities. Office workers and domestic employees were excluded from some of the benefits of the protective legislation, such as time for nursing. Argentine employers began to hire single women and to fire those who got married. In 1938 Socialist Alfredo Palacios proposed a bill forbidding that practice. In this effort he received the support of none other than Monsignor Gustavo Franceschi, the most distinguished member of Social Catholicism.[94] In 1934 Uruguayan physician Augusto Turenne, a staunch advocate of state regulation of women's work, denounced the dismissal of pregnant women from their jobs when their pregnancies became visible. He suggested state maternity insurance and the rigorous enforcement of paid pre- and postnatal leave. Insurance would guarantee women the financial aid they needed and would protect them from callous firing practices.[95] In 1941 another Uruguayan deputy complained that the 1918 law to provide chairs for working women was not enforced. The Labor Office was denounced for not carrying out its oversight duty, while women employees had to stand for over eight hours. The foul hygienic conditions in some factories dealing with animal bristles and employing minors and women were reported to one of the first elected Uruguayan female deputies two years later. She was able to gather other deputies' support to request that the National Labor Office establish a department to supervise women's and minors' labor.[96]

The meticulous reports submitted by early twentieth-century labor inspectors remain exceptional; there are few accounts of the working conditions in factories employing women in the 1930s. One report of a pottery factory in Penco, Chile, described a workforce of over 800 women earning just over 2 pesos a day. Men and women moved boxes of pottery in and out of the furnaces without protective gloves, and women and children carried pottery and charcoal in wheelbarrows. The male worker reporting this commented that such tasks were more appropriate for men than for women, but the only distinctions between the sexes were that women wore dresses and earned much less.[97] In the late 1930s the labor-oriented women's newspaper *La Mujer Nueva* devoted attention to the lack of compliance with labor legislation in Chile. The large textile company Yarur Hermanos, it reported, still required a ten-hour day. Another textile manufacturer, La Cordillera, ran a twelve-hour night shift in unheated plants. In 1940 the newspaper was bitter about the lack of compliance with labor legislation dealing with women. The recently enacted law establishing a minimum wage for private employees was disregarded.[98]

By the late 1930s some female industrial workers struck to protest the lack of enforcement of labor legislation. In Argentina female garment workers, including those working at home, began to make successful claims for a minimum wage. But apart from sporadic coparticipation in strikes, women did not assume their full potential within the labor movement in any of the three nations.[99] Possibly the best-enforced law was the Argentine pre- and postnatal compensation. In 1940, 133,144 women contributed to the fund and 14,972 received benefits: over one-third were textile workers either in Buenos Aires or in Buenos Aires Province. The median financial subsidy ranged from 175 to 200 pesos. The prescribed service by a physician or a midwife had been supplanted by an additional 100 pesos cash subsidy.[100]

Rationalizing Women's Work: Pros and Cons

Women's incorporation into the labor force posed numerous ideological and pragmatic challenges for men and women of all social classes. Old prejudices about women working outside the home were not confined to middle-class women. Poor women and their families worried about the exploitation of female labor, the "risks" of the streets, and all manner of danger surrounding women away from the shelter of home. The threat to women's health was another important issue shared by labor leaders, feminists, and public health experts. Women's competition for jobs inspired bitter attack and defense from several sides. These topics were debated for four decades and at the end of the 1930s, when the process of female incorporation into the labor market was irreversible, the debate had come to a standoff in which no ideological position could claim a victory. The solutions offered to the many questions posed by female workers formed a body of thought that can be only briefly explored here, since labor history is beyond the scope of this chapter, but the following sections will explore how issues raised by women's work affected gender relations during this period.

Work as Exploitation of Women

In the first years of the twentieth century socialist and anarchist labor leaders viewed women's labor as "toil and sweat." In 1901 in *El Trabajo*, a Uruguayan socialist newspaper, gave a typical negative portrayal of female workers:

> Poor little needleworkers who leave pieces of their souls in their machines to finish the rich dresses that the great ladies will show off; unhappy seamstresses who will see the sun rise after working all night, to earn the miserable crumb that will appease the hunger of their families; unlucky tobacco workers who will be obliged to breathe the dust that harms them; young shoe workers who sacrifice their youth and beauty in painful labor; despised servants who suffer insults and impertinences from their masters.[101]

Argentine socialist Juana María Beguino, writing for a Uruguayan labor newspaper in 1902, called on men and women to support each other to create a better world for workers while regretting that women workers were condemned by fate to forgo the emotional warmth of their own homes.[102] Several years later, when she spoke at the First International Feminine Congress in Buenos Aires (1910) on the condition of working women and children, Beguino's speech bore traces of the conflict between earlier attitudes and new realities. She was still unsure that women's new "economic freedom" justified the physical demands made on them by unregulated labor, and she called for a return of married women to the home, "to lull their children into sweet sleep with loving songs."[103] Beguino could not forget women's vulnerability under harsh working conditions and the loss of their nurturing roles as mothers and wives. Chilean Esther Valdés de Díaz, as editor of *La Alborada,* acknowledged women's humiliation and exploitation as labor, blaming the unquenchable ambition of capitalists. She believed that women's "physical constitution" was weaker than men's and condemned those who made them work longer hours.[104]

Resisting capitalist exploitation remained a key theme among the most radical members of the socialist and anarchist groups in the first two decades of the century.[105] Those yearning for women to return home had to yield to the economic reality that men's wages were not sufficient to meet the needs of a family. The inevitability of female labor was increasingly though often reluctantly acknowledged. Calls for the union of workers of both sexes were followed by demands for legislation to reduce economic discrimination against women. The first Chilean Socialist Party's program (1897) did not address the issue of female work, but by 1901 the Democrat-Socialist Party of Valparaíso called for regulation of women's work as part of legislative protection for both sexes.[106] In Uruguay the Colorado Party endorsed labor regulation and protective legislation, but it faced strong political challenges from the Blancos of the Nationalist Party. There was room for anarchist and socialist propaganda and activity, however. Early Uruguayan labor newspapers such as *El Amigo del Pueblo, Despertar,* and *El Trabajo* supported female workers' rights.[107]

At the opposite end of the political spectrum conservatives of several shades, and the Catholic Church, shared the concern of the ideological Left for working mothers, guided by Pope Leo XIII's *Rerum novarum.* Women should not work outside the home, but if they were obliged by circumstances, the church directed them away from mutualist societies with leftist ideologies.[108] Conservative economists were aware of the value of women's work but preferred not to factor it into their assessments of the national economy, thus perpetuating the concept that it was not central to the economy of family and nation. Alejandro Bunge adopted this position in his 1917 study of the Argentine economy.[109]

As long as wages remained low and regulatory legislation fell short of expectations and went unenforced, there were plenty of reasons to write about female labor exploitation. In the 1930s the pages of Chilean *La Mujer Nueva* and Argentine *Vida Femenina* privileged the discussion of working women's issues. *Vida Femenina* mostly discussed inequality in female wages and the lack of social welfare. Women workers were exhorted to join in union activities. Labor itself was not decried; it was still regarded as the "route to equality" with men.[110] *La Mujer Nueva*, the publication of the Movimiento Pro-Emancipación de la Mujer de Chile (MEMCH), repeatedly denounced the exploitation of female industrial, agricultural, and domestic workers in sharper tones than *Vida Femenina* and campaigned for broader welfare coverage.[111] At its 1940 meeting MEMCH reconciled the tension between equality and protection by resolving that gender equality in the labor market meant equal protection for men and women. Night work should be open to both men and women in good health, and women should physically prepare to undertake the same jobs as men by practicing sports.[112]

For several months in the mid-1930s *Acción Femenina*, a Chilean middle-class feminist magazine, carried on a workers' agenda under what appears to have been a leftist editorial stewardship. In addition to urging continental workers' solidarity, the magazine published essays on the exploitation and devaluation of women's work and the gap between men's and women's wages in department stores. Author Grace Thorni urged women's associations to denounce the situation and demand the services of social workers and labor inspectors. Women's work, whether a choice or a necessity, deserved respect and protection.[113] Women's participation in several key strikes in the 1930s, such as the Argentine textile strike of 1935, gave them a sense of their own worth, but the small benefits received by one sector of the labor force had no effect on the others. In fact, as we will see later, there were several nasty backlash attacks against women workers.[114]

Work, Health, and Honor

High among the preoccupations of the early labor leaders, public health specialists, and feminists was the perceived threat that industrial labor posed to women's health and reproductive abilities. Before the twentieth century the only women who received public health attention and methodical regulation of their activities were prostitutes.[115] Since 1891 the Argentine socialist labor federation [Federación Obrera] had explored the industrial plants where women worked under the assumption that abuse of women in the workplace threatened their health and endangered the family. In 1894 this organization identified the employment of women and children in factories as "the source of many ills in the family, and of decline in the already meager salary of men."[116]

In a 1903 pamphlet, socialist-feminist Gabriela Laperrière de Coni warned women about the hazards of labor in poorly lit and ventilated rooms and the dangers of posture-constricting work that deformed their bodies and possibly affected their reproduction. She advised women to forgo that type of labor unless forced by economic need. It was their duty as workers and women to protect their own health and that of future generations.[117] Given what we know about the working conditions of the period, her concern was justified. In 1904 she wrote a bill to regulate women's work in which she proposed prohibition of night work and work with heavy machinery and advocated paid leave after childbirth. This bill was later endorsed by Alfredo Palacios, whose name has since been attached to it.[118]

Socialist physician and public health advocate Dr. Angel Giménez lucidly analyzed the health conditions of working people in Argentina in his 1901 medical dissertation. His ideas were similar to Gabriela Coni's and were based on contemporary medical knowledge of the effects of noxious matter on the human organism.[119] He was particularly concerned about match workers because of the poisonous substances used in manufacturing. His approach, although strictly medical, had a marked social bent. He endorsed the eight-hour workday, better wages, and improved quality of life for the working population. Dr. Juan Bialet Massé, already discussed, must also be counted among those who voiced the opinion that women suffered considerable stress working either at home or in factories. Despite the early interest of some labor organizations, many labor newspapers had little to say about health, being more concerned with the propagation of their ideas and the mobilization of the workers. By the mid-1920s concern with public health had broadened owing to the increasing popularity of eugenics concepts and included all women. Women workers benefited from laws regulating working hours and restricting their labor in jobs considered threatening to their health or beyond their physical capacity. For some, regulation made industrial work preferable to work at home. If the laws were enforced, a factory was a more healthful place to work than the dirty, dark, and unhygienic homes of poor people.[120]

Work outside the home was also regarded as jeopardizing women's morals. The vulnerability of working women to sexual abuse elicited a strong response among men and women on the Left. Ethical considerations were important for some of the early female leaders, who denounced some occupations as a risk to women's virtue. Since 1896 the Argentinean Socialist Party's program had included the prohibition of any employment that endangered women's morals.[121] The topic was discussed in *La Vanguardia;* in 1905 the newspaper reported how a manager recruited female scabs "in less than honest places" to replace women strikers in a shoe factory.[122] The fiery

Uruguayan anarchist María Muñoz saw the greatest moral threat in the suave factory manager and some male workers. She was concerned about women workers who "made a mistake" to satisfy a man's whim, but she was equally aware of abusive husbands.[123]

Women themselves expressed anxiety about male advances. If working conditions exposed women to "corrupting" influences, editorialist and working woman Esther Díaz favored eliminating the opportunity altogether. Women should not be forced to leave work late, "exposed to compromise their virtue in the shadows of the night." Díaz painted a dark picture of lusting male "wolves" waiting outside factories for innocent workers who, treated like beasts at work, fell for the sweet enticements of those scoundrels.[124] The Chilean newspaper La Alborada supported the municipality's prohibiting jobs for women in bars in Santiago. Although it had deprived 3,000 women of jobs—claimed a 1906 editorial—economic suffering was preferable to the immorality fostered by such an occupation.[125]

Anarchists advocating less conventional sexual relations implicitly acknowledged that poor working women were exposed to compromising situations, but they would not defend conventional "morality." Writing for the Buenos Aires anarchist newspaper La Protesta Humana in 1898, José Nakens drew a bitterly satiric picture of the young female worker who, faced with a life of hard work, hoped that prostitution would enable her to become the "cocotte" of an old rich man and accumulate enough money for her old age. He attempted to exonerate those women who, despairing of labor's meager reward, either "fell" into or chose prostitution.[126] In his report Bialet Massé suggested that in some provincial establishments owners carried on sexual relationships with female workers and that some seamstresses who worked at home were sexually exploited by employers. A 1917 report on the occupations of prostitutes before they engaged in commercial sex cited sewing as the most common trade.[127] When Celia La Palma de Emery carried out the first inspection of Buenos Aires's industrial sector, she was worried about the "competence and the morals" of the female worker. She objected to hiring women with police records or lacking in education. She argued for comfort in the work place because it enhanced welfare and morality, which she understood as orderly and peaceful behavior among the workers.

Concern for women workers' morals appeared in the most unlikely sources. The 1921 Chilean labor code bill had two articles addressing "morals." No widower or single male employer could take on female apprentices under age twenty-one. A female apprentice could rescind her contract if the contractor's wife or the employer's female representative died.

These prohibitions would eliminate women's working for single men, creating situations "compromising" to their reputations.[128] In 1921 Argentine President Hipólito Yrigoyen submitted a bill for a labor code. Article 99 assumed a moralizing tone stating that "the regulation of female industrial and commercial work in the country should be subject to rules protecting their morals, security, and health."[129] That was the trinity of values that would make labor acceptable for all women.

The state, organized labor groups, and feminists assumed the role of protectors and defenders of women in the two areas they deemed crucial for maintaining social order: health and morals. Both were related to women's sexuality and reproductive capacity. As future mothers, young women should be healthy to produce healthy citizens, but their "morality"—their conduct with the male sex in public areas where the protection of the family was absent—was no less important. Promiscuity was a threat to the family: traditional attitudes about women's honor died hard.

Labor as Economic Independence: An Ambivalent Reality

As seen above, socialists made the first efforts to counterbalance the exploitation of women's labor with the benefits they and society derived from their labor. This double allegiance to potentially antithetical themes made their message ambivalent at times. Middle-class feminists held a more consistently uplifting view of labor as a positive contribution to the nation and to their own gender. Rising inflation and the several economic crises between 1915 and 1930 forced many middle-class women to seek employment outside the home. By the mid-1920s professional men and women were ready to admit that many male household heads were unable to provide fully for the needs of the family and, more important, that many women were heads of families or had no man or family to sustain them.[130] This apparently "universal" expansion of women into the labor force, which now contained a significant number of white-collar workers, was translated into a constructive view of women's work. Middle-class rhetoric presented working women as industrious little bees helping to create a better nation. Some men who professed to disdain the banality of upper-class women extolled the labor of female proletarians and praised middle-class women who acquired a degree or a profession to ensure their economic independence. "Thus we see in our midst thousands of women in the conquest of an independent position, invading the spheres of men's labor, a beautiful renaissance of women's efforts," wrote Uruguayan José Virginio Díaz in 1916.[131] Young industrial workers were compared to colorful butterflies by a Chilean writer, who waxed poetic on women workers receiving their weekly paychecks. Working long hours was hard, but women took pride in helping their families, contributing to national progress, and being useful citizens. Work helped women to achieve personal equality with men and to marry for love rather than for money.[132] Even those who opposed suffrage and distrusted radical feminism regarded paid work as empowering women. "Labor's legal strength is the headstone of feminism," wrote Argentine María Teresa León de Sebastián in 1928.[133]

An astute observer of his own times, Argentine jurist Juan Carlos Rébora, surveying the social changes in the first quarter of the century, also associated women's work with economic independence and feminism. Women, he posited, had been attracted by the office and the factory, and by 1914 they predominated in about fifteen occupations. Although he noted the absence of women from the vast majority of occupational categories, he ignored the heavy dependence on traditional occupations such as washing and ironing, weaving, and sewing, concluding that "the economic emancipation of women was a consummated fact." This economic emancipation was the real social change supporting the demand for the legal changes necessary to redefine women's role in society.[134]

Not all middle-class feminists believed in a female professional paradise, but even those who recognized the problems implicit in women's employment, believed the future lay in expanding professional careers on equal terms and in lifting legal obstacles to women's administering their own income. Thus Elvira Santa Cruz Ossa (writing as Roxane), a well-known and respected Chilean writer of the 1920s who professed to be a feminist "in word and deed," defined feminism as mostly "economic, and requiring three factors for its resolution: [access to] labor, . . . equal wages, and free disposition of one's properties and earnings."[135] Middle-class optimism about the unbounded possibilities for women to change society through their work was fully shared by neither socialist feminists nor the labor press and, above all, did not reflect the realities of the laboring classes as portrayed in the reports of the labor departments of the three nations. The articulate middle class created and projected its own image of female labor, based on its experience with white-collar jobs and professional education. But whether presented as a panacea for independence, a reckless form of exploitation, or a necessary catharsis that could open new horizons for women, the figure of the working woman still evoked rancor and opposition among many men and women.

Bitter Fruit: Women's Labor under Attack

Regardless of the efforts of the most inspired socialist and anarchist leaders to support an ideal of justice for female workers, anxiety over labor competition would not go away. Among the earliest commentaries on gender rivalry for jobs was one by Chilean needleworker Esther Valdés de Díaz. In 1907 she stated that "women who work in factories, pushed by the need to earn their daily bread, not only are not in their place but, without realizing it, are competing with men and, in doing so, becoming victims of capitalism. . . . When women replace men in the workplace, they contribute to the devaluation of men's work." [136] Such mixed feelings were not easy to uproot from labor circles and were largely due to women's depressed wages. [137] In 1922 the threat of female workers to themselves and to society was discussed by an anonymous Argentine in the anarchist newspaper *Nuestra Tribuna*. The writer denounced capitalists' praise of working women as a trap. They really wanted to devalue the work of men and displace them with cheap female labor. [138]

Most middle-class people were unaware of anarchists' critiques and continued to believe that women's work had more than economic value. Indeed, it had political potential that began to be appreciated in the 1920s, when the campaign to reform the civil codes was in full swing in the three nations. Those supporting reform underlined working women's need to gain full control of their own earnings. Lifting the legal restrictions on women's managing their wages would weaken men's power over their wives, an important watershed in gender relations. The Civil Code was reformed in Argentina in the mid-1920s, and twice revised in Chile by 1934 to give married women financial autonomy and greater authority over their children. The strength of the moral argument carried by feminists and socialists was largely based on the reality of female work.

Even though the image of women's achievement through labor and economic independence was not accurate, it was successful enough to backfire as the economy changed in the 1930s. By the mid-1930s the specter of women taking the place of jobless male family heads returned. The call for women to join unions and strike to combat poor wages, inflation, and the hiring of teenage girls was sounded again, but with the ominous theme of defending the territory gained thus far. In 1934 Alicia Moreau de Justo remarked on the "continuing incorporation of a new contingent of women [to industry], often displacing men on account of their lower salary." She urged rewriting protective legislation for women. To avoid gender conflict she suggested raising women's wages and maintaining separate spheres of labor. These measures would make men comfortable with women's access to the labor market. [139]

The backlash against women's share of the labor market had two fronts: ideological and legislative. Neither was ultimately successful, but both left some bitter memories. The ideological front was maintained by conservative or right-wing writers and politicians. Female labor outside the home was resurrected as a threat to the stability of the family. Analyzing the causes for the increasing number of broken homes, the Chilean José Luis López Ureta blamed the "crisis of the family" on several "dissolving causes," among which he placed women's "industrialism." Even though he dealt with abandonment by men, he cited women's work as partially responsible for a male crime.[140] Women were having fewer children and taking men's jobs in factories, offices, and schools, claimed an anonymous analyst in the Chilean newspaper *Zig-Zag*. "Men are feeling walled in by feminine competition, and everyday life is harsher for them."[141] Women were put on the defensive, having to demand respect for their labor and to demonstrate that if they were deprived of their work the economic situation of the family and the nation would worsen.[142]

Would it be possible to rechannel women into certain occupations and create clearly separate spheres of interest that would allow each sex its own turf and retain some traditional values within the reality of change? This idea was backed by Machiavello Varas, a Chilean professor of political economy. Unlike others, he believed feminism was a good thing, having delivered the death kiss to *empleomanía*, or oversupply of male bureaucrats. Women's access to public and private jobs *should* displace idle men. He pressed his point by suggesting that the government draw up a list of positions open *exclusively* to women in post offices, savings institutions, hospitals, notaries' offices, and telegraph stations. The displacement of men from some occupations was a welcome incentive for them to look for other jobs less bound to routine, more entrepreneurial, in tune with the complexities of modern life, and most important, more appropriate to their sex. Another Chilean, Amanda Hermosilla Aedo, backed these ideas and suggested that women should be given exclusive control over primary school teaching and lower-rank bureaucratic positions. The first of those wishes was almost a reality in the three nations; the second was on its way. Hermosilla Aedo accepted the lower rungs of the bureaucratic ladder as an appropriate field for women's labor. Pursuing economic security, some women clipped the wings of other women's hopes to obtain challenging jobs instead of positions discarded by men.[143]

The more pragmatic opponents of women's invasion of certain occupational sectors attempted to draw the line. In Chile a couple of bills to curtail their work alerted women from several walks of life to a conservative male backlash. In 1936 President Alessandri, backed by the Labor Ministry, proposed to restrict women's employment in government and municipal offices, establishing a 20 percent quota for them to offset male displacement from the labor market. Another bill to establish a minimum wage, but only for men, responded to a Labor Code article that allowed a gender difference. Between 1933 and 1935 Chile had suffered a great economic crisis: unemployment was high, the cost of living had risen, and the value of the peso had declined. Women were unwelcomed competitors in the labor market.[144] Chilean women, who already could vote in municipal elections, were outraged by the proposed legislation. All feminist organizations joined in a public opinion campaign to influence the members of Congress. Protests were signed by the Radical Party, the Partido Cívico Femenino, the Inter-American Commission for Women, the Unión Argentina de Mujeres, Argentine writer Victoria Ocampo, and the Movimiento Pro-Emancipación de la Mujer en Chile, a feminist umbrella organization. The deputies rejected the bill.[145] Data released by the National Statistics Office in 1936 showed that working women were at the bottom of the earnings ladder. A survey based on 9,499 privately employed women who contributed to labor benefit funds reported that 67 percent earned less than 300 pesos a month. Only 9 percent earned over 500 pesos.[146]

In Argentina an intellectual backlash was carried out by the proponents of juridical eugenics, among whom Carlos Bernaldo de Quirós was the most outspoken. For him women were "an irreplaceable embryogenic, maternologic home, social and demographic capital." Dissipating that potential could only be negative for any nation. The exploitation of women's labor by irresponsible capitalists had to be stopped by protective legislation. At the same time the state should organize female labor, keeping in mind that the highest service of womanhood was maternity. After an extensive exposition of questionably used statistics on sickness, death, and fertility decline in working women in several nations, he proposed enticements to keep fertile women at home, away from factories. Only those women whose "genetic value" to the nation was already over (those older than fifty or infertile) should be allowed to compete with men in industrial work. He supported revision of existing laws to remove all pregnant women from work after the sixth month. He showed himself magnanimous by not opposing the work of professional women or those who were the only support of their families.[147]

Carlos Bernaldo de Quirós belonged to a generation preoccupied by the decline in the birthrate and obsessed with eugenics. Others who shared his ideas about an impending demographic crisis proposed legislation that would encourage births by offering working families a bonus for every child. Although such bonuses already existed in Argentine private firms in the late 1930s, bills providing similar help by the government had been discussed since the mid-1920s without much success. In May 1938 Socialist senator Alfredo Palacios picked up the idea and put forward a bill to give fathers of large families preference in state employment, especially those married to employed women "who would leave their work to devote themselves entirely to their families." Although Palacios may have spoken for himself and not for socialism in general, it is clear that thirty years after he endorsed the first bill to protect women in the workplace, his stance was no longer in harmony with that of the women in his party. That same year a deputy sponsored yet another bill to provide a 10 peso bonus to state employees, or a higher one for those earning less than 180 pesos monthly, "as long as the women remain in the home taking care of the family." [148] These incentives for working women to return home were not sizable enough to compensate for their economic need or to tempt them to abandon their work, but the bills are eloquent in their intentions.

Unquestionably middle-class men in the 1930s still harbored doubts about women's increasing participation in social and political activities as well as in the labor market. They argued that work deprived women of their emotional wealth, ignoring the realities behind women's decision to seek employment, which had not changed since the turn of the century. [149] A 1938 inquiry among 424 female workers in the Chilean textile company Yarur Hermanos revealed that 32.5 percent contributed their entire wages to the maintenance of the home. Three hundred (71 percent) had to work because either the father's or husband's income was missing (180) or insufficient (120). Only 46 said they worked to become economically independent, and 5 worked to improve their standard of living. Among those 180 who had no male supporter, nearly half (72) had been abandoned by father or husband, while almost one-third more (62) had lost one by death. [150]

Summing up the experience of four decades, in May 1940 socialist feminist Argentine María L. Berrondo appraised, with a mixture of sadness and irony, male critiques of feminism and women's incorporation into the labor force. Many women worked to help their families and exchanged efficient and hard work for low wages. She discerned that some men saw this as a just punishment. Women had demanded work, had displaced men, and were now killing themselves for paltry sums. It served them right. But Berrondo had no patience with such accusations, especially from learned sociologists. What on earth, she wrote, had feminism to do with the "management voracity" that hired women precisely to pay them less? Feminism did not advocate unfair competition. It had taught women to fight for themselves, and had it been fully successful, women would have become members of all unions and political parties, helping men promote human dignity. It was imperative that both men and women understand the economic need that pushed some women to work. The verbal punishment must stop: women had carried a heavy load of guilt throughout history and needed no more. Fed up, she challenged men: "How happy would men be if they were alone in this world? But until that divine solitude is theirs, and while the problem remains on the same premises, [men] could choose between helping women to grow intellectually and motivating them to join the unions and political parties to defend their common interests, or sweeping them [away] Hitler-style. Women wait for their decision."[151]

Berrondo's bitterness and disillusion may not have been shared by all working women, but it reflected the disenchantment of those who, looking back on four decades of activism, felt betrayed by a reality that no protective legislation would mask. Neither class nor gender had been redeemed from prejudice and abuse. Socialism, anarchism, and feminism had joined hands early in the century to lift working women up from need and exploitation. Class and gender had for once come together in the ranks of these ideologies as they shared objectives of redemption. When socialists and feminists agreed to downplay class to obtain protective legislation, anarchists then withdrew. The emphasis on protection, however, left women in "their place." In 1940 women remained trapped behind superficial praise of their work and experienced the reality of unenforced legislation while still facing the same economic needs that had led them to jobs in factories and offices.

CHAPTER 3

Puericultura, Public Health,
and Motherhood

Although labor was a signifier of change for women at many levels, public health and child care constituted a unique arena where feminists could make a case for women's special role in any scheme of social change. Inferior housing, lack of potable water, and poorly developed sewage systems were a few of the environmental problems facing people in the rapidly growing urban centers.[1] Tuberculosis permanently affected a significant number, and infectious diseases and infant mortality regularly visited poor neighborhoods. How disease and poor working conditions affected women's and children's health was one of the most important issues raised by physicians and by feminists, who found in the care of children a key source of legitimation for women's emergence into the public arena. The traditional view of women as mothers, nurturers, caregivers, and healers gained new relevance when it was put at the service of the nation. The female professionals graduating from the universities in the first decade of the century won much male support because they were dedicated to social problems that did not detract from their femininity and modeled acceptable female behavior.

The urbanization and population growth experienced by the Southern Cone nations between 1890 and 1910 resulted partly from a vast wave of immigration in Argentina and Uruguay and from internal migration in Chile. Desirable as this growth was, it was plagued by alarming health problems that reflected badly on nations wishing to join the mainstream of Western "progress." One way of demonstrating "civilization" was to control the embarrassing social and medical problems affecting their cities. In the early 1880s a few concerned physicians made the first efforts to replace charity with preventive medicine and to educate the population on critical health issues. The full impact of public health plans and debates was not felt until after 1910, however, when the governments of these nations began to respond in earnest to medical pressure.

The protection of motherhood and childhood fell to those who called themselves *higienistas,* a corps of physicians and social scientists who saw in public health programs a means to improve the urban health profile and make their countries conform to European and North American standards of social progress. Social hygiene was the product of research carried out in the last decades of the nineteenth century on the relation between disease, the urban environment, and people's living and working conditions. Public health specialists made these elements relevant to long-term state policies that would ensure some lasting control over morbidity and mortality. A Uruguayan health official later defined the new orientation in public health as seeking to "accommodate the new scientific orientations on the preservation of health through early diagnosis and the improvement of the conditions of life owed to social solidarity."[2] From 1900 to 1940 the banner of *higienismo* was carried mostly by male physicians, with a few women joining them in the 1920s. Among the most notable *higienistas* of their time were Argentines Emilio Coni, Telémaco Susini, José Penna, and Domingo Cabred; Chileans José F. Salas, Eduardo Moore, Pedro Láutaro Ferrer, Manuel Camilo Vial, Roberto Dávila Boza; and Uruguayans Joaquín Canabal, Ernesto Fernández Espiro, Alfredo Vidal y Fuentes, and Julio A. Bauzá.[3]

The improvement of public health rested on several strategies, and preventive care was a key element. Social hygiene aimed at surrounding people with a clean environment, teaching them basic rules of personal care, and changing their habits to prevent diseases and ensure the health of future generations. The increasing influence of *higienismo* brought the first institutions to control disease and promote national health. In Chile the establishment of a Consejo Superior de Higiene Publica was proposed to the Chamber of Deputies in 1881 and officially approved in 1882 along with an Instituto de Higiene.[4] Unfortunately, lacking political and economic support from the government, they had little impact on the health of the population at large. Furthermore, medicine was only then discovering the source of diseases, and many remained beyond effective cure. After much debate and delay, the first Código Sanitario was enacted in 1918, compiling the legislation on public health.[5]

In 1925 this code was superseded by another designed by United States *higienista* Dr. John D. Long. Despite the country's constitutional crisis, a March 1925 decree created a division of social hygiene in the Ministry of Health, Social Welfare, and Labor. That legislation set up clinics to control venereal diseases and provide gynecological and pulmonary services.[6] The teaching of "social hygiene" was made compulsory in all primary schools.[7] In 1931 yet another sanitary code replaced the 1925 legislation, which had remained unenforced. The 1931 code retained many of the former code's provisions for the care of public health and created a National Public Health Service entrusted to a director general of public health.[8] The reorganization of the public health system ushered in a new era of centralized services and, more important, reflected the state's intention to increase control over the medical needs of the nation. Throughout the 1930s ad hoc legislation began to implement the mandate of the National Public Health Service.[9]

In Uruguay bills enacted in 1892, 1894, and 1895 proposed a National Council of Hygiene. The last one succeeded, and the council was approved by the executive in October 1895,[10] charged with controlling contagious and infectious diseases, prostitution, and the activities of the medical profession.[11] In 1927 an administrative reorganization resulted in the foundation of a National Council of Public Welfare [Primer Consejo Nacional de Asistencia Pública].[12] In 1931 the Board of Public Health [Consejo de Salud Pública] consolidated the services previously given by the National Council of Hygiene and the Institute for the Prophylaxis of Syphilis.[13] When the Ministry of Public Health was founded in 1934, it supervised established aspects of public health and also new ones such as drug addiction and prenuptial certificates.[14]

Public health was officially introduced in Argentina in 1852 with the foundation of the Council for Public Hygiene and was firmly established as a discipline by Dr. Gillermo Rawson, who began lecturing on public health at the University of Buenos Aires in 1873. Rawson forged a generation of public health specialists, among whom were Emilio Coni and Telémaco Susini, who carried his work into the twentieth century. Several temporary councils operated rather inefficiently at the municipal and national level until the federal government created a National Department of Hygiene in 1880. Because of internal squabbles between municipal and national authorities, the authority of the National Department was expanded by an 1891 law, implemented in 1900, entrusting it with all matters relevant to public health. This institution directed public health policies until 1943, when it was replaced by the Dirección Nacional de Salud Pública y Asistencia Social.[15]

Child Mortality as a Health Problem and a Social Problem

The three Southern Cone nations had extremely high child mortality at the turn of the century. Social reformers and *higienistas* called for effective state health policies, since child mortality affected the ultimate welfare of the nation. A high death rate among infants and children was regarded as reflecting failure to protect future generations. Because women were the key caretakers of children, they were an essential element in the design of any policy addressing their needs as mothers as well as the needs of their children. A survey of the policies on child care adopted by Southern Cone nations will help us understand the new cooperative role women were assigned in *higienismo.*

About 1900 there were two main causes of the high death rate in the Southern Cone nations: tuberculosis and child mortality. Respiratory and gastrointestinal diseases affected both children and adults, but children suffered most, accounting for 52 percent of all deaths in the city of Buenos Aires in 1875.[16] Emilio Coni claimed that before 1907 116 per 1,000 infants under one year of age died annually. Thanks to increased efforts in public child care, that figure was reduced to 102/1,000 between 1913 and 1915.[17] To its credit, Argentina succeeded in further reducing infant and child mortality in the ensuing years, and by the mid-1920s the death toll for children under one year had declined considerably. Nonetheless, in 1924 the province of Buenos Aires reported that babies under one month old were still dying at the rate of 69/1,000 and children under one year at 105/1,000.[18] Although this was an improvement over the previous decade, the toll was still high. At the end of the 1930s the death rate in that province remained stationary at 65.5/1,000 for infants between one month and one year of age.[19] The death rate was much higher in some of the distant poorer provinces such as Jujuy, where it was 199/1,000.

The Chilean child death rate was appalling, especially in Santiago. Between 1871 and 1908 it rose from 273/1,000 to 325/1,000, with a peak of 340/1,000 for 1891–95.[20] The figures reported in 1905 for children under five represented 49.3 percent of all deaths, almost the same as that of Buenos Aires in 1875. The rate had declined slightly two years later (1907), to 37.9 percent.[21] Child mortality decreased throughout the first two decades of the twentieth century, but it was still very high compared with that in Argentina, Uruguay, and other countries in the Western world.

Long-term statistical data between 1900 and 1930 show that infant mortality in Chile had peaks and troughs, with a slow decline over the years. Two peaks in 1905–9 and in 1919, at 302/1,000 and 306/1,000 respectively, mark the highest incidence, but the death rate declined between 1915 and 1930 from 254/1,000 to 234/1,000.[22] From 1931 to 1935 the situation did not seem to improve significantly, since in 1935 the national infant death rate was still 250/1,000 and only slightly less in the urban centers.[23] The figure for 1936 was 252/1,000. At that point Chile had one of the highest child mortality rates in the world, being at the top of a list of twenty-six countries, none with over 200/1,000 deaths.[24] Figures for outside Santiago verify the intensity and breadth of the problem. In 1928 *El Mercurio* of Santiago quoted child mortality at 29 percent of all births in the northern city of Iquique.[25] More depressing was the figure released in 1935 by the city of Chillán, where only 20 out of 100 children survived their first month.[26]

Uruguay had half of Chile's child mortality, but in 1920 pediatrician Julio A. Bauzá despaired of the slow progress in curtailing it. Infant mortality was 11 percent of all deaths in 1905–10 and 12.5 percent in 1911–15. In fact more infants died of gastrointestinal complications in 1911–15 than in 1901–5.[27] Statistics for the second decade of the century were no more hopeful. In Montevideo infant mortality was at its highest in 1915, when it reached 147/1,000, and lowest in 1921, when it was 100/1,000. The national rates of infant mortality fluctuated between 1911 and 1921 but were never below 93/1,000 (1912) and reached 124/1,000 in 1916.[28] Despite all the efforts to provide health care to babies and mothers, in 1927 Uruguay recorded 4,500 deaths out of 19,939 children under one year of age (22.5 percent). In that same year 1,392 babies were stillborn. The average child mortality for the country at that point was 110/1,000.[29]

Ten years later there was a significant improvement. Between 1938 and 1939 the national rate dropped to 82/1,000. As in Argentina, rural departments had much higher child mortality. Such was the case in Rivera, Cerro Largo, and Artigas, where death rates fluctuated between 114 and 131/1,000. In Canelones, however, the rate was only 52/1,000. Montevideo held close to the national average with 81/1,000. The hope of public health officials, pediatricians, and eugenicists that pre- and postnatal care would make a difference seemed closer to reality when in 1943 child mortality was reported to be 69.3/1,000 outside Montevideo and 30.7 in the capital.[30]

The statistical data for the three nations underline the urgent nature of this public health problem. The infant and child death tolls in the mid-1930s compared unfavorably with those of European nations such as Switzerland and Sweden and placed the Southern Cone closer to Eastern European nations and Northern Ireland. Yet the Southern Cone fared differently from other Latin American nations. In 1930 Chile, with the highest rate of child mortality in the Southern Cone, was well above Mexico, Colombia, Costa Rica, and El Salvador. On the other hand, Argentina and Uruguay compared favorably with Colombia and Costa Rica, where mortality was higher.[31] According to a eugenics source, in 1941 Chile and Costa Rica remained among the world's nations with the highest infant mortality, while Uruguay was in the category of "moderate" infant mortality, and Argentina, along with Venezuela, Ecuador, and Mexico, was among those with high rates.[32] The 1930s decline in the birthrate coupled with a high rate of infant mortality in the three nations made for a somber forecast. Immigration had ceased to increase population, and some politicians and eugenicists feared their nations would "weaken" and fail to fulfill their social and economic potential. This climate of opinion must be kept in mind if we are to appreciate the meaning of policies addressing the protection of motherhood and childhood.

The health of pregnant women was another source of medical concern. Most women had no effective means of birth control, and many suffered complications throughout pregnancy and at delivery. To control their fertility some resorted to abortions that sent many to "maternity" wards, if not to the grave.[33] Prenatal care was rare: maternity hospitals rendered services at birth and during a brief postpartum period, but the limited number of hospitals obliged most women to deliver at home, aided by a midwife. During the first decades of the century most women preferred to do so. Only when the home was totally unsuitable were they advised to go to a hospital, in the belief that mothers should not abandon their children and families for delivery.[34] In the mid-1930s the personnel available for prenatal care and delivery in the three nations was still inadequate. In the 1935–39 roster of medical professionals rendering services within the Chilean social security system there were 42 obstetricians and 198 midwives. In the Argentine province of Catamarca there were only 3 certified midwives, resulting in high mortality at childbirth and bad health throughout pregnancy.[35] In 1939, out of a total of 166,251 pregnant women in Chile, the Ministry of Health estimated that 91,650 relied on their own means for prenatal care, not using any state facility. Generously assuming that a third of them had enough money to pay for medical services, over 64,000 were assumed to lack any medical care — over a third of all pregnant women.[36]

The Role of Women in Promoting Social Hygiene

The appalling health problems facing women and children explain the *higienistas'* interest in developing a health care system more accessible to those in need and, preferably, served by women. Social hygiene had two agendas for women: to teach other women how best to perform their roles as mothers, and to serve the nation as health care professionals. When the education of women became a national issue in the 1880s, most voices claimed "higher" education to allow women to go into professional careers. Many educators, however, did not lose sight of the need to prepare women for less sophisticated objectives such as the efficient management of the home and the "scientific" care of children.

The discussion of women's education had philosophical as well as pragmatic components. Educators of the period regarded women primarily as future mothers, having significant educational and moral influence on children and the home and best served by an education geared toward those ends. Thrift in housekeeping would be improved by learning mathematics; chemistry, physiology, and hygiene would allow mothers to understand the rules of health and maintain their families' well-being.[37] One of the new subjects to be introduced in women's education was child care, or *puericultura*. Training women to provide better care would save children's lives and give mothers a sense of responsibility and pride about their role. The scientific care of children was a logical corollary to the pedagogical reform of the late nineteenth century, when the science of preserving health was directed toward those "called to undertake the high and sacred duties of maternity."[38]

In the mid-1910s *puericultura* also meant the teaching required to give proper care to mothers and children in hospitals where obstetrical services were furnished. The Chilean government founded the Institute of Puericultura in 1906 to offer medical services to pregnant women and to children under one year of age. In Santiago a school for obstetrics and *puericultura* was founded in June 1913.[39] Similar services were offered by the Institutos de Puericultura in Buenos Aires by 1912, which originated in one clinic founded in 1907 by Dr. Enrique Foster that had expanded into six clinics with the aid of Asistencia Pública and that eventually became child-care centers.[40]

One of the best treatises in domestic education was published in Chile in 1909. It devoted one chapter to the care of babies and to identifying the most common diseases of infancy. A full text on child care was published in 1929.[41] In Argentina, the Ministry of Education authorized a course in infant hygiene in July 1897.[42] One of the first books to make child hygiene accessible to mothers was published at the turn of the century in Buenos Aires by an eminent pediatrician and *higienista*, Gregorio Aráoz Alfaro, who began writing on the subject in 1893, and spent the rest of his life promoting child care and public health. His *Libro de las madres*, published in 1899, covered the ground from prenatal care to late infancy. It was still recommended as a mother's manual in 1919 by none other than Dra. Alicia Moreau.[43]

Responsible and scientific child care imparted special prestige to mothering. Women would help to abate infant and child mortality, an urgent mandate of public health, and would serve as agents of social progress — powerful concepts in the first decade of the century. In Argentina *puericultura* was the catalyst for the formation of several women's groups to promote the protection of mothers and children. The Club de Madres was such an institution. Founded in 1912 by a group of upper-class women, the Club hoped to develop a broad plan of "hygienic" activities to improve children's health. Their first efforts, however, followed the traditional activities of donating food and clothes to *conventillo* [slum] families.[44] Far more important was the foundation of Unión y Labor by a group of feminist and socialist women whose purpose was "to work for feminine progress and the protection of childhood."[45] The association published a magazine by the same name, and proceeds from its sale were channeled toward a child-care center (Casa de los Niños) for infants.

The contributors to the magazine were intellectuals of Buenos Aires, and though not sharing the same political views, they had a common recognition of women as a key factor in social change. Some of them, like physician Elvira Rawson de Dellepiane, were full-fledged feminists committed to the emancipation of women.[46] Sara Justo was a socialist and shared with Rawson de Dellepiane the hope of founding children's homes and *hogares maternales* to provide services for poor mothers and their babies.[47] The society received a plot of land on which to build a children's home in 1910, but though they had assets of up to 25,000 pesos by the end of 1911, we do not know whether they ever built it.[48] In mid-1913 Unión y Labor expressed its support of teaching *puericultura* in the normal schools.[49] Unfortunately the magazine ceased publication shortly after the First Congress on the Child (see below), and there are few traces of its staff thereafter. The activities of Unión y Labor did not revolve exclusively around the medical care of infants and children. Its members supported social services for poor mothers and street children. They saw this as part of a feminist contribution to society that would change women's status without disrupting their roles as mothers and would support children's rights to welfare and happiness.

Puericultura was one of several important topics at the 1910 First International Feminine Congress in Buenos Aires. Elvira Rawson de Dellepiane addressed child care in a paper describing the depressing picture of congenitally weak children and requesting special schools for the mentally retarded and for normal but sickly children. In describing the product of negative heredity she used the realistic language of a physician exposed to hospital cases to advance the concept of social prophylaxis. Although not referring directly to venereal diseases, she made it clear that a "sad morbid inheritance" was to be blamed for the wretched condition of the children. Rawson de Dellepiane outlined the regimen that should be followed with sickly children, which consisted of careful and continuous medical supervision, a nutritious diet, and a healthy environment.[50] Other delegates to the congress brought the subject of child care into their papers or into the discussion of other topics. The most important statement on *puericultura* was that of the Science Commission, which endorsed teaching child care to women between fifteen and twenty years of age.[51]

The Congresses on Childhood and the Cult of Motherhood

The endorsement of "scientific" motherhood by the First Feminine International Congress was central in its acceptance by forward-looking women interested in social service. With the approval of physicians and feminists, child care and the role of women in changing the demographic future of the nation were discussed as policy issues in the national congresses on children that took place in Chile in 1912 and Argentina in 1913. The Chilean National Congress for the Protection of Childhood [Congreso Nacional de Protección a la Infancia] took place between 21 and 26 September. It centered largely on medical and juridical issues. Child mortality was central, but it was understood that women were the lightning rod. Pre- and postnatal care, along with health instruction to pregnant women and nursing mothers, were regarded as essential and were discussed in great detail. Dr. Víctor Körner, a participant, supported total maternal care and recommended legislation forbidding pregnant women to work for one month before delivery and forty days afterward.

One of the two women listed as "attending" the conference commented that the male physicians had failed to stress sufficiently the economic needs of working women, and she suggested that any legislation to regulate women's work should make factory owners establish a fund deducted from the female workers' salary to provide for their care when they became "sick." Rafael Edwards was the only participant who focused on state regulation of children's and women's work. He acknowledged the need to protect female workers and raise their wages. To him such policies were not a choice but a duty. Regulation prohibiting work for expecting mothers had to be countered by free health services and the creation of mutualist societies to provide services for working women. Edwards went only halfway to meeting women's needs because he was reluctant to enforce regulations on factory owners.

Participating physicians confined their remarks to "poor" or "indigent" children, aware that the problems they were discussing were usually suffered by poor people. They recommended the collection of better statistics to correlate mortality with social problems, to protect abandoned children, and to provide rest for working mothers, regulation of commercial wet nurses, and more maternity wards in general hospitals. Not a single woman officially participated in this congress. Women were still a tiny fraction of medical students; by 1907 there were 4 female and 305 male physicians in the province of Santiago. In 1915 there were 30 female and 433 male physicians. In contrast, there were 142 midwifery students. Although the number of women doctors was growing, in 1912 they did not have enough prestige to be asked to participate in the congress. It is therefore not surprising to see the social problems of motherhood and infancy addressed as legal matters, such as criminality, adoption, and legal protection. The image of women emerging from this congress was of mothers engaged in the physical task of giving birth, nursing, and caring for children while the state assumed an ever expanding role of protector.[52]

The Argentine congress took place in Buenos Aires in October 1913 and was attended by Uruguayan guest participants. In contrast to the medical orientation of the Chilean congress, this was an intellectual as well as a medical event, gathering a brilliant array of sociologists, physicians, public health specialists, educators, and feminists. It received advance publicity in journalistic and academic circles, and many personalities and institutions expressed support. When the congress met in its inaugural session on 13 October it became a forum for the discussion of the most advanced theories of education, legal reform, child psychology, and child care.[53]

The congress was presided over by the well-known "freethinker," social activist, and feminist Dra. Julieta Lanteri. The official secretary was socialist educator and reformer Raquel Camaña. Dra. Paulina Luisi represented Uruguay and the physicians in charge of elementary school children of her nation. Other notable women of this generation participating in the congress were Carolina Muzilli, Dra. Elvira Rawson de Dellepiane, Dra. Petrona Eyle, Elvira López, and Dra. Alicia Moreau. The Asociación de Universitarias Argentinas and Unión y Labor were among institutions supporting the event. That a woman was allowed to be the presiding officer was partly a matter of male "gentility" but also a recognition of the intellectual stature of the female participants. Although in the minority, the professional women attending took part in all debates and read important papers that received wholehearted support from the congress.

In the inaugural session Lanteri traced the idea of the congress to the Argentine League for Women's and Children's Rights [Liga para los Derechos de la Mujer y el Niño], founded in Buenos Aires in January 1911. The League was yet another expression of the interest this first generation of feminists had in the welfare of children. Its members sponsored public lectures on children's issues, wrote letters to the authorities protesting the abuse of child labor, suggested projects to provide care for poor children, cosponsored the foundation of schools, and supported the candidacy of women in the National Council for Education.[54]

Shortly after its foundation the League had set out to organize a congress to discuss important social issues related to childhood. It had sought the support of many distinguished men—not because women did not believe in their own organizational capabilities, explained Lanteri, but because the future of children was in the hands of both sexes. With this strong affirmation of the need to preserve cooperation and harmony between the sexes, the congress discussed a variety of subjects in its sessions on education, hygiene, law, and psychology.

The papers read defined women's role in child care as a national and an individual task. Women were urged to participate in public health projects for children's health and hygiene. Although professional women had engaged in public health efforts for several years, it became obvious in the congress's discussions that there was a level of professionalism men were not ready to accept. Dr. Rafael Sedano Acosta proposed that female physicians should have a privileged place in primary school medical inspections, since women had special didactic capacities and a great "affinity for work." Furthermore, he argued, it was "morally and socially desirable" that women undertake that role. His remarks triggered a heated debate by some who thought that the "dignity of the male doctors" would be hurt if female doctors replaced men in the inspections. Sedano Acosta rebutted that argument by explaining that visiting doctors examined mostly female teachers and pupils, who would probably prefer to be examined by a woman. Dr. Lanteri "vehemently" supported Sedano Acosta in a high-pitched exchange. By 1913 women professionals had assumed they had professional acceptance and a niche in their disciplines, but the egos of many male *higienistas* were uncomfortable with the idea. Nobody argued that teaching child care should not be reserved for female teachers: in 1913 the typical teacher in Argentina was a woman. Teaching was becoming "feminized," but medicine remained a male domain. The difference in professional status between a female physician and a teacher was significant. It was acceptable that a teacher, as a woman in a female profession, was most suitable to teach younger women to care for infants. To inspect a school district in a capacity previously assumed by a man, however, was as yet an unacceptable role for women.

At a personal level, the teaching and learning of child care was part of the ideal education of all women as future mothers. A proposal to make *puericultura* a compulsory subject in the normal schools for teachers was unanimously approved by the congress. Dr. Enrique Feinmann had already suggested such a proposal to the Board of Education in 1912, and the congress's endorsement constituted a public and intellectual seal of approval. Drs. Pedro Rueda and Mariano Etchegaray agreed that Argentine women were in dire need of learning the principles of infant hygiene. Rueda supported the role of female physicians for such a task, backing Sedano Acosta's recommendations of women for some public posts. Etchegaray encouraged the rehearsal of maternal functions from the earliest years, tying it to the latest advances of social and personal hygiene. Schoolgirls of eight to ten would play with their dolls to learn about their tasks as mothers. "When all mothers know well their responsibilities toward their children, the Argentine Republic will have moved a giant step toward progress and the improvement of the race." [55]

The defense of childhood hinged on teaching child care within the public school system. Feinmann suggested courses for all girls over twelve, whether they attended normal schools or high schools [liceos]. All girls should be educated in the care of their younger siblings, since in modest homes older sisters often took on this task while parents worked. Feinmann concluded with a proposal for a national institute for maternity and child care that would educate single as well as married mothers.

Child-care advocacy, linking all women to social hygiene through motherhood, received a decisive promotional blessing three years later in the First American Congress on the Child in Buenos Aires in July 1916. A large number of distinguished intellectuals, physicians, educators, and lawyers from the Southern Cone attended. As a sequel to the 1913 National Congress on the Child it lacked the innovative thrust the earlier event had attained, but this congress aspired to a continental scope and received delegations from practically all Latin American nations. Ironically, the government of Argentina, celebrating the centennial of the declaration of independence that very year, neither included the congress among its official events nor provided funds for it.

The first generation of feminist and activist women was well represented in this congress, and women's participation was more extensive than in 1913. Argentina had the most women present. The Uruguayan delegation included Paulina and Clotilde Luisi and nine other female educators or directors of women's charitable organizations. The Chileans did not send a single woman. Dra. Julieta Lanteri Renshaw was called on again to chair the congress as a doctor and as president of the League for Women's and Children's Rights. Other female educators, feminists, lawyers, and physicians present were Dra. Alicia Moreau, Elvira López, Francisca Jacques, María Angélica Barreda, Ernestina López de Nelson, Dra. Elvira Rawson de Dellepiane, and Petrona Eyle. Socialists were represented by Carolina Muzilli, Dr. Enrique del Valle Iberlucea, Dr. Angel M. Giménez, and Deputy Alfredo Palacios. Among other notables were José Ingenieros, Carlos Octavio Bunge, Alejandro Korn, and the Uruguayan writer Carlos Vaz Ferreira. The presence of these distinguished intellectuals demonstrates their concern with childhood as a symbol of the future, and their faith that the physical and social sciences could chart a new course for society. The program reflected *higienista* and feminist concerns for children: the organization of a ministry for minors, the investigation of paternity, delinquent abandoned children, and treatment of children in the Penal Code. The delegates considered a bill for regulating children's and women's labor and putting-out work, health hazards in industrial establishments employing women and children, and child-care centers. The session on social issues dealt with physical and intellectual education and the teaching of hygiene in intermediate school (eleven to fourteen years). A session on mothers' and children's welfare discussed the protection of motherhood and special education for women. The creation of mothers' clubs and children's clubs and the need to favor and protect industries "appropriate for women" were also discussed.

Argentine socialist Carolina Muzilli reported on child labor and demanded its regulation, a proposal unanimously approved. She also suggested that women be given time to rest during their menstrual period, revealing the current attitude toward a "unique" feminine problem. At her suggestion the congress approved a recommendation that working women could take three days off work each month without having to give their employers an excuse. Participants in the congress, feminists and otherwise, remained unperturbed by a measure that underlined the physical differences between men and women and could further contribute to devaluing women's work. For the social reformer, the important issue was a healthy worker and protection for what was then regarded as an inconvenient and exhausting physical female problem. The congress had also a session on eugenics as a biological, social, and "ethnological" concept and on the role of the state in the achievement of its goals.

The Congress on the Child was not simply a conference on children; it marked a departure point for considering the state as responsible for the protection of children and women. It reflected the concerns of social reformers in several walks of life and their convictions about the vulnerability of the "weaker" members of the social body. Some members of the congress, such as the socialists, intended to enhance and legitimate their role as defenders of womanhood and social reform. The interests of the women were more pragmatic. As educators, physicians, and lawyers, they dealt with mothers and children daily, and they wanted their governments to take definite steps toward their welfare. Their presence was politically meaningful insofar as the espousal of their cause by eminent men reaffirmed their role as builders of the future and participants in social change.

The Montevideo Congress of 1919 continued the discussion of themes such as child abandonment, nutrition, protective societies for children, and regulation of work for boys and girls under fifteen. Street vending was condemned, and a proposal to ban it for girls suggests concern over its becoming a steppingstone to prostitution. Child abandonment was discussed because a social stigma attached to unwed mothers and the state's failure to support women who, married or not, had to raise their children by themselves. The state's responsibility for supporting mothers and children was reiterated in several papers on subsidies to nursing mothers in order to eliminate institutional wet nurses, cash bonuses to families raising children, and the allocation of money for more child-care instruction.[56] Infant mortality was still blamed largely on maternal ignorance of child care and hygiene. Uruguayan physician Dra. Isabel Pinto Vidal lectured on the social causes of juvenile delinquency. The congress ended with a dramatic final statement from the Uruguayan Chamber of Deputies on the state's right and duty to protect women and children and regulate their working conditions.[57]

This and other congresses on childhood buttressed the role of the mother, albeit an educated mother, in the protection of children, and encouraged the participation of the state in the design, funding, and maintenance of demographic and health policies. In theory as well as in practice, child care received its imprimatur in the late 1910s. Thereafter it would be intimately associated with public health and eugenics, although the connection was not always clear.[58] Chilean Normal Schools 1 and 2 in Santiago did not adopt the teaching of *puericultura* until the mid-1930s.[59] By 1915 Argentina had begun such instruction in the Normal Schools with the institution of the subject in professional schools.[60] Although child care was retained as a subject in Normal Schools in Argentina, it had a more troubled fate in professional schools. It is unclear whether the appointment of a male professor in 1914 was abrogated later on, since the course in *puericultura* was reestablished in two professional schools in June 1924. In 1931 the subject was again abolished at the recommendation of a female school inspector who considered such courses "immoral."[61] The socialists took that opportunity to point out that child care was still taught in the *liceos* and normal schools and considered the irony of having the subject suppressed in schools attended by women from modest homes, especially while Argentina still had very high child mortality. Several years later the socialist deputy Américo Ghioldi made a case for the introduction of child care as a subject in the male normal schools.[62] This suggestion did not succeed because it was ahead of its time; child care was still regarded as an exclusively female occupation.

The popularity of *puericultura* throughout the 1920s and the 1930s suggests that despite the increasing presence of women in the labor force and the realization that their roles in society were changing, biological destiny was still the most important concern of educators of both sexes, politicians, and many women in the feminist camp. Like motherhood, *puericultura* was eminently acceptable to feminists. It tied up with several social causes and satisfied the ethos of service, morality, and edification of womanhood that they embraced. There would be no cleavage between social change for women and the exigencies of their own gender. Dra. Elvira Rawson de Dellepiane, for example, had taken upon herself the administration of the health care of a kindergarten in the populous neighborhood of La Boca. She realized that supplying food was not enough and organized a mothers' committee to provide baths and clean clothes as part of a program to teach children the principles of hygiene.[63]

In 1920 the National Council of Women in Uruguay explained its support to pre- and postnatal child care by arguing that the causes of infant mortality were illegitimacy, poverty, and ignorance. The problem of illegitimacy could be addressed by adopting a single standard of morality. Unwed mothers were often poor and ignorant. Although poverty could not be immediately resolved, it could be remedied by teaching the mother about "intrauterine" or "obstetric" child care (prenatal care) and care of infants in the first critical months of their lives. The council urged the state to vote subsidies that would allow mothers to care for their children without economic pressures.[64] The concern of the best-organized feminist group in Uruguay for the health of what was then called the "mother-child dyad" reflects the importance child care had as a means of legitimizing women's new role in society. *Puericultura* provided the stimulus for their greater participation in the national health systems and gave them higher visibility and a claim for a more active role in national life.

By the time the Fourth Pan American Congress on the Child took place in Santiago in October 1924, there was a solid body of pediatric and health studies behind the concept of child care as an essential element of social hygiene, and women had been consecrated by feminists and nonfeminists as the priestesses of the new subject, though men remained the policymakers. Well-known and mostly male pediatricians and *higienistas* of the three nations participated in this congress: Gregorio Aráoz Alfaro and Emilio Coni from Argentina; Luis Morquió, Pedro Blanco Acevedo, Dardo Regules, and Augusto Turenne from Uruguay. Several notable women from the three nations played major roles, and though they were less prominent than in the Buenos Aires congress of 1916, that Dra. Ernestina Pérez, a Chilean doctor, presided over the congress marked a significant change from the first congress in Santiago twelve years earlier. Dra. Cora Mayers, Amanda Labarca, and Enriqueta Aliaga de Silva, among others, represented Chile. The Sociedad de Puericultura of Valparaíso sent representatives. The Uruguayan delegation was mostly male and had no notable female participants. Dra. Elvira Rawson de Dellepiane, Esther and Felícitas Smith Bunge, and Dra. Ernestina López represented Argentina.

Some topics had become fixed features of these congresses, such as institutions for unwed mothers, milk services for poor children, infant child care, abandoned children, clinics for mothers and children, mothers' rights over their own children, and projects to create schools for mothers.[65] Argentine Enrique Feinmann continued to support the concept of teaching child care in secondary schools, and visiting nurses who specialized in child care were also recommended. On closing, the congress recommended the creation of offices to coordinate eugenic measures, the foundation of medical-pedagogic centers for child care, and the methodical expansion of the practice of *puericultura*. Several women's groups held gatherings before and during the congress and sent petitions to the government for changes in the status of women. A few days after its closing the Chilean Gran Federación Femenina announced its participation in a planned crusade against infant mortality, organized by popular clinics.[66]

At the Service of Motherhood and Childhood

The advocacy of *puericultura* in national and international congresses boosted private and public efforts to offer adequate care to mothers and children, not in the spirit of charity as had been customary in the first decade of the century, but as a civic service to the nation. In the early 1920s Cora Mayers, a strong advocate of social hygiene, sex education, and child care, became head of the Chilean Department of Sanitary Education. One of her achievements was the organization of the League of Little Mothers [Liga de Madrecitas], which followed an idea first tried in the United States as part of a broader outreach program designed to popularize health care.[67] Argentine Emilio Coni had also been aware of the existence of League of Little Mothers in the United States but had been unable to foster the idea in his own country.[68]

Mayers proposed to train girls with younger siblings in child care, to encourage them to become their mothers' helpers. Such home care would follow the rules of basic hygiene, giving infants a greater chance of survival. The League would accept girls over twelve who could practice with a child in their own family. The League taught them about baby feeding, bathing, early detection of illness, milk sterilization, appropriate clothing, and so on. The plan assumed that all girls would one day be mothers themselves and that learning child care early in life would be a great asset to them as well as to society. The Liga de Madrecitas was adopted in some secondary schools.[69] Other Chileans were ready to approve this or any other plan that would include child care in women's education, which *had* to be different from that of men, argued a physician who wished to see the subject taught in all secondary schools.

A 1923 Argentine presidential decree provided for the creation of a Children's Bureau [Asistencia a la Infancia] in the Department of Hygiene.[70] The bureau would study the problem of infant diseases and mortality, protect mothers, and promote child hygiene at home and in schools. Its top-heavy structure was symptomatic of the bureaucratic orientation of such government offices, which in the Southern Cone nations moved only too slowly toward achieving their agendas. Private organizations helped compensate for the slowness of the state. In 1924 Dr. Gregorio Aráoz Alfaro traveled to the province of Catamarca to help establish centers for infant care, and day nurseries and children's kitchens were organized in Buenos Aires's most populous neighborhoods.[71] The Hogar Infantil opened in November 1925 to shelter forty children of both sexes aged six to twelve. In 1926 the National Council of Women joined the trend by organizing a White Cross Child Welfare Commission to help institutions and associations reach needy children and to educate girls and women on child care.[72] The promotion of motherhood and child care were further popularized by special events such as a Baby Week sponsored by the Buenos Aires Mothers' Club, which included lectures in baby and child care, discussing the benefits of well-prepared baby formula and proper clothing as well as the connection between infant mortality, venereal disease, and alcoholism. A parade of healthy children, and the closing of several streets to be used as temporary playgrounds, brought the message to the heart of the city's neighborhoods.[73]

Chile and Uruguay were not left behind in the wave of activities extolling healthy motherhood and childhood. Chile adopted Mother's Day in 1924.[74] Among the special events were prizes for mothers of five or more children and for the best looked-after worker's home. A similar Baby Week was celebrated in Montevideo in 1925, with 4,000 children participating in a parade under the auspices of the Uruguayan Association for Child Welfare [Asociación Nacional de Protección a la Infancia], founded in 1924.[75]

In 1925, the same year that a law for the protection of working mothers was approved, the Pediatric Society of Chile began offering child-care classes to working-class mothers. The Department of Sanitary Education sponsored a series of public lectures by Cora Mayers in 1926 to encourage parents to support efforts by the government to provide physical examinations for children.[76] The medical profession's support for *puericultura* was strengthened by the efforts of the National Maternity Council, founded in 1926 to work on the prevention of venereal diseases and promote healthy motherhood. Clinics to treat syphilis and facilities to offer prenatal classes and infant health services were part of its program. Its director was Dr. Carlos Monckeberg, later involved in a controversy over legalization of abortion in Chile.[77]

By 1928 *puericultura* had become a household word in the Southern Cone. Santiago's *El Mercurio* reported a well-attended lecture given by Berta Gaudie de Ortiz titled "*Puericultura* and Skim Milk," which turned out to be on the benefits of breast-feeding. The lecture was illustrated with a film on infant and child care. Behind this and similar lectures was the assumption that mothers' ignorance condemned their babies to death. The target was, predictably, the working mother or the working-class mother—most often the same person. Members of the audience wanted this film shown in working-class neighborhoods to help the wives of workers learn the duties of their "delicate mission."[78] An implicit acknowledgment of the differences created by wealth and class was behind such comments and all the schemes to remedy the situation. To the class consciousness of some of these programs we must add the aspersions that some commentators cast on "modern women." Stressing healthy habits, these campaigns condemned certain social habits associated with the "liberation" of women, such as smoking and drinking, described as the results of the "modernization" and definitely censured by the advocates of *puericultura*.[79]

Mother's milk played an important role in campaigns advocating prenatal care for expecting mothers, child care, eugenics, and public health awareness. Providing hygienically processed milk to nursing and postnursing mothers was a popular cause certain to gain at least some administrative support. Nursing itself was becoming something of a health fetish. In 1909 the Center for Propaganda against Tuberculosis organized a one-year competition for nursing women in Valparaíso. Prizes were awarded to the mothers of the healthiest breast-fed one-year-old children: 349 mothers registered, 160 finished the contest, and only 4 deaths were recorded among those originally registered. This is the point the doctors wished to prove. During the year the children were examined to ascertain weight gain and general health, and cash prizes were awarded to the children who had gained the most. This competition was reported at the 1912 congress for the protection of childhood as a successful means of instructing mothers and having them bring their children for regular medical checkups.[80]

Women who denied their babies the precious liquid began to be condemned by physicians. Dr. Emilio Coni sang the praises of the food and health-care services to nursing mothers operating in Buenos Aires since 1916 as helping to fulfill "an imperious demand of mother nature on behalf of the interests of mothers, children, and the social order."[81] An advertisement for a malt drink appearing in 1916 in *La Nación* of Buenos Aires used World War I views of soldiers, death, and coffins to remind mothers of the ongoing war and urged them to use the product to improve their milk production. A mother who used artificial milk substitutes exposed her baby to more risks than a soldier in the battlefield. A decade later a Chilean cartoon showed a mother holding a baby who addressed a cow, saying: "I don't need you; I have a mother."[82]

Mother's milk was not always available, since many working mothers could not — or would not — take time to nurse. Furthermore, children needed safe milk beyond the nursing years. Feminists and public health experts thought the state should solve these problems. In the late 1910s Uruguay dispensed free milk through a Public Charity Commission that purchased milk to be distributed through *gotas de leche,* milk stations where poor mothers picked up hygienically processed milk for their children. In 1918 they were under the supervision of the National Hygiene Council. They also employed healthy wet nurses to provide breast milk to needy children.[83] Milk stations became popular and began to spread, often annexed to a hospital, like that functioning in the Chilean city of Talca since 1921.[84] The Chilean Patronato de la Infancia, a charity institution founded in 1901, began to distribute milk to poor children in 1908. Another private institution, the Protectora de la

Infancia, also began a milk service about 1915 and reported serving 3,047 children a month in 1924, in addition to giving lectures on child care in several neighborhoods of Santiago. Similar institutions operated in Valparaíso and Concepción.[85] In 1930 the *gotas de leche* were distributing over 600,000 liters of milk each year to more than 13,000 children, mostly in Santiago.[86]

Argentina had *gotas de leche* and *copas de leche* programs. In 1904 Dr. Emilio Coni, in his role as municipal physician, approved the creation of the *gotas de leche*, a program suggested by another higienista, Dr. Enrique Foster. The municipality sustained a clinic that provided milk to fifty needy children. In 1908 this project was taken over by Asistencia Pública, which opened six outlets by 1912 and also inspected the health of wet nurses hired to provide milk.[87] In 1912 the gotas de leche were complemented by pre- and postnatal public services.[88] The *copas de leche* was a slightly different project, first tried in 1905 to provide milk to children attending public schools. The idea was so successful that when Ana C. de Uranga, director of a girls' secondary school, founded the Society for the Protection of Childhood [Sociedad de Protección a la Infancia] in 1907, one of its purposes was to help assemble the *copas de leche* program. By 1915 the program distributed three million glasses of milk during the school year.[89]

Mother's Week, celebrated in Santiago in November 1929 with lectures on child care, social prophylaxis, and eugenics, glorified the role of mothers and the interest of the Chilean state in protecting mothers and children. President General Carlos Ibáñez attended the inaugural conference, and *El Mercurio* sang the praises of *puericultura*. One headline stated that "a mother's heart and mother's milk do not have substitutes," and the Ministry of Welfare [Beneficencia y Asistencia Social] opened a new subsection with offices in key cities to centralize the welfare services for mothers and children.[90] To ensure adequate child care, the Pediatric Society proposed that an instruction sheet be attached to the birth certificate issued by the Civil Registry.

In Uruguay a Child Welfare Association was founded on 19 March 1924. Like the Chilean Patronato de la Infancia, it was an umbrella organization that received both private and government funding.[91] A government-supported Child Welfare Department provided shelter for children and mothers and for children whose mothers employed themselves as wet nurses. Eight Infant Welfare Centers in Montevideo provided physical examinations and treatment for sick children. In 1924 they claimed to have treated 4,000 children. Such centers were primarily concerned not with teaching child care, but with providing services, especially milk.[92] Instruction on child care was given by visiting nurses or workers trained by the Child Welfare Association, which in 1926 began to place its social workers in the government's welfare centers to do social casework with the mothers who took their children there. By 1926, as in Buenos Aires, the government supported children's canteens in the poorer quarters of the city, but they were able to feed only fifty children that year.[93]

Other charitable institutions catering to mothers and children in the Southern Cone were the cantinas maternales [mothers' canteens] founded privately in 1915 by a wealthy Argentine philanthropist, Julia Elena Acevedo de Martínez de Hoz, and supported by women of the upper classes.[94] By 1924 there were six canteens, providing two meals a day to expecting mothers, wed or unwed. A doctor and a nurse made daily rounds to provide health advice. After childbirth the mothers were visited for ten days by a nurse who gave them one peso for daily needs. Two weeks after birth the mother could return for meals until her child was two years old. Children were given a weekly physical examination by a doctor. Schoolchildren between six and twelve received lunches if their teachers gave them a card.[95]

Several food kitchens operated in 1924 in the populous neighborhoods of the city of Buenos Aires (Boca, Barracas, Nueva Pompeya, Villa Crespo) where poor children could get lunches for 20 centavos. These lunch services, supported by the municipality, had opened in 1925, serving 150 children.[96] These endeavors show that women were indeed creating more room for themselves in their assigned motherhood niche. The international League of Iberian and Spanish American Women, a feminist organization aspiring to create bonds between women in Spain and Latin America, joined the childcare drive when, in 1926, it decided to hold a congress to discuss "women as an influence in moral and material reconstruction in every country," civil and political rights and educational improvement, and also the issues of protective legislation for working women, maternity benefits, and day nurseries.[97]

Charity, however, was beginning to go out of fashion in the 1920s. Argentine president Hipólito Yrigoyen, not known for his social sensitivity, could not escape the attraction of motherhood and childhood and signed a presidential decree on 12 November 1923 creating the Department of Asistencia a la Infancia [Childhood Assistance], a branch of the Department of Hygiene.[98] Not wishing to show less concern, in 1924 the Labor Department recommended establishing a home maternity service.[99] That such services required more than decrees must have been obvious to all. Some of the programs were implemented; others had to wait for the budget allocations and, above all, for the organization of the needed human resources. In 1926 the Medical

School Board requested that the National Council of Education include in its budget funds to maintain seventy-five elementary school health advisers. They were members of a recently created body of teachers who had taken a two-year course given in the School of Medicine to enable them to check children's dental health and give lectures on hygiene. This task increased the visibility of women in public health projects, although the limited training of the visitors defined them as helpful aides rather than as professionals. Also in 1926 the National Council of Women founded a "White Cross Welfare Commission" to help institutions locate needy children, in addition to advising girls and women who wished to specialize in child care.[100]

Social hygiene and interest in child care generated a new career for women as *visitadoras sociales* [social workers]. In 1920 Emilio Coni suggested a corps of infant hygiene nurses and social workers patterned after those in the United States. He regarded these women as the natural assistants of physicians and *higienistas,* extending their reach into the community. At the same time other Argentine pediatricians were recommending a corps of visiting nurses patterned after a British model. Dr. Alberto Peralta Ramos claimed that only women had the temperament and psychological qualities to establish a network of mothers and wet nurses. This corps was expected to be self-sacrificing and capable of undertaking the job with love, dedication, tact, and discretion to convince "oftentimes ignorant and ill-disposed women" to learn the saving rules of hygiene. Some of these doctors continued to see negative qualities in women of the lower classes, implicitly casting middle-class nurses as torchbearers of enlightenment to their less educated sisters.[101]

In the late 1920s social workers received their official blessing in Chile and Uruguay. Despite a constitutional crisis in 1925, the Chilean School of Social Service was founded in that year. It followed a Belgian model and was directed by a Belgian specialist. Students took courses in social hygiene, political economy, civic education, accounting, nutrition, domestic economy, and other subjects relevant to their mission. The Chilean social workers were a health and social-support cadre who visited working mothers and their families, teaching them elements of *puericultura* and contagious disease, which it was assumed would have a large role in helping poor families sort out their problems. The students were trained by Asistencia Social, a state agency that looked after the welfare of working-class families. The first graduates found jobs in a newly created institute to care for the health of elementary school children (Instituto de Salud Escolar), in hospitals, and as advisers to delinquent children. Other government offices, such as the

Labor Department and the Office of the Presidency, began to use their services by 1930. Unquestionably social service provided Chilean middle-class women with a rewarding employment opportunity.[102] By 1939 these professionals were taking courses in statistics, psychology, and criminology that went beyond the original task of providing mother and baby care, although they remained bound to family service.[103]

Uruguay took special pride in its social workers. In 1927 it graduated its first twelve *visitadoras,* after two years of study at the Institute for Experimental Hygiene of the Faculty of Medicine. Twelve others were added as honorary members, to form a corps of social workers for the Division of Hygiene and School Services.[104] In 1934 a school of Public Health and Social Service was created to supersede the medical school in this task. The new school required more preparation from the applicants. Whereas the first *visitadoras* had needed only a primary school certificate to begin their training, starting in 1934 all applicants were required to have a secondary school or normal school certificate. More girls than ever were finishing the secondary education and the authorities were sure they would see the advantages of a "short career" that would guarantee them employment after graduation.

The new curriculum included courses in hygiene, *puericultura* and maternity, domestic economy, and laboratory training. Many of the doctors offered free instruction, to cooperate in preparing the social workers. Uruguayan public health authorities showed more than modest pride in reporting that the *visitadoras* attended courses in the School of Medicine and were well prepared in matters of public health and hygiene.[105] In 1941, after the government approved the regulations for the state care of children between three and fourteen years of age (*segunda infancia*), female social workers were considered an essential part of the project. Furthermore, plans for the establishment of maternal schools to give total care—food and schooling—to children between two and seven years old were praised as a "new source of feminine employment," an ideal shared by the Argentine doctor Gregorio Aráoz Alfaro.[106] Male authorities insisted on seeing women in the social welfare field as playing a motherly role in the institutions they worked for. Women employees would provide a warm home atmosphere, as sources of advice and understanding.[107] The cultural mores of the 1930s retained this traditional view of women: old and new coexisted in a peculiar relationship under the cult of motherhood.

By the late 1930s Uruguayan health authorities had extended the teaching of child care to the countryside through clinics and milk service. They had come to the conclusion that *puericultura* was essential to help curtail infant mortality and suggested increasing the number of social workers living in rural communities and working as a team with the local teachers. Such plans show how far social hygiene, child care, motherhood, and womanhood had become partners in forming new health care policies in the Southern Cone.[108] The elevation of *puericultura* to a science, however, further polarized gender roles. Femininity was overcoming feminism in the technical field.

The Legal Mandate for the Protection of Children

Two decades of medical directives, public policy, and cultural reinforcement on the benefits of child care resulted in the enactment of the 1934 Código del Niño in Uruguay and protective legislation in Argentina and Chile. The concept of the declaration of a charter of children's rights was proposed by a Swiss female physician and adopted by the League of Nations in 1924. A Cuban Congress on the Child approved a declaration of the rights of children in 1927, and the Chilean Medical Corps formulated a Decalogue of Children's Rights in 1928. In 1927 the Fourth Pan American Conference ratified the International American Institute for the Protection of Childhood with residence in Montevideo.[109]

Neither Chile nor Argentina enacted a children's code, but the three nations attempted to establish a legal system of protection for needy children and their mothers. In essence they aspired to find a viable answer for the important social problem of out-of-wedlock births. Although the code did not tamper with the established patriarchal family, it was an acknowledgment that not all was well with gender relations and the care of children. Missing from most of the legislation and state-initiated measures was the father, who was hardly ever mentioned. The official and private initiatives completely ignored the duties and responsibilities of fatherhood. Although the concerns of early twentieth-century feminists finally were formally addressed in an official manner as the state decided to assume its share of responsibility for the future generation, the dialogue on the subject was carried out between women and the male doctors who represented the state.

The Uruguayan Código del Niño mandated the creation of a Council of the Child, a body in charge of "guiding all matters relative to the life and welfare of minors from the gestation period through the attainment of legal majority."[110] This sweeping jurisdiction was watered down by many circumstances such as budget constrictions and the protracted process of obtaining approval of the proposed offices. By attempting full pre- and postnatal coverage the code aspired to advise on the "eugenic" behavior of the couple before marriage and encourage them to visit the "prenuptial" clinics of the Ministry of Public Health. For the Uruguayan authorities women became mothers at the moment of conception, and the state should assist them throughout pregnancy and childbirth.[111] Protection of children, acknowledged the council, had to include the needs of mothers and families. An important right for working mothers was spelled out in article 37, which guaranteed all pregnant women one month of leave before childbirth and one after. The mother received half pay during those two periods and was entitled to retain her job, even though she might not be able to return to work after a month for medical reasons.

The report of the council's first six years indicates that Uruguay gave this essay in social reform a fair trial. Several established private charitable institutions lent a hand. Adolescent unwed mothers could seek shelter in La Bonne Garde. The Casa del Niño received mothers while seeking employment for them as domestics, a sign that most of the women seeking help were poor and unskilled. A network of maternal canteens and clinics provided free meals for expectant mothers. Pro-natalist policies guided the public health officials, who complimented some matrons of a shelter home for encouraging first marriages, regularizing "relationships," and fostering adoptions. The separation of children under three years from their family was to be carefully regulated, and the División de la Segunda Infancia had the duty to investigate the civil status of the children under its care.[112] This meant that illegitimacy had to be acknowledged but that the state would protect the health of all children, regardless of birth status.

Although Chile did not enact a children's code, protection of children and mothers was part of the 1931 Sanitary Code and the Labor Code. An effort to enact a children's code was made in August 1935, when a bill for the creation of a council for the defense of the child and a defense charter for unprotected children were unsuccessfully brought before the Chamber of Deputies.[113] A law for the protection of working mothers had been enacted in March 1925, providing for sixty days of leave after childbirth and preserving women's jobs after that period. The Labor Department was in charge of compliance to this law and of ensuring that factories informed their female workers about the legislation.[114] State and municipally supported plans to offer medical and financial aid to pregnant working women, as well as economic support for four months after delivery, were laid out in 1929 during the administration of Carlos Ibáñez. These measures were incorporated into the Sanitary Code that guaranteed state protection to pregnant women from conception through pregnancy and until six months after the birth.[115] This protection was understood as medical (hygiene) and social (welfare aid) and would be free for those who could not afford to pay. The Labor Code mandated six weeks each of pre- and postpartum leave for women workers. The state and the employer would both contribute to a maternity fund that would pay the woman half her salary throughout her leave.[116]

In Argentina a bill to create a National Children's Bureau was submitted to the Chamber of Deputies in 1932, but no action followed.[117] An Association for the Rights of Children was founded in October 1935: a feminist and an expert on juvenile delinquency, Ernesto Nelson, was the speaker. The association advocated the study of childhood and offered intellectual and moral support to institutions caring for children.[118] By 1937 it had gained legal status and had printed "statutes" outlining the nine basic rights of children. The first asserted that all children have a right to life, to maternal attention, to the legal recognition of the father, and to the vigilance of the state. The protection of the future generation began with preserving life, a health issue, but the inclusion of the father and the state in the care of children was an innovative element addressed directly to the debate on the investigation of paternity and the increasing role of the state as surrogate father.[119]

Another key actor in the development of child-protection advocacy was the Argentine Socialist Party, which since the first decade of the century had raised numerous child health issues. Its main advocate of protective legislation for women, and especially for pregnant working women, was Alfredo Palacios, who in 1907 proposed the first law to provide compulsory leave for mothers. Understood as "intrauterine *puericultura,*" this legislation cared for the fetus as much as the mother. The law was approved in 1908, but it did not receive its mandatory implementation until 1913 and remained a dead letter for five years. In 1915 Socialist deputy Enrique Dickmann took the concept of protecting motherhood one step further and proposed paying a subsidy to expecting mothers during the mandatory leave. Radical Party deputies Rogelio Araya and Leopoldo Bard submitted bills concerning a similar subsidy in 1918 and 1925.[120]

Despite the support of many *higienistas,* notable socialist-feminist women such as Alicia Moreau, and other members of the Radical Party, none of these bills went into effect. The antilabor stance of Yrigoyen's and Marcelo T. de Alvear's administrations effectively blocked social legislation. The concept of paid leave was eventually adopted on 14 June 1934, when the times were more propitious and conservatives lent their support, probably under the influence of current eugenics theories. Law 11.933 took effect in 1936. Working mothers and their employers made compulsory contributions to a fund to compensate mothers postpartum. Women, in fact, were not receiving a "free" service: they were helping to pay for it. Those who earned very low wages were exempted from the maternity deduction. In August of that same year Palacios proposed another law (12.341) calling for a National Department of Maternity and Childhood [Dirección de Maternidad e Infancia] to "encourage the improvement of future generations . . . by combating infant mortality and its causes and protecting women in their condition of mothers or future mothers."[121] The law was approved by the deputies on 21 December 1937. Among its objectives were prenatal care, a national health survey of children since birth, shelters for unwed mothers, health centers, kindergartens, and vacation centers for infants and children.

Another objective of Law 12.341 was to control professional wet nurses. It achieved this goal by making mother's milk mandatory for all nursing infants. The law categorically established that all mothers had the duty to nurse their children. No mother could nurse any other child until her own was five months old. The legislation exempted mothers unable to nurse. A bill promoting the same idea had been proposed in Congress by Radical Party deputy Leopoldo Bard in 1926, which prohibited nursing any other child until the wet nurse's own baby was four months old. Children were born with a "right to their mother's milk," but not until the mid-1930s did the state feel ready to make a statement on that right.[122] The Department of Maternity and Childhood ascribed to itself the power to issue health certificates to women engaged in commercial wet-nursing. In turn, wet nurses would be protected by a certificate stating that the child in their charge was free of contagious diseases. Parents and wet nurses had to register their contract in order to initiate the department's supervision. Given the steep decline in the demand for wet nurses preceding the enactment of this law, it can be interpreted more as lip service to motherhood than as an effective form of health control. Ideologically, however, wet-nursing received the kiss of death as an occupation debasing motherhood.

The legislation to pay for postpartum leave seems to have been successful at least in creating a fund. In 1942 Alicia Moreau was campaigning for an increase in the benefits provided by the law, given that the fund had a surplus. She proposed longer periods of paid leave and an increase in the premiums for mothers who had several children.[123] At the end of the 1930s the Socialist Party reiterated its traditional pro-motherhood and childhood policy by advocating state support for "prolific mothers" and municipal financial and health protection until the end of primary schooling.[124]

The philosophy of protection embodied in the legislation of the 1930s was a fitting end to several decades of promotion of motherhood supported by the *higienistas,* feminists, socialists, and even anarchists. "Motherhood as a social function should not just be surrounded by the aura of dignity and respect, but should also receive the aid of the state when economic conditions demand it," stated a Chilean social scientist in 1941.[125] In conceptualizing the rights of children and the enactment of protective legislation, the preciousness and fragility of the child's life was regarded as at stake. This was consistent with the health and child-care ideas advanced at the beginning of the century and with the debates over the definition of conception and abortion that took place in the mid-1930s. The lives of mother and child were indissolubly tied at all times. "Protection to the maternal womb" was a sacred undertaking supported by *higienistas,* social reformers, social workers, and finally the eugenicists of the 1930s. Who was at the center of the multiple efforts of policy definition and execution — the mother or the child? The tension was resolved by adopting the concept of "mother-child dyad," a phrase often cited in political, legal, and medical circles to support measures on behalf of motherhood, childhood, and the family. Mothers and their children were welded in a tight ideological unit that left motherhood intact as the paramount role for the female sex. Women remained object and subject of the cult of motherhood. They were the recipients of social legislation that redefined them as actors in the role of caregivers but also defined them as subjects in need of protection in the exercise of their biological functions. The absence of men from these plans is significant. The state became a surrogate father through the services of physicians, whose loving and constant attention to babies and their mothers helped fill the void left by the absence of the real fathers from the nursery and sometimes from the home.

CHAPTER 4

Feminism and Sexuality: An Uneasy Relationship

─────── Human sexuality was not a new theme in medical circles in Southern Cone nations in the late 1890s, but its discussion in public or in the women's press was a challenge that only a few brave spirits undertook. Physicians and public health specialists began discussing sexuality in the late 1880s to assess the impact of venereal diseases on public health. It was natural that the men who monopolized those fields took a male viewpoint and, after focusing on prostitution as "the" source of venereal diseases, they directed their efforts against the women engaged in that occupation. Prostitutes became the target of medical probes as well as police harassment for the next several decades.[1] Other forms of female sexuality were discreetly expunged from daily discussion in journalistic, legal, and educational literature. They would not become a subject of public interest until they could be dissociated from the shady connection with sin, degradation, and vice. The association of female sexuality with commercial sex was not easy to transcend, but the transition was made possible by the growing interest in human reproduction and by the challenge to traditional sexual mores, posed largely by anarchists and feminists. Eventually educators, jurists, and policymakers became involved in the discussion of human sexuality in the 1920s, when it became obvious that social reforms could not be accomplished without addressing the sexual bases.

Feminists' interest in sexual behavior was not triggered by a desire for liberation of female sexuality. It rose instead from concern over the double standard of morality, which they saw as one of the sources of gender inequality. The equality of the sexes had to be defined by the law, but legal answers alone did not solve the social and ethical issues raised by traditional male behavior. Feminists were concerned about the vulnerability of unwed mothers and their offspring and the minimal responsibilities assigned to men in the care of children conceived out of wedlock. They believed high rates of child mortality were related to illegitimacy and to the marginalization of single mothers. As men evaded the responsibilities of paternity they forced the state to protect abandoned women and children. Sexuality was not only a private issue; it was also a public matter. Thus, while physicians focused on prostitution as a source of disease and as a health issue, feminists of both sexes addressed it as the consequence of poverty and lack of proper sex education. Prostitution was not a disease but a sympton of broader social and sexual mores in need of reform.

The feminists' focus on the social aspects of sexuality stressed sex education and solutions to the stigma of illegitimacy. This does not mean they ignored its physical aspects. Female physicians like Paulina Luisi and Alicia Moreau were involved in health campaigns that required dealing openly with venereal diseases and prostitution. Other feminist writers acknowledged that the sex drive lay at the bottom of gender-related social problems, but they were restrained by canons of "good taste" and etiquette from a frank discussion of sexual matters.

Women, Feminism, and Sex Education

Although women's honor depended on proper sexual behavior, most women knew little about their sexuality. Discussion of prostitution and its medical aspects did not create an auspicious atmosphere for teaching women about their sexual functions and the process of reproduction, because prostitutes epitomized the wrong type of female sexuality. Neither the function of female organs nor sexuality was discussed in social or family circles, much less written about in women's magazines or newspapers. At no point in the educational system did children or young adolescents have the opportunity to learn about human reproduction. The "facts of life" were something most parents and teachers were unprepared or unable to address, and children often learned through experience and gossip.

To complicate matters, Roman Catholic moral canons permeated the education of most children.[2] A young woman was subjected to traditional concepts of honor that separated the good from the bad according to the preservation of virginity. A woman's family had to see that she remained respectable, because her personal honor involved the honor of the family as well. These concerns were voiced by members of the middle and upper classes more often than by the working poor, although poor women were more vulnerable to a "fall" forced by economic circumstances. Sexual mores generated even more tension when, with increased urbanization and education, middle-class women abandoned the shelter of the home and took jobs that brought them into daily contact with men. Argentine Alicia Moreau de Justo recalled, "In those days [ca. 1900–1905] a young woman who went out alone, especially at night, was labeled [as a bad woman]. . . . not only by men, but also by other women."[3]

The rigid privacy surrounding the development and exercise of sexual functions made these subjects strictly medical issues and, as such, under the control of men. When women were admitted to medical schools in the late 1890s, however, they finally had the opportunity to study and discuss their bodies in medical terms as well as in terms of social consequences. Medicine became one of the most popular professional choices among the first generation of university women. The first women doctors treated mostly female patients and practiced family medicine. They learned of the extensive damage done by venereal diseases to the generative organs of their patients and witnessed the sad results of congenital diseases in stillbirths or defective babies. Supported by the prestige of their career and the immunity it gave them in speaking about otherwise "embarrassing" topics, women doctors could address women's sexuality, the reproductive system, the physiological and health aspects of pregnancy, the problems of unwanted pregnancy, and abortion.

The first effort to teach about female sexuality from a woman's point of view was that of Elvira Rawson de Dellepiane, who in 1892 wrote her medical thesis on "women and hygiene," initiating a long career devoted to female health and to feminist and women's issues.[4] Rawson de Dellepiane studied the life cycle of women and their physical, educational, and moral needs. Very much a middle-class woman of her generation, she sought to preserve healthy and moral womanhood, on the assumption that women's individual dignity depended largely on their personal and social ethics. Thus, even though she wrote from a medical viewpoint, she proposed models for acceptable social and personal behavior.

Knowledge of the body's functions was indispensable to learning how best to care for it. In her thesis Rawson de Dellepiane dealt with the problems of puberty, marriage, pregnancy, childbirth, and breast-feeding. Although never explicit in her description of body functions, she tactfully suggested the need to understand the physical and mental changes of each cycle. Puberty was a disturbing change for most girls owing to ignorance of their own bodies. Poor women were also subjected to a hostile urban environment, and promiscuity in the crowded tenements of Buenos Aires could be compounded by physiological damage to the reproductive systems from working in unsanitary or makeshift factories.

She addressed women's physiological problems in marriage with finesse and experience — she was the mother of several children. She disapproved of early marriages because of the negative physiological effects that pregnancy had on immature young women, and she condemned the closely consanguineous marriages reported in provincial populations. Rawson de Dellepiane was also concerned with the growing incidence of venereal disease in Buenos Aires, posing a threat to healthy offspring. Yet in her book she offered no suggestions on how to deal with that health problem. She recognized female sexuality by stating that marriage "brings the satisfaction of sexual desires [which have a favorable] effect on women's health and contribute to lenghthening her life."[5] This led her to comment on the problems facing frigid women, who accepted the duties of marriage as a repugnant burden. As with venereal disease, she sidestepped this issue and offered no solutions. Her focus was on the positive aspects of marital hygiene and motherhood, and she advised married women on how to care for their sex organs and how to carry out a healthy pregnancy by exercising and by regarding their state as natural, not as a disease. Rawson believed women should nurse their children and recommended abstaining from sexual relations during the nursing period, arguing that "such repeated emotions" could affect the baby. Furthermore, fear of a new pregnancy could have a negative psychological effect on the nursing mother.

Wrapped in euphemisms, but still objective and terse, these comments and advice from a newly graduated female doctor who in the ensuing years would become an active feminist indicate receptivity and sensitivity to sex-related topics. Elvira Rawson opened the door to further discussion of subjects considered "delicate" by ably blending physiological, educational, and moral themes. Acknowledging female sexuality, she and other female doctors of her generation dispelled the traditional image of women as angels of spirituality and introduced women's voices into the discussion of sexual functions. Although she did not express strong views, just commenting on these topics marked a departure from the assumption that they were unladylike.

Despite the publication of this work and its author's active participation in feminist activities, other feminists were still not encouraged to deal with female sexuality openly or consistently. Female doctors could write and speak on sex-related subjects with greater ease than nonprofessional women: their status gave them authority. Feminist men and women routinely tied the sex drive to motherhood and family formation and found it difficult to define or discuss sex as a source of pleasure. There was, however, an important and vigorous departure from the mainstream of middle-class feminist thought on sexuality. Strongly influenced by class and economic factors, it was voiced by the increasingly self-conscious anarchist groups that thrived for over two decades in the cities of the Southern Cone. Though anarchists refused to share the feminist discourse, their views on human sexuality influenced medical, legal, and public opinion. Their ideas were discussed during the congressional debates on divorce and abortion and were even ascribed to feminists by feminism's opponents.

Anarchism and the Left on Sexuality

Releasing human sexuality from its rigid confines was part of the anarchists' quest for personal freedom. They saw social and religious restraints on the free expression of the sex drive as artificial impositions on the individual by state and church. They challenged monogamy as a social institution, restated the right of men and women to choose the sexual partners of their liking, which they described as "free love," and discussed the meaning of reproduction of the working class in a capitalist society.

Argentine anarchists initiated the discussion of sexuality, love, and free unions in their publications. Challenging the prudish journalistic silence on sexuality, *La Protesta Humana* published articles on sexual love and sexual unions that defied traditional Catholic views on the irrevocability of marriage and celebrated relationships based on love and companionship. Anarchists claimed that bourgeois society and the church exploited women by forcing them to marry for financial security. Unable to become economically self-sufficient, women "sold" themselves into matrimony.[6]

Anarchist literature stressed that "sexual needs vary greatly between men and women and from one individual to the other."[7] If such needs could not be totally satisfied through a monogamous and indissoluble relationship, people should have other chances. Love had limits and often an end, claimed one writer, and individuals were attracted by different qualities in other persons throughout life. Implied was the possibility of changing partners, although the message was not deliberately blunt.[8] Opponents of free love argued that freedom in choosing a sexual partner fostered prostitution and created "fallen women." One writer denied this, claiming that women who loved freely and willingly would remain "chaste" — not promiscuous — suggesting that even some advocates of free sex expected women to be faithful.[9]

Despite ideological commitments, the need for a family was recognized by many writing for the anarchist *La Protesta*. To reconcile individual and sexual freedom with aspirations for a homelife, anarchists proposed redefining the power relations of men and women within the family. The goal was to end the "brutal pretensions of the male to become the owner of the female."[10] To do so people had to understand that sexuality was a means for establishing an equal relationship in which partners shared feelings and obligations. Ultimately, one writer stated, the perception of the female body as an object to satisfy "male lasciviousness" had to vanish.[11]

Despite their intense propaganda against exploitation of the female body, Argentine anarchists reflected a masculine perception of sexual relations. Their message was addressed to women but was written by men. Some writers assumed that men made women beautiful by making them fecund and helping them fulfill their "sacred mission" of motherhood.[12] Anarchists were the only political writers of the period to celebrate the pleasure of physical love. Luis A. Rezanno eulogized it in turgid prose, praising the force attracting the sexes and imagining the pleasures women experienced in physical love. "No law is capable of stopping the pleasure experienced by the female in the arms of the male, under the burning caress of his kisses, and from the warm spray of the seminal seed."[13]

In Chile leftist women participated in the dialogue on sexuality more often than in Argentina, and the discussion was more directly focused on reproduction. Early Chilean working women's newspapers discussed birth control, adopting a fierce class approach. The anarchist dogma that the working classes were exploited through the unchecked birth of more working people was an adaptation of the neo-Malthusian fears of the late nineteenth century.[14] In its August 1908 issue *La Palanca,* an ephemeral newspaper published by Santiago's needleworkers, published a powerful article by "Yedra" that delivered both a neo-Malthusian and a feminist message. The writer commented on the multiple births to one working woman and the despair she expressed at the prospect of having to support three more children. "Yedra" attacked the two sources of unwanted pregnancies: men, in the "selfish, brutal, and mechanical" satisfaction of their own sexual needs, and scientists, whose criminal indolence and lack of sensitivity deprived women of knowledge of their own bodies and especially their reproductive functions. Infanticide was the unfortunate answer to irresponsible procreation. Chileans, argued the author, should follow European models of hygienic and scientific birth control methods. Whether or not "Yedra" represented the feelings of all working women, this article proved that some of them had strong opinions on women's need to control the size of their families.[15]

Class struggle was more forcefully delineated by another Chilean writer. In 1913 Clara de la Luz read a paper at the socialist Centro Demócrata in which she discussed the relation between poverty, capitalism, and procreation. Following the ideas of Franck Sutor and Luis Bulffi, she accused the church and capitalists of encouraging the blind procreation of the proletariat in order to maintain a plentiful supply of cheap labor. The living conditions of the proletariat were dismal and likely to push workers into despair. The solution, she suggested, would be a "strike of wombs" until women could take control of their own bodies.[16] The urgency of the struggle between capitalism and the proletariat rang through this book. Capitalism, clericalism, and blind procreation conspired against working-class women. To escape their wretched working and living conditions, they had no choice but to learn the principles of "scientific procreation." Large families exacerbated workers' poverty and riveted them to a life of physical and emotional despair. Those pursuing an ideal of social justice had to agree that "children in large numbers are a source of suffering and bitterness for poor parents, who are incapable of providing well for them and are deprived of the greatest satisfaction of all loving parents." She urged Chilean mothers to consider having fewer offspring, though she was convinced this goal could not be achieved until Chilean authorities agreed to teach workers about their sexual functions. "Those who love humanity have the duty to teach the ignorant. Responsible parenthood allows children to grow happily by the side of their parents." Thus family planning was equated with an act of social justice that would ultimately allow all people a reasonable share of land and bread.

These writings showed a clear understanding of the relation between class, poverty, and reproduction among Chileans writing for female workers. Such articulate arguments on planned parenthood among workers were published only in the most radical newspapers. Could this position reflect the strong class feeling of Chilean labor? Though it would be desirable to support this argument, a survey of the influential socialist newspaper *El Despertar de los Trabajadores* reveals much less emphasis on sexuality or family planning. An essay published in February 1913 criticized those who had children when it was impossible to feed and educate them. The male author recommended limiting their numbers to suit the family's economic means. More important, he stated that the choice of procreation belonged to the woman, regulated "by her will through the use of suppositories [contraceptives]."[17] Allocating birth control to women was not a new idea, since despite prohibitions, women have assumed that task for centuries. Proposing a scientific medical approach to the subject rather than abortions or the use of folk medicine, however, was an important departure from the methods widely used by Chilean women at the time. Motherhood at will, sheltered by the safety of medicine, was a revolutionary idea.

In 1926 the anarchist *El Sembrador,* published irregularly in Valparaíso, carried a few articles on birth control, free love, and planned motherhood. The author explained that the word "proletariat" meant "maker of children" [*prole*], and underlined the negative correlation between poverty and number of children. He struck a new chord by presenting a male viewpoint on unregulated fatherhood. Men suffered when they begat children they were unable to feed properly, and they were driven to drinking and alcoholism. The ill-fed and sickly children of the poor were abandoned by their parents or exploited by others. Such circumstances legitimized information on contraceptives. He also pointed to the "feminist" consequences of freedom from pregnancy. "A woman will never be the mistress of her own body if she cannot choose the moment she wants to become a mother and will never be free if she does not know about contraceptive methods." Class gave elite women the knowledge and means to regulate their conceptions; poor women should have the same right. Only when women liberated themselves from the tyranny of nature—from being mere breeders—did they become free from men and from laws designed to keep them in submission. Apart from the fact that this message was delivered in the name of a political ideology, its strong support of women's control over reproduction was consistent with the individualistic feminism endorsed by the most radical wing of anarchism. But it was a position with few followers and far ahead of its time.[18]

Although at the beginning of the century the message of birth control was more heavily underlined by class consciousness, the triumph of science over nature symbolized by contraceptive methods was more topical in the 1920s. When Chilean anarchists began to distribute a pamphlet titled "Conscious Generation," they came under attack from the head of the Chilean Junta Sanitaria for conspiring against "morality, honest customs, dignity, and the progress of the motherland." The anarchists had the law on their side, since they had legal permission to sell the pamphlet. This encounter was partly political and partly ideological. It reveals that government officials, despite endorsing public lectures on sex education, were not at ease with having a group of political radicals distribute contraceptive information. The bureaucratic response reflected most people's views that sex education related to issues of disease and its prevention, not to the "evasion" of motherhood represented by contraceptives.[19]

There was little if any discussion of birth control in the Argentine anarchist press of the 1920s. Early in the decade Juana Rouco Buela's *Nuestra Tribuna* advertised three books dealing with sex and planned parenthood.[20] Apart from a couple of articles on free love, however, this newspaper added no new dimension to the discussion of birth control or sexuality.[21] Anarchists were neither popular beyond their own group nor totally committed to this aspect of social and sexual liberation—some writers seemed to have shied away from their radical colleagues' stance. Birth control and contraceptives were not acceptable to the more "conventional" socialist labor leaders or to the bulk of workers of either gender. The cult of motherhood never lost any of its power despite all the concern with human sexuality and the new technology for controlling its consequences.

The Issue of a Single Morality for Both Sexes

A single morality for both sexes (*moral única*) became one of the most important ideological foundations of sex education, the abolition of regulated prostitution, the establishment of clinics to check venereal diseases, and divorce. It also supported demands for the investigation of paternity and the legal recognition of children born out of wedlock. Its adaptability to a variety of causes made *moral única* one of the most persuasive ethical weapons wielded by feminists.

Feminists began to discuss the injustice of a double standard of morality for men and women before they felt confident enough to address the specifically sexual topics it logically introduced. Morality was an abstract concept that could be examined with no references to sexuality and used to support the justice of social causes. Women found it difficult to discuss sex education openly for many years, because it was bound to require explanation of body functions and concrete references to venereal diseases and prostitution. But *moral única* was a safe arena for discussing gender relations.

An exception to the rule of keeping the topic of sexuality out of the parlors of respectable homes was the writings of María Abella de Ramírez, the first nonmedical efforts to bring the subject out of the closet. In 1902 Abella de Ramírez first discussed the blatant injustice of codes of honor defining male-female relationships.[22] It was unjust to teach women that they were more accountable for "virtue" than men, and to allow men greater freedom to express their sexuality. Such exemptions debased the principles of personal accountability and responsibility. She reiterated her condemnation in a short story written for *Nosotras,* the feminist magazine she founded in 1902 in the Argentine city of La Plata. Literature was an acceptable way to approach a touchy subject. In "The Temptation," an educated young woman of good family feels an electrifying physical attraction to her cousin. Although the couple resists the temptation, the author warns that passion could easily overcome any "virtuous" woman; the physical impulses of young love are experienced by all women regardless of social class. Those who cannot resist are seduced and labeled "fallen."[23] The story found a sympathetic ear among the readers. Still worried by publicity, a woman from La Plata writing under a pseudonym expressed her frustration over social prejudices that barred single, widowed, and even some married women from fulfilling their natural instincts while others fell into prostitution to satisfy the passions of men.[24]

Other feminists would later argue that when two persons engaged in an activity by common consent, it was only just to allocate equal responsibility to both.[25] Women had the right to demand from their husbands the same moral and physical standards they were held to. Thus feminists envisioned a single standard of morality by which men had to rise to the expectations already imposed on most women. Summing up three decades of discussion, in 1933 Chilean Aurora Estrada y Ayala tersely condemned the social and legal codes that "gave men impunity and women responsibility."[26]

What could women do to raise social and moral expectations for men? Several writers urged women not to resign themselves to behavioral codes designed by men and applied only to women. Blanca C. de Hume, realizing that many women were not prepared for public activism on such issues, encouraged her readers to educate their children in the new ideas.[27] Estrada y Ayala also urged women to remember their social duties as mothers, and encouraged them to participate in moral change. The message of commitment to reform of moral and sexual norms was not one that many women adopted readily, but it found a warm reception among a group of vocal and influential social feminists. The themes that drew the most intense response concerned the correlation between sex education, personal attitudes about the opposite sex, and venereal diseases as a public health problem. Through sex education these activists hoped to help change the double standard of morality and gender relations.

Single Morality and Sex Education: The Debate

One of the most important offshoots of the campaign for a single moral standard was the belief that sex education could create healthier attitudes about sexuality and procreation. This discussion was sometimes vexing and challenging but was regarded as crucial for personal and social health. Sex education had had two perspectives since the first decade of the century: instruction of both sexes about their roles in the reproductive cycle to teach responsible sexual behavior, and sex education as a necessary basis for eradicating the social diseases mortgaging the future. These approaches developed separately at first but met in the writings of some feminists and *higienistas* by the second decade of the century.

Sex education was first advocated by dissident groups such as the anarchists and self-appointed freethinkers. These groups sought a more honest approach to the "facts of life" to prepare men and women for their duties as spouses and parents, as did María Abella de Ramírez.[28] She often shocked other women, and her ideas were not adopted by her generation.[29] At the First International Feminine Congress held in Buenos Aires in 1910, the Peruvian feminist Dora Meyer reported on sex education, and her paper was fully endorsed by the congress. Meyer approached the subject by scrutinizing male behavior according to the standard of a single morality. Most men, she argued, abused their procreative faculties. Many husbands gave little consideration to their wives' needs as persons. Women subjected to this endured continual pregnancies and became little but reproduction machines or, at best, nannies to their own children for the rest of their lives. Other men practiced irresponsible procreation outside marriage. Meyer denounced the assumption that men had the right to engender lives they did not plan to foster and protect, whether within or outside marriage. She called for moderation and sexual control on moral and social grounds. Like many other women of that period she stopped short of practical advice, satisfied with addressing the issue and suggesting changes.[30]

A different approach to sex education, although not necessarily antagonistic to that of Abella de Ramírez and Meyer, stressed public health issues and the consequences of venereal disease for individuals and their progeny. One of the first to follow this line of thought was the Argentine socialist and activist Raquel Camaña. Though she never called herself a feminist, her interest in educational reforms, health matters, and social justice for workers was very similar to contemporary feminists'. Camaña was a graduate of the normal school of La Plata and a student of Mary O. Graham, one of the most popular North American teachers brought to Argentina by educator Domingo Faustino Sarmiento. She represented Argentina at the 1910 Paris Congress of Educational Hygiene [Higiene Escolar]. Advocating sex education in the primary schools, she stirred great interest. After the congress she traveled in Belgium and Spain lecturing on the topic. On her return to Argentina she applied for a position on the Faculty of Philosophy and Letters at the University of Buenos Aires but was not deemed an appropriate candidate. Camaña wrote extensively on a variety of educational subjects. Her untimely death from tuberculosis in 1915 cut short a potentially brilliant career.

Camaña combined traditional and modern attitudes, but she was viewed as a radical by many of her contemporaries. She was traditional insofar as she believed that woman and mother were synonymous; she was radical because she proposed that women needed sex education to fulfill their social duty as mothers. Learning about each other's sexual functions would kindle respect between men and women and help young people understand the beauty of the laws regulating the multiplication of the species.[31] Sex education should start at home and continue throughout primary and secondary school. Because she believed that puberty was a difficult stage in life, she did not support mixed sex education classes. She suggested that universities give public sex education classes, using their students and faculty to lecture on responsible paternity, sexual morality, pregnancy, and child care.

For Camaña the ultimate object of sex education was the health of the unborn child, reflecting the concern of her generation with what was then termed *puericultura intrauterina* [prenatal care]. She stressed the social and personal responsibility to conceive healthy children, free of the mental and physical handicaps produced by venereal diseases. She was also an early supporter of eugenics to prevent the proliferation of communicable diseases and the reproduction of individuals carrying them or affected by them. Camaña recommended that sex education be incorporated into the biology and ethics curriculum but gave no specific guidelines on how to teach it. She described sex education as "living poetry" that would solve such social problems as alcoholism, prostitution, criminality, and infant mortality, and foster a new social religion in which the supreme ideal would be the improvement of humankind through the creation of healthier new lives.

Camaña spoke on sex education at the 1913 Argentine National Congress on the Child and provoked a heated discussion. Not only did she endorse coeducation, still a controversial subject, but she supported compulsory sex education in public schools for children under ten. Her proposal on sex education was voted down as immoral, and the gap between supporters and opponents remained unbridgeable.[32] Three years later the idea received warm support at the First American Congress on the Child, but Camaña was already dead.[33]

Despite its volatile nature, sex education became a more open topic through the combined influence of social hygienists and eugenics advocates within the medical profession. Their approach differed from that of the women and feminists who first wrote on the subject. For the *higienistas* sex education above all taught how to practice medically safe sex. The more immediately obvious benefits of their approach gave it an advantage over the educational goals of women such as Abella de Ramírez and Camaña. In 1905 Uruguayan *higienista* Alfredo Vidal y Fuentes wrote a small "educational" booklet to alert young men to the dangers of venereal disease and teach them how to protect themselves on their visits to prostitutes.[34] The medical profession continued to regard sex education as a topic for men only.[35] By 1914 a few bold individuals began to discuss sex education for youngsters as part of general education. A booklet circulating in Argentina told parents to teach their children about sexuality before they learned half-truths from friends or servants. Clandestineness fostered pornography rather than a healthy attitude on sexual relations. Parents should talk about the sexual organs as naturally as they spoke about other parts of the body and should begin sex education as soon as the child could read. Sex education for girls was described as an urgent need. Girls should learn about male seduction, prostitution, and the "degeneration" produced by alcoholism and syphilis. Above all, women had the right to marry knowing that their children would not be born deformed or sick.[36]

Sex education as discussed at the 1910 Paris Medical Congress, and French ideas on public health, had a strong influence on Argentine and Uruguayan doctors, who in the following decade found inspiration in its guidelines on how to deal with human sexuality and health. The spread of venereal disease was regarded as an effect of prostitution, which in turn was sustained by the white slave trade.[37] Public opinion was stirred by the discussion of whether prostitution should be regulated—put under the control of the police and health authorities—or whether such control should be abolished. Abolition was supported by a significant number of physicians. The "abolitionists" had an informal alliance with some feminist women doctors who saw state control of prostitution as offensive to all women and an ineffective way of combating venereal disease.[38] The debate kindled interest in all matters related to venereal disease, and the preventive benefits of medically oriented sex education were regarded as paramount in public health policies. The 1917 First Uruguayan Medical Congress endorsed the concept of sex education as necessary for the containment of syphilis.[39]

The creation of the Argentine-Uruguayan Abolitionist Federation in 1918 gave a boost to the discussion of sex education as critical to abolishing regulated prostitution. The founders were doctors who underlined the medical aspects of venereal disease and approached sex education from a clinical angle. They also believed they were protecting national health. The Federation held its first sex education conference in Montevideo in October 1919. Argentine physician Juan A. Senillosa proposed creating an Institute of Sexual Ethics, but the idea did not prosper. Yet lecturing on the subject was becoming more acceptable, and none other than the Uruguayan Consejo Nacional de Mujeres sponsored a lecture on sex education the following year.[40] The lecturer, Dr. Santín C. Rossi, argued that sex education was an important part of social equality for women. This idea was shared by Dr. Fernández Verano, who supported feminism to promote women's economic independence and personal freedom to choose a healthy partner rather than marrying for economic interests.[41]

The foundation of the Liga Argentina de Profilaxis Social (1919) and the Liga Chilena de Higiene Social (1917) brought sex education to the attention of a larger audience. The Chilean League met in September 1917 to issue a "Declaration of Principles" and shortly thereafter sent a message to the Chamber of Deputies expressing concern over the high incidence of venereal disease and the lack of any scientific organization to combat it. It proposed creating an institution to control venereal diseases and urged allocation of funds for such purposes in the 1918 budget.[42] In subsequent years some deputies supported public health policies to eradicate venereal disease. Wenceslao Sierra, for example, condemned the "social silence" on the topic, advised instruction for young men, and backed a bill to send five physicians to Europe to learn the latest techniques for control. One of those physicians had to be a woman, to serve the needs of women and children in Chile.[43]

Aiming at mass communication, the Liga Argentina printed fliers and organized conferences on sexual topics, although no explicit information on sexual functions was ever imparted in these first efforts to reach the public. These fliers dealt with such subjects as prenuptial certificates, child care, sex education in the schools, and sexual hygiene for members of the armed forces. It began to use slides and films to fight "the ignorance bred by social prejudice." In 1926 the Argentine Liga claimed that 14,000 persons had attended its public lectures.[44] Its annual report for 1934 claimed an attendance of several thousand persons at lectures in Bahía Blanca and La Plata.[45] Dra. Alicia Moreau was a member of the League's consulting board in 1934 and participated, along with several well-known women doctors, in the annual lecture series.

The Chilean League also attempted to remedy what a medical professor lamented as a total absence of instruction in sex hygiene in schools as well as general ignorance of the subject.[46] In 1924 the League reported distributing 35,191 pamphlets and 13,296 handbills, giving forty-four lectures to audiences totaling 19,600 persons, and exhibiting ten films borrowed from the American Social Hygiene League in the United States.[47] In 1925 the Chilean Department of Social Hygiene, then under the Ministry of Health, began a campaign to educate the public on "social" diseases, targeting small towns and working-class associations.[48] On 17 March 1925 Chile approved a decree to combat syphilis, tuberculosis, alcoholism, and prostitution. To back such an agenda the decree recommended sex education in the primary and secondary schools.[49] This suggestion remained a dead letter, because most parents did not approve of such teaching. On the other hand, medical education on venereal disease—still addressed as sex education—was gaining general support. The Dirección General de Sanidad endorsed that type of education, and beginning in 1929 it began a campaign supported by the national press.[50]

The cooperation of several well-known feminist physicians in these attempts to reach the public helped stimulate interest among women, and it definitely enhanced the role of women in public health. Dra. Ernestina Pérez, an 1887 graduate of the University of Berlin and a specialist in gynecology and nursing, attended the 1921 Berlin Congress on Sex Education, which endorsed her proposal for compulsory sex education for all children. In 1923 and 1924 she gave a series of slide-illustrated public lectures in Santiago on the prophylaxis of "social diseases." Cora Mayers also lectured on infectious and inherited diseases, promoting sex education as part of a medical program on public and personal health.[51]

Sex education in Uruguay received its share of attention largely as the result of Paulina Luisi's forceful support. An uninhibited public debate on such matters by a woman was bound to catch the public eye. Luisi was not, however, the sole standard-bearer for sex education in Uruguay, though she gave herself the distinction of having initiated it and resented that some male physicians never credited her with opening the debate in Uruguay. One of those men, Dr. Mateo Legnani, recognized Luisi's contribution, but apparently she felt he had borrowed her ideas. Early in 1923 Legnani engaged in a heated debate with conservative Dr. Juan B. Morelli, author of a cheap, widely available pamphlet opposing sex education in the name of morality and religion. In a series of articles in *El Día* Legnani rebutted Morelli's arguments, citing the sexual content of the Old Testament, noting how sex education was taught in the United States, and supporting sports as a better alternative to sexuality than the chastity recommended by Catholic conservatives. He praised Paulina Luisi's work and cited others interested in the topic.[52] By the mid-1920s sex education was out of the closet. In subsequent years it was incorporated into the broader agenda of social prophylaxis and social eugenics.

Women's Views on Sex Education

The most distinguished feminist women doctors to support sex education and the League of Social Prophylaxis were Argentine Alicia Moreau de Justo and Uruguayan Paulina Luisi. Both believed the solution to many social problems rested on new pedagogical methods, including sex education. Luisi had the more consistent interest in the topic. Moreau de Justo wrote on it only occasionally, although her interest can be traced back to her first writings. For her the subject transcended medical boundaries and became a social issue. Doctors and legislators had the duty to search for a permanent solution to the medical problems caused by prostitution and venereal disease. Physicians should become educators and provide parents and teachers with information and support for imparting responsible and truthful information through the family and in the schools. Legislators should defend sex education programs with supportive laws. Moreau de Justo believed that childhood sex education was essential to creating sexually and ethically responsible adults. "This is what we understand by sex education. It is not the mere acquisition of knowledge, but the formation of feelings that dignify life." [53] Her ideas accurately reflected a feminist viewpoint that injected a pedagogical ethos into social reform.

Moreau de Justo's moral view of sexual behavior was also the backbone of Paulina Luisi's theories on sex education. No other Southern Cone feminist devoted so much time and energy to the problems of gender relationships and sexuality, and none developed a fuller set of ideas. That her ideas had many internal ambiguities and contradictions does not detract from their merit as expressions of a deeply felt personal ideology and a reflection of contemporary trends in sex education.

Luisi was a normal school teacher who became the first woman doctor in Uruguay in 1909. Interested in sex education since her earliest professional days, in 1906 she became acquainted with the ideas of French doctor Alfred Fournier. She tried to persuade the director of the Public Instruction Board to purchase and distribute Fournier's manual on sex education to boys in the senior classes of the primary school (twelve to fourteen years of age) and the normal school (fourteen to eighteen). Her suggestion was characterized as "anarchist" and "immoral." [54]

Luisi visited Europe in 1913, just after the first Congress on School Hy-

giene in France. This congress had set guidelines on child health and education, and Luisi was encouraged by the director of Uruguayan public instruction to learn all she could about sex education. When World War I cut her
travel short, she returned to Uruguay convinced of the need to teach about
human sexuality to the public at large under one educational plan. Between
1916 and 1919 she laid the basis of her own stand on human sexuality: the
abolition of regulated prostitution, and sex education.

At the 1916 First American Congress on the Child sex education was not
among the official themes. Nonetheless, Luisi spoke on her plan for child
sex education, and it received the congress's approval at its plenary session,
unlike a similar proposal Raquel Camaña made three years earlier before a
national group of doctors and educators.[55] Perhaps the presence of a significant body of international participants was influential in 1916. Attempts to
gain official recognition for sex education were on Luisi's agenda throughout the decade. She had the support of the medical profession and acted as
a medical doctor within the abolitionist campaign, advocating a program of
social prophylaxis. However, her objective was above all pedagogical, and
she continued to seek the endorsement of Montevideo's authorities to approach sexuality as part of a comprehensive educational experience.[56]

In 1921 her presentation on sex education at the Ninth Medical Congress
of Uruguay earned her the opposition of Catholic Action and the Catholic
press and eventual condemnation by the Roman Curia. This and her participation in the 1922 Paris International Congress of Propaganda for Social
Hygiene, Prophylaxis, and Moral Education made Luisi the uncontested if
controversial leader of sex education in the River Plate area. Her influence on
the educational system was limited, however. The normal school in Montevideo offered its students lectures on sex education for voluntary attendance,
and eventually a chair of social hygiene was created. In 1922 Dr. Mateo Legnani proposed a national sex education plan. Luisi did not support this draft
because it approached the subject only from a medical viewpoint, ignoring its social and ethical aspects. By this time Luisi was chiding the faculty
of the School of Medicine for confusing sex education with the reeducation
of prostitutes and for supporting centers for "sex education" that addressed
only the physical aspects of sexuality.[57]

During the late 1920s and into the 1930s Luisi's ideas on sex education
jelled into a system that incorporated technical knowledge of the reproductive process, the consequences of sexual activity, and strict personal ethics.
Sexuality, in her view, was a collective issue, not an individual one, because
its consequences affected society as a whole. The health of future genera-

tions was directly related to the health of the reproducing couple, and the exercise of human sexuality demanded utter respect and a strong sense of duty and responsibility. Luisi believed that sexual instinct could be brought under control, but only when sex education went beyond the physical and became an intellectual and moral experience. Sex education should begin at an early age and form the character of individuals by convincing them to respect the laws of life and to make conscious and deliberate choices in their sexual behavior.

The moral goals Luisi pursued were not abstract entities. Arguing against a double standard of morality for men and women, she sought to correct the assumption that procreation was predominantly a female responsibility. Parenthood involved both sexes, and men's obligation to future generations and to society should not be neglected without punishment. Sex education would prepare men to assume their responsibility as fathers and alert society to the injustice implicit in seduction, abortion, infanticide, and the stigma attached to single motherhood.[58] In addressing these issues, Luisi pointed out that one of the most important problems in gender relations was the rigid demarcation between male and female roles within and outside the family. Strict gender-role separation put the burden of homelife and raising children on women and left men unwilling to acknowledge moral responsibility for the offspring of extramarital affairs. Many women became involved in such relationships either through lack of family protection or for economic reasons.

Luisi believed that the ethics of procreation hinged on its physical consequences. Diseased parents should not beget new lives. All should be aware of the harmful effects of heredity and infectious diseases. Like most doctors of her period, she believed in the possibility of ridding society of pathological strains, but to accomplish its goal, social hygiene had to be complemented by moral hygiene. Moral hygiene would teach men the discipline to avoid prostitutes, and would also teach children and adolescents how to curb their sexual instinct and use it only for procreating healthy new generations.[59] Summing up the purposes of sex education, she saw it as helping spiritual forces tame the instincts and impose a discipline that would ultimately benefit the species.[60]

Building on those premises, she denounced the trivialization of sex in the pursuit of pleasure for its own sake.[61] In the 1930s Luisi decried the increasing message of sexual pleasure in public advertising, entertainment, and even fashion.[62] Although pleasure was an admissible part of the sex act, she claimed, it was not its primary goal. She believed the emphasis on hedonism led to ephemeral physical encounters in which procreation was carefully avoided. Such practices debased the couple's physical and spiritual responsibility for creating a new being. Moving forward on the path of personal and social ethics, Luisi directed sex education toward "purity." Men and women alike could and should be taught to preserve their mental and physical chastity until they were ready for the high task of reproduction.

This emphasis on chastity brought her close to the teachings of the Roman Catholic Church, one of her archenemies. Luisi used language permeated with religious connotations and with the evangelical message of a new morality.[63] Much as she decried the political oppression of fascist regimes, she endorsed state interference in population matters. Assuming that procreation was not "an individual right" but a racial and eugenic duty to be fulfilled in a healthy and efficient manner, she gave society the right to supervise it for the benefit of the species. Yet, she opposed state regulation of prostitution because the state was then pursuing the wrong health policies by focusing on a single source of transmissible diseases.[64]

The eugenicist and the feminist in Luisi carried out a dialogue in which the need for control of transmissible and hereditary diseases alternated with the ethical imperative of protecting motherhood and childhood through application of a uniform moral code.[65] Luisi never addressed the sexual instinct once the desired number of children had been born, suggesting that she was more interested in reforming sexual behavior before marriage than in dealing with sexuality in married couples. Like others engaged in purity campaigns, she defined sexuality in terms of channeling its force into culturally and socially acceptable parenthood.

The feminist press did not address sex education until the 1930s. Until the mid-1920s discussing sex education in the mass media, especially in publications dedicated to women, was not acceptable. Even in the mid-1930s women preferred not to be seen attending public lectures on sexual issues, which were also considered "improper."[66] In Argentina *Vida Femenina* carried two articles in 1933 and 1936. In Chile *Acción Femenina* and *Nosotras* ran one article each, in 1935 and in 1934. Martha Licyh in *Vida Femenina* discussed sex education as it concerned family planning. Her message was largely neo-Malthusian and addressed the burden of unwanted motherhood on middle-class and working-class women, and it echoed Luisi's views on sex education as a means of restraining instinct. Argentine Dra. Thelma Reca, writing in *Vida Femenina* in 1936, also showed Luisi's influence, advising sex education for children although aware that many parents needed more information as well. Neither the Chilean nor the Argentine feminist press improved on

Luisi's ideas or offered any specific methods of teaching about sex.[67] In the 1930s sex education was in principle accepted by *higienistas*, eugenicists, and feminists but not widely accepted as a subject for minors.

At the close of the 1930s the debate on whether sex education should consider the ethical as important as the physiological remained unresolved, but Camaña's and Luisi's ideas were not completely forgotten. In 1940 Chilean Dr. Waldemar Coutts, a respected public health specialist, recommended sex education from childhood on.[68] But the medical view was the one that gained recognition through legislation. Argentine Law 12.331 proscribed legalized prostitution and mandated venereal prophylaxis. It also provided for a national hygiene department that would develop a plan for sex education. In the meantime a Venereal Museum in Buenos Aires would provide such education. As of 1940 those mandates remained unfulfilled.[69] The feminist message was derailed into the eugenics camp, where it became ancillary to supervising the propagation of the species.

The Issue of Illegitimacy as a Feminist Cause

The rate of illegitimacy embarrassed social commentators and development planners and was related to the question of health. Feminists, physicians, and experts on public health argued that children born to unwed mothers were more likely to be prey to disease and death because their mothers could not give them adequate care. The correlation of illegitimacy with syphilis (identified as "congenital" syphilis or "congenital weakness"), alcoholism, and child mortality was taken as fact in the First National Congress on Childhood in Chile (1912) and became part of *higienista* and feminist lore throughout the following decades.[70] In 1912 Uruguayan Colorado deputy José Espalter cited "statistics everywhere" showing that more out-of-wedlock children died.[71] These claims lacked a statistical basis: they simply cited high rates of child mortality and illegitimacy side by side, without cross-tabulation. Only data linking birth status to mortality figures could lend certainty to these claims, and rarely did the three nations record the birth status of deceased children. In 1920 the Argentine province of Tucumán, where high rates of illegitimacy prevailed, cross-tabulated mortality and illegitimacy rates for infants under one year of age. Of 2,595 children who died, 1,233 were illegitimate and 1,362 legitimate. This example suggests that *direct* causal relationship between illegitimacy and child mortality was difficult to prove despite repeated claims.[72] Lacking precise data, we can only surmise that the testimony of feminists and physicians was based on their experience and that whether or not they were correct, their intention was to condemn a widespread injustice.[73] Illegitimacy, child mortality, and child abandonment demanded attention and remedy, and tying them to an ethical issue strengthened the case.[74]

Measuring Illegitimacy

Illegitimacy rates for the Southern Cone were high at the turn of the century, and they became even higher in subsequent decades. Whether this was a temporary aberration or represented a trend with deeper historical roots remains to be tested by long-term studies.[75] Civil marriage enforcement was cited as one possible cause for the rise in illegitimacy. People, it was argued, neglected to register their unions or refused to do so as a protest against the civil marriage law. The low rate of marriage and the high illegitimacy rate led some opponents of divorce to argue that the only social reform needed in the Southern Cone was more effective enforcement of marriage.[76] Other commentators saw high illegitimacy rates as a sign of increasingly loose female morals.[77]

Statistical data for Chile between 1850 and 1948 provide a realistic base for judgment (see fig. 1). Although in the mid-nineteenth century 22.3 percent of all births were out of wedlock, in the 1890s the rate climbed above 30 percent, reaching a peak by 1929. In the 1930s it began to decline, and by 1948 it was close to the 1850 figure.[78]

In Uruguay the illegitimacy rate was lower than in Chile, never rising above 30 percent of live births (see fig. 2). The profile differed from Chile's in some details. Whereas Chile showed a steep rise and a dramatic decline, Uruguay's increase was steady and commensurate with the growth of the population. For several years it lingered on a plateau. As in Chile, it began to decline slowly in the mid-1930s. The differences, however, were more of degree than substance.[79]

Argentina's figures offer contours similar to those of Uruguay and Chile. The rate of illegitimacy between 1910 and 1938 varied with geographical location, increasing except in the capital city of Buenos Aires. All national averages masked information for provincial rates, which were significantly higher for all three nations. For example, while the national average in Uruguay in 1939 was 27.38 percent, the northern provinces of Paysandú, Salto, and Artigas had rates of 41.8, 48.7, and 45.6 percent, respectively. At the other extreme the province of San José, contiguous to Montevideo, had a rate of 16.6 percent.[80] The disparity in illegitimacy rates between urban cen-

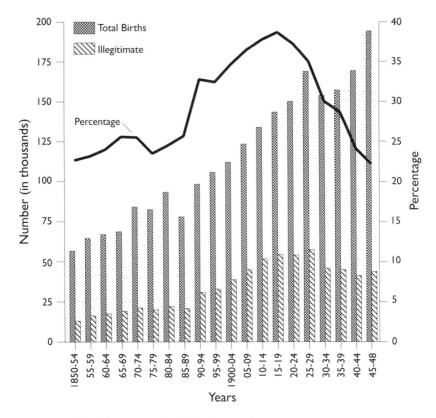

FIGURE 1.   Illegitimacy rates in Chile, 1850–1948.

ters and the provinces, and even provincial capitals and their departments, remained constant through the 1930s.[81]

In 1917 the rate in the main provincial cities and in the city of Buenos Aires showed significant differences: Corrientes, Salta, and Jujuy, led the nation with out-of-wedlock births above 35 percent of total births (see figs. 3 and 4).

In 1917 an essayist for Buenos Aires *La Prensa* commented on the high illegitimacy rates in the provinces of Salta, Jujuy, Tucumán, Catamarca, and Corrientes. The anonymous writer explained the difference between the capital and several provinces in terms of the predominance of *nativos* in those areas. Their poor morals and bad health were a national blemish, a situation embarrassing for the "national aspirations."[82] The cosmopolitan residents of Buenos Aires felt humiliated by the provincial illegitimacy

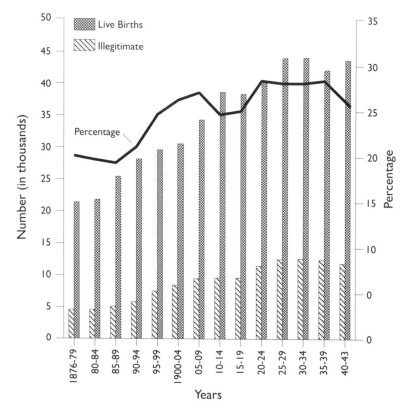

FIGURE 2.   Illegitimacy rates in Uruguay, 1876–1943.

figures, not realizing that a rate of 15 percent for the capital was high compared with central European figures. References to "natives" implied that the
Indian or mestizo element had lower standards of socioethical behavior, revealing the implicit racism of the Europeanized capital.[83]

The feminists viewed the problem using a more complex set of ethical
values that paid great attention to gender relations and to the social accountability of national leaders. Irresponsible legislators who refused to change
the legal conditions that fostered illegitimacy were one of their targets.
Feminists believed a nation that allowed its children to die in such numbers
showed no respect for its citizens, and illegitimacy also reflected the abandonment of pregnant women and conditions in homes based on unstable
relations. At bottom they also saw illegitimacy as a consequence of the shady
legal basis of gender relations.

TABLE 12   Argentina: Illegitimacy Rates per Thousand Births

	1910	1920	1925	1931	1935	1938
Buenos Aires Province, Santa Fe, Córdoba	143	159	161	169	184	189
Entre Ríos, San Luis, Santiago del Estero, Mendoza, San Juan, La Rioja, Catamarca	346	349	339	343	349	355
Corrientes, Salta, Jujuy, Tucumán	457	472	481	476	484	474
Buenos Aires	126	126	112	108	107	114
Territories	329	n.a.	n.a.	393	447	468
National average	220	n.a.	n.a.	254	277	282

Source: Alejandro E. Bunge, *Una nueva Argentina* (Buenos Aires: Kraft, 1940), 169. The territories were Chaco, Chubut, Formosa, La Pampa, Los Andes, Misiones, Neuquén, Río Negro, Santa Cruz, and Tierra del Fuego.

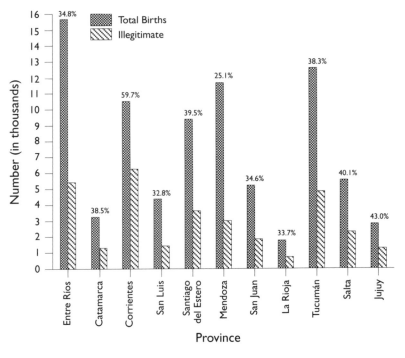

FIGURE 3.   Argentine provincial illegitimacy rates, 1917.
La Prensa (Buenos Aires), 18 May 1919, 5.

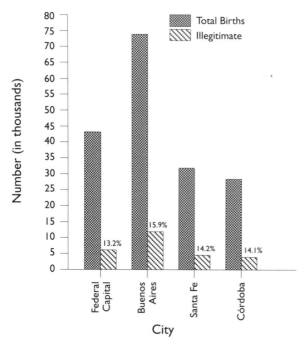

FIGURE 4.   Illegitimacy rates in the major Argentine provinces, 1917.
La Prensa (Buenos Aires), 18 May 1919, 5.

Illegitimacy and the Acknowledgment of Paternity

Although the literature dealing with child mortality and "illegitimacy" used that term as a general signifier, its legal definition was no simple matter. Many of those who spoke or wrote on illegitimacy for popular consumption ignored legal nuances. Legally, illegitimacy was a condition of birth that could be changed, but the judicial process was complex. The definition of children born out of wedlock was rooted in Spanish colonial legislation, which in turn had medieval and Roman roots.[84]

The definition of illegitimacy was found in the civil codes. The meaning of the term is very close in the three nations, and I will use the Uruguayan Civil Code to illustrate. In Uruguay *hijos naturales* were the offspring of two single persons who were not married during the "act of conception." Nonetheless, children were not so classified until they were recognized as such by the parents in a public, legally binding document or in a will. Either the mother or the father, or both together, could recognize a child as "natural." If only one parent did so, only that parent was acknowledged, and the name of the other parent could not be revealed. The parent who recognized the child had *patria potestad,* or complete control during the child's minority. Unless a couple agreed to share responsibility for the child, recognition by only one parent left the other entirely free of accountability. On the other hand, parents could lose their parental rights on grounds of mistreatment, repeated delinquency, corruption of minors, and other criminal activities.[85]

Natural children thus recognized could not claim the rights of legitimate or "legitimated" children.[86] Only marriage of single parents to each other legitimated natural children. Without recognition natural children and their mothers faced strong obstacles in claiming legal paternity. Investigation of paternity was forbidden by the 1868 Civil Code and its subsequent editions in 1893 and 1924.[87] Several laws approved between 1914 and 1916, under the influence of *batllista* social reforms, gave recognized "natural" children a broader right to share in the inheritance of their parents, but not complete equality with legitimate offspring.

A 1911 bill by Ricardo J. Areco, an ardent social reformer, proposing the recognition of paternity out of wedlock was approved in September.[88] This bill allowed paternity to be established in a variety of circumstances, and the most important ones for women were those not stated in the Civil Code. Women could initiate the investigation of paternity in the following circumstances: in demonstrable cases of rape or seduction at the approximate date of conception; when the presumed father had provided for the child for over a year, implying legal acknowledgment; when the alleged father was living in concubinage with the mother at the time of conception. Men would be protected from possible fraud if the mother lived "dishonestly" during conception or maintained sexual relations with another man. The process for claiming paternity had to begin within two years of the child's birth or be undertaken by the child within five years of becoming a legal adult.[89]

Uruguay reasserted the right to investigate paternity with the enactment of the Código del Niño in 1936. The code stated that all children were entitled to learn who their parents were. The new legislation entitled the natural child to financial support and the use of the father's surname, but not to any share of the father's property unless legally recognized as stated above. There were boundaries the state did not feel it could cross even for the benefit of children. The legally constituted family was still the goal of legislators, feminists, and reformers, and any right to share the property of legitimate children would weaken the case for the legitimate family. Thus legislators reaffirmed the father's will to maintain the stability of the legal family: the patriarchal system protected its ultimate bastion.

The Argentine Civil Code was much tougher than the Uruguayan on the issue of recognition. In cases of contested paternity, the mother's word had no legal standing whatever. The father could not deny the legitimacy of a child born within 180 days after marriage if he knew of the pregnancy before the marriage or consented to give his name to the child, but only he could make a legal claim on the legitimacy of any child born within marriage. The wife's testimony was not acceptable.[90] To counterbalance, married women were protected from being assigned a child by a clause forbidding the investigation of maternity. In both instances the object was to protect the institution of marriage from any party outside it. If parents were single at the time of conception they could legitimate their offspring only through marriage, and they had to acknowledge their natural children before marriage for the legitimation to be valid. A natural child could request to be recognized by the father (but not legitimized) if there were enough legal proofs. This request could be enforced even against the will of the alleged father. Any legal recognition of natural parenthood was irrevocable, and the parents of such children had the same rights over their children as legitimate parents.[91]

The Chilean Civil Code was similar to the Uruguayan in its definition of legitimacy. It denied any means to approve or disprove illegitimacy or the investigation of paternity and paternity claims. Registering children as natural was also the only legal way to give them that status. Out-of-wedlock children were those whose fathers were proved in court to have fathered them. Such children were entitled to a minimum of support, but there the father's responsibility ceased.[92] In the mid-1920s, possibly under the influence of feminist arguments, ad hoc legislation attempted to alleviate the situation of illegitimate children. A law on labor accidents enacted in 1925 considered legitimate and registered natural children equal before the law for receiving accident benefits.[93]

Legal recognition of paternity and legitimation were not idle processes in the Southern Cone. There are no studies on the subject, but data available for Uruguay allow us to take the pulse of a very fluid relationship between birth outside marriage and the possibility of changing legal and social status through parental recognition (see fig. 5).[94]

There are grounds for thinking that recognition and legitimation helped buffer the disintegrating social force of illegitimacy. Early in the twentieth century the number of out-of-wedlock children legitimated or recognized by either parent was small. Between 1929 and 1943 legitimation and legal recognition increased steadily while the number of illegitimate children began to drop slowly. The yearly figures on legitimation and births out of wedlock do

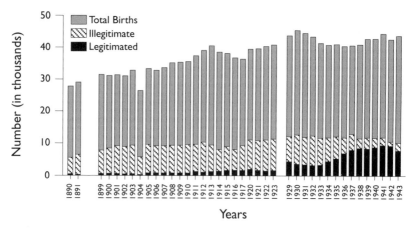

FIGURE 5.   Illegitimate births and legitimations in Uruguay, 1890–1943.
Uruguay, *El movimiento civil y la mortalidad en la República Oriental del Uruguay*
(Montevideo: Imp. National, 1890–1943).

not correlate. They indicate a trend toward acknowledgment of parental responsibility and should not be linked to the annual number of illegitimate
births. Children could be recognized anytime between one and ten years of
age or even later. Data for Uruguay show that it was more common for children to be recognized when they were over five years old. Even though long-
term statistical data suggest that the rate of legally acknowledging children
under one year rose steadily throughout the years, and rose dramatically in
the 1930s, the younger children were more vulnerable and less protected by
the legal umbrella of recognized affiliation (see appendix 1).[95]

Data on children born out of wedlock in Tucumán in 1920 offer another
glimpse into legitimation. That year 3,787 children were registered as having
been born out of wedlock, while 2,306 were recognized or legitimized by
the father and 1,291 by the mother. Only 190 were recognized jointly by both
parents. Fathers were taking the initiative in legal recognition, but this was
expected given the nature of the laws. Maternal recognition meant that the
woman was willing to assume all responsibility for care and education. Most
likely unwed mothers would put pressure on the natural father before taking
that step. These figures also corroborate the Uruguayan situation, insofar as
the number of legitimations almost equals the number of children born out
of wedlock. Unquestionably, many children never overcame the marginality
signified by lack of recognition or legitimation, but a considerable number
did receive the benefit of late legal acknowledgment, though it was a nomi-

nal move unless backed by economic support or the eventual legalization of the union.[96]

Recognition of natural children was not the only issue related to illegitimacy. *Patria potestad*—the right to determine children's fate and to administer and benefit from their properties or labor until they reached legal majority—was a key element in family law that also came under scrutiny during the 1920s. The Uruguayan Civil Code granted *patria potestad* over natural children to the parent who had legally acknowledged them. Up to the adoption of the Código del Niño, if both parents had recognized their child as natural the mother had the right to keep him or her until age five. At that point the child would pass to the father's care. Should this automatic transfer be challenged, a judge would determine the child's fate. This proviso was enough to deter any joint recognition of parenthood, because the mother would face the loss of the child or require a legal suit to prevent it. The Código del Niño abrogated the automatic transfer and allocated all such cases to judicial judgment.[97] However, it did not abrogate the clause stating that a married person who recognized a natural child could not bring the child into his or her home without consent of the spouse.

The 1926 reform of the Argentine Civil Code created one problem of jurisdiction over children born out of wedlock. Its wording allocated equal shares in *patria potestad* when both parents recognized the child. The potential conflict created by the ambiguous wording had to be resolved by the judge. As early as August 1926 a judge facing such a case decided that the mother of a natural child could not be deprived of *patria potestad* without sufficient reason.[98] This decision rested on the assumption that the mother had that right all the time.

Advocates for Change: Gender Relations and Illegitimacy

For feminists, out-of-wedlock births, illegitimacy, and the need for acknowledgment of paternity revealed that unwed mothers had a very weak position before the law. Simply stated, they were at the mercy of men's will to acknowledge fatherhood. Socialists and anarchists supported the investigation of paternity in all cases of abandonment of the mother and out-of-wedlock births and urged legislation to make fathers accountable for all their children. Their solution had no hope of being accepted by any legislature. Abrogating the proscription of paternity investigation was unthinkable for most male jurists and legislators.

The first arguments heard against the civil codes' prescriptions contended that the right to investigate paternity was an act of reparation and protection for the child. Opponents defended the privileges granted by legal marriage as a just means to stop illegitimate unions, constant sources of "disorder and immorality."[99] No legislation was completely successful in erasing the differences in birth, but Uruguayan Ricardo J. Areco obtained legislation recognizing paternity in several circumstances. His arguments illustrate a feminist and social reformist position: he argued for change without directly challenging the sanctity of marriage. He clearly stated that he did not wish a blanket equality, because inequality "is another form of justice, the guarantee of public order and of the dignity of marriage." Nonetheless, he found the prohibition on investigating paternity unacceptable because "it consecrates the irresponsibility of one person who causes damage to another." The child had the right to be provided for and educated, and the mother should not bear this responsibility alone.

Areco assumed that women suing men in paternity cases had been the victims of seduction, and he was no friend of seducers. By favoring seducers the Civil Code had placed the future of society in the hands of men subject to caprice and lust and willing to sacrifice the weak, "opening the gate to vice, crime, prostitution, and suffering." His bill would alleviate those social and moral problems, and he hoped it would reduce the many abortions and infanticides resulting from the lack of protection to seduced women. He also believed Uruguay could not afford to rely on a future labor force composed of men who had suffered a deprived childhood.[100] Stirring up sympathy for abandoned women, Areco appealed to the sense of honor and respect owed to motherhood and childhood. At the base of his argument was "compensatory feminism," stretched to argue that children also deserved compensation for their social handicaps. Areco was not ready to consider reasons for illegitimacy other than seduction — a palliative to explain the fall of decent women — and was obliquely defending the solidity of marriage.

The arguments used by legislators and opponents to any legal reform of legitimacy and paternity laws were a matter of personal opinion based on their own experience. Data gathered by social scientists further complicate the discussion of illegitimacy and gender relations. In 1934 Chilean Luisa Daco made a case for protecting illegitimate children by noting that of 300 children in one of Santiago's children's homes, 236 were born out of wedlock.[101] These figures favored the feminists' moral argument, but they were countered by another Chilean study based on data from the Minors' Court [Juzgado de Menores]. Between 1929 and 1931, 5,524 cases of abandoned children showed that out of 4,738 children, 3,270 (71 percent) were legitimate.[102] The difference between the two studies lay on the nature of the abandonment and the origin of the data. Most of the children who landed in charitable institutions were illegitimate and destitute, and we may speculate that their parents either did not wish to assume responsibility for them or could not. Most cases reviewed in the courts concerned legitimate children and were brought up by mothers resorting to the law to claim paternal accountability. Whether addressing outright abandonment by both parents or legal abandonment by one, the laws were not effective in protecting all women and children.

Facing that stark fact, some social workers demanded more attention to the social and economic dilemma of unwed mothers and more services to them rather than further discussion of moral issues. Illustrating this position was the report of a study of 100 unwed mothers carried out by Dr. José Beruti and María L. Zurano, presented at the 1937 Argentine First National Conference of Social Welfare. At that point the objective of social work was to change the meaning of unwed motherhood from a "moral" problem to a medical and social problem. Of the 100 unwed mothers interviewed, 80 percent were native-born Argentines, and 60 percent (75 women) came from the provinces. Half were under twenty-two, and the rest were twenty-three to twenty-six years of age. Forty-two percent were illiterate, and another 47 percent had only four years of education. Nearly half were either orphans or natural children themselves. Only 18 percent received support from their children's father. Fifty-five percent were domestics, 20 percent were industrial workers, and 20 percent were homebound. The rest were students, teachers, or employees.[103] This general profile of young provincial migrants without family protection, with little education, and mostly unskilled may have been the archetype of the unwed urban mother. Lacking other studies either in Argentina or elsewhere, I can only suggest that this prototype seems to fit the picture conveyed more impressionistically by other sources.

The Beruti-Zurano study was used by the socialist members of the Buenos Aires municipality to seek an ordinance, approved on 21 December 1937, to open five maternal shelters [hogares maternales] in the city, caring for 100 mothers each. Admission was to be granted if the women would sign a contract to stay in the shelter for six months to nurse their babies. In the meantime the administration would seek employment for them in "homes where they could bring their children." In other words, their fate was to remain domestics. The shelter sought to provide the mothers with temporary relief in exchange for the commitment of nursing the children. This, health experts believed, would most likely guarantee the children's survival.

Anarchists and some socialists would have seen in the Beruti-Zurano study a textbook example of capitalist exploitation. Feminists could see a gender issue that pitted women against men regardless of class. Gender was the element that could render a woman of the upper class and a factory worker equally "fallen" and dishonored if they made the same sexual mistake. Early in the twentieth century the first feminists urged legalization of the paternity investigation as redress for abandoned and cheated mothers, but by the 1920s their arguments expanded to include children more explicitly.[104] Maternity was a noble mission and should not be debased by the stigma of illegitimacy. All mothers and all children were equally deserving in the eyes of socialists, feminists, and social reformers.

The introduction into the debate of children's rights and the celebration of maternity was double edged. Should legally married mothers be threatened by claims that would reduce the patrimony of their children? Many women thought the only protection they had against their husbands' philandering was the legitimacy of their union and the security it provided for their children, and they rejected any legislation that would endanger either. What many of these women wanted was greater control over their legitimate children. Viewed this way, illegitimacy and paternity claims pitted women against women while relieving the pressure off men.[105] Staunch feminists continued to make a moral and emotional case for out-of-wedlock children. In 1935 Amanda Labarca tried to stir the conscience of Chilean women, urging them to consider illegitimacy as an ethical issue. Such social welfare as child-care centers, milk distribution, asylums for orphans, and similar measures helped save lives but did not meet the social needs of a generation of weak and unloved children. Parental responsibility was essential to bringing up children. If one parent failed to assume responsibility, the outcome could be expected to be neglect of the child's basic needs. As long as a double standard of morality permitted men to father children without marriage or caring for them, the nation would pay. The nation needed healthy children for a better future, and it should pursue this objective by forcing fathers to provide for their children whether legitimate or not.[106]

Statistical data shed some light on parental accountability. The registration of children born out of wedlock by either mother or father suggests some changes in the assumption of legal responsibility for children at the time of birth. Children could be registered as of "known father and unknown mother" or of "known mother and unknown father." In the first case we assume that the father wished to exercise his *patria potestad* and the woman preferred to save her name for reasons of "honor." In the second case the woman publicly and legally assumed the care of the child and the father was freed from any responsibility. Children registered as "of unknown parents" were totally devoid of legal parental care. We do not know whether another member of the family took care of them or if they were abandoned in charitable institutions.

Registering the child was an affirmation of legal and social responsibility that changed throughout time. Data for Uruguay show that although in the first decades of the century slightly more men than women registered their children without acknowledging the other parent, this pattern began to change in the 1920s, when the percentage of women registering their children as "of unknown father" began to rise. By 1943 that number was twice as large as the number of men assuming responsibility alone. More than half the children born out of wedlock were registered as their mothers' sole responsibility (see appendix 2).[107]

As time passed and more women were willing to acknowledge their children, men's responsibility—or willingness to recognize their children—declined. Was this rise in female recognition the result of "women's sexual liberation," or did it indicate a decline in the censure of unwed motherhood? The trend coincides with increased welfare services to children and mothers. One could see in these figures a change of attitude, the result of a more flexible social stance on illegitimacy enhanced by state incentives. In the early 1940s Uruguay planned incentives for marriage that dovetail with the slight declining trend in illegitimate births for that period. The nation was considering using its maternal clinics as centers of social reform. Reporting on rural maternity care centers early in 1941, Manuel Gortari recommended that they "assume the role of legal offices for the protection of abandoned mothers, seeking the means for the investigation of paternity to establish the degree of responsibility and obligation for protection that the law imposes on fathers."[108] Attempting a final solution for illegitimacy, in December 1943 a Uruguayan deputy proposed a bill to encourage marriage among consensual couples with children. The bill proposed to grant any woman who had lived with a man for over ten years the same rights to conjugal properties as those of legal wives. The presence of children reduced the waiting time to five years.[109] Another bill introduced that same month proposed to encourage marriages—and legitimate births—by granting couples of limited income loans to set up homes, payable in one hundred monthly payments. If the couple had children before the end of the repayment term, the loan would be slashed by 30 percent.[110]

Regardless of the amelioration some perceived, the situation had changed only in degree, not substance. Many women remained dissatisfied with legal inequalities affecting unwed mothers, and many men continued to admire sexual prowess and seduction.[111] Rather than challenging the legal protection afforded the fathers of natural children, the legislators of the period chose to apply palliatives under the guise of protection. Unable to change the laws forbidding the investigation of paternity, most feminists accepted the remedy offered by the state to protect women as a means toward a nobler and more just future. Some did not relent, however. Sara Rey Alvarez, founder of the Uruguayan Partido Independiente Democrático Feminista, placed the investigation of paternity and the legal equality of natural and legitimate children second in the party's program, preceded only by legal equality of women within marriage.[112]

On the whole, illegitimacy and paternity were a great challenge to feminism in the Southern Cone and a persistent reminder of the strength of sexism and patriarchal domination. By 1940 female sexuality had been acknowledged, discussed, and subjected to state regulation in cases involving public health and prostitution, although it was not recognized as an appropriate topic for public discussion. Sex education continued to be regarded as a medical subject. In its connection with reproduction, female sexuality continued to be strictly regulated, as we will see in the following chapter, in the continued denial of legalized abortion. In contrast, male sexuality remained free to express itself. Men suffered no restrictions on their ability to help conceive as many children as they saw fit, legally or "illegally."

Social relations between men and women in 1940 were not as strictly codified as in 1900, but mores had not changed profoundly. Most people were not ready for open discussion of sexuality and sex education for minors and women. The feminist proposal to make sex education part of a moral plan to put gender relations on a more equal footing did not succeed. The problem with the feminist agenda was that it attempted to curb male sexuality and raise gender relations to a spiritual and ethical level that most men were unwilling to accept. Bound to uphold the sanctity and validity of all forms of motherhood, feminists settled for state protection of mother and child to solve the problems created by the deeply rooted double standard of morality. Such protection, however, freed men from assuming their full sexual and paternal responsibility before begetting children. Gender equality remained a hope for the future.

CHAPTER 5

The Control of Reproduction:

Gender Relations under Scrutiny

Feminists had a strong concern for the social consequences of male and female sexuality. Ironically, feminists had no power to change the course of that discussion or to shape the legislation that controlled socio-sexual behavior. Reproductive health, prenuptial certificates, and abortion were in the hands of doctors and jurists, many of whom used feminism inferentially but kept feminists out of the decision making. Yet feminists influenced all discussions of human sexuality; their insistence on including women as both actors and objects in social programs of any nature changed gender policies forever. Women did not automatically benefit, nor were gender roles changed greatly through discussion of reproductive policies, but their study is essential to understanding the complexities of women's lives in the period.

At the turn of the century, genetic studies of plants and animals began to unlock the mysteries of life and led some scientists to assume that genetics could be put at the service of humanity through social engineering. The resulting body of pseudoscientific analysis of human reproduction was eugenics, an offshoot of scientific positivism that applied the principles of heredity to people. It promised improved humans through planned reproductive strategies that isolated desirable biological and social characteristics and created physically and morally superior individuals through evolution. Social policies favoring the healthiest and strongest would eventually create a "better" human race.[1] Combining of medical and biological knowledge with sociological theories created a powerful mixture that fueled public health programs as well as precarious and even dangerous schemes to promote perfection in the human species. The principles of eugenics found avid readers in South America. Southern Cone physicians, lawyers, educators, and sociologists kept well informed about medical developments in England, France, and the United States. How these men and women interpreted eugenics is central to understanding the medical and social goals these nations adopted and how they affected gender relations in the 1920s and 1930s.

What made eugenics appealing to South American professionals was the hope it offered for demographic growth and for eliminating the health problems that had plagued their nations. The concern with public health was paramount in bringing some physicians within the fold of the "new science."[2] *Higienistas,* liberal social reformers, socialists, and anarchists warned of the problems caused by demographic growth in urban centers and backward rural areas and the collective and environmental threats posed by disease. Eugenics added personal and nationalist dimensions. Women could be infected with venereal disease by their husbands and be condemned to infertility or birth of sick children, warned a Uruguayan *higienista.* Their milk could carry disease rather than nurture life. Syphilis and gonorrhea affected new generations and the future of the nation.[3] These notions were based on neo-Lamarckian eugenics that accepted the inheritance of acquired characteristics and stressed the influence of environment on the development of individuals and societies. To a generation brought up to believe in the expanding power of medicine, the urgency of preventing these dangers by education, public policy, and social legislation was patent.

The neo-Lamarckian eugenics design had social objectives that infringed the individual rights of men and women. If venereal diseases affected the genetic makeup of future generations, should penalties and restrictions be applied to those who carried such diseases or helped transmit them? Should individuals born with hereditary weaknesses or affected by what were assumed to be debilitating diseases be forbidden to reproduce? Should men and women be tested before marriage to assess their reproductive health? Many thought the state had a social responsibility for the health of its citizens, present and future, and also the power to answer such questions. By the early 1920s the state received help from medical and legal circles. Physicians, lawyers, and legislators designed policies and helped enact laws to curtail the transmission of venereal disease and protect the health of mothers and children.

The creation of a "eugenics mentality" was the labor of second-generation *higienistas,* active between 1915 and 1940, who made sexuality and its social consequences the basis for social and health reform. One of the most articulate and enthusiastic eugenicists of his time was Dr. Alfredo Fernández Verano, a member of the Argentine League of Social Prophylaxis. He was best known for his indefatigable campaign against venereal disease, although his understanding of how to treat the problem of prostitution was by no means universally accepted. In 1931 he published a slim book that reflected his long-held ideas about public health, human sexuality, and population policies. Because his views were shared by other doctors of his generation, his definition of eugenics will serve as a prototype for all. He followed the premises established by Francis Galton, defining eugenics as the "science that studies all the influences that may potentially affect reproduction, with the purpose of preventing degeneration and attaining the improvement of the human species."[4] Without deviating from the established understanding, he identified eugenics' positive and negative modes. Positive eugenics pursued the selection of those who were more "apt" for healthy reproduction, whereas the attempt to prevent the reproduction of weak, infirm, or sick individuals was known as negative eugenics. Unlike some European and North American doctors of the 1930s, South American physicians such as Fernández Verano opposed sterilization as a means to prevent the reproduction of people presumed to be "inferior." Such methods were described by him as "repugnant to our feelings" and had failed in those countries where they had been tried. He proposed instead what he called "conjugal prophylaxis," the medical examination of engaged couples to detect any disease capable of being transmitted to the partner or to their offspring. If the finding was positive, he recommended that marriage be prevented. He did not specify how this should be carried out, however, and in fact did not linger on the point, choosing instead to restate his case for prenuptial health examinations.

In 1931 Fernández Verano voiced what seemed already to be accepted convictions among male and female doctors in the Southern Cone. The Chilean *Boletín del Ministerio de Higiene, Asistencia, Previsión Social y Trabajo* explained in its October 1927 issue the objectives of eugenics as officially sanctioned in that country. Eugenics was presented as an effort to enhance the quality of life by preventing the transmission of harmful hereditary characteristics while stimulating the useful and positive. As with many other eugenics writings in South America, there was no clear definition of positive and negative characteristics. By inference, diseases and handicaps were negative conditions, and insanity, delinquency, and mental retardation were negative traits. Eugenics' ultimate objective was described as the extension of life in the best physical and psychic condition. The *Bulletin* declared the same distaste for the suppression of handicapped persons expressed by Fernández Verano. "The human species cannot be treated as plants or animals that benefit from the removal of diseased specimens." Human life demanded defense and protection. Although weak persons might make poor soldiers or athletes, they could have excellent mental qualities from which humanity could benefit.[5]

Although it was not immediately apparent, social hygiene and eugenics helped legitimize women's participation in social reform, insofar as they involved reproduction and the care of the population. While connecting sex education and children's health, eugenics also stressed women's health and gave them equal importance with men in reproduction. That eugenics also helped to fix certain gender stereotypes by making motherhood the centerpiece of women's physical participation in its social utopia did not seem to bother feminist sympathizers and women supporters, who regarded motherhood as a natural and proud female function and wanted nothing more than to improve it. As eugenics became part of the vocabulary of social and health reform, women were of necessity included as recipients and caretakers of plans for hygiene and prophylaxis.[6]

Women's Views on Eugenics

The first women to write on eugenics was Elvira López, who in 1912 published an informative article in the magazine of the Museo Social Argentino on Francis Galton and his "new science." López, however, did not pursue the subject and apparently acted as a disseminator rather than as a eugenics supporter. The task of identifying eugenics as an arena for social reform was taken on by two socialist women, Raquel Camaña and Carolina Muzilli. They gave eugenics a unique twist that saved its diffusion in the Southern Cone from becoming an elitist construction. This astute manipulation was initiated by the fervent Argentine educator Raquel Camaña, who, as a socialist favored a different approach to human selection. She suggested that the masses be taught the conditions necessary for healthy reproduction to overcome the handicaps of poverty and ignorance. The state should circulate eugenics concepts and exercise some control over alcoholics, the mentally ill, and those afflicted with tuberculosis or syphilis, to eliminate those scourges of humanity.[7]

Another exponent and supporter of eugenics was socialist writer and activist Carolina Muzilli. The daughter of Italian immigrants to Argentina, and a seamstress by occupation, Muzilli lived a short but intense life, dying of tuberculosis in 1917 at the age of twenty-eight. She set forth her eugenics ideas in four articles for La Vanguardia in mid-February 1917, shortly before her death.[8] In those essays she discussed the decline of the health and the moral fiber of the working class. Muzilli inveighed against the misuse of Darwinian concepts by the ruling elite, who assumed that their social and economic success showed they were the fittest of the human species and validated their exploitation of the working class. She also censured racist theories and scientific experiments aiming at creating superior races.[9] As she saw it, eugenics could be taken to undesirable extremes in the hands of such people. She feared they would attempt to restrict the reproduction of those they believed inferior, most likely working people.

Muzilli assumed that class conflict generated and aggravated health problems. Working people were ill fed and tired. As parents they were likely to procreate without thinking of the consequences, in a state of exhaustion and unfitness that precluded any thought of prenatal care and boded ill for the new generation. Children of working parents often looked old and tired. Workers were not to be blamed for this situation: society could not expect a healthy generation from people who were denied good nutrition and the most basic comforts of life. Workers deserved preferential attention from those who wanted to better humankind. Thus Muzilli, like Camaña, used Darwinism as a tool to defend the working class. A well-understood science of eugenics, she argued, adopted measures to guarantee the welfare and improvement of all people, especially workers, the group contributing the most to social wealth. Muzilli also considered the shared interests of both genders in the success of sound eugenics practices, which, she stated, would benefit "the human species, male and female."[10]

Women doctors also began to explore eugenics and social hygiene. Between 1916 and 1919 Paulina Luisi examined the potential of eugenics legislation to solve intractable health problems. Her viewpoint combined the physician, the feminist, and the socialist reformer under the influence of French neo-Lamarckian doctor Adolphe Pinard. She was sensitive to the physical strain of poor working conditions that weakened workers as potential parents. Eugenics legislation must improve the workers' living conditions, attack drug and alcohol addiction, and establish services for venereal prophylaxis. In 1916 she was willing to consider state intervention to prevent the reproduction of those with transmissible diseases that affected the physical or mental well-being of future generations, and by 1919 she was still in favor of regulating their reproduction.[11]

The relation between child care, women, public health, and eugenics was apparent not only to distinguished women doctors but to leading intellectuals of the 1920s and 1930s. In 1926 one of Chile's most celebrated women, the future Nobel-laureate poet Gabriela Mistral, expressed her concerns in a small essay on social hygiene in Latin America. Although Mistral never called herself a feminist and never joined any feminist organization, her ideas on social eugenics mirrored those of the *higienistas* and feminist doctors of her generation and no doubt were grounded in her Chilean experience.[12] She praised the transformation of "unorganized charity" into organized public welfare, a movement that would enable Latin American nations to face the problems created by venereal disease. The "quality of the new generation" was at stake. Governments must take steps to combat the threat posed by the three most common scourges in Latin America: syphilis, tuberculosis, and alcoholism.

She proposed the concept of "biological patriotism" to support endeavors against health hazards and negative heredity factors. Biological patriotism, she said, was a concept of a "more objective and abstract nature [than that] of nationality (or race)." Old-fashioned epic stories and sentimental concepts of national identity should be discarded. What nations needed most were healthy citizens, good housing for working people, welfare support, sex education free of social prejudice, campaigns against tuberculosis, laws against alcoholism, sports programs, and a better penal rehabilitation system. Women had a special place in her scheme as social workers. The female social worker would observe and report poor living conditions, secure state help, and teach the poor. "By giving a mission of this kind to conscientious and mature women," governments gained valuable information about their own people. Thus women would be facilitators, bearing the missionary flag that others had already put in their hands. Mistral's ideas on women's role in national health schemes would shortly thereafter become a pedagogical and policy reality as Southern Cone nations launched schools of social work and increasingly entrusted their graduates with roles similar to those she suggested.

Mistral was not the only Chilean endorsing eugenics solutions in the mid-1920s. In 1924 Chilean labor and socialist leader Moisés Poblete Troncoso lamented in *El Mercurio* that the many health problems besieging Chile were "leading the nation to depopulation." He suggested consolidating all welfare institutions under a systematic plan to save the motherland and advocated adopting eugenics principles.[13] Eugenics, cloaked by social hygiene, was behind the organization of an Assembly for the Preservation of the Race [Asamblea de la Salvación de la Raza] in Santiago, dedicated to enlightening workers on the dangers of venereal disease.[14] The efforts of the Chilean League of Social Hygiene were praised in 1921 by a workers' newspaper, *El Nuevo Régimen*, the mouthpiece of socioethic association Pro Patria y Hogar.

Saving the race from alcoholism, venereal disease, and prostitution was a patriotic duty that fell to all, but especially to the men at the helm of government. Women, suggested *El Nuevo Regimen,* helped by influencing their husbands' political choices.[15]

The endorsement of social prophylaxis and the resort to eugenics to solve national health problems found support among people in all walks of life. Muzilli's and Camaña's class-conscious eugenics was not popular after the mid-1920s. Socialists physicians such as Alicia Moreau and Paulina Luisi did not emphasize class distinctions or focus exclusively on workers' needs. Although they did not lose sight of the poor, they regarded eugenics as applicable to all. Dr. Cora Mayers, a distinguished Chilean supporter of "social hygiene," also leaned toward a pragmatic application of eugenics concepts in public health schemes to benefit those in greater need. Although implicitly these were the poorer segments of the population, she did not carry a political message in her public life. In health programs, as in politics, selfless altruism and nonpartisanship sustained female participation in any social scheme beyond the home.

Alicia Moreau was among the few early supporters of eugenics who carried her message throughout the 1930s. One of her few recorded lectures on eugenics was broadcast in 1932.[16] After explaining the failure of Prohibition in the United States, she discussed genetic control of future generations. Although genetic manipulation of animals was desirable, she did not consider it acceptable for humans. "We in eugenics," she stated, pursue "immanent perfection." The first task was to prepare people's minds by eliminating negative influences implanted by education, religion, class concepts, and so on. These steps would lead to that perfect future of healthy individuals in healthy nations. Her broad blueprint for social change based on eugenics comprised women's civil and political emancipation, regulation of working hours, and protection of workers of both sexes as well as children. These measures, and coeducation of the sexes, would lead to a better understanding of sexuality and a greater respect for human life in its most harmonious expressions of beauty, health, and intelligence. When most people's minds were freed of prejudice and error, eugenics legislation could be adopted. Her utopia was in the future: the present called for more education. Casting eugenics as an ideal prospect, Moreau removed some of its most controversial aspects.

Stronger eugenics policies were advocated by Amanda Grossi Aninat, a Chilean scientist and convinced eugenicist who in the mid-1930s recorded developments and supported several proposals for legislative and social reform. Grossi supported the creation of a National Institute of Eugenics where jurists, *higienistas,* sociologists, economists, educators, and scientists would work together to translate information on hereditary and sociology into social planning for future generations.[17] She shared the belief that "defective offspring injure the biological physiognomy of future societies and hinder progress."[18] The cost to society was economic and moral, and the state had the responsibility of fostering quality in the human species. In her view Chile had failed to assume such an obligation. She regretted that the Chilean Civil Code, as a regulator of people's lives, had no jurisdiction over procreation or the health of a marriage partner, two subjects central to eugenicists. Although Grossi showed some interest in the German racial legislation of the mid-1930s, she joined other Latin American physicians in denouncing the lack of scruples shown in the attempt to create a better race and condemned sterilization, stating that "the Latin American criterion is very distant from German and North American thought."[19]

Opinions on eugenics measures adopted elsewhere in the world varied among the few other women who wrote on the topic. In 1934 *Unión Femenina de Chile,* the journal of an umbrella organization by the same name, reprinted an article from the Uruguayan newspaper *Ideas y Acción* that seemed to endorse German laws obliging persons with presumably hereditary mental and physical conditions to register with a hygienic bureau. The Uruguayan article lauded prenuptial health certificates and birth control to counter the weakening influences of alcoholism, syphilis, and tuberculosis. Since it was reprinted under the title "Eugenics at the Service of Racism," it seems apparent that the Chilean organization condemned its message.[20] The hard-line North European version of eugenics was not generally endorsed by women writers in the Southern Cone nations. Whether feminists, journalists, or social scientists, women approached eugenics cautiously, endorsing its benefits for social, health, and ethical reform.

Eugenics and the Attempt to Reform Marriage Legislation

Since the mid-1920s, legal experts began developing the concept of juridical eugenics, an idea that led some Southern Cone jurists close to theoretical support of state-controlled reproduction. Juridical eugenics was defined as a body of laws to conserve and defend life and essential human rights by promoting the harmonic development of the individual.[21]

When the medical and legal aspects of eugenics began to influence policy-making in the mid-1920s, they were bolstered by the recommendations of many *higienistas* eugenicists. The principle of state intervention and legislation in the several fields of eugenics required a body of legal thought to validate it. Eugenics jurisprudence was often cloaked in either nationalism or patriotism.[22] "The greatness of any nation derives from the principle of racial vigor," stated a young Chilean jurist, adding that "a state that neither supports the study of the measures that medical science proposes to prevent the propagation of [social] plagues, nor organizes services to eradicate them, nor introduces legislation to defend the race . . . fails the most elementary duties of humanity and patriotism."[23]

By the mid-1920s the state had already assumed the right to intervene directly in social affairs by legislating labor contracts, labor conditions, and social welfare. Therefore it could legitimately legislate on individual sexual mores to protect public health. Individual liberties, eugenicists argued, could be either reduced or denied for the public good and to benefit the health of future generations. Calls for legal impediments to marriage on account of venereal diseases, the acceptance of venereal diseases as a cause for divorce, and recommendations for prenuptial health certificates appeared in print and in legislative discussions during the mid-1920s.[24] Eugenics interest in the Southern Cone mirrored a general interest in Latin America.[25]

One aspect of eugenics that most Latin Americans rejected was sterilization. This topic was discussed in 1934 at the Second Pan American Conference of Eugenics and Homiculture in Buenos Aires. Chilean representative Waldemar Coutts repudiated forced sterilization as being unscientific and possibly creating human mediocrity. He was joined by two pediatricians, Argentine Gregorio Aráoz Alfaro and Uruguayan Gregorio Berro. They doubted that the state of genetic knowledge warranted any sterilization scheme and saw ethical problems in the allocation of power to carry one out. The Cuban delegate, on the other hand, supported "voluntary" sterilization, and though the debate reached no conclusions, it was evident that the consensus was strongly against it.[26]

Although most mid-1930s eugenicists rejected sterilization, eugenics principles were moving some nations toward considering legal methods to control hereditary diseases, either through restrictions on commercial sex or through preventive measures such as prenuptial "health" certificates. Opinions remained divided on imposing state regulations on marriage. In 1937 a Congress on Civil Law in Córdoba, Argentina, supported a declaration that leprosy and venereal disease should be impediments to marriage. The inclusion of restrictive articles in the Civil Code was the goal of some eugenicists, who bemoaned the resistance of their colleagues. Argentine Enrique Díaz de Guijarro took the members of the First Congress on Population (Buenos Aires, 1940) to task for rejecting the principle of family eugenics. He praised Peruvian eugenicists for supporting the concept in the First Peruvian Conference on Eugenics.[27]

The most forceful eugenicist of the period was Argentine lawyer Carlos Bernaldo de Quirós, professor at the University of La Plata and the School of Biotypology in Buenos Aires.[28] Bernaldo de Quirós criticized existing legislation and population policies for not protecting the family, which he wished to see under the jurisdiction of public law and state supervision for the benefit of society. He argued that the Civil Code's blanket endorsement of individual freedom and its emphasis on property had led to all sorts of individual and social "aberrations," worsened by the lack of proper sex education.

Bernaldo de Quirós supported state intervention in marriage and the definition of several types of "undesirables" to guarantee healthy offspring. Any individual who could not perform an act of "positive procreation" that would bring forth a healthy new human being should not be allowed to reproduce. Although he officially repudiated Nazi excesses, his writings bear a distinct air of fascist intolerance. Sharing with other Southern Cone eugenicists a fear of demographic stagnation, he favored early marriage, the return of women to the home, and a broad definition of diseases that precluded marriage. The health of future generations did not depend solely on good sexual habits or following the medical rules of hygiene and disease prevention; it also meant a commitment to combat transmissible diseases that could affect the unborn.

The compulsory requirement of a certificate of venereal health before marriage was a key component in eugenicists' marriage policies. As *higienismo* began to associate with eugenics and the campaign against legalized prostitution began to win the support of distinguished medical professionals, the prenuptial examination seemed a natural element of the eugenics package. Although efforts to have the tests accepted proved futile for many years, the debate involved jurists, physicians, and policymakers and was crucial in redefining the sexual and reproductive responsibilities of both genders.

Argentine Emilio Coni, always pioneering public health measures, spoke on the need for prenuptial certificates at the Pan American Congress held in Santiago in 1907.[29] In 1919 he presented a bill to the executive board of the Argentine National Hygiene Department [Departamento Nacional de Higiene] to adopt a medical prenuptial certificate.[30] The League of Social Prophylaxis, a private organization founded by Argentine doctors in May 1921 to disseminate knowledge on venereal disease, promoted prenuptial examinations.[31] Inspired by men such as Fernández Verano, the League argued that if the municipality demanded a health certificate for attending school or selling merchandise, it should also demand one for marriage. If military service could not begin without medical examination, neither should marriage be entered on without it. In 1931 Fernández Verano claimed that feminists adhered to eugenics ideology because they understood the important family and social consequences of the prenuptial health certificate. He did not identify either persons or groups.

In 1925 Radical Party deputy Leopoldo Bard presented a bill for the adoption of a prenuptial certificate[32] that required a medical examination and a certificate of venereal health fifteen days before the wedding from every man intending to contract marriage. It punished with a prison term any civil bureaucrat issuing a marriage certificate without a medical examination and would abrogate the medical rights of any physician giving false testimony. The bill was not approved, and this failure became a source of discomfort to Argentine eugenicists when Chile, where municipal venereal clinics opened in 1913, took the lead in adopting a "health" certificate for all men before marriage.

Early in 1924 Dr. José Santos Salas, an energetic *higienista* and military doctor, undertook a personal campaign to disseminate knowledge about venereal disease in Chilean small towns. One year later, as minister of public health, he was instrumental in writing a decree later dubbed Ley de la Raza — "Law of the Race" — adopted on 17 March 1925, which created a Division of Social Hygiene to combat "diseases of social transcendence." Article 1 established it as the state's duty to fight any disease or social custom leading to the degeneration of the race and to adopt the means necessary to improve and invigorate national health. Syphilis, tuberculosis, alcoholism, and prostitution were identified as social diseases. The legislation offered a complete health package and provided guidelines for the compulsory treatment of syphilis and other venereal diseases as well as for testing. Article 87 established that before marriage all men must present the Civil Registry official a certificate of venereal health issued by the appropriate hygiene authority. Nobody should be married without that certificate. A health certificate for women would require only a blood test unless they had a "clinical antecedent" — a medical record of venereal disease — that would make further tests desirable. Disregarding this decree would carry fines of 100 to 1,000 pesos.[33]

Ley de la Raza was supposed to be put into effect as soon as the testing services were in place. Tests would be paid for by the applicants on a sliding scale. The Ministry of Hygiene, in charge of enforcing a Sanitary Code

enacted in 1925, moved the surveillance of venereal disease from the municipality to its division of Social Welfare [Asistencia Social], which, according
to a source of the period, stalled the effective enforcement of the decree.[34] The
assumption was that the necessary bureaucratic infrastructure was missing.

Clinics offering prenuptial examinations in three Chilean cities (Santiago,
Valparaíso, and Antofagasta) in the early 1920s met little success. According to a report from the Ministry of Social Welfare (previously Ministry of
Hygiene), they received relatively few service requests and were rarely used
by the public. They seem to have had little effect on the control of venereal
disease, although the need was evident if the numbers provided by the Ministry were accurate. In 1929 the Ministry of Social Welfare's *Bulletin* stated
that in the estimate of physicians and venereal disease experts, 10 percent of
the population suffered from syphilis in 1927. A study of 1,200 enlisted men
in 1925 showed that 25 percent had "hereditary syphilis" and 9 percent had
"acquired syphilis." [35] There was no decline in the number of new cases (male
and female) treated in the clinics of Santiago between 1929 and 1930.[36]

Argentina's Leopoldo Bard, inspired by China's new policy of "social hygiene," redrafted his 1925 bill in 1927 to establish a "social prophylaxis" plan
that would include, among other measures, reforming the Civil Code to
establish a compulsory prenuptial certificate and criminalizing venereal disease. Persons who knowingly exposed others to venereal disease would be
fined; those affected could be obliged to undertake treatment. "Once social
and political unity is achieved, the first duty of a modern state is to protect public health," stated Bard in support of his bill.[37] Legislation for a *ley
de la raza* was introduced on 15 June 1927.[38] This bill was not adopted, and
no effective service for prenuptial testing was available until the Argentine
League for Social Prophylaxis opened a free clinic for voluntary screening in
1931. The adoption of eugenics legislation and practices was slow despite the
support they enjoyed among physicians and jurists.[39] Eugenicists had a long
road ahead in convincing the national authorities to adopt compulsory prenuptial tests for venereal disease.

Significantly, the onus of venereal disease transmission was switched from
women to men. Late nineteenth-century public health experts had zeroed
in on "fallen" women as the foci of infection. The "regulation" of prostitution had been their answer to the spread of venereal disease. Thirty years
later, the advocates of prenuptial tests openly admitted the role of men as
carriers. Leopoldo Bard pointed out in 1927 that existing legislation ignored
men's part as vectors of disease. In Chile Dr. Juan Astorquiza Sazzo, serving
in the national health service in Bío-bío, stood up for women infected by

their husbands. He claimed that over 60 percent of sterile women owed their condition to gonorrhea transmitted by the husband. Miscarriages and sickly children should rightly be blamed on the fathers, and this reality was behind his support for testing men.[40]

The Chilean Sanitary Code approved in May 1931 endorsed prenuptial consultations but failed to make them compulsory.[41] It was unclear whether men, women, or both sexes were to take such examinations, but the code relied on voluntary action.[42] In its annual report for 1934 the Argentine League for Social Prophylaxis said it had tested 612 persons in 1931 and 585 couples in 1934. Obviously the premarital tests were far from receiving wide public endorsement.[43] Public apathy was also apparent in Uruguay, where since the mid-1920s Dr. Alejandro Gallinal had endorsed a bill to require compulsory prenuptial certificates for all men.[44] No action seemed to have been taken on this draft, but the Uruguayan Ministry of Public Health opened a prenuptial clinic in October 1932 with the full endorsement of the government. In two years of offering voluntary and free tests, the statistics showed that only 277 men and 26 women had taken them: 56 had been found suffering from syphilis or other venereal diseases.[45] The small number of people taking the test, especially women, reflects the ineffectiveness of the legislation.

The most common critique of all bills for prenuptial tests was that only men intending to get married were liable to screening, leaving out those who lived in open relationships. In Uruguay, Socialist deputy Emilio Frugoni denounced voluntary prenuptial testing as ineffective and ideologically unjustifiable. Along with other Socialist deputies, he supported tests for both sexes.[46] Medical authorities pointed out that even testing for venereal disease before marriage had its drawbacks. The timing of the test was critical: venereal disease could be masked by treatment, and a man could still be infectious while apparently "cured." A test carried out too long before the wedding could not ensure that the man would be healthy at the time of the ceremony. Equally, a test carried out just before the wedding might not detect an infection recently contracted. Testing was ineffective because it did not prevent the marriage, regardless of results, and a diseased individual who remained single could continue to transmit the disease. Such doubts were aired by many responsible physicians who refused to endorse prenuptial tests as a panacea.[47]

At stake was also whether the state had the right to forbid marriage on reasonable grounds. Certain restrictions already in effect through the Civil Codes forbade the marriage of lepers and the insane. They also considered lethal infectious diseases grounds for divorce. No legal mechanisms, however, authorized any of these nations to prevent the marriage of two people who wished to marry even though they knew they were affected. *Higienista* propaganda dispelled the initial doubts of some physicians such as Alfredo Fernández Verano, who had stopped short of endorsing a prenuptial examination in his 1918 doctoral dissertation. In 1938 he heartily endorsed the idea.[48] During the Second Pan American Conference on Eugenics and Homiculture the discussion of prenuptial certificates found some doctors still unready to support mandatory tests. Argentine José Beruti felt that Latin American countries were economically and medically unprepared to enforce them. Victor Escardó, a Uruguayan physician opposed to the idea, found a way to connect feminism with the prenuptial certificate and cast a bad light on both. He stated that some doctors "followed very advanced *feminist* ideas . . . that demand the certificate from both men and women," but he was of the opinion that in matters involving "feminine modesty" all doctors should exercise caution.[49]

Between 1936 and 1940 "eugenics weeks" and "antivenereal days" sponsored by the Argentine and the Uruguayan Leagues of Social Prophylaxis encouraged further discussion of the prenuptial test. This meant examining the groom and issuing a certificate of venereal health within a fixed period before the wedding, the only formula acceptable to sanitary authorities. Doctors, sociologists, and eugenicists were aware that most women were unwilling to submit to any test that questioned their morals. The social assumption was that "honorable" women had not engaged in intercourse before marriage: only prostitutes caught venereal diseases. On the other hand, most men were assumed to be sexually active before marriage and vulnerable to such infections.

Argentina eventually took the decisive step of legislating a prenuptial certificate in 1936 as part of its Ley de Profilaxia Social [Law of Social Prophylaxis], which also ended all licensed prostitution. The law was enforceable beginning June 1937. It entitled duly appointed "sanitary authorities" to promote prenuptial medical examinations. Doctors in national medical services or appointed by sanitary authorities issued free prenuptial certificates at least fifteen days before the wedding ceremony to all men contracting marriage.

Criticism of this legislation was thorough and came from all fronts. Juridical eugenicists found it narrowly conceived and lacking the strength to address the nation's health problems. Carlos Bernaldo de Quirós and Nicolás V. Greco expressed the sentiments of many others,[50] regretting that the law had not been incorporated in the Civil Code and given a stronger legal base and higher social purpose. As enacted, they argued, its objectives remained closer to social prophylaxis than to eugenics, and it lacked the appropriate support of sexual education and public awareness. The legislation was also vague about medical supervision for physical exams and blood tests. Bernaldo de Quirós endorsed the concept of marriage as the responsibility of both partners and would not settle for the compulsory testing of only one sex.[51]

The last attempt before 1940 to legislate a prenuptial test took place in Chile. In 1934 a bill endorsed by Dr. Miguel Concha criminalized venereal diseases, punished those who consciously spread them, and demanded a compulsory prenuptial test.[52] This bill was neither discussed nor approved. Among the women's groups, only the Valparaíso-based Agrupación Nacional de Mujeres de Chile supported the legislation. Its program called for the enforcement of prenuptial certificates and compulsory treatment of "social diseases."[53]

In 1938 Dr. Salvador Allende, then minister of public health under Pedro Aguirre Cerda's coalition government, supported a certificate of venereal health to be secured by any couple seeking to marry. This is a clear indication that the much touted 1925 Salas Law had remained a dead letter. He supported a bill whereby a venereal health certificate would be issued by the National Council on Public Health [Consejo Nacional de Salubridad] and could not be dated earlier than three days before the wedding, to prevent a period of recovery or "whitening" before marriage. Several qualifications would void the requirement of the certificate. One was rape followed by pregnancy; another was the legitimation of a consensual union with offspring. In those cases the couple was still be obliged to seek a health certificate thirty days after their marriage. Officials of the Civil Registry performing a wedding without the certificate would be put on administrative leave for six months.[54] Like its 1925 precedent, and unlike the Argentine legislation, this bill applied to women. Those who saw such a requirement as offensive were dismayed, but the bill did not become law. Neither this nor any other bill denying the right to marry to those suffering from venereal diseases, tuberculosis, sexual impotency, epilepsy, and so forth and requiring a prenuptial certificate was accepted in the Southern Cone by the close of the 1930s.[55]

Mainstream Feminism, Reproductive Issues, and the Debate over Abortion

As stated, women only occasionally discussed female sexuality openly, even in the late 1920s when the constraints on what was considered "appropriate" were somewhat relaxed. The Chilean Zulema Arenas Lavín, writing for *Acción Femenina* in 1923, stated that divorce would give women the opportunity to remarry and find a channel for their "genesic [sexual] inclination." After legal separation a woman remained apt to fulfill the "sacred mission that natural laws imposed on her," because nature did not make exceptions for the female sex. To deny women remarriage amounted to disfiguring their moral and physical life, she stated, and created an inhuman, even immoral situation.[56] It took more than a decade for another Chilean feminist, the poet Cleophas Torres, to allude to the "biological imperatives" of women and to tie illegitimacy to sexuality. Woman, she said, was a concert of energies and aptitudes oriented toward procreation and motherhood. The biological imperative was irresistible and natural once woman reached sexual maturity. She would not be stopped because a given man was unwilling to take her to "sign a register together." The result was unwed motherhood, a social problem for which women alone should not be condemned, since this biological process involved men as well.[57]

Although female sexuality was openly acknowledged by a few bold women, for most people, feminists included, birth control and abortion remained discreetly hidden behind the discussion of sex education and the double standard of morality. Feminists shared the widely accepted cultural assumption that motherhood was predestined and was the true fiber of womanhood. Few had a clear idea how to reconcile actions that had very negative social and cultural connotations, such as birth control and abortion, with the new ideas of social justice and female liberation.

The few women who addressed contraception and abortion in feminist magazines of the 1920s and 1930s castigated those who practiced the first or committed the second. In 1923 Juana Riffo de Mayorga, a professor of physical and biological sciences in Concepción, Chile, and the first woman to become a member of the municipal board of education in that city, attacked contraception in *Acción Femenina*.[58] "Nature," she said, "by some unknown means, will punish the unhappy and degenerate authors of such crimes." Equally against contraception was Argentine Socialist Alfredo Palacios, a staunch supporter of motherhood. Seeking approval of social legislation to grant maternity benefits to working mothers, in 1933 Palacios delivered a strong attack on men and women who "denied themselves to procreation." He felt it appropriate to quote Theodore Roosevelt's opinion that voluntary sterility was a behavior adopted by nations in decline.[59] But whereas Palacios spoke with the strength of a life devoted to the cause of the working classes, the conservative position of one female writer in Chile betrayed class consciousness reeking with prejudice. A Dra. Kelts, as she signed a 1935 article on infant mortality, slipped in her opinion on contraceptive measures. The worst aspect of this new practice, she said, was that it had made some inroads in the "popular" classes, "the main national reserve for men."[60] She was expressing the pro-natalist right-wing ideology of the 1930s in a Chile increasingly stirred by the activities of Nazi, socialist, and communist groups.

An exceptional departure from this line of thought was the opinion of Dra. Marta Licyh. Writing for the Argentine magazine *Vida Femenina,* she echoed the anguish of many middle-class and working-class women burdened by a large family and unable to provide their children with a minimum of material and spiritual comforts. Why should women always bear the brunt of limiting the number of children? Even the right to abortion, regarded by some as an index of women's liberation, looked to her like another form of sexual brutality. Abortion could be right or wrong from a moral and demographic point of view, desirable or not from a medical point of view. Licyh subtly suggested that for some women those were moot points. Real liberation consisted in voluntary motherhood illuminated by an understanding of women's own sexuality and complemented by their civil, political, and economic emancipation.[61]

Discussion of voluntary motherhood and contraception led inevitably to the issue of abortion. Immediately after the First World War abortions increased throughout Europe and began to be discussed in medical and feminist circles. Statistics were hard to gather, but the few doctors who discussed this issue in the late 1920s and early 1930s considered it an alarming public health problem. In the Southern Cone abortion was a crime punishable by law, and few of those involved volunteered any information. The penal codes imposed jail on those engaged in abortions. The 1874 Chilean Penal Code did not undergo any reform on this issue until the 1940s. It established several nuances of guilt and punishment, whether abortion was forced or carried out with the consent of the woman involved. If the woman sought an abortion to hide her dishonor, she was still liable to a jail sentence. Doctors performing abortions were liable to "medium degree" punishment.[62] The 1931 Sanitary Code allowed several exemptions in enforcement, especially if the mother's life was threatened. The Argentine Penal Code, revised in 1921, also established a jail sentence for doctors, midwives, and pharmacists taking part in an abortion. However, it made exceptions for abortions performed to save the mother's life, for health reasons, to end a pregnancy caused by rape, or in a mentally deficient or insane woman. A woman who willingly submitted to an abortion was punished with a maximum of four years in prison.[63] The

Uruguayan Penal Code punished self-inflicted abortion with up to eighteen months in jail and meted out two to four years to any accomplice.[64]

A notable woman feminist who discussed abortion was Dra. Paulina Luisi. Having worked among poor women and prostitutes, Luisi had learned about the intimate tragedies of unwanted motherhood. She first supported abortion for medical reasons. Later in life she shifted toward a redefinition of the purpose of sexuality. In 1917, however, attracted to eugenics, she stated her belief that children conceived in negative circumstances and likely to be either mentally or physically unfit should not be born.[65] Luisi considered abortion of healthy fetuses a crime but understood the economic pressures that obliged underpaid and overtired working women to seek abortions. Maternity was an option a working woman could control. In the struggle for survival she could not give up her job, but she could give up maternity.[66] As a socialist feminist, Luisi had another solution. State economic aid would allow working mothers to enjoy their maternity rather than reject it. By 1920 Luisi had developed a firm position on the dual responsibility of men and women in creating a new life. If abortion brought punishment to an abandoned woman, it should entail a similar treatment for the man who helped create the new life, for failing to assume his responsibilities and denying the child's rights.[67]

Luisi's stern moral position on the sexual accountability of men was unlikely to be totally acceptable to a male-dominated society. Her message on abortion, however, did not go unheeded by the medical and legal communities, which began to debate the issue in Uruguay in the early 1920s. Their objective was to establish clear guidelines for abortion as a public health problem, and they eventually became political. Some of those who participated in the debate were clearly influenced by changing attitudes about human sexuality and an increasing sensitivity to the burden that double standards of morality put on women.

Abortion in Uruguay: An Unusual Debate

Between 1922 and 1938 the debate on pregnancy and abortion evolved from a theoretical issue into a political one as medical doctors, legislators, and the Roman Catholic Church entered public debates generated by medical exposés of abortion practices, the results of a medical congress in Valparaíso in 1936 and the enactment of a new Penal Code that implied the decriminalization of abortion in Uruguay. Argentina did not face any head-on confrontation on this issue during this decade. The reexamination began in Uruguay.

Among the first to speak was Dr. Miguel Becerro de Bengoa, who argued in 1922 that women had already made a de facto choice to control their reproductive functions by practicing abortion despite the existing legislation.[68] Well informed on current feminist thought, Becerro de Bengoa suggested reforming the law to hold men accountable for the children they fathered with single women. Accountability for out-of-wedlock paternity could be a strong economic deterrent to consensual unions and extramarital affairs. Becerro de Bengoa refrained from unqualified endorsement of abortion: he supported the punishment of any person—physicians included—who induced abortions in married women without medical reasons. His stand was against philanderers and irresponsible men, and his goal was to protect single, not married women.

The discussion moved a step further when Dr. Augusto Turenne, a well-known obstetrics professor and an official in the Ministry of Public Health, published a pamphlet on planned parenthood and the need for a policy of "social obstetrics."[69] His long medical practice in the Montevideo tenements had acquainted him with abortion among poor women. He estimated that between 40 and 50 percent of maternity-ward beds were occupied by women whose poor economic circumstances had led them to abort. There was no way of knowing how many unreported abortions took place yearly. Such stark reality demanded reflection on contraception and planned parenthood, which had to rest on women's inalienable right to determine whether a new human being should develop inside them. These were the only alternatives to abortion.[70]

The physicians involved in the abortion debate were concerned above all about the health issues raised by badly performed or self-inflicted abortions. In the early years of his practice before the turn of the century, Dr. Turenne claimed, only 2 percent of the women treated in the public maternity hospital had come for abortion treatment. Between 1898 and 1925, however, he had seen that figure rise to 40 percent. The increase was among poor women, since it was common knowledge that well-to-do women either used contraceptives or went to private clinics.[71]

Since abortion was defined as a crime by the Penal Code, Uruguayan jurists debated definition, allocation of responsibilities, and determination of culpability. Induced abortions—as opposed to miscarriages—were under legal scrutiny to determine whether they were criminal or were justifiable in certain circumstances. Abortions were "justifiable" to save the woman's life or preserve her health. Another justifiable category was the "eugenic" abortion, when it was feared that the child carried a negative genetic inheritance that would make life unbearable and lead to degeneration of the human race. Abortion in a demented woman was justified as a eugenics measure. "Compassionate" abortions were carried out after rape or incestuous relationships. Economic penury was an acceptable excuse to save poor families the burden of more children. Also excusable was an abortion for the sake of "honor," to hide the fruit of an illicit relationship that should remain undisclosed to prevent personal or family dishonor.[72] But even in a country that was disposed to regard certain personal and economic circumstances as excusing abortion, the issues raised in the early 1930s put those men who defined health standards for women — doctors and lawyers — to a tough test to change traditional attitudes about women's reproductive rights.

In 1930 the minister of education assigned José Irureta Goyena, an eminent and politically conservative jurist, to revise the obsolete Penal Code.[73] Irureta Goyena had previously submitted a legal opinion arguing that before birth the fetus had life but lacked juridical personality. Rights were the attribute of juridical persons, and though the law recognized life in the unborn, it could not recognize a legal person.[74] The new code was ready in 1933. Its article 44 established that an injury [lesión] caused with consent was not punishable unless it was carried out to exempt the patient from obedience to the law or inflicted injury on another person.[75] This article did not intend to focus on abortion, but it was quoted by those who assumed that an abortion performed on a consenting woman fell into this category. This interpretation was reinforced because only abortion without consent was mentioned in the code.[76] The cautious but positive support that many physicians had given to legal abortion may have helped key jurists and legislators to conclude that the medical consequences of ill-performed abortions were damaging enough to warrant its decriminalization. They assumed the new code allowed the measured intervention of the medical profession to provide safe abortions.

No sooner were the terms of the new Penal Code known than it was subjected to strong political criticism and caused uneasiness among conservatives concerned about euthanasia and abortion.[77] Horacio Abadie Santos, defending the new code's innovative character, proposed that the 1889 code remain in force through 31 July 1934 to allow further study of the new articles and their legal implications. His suggestion was accepted. The Penal Code went into effect on 1 August 1934. Further discussion of possible amendments could be pursued after the code had time to be tested.

Time was not something conservative deputies wanted to waste. In September the deputies voted to submit several articles of the new Penal Code to review by the Laws and Codes Congressional Commission. In the meantime, that commission rendered a technical report on the redefinition of some forms of lesions and its punishment. The Supreme Court also made some technical recommendations. By September 1934, one year after its submission, the Penal Code was subjected to both attack and defense. Deputy Horacio Abadie Santos extolled its flexibility and its modernity in the definition and punishment of political and civil crimes, but conservative deputies continued to stew over abortion. An opponent of the new code, Dardo Regules, proposed extending the old code to March 1935 and submitting the new one to a legal commission. In Regules's opinion the Penal Code had not been properly discussed, since the Senate had introduced fifteen revisions and the Chamber of Deputies had proposed twenty-five. He argued for postponement, adding that abortion had no roots in Uruguayan society. The facilities given to abortion contradicted the social legislation of the 1930s for the protection of mothers and children, such as the Código del Niño. Abadie countered Regules, stating that a code already in effect should not be postponed. He countered that responsible motherhood was a concept already accepted in Europe, whereas in Uruguay the reality for women who resorted to abortion with nonprofessional practitioners was disastrous. He made an emotional appeal to his colleagues raising the specter of women pregnant after rape, and finished by stating that if a woman had the right to commit suicide, she also had the right to remove a part of herself.[78]

Socialist Emilio Frugoni accepted that abortion was impossible to uproot, regardless of any legislation. His opinion was that "the elimination of intrauterine life may be justified as a right of the mother, just as are measures to prevent conception."[79] Given the irreconcilable positions on abortion, the deputies approved the creation of yet another commission of two members of the Supreme Court, a criminal attorney, a member of the bar association, and Professor Irureta Goyena, the author of the Penal Code. The commission would suggest reforms after two years.

The government, then under General Gabriel Terra, was not convinced by arguments for further study. Charging that abortion was a "repulsive and unnatural act" conspiring against the "organic and functional integrity of women," the Ministry of Public Health determined on 15 January 1935 that the new legislation was contrary to the interests of society and the individual, and it forbade abortions in all institutions under its control except when necessary to protect a woman's life or health.[80] This motion blocked abortions on demand in institutions funded by the state.[81] But echoing widespread public opposition, the regime moved fast to make the legislation difficult to enforce and pave the way for its abrogation.

El Día, the influential Colorado Party's newspaper, stated its position on 14 February 1935. It considered abortion morally censurable and dangerous to women's health but thought it should not be severely punished. Abortion was a complex problem with deep roots, and the Penal Code was not the instrument to solve it. "Only conferring dignity to all motherhood, legitimate or not . . . would lead to permanent solutions." *El Día* suggested that improving economic conditions among the poor and ending moral judgments would eliminate most reasons for abortion. The new legislation did not change the social situation, but it was a step in the right direction. *El Día*'s middle position made much sense by pointing to the economic roots of the problem and supporting motherhood, yet with understanding for women who resorted to abortion out of economic necessity.

On 15 March 1935 Deputies José María Tarabal and Dardo Regules submitted a bill to abrogate article 37 of the Penal Code on euthanasia and to reform article 44 to make abortion explicitly punishable. Their bill proposed fifteen to eighteen months in prison for any woman performing an abortion by herself or allowing others to perform one. If abortion was induced to save her "honor," it carried a three- to six-month sentence. Any person helping a woman abort received a two- to four-year prison term. Should the woman die the punishment would be increased.[82] The Tarabal-Regules bill loomed over the discussions held by the special commissions designated to study the reforms to the Penal Code. In July 1935 the Hygiene and [Social] Assistance Commission joined others studying the reforms under consideration by the Law and Codes Commission. In August Dardo Regules had the deputies agree that the Law and Codes Commission and the Hygiene and Assistance Commission should issue a joint opinion.[83]

All these tactical maneuvers failed to bridge the differences among the deputies. The confrontation came to a head when the Law and Codes Commission rendered its report, an adroit mixture of medical and feminist arguments that was the more surprising for not having input from the women who claimed leadership in the country's feminist movement.[84] It supported the decriminalization of abortion, claiming to have taken into account the socioeconomic changes responsible for greater freedom in the relations between the sexes and the principles of the "feminist movement." A decline in the prejudices about women as "sexual beings" had forced men to reassess their traditional ideas. Women, the report argued, had become more independent and no longer regarded marriage as a solution to their economic problems or as the institution to which they had "to subordinate their sexual impulses." Neither was motherhood their only concern. In fact maternity was in many instances an obstacle to potential occupations in offices

Above. 1. Elvira Rawson de Dellepiane and children.

Left. 2. Cartoon from the Argentine periodical *P. B. T.*: "Go away! What is politics to women?" (Biblioteca Nacional, Buenos Aires.)

LA PALANCA

PUBLICACION
FEMINISTA
DE PROPAGANDA EMANCIPADORA

10
Cts.

REVISTA MENSUAL, ORGANO DE LA ASOCIACION DE COSTURERAS
Directora: Esther Valdes de Diaz Redaccion: Copiapó 782

EPOCA 2ª ÉPOCA DE "LA ALBORADA"

AÑO I.   SANTIAGO DE CHILE, JULIO de 1908   N.º 1

El Deber presente

La saliente i prolongada huelga ferrocarrilera, es un hecho ante el cual todos los que trabajamos, todos los que aportamos el continjente de nuestro brazo, de nuestra intelijencia, enerjía i conocimiento al impulso de la industria o del capital público o privado, debe interesarnos como cosa propia; por cuanto el triunfo o derrota de esa colosal huelga, puede ser para la colectividad proletaria, triunfo o derrota moral i material. Triunfo moral, porque el triunfo significaría valor e importancia a la organizacion gremial obrera. Derrota material, por cuanto «la derrota» de nuestros hermanos ferrocarrileros, seria una derrota i un fiero golpe material para la organizacion i disciplina de la organizacion gremial obrera.

Analicemos este importante problema.

Desde que la colosal i solidaria huelga anterior obtuvo por valioso triunfo, el pago de los jornales de los operarios ferrocarrileros al tipo de 16 peniques, el Gobierno i la Direccion de los Ferro-carriles, han quedado molestos, porque ese triunfo obrero denotó que existia una fuerte i solidaria organizacion obrera.

Es por esto, que desde entónces el gobierno i el capital, fraguan en silencio maquiavélicos planes para arrebatar el triunfo obrero i dar un golpe de gracia a la organizacion i disciplina gremial obrera.

En efecto, como un gran complot fraguado contra la organizacion del gremio ferrocarrilero, se clausuró la Maestranza Yungai.

Esta violenta clausura, que dejó en la calle a mas de 500 familias i a muchos meritorios trabajadores con mas de años de trabajo en la Empresa, no solo fué censurada por la prensa toda del pais, sino tambien por el criterio sano i elevado

Opposite. 3. Masthead from 1908 issue of *La Palanca: publicacíon de obreras,* periodical of the Chilean needle-workers' union.

Above left. 4. Uruguyan Paulina Luisi, in 1909 the first woman to graduate from the School of Medicine, with her classmates. (José Pedro Barrán, *Medicina y sociedad en el Uruguay del Novecientos: El Poder de curar.*)

Above right. 5. Ernestina López with her students, ca. 1907. (Archivo General de la Nación, Buenos Aires.)

Below. 6. Carolina Muzzili (here spelled Muzilli), Argentine Socialist and champion of working women. (Archivo General de la Nación, Buenos Aires.)

Above. 7. Raquel Camaña, left, and Dra. Julieta Lanteri de Renshaw, right, with their printing press. (Archivo General de la Nación, Buenos Aires.)

Below. 8. Amanda Labarca Hubert, Chilean Educator.

Opposite. 9. Alicia Moreau de Justo, from *Nuestra Causa*, ca. 1920.

NUESTRA CAUSA

REVISTA MENSUAL DEL MOVIMIENTO FEMINISTA

Dra. Alicia Moreau

Acción Femenina

W. Barbier

Santiago, Enero de
N:o 5

Precio: 40 C

Above. 11. First graduating class of Enfermeras Sanitarias (public health nurses), Santiago, Chile. Dra. Cora Mayers is second from left in the second row, with corsage. Sara Adams, head of the public health nursing school, is at center with cap. (Biblioteca Nacional de Chile.)

Left. 12. Warning poster from the Liga Argentina de Profilaxis Social, advising prenuptial medical examinations: "Two intruders who all too often form part of the wedding party —gonorrhea and syphilis."

Opposite. 10. December 1922 cover of *Acción Feminina*, Santiago de Chile. (Sara Guerin de Elgueta, *Actividades femeninas en Chile.*)

13. Mother: "Who are you going to vote for, dear?"
Daughter: "I don't know yet—I haven't seen the photographs [of the candidates]."
(Anti-suffrage cartoon from *Topaze*, Santiago.)

14. "Today's Electioneering Women." (Anti-suffrage cartoon from *Topaze*, Santiago.)

15. Symbol of the First Congress of the Movimiento Proemancipación de las Mujeres Chilenas (MEMCH), 1937. (Biblioteca Nacional de Chile.)

and industry. Sex education and contraception had broken down many traditional taboos on sexual behavior. Women were increasingly conscious of their personal liberation, and it made no sense to force them to become mothers against their will. Furthermore, traditional views on women's pregnancies reflected egotistic male attitudes. Sexual pleasure lasted minutes for men, but the consequence for women was months of pregnancy and a lifetime of responsibility for raising the child. Opposing abortion was like using motherhood to punish women for men's sexual irresponsibility. Adding a legal-social note, the commission pointed to the failure of antiabortion legislation and the tragedy of clandestine abortions for poor women.

The issue of whether the fertilized egg and then the fetus should be considered a differentiated life after conception, with a "right to life," was considered and dismissed, following European medical authorities who gave women broad discretionary powers. Making therapeutic abortion admissible on grounds of rape invalidated any argument against abortion per se. The commission determined that before the third month the fetus was an undefined entity because the placenta and the fetus were closely bound. Between the third and the seventh months the fetus was assumed to become a separate being, but the commission did not define whether abortion at this time should be punishable. After the seventh month abortion constituted feticide, and after the ninth month it became infanticide. Thus the commission recommended that abortion not take place after the third month and that it be performed by a physician, not by a midwife or an untrained person. It also endorsed therapeutic abortions. Having authorized medical abortion, it sought to eliminate clandestine abortions by ruling that any woman found guilty of self-inflicted abortion beyond the defined circumstances be liable to up to eighteen months in prison. Before sentencing, judges should consider "the preservation of honor as an alleviating circumstance." If the woman died as a result of abortion, the physician involved was liable to a maximum of four years in prison.

The commission concluded by endorsing the use of contraceptives and recommended sex education, sports, restriction of nudity, sexual continence, and moral cinema as conducive to a healthier social and sexual climate. It also expressed its wish to negate the exaggerated value ascribed to "honor" and "dishonor," which forced many women to take dangerous measures to protect their reputations. All these points had been discussed by feminists since the turn of the century. In a sense their endorsement by an official body reflected the evolution of attitudes fostered by two decades of social and economic change and vindicated feminists' opinions.

The report did not have the endorsement of all the legislators. As expected, Dardo Regules, a member of the joint Commission, cast a dissenting vote. He received support from jurists and physicians José M. Tarabal, Salvador García Pintos, and José Pou Orfila.[85] They held to the sacredness of the fetus's life at any point throughout its development, as a life independent from that of the mother. Abortion was an offense to nature and social stability. García Pintos avoided using religious references in his writing and simply underlined the legal issues, such as recognition of the unborn child's right to inherit, which expressed his argument that "the contained could not be absorbed by the container." Pou Orfila, a gynecology professor at the School of Medicine, was not a supporter of natalist theories, but he considered abortion a violation of biological laws. He declared himself an enemy of contraceptives and would tolerate abortion only on therapeutic grounds.

Dr. Augusto Turenne, a supporter of "social obstetrics," found himself in the middle, between the defenders and opponents of unrestricted and decriminalized abortion. In 1935 he stated that the unborn had a different and separate juridical and biological personality, yet, he maintained his position against openly fascist and Nazi pro-natalist policies. Turenne also continued to criticize the religious authorities for emphasizing sexual continence but failing to note the responsibilities of procreation.[86]

In January 1935 the Comité Uruguayo de Eugenesia y Homicultura, led by Turenne, made a public statement on abortion. Abortion for reasons other than the health of the woman did not mean the act was not contrary to moral laws, the preservation of life, and the "biological potential" of women. The committee thought that repeated abortions undermined women's physical and mental health and favored legislated solutions to the myriad economic reasons behind abortions. Signing with Turenne were such well-known doctors and professors of medicine as Luis Morquió and Roberto Berro.[87] Turenne believed the legislation relaxing punishment of abortion would not lead to an increase in demand. In fact, fewer abortions were registered six months after the reform of the Penal Code than before.[88] Some members of the medical profession had a difficult choice to make between the strong cultural support of motherhood and their view of desirable health policies.

Also in 1935, several faculty members of the School of Medicine issued a carefully worded report. They believed that repeated abortions—especially those not based on medical need—were unsafe and socially undesirable. For Uruguay a decline in population was neither demographically nor economically advisable. The report took the state to task for neglecting instruction in sex education and failing to foster development of a physically strong population. It also criticized men who abandoned the mothers and babies to their own fate. Given that the nation was not yet ready to provide economic help to poor families, the report encouraged the "prudent" dissemination of contraceptive knowledge. It also recommended that only physicians be allowed to perform abortions, to ensure the safety of the operation.[89]

The Regules-Tarabal bill did not make any headway until it was reintroduced to the Chamber of Deputies in 1937. The bill argued that not even the Russian penal codes of 1922 and 1926 established as much freedom in the choice of abortion as the Uruguayan code. The deputies appointed a commission to study the proposed bill. Its report was not unanimous, since Dardo Regules continued to oppose abortion, but it allowed abortions performed up to the third month of pregnancy and under medical supervision. Therapeutic abortions continued to be legal. In 1937 the Terra administration sent its own bill to the Chamber of Deputies, signed by Terra and his minister of Public Health, Juan César Mussio Fournier.[90] This bill represented the official posture against abortion, halfway between condescending compassion and moral admonition. The bill acknowledged the injustice to women seduced by irresponsible men, but the Ministry persisted in wanting full legal punishment for those who instigated and abetted abortion. Women who aborted willingly for reasons other than those given (honor, poverty, or disease) were to be treated with less compassion. Addressed as "modern women," they were portrayed as an "antiwoman" type — afraid of maternity, reneging the virtues of their sex and aspiring to copy and enjoy the freedom that had previously been a male prerogative. They had committed the unforgivable "biological and moral error" of wanting to control their sexual life on the same terms as men. Such women were "morbid and frustrated" examples of "a psychic and moral feminine intersexual" type, identified as under the influence of "the promoters of feminism."[91] The biological differences between men and women dictated a different sexual morality for each sex. "Biology imposes a moderate, contained, and sheltered [recatada] sexual behavior on women. This is not the case for men."[92]

The feminist angst for tearing down the double standards of morality found a resonant denial in the administration, which openly stood behind traditional male sexual prerogatives. Terra and Fournier adhered to the late-1930s conservative view that women were destined for a social role through maternity, requiring that all their physical energies be devoted to that task and demanding acquiescence to the predestined roles and behavior of the sexes. The administration's draft argued that abortion was not the mother's right but a social crime. Yet it declared that the mother was sufficiently punished by the loss of the child, and the state would impose a penalty only when *habitual* abortions indicated "a systematic desire to avoid childbirth." Those who collaborated in abortion — including physicians — were to be punished for a crime against society.[93] The Terra regime had succeeded in identifying feminism with abortion.

Given the sensitivity of the subject and its importance for women, it is surprising that few participated in the debate. Among the few was Dra. Sara Rey Alvarez, founder of Partido Independiente Democrático Feminista. She was a woman of convictions, and on the abortion issue she sided with motherhood. In August 1935 *Ideas y Acción* editorialized against the dangerous innovations introduced by the Penal Code. Rey Alvarez was invited to be a member of the commission studying the code, and she was ambivalent about the choices offered. She favored legislation to allow abortions for therapeutic reasons, in cases of rape or incest, for unwed girls under fifteen, for mentally defective women, and even for the destitute. She believed that women should not be made to bear the burden of men's faults. But though she endorsed responsible and voluntary maternity — family planning — she strongly opposed any legislation that ignored the embryo's rights.[94] Rey Alvarez supported the 1937 Terra-Fournier bill. In her opinion, complete pregnancy control by the mother sent young people a negative signal — that sexual unions could be fleeting and inconsequential.[95] It is difficult to judge whether Rey Alvarez's position on abortion hardened between 1935 and 1937. She seemed to share her generation's vision of idealized parents joyously procreating the appropriate number of children with a sense of social mission and personal fulfillment. Motherhood should not be desecrated, she wrote in a 1937 editorial. As a feminist who deplored restrictions on women's work and supported a single moral standard for both sexes, she could not reject the legitimacy of abortion for some women, but neither could she support complete sexual freedom.

Feminists in a culture so strongly in favor of motherhood were forced to adopt an ideologically meandering course that helped maintain the status quo. When the First National Congress of Women met in Montevideo in January 1936, it did not discuss abortion at all but advised that the state disseminate information on contraceptives so women could learn their advantages and that it support research to perfect contraception.[96] This position expressed the choice of a significant group of women not only from Uruguay, but from several countries. The venom spewed on feminism by the government probably kept others from making public statements. If they disagreed with government policies, they had little to gain by defending their point of view, and it was unlikely they would influence the administration. Most Southern Cone women probably shared Alvarez Rey's point of view and sided with motherhood.

The debate spurred by the 1937 bill went on for several years. Some of the arguments of the leading participants bear closer examination as mirrors of current opinion on abortion, womanhood, and motherhood. In December 1937 Socialist deputy Emilio Frugoni defended abortion in the Chamber of Deputies.[97] He recalled the careful assessment of individual and social circumstances made by the faculty of the School of Medicine in 1935 and reaffirmed their conclusion that abortion was a moral act subject to personal decisions and not to legal repression, especially when experience had demonstrated that no amount of legal restriction could control it. Supported by Deputy Lucio Malmierca, he reminded his colleagues that the repression of abortion was based on a double standard. Women were punished; men escaped all responsibility. Any restriction on medically supervised abortions encouraged self-performed or clandestine abortions and contradicted the Civil Code reform's intention to put abortion in the hands of qualified professionals.

Pressed for a solution, the commission in charge of studying the administration's bill submitted a modified version of the Terra-Fournier project, but in the end those who favored criminalization succeeded. Both the deputies and the senators approved a new law issued on 28 January 1938 that modified the 1933 Penal Code and declared abortion a crime punishable by a minimum of three months in prison for the woman and six months for any collaborator. Longer terms were prescribed for those who forced abortion on a woman or inflicted severe medical damage. However, even forced abortion had mitigating circumstances. The 1933 Penal Code and the 1938 reform allowed judges to reduce the punishment or absolve the participants when the abortion was forced to save the honor of the husband or the wife or to avoid the consequences of rape. Saving the honor of the woman or the husband operated as a mitigating factor even in the case of voluntary abortion. Performing an abortion to save a woman's life, even without her consent, was a strong extenuating circumstance for the doctor.[98]

Uruguayan legislators found it comforting that even Minister Mussio Fournier acknowledged that, though restoring criminality to abortion, the law was willing to overlook instances motivated by compassion for the woman. Women were to be left at the mercy of their judges' understanding as long as they could prove they did not practice abortion "habitually." The 1937 phrasing of the Ministry's position irately condemned men who urged women to abort. The truculent melodrama of abusive, immoral men and seduced, cheated, and suffering women, perhaps under the pernicious influence of feminism, returned the issue of abortion to its familiar pre-1930s grounds.

Several amendments to the law were introduced in May and June 1938, October 1939, and December 1941. They established the legal procedures for interrupting pregnancy, abrogated some mitigating circumstances, and warned doctors that judges would have the right to determine whether the justification was acceptable.[99] The 1941 amendment established that doctors had to submit pathological evidence after an authorized abortion. If a woman died after an abortion in any state medical facility, an autopsy was to be done. These amendments tightened the law and served notice that physicians were under strict medical surveillance and legally accountable.

In the 1930s few men were ready to concede women's legal right to determine the fate of conception. That some jurists and physicians allowed mitigating circumstances or a consensual agreement between the woman and her physician did not change mores in the Southern Cone. This was a tragic situation, given that women were making the risky choice of abortion with unusual frequency.

Discussion of Abortion in Chile and Argentina

Medical concern with clandestine abortions similar to those in Uruguay led to the discussion at a medical convention that took place in Viña del Mar, Chile, in January 1936. A group of doctors meeting in the city of Concepción for a medical week had called for legalized abortion to reduce the high rate of death and complications from clandestine abortions performed by midwives and amateurs. Although data for the early 1930s are not available, the magnitude of the problem may be gauged from information for 1936 and 1937 supplied by several medical sources and by private and public hospitals. Five hospitals reported 10,514 treatments for abortion in 1936.[100] This was a partial number, since private clinics did not report. The Ministry of Health reported in 1937 that 13,351 out of 57,049 women (24 percent) in the public maternity hospitals were admitted for complications of botched abortions.[101] Dr. Víctor M. Gazitúa, obstetrics professor at the University of Chile reported that in a maternity ward under his supervision a median of 1,400 abortion cases were treated; between 60 and 70 percent were induced. Gazitúa also reported a second group of 1,002 terminated pregnancies, of which 571 (56.4 percent) were miscarriages and 451 (43.6 percent) were induced abortions. In San Borja Hospital, 36.7 percent of deceased females died from abortions. Of 1,900 autopsies practiced in three years, 84 women died during childbirth and 282 owing to botched abortions. The latter figure represented 14.8 percent of *all* deaths. In Barros Luco Hospital another physician reported that in 307 female autopsies, 91 deaths were due to abortions.[102] These were mostly women of the poorest social strata, avoiding the economic burden of still more children. These 1930s figures were just the beginning of a trend that would continue its ascending curve through the 1960s.[103]

The doctors endorsing the recommendation suggested opening clinics to provide free abortions to single mothers and poor women with large families. They also supported education in contraceptive methods and planned motherhood as long-run solutions. Behind these recommendations was a consensus that the social aspects of medicine deserved more state attention: the health needs of the working classes should be more closely monitored by creating statistical information on housing, nutritional needs, mortality, and so on.[104]

Abortion on demand and contraceptive education were explosive subjects in the Chilean press. Hardly five days after the discussion at the medical convention, Archbishop José Horacio Campillo condemned abortion, sterilization, and contraception.[105] The signatories to the Valparaíso Medical Convention received both support and attack. Those in favor derided the hypocrisy of well-fed and well-to-do people who could afford to stand by the church and against the tragic reality of the poor. Those against reviled what they considered murder in the womb.[106]

A group of over twenty doctors protested the medical convention's position as against medical ethics. Dr. Carlos Monckeberg, an obstetrics professor at the University of Chile, led the attack against the convention's resolutions. He condemned abortion on demographic and moral grounds, criticizing his colleagues' ethical ambivalence. Chile, he claimed, was not an overpopulated country where abortion made sense. He saw abortion leading to personal and social deterioration, divorce, and the eventual dissolution of the family. Women as mothers and "queens of their homes" were defiled by the medical congress. Monckeberg urged social welfare measures to teach women to be better mothers and to help poor families care for their children. He showed empathy toward unwed mothers, urged more tolerance toward issues of honor that compelled single women to seek abortions, and endorsed educating men in sexual responsibility.

A nationalist tone was injected into his arguments when he appealed to the truly Chilean doctors—those with Chilean racial and mental character-

istics as opposed to "naturalized ones" — to think of the potential annihila-
tion of the Chilean race, replaced by "foreigners." Whether or not this was
an implicit anti-Semitic allusion, a few Jewish doctors made a public statement against Monckeberg's remarks, adding that Jewish doctors also opposed abortion.[107] This debate exposed the tension created by opposite and
equally valid sociomedical arguments. Uncounted female deaths from unsafe abortions were a stark reality among the Chilean poor. Infant mortality
was staggering, and legal abortions were not the answer for a country with
that problem. Legislated welfare and protection of motherhood, sponsored
since the turn of the century and being enacted and implemented in the
1930s, were the only ways to accommodate the objectives of both sides.[108]

Unlike the situation in Uruguay, the controversy over abortion was not
ignored by Chilean women. *La Mujer Nueva,* the journal of the Movimiento
Pro-Emancipación de la Mujer de Chile (MEMCH), took up the challenge to
discuss abortion from a gender and class perspective. It revived the issues
of class, poverty, and maternity among working women that had first been
aired in *La Palanca* several decades before. From its first number in November 1935, the journal took a stance favoring contraception and abortion,
consonant with MEMCH's program for female emancipation, including freedom from compulsory motherhood. MEMCH placed strong emphasis on
class and gender to bring home the social critique to the ruling elite. Male
workers' salaries were so meager, argued *La Mujer Nueva,* that women and
children were forced to work as underpaid and undernourished domestics and washerwomen to help feed their families. Poor nutrition and lack
of health care were chronic problems and explained high infant and child
death rates. Under those conditions motherhood could bring no happiness. Society had no right to demand children from women condemned to
poverty in the name of "morality." Unless society provided minimum protection to the working woman, she was entitled to liberate herself from the
slavery of unwanted children.[109] MEMCH called for a more active government role in protecting all working women, regardless of their occupation.
Enforcement of maternal leave, underwritten by unions and employers, and
nursing facilities for mothers at the workplace should be made available to
industrial workers, teachers, domestics, and agricultural workers.

MEMCH's official position eventually shifted toward endorsement of standard welfare measures. Women's control over their own bodies was not
carried to its logical conclusion: even the most radical feminists of the period
could not give up the concept of protecting motherhood. The philosophy
behind all those men and women who discussed abortion and maternity in

the 1930s was best reflected in the writings of Dr. Juan Astorquiza Sazzo. He maintained that false social ethics condemning unwed mothers and the lack of a proper education in the dignity of women's role as mothers were to blame for the frequency of abortion, which would never be eradicated by repressive means. Maternity should be regarded not as "infamous," but as the willing acceptance of a mission.[110]

Argentina did not experience any striking controversy over abortion during the 1930s, but the subject had been discussed by several male authors in previous years. Dr. Osvaldo Bottari, a faculty member of the Buenos Aires School of Medicine, probably represented the standard medical opinion in the second decade of the century. He condemned abortion at the First National Congress of Medicine in 1916. Bottari assigned society the right to protect the embryo from its inception and criticized contraception and abortion at will as selfish unless strong economic and medical reasons justified them. Encourage marriages and eliminate the social stigma of out-of-wedlock children, he advised, and illicit liaisons will decline. Protecting unwed mothers was a form of "moral prophylaxis" because children were a social investment.[111] Early in the 1920s abortion was condemned by eugenicist Dr. Alfredo Fernández Verano. A pro-natalist position seems to have been most popular in Argentina, where eugenics had its most ardent proponents.[112] Even such men as the Socialist Alfredo Palacios, not a eugenics supporter in the 1920s, veered toward a strong pro-natalist position in the mid-1930s, endorsing the concept of "intrauterine child care" and proposing a series of bills to protect the unborn and expectant mothers.[113] None of the main Argentine feminist publications of the 1930s took an open position on abortion.

After an extraordinary population expansion at the turn of the century, some demographic experts were concerned about slow natural growth in the 1930s. Fears of "denatalism" worried some national statesmen and eugenicists.[114] Carlos Bernaldo de Quirós estimated there were 100,000 abortions in the federal capital alone and felt the problem demanded strong measures.[115] He regarded abortion as the result of failed policies of sex, eugenics, and maternal education and condemned it as a mockery of social ethics and the law itself.[116] His proposed solution, never carried out, was to establish a national register to record all deaths before, during, and after premature births, regardless of "intrauterine age." This, coupled with sustained surveillance of public and private maternity clinics by the National Department of Hygiene, would curtail abortion. Remarkably, his idea for a register of fetal deaths had been approved in the First Argentine Congress of Population in

1940.[117] Although other men and women involved in the abortion debate during the 1930s did not agree with his methods, many shared his goal of encouraging motherhood to revitalize demographic growth.

Several other opinions were expressed on the nature of abortion and how to bring it under social and medical control. The state of Córdoba submitted a bill to its Chamber of Deputies to allow therapeutic abortion with the approval of two doctors, who would determine if the life or health of the mother was imperiled. A medical adviser to the government thought Argentina should adhere to the Medical Ethics Code approved by the Sixth Medical Congress in Santiago in 1928, which allowed therapeutic abortion under similar conditions.[118] The Third Pan American Scientific Conference (Lima, 1934) recommended that all nations reform their penal codes to allow abortion for raped women.[119]

A respected Spanish jurist of the period, Luis Jiménez de Asúa, whose lectures on abortion, euthanasia, eugenics, and legal reform took the Southern Cone by storm, represents the most widely accepted juridical and moral position of the 1930s. In 1942 he lectured in Bolivia, while revising a very popular book in which he advocated relaxing sexual taboos and posited the feasibility of euthanasia.[120] His legal opinion represents the analytical process that led many of his generation to accept the concept of therapeutic abortion without advocating its decriminalization or recognizing women's right to control their own pregnancies. Jiménez de Asúa was well aware of the distinctions created by class. Despite restrictions, rich women had abortions, creating a situation where the law was enforced only against the proletariat. Having carefully examined the penal codes of several nations and considered all the pros and cons expounded by European jurists, Jiménez de Asúa stated that he had come to accept abortions to prevent the birth of a sick or impaired child. However, when he asked himself whether "women, in the exercise of their rights to a responsible motherhood, may undergo an abortion as a voluntary rejection of maternity, or when they wish to cut the number of their children," he was not prepared to go that far and felt cultural norms should be respected. Because most people regarded abortion as reprehensible, he could not endorse the destruction of a human being once conceived except in therapeutic, eugenics, or "honor" cases. He favored punishment for abortion, indicating that other measures could slow its practice. Social and economic help to unwed mothers, the use of contraceptives, and reduced penalties should be considered as alternatives to complete decriminalization.[121]

In the end, abortion remained a crime committed by thousands of women. The rejection of change in the legal concept of abortion reflected cultural fears of any challenge to traditional values and ethical norms about "intrauterine" life. The cult of motherhood was hardly dented by the abortion controversy. The endorsement of moderate control over the termination of pregnancy by radical feminists, and the opinion of a select but limited group of physicians and jurists troubled by the appalling number of clandestine abortions, did not garner much support from the population at large or, ironically, from most women's and feminist organizations. At the end of the 1930s the prospect of state support for motherhood and the needs of infants and children seemed to offer reasonable hope that correcting the social causes of clandestine abortion would eliminate it.

―――――――

Eugenics, as understood by Southern Cone adherents, provided a strong foundation for public health schemes that early social reformers and feminists endorsed as a just solution to the problems of the urban poor while bolstering the role of women in such schemes. Implicit in the social message of juridical eugenics, however, was the understanding that women were largely meant to be healthy reproductive vessels. This message gained strength in the 1930s and did not help feminists to forge the image of women as independent and responsible agents of health care with the right to demand sexual accountability from men. It reinforced the image of mothers at the service of the state. To be accurate, some feminists had themselves supported the idea of motherhood as a social function, but they did not confuse service freely rendered to the nation with the obligations eugenicists imposed. Fortunately, none of the worst aspects of eugenics, as practiced in Nazi Germany in the late 1930s and early 1940s, were ever applied in Latin America. Its most positive service was to call attention to the fact that men were also vectors of venereal disease and coparticipants in procreation, and that state policies designed to improve public health by regulating sexual behavior had to include both genders.

The discussion of abortion mirrored most people's feelings about the appropriate role for women. There was cultural prejudice against any challenge to the traditional concept of women as mothers, even though thousands chose not to be mothers at the risk of their lives. Abortion was defiance against the natural order of things, and in the eyes of many showed lack of respect for life itself. That women—the vessels of life—should be able to control their reproductive function, let alone deny it, was an affront to the patriarchy, represented by physicians, clergymen, and jurists. Those three groups were not ready to relinquish their power over the female body. The pervasive strength of gender roles continued to uphold a situation in which the only option open to women was the practice of a criminal activity.

CHAPTER 6

Reform of the Civil Codes:
The Pursuit of Legal Equality

The civil laws defining individual and family rights in the Southern Cone nations changed little with independence from Spain, nor were the regulation of the internal affairs of the church and its relationship with the state altered. Between 1858 and 1879, however, Chile, Argentina, and Uruguay revamped their juridical systems and adopted civil codes inspired by the Code Napoleon and contemporary English law, both much admired by South American lawmakers.[1] These new civil codes severely restricted the rights of married women and of women as minors and enforced a patriarchal system in which the authority of fathers and husbands had few legal challenges.[2] The wisdom of those laws was questioned as time passed and the nations began to move toward European models of industrialization and technological advance.[3] The legal subordination of women to men as daughters and wives was not compatible with the new concept of equality of the sexes under discussion in Europe and North America, much less with the concept of "progress" those nations endorsed.

Many gender issues were considered private matters within the family, and the state had entrusted the formation of the family to the church. The Civil Codes endorsed the concept of a state religion regulating the basic events of life: birth, marriage, and death. To redefine the juridical personality of women within the family and society, jurists first had to redefine the church-state relationship. The state had to assume a new role in the control of its subjects and secularize many institutions. No change in gender relations could take place until this issue was resolved.[4] Divesting the church of its control over marriage was paramount. Uruguay, Argentina, and Chile undertook this task between 1884 and 1889 as part of sweeping reforms planned and carried out by a generation of liberal legislators and politicians.

These reforms were not directly linked to women's rights but were regarded as essential for moving their nations into the mainstream of European and North American "modernity."

The laws defining marriage were the key to defining and controlling gender relations in the family. Marriage, stated the Chilean Civil Code, was "a solemn contract whereby a man and a woman are indissolubly united for life, to live together, to procreate, and to lend each other mutual help."[5] Although a legal contract, marriage was carried out by the Roman Catholic Church and followed canon law; priests performed the ceremony and kept the official records. Only death or a special annulment could separate a couple. Though such separation was called "divorce," it barred remarriage, and a complete dissolution was difficult to obtain.[6] The Civil Codes acknowledged these canonical foundations and built on them to define the legal obligations of a married couple. The efforts to dismantle the legal restrictions on married men and women imposed by the church and sealed by the Civil Codes were of prime importance to feminists of both genders.

Submission of female to male within marriage was carefully delineated by the law. Husband and wife, the codes established, owed fidelity to each other, and any transgression was a cause for separation. The Civil Codes gave the husband the right to establish the couple's residence; the wife was obliged to live wherever he chose. If living together posed a threat to the wife's life because of continual ill treatment by her husband, she could abandon the home, duly notifying a judge and sue her husband for a separation (divorce). Although a man could force his wife to live with him, no such obligation applied to the husband. According to the Chilean and Uruguayan codes, a wife had the right to "be received by her husband in the home." Since the man as the head of the home was entitled to make his wife live with him, the right to be received in his house mostly covered any attempt to evict his wife from the home.

Husbands held total administrative control over the wife's property, which included what she owned before the marriage and what she acquired after it. The determination of what was his and hers, as distinct from what was theirs, was very important. To retain dominion over her property a woman had to legally establish what she owned before the marriage, so that her property was described and "separated." After marriage the system of communal property [bienes gananciales] went into effect and applied to all property acquired, or profits earned during the marriage. These belonged in equal shares to husband and wife, but the husband had the legal right to administer them.

The separation of property before marriage not only safeguarded property that the wife's family wished to preserve as exclusively hers, but also retained for the woman the only vestige of juridical personality she could have. Only widowhood or a legal divorce restored her full rights to administer her property and receive her share of property acquired by marital community. If the woman was the guilty party in a divorce suit based on adultery, however, she lost her rights to her share of the marital community property.

Women could not enter into any legal action, assume or relinquish a contract, or sell or mortgage their property, whether "separated" or not, unless authorized by their husbands or under the few exceptional conditions established by the codes. The Argentine code gave the wife the right to administer any property she received after marriage if that condition was imposed by the donor. Even in this case she had to receive authorization from her husband or a judge.[7] Any suit against a married woman was addressed to her husband; she could not enter into a legal suit against his will, unless authorized by a judge.[8] The right of a husband to represent his wife was lost in cases of prolonged absence, mental alienation, or incapacitating disease. In such circumstances the state, represented by a judge, could authorize the wife to act independently.[9] The Uruguayan code gave the woman the right to challenge her husband's denial of authorization.

The codes presumed marital acquiescence when women acted independently as landowners or in business or simply worked outside the home. Under this assumption they fulfilled the duties and the legal obligations such occupations entailed. Husbands retained the right to oppose their wives' activities and obtain an injunction against any commercial or professional transaction. The Argentine code specified that a woman employed in commerce with her husband's permission or acquiescence could not mortgage either his property or that held communally. The husband's right to control his wife's actions and her earnings was to become one of the key issues in the campaign for the reform of the Civil Codes.

The protection married women were entitled to receive from their husbands to compensate for the loss of their personal independence was broadly defined. Husbands had the duty to provide for their wives and children, but the limitations on women's independence were almost as sweeping as those for minors. An Argentine jurist said that women were held in the "concept of a minor because the husband is like a curator, the head of the conjugal society." Married women's disabilities were described as incapacities, and they were *incapaz*, or rendered legally incapable of taking a number of legal actions.[10] In 1891 the Argentine Supreme Court stated that "as long as marriage lasts, women in general lack civil capacity and are under the tutelage and power of their husbands, forming in the eyes of the law a single juridical personality with them."[11] The wife's subordination to her husband's will, and her economic and administrative dependence, were unambiguously described as "obedience" by the Uruguayan and Chilean Civil Codes in the preamble to the section on the rights and duties of husband and wife. Although the Argentine code did not speak of obedience, it "punished" a woman who refused to live with her husband by revoking his duty to feed her. Despite the obvious restrictions imposed on wives by the Civil Codes, some jurists did not regard women's situation as oppression. In his 1893 commentaries on the Uruguayan code, Alvaro Guillot, quoting other legal experts' opinions and adding his own, explained that the law did not confer upon the man absolute authority over the woman. He and others saw "obedience" as a pragmatic solution to assigning the guiding role in a society of two persons implicitly assumed to be equal.[12] Guillot had no qualms about accepting the implied subordination imposed on the wife by the duty to obey. This subordination was softened because it was based on a special relationship: it certainly did not imply blind obedience, and it excluded punishment or humiliation of the woman.

Another crucial area was control over the children. Both parents were responsible for raising and educating their children, but their legal representation was the father's privilege. *Patria potestad,* the rights the law conferred on a father over the persons and property of his minor children, was relinquished to the wife only in the absence of the father, either by death, abandonment, neglect of parental duties, or when a woman was the only acknowledged parent—the mother of children born out of wedlock.[13] In normal circumstances "such rights do not belong to the mother," stated the Chilean code. Single mothers retained parental rights over their children, but this exception did not recognize women's ability to carry out such tasks; it was a concession to special circumstances. For example, a woman who violated marriage's moral codes was saddled with the responsibility of raising and providing for her child. *Patria potestad* in this case was not a privilege; it was an escape valve for the man and a punishment for the woman. Fathers of out-of-wedlock children remained free of any legal obligation unless they acknowledged their paternity and were willing to share authority and responsibility. The assumption that both the mother and the father assumed *patria potestad* over the child in this situation bothered some legal minds. They saw it as a source of many personal problems because they could conceive of social order only as the result of a single dominant will, that of the father.

Divorce, as accepted by the church and the Civil Codes, involved allocating parental care of children. The codes resolved this thorny problem by establishing an age and gender division of custody, leaving a margin of decision making to the judge. The Chilean code established that the mother would take care of all children under five years of age, regardless of sex, and of all daughters, regardless of age. The husband would undertake the care of boys over five years old unless decided contrariwise by the judge. A woman convicted of adultery automatically lost authority over all her children.[14] That possibility was not fixed in the Argentinean code, and as of 1929 there was no unanimity in the decisions taken by several judges.[15] The Uruguayan code established that in case of divorce children over five years of age would remain with the innocent party, unless their legal representative requested otherwise. All children under five would remain with the mother. The guilty partner would be responsibile for the expenses of raising and educating the children.

The loss of control over their persons, their property, their movements, their ability to exercise their own will, and their children was the main source of discomfort for married women at the turn of the century. Gender and civil status, not class, placed all women in the same circumstances. Whether factory workers or university professionals, married women were equally restricted by the law.

Changing Realities: Reforms under Discussion, 1880–1915

The ideal of domesticity that the Civil Codes either reflected or wished to impose or reinforce may have suited mid-nineteenth-century society, but it came to be out of tune with the realities of the early twentieth century. The greater educational opportunities for women from the 1880s onward created a body of female wage-earning professionals by the first decade of the twentieth century. And a constant increase in women employed in urban factories made the female industrial workforce a significant labor element by 1925. Should a married working woman be obliged to surrender administration of her wages to her husband, to whom the law stated that such a right belonged? Could a university-educated woman be denied legal authority over her children? Why should a wage-earning married woman be denied the right to be a legal witness or be obliged to request permission from her husband for pursuits related to her work? These economically "independent" women created new legal circumstances not previewed in the codes, demanding a review of the existing legislation.

The feeling that it was desirable to soften the restrictions on minor and married women began to develop after the adoption of civil marriage. Having wrested from the church the exclusive control of marriage, liberal jurists felt the ground had been broken for a reexamination of the legal inequalities imposed on married women. Reform of the Civil Codes was a lengthy and arduous matter. Changes had to be studied and approved by the Senate and the Chamber of Deputies and signed into law by the president of the nation. Achieving a propitious conjunction of so many wills demanded support from cooperative members of the legislature and a communal feeling that change was necessary and timely. A review of the legal opinions calling for a change in the Civil Codes before 1910 will help in understanding the difficulties.

On 28 July 1887, Julio Zegers denounced in the Chilean Chamber of Deputies the principle of requiring parental consent to the marriage of any person under twenty-five years of age.[16] Zegers sought to lessen the monopoly of authority that *patria potestad* gave the father by establishing a formula whereby in certain situations created by litigation [*disenso*] between members of the family the mother's opinion should be taken into consideration. He demanded more flexibility in dealing with the rights of women as individuals, because the forward movement of "civilization" was leading toward their greater personal freedom. In dissent cases, the opinion of the mother would balance the father's legal right to make the decision. A judge would determine the outcome, but Zegers favored a division of authority based on gender. The mother would have a leading voice in the marriage of female children, and the father in that of male children. This solution would inject into any dissent case the love of the woman and the "judgment" of the man, implicitly assuming that men and women had specific biological traits. Men—as fathers—were rational and could be stern and capable of putting economic or personal interests ahead of their emotions. Mothers would protect the emotional interests of their offspring. Zegers never questioned the authority of parents or their right to influence the marital decisions of their minor children.

Zeger's proposal for limiting the scope of male *patria potestad* for special dissent cases was a lateral movement in gender relations rather than a step ahead. He continued to assume that it was "natural" for the family to have a male head because the original man of creation "saw first the light of the world." Based on such biblical metaphors, Zeger's proposal was ultimately inconsequential. Had it been ratified it would have affected a few cases of a legally infrequent situation.[17] The Constitutional, Legislative, and Justice Commission took ten years to endorse Zeger's proposals, and then no action was taken. In fact no reforms of the Civil Code affecting women's rights would take place in Chile for another forty-seven years.[18]

Were male jurists prepared to reject the principles embodied in the codes by the venerated founders of national law? In the late 1880s, when the first doubts were cast on the Civil Codes, the intellectual picture of the Southern Cone nations was complex. Positivists, liberals, anarchists, and socialists argued their positions in the main urban centers, drawing support from several social and economic groups and pitting their opinions against the conservative supporters of the status quo and traditional values. Positivists were most often the new academic and bureaucratic middle class, enamored of the idea of incorporating their nations into the mainstream of technology and international trade. Although enthusiastic about progress, they had doubts about women's abilities and role in society.[19] Liberals were often middle-class intellectuals, strongly anticlerical and eager to eliminate any doctrinal connection with the church. They found inspiration in the works of John Stuart Mill and in eighteenth-century rationalism. In 1883 Uruguayan Nicolás Minelli recalled Montesquieu as he concluded that the differences between men and women were imposed by men themselves rather than by nature. To each according to his abilities, he preached. A division of functions and authority would naturally emerge in any marriage, which he compared to a commercial society, not a political entity. As such it needed not a "head," but a good partnership.[20]

Conservatives, liberals, and positivists were the backbone of the political elite at the turn of the century. Anarchists and socialists, a small cadre firmly committed to social reform, were busy organizing the workers of the urban centers. Although anarchism rejected political participation, socialists struggled to gain a share in political power and to influence the political decisions of the ruling minority. These leftist ideologies injected important elements of analysis into the study of the female condition. Socialists quoted August Bebel, anarchists quoted Marx, and both took an ideological stand that openly supported female legal and political equality. Liberals and anarchists had very few political objectives in common, but socialists and liberals did bridge some ideological gaps for the sake of legal and social reform. In the following three decades these two political groups found common grounds to support a reform in gender relations by revising the Civil Codes.

The assimilation of these diverse ideas is illustrated by a debate over the legal rights of married women in Argentina. In 1882 Luis A. Mohr and Julio Llanos considered founding a magazine to debate and defend married women's legal equality.[21] They consulted one of the outstanding legal minds of the period, Santiago Vaca Guzmán, a Bolivian by birth and a longtime resident of Buenos Aires, who responded with a full-blown essay on women's civil and political rights. His point of view reflected the positivist interpretation prevailing among educated upper-class males. Vaca Guzmán deprecated the controversy around "women's liberation," which he thought was fueled by the exaggerated sensibility of some literary writers. Women, in his opinion, had intellectual capacity that could be expanded through education; most were as intelligent as the average man. But female intelligence had boundaries resulting from women's own physical attributes. If equality was the objective, it should be defined as giving all people the opportunity to use their abilities. Nature determined that some would go further than others, just as eagles fly higher than sparrows.[22] Was Vaca Guzmán suggesting that women were like sparrows? His opinion remained veiled by his metaphors, but he expressed himself clearly in less controversial matters. He would not support the expansion of women's rights into the political arena. The burdens imposed by "periodic accidents" and by their reproductive duties barred them from civic and political activities. Should women attempt to take part, the emotional pressure could compromise their reproductive capacity. No man could ever replace a good mother, and no mother should aspire to become a mediocre statesman. The interests of humanity and the state lay in preserving women for the task that best suited their nature. Most conservatives and traditionalists would follow this line of thought to endorse the status quo in gender relations.

Mohr was not persuaded by Vaca Guzmán's arguments. Although the proposed journal did not appear, eight years later Mohr published a book contesting the arguments of "reactionaries" and reaffirmed his belief that females could participate fully in civic affairs. He endorsed political rights for women, and to prove his point he printed the political speeches of two women who had taken part in the 1890 coup mounted by the Unión Cívica Radical against the Argentine government on grounds of electoral fraud — Eufrasia Cabral and Elvira Rawson.[23] Cabral seems to have been a fiery activist who strongly argued for women's duty to participate in politics and their right to freedom from the home. Although Cabral's name does not appear later on in the ranks of feminism, she must have been an exceptional woman, and the brief memory of her political initiative suggests that by the turn of the century a few Argentine women were ready to accept the challenges of political activism. Rawson, whose part in the 1890 events was more subdued, matured into an active feminist after the turn of the century.

Mohr's endorsement of women's capacity for political activity anticipated the posture of anarchists and socialists only two decades after the publication of his book. Chile offered a more subdued but comparable example of female activism during a constitutional crisis in 1891 that pitted the elected president against the Congress. Women favoring the congressional party gathered money, acted as spies, and covered up for the men in *tertulias,* or literary evenings, where political strategies were discussed. None of them left the home as their base, and they did not speak publicly like the Argentineas Cabral and Rawson.[24] Exceptional circumstances and female personalities inspired Mohr but did not give most male jurists enough assurance that women were ready to carry out civic efforts outside the home. Political equality was an emotional issue that most men were unready to accept. Yet reforms aiming to create greater equality within the family without disturbing the internal hierarchy that held man at its head had a much better chance of a hearing.

Discussions and debates on drafts to reform the restrictive clauses of the Civil Codes gained momentum in the first decade of the century as sensitivity toward the civil status of women matured. Argentine jurist Luis María Drago drafted the first initiative to reform the civil rights of married women in his country. He focused on property rights and argued that marriage should not put women under the total financial control of their husbands. By protecting married women's property the law would ensure their equality within marriage. By equality he understood not the legal equation of the sexes, but the respect owed to the civil or juridical identity of the wife, then totally submerged in the husband's.[25] His bill was strictly oriented toward "separation of properties," [*separación de bienes*] which guaranteed women ownership of all the property they owned before marriage or acquired in their own name afterward. Women would gain the right to sign contracts and dispose of any of their property. Husbands would not automatically become responsible for their wives' debts or vice versa. Drago's bill also protected the right of women to control their own earnings and the income from property of children from a previous marriage. Drago's bill was introduced in the Chamber of Deputies in 1902 and again in 1914, but it raised no response on either occasion. Later Socialist deputy Mario Bravo praised its meticulous legal methodology as one of the most carefully devised law drafts he had read. The strictly economic nature of this reform ignored control over the children and other aspects of family law, but it was praised by the Socialist Feminine Center, then at the vanguard of social reforms, as a step toward female economic independence.[26]

In late August 1905 Argentine deputy Juan Antonio Agerich sponsored a bill to streamline the dissolution of conjugal property. In September 1909 he drafted yet another bill to grant divorced or married women the right to administer their own property, act as guardians of their children in a testamentary adjudication, and retain *patria potestad* over the children of a first marriage.[27] Agerich's second proposal was more socially conscious because it was based on a bill introduced by Socialist deputy Alfredo Palacios. In his first term as the first Socialist in the Chamber of Deputies, Palacios and his party endorsed a host of reform bills. The bill to broaden women's civil rights, proposed in 1907, would have given them the right to enter into legal contracts without their husbands' permission; to be witnesses in the same circumstances as men; to administer their properties after divorce; to engage in any profession of their choice, and to administer their earnings. Single aunts and uncles could become guardians of their minor nieces or nephews.

Palacios acknowledged that this bill had its intellectual origin in the female feminist wing of the Socialist Party. Yet like other men of this period, he was still unsure of the meaning of feminism. Palacios shared with other social reformers of his time a feeling that women's equality could be achieved through juridical changes that would not challenge current notions of gender roles. The law was to be used as leverage to eliminate some inequalities stemming from gender and class that stifled women's intellectual and economic abilities. Palacios's bill was not acted on. He introduced another bill for the reform of the Civil Codes in 1915 with similar results.[28]

The Drago and Palacios bills focused on economic "liberation." Drago's bill was a "patrician" or middle-class interpretation of desirable changes to help married women protect their property. Palacios was no patrician, but four out of seven of his bills' articles addressed the administration of money.[29] He sought sharing of *patria potestad* to let the mother administer the inheritance of any children from a previous marriage. Palacios claimed his bill sought the "economic emancipation of women" and explained its utility for the poor as well as for the rich. Time only strengthened the economic arguments in subsequent bills. Socialist deputy Antonio de Tomaso, in an impassioned defense for the reform of the Argentine Civil Code in 1926, emphasized women's work and the need to free working women from legal bonds. De Tomaso cited the figures of the 1914 national census as testimony to women's role in the labor force and pointed out that the law had already begun to change under the weight of reality. In 1914 the postal savings bank allowed women to deposit and withdraw funds without their husbands' authorization. De Tomaso came to see the juridical reform of the Civil Codes as a step toward the exercise of political rights. Once the economic bases of women's authority became equal to those of men's, he argued, they would be ready to assume a political role in the nation.[30]

Chileans and Uruguayans lacked any bill similar to Drago's, but they discussed theoretical arguments for the reform of the Civil Code, sometimes in law theses. These academic pieces illustrate the direction of legal thought among younger men. All of them were dissatisfied with the defined status of women and agreed that the higher level of female education and women's participation in the workforce called for an end to their legal subjection. Luis A. Constela, acknowledging feminist influence on Western juridical thought, proposed that equality with men was not what he sought, since neither all men nor all women were equal in their capacity or ability. Constela proposed juridical "equivalence" of the genders to obliterate juridical restrictions. Alberto Ebensperger accepted the tenets of feminism as long as it did not seek goals that were "absurd and incompatible with the nature of women." In his view some hierarchy should be retained in the family, which required a head like everything else in society.[31]

In 1912 Luis Claro Solar proposed the first bill to challenge the Civil Code in Chile. Following the juridical trend of the period, it dealt with married women's property rights. Claro Solar, a middle-class social reformer like Alfredo Palacios in Argentine, was not so much interested in middle-class women as in married working women who remained in the legal custody of their husbands. To him working-class husbands were less than responsible in respecting their wives' earnings, and his objective was to ratify female economic independence.[32] His proposal went nowhere. Civil Code reform in Chile remained on the back burner.

The discussion of women's civil rights in Uruguay took place in a heavily politicized arena where the ideological position of the Colorado Party played a major directing role. The strong secular drive and anticlerical feelings of José Batlle y Ordóñez's followers were focused on the divorce issue. The first attempt to legislate changes in women's civil and political status was too brief and sweeping, responding more to conviction than to reasoning. The one-article bill sponsored by Héctor Miranda in July 1914 called for the recognition of women's civil and political rights and had its ideological basis in John Stuart Mill's ideas and in current feminism. Miranda's bill focused largely on political rights, and it was never discussed.[33] Miranda's untimely death closed the first legislative chapter in the history of reform, but the story continued to unfold after 1915.

Women Speak for Themselves

Men carried the banner of legal reform because they were the only ones with the political power to do so, but women did not lack opinions on their own condition. As early as 1901 Argentine Elvira V. López acknowledged that the legal inequalities prescribed in the Civil Codes were a thorny subject, and she believed the time was ripe for their reform. Although she regretted that legislation tied the hands of married women on issues such as *patria potestad*, she also lamented the impediments to female economic freedom affecting working women. Legal restrictions burdened *all* women, regardless of class. Middle-class women suffered from constraints on the exercise of their professions, and though a few women had won legal battles to engage in their professions, those victories had not created a favorable climate for others. Reforms in the Civil, Commercial, and Penal Codes were necessary to establish firm grounds for all women.[34]

Other women agreed with Elvira López. In June 1903 *Nosotras*, María Abella de Ramírez's feminist magazine, published an article on women's ignorance of the Civil Code. The essay identified married women's most common complaints and aimed at helping them find a solution within the existing law. Socialist Justa Burgos Meyer denounced the unjustified legal control over their wives' wages that the code gave husbands. Responding to the 1902 reforms proposed by Luis María Drago, she remarked on the incongruity of the situation created by the growing number of working women whose profligate or alcoholic husbands could appropriate their wives' earnings. These early denunciations went beyond the mere economic vulnerability of working women and exposed the central theme of women's discontent: their humiliating legal dependency. As long as men had the right to control their wives' wages, it was irrelevant whether they were generous enough to allow women to keep them. Women wanted justice, not gallantry.[35]

The National League of Women Freethinkers and the Liga Feminista Nacional placed married women's civil rights reform above political rights, an ideological position shared by most activist women of the period. Liga Feminista's top objectives were the ratification of women's right to set apart their property before marriage, and a marriage contract in which the husband allocated an allowance for the wife's maintenance. The next two points called for the wives' right to set their domicile "in common accord" with their husbands and not to be legally compelled to return to their husbands if they left of their own free will. These suggestions predated those of male feminists such as Uruguayan Baltasar Brum, a clear indication that women did not have to be taught what gender equality meant within marriage.

These four points also reflected the individualistic character of the early feminist nucleus established around Dra. Julieta Lanteri and María Abella de Ramírez. Their focus was on redefining women's *personal* freedom vis-à-vis men and the institution of marriage. Abella de Ramírez often mentioned "slavery" in describing the legal situation of women in Argentine (and South American) society. She was struggling against contentions that it was futile to grant women any rights because their natural destiny was to be married, and a successful marriage required that the male hold power. She argued that marriage, an institution still bearing the trace of "remote times of barbarity and oppression," did not have to be inimical to freedom. It had to be modified to suit "modern times" and become more compatible with the new concept of women's independence. The reform was up to enlightened and liberal men."[36]

In 1910 Elvira Rawson de Dellepiane drafted a reform of the Civil Code that contained the major legal changes already identified by male jurists as essential for a change in women's status within and outside marriage. She presented it to the First International Feminine Congress, and the Centro Feminista adopted it. After having it assessed by a group of lawyers, the Center presented it to Deputy Palacios for his endorsement and for consideration by Congress. Acting behind the scenes of national politics, women received little official recognition for their ideas. This is probably the bill Palacios introduced in 1913, but Rawson saw the draft much "mutilated" by the examining commission, which "found it too comprehensive . . . and preferred to suppress all articles that threatened masculine interests."[37]

At the 1910 First International Feminine Congress in Buenos Aires, Ernestina López broached the subject of legal subordination by defining justice. Assuming that justice meant equality of rights and duties, she noted that though the Penal Codes made no special concessions to women in the application of criminal law, the state curtailed their rights in the Civil Code. This ran against the concept of natural law that entitled all humans to a basic set of rights. Applied to the female sex such rights meant, simply and squarely, equality before the law. López saw the roots of inequality in women's economic dependence on men. Like other educated women of her generation, she was anxious to match women's labor and economic ability with recognition of their juridical personality.[38]

Other participants in the congress agreed on the need to bring all legislation into agreement with the changed realities of women and society. Chilean lawyer Mathilde S. Throup underlined the irrationality of recognizing rights and legal capacity in single women only to deny them after marriage. The only reason was flimsy "social traditions." Legislators had irrefutable proof of women's capacity, she said, but they persisted in considering women weak or inept. Equity justified a change of the situation. Ana A. de Montalvo, an Argentine, spoke on civil and political rights and urged women to form a Latin American confederation to defend women's and children's rights.[39] Behind these educated middle-class women's defense of justice and equality of opportunity was a plea for access to the same occupations in which men had gained economic and social influence. In 1910 the limitations on professional women's activities were real. The very same year this congress met, *La Vanguardia* reported that the general attorney for the province of Buenos Aires had denied two women the right to act as notaries because only citizens could occupy the position, and women did not have citizenship.[40]

Let Woman Be Equal to Man before the Law

Between 1915 and 1920, social reform was high on the agenda of populist parties of the center and the Left. They argued that national progress and industrial growth could not be achieved unless the benefits were shared by a broader population base, which called for including women. By the mid-1910s women's civil rights and suffrage became "political" issues stretching beyond the learned debates of a handful of supporters in Congress and in law schools and finding a response in the press. Women themselves began to participate more actively in the debate.

Women's civil equality before the law was a complex technical issue amenable to debate among lawyers and judges but raising a very limited emotional reaction among the general public. To counterbalance the dullness implicit in the legal nature of the reform, most supporters from the mid-1910s onward discussed civil and political equality as complementary parts of a reform package, or as closely related issues that could follow each other. Equality was an abstract term that might make more sense to more people if it was tied to daily activities that women could perform but that were denied to them by the law. If a woman was entitled to earn and administer wages, retain control over her property, and share the rights and responsibilities of raising her children, was she not entitled to all the rights of a citizen? Equality could not be granted piecemeal. Héctor Miranda and Baltasar Brum in Uruguay and Leopoldo Bard in Argentina proposed simultaneous bills for civil and political rights. When Chilean conservative Luis A. Undurraga proposed a bill to enfranchise women, he also admitted the need to reform the Civil Code to allow married women to administer their own property.[41]

Opponents of women's political rights were conscious of the significance and consequences of any change in the legislation redefining women's civil rights. Concerned that modification of the status quo of gender relations was

taking place too fast, they withheld their support from reform bills or constitutional changes calling for broad changes and obliged their colleagues in
Congress to choose between support for suffrage and for civil rights. Doubtless the latter was the lesser of two evils in the traditionalists' opinion. Reforms in family law remained within the contained space of the home and
did not affect national politics. As a less emotional issue, it was resolved with
greater ease than suffrage in Chile and Argentina, where politics were plural-
istic and reform was evolutionary. In Uruguay, by contrast, under the spell of
a party strongly oriented toward political reform and politically constrained
in a de facto two-party system, the emotional appeal of suffrage eventually
carried the day. Although suffrage was not adopted by the 1917 constitution
it remained pending, a mesmerizing near reality for many men and women
who privileged it on their reform agendas. A favorable vote was reached in
1932, long before the technical changes of the Civil Code could be achieved.

Two themes were central to all debates on reform of the Civil Codes: the
need to raise married women's status to make them equal to their husbands
within the family, and the need to give married women the legal economic
leverage they required in their new role as wage earners and as intelligent
and capable administrators of their own property. One argument demanded
that woman's individuality be recognized in its own integrity, not as an appendix of the husband's. The other addressed women's economic role. The
two were intimately tied. Most jurists and legislators were convinced that
"female economic emancipation" was a compelling factor moving the law
inexorably toward change and that economic reasons were just as important as female intellectual capacity in justifying reform.[42] This attitude was
best summarized at the closing of the 1920s by Juan Carlos Rébora, a noted
Argentine jurist. He regarded reforms in the Civil Code as a natural result of
women's economic independence. Like de Tomaso before him, Rébora cited
the figures yielded by the 1914 census and argued that since the middle of the
second decade of the century the civil restrictions on women had become
inadmissible.[43] They were right about the legal incompatibility of work and
submission, but their perception of independence was incomplete insofar as
it considered only women's ability to earn money, and not the true value of
those earnings in the economy of the family.

The theoretical understanding of legal qualification meant ability to exercise a function fully, without constraints. All proposals for reform of the
Civil Codes were based on the assumption that women should have the same
rights as men under a set of carefully spelled out conditions.[44] They per-
tained mostly to spheres of activity shared by both genders and to activities

undertaken by women without any recognition from male-centered codes of law. Promoters of female civil rights made frequent allusions to conferring dignity on women in their many roles by allaying doubts about female capacity that underlay existing restrictions. Women had "grown up" enough to be men's equals. The inclusion of *patria potestad* in the debate over the reform of the Civil Codes pressed the issue of women's judgment based on intellectual ability. If women could undertake the responsibilities of work and solve financial problems, it followed that they were competent to share legal rights over their children.

No reform legislator in the Southern Cone supported radical change in gender roles, let alone change in gender behavior within or outside the family. The traditionality at the base of proposed reforms must be recognized to understand their limitations, as well as the limitations of those who opposed them. Not a single reform-oriented male legislator failed to express his regard for women's femininity or extoll their role as mothers. Justice for them was the recognition of women's special contribution to the family and the nation. None of the proposed changes, they became convinced, would alter gender relations. This reassurance was important for male legislators and was promoted by female proponents of married women's legal equality within the family. Reform would strengthen women's faculties as mothers but would not undermine husbands' rights or authority as head of the family.[45] No reform program could have advanced an inch had it been based on women's independence from family and motherhood.

Women's civil rights and entitlement to full equality before the law received an important boost when they were brought up before several continental conferences, such as the Pan American Women's Conference held in Baltimore in 1923, the Fifth Inter-American Conference in Santiago (1923), the Sixth Inter-American Conference in Havana (1928), and the Seventh Inter-American Conference in Montevideo (1933).[46] No conclusive causal relation can be established between these conferences and the adoption of reforms in the Civil Codes of Argentina and Chile, but it would be unwise to deny that discussion of women's legal equality in the international arena sparked change in attitudes.

Reforming the Civil Codes, 1920–46: National Surveys

In 1926 Argentina became the first Southern Cone country to introduce significant reforms in its civil code. Chile adopted several reformist measures in 1925, but they were so limited that further reforms were sanctioned in

1934. Uruguay did not accomplish its own revisions until 1946. For clarity, I will present a chronological country-to-country survey of the reforms.

Argentina

After the snubbing of the third Palacios bill for women's civil rights in 1915, another socialist, Senator Enrique del Valle Iberlucea picked up the issue in May 1918. His bill struck down all legal impediments barring women from public employment and professional occupations, recognized *patria potestad*, and preserved women's nationality if they married in Argentina. The last was discussed in international feminist conferences, but with the exception of this bill it was not considered an issue in the reform of the Civil Codes in the Southern Cone before 1940. Under this proposed legislation women would continue to control any object of their personal use, their tools, and any legacy in their name, regardless of their acceptance of community of ownership with their husbands. A husband could sue a wife or vice versa if they had chosen "separation of property," and they could also arrange contracts between themselves as if they were not related. This arrangement was decried by other deputies and jurists as the extreme individualization of marriage partnership.[47] Although the bill was twice approved by the Senate's Commission on Codes, it was never debated on the floor. Stalling was a common and effective practice against reform legislation.

Between 1918 and 1925 several other bills were introduced. The administration of Hipólito Yrigoyen was not opposed to some social reforms, and the Radical Party had some staunch supporters of women's and children's rights. Deputy Carlos F. Melo introduced two bills in July and September 1919. By this time the principle of the inalienability of the wife's income was accepted by all jurists, and Melo's bill did not substantially change the substance of previous ones. Bills introduced between July and August 1924 rephrasing previous proposals were overshadowed by legislation introduced jointly by Socialist senators Mario Bravo and Juan B. Justo, and another by Radical Party deputy Leopoldo Bard. The legislature definitely was intent on reforming the Civil Code. To solve the issue of two parallel bills, an interparliamentary commission formed by members of the Senate and the Chamber of Deputies reviewed the reforms proposed by both and reached a consensus to combine them into one bill. Conservative deputy Angel Sánchez Elías helped move the bill through Congress in a display of unusual accord.[48] The resulting bill was discussed, approved by the Senate in 1925, and handed down to the deputies, who discussed and modified several articles throughout August 1926. The reforms to the Civil Code were approved on 22 September 1926, bearing the number 11.357, and dubbed the "law of women's civil rights."[49]

Law 11.357 enabled women of legal age, regardless of civil status, "to exercise all the rights and civil functions that the laws granted men of legal age." It confirmed unwed mothers' *patria potestad* over their children. Fathers who acknowledged out-of-wedlock children would exercise the same right. Married women over twenty-one could retain *patria potestad* over their children by a previous marriage. They also could take any employment they chose and administer their earnings as they wished, belong to any civil or commercial association or cooperative, and administer the property of children of previous marriages independent of the conjugal society formed through their second marriage. Women were also entitled to participate in civil and criminal suits affecting themselves, their property, or that of their children by a previous marriage and act as guardians, executors, and witnesses.

A woman's own property, or that acquired throughout marriage, would not be liable to her husband's debts, and the same applied to his property. The only exception was for debts contracted to educate the children, to sustain the home, or to preserve property held in common, for which both spouses were liable. Minor married women had the same civil rights as women of age, but they needed their husbands' consent to dispose of their property if the men were of age. Should both be under age, a judicial authorization was required to validate the woman's actions. Adult women could also be guardians of minor siblings if parents were declared incapable of caring for them and neither older brothers nor grandparents could assume the responsibility.

This law reflected many years of debate and incorporated the essential elements of female juridical emancipation as understood in 1926. Although its objective was to free women from legal impediments, it still left significant concessions to the husband. The most important was that the husband exercised *patria potestad* over the children in preference to the wife except in his absence, by default, or by special adjudication. It was also presumed that a husband had the right to administer his wife's property without accounting for it if she failed to register her will to the contrary. The law also privileged the male over the female as a guardian for siblings.

Years after enactment of the law, jurists uncovered all sorts of technical problems with the text, but such technicalities did not affect the immediate consequences of its application. Within three years women had begun to act as notaries in the province of Buenos Aires. They were also stockbrokers, auctioneers, and public employees. Remarried women sued to re-cover *patria potestad* over their children, since the law was made retroactive in this regard.[50] In 1929 Juan Carlos Rébora and Alberto Escudero reviewed the jurisprudence of the law and showed that women had made considerable legal gains in a relatively short time. In other areas, such as the acceptance of a joint domicile, divorces obtained outside the nation, and disposition of conjugal property in complex litigations, the situation was fuzzy and vari-ously interpreted by several judges.[51]

In his final assessment, Rébora pointed out that the law paved the way for women's political rights by removing all gender obstacles to exercise of the civil functions men enjoyed. If women could be judges and adminis-trators and assume occupations and functions for which citizenship previ-ously was required, they had become de facto citizens. Rébora concluded that the term "citizen" belonged to anybody who had Argentine nation-ality. Having nationality and citizenship, women were entitled to vote. Even though neither the Senate's nor the Deputies' revisions had an apparent con-nection with suffrage, during congressional debates reform supporters such as Mario Bravo had taken great care to dispel the suspicions of conservative colleagues that "civil functions" could apply to suffrage. The conservatives' apprehension, in Rébora's view, was well founded. The wording of Law 11.357 had left the door ajar for suffrage. In his opinion virtually all legal impedi-ments had been eliminated, and all that was required to win it was that "the Ministry of Justice be occupied by men enthusiastic on social doctrines, or some sentimental dynamism for individual action."[52] Three years later the Chamber of Deputies assumed that role, but the Senate rejected the chal-lenge. Unfortunately for Argentine women, favorable circumstances did not materialize again until 1947, when a special doctrine, *justicialism,* injected the type of emotional dynamics Rébora prescribed for success.

Chile

In Chile the reform of the Civil Code was less complex and much nar-rower in scope than in Argentina and Uruguay. The Claro Solar bill men-tioned earlier was tightly focused on the economic rights of married women. Unlike the case in Argentina and Uruguay, no outstanding legal debate or thorough examination of the code preceded its first reform. The conser-vative political ideology dominating Congress conspired against any legal challenge to family law before it began to weaken in the mid-1920s. Further-more, no middle-class feminist leadership developed until the late 1910s, and for working-class feminists of the early twentieth century, economic reforms had priority over other considerations.

Chilean social reformers were aware of the trend toward abrogating civil restrictions on women. Argentine and Uruguayan debates and contemporary discussion in Europe were well known in Chile. Nonetheless, in 1918 many political figures were taken by surprise when the Conservative Party included women's civil and political rights in its platform.[53] Conservatives had nothing to lose and much to gain by courting women at a period when the emergence of popular elements in national politics seemed inevitable. A younger conservative generation hoped their party would catch up with these social shifts. Women could become the best supporters of conservative candidates.

Conservative feminism was at the bottom of Carlos Calderón Cousiño's concept on how to reform the Civil Code. Defining himself as an admirer of feminist ideas, in 1919 he endorsed a moderate version of feminism that would preserve the inner stability of the family without undermining the authority of the husband. A mathematical equation of men and women was unwise, given their different functions. Calderón Cousiño favored the economic independence of single women but wanted to retain male control of the married couple's property.[54] The first attempt to reform the Chilean Civil Code mirrored this brand of cautious conservatism that accepted feminism as an ideology of justice, but did not want to change social structures too rapidly.

Arturo Alessandri's ascent to the presidency of the nation in 1920 signaled the advent of political populism and with it an opening for executive experimentation with social reform. Owing to an intense power struggle between the Congress and the president, concrete changes in the social system were hard to achieve, but ideas that had seemed utopian a decade earlier gained in strength, if not in legislative reality.[55] In the early 1920s Chileans feminists of both sexes regarded feminism as an avenue of legal change. Alejandro Valdés Riesco, writing in 1922, stated that "true feminism" had two aspirations: to strengthen women's rights and to give them greater legal protection. Rights and protection would allow women to fulfill their mission in life. No conceptual antagonism was perceived between expanding women's rights in some areas and enclosing them in behavioral and legal niches in others. Protection suited traditional concepts of gender roles, while equal civil rights satisfied the quest for modernity.[56]

Midway through Alessandri's administration, opinions on the desirability of reforming the Civil Code began to converge. Eleodoro Yáñez proposed a reform that, though not successful in the Chamber of Deputies, paved the ground for discussing women's rights. Speaking for the magazine *Acción Femenina*, the president of the Liberal Democratic Party advocated equal civil rights for all women, especially for working women.[57] *El Mercurio* of Santiago published two editorials in February 1922 explaining to its readers—ten years later—the meaning of Luis Claro Solar's proposed reforms to the Civil Code and noting the "increasing sympathy" for a reform that would benefit married women.[58] Alessandri's own Radical Party timidly joined the "campaign" for women's rights. Alessandri had given attention to women's issues during his presidential campaign and continued to show some interest.[59] In 1923 Radical Party member Mariano Bustos Lagos, in a partially anticlerical tirade, claimed for his party a well-established record on behalf of women's rights since the nineteenth century.[60] Clarisa Retamal Castro argued in her 1924 law thesis that Chilean women's redemption from their embarrassing subordination was almost a sacred duty for her generation. She quoted Alessandri's promise during his campaign to seek full civil rights for women and urged him to act on his promises.[61]

Partido Cívico Femenino, one of the first women's feminist organizations in the nation, assumed increasingly bolder views on civil and political rights from 1922 to 1923.[62] Under different leadership by 1923, it still backed legal reform, hoping that Alessandri's "frank feminist tendencies" could help women achieve their rights.[63] Although the party did not want to be misrepresented as a radical feminist organization, its refurbished magazine, *Revista Femenina*, printed articles by influential mainstream feminists such as Elvira Santa Cruz Ossa (Roxane). Roxane professed to be a feminist in word and deed, and her understanding of feminism was representative of her period, "requiring three elements for its resolution: labor . . . equal wages, and free disposition of one's properties and earnings."[64] She supported women's equal access to the professions and equal civil rights before the law. She criticized the Civil Code for restraining "women's legitimate aspiration of equality and social justice" and recommended not only a reform of the Civil Code but employment of women in the ministries. She was not ready for equal political rights and thought most men were unready too. Although strong and hardworking, women were too impulsive for political activities. Her distrust of suffrage was not shared by other feminist organizations, but Chilean political life was too convulsed in the mid-1920s to give attention to female suffrage, and mainstream feminists such as Elvira Santa Cruz and Amanda Labarca saw a more realistic option in the reform of the Civil Code.

The confrontation between Alessandri and his Congress came to a head in mid-September 1924 when, under fire from the military and alienated from the divided Congress, he stepped down and left the country. Alessandri was replaced by a Junta de Gobierno, which called for a new constitution and summoned Alessandri back in 1926. The campaign for Civil Code reform went ahead despite the constitutional crisis, and before he returned the junta approved several important reform laws. Two conservative women's organizations, the Patriotic Union of Chilean Women [Unión Patriótica de Mujeres de Chile] and the Feminine Catholic Youth, took the opportunity of the Third Congress of the Child in Santiago in October 1924 to issue statements favoring legal reform to allow women a more active role in society, and both organizations petitioned the Junta de Gobierno for such reform. The Unión Patriótica asked for civil rights and suffrage so its members could participate in government by voting and running for election. In a more restrained tone, the Catholic association said its members wanted to see women fulfilling the "providential mission" for which they were prepared. They disclaimed any desire to destroy the integrity of the family and called for more female teachers and social workers.[65] Catholic organizations' support for women's rights was important and would deliver political benefits to conservatives in the following decade.[66]

Alessandri's temporary removal from power yielded an unexpected benefit for women's rights. A bill submitted by Deputies José Maza and Roberto Sánchez, reflecting a petition by the National Council of Women, was rescued from oblivion and reactivated by Maza, who had become a member of the temporary government [Junta de Gobierno]. The result was the approval of a law decree of 12 March 1925, enacted a few days before Alessandri's return from political exile. The decree eased some of the restrictions on married women's property, giving them the right to administer property legally "separated" from conjugal administration. It did not significantly alter the terms of *patria potestad,* which mothers could exercise only on the husband's death or incapacity. The 1925 reform's main contribution was to entitle women to act as guardians, executors, and witnesses and to grant married women freedom to exercise any occupation and administer their incomes unless their husbands objected.[67]

Despite the shallowness of the changes adopted, this decree was well received by feminists, who overlooked its shortcomings. In May 1924 the dean of the Law School of the University of Chile appointed a commission to study a reform of the Civil Code in all matters related to discrimination against women, especially *patria potestad* and the administration of the property and income of married women and of women permanently separated from their husbands. "Public opinion and the new social needs," were among the reasons cited for the study.[68] The commission proceeded with its work despite the 1925 reforms, demonstrating their inadequacy. It sent its first draft to a subcommission of senators and deputies for their sugges-tions. The commission's further reforms did not receive Congress's attention until November 1933, after Arturo Alessandri had returned to the presidency for the second time and the country had weathered another constitutional crisis. At that point, Alessandri pushed for the revision, and the Chamber of Deputies studied the draft in December 1933, aided by jurist Arturo Ales-sandri Rodríguez. There was no debate. This second and more thorough set of reforms was accepted unanimously by the Deputies in January 1934. The Senate made several modifications in November that were accepted by the Deputies on 4 December. The resulting body of reforms was declared law by President Alessandri on 14 December 1934.[69]

The 1934 reforms were an improvement, but far from revolutionary. They gave women a modicum of freedom but preserved gender hierarchies and men's legal authority within the family. For example, a woman wanting to remarry had to request a guardian for her children or her second husband's authority would automatically extend over all her acts as guardian. Mar-ried women still required their husbands' authorization to assume a debt and to receive or reject a donation or an inheritance. They also needed male consent to accept a lien and to buy or sell property. Nonetheless, the very same married women could engage in any profession or employment unless their husbands explicitly forbade it. Barring any stated objection, women maintained control over their earnings as if they were legally "separated." Employers hiring women were protected from any demand by the husband, since only the woman's property was liable to a suit. Equally, men's prop-erty was not liable to a suit for their wives' debts. Women under twenty-five needed judicial authorization to put liens on real estate. Women divorced in perpetuity were in full command of their property. *Patria potestad* was shared by both parents, but, fathers had precedence over mothers in the ap-pointment of a guardian or executor.[70]

No further reforms to the Civil Code affecting women were carried in the period under study. In 1940 Arturo Alessandri Rodríguez, adviser to the 1934 reforms, had second thoughts about the restrictions still in force over conjugal property rights. He confessed that his previous advice had been narrow and sprang from his concern for maintaining order and peace in the family. Confiding the administration of conjugal properties to the hus-band left female subordination unaltered — the price for social order. The only consolation for women was that the 1931 Labor Code was reinforced by the revised Civil Code. Working women received their wages without intervention of their husbands, and if they were over eighteen they did not need marital authorization to join a union. This legal protection, he stated, tempered his regrets about the incompleteness of the Civil Code reform.[71]

Uruguay

The reform of the Civil Code was a real struggle in Uruguay, an ironic historical twist for a nation that took pride in far-reaching political and social reforms. Efforts stretched for over thirty years after Héctor Miranda's first attempt to change the law in 1914. The conservative National Party acted as a curb to many of Batlle's reform plans, and it could not be persuaded that catapulting women into civic and political life would benefit the nation. Colorados themselves were divided over the wisdom of some of Batlle's proposed reforms. Before 1916 women had little influence over reformist male politicians. This situation began to change when the National Council of Women was founded in 1917 and assumed a leading role in bringing women's issues into the public forum. The council made public statements on civil rights and organized working committees to study reform of the Civil Code and dismiss the illusion that Uruguayan women lived in a very liberal society.[72]

When the Colorado Party convened to draw up a new constitution in 1916, it was plagued by internal division and unable to press for a radical change in women's rights, either political or civil. The Socialists, represented by Emilio Frugoni and Pablo Celestino Mibelli, proposed to substitute "person" for "man" in relevant passages of the constitution, to pave the way for recognition of women's rights.[73] Carrying the banners of female suffrage and equality in civil rights seemed a normal procedure for some batllistas and for the socialists, but in fact this double purpose seemed to hurt more than help the issue of civil rights. The 1917 assembly in charge of redrafting the national constitution failed to adopt either one.[74] After this constitutional defeat, the more dedicated reformers among the batllistas continued their ideological course with feminist support. In 1919 Baltasar Brum, a convinced supporter of women's rights, was elected president of Uruguay at age thirty-five. As a minister in the administration of Feliciano Viera (1915–19), Brum had spoken openly of his hopes to eliminate from the Civil Code all "absurd inequalities."[75] As president he continued to support what he rightly identified as feminist reforms, but he needed parliamentary backing. To expedite reforms, he lent the Colorado batllistas his intellectual power.

In 1920 *batllista* Colorado legislators formed a weekly discussion group to examine the issues before the chambers and devise bills and strategies for achieving the party's reform program. President Brum participated in such sessions. In 1921 the group decided to lend its full support to the campaign for women's civil and political equality, and it asked Brum and two other deputies to write a report on the subject.[76] Brum's legal talents and "feminist opinions" would help them draft a bill to introduce in the chambers. The result was a thorough reexamination and redrafting of all the articles of the Civil, Penal, and Commercial Codes that restricted the full liberties of women.

As a blueprint for change the report was brilliant and had no rival anywhere in South America. The reasoned justifications backing each proposed change were ringing defenses of gender equality regardless of civil status.[77] Included in the proposed reform were all articles dealing with marriage relations, de facto separation, establishment of paternity, exercise of *patria potestad* and right of guardianship, administration of property in common, and property legally "separated" by either of the spouses before marriage. The reforms to the Penal Code addressed the punishment of adultery. The draft also covered civil procedure, that is, the code's definition of the legal capacity to exercise professions and to initiate legal suits. For example, Brum wanted to change article 11, which forbade women to be judges. Women were already graduating from law school, and there was no reason to deny them access to the judiciary, especially when they might show special aptitude for dealing with problems such as delinquent children. His suggested reforms also eliminated restrictions preventing women from becoming notaries.

All legal deterrents to women's professions or commercial endeavors would be struck down by simply eliminating any reference to gender. A radical proposal was to require women to serve in the national guard, without specifying how they might be used in wartime. The breadth of Brum's study was stunning, and the means he proposed were simple in their conception. Any article containing gender-specific restrictions, which in all cases favored men and denied women a given right, were rephrased to include both sexes. "Man" was replaced by "person," or the sentence was made neuter. The result was a clear symmetry of rights and duties for both sexes, restoring the dignity of opinion and consent to women.

A few key examples of Brum's proposed reforms will illustrate how he contemplated achieving symmetry within marriage. Article 128, stating that men owed protection to their wives and wives owed obedience to their husbands, would be changed to read that "spouses owe each other reciprocal respect and protection." Article 33 and article 129, which gave husbands the right to oblige wives to reside wherever they determined, would be changed to state that husband and wife would agree on a common domicile and that each had the right to be received by the other. Articles dealing with the administration of property and the right of women to keep their earnings received special attention in Brum's revisions. He acknowledged that these articles posed some of the issues most debated by feminist followers and sympathizers in the Southern Cone. To Brum, men's lordship over their wives [señorío] had justified women's loss of administrative rights after marriage. The rejection of the concept was indispensable for restoring women's rights. At a time when women's political rights were recognized by many countries, their right to share administration of communal property could no longer be questioned. The capacity of the woman to administer her earnings was fully recognized by using the word cónyuge, which could apply to either gender. Brum discarded the specific mention of married women in the existing code to avoid its sexist connotation. He also assumed that although the code gave couples the option of separating their property by judicial procedure, this was an impractical situation for poor or working couples, who had no property and would never resort to that legal device.

Mindful of the sensitivities that could be raised by a change in article 130, dealing with the administration of conjugal property, Brum proposed an oblique rather than a frontal modification. He proposed three choices: that women "separate" their property to retain control throughout marriage; that they let their husbands administer their property as well as the conjugal property, with their tacit or expressed consent; or that they coadminister with their husbands. Regardless of choice, equality should be maintained by making wives answerable for any excesses and denying both husbands and wives the choice of renouncing any of their rights. A wife's tacit delegation of power to her husband did not revoke her right to reclaim it; if she trusted her husband's administration she was not obliged to take any action. Brum's formula was a practical face-saving solution for both men and women. Other articles on the administrative relationship of husband and wife (article 1970, 1978, 1985–97) followed the same gender-neutral formula to achieve equality for the woman.

Brum also tackled the double standard of morality of article 148, which sanctioned separation because of the wife's adultery in all cases, but only because of the husband's scandalous concubinage. He simply struck down the reference to the wife, stating that adultery was a justifiable cause for divorce. The Penal Code would stop considering the wife's adultery a mitigating circumstance for violence against the adulterous parties.[78] On the subject of *patria potestad* (article 252) Brum gave both parents rights and duties and made this institution "simultaneous," eliminating the hierarchical arrangement in which the mother "succeeded" the father in the execution of rights. If two legal partners could share all administrative responsibilities, argued Brum, the simultaneous exercise of *patria potestad* was not unreasonable.[79] Brum considered the reforms he proposed part of the "social reparation" program of the Colorado Party. "Men," he stated, "have always feared women's competition, and being entitled to make and unmake the law without women's consent, have reserved for themselves the lion's share, adjudicating themselves a series of privileges they refuse to give up."[80] His feminist proposals reconciled innovation with the sound customary social usage of his country without sacrificing the principle of gender equality.

Brum's plans to reform the Civil Code had a warm reception among feminist organizations and legislators within and outside Uruguay and remained a benchmark for other Civil Code reform bills proposed thereafter.[81] Unfortunately, after the bill was submitted to the Congress in 1923 by two *batllista* deputies, the rest of the chambers failed to recognize its significance and paid it no further attention. The growing internal divisions of the Colorado Party, the expanding strength of the conservative Nationalist Party, and a division within the feminist ranks, which eventually rallied behind suffrage, may explain the neglect of Brum's reforms. Uruguayan feminist women cherished Brum as the most outspoken supporter of their cause, but they realized that the campaign for civil and political rights needed further bolstering.

In the early 1920s, legal issues affecting women were tackled through piecemeal changes in the legislation. Uruguayan women successfully challenged the prohibition on acting as notaries. After obtaining her professional degree, María Luisa Machado Bonet, a member of a feminist family, had the National Council of Women petition the legislature to abrogate all impediments to female notaries. Under the law, all public employees had to be registered citizens—capable of exercising all the rights of citizenship. Women lacked the right to vote and so were not considered citizens. The law was openly disregarded, and there were hundreds of female employees in a situation ostensibly illegal. Machado Bonet and the National Council of Women were successful in their drive, and women notaries were legalized,[82] but at the end of the decade Uruguayan female lawyers still had to have a male countersign any document.[83]

The mid-1920s marked an impasse in the feminist movement, but there was a gain as some Catholic writers joined the ranks of those favoring civil rights reform. Writing as a representative of Catholic women, María Nélida Madoz Gascue argued for both the vote and the reform of the Civil Code. She said that if humankind was ruled by one divine law, Catholic women could and should aspire to equity in human laws. In that vein, she listed all the articles of the Civil Code that required reform and joined other men and women in demanding female economic autonomy and jurisdiction over children.[84]

In 1930 the Senate began studying a bill to adopt substantial reforms in the Civil, Penal, and Commercial Codes using Brum's blueprint. This renewed interest in legal reform was presumed to commemorate the centennial of Uruguayan independence by granting women an equality more consistent with the times.[85] Socialist senator Pablo María Minelli moved the project to the Senate's Constitutional and Legislation Commission and obtained its approval on 22 June 1932. This bill created a so-called Code of Civil Rights of Women, a set of articles to replace those in the Civil, Commercial, Civil Procedure, and Penal Codes.[86] The Senate's bill lingered in the Chamber of Deputies. Other "distractions" such as the growing debate over the reform of the Penal Code and the campaign for suffrage captured the attention and time of Congress as well as public opinion. Female suffrage was approved by the Deputies in December 1932, and in the elation of the victory the reform of the Civil Code was shelved again. Legislators and the public alike disregarded the flagrant contradiction of enabling women to vote while their civil rights remained severely curtailed. Ironically, as women were readying themselves for their first political participation, a coup d'état in March 1933 to end the "collegiate" presidency delayed their opportunity until 1938.

The tarnished image of the Terra administration among liberals and social reformers was partially redeemed by one of the female leaders emerging in the 1930s, Sofía Alvarez Vignoli de Demichelli, a lawyer and an advocate of political and civil rights, but unsympathetic to the plural presidency. At the Seventh Inter-American Conference (1933) she asked for a continental endorsement of women's civil and political rights.[87] Her speech cited the irrepressible force of feminism, and while congratulating her country for having granted women political rights, she reminded her audience that Latin American women still lacked some fundamental civil rights. The conference paid lip service to the cause with a declaration of sympathy from a majority of the representatives, acknowledging the validity of the concept, but it did not vote any binding recommendation because it thought each nation should find its own formula for the necessary legal changes. Only Cuba, Paraguay, and Uruguay supported Alvarez Vignoli's recommendations.[88]

When Civil Code reform was discussed again, Uruguayans were under a new constitution approved in 1934, but the Colorado Party was absent, having abstained from national politics for several years. Some delegates to that constitutional convention proposed establishing the legal equality of men and women by replacing "men" with "persons" in article 8, thus rendering all individuals equal before the law.[89] But more than words were necessary. Although the Colorado Party's 1936 platform contained a reference to women's eligibility for all public and political positions, it did not cover other important civil rights. Most of the party's statements on women concerned protective legislation. The party also backed female suffrage, a right women already had.[90]

Lack of civil equality was to become an obsession among feminists, *batllistas*, and socialists. By 1936 Uruguayan women counted a host of feminine organizations and one feminist independent party. At the First National Women's Congress in Montevideo in April 1936, the recently organized Independent Democratic Feminist Party stated its views on the reform of the Civil Code. Represented by its founder Dra. Sara Rey Alvarez, it endorsed legislation still pending in Congress. Her party subscribed to a program of civil rights based on Brum's 1921 blueprint.[91] The Women's Congress endorsed the Independent Democratic Feminist Party's stance on civil rights, but its main interests were war, peace, and fascism.[92]

In 1937 the reform of the Civil Code returned to the Chamber of Deputies under the sponsorship of Socialist deputy Emilio Frugoni. Passage seemed easy, given that the Minelli-Brum project had been approved by the Senate in 1932. However, the new constitution demanded that bills not approved by both chambers before 1934 be reintroduced. The Senate took the initiative again with a bill sponsored by Martín R. de Echegoyen, which was approved on 26 December 1938.[93] The Echegoyen bill was a pale shadow of Brum's thorough proposals. It granted full juridical capacity to adult single, divorced, or widowed women. It also granted women the right to exercise any profession, to administer and freely dispose of their income, to be a party to civil or criminal suits, to accept inheritances or donations, and to exercise *patria potestad* over their children by a previous marriage. Several key flaws weakened the bill, however. It allowed husbands to challenge their wives' right to work and to accept inheritances. Husbands could take their wives to court for a hearing. A married woman not expressly stating her will to administer her property and registering her claim had that right suspended. The "separation" in the property administration could be revoked at the request of both spouses. Echegoyen assumed it would be "excessive and inconvenient" to impose administration of her property on an unwilling wife. He did not believe in "separation of property" and posited that, ideally, society would progress toward an "absolute community or total fusion of the [conjugal] administration" in which husband and wife would consult each other and regard each other as equals. The problem was that he made the "fusion" mandatory for only one partner.

Echegoyen argued that married women should have rights "compatible with their condition, that is, with the psychological and moral base of marriage." To justify his position he quoted Gregorio Marañón, a Spanish physician whose pontifications on gender and psychology were very popular in Spanish America in the mid-1930s.[94] The senators who favored the reform praised its "minimum of discreet modifications" and the "prudent criteria" used to follow the rhythm of social and economic changes. They acknowledged that although equality was not established, the wife's duty of obedience was significantly diminished. This was perfectly satisfactory to the Senate, betraying its conservative and patriarchal leanings. In effect, the options established by Brum in 1921 were sadly narrowed by the Echegoyen bill seventeen years later. Proudly, the senators concluded that the reform would not create new habits and that married life would continue "as usual."

Life "as usual" was no longer an option for committed feminists. Sara Alvarez Rey criticized the Echegoyen bill as a "timid, limited, and anodyne." It gave the illusion of modernity by granting rights to single or widowed women while blocking any real change in married women's rights.[95] This conservative bill was unlikely to pass the Deputies' scrutiny. In 1939 Emilio Frugoni took up the challenge and introduced a bill modifying the 1932 Brum-Minelli draft that, he claimed, would bring about reforms closer to Brum's original plans. Frugoni assumed that gender roles within marriage were not equal and that the law should reflect differences in behavior and expectations. He proposed a rather unusual interpretation of conjugal rights based on the premises of compensatory feminism. Frugoni argued that the property of each spouse, whether inherited or earned during marriage, should be administered separately. Yet the husband's profits or earnings should be considered "conjugal," or shared, whereas those of the wife would be "reserved," or hers alone. In other words what was his was theirs, but what was hers was hers. He justified this imbalance in favor of the wife with a special doctrine on the value of each spouse's contribution to the home: Frugoni expected men to bear its economic responsibility and women to administer it. The wife was entitled to her share of conjugal profits for performing her tasks. If in addition she worked outside the home, she was undertaking a double burden for the sake of the home economy. Therefore she should be able to retain her earnings without sharing them with the husband.

Frugoni's logic followed a pragmatic compensatory line in tune with his compatriot Carlos Vaz Ferreira's earlier views on feminism.[96] Equality for its own sake was impractical in the view of men of Brum, Vaz Ferreira, and Frugoni's generation. Women needed protection because they were more vulnerable than the man and often did more for the economy of the home. As a socialist, protecting the working wife was Frugoni's uppermost concern, but he was also convinced that his proposal went beyond class and addressed the needs of all women. Whereas in the past married men "lived like owners and died like associates," under his proposal women would share in the administration of conjugal property, thus gaining new rights. He extended women's traditional control over their dowries—an obsolete legal institution—to what mattered in the twentieth century, their earnings. This was his understanding of female liberation from economic subordination within marriage and a unique Uruguayan interpretation of women's rights.

Frugoni's bill, understandably, was not approved, and subsequent bills dropped his proposed asymmetry in favor of the woman. As it unfolded in the 1940s, the Uruguayan civil rights debate was different from others in the Southern Cone, and in the rest of Latin America, in that it included women. In 1942 women were first elected to Congress. Sofía Alvarez Vignoli de Demichelli and Isabel Pinto Vidal, Coloradas, were elected senators, while Magdalena Antonelli Moreno, Colorada, and Julia Arévalo Roche, a communist, became the first deputies. These women were committed to obtaining the revision of the Civil Code. Alvarez Vignoli and Antonelli Moreno introduced two bills in 1943. The Antonelli Moreno version was the one to be discussed and to succeed.[97] For the first time in Southern Cone history, a woman carried the banner of civil rights in the last stretch of the battle. The Senate approved her bill in 1944, and the Deputies discussed it between November 1945 and March 1946. It became Law 10.783 on 18 September 1946.

The Uruguayan Civil Code reform was long overdue. When the bill was discussed by the Deputies in 1945, all ideological arguments had been exhausted. Lawyers and notaries expressed their support through their associations. The Supreme Court of Justice reviewed the proposal and suggested some minor cosmetic rephrasing for clarity. The text reiterated the principle of gender equality before the law using the formula of "civil capacity" empowerment. Married women were given freedom to administer and dispose of their property and its income, their earnings, and any property they would acquire. This control did not curtail their right to consent to or disapprove of the disposition of conjugal property. Creditors could sue for only the personal property of either husband or wife, or his or her share of conjugal property. Husband or wife could request the dissolution of the conjugal society at any time, not being bound for life by any agreement carried out before marriage. The domicile was set by common agreement, and both spouses were assumed to contribute in their own way to the support of the home. *Patria potestad* was to be shared, and if minor children owned any property, its administration was determined by common agreement. Brum's spirit was behind this bill.

Thus ended the long chapter of debate over female civil capacity in Uruguay. The Uruguayan Civil Code attempted to combine protection and independence for women with shared obligations for both spouses. In a long and well-reasoned defense of the bill, deputy Magdalena Antonelli Moreno acknowledged that her 1943 bill stemmed directly from Brum's study, but she introduced elements responding to the needs of women in her own times. An important one was the concept of "democracy" within the family. Witnessing a worldwide conflagration fought in the name of democracy, Antonelli was quick to realize that the political concept of representative government also applied to the family. The liberty, equality, and justice that the reformed Civil Code would bring into the home epitomized true democracy. Children brought up in homes where each person's rights were respected could not fail to become good citizens.[98]

She also rekindled the fire of motherhood. Her bill went beyond recognizing the juridical capacity of married women, she stated: it "validated the rights of mothers, which is also to say the rights of children." Her identification of the rights of married women with the rights of motherhood followed the principles Frugoni expressed in 1939. She favored the legal interpretation that recognized the efforts of mothers on behalf of the home and entitled them to half of the conjugal property, and she was disappointed with the Senate's version that ignored this principle. The reform of the Civil Codes ended with a paean to motherhood within democracy. It was a fitting end for a country whose main twentieth-century reformer, José Batlle y Ordóñez, had once stated that "the woman as a mother, regardless of her status, deserves only good from the nation."

In retrospect, the legal equality mandated by the three countries bore the imprint of their times and their political situations. The Argentine Civil Code rode the wave of feminism and satisfied in principle the claim for economic equality before the law, dismantling most of the husband's dominion over the wife in that area and giving women serious recognition as economic agents. The sharing of rights over the children was enhanced, though it remained subject to a subtle form of male domination. The reforms of the Chilean Code suffered from the legal conservatism of that nation, and those carried out in the depression years suggest male economic insecurity. Bills proposing female quotas and incentives for family earnings suggest that legislators felt the pulse of such gender tension. Many legislators regarded the protective legislation encoded in the Labor Code and reaffirmed throughout the 1930s as appropriate counterbalance to the rights still missing in the Civil Code. The result was a partial reform that fell short of full recognition of women's rights while validating patriarchal rights over the family and the children. For its part, the protracted Uruguayan reform process suffered from a return to political conservatism in the 1930s and was also delayed by the existence of an extensive protective legislation. Yet it had behind it the finest philosophical argument for female equality before the law and was enhanced by the introduction of the concept of democracy. It came closest to fulfilling the hopes of early twentieth-century feminists.

The revisions of the Civil Codes underwent an important evolution from being blueprints for economic equality and expressions of recognition of female intellectual ability to recognizing women's equality to men within the family and in most situations of social life. Men like Drago and Palacios assumed that civil equality would emerge from economic equality: both represent cautious approaches to gender relations. In sharp contrast, women like Elvira Rawson de Dellepiane, María Abella de Ramírez, and Julieta Lanteri stretched the meaning of reform to include other rights more closely related to women's role within the family. Once the rights of married women as mothers became an issue, the reform of the Civil Codes became more broadly a family issue. Sharing responsibility for the children became a symbol of women's equality. The legal recognition of the values of motherhood fulfilled the cultural assumption that this was women's greatest mission in life. If these rights remained unfulfilled, in feminists' view, reform remained shortchanged.

From the time feminists began to write on the reform of the Civil Codes at the turn of the century, it was clear they did not want to obliterate the distinctiveness of female psychology. Their objective was sharing with men the rights they required to perform their "sacred duties,"[99] which were female and maternal. The right to escape the husband's legal privilege to control the wife's earnings was defended as the mother's right to use her money to feed her children, and the right to share *patria potestad* was defended as mothers' right to assume their responsibility in raising their children. Few challenged such generalized perception of the objectives of Civil Code revision.[100] Most feminists wanted equality before the law to bring women out of an intellectually and economically humiliating situation of subordination and to look men in the eye, not to disengage themselves from the duties of motherhood or to challenge the roles in which they felt most comfortable.

CHAPTER 7

Divorce: The Triumph and the Agony

The liberal reformers who undertook the revision of church-state relations argued that the fundamental task of the state was to maintain individual freedom in all aspects of civil and religious life. To ensure such freedom the state should not delegate to the church the guardianship of institutions that affected all citizens,[1] just as the state should not determine what a person should believe or how to conduct the rites accompanying the key moments of life. It was on these bases that liberal politicians began debating the secularization of marriage in the early 1880s. The Catholic Church adamantly opposed any infringement on its territory, and though it eventually lost the battle, its defeat was not complete, since the indissolubility of marriage was not abrogated. The civil marriage legislation approved in the Southern Cone nations was a compromise between the trend toward secularization and traditional values inherited from the colonial period.

Civil marriage was adopted in Chile in 1884, in Uruguay in 1885, and in Argentina in 1888–89, after many debates and possibly against the will of most people.[2] In Argentina the Santa Fe provincial government had adopted civil marriage in 1867, but conservative and ecclesiastical opposition was so strong that the governor was deposed and the law rescinded.[3] Secular marriage was a civil contract. To be valid, a wedding had to be performed and registered by a civil servant appointed by the state. This assumption did not exclude a religious marriage ceremony, but a wedding performed by a priest without registration in the civil records was null, and children born from it were illegitimate. In no circumstances, however, was there any escape from the bond of marriage, whether celebrated by the church or by the state. Divorce under the Civil Codes meant separation of the spouses based on conditions approved by ecclesiastical authorities many centuries before.

The adoption of civil marriage begged the question of dissolution. Theoretically the new definition of marriage included its possible termination, like any other civil contract. In practice it was denied, since marriage was assumed to be a *special* contract. It was predictable that some bold jurists would try to complete marriage secularization by challenging the official solution and pushing forward the discussion of divorce.

The Catholic Church did not relent in arguing that marriage was a sacrament and not a simple civil contract. For the ecclesiastical authorities the church ceremony was the only legitimate form of marriage.[4] The indissolubility of marriage had slowly been elaborated as a canon throughout the Middle Ages and had finally become a doctrine of the church between the late eleventh century and the mid-twelfth. Only in carefully defined circumstances could a couple divorce after the consummation of marriage. Remarriage during the life of the "divorced" spouse was exceptionally difficult, demanding exhaustive investigation of the case to meet the strict requirements of the church. If such requirements were not met but the ecclesiastical authorities agreed to "divorce," separation was defined as "of bed and table," without the possibility of remarriage. Even such divorce required a lengthy and rigorous examination of all marital circumstances by an ecclesiastical authority. Remarriage could take place only after the death of the spouse.[5]

Indissolubility remained unchallenged after the adoption of the civil marriage laws because it guaranteed social order. A marriage that could not be easily undone was perceived as strengthening the family, preserving the moral value of wedlock, protecting the status of women within marriage, and offering the continuity and stability necessary for raising children. For these reasons the challenge posed by absolute divorce generated protracted and emotional debates, and it succeeded only in Uruguay, under the strong pressure of the Colorado Party after its empowerment in 1903. Argentina and Chile never had a ruling party driven by such strong secularizing force as the Uruguayan Colorado Party, or with so much power to exercise it. No Chilean or Argentine president had ever declared himself in favor of divorce. There was no clear majority for it in Congress, and though it is difficult to assess public opinion in the first quarter of the century, the church was influential enough across all segments of the population that we can assume divorce was not a popular issue politically or socially. Nevertheless, it was heatedly debated as part of the social and gender relations reform urged by liberals, leftists, and feminists. Liberals of various shades campaigned for divorce as part of an anticlerical and secularizing program; anarchists advocated free unions with no religious mediation and detested the church;

socialists, strong supporters of the family, favored it because they were anti-clerical, regarded divorce as a break with bourgeois social structures, and favored women's liberation from the church's influence. Feminists adopted it as part of the process of achieving female equality before the law and as a solution to the age-old problems plaguing gender relations.[6]

The Debate over Indissolubility and the Uruguayan Solution

The debate over divorce in the Southern Cone was sustained between urban middle-class liberal reformers and Roman Catholic traditionalists. The main arguments were drawn in the early years of the century, and though this debate continued beyond the late 1930s, the ideological positions changed very little. In Uruguay the intellectual discussion of complete dissolution of marriage was already under way in the early 1890s. In 1892 a thesis for a degree in jurisprudence established that civil marriage implied the logical possibility of dissolution and suggested that divorce was a "moral solution for a cultivated society." The "moral" problem at the bottom of divorce was obviously adultery, a touchy issue for ecclesiastic as well as secular authorities. The solution offered as worthy of urbane society was far from novel: female adultery was grounds for divorce in all cases, male adultery only when accompanied by public scandal. After divorce the adulterer could not marry his or her accomplice, and nobody could divorce twice on the same allegations. These restrictions aimed at preventing serial marriages based on successive infidelities.[7] Traditional social and moral codes that condoned less responsibility for the man while punishing the woman unduly remained unchanged except that, as proposed by this thesis, the marriage bond would be broken, freeing husband and wife from a lifelong attachment. Adulterers would be punished by prohibiting their remarriage.

The cautious approach of this study was symptomatic of others carried out in Chile and Argentina at the same time and did not intimate rapid change. As the century turned, however, the debate on divorce flared up in Uruguay and Argentina, perhaps reflecting the great social pressures building up in the two nations. In 1902 Uruguayan deputy Setembrino Pereda introduced a bill for the dissolution of marriage with an emotional appeal. He saw in divorce a guarantee of family peace by providing an escape valve for marriages in which love had been exhausted. A marriage was not made by the law; it was guaranteed and protected by the law. If its basis—love—did not exist, the law should not perpetuate it. The Penal Code prescribed adequate punishment for adulterers, which would continue to act as a deterrent

after divorce was approved. This project accepted the traditional and unequal evaluations of guilt and responsibility for the two genders but offered
the possibility of a complete break. A contract entered by free will should
preserve the option of being released by free will if it was to retain its moral
validity.[8]

This tempered interpretation of divorce was anathema for Mariano Soler,
first archbishop of Montevideo, who issued a pastoral letter in 1902 to
counter the Pereda bill.[9] Although the Catholic Church in Uruguay maintained cool but not unfriendly relations with the government, it was ready
to defend its turf against the growing assault of anticlerical ideologies. Soler
was aware that other nations had already adopted absolute divorce and that
defenders of divorce used them as examples of dissolution without social
breakdown. Absolute divorce was unacceptable to the church and a last resort adopted by some nations with corrupt domestic situations. He did not
accept comparisons with other nations as applicable to Uruguay, although
he used French and English data to establish that divorces continued to increase in other countries. The Pereda bill failed to gather support among the
deputies, but this did not cool the enthusiasm of pro-divorce reformers.

The opposition was strong and ready for further assaults. In 1905 and 1906
Pius X spoke against liberals and utopian socialists and urged Catholics to
organize against the threat.[10] In Uruguay the growing liberalism suspected
by the pope was embodied in young reformist deputies, eager for social
and political change and unafraid of political controversy. Carlos Oneto y
Viana, a youthful newcomer, introduced his divorce bill in 1905.[11] The Oneto
y Viana bill received a majority of favorable votes in committee and was
sent to the floor for debate in October 1905.[12] The committee described it as
"a self-evident [act of] progress in the spheres of public and social order."
It was a daring and controversial bill that created much social friction. The
Ateneo, a private intellectual club wishing to foster public debate on divorce,
was forced to cancel a public lecture on it because of the bitter debate in the
chambers.[13]

Discussion of the divorce bill lagged for two years in Congress, and much
of its thrust was directed at the nature of marriage itself. Some deputies supporting the bill attempted to eliminate odious nuances of irreligion or athe-
ism from the debate to elevate it above base emotionalism. Deputy Pérez
Olave, in a cogent defense, acknowledged the long-standing struggle between church and state to control the institution of marriage, but he argued
that accepting state intervention in marriage did not amount to denying the
existence of God or forsaking the church. The state was not atheist, it was
simply secular. For him marriage was a sui generis civil contract that should

be undertaken in the hope that it would last forever. Since human weakness prevented that ideal, however, it became an empty civil formality if the conditions that led to marriage disappeared in either party. Divorce, he claimed, should be regarded as an option neither independent of nor opposed to marriage, but part of its possibilities.[14] Significantly, Pérez Olave mentioned the increasing influence of feminism as a factor in women's reaction against the legal subordination implicit in most marriage legislation.

The Oneto y Viana divorce bill became law in October 1907,[15] a political triumph for the Colorados. The law established the following grounds for divorce: female adultery in all cases and male adultery when it caused public scandal; attempts by one spouse against the life of the other; grave and repeated physical injury; a penal sentence of ten years or more imposed on one of the spouses; voluntary abandonment of the home for over three years by one of the spouses; and mutual consent after two years of marriage. This was a significant innovation over previous bills and proposals. Nobody could divorce more than twice. Divorced women had to wait 301 days after the dissolution to contract a new marriage, to prove there was no pregnancy by the previous husband. All children under five years of age would remain with their mother; custody of those over that age would be determined by the judge. Both parents remained responsible for the children's education. The father retained *patria potestad,* the right to determine the fate of minor children; in his absence it passed to the mother.

The ethical assumptions behind this bill were traditional, and apart from the possibility of personal freedom, women remained at a disadvantage before the law. To redress this situation, a major refinement was approved in the Senate in August 1912 and in the Chamber of Deputies in September 1913. This amendment was called divorce by the sole will of the woman [*por la sola voluntad de la mujer*], and allowed women to initiate a divorce suit without having to prove any of the circumstances defined as prerequisites by canon and civil law. Once the woman petitioned for divorce, she was questioned periodically on her intentions, and if she persisted the divorce was granted after a year and a half. The 1913 divorce bill was one of the most advanced in the world and put Uruguay at the cutting edge of gender legislation.[16] The revised bill was based on legislation proposed by the French brothers Paul and Victor Margueritte during the 1900 International Congress on the Rights of Women. The Margueritte plan allowed dissolution by the expressed will of either party, stated three times over a period of three years. It was understood that President Batlle y Ordóñez viewed the change with sympathy, since he had long advocated reform of family legislation.[17]

Divorce by the sole will of the woman was formulated and put forward by Batlle's collaborators Senators Ricardo Areco and Domingo Arena. The bill first presented to the Senate established that divorce could be initiated by either the man or the woman, following the Margueritte brothers' model. This formula aroused the strong opposition of two members of the informing committee and other deputies, who assumed that it paved the way for easy divorces initiated by men. Halfway through the debate Arena proposed a change in the wording whereby the woman would be the only one with the legal right to initiate divorce. Arena confessed to being influenced by Carlos Vaz Ferreira, the formulator of compensatory feminism. Vaz Ferreira argued that men already had easier access to divorce under the mutual consent formula. If the deputies' purpose was to protect women, they should adopt a formula that would do so openly. Arena accepted this revision, and after conferring with Batlle y Ordóñez he presented it to the Senate with Areco's support. Their desire to achieve personal equality within marriage by giving women the right to initiate divorce was really nonegalitarian, since it denied men that right. The legislators favoring this draft were keenly aware of the criticism, yet they argued that such inequality was based on justice rather than on any elegance in the conception of the law. It was meant to redress the advantages men had always had within marriage. The principle of protecting women answered to their understanding of the law as a tool to serve the weak. The law bypassed the "intrinsic immorality of [having to offer] proof" and helped women preserve their privacy.

In supporting the divorce formula that let women begin and sustain a no-fault divorce case, Domingo Arena argued that this formula would simply raise women to men's legal level and would therefore establish symmetry in their relations. Arena aspired to subvert some of the stereotypes used by opponents of divorce, which portrayed men as taking advantage of women they no longer loved. This divorce bill would put men on the defensive, he argued: husbands would have to be better companions to their wives. Married women were not to be regarded as definitive conquests; they could strike back. Marriage was a very special contract that had to be "constantly renovated." Arena also attempted to expose the intellectual flaws in the Civil Codes that, in his opinion, condoned the subordination of women. He wanted an essentially feminist legislation to set a "beautiful example" for the rest of the world.[18]

The Debate in Chile and Argentina: An Unfinished Story

Debates on divorce legislation in Chile and Argentina began as early as those in Uruguay, but the results were much different. The Chilean chambers heard the first discussion of divorce from liberal Valentín Letelier in June 1875.[19] Letelier's bill did not permit marriage dissolution, let alone remarriage, but in supporting civil marriage he studied the possibility of divorce and characterized marriage as a civil contract. That it would be subject to dissolution like any other civil contract was a corollary that did not go unnoticed by liberal Chilean legislators. Letelier's proposal was studied by a committee that simply shelved it until 1883, when Liberal deputy Manuel Novoa, inspired by French divorce advocate Alfred Naquet, reopened the debate. Whereas Letelier had preserved the traditional proofs of wrongdoing by either spouse as causes for "divorce" (legal separation), Novoa wished to "decriminalize" it by accepting mutual consent as a valid cause for separation. This concept was rejected outright by Chilean deputies as an opportunistic maneuver by the proponent. They were unwilling to accept any course of action that did not follow canon law requirements to prove a moral crime (adultery) for the woman or scandalous cohabitation with another woman by the man as the basis for legal separation.[20] Divorce was not discussed in Chile again until 1924.

The early twentieth-century dialogue on divorce in Argentina and Chile benefited from the general perception that women had taken on a new social role with their incorporation into the labor force and that all matters related to their rights deserved revision. The danger of falling behind reformist trends elsewhere in the "civilized" world was a matter of national pride motivating some supporters. Nonetheless, in the intellectual debate over divorce the advantage lay with the traditionalists. They had the existing laws in their favor, as well as the support of key political figures and the Catholic Church.

When a divorce bill was discussed in Chile in 1924 the church arranged for a strong opposition campaign. Students of church-state relations in Chile argue that though there was no strong antagonism after the debate over civil marriage had cooled down, the Roman Catholic Church was far from sanguine about growing pressure for an official separation of church and state. The church actively supported the Conservative Party in national politics and took a strong interest in labor organization. When Crescente Errázuriz became archbishop of Santiago in 1919, he adopted a new policy of abstaining from open participation in electoral politics, but he did not withdraw from his duty to defend the church.[21] His response to the divorce bill was forceful and fast.[22] Nations that had adopted divorce laws, he insisted, had deviated from the norms established by God and natural law. Divorced and remarried people anywhere in the world lived in "perpetual adultery" and were not entitled to the ministries of the church. The archbishop characterized the proposed legislation as promoting social disorder and the destruction of the home. Religion gave Christians strength for the sacrifices necessary to maintain a family. His pastoral letter eulogized the beauty of mature women surrounded by several generations of descendants. A family made strong by its internal and undisturbed unity was the prize for a life devoted to virtue and abnegation.

Chilean jurists adopted a traditionalist view on divorce during this period. There was a quasi-consensus among the middle and upper classes on the undesirability of absolute divorce, and the political and economic situation of the middle and late 1920s was too unstable to warrant any legislative initiative on such a touchy subject. The political thrust for social reform had a weaker base in Chile than in Argentina, where the socialists injected their intellectual acumen into the discussion of divorce. Feminism, just beginning to mature, lacked the support that socialism lent it in Argentina. Any divorce legislation preceding or immediately following the 1925 separation of church and state faced a public totally unprepared for it and quite likely to reject it. That rejection had as much to do with religious observance as with the limited economic choices available to women lacking male support.[23]

Chilean women writing in the early 1920s, unlike their Argentine counterparts, were not inclined to endorse divorce, but some pro-feminist men supported divorce as part of a general plan for "female emancipation." In 1923 Mariano Bustos Lagos, speaking for a local chapter of the Radical Party in Linares, voiced a broad endorsement of social reform measures focused on women and the family.[24] Citing Manuel A. Matta, Enrique McIver, and Pedro Gallo (notable nineteenth-century reformers), he called for the end of religious tutelage over the home. He endorsed divorce in the name of freedom and progress and to end the immorality of adultery that also carried the threat of venereal disease. This allusion to *higienista* concerns shows how feminist themes merged with political, social, and health preoccupations to become a total reform program.

Divorce was not discussed again until the mid-1930s. By then church and state had separated, not without ecclesiastical protest, but with a minimum of political discomfort for President Alessandri. Ecclesiastical resentment smoldered for several years over the need to register a civil marriage before a religious ceremony, but a law issued in February 1930 settled this question definitively in favor of the state. By 1934 the nation had successfully weathered a constitutional crisis, and confidence in the political process was restored. Women had obtained the right to vote in the municipal elections, and President Juan Esteban Montero, showing willingness to move forward, supported several reforms in the Civil Code that gave Chilean women greater legal equality with men. Such modest advances in gender legislation made no impact on the view some men still held on women's role in society. In a book on divorce published in 1934 Luis María Acuña argued that men had greater intellectual ability and physical strength than women and so were obliged to tolerate their defects and weaknesses and protect them with "love, abnegation, and tenderness" in indissoluble marriage.[25]

In June 1933 the Chilean Radical Party introduced a divorce bill in the Chamber of Deputies. The reasons remain difficult to explain. The party may have been attempting to project an image of social "progress" much needed in a period of crisis and congruent with the party's alleged social interests. The opinions recorded in the national press were polarized. *El Mercurio* of Valparaíso claimed to have taken a "poll" on divorce and concluded that the few responses received indicated its lack of popular support. *Nosotras,* Unión Femenina de Chile's mouthpiece, disagreed and reprinted the editorials of a variety of newspapers in the capital and the provinces. Most of the opinions recorded favored divorce, although for different reasons.[26] Iquique's *La Opinión* and *Crítica* anchored their support in their ideological opposition to conservatism. Tocopilla's *La Opinión* and its namesake in Illapel supported the divorce bill but were suspicious of the Radical Party's motives. The Tocopilla journal believed the Conservative Party's cautious silence on the topic reflected its interest in preserving the status quo for the rich. *El Yunque,* of Antofagasta, favored divorce to legitimize thousands of homes and to weaken the influence of religion. San Felipe's *El Trabajo* predicted happiness for the marriages of the future. Opposing divorce was La Serena's *El Obrero.* It accused radical masons of being behind the bill. Santiago's Catholic *El Imparcial* decried the abuse of a sacrament established by God.

Apparently this bill was not acted on, and another divorce bill was discussed in July 1935. The feminist magazines *Nosotras* and *Acción Femenina* expressed their support. A collaborator for *Nosotras* declared her wish for a divorce that, though not easy to obtain, would offer escape to those in an intolerable relationship.[27] *Acción Femenina* made a case for facilitating divorce for the poor, who lacked the options the rich had for solving their personal problems. Having made a class pitch, it discussed the inequities women were subject to under the existing law. Opponents of divorce argued that women preferred to be protected in old age. *Acción Femenina* found much humiliation in such protection and contended that the only valid foundation for marriage was love. Women feared for their children's fate in case of divorce, but no woman, it claimed, would deny her children her love, whether divorced or remarried. As long as the mother-child dyad was maintained, the home was preserved. The inference that neither father nor husband was essential to the home was not offensive for a feminist magazine in a country with high rates of consensuality and out-of-wedlock births, and in a period that glorified motherhood.

Santiago's Roman Catholic newspaper *El Imparcial* rekindled its previous campaign against divorce, and in July and August 1935 it ran several interviews with educated professional women who opposed divorce. These women reverted to atavistic fears of family dissolution. Divorce made the abandonment of children and wives easy and tempted wives to leave sick husbands. Divorce could entice amoral women to seduce other women's husbands.[28] Earlier images of men abandoning their wives and seducing other women were reversed to picture a seductress. Implicitly this reversal reflected a degree of "liberation" from the old victim mold and the possibility of aggressive sexuality in women. To the Catholic press, such behavior amounted to immorality, and no effort should be spared to prevent it. Acción Patriótica de Mujeres de Chile, a Catholic women's association, joined the campaign against divorce through its magazine *Voz Femenina*.[29] Although opinions were exchanged throughout this decade, the divorce bill did not advance and eventually disappeared from sight. Opponents of divorce found a new ally in the admirers of eugenics, which had interested students and propagandists in Chile. Eugenicists strongly supported marriage, motherhood, and the family, and their opinion was aptly summarized by Amanda Grossi Aninat as she wrote in 1941, "From the point of view of eugenics, divorce is a secondary issue. It is wiser to marry well than to seek redress through a second marriage."[30]

Divorce in Argentina

Divorce was debated and defeated in the Argentine Congress on seventeen occasions from 1888 to 1932. In 1932 a bill allowing complete dissolution was approved by the Chamber of Deputies and forwarded to the Senate, which shelved it and successfully resisted all urging from the Deputies to discuss it.[31] This long story of failed attempts began with the first "complete dissolution" bill by Liberal deputy Juan Balestra in 1888. He intended to incorporate divorce in the Civil Code, and he may have planned to complete the move for civil marriage, approved that same year. His bill was groundbreaking: it put both sexes on the same level of legal accountability. Adultery, which weighed heavily against the woman in current canon and civil law, was cause for divorce without mitigating circumstances for the man.[32] The bill's wording strongly suggested that women were empowered and vindicated. Appearing on the heels of civil marriage legislation divorce had a dim future, and this quixotic bill was never discussed. Thirteen years later a second bill was submitted by a young deputy, Carlos Olivera. His 1901 bill adopted Balestra's stance that adultery in *either sex* was cause for divorce. Unlike its predecessor, Olivera's bill got a hearing in the press and before the public. The Catholic Church moved to the defense, and the bishop of Buenos Aires led the ecclesiastical hierarchy in a request to respect tradition and beliefs and save the nation from falling into irrevocable immorality. The bill passed from the legislative commission for full debate on the floor where, surprisingly, it lost by two votes (fifty to forty-eight).[33] Olivera reintroduced his project in 1903, but there was little fire left from the preceding session. The climactic support reached in 1901–1902 was held back by the continuous delay tactics by divorce foes in the chambers. Thirty years passed before divorce would again muster enough votes in the chambers to supersede its status of "bill under discussion."

Up to 1902 divorce was a liberals' issue, but in 1903 the Socialist Party endorsed dissolution of marriage as part of its plans for social change. Socialists shared with liberals an anticlerical stance. In August 1903 Alfredo Palacios gave a conference at the Centro Socialista on clericalism and divorce.[34] He placed a divorce bill on the congressional agenda in 1907. Palacios took Balestra's and Olivera's bills as models on the adultery issue but copied the recently approved Uruguayan divorce law by introducing the concept of mutual consent after a six-month waiting period.[35] In another departure from legal practice—and in recognition of women's rights—his bill allocated *patria potestad* to the party who was granted the child by judicial decision.

Palacios returned to the Congress with divorce drafts in 1913, 1914, and 1932. Other deputies and senators presented their own variations. In 1911 and 1913 Deputy Carlos Conforti submitted drafts not acted on.[36] In 1913 Deputy Víctor Pesenti submitted a draft incorporating Uruguay's latest refinement, divorce by the sole will of the wife, but distorting it to the sole will of *either* spouse after two years of marriage, a change that contravened the original intention of the Uruguayan divorce bill. Palacios's 1913 bill did not make that mistake; it changed nothing in the Uruguayan model. Deputy Conforti withdrew his draft before the end of the year, tired of his colleagues' postponements and what he regarded as the cold and rigid dogmatism then reigning in the chambers.[37] The socialist *Humanidad Nueva* published a study of the Palacios and Conforti bills in 1913, signaling the party's decision not to abandon this issue.[38]

Socialist deputy Mario Bravo picked up the divorce bill for his party in

1917 and carried it for several years—1918, 1920, 1925, 1927, and 1932—either as author or as cosigner.[39] Bravo made some adjustments to previous proposals. His 1917 bill ranked mutual consent as the first ground for divorce. The sole wish of the woman, if she was of age and a mother, and the adultery of either the husband or the wife ranked second and third. Divorce by the sole will of the woman could take place after six months and six days. He also allowed a traditional separation if dissolution was not desired and gave the woman complete freedom to choose her residence once the suit was initiated. Bravo's bill was cosigned by several nonsocialist deputies, who wished to see the legal implications of civil marriage come to fruition.[40]

Speaking in Santa Fe in 1919, Mario Bravo defended his party from accusations that its policies conspired against the stability of the family.[41] He questioned social and cultural patriarchalism and the conventional "social lie" about the Argentine family's stability. He claimed that reality disclosed children living with alcoholic, chronically sick, or criminal parents. Legal separations based on incompatibility and accepted by the church and society helped to reinforce clandestine families thriving by the side of those legally formed. Divorce should be a redeeming law, not a destructive one. It did not create family problems, it helped resolve them. Bravo's statements became the party's program. In ensuing years Enrique del Valle Iberlucea, Antonio de Tomaso, Juan B. Justo, Silvio Ruggieri, and Alfredo Palacios returned to Congress with divorce bills in unflinching challenge to their colleagues.[42] No other political party conducted such an intense campaign on behalf of this issue.

Radical Party deputy Leopoldo Bard was the only nonsocialist deputy who attempted more than once to persuade other deputies on divorce, submitting his own bills in 1922, 1924, 1926, and 1928.[43] Bard's bills proposed mutual consent for legally adult spouses and, picking up a social hygiene concept, included sexual disease as an admissible cause for divorce.[44] The 1928 Bard bill demoted adultery to fourth place, giving priority to imprisonment of a spouse and to unmitigated physical abuse. However, he retained the old formula that viewed women's adultery as a cause for divorce in all cases. Other bills submitted in the 1920s by members of several parties represented personal convictions, but unlike the socialists' bills, they did not enjoy the blessing of their parties. President Hipólito Yrigoyen (1916–22), made it clear that he would never endorse a law threatening the stability of the family, considerably reducing the chances of a serious parliamentary debate during his administration.[45]

After three decades of debate the eminent jurist Juan Carlos Rébora assessed the divorce issue.[46] Neither a feminist nor an outright traditionalist, Rébora accepted and cogently explained the economic underpinnings of women's new role in society and supported divorce as a social change beneficial for Argentine "modernization." Critical of the lack of internal coherence in the laws and their interpretation, he argued that the existing Argentine jurisprudence on "divorce" allowed the judges determining separation cases between 1926 and 1929 to engage in serious inconsistencies between the theory inscribed in the Civil Code and reality. In some adjudications the law benefited women; in others it restricted rather than amplified their rights. Judges had begun to accept the doctrine that women who left their homes after their husbands' repeated infidelities did not incur legal abandonment. Women were also leaving the country during divorce suits. This ran against the legislation still in effect, which required that the woman be "deposited" in an honest home during the "divorce" trial. Rébora was sympathetic to new practice as a reaffirmation of women's expanding freedom.[47]

Perhaps Rébora's most important commentary was on the predicament of thousands of Argentines who traveled to Uruguay to take advantage of the divorce legislation there and who returned either remarried or ready to "marry" a second time. Argentine judges consistently denied the validity of those unions, considering those involved adulterers and bigamists if their previous spouses were still alive.[48] The flight to Uruguay had become inevitable once Argentines realized that the divorce bills repeatedly discussed in the Chamber of Deputies had no chance of being approved. He foresaw numerous problems on establishing inheritance and recognizing children's legitimacy in such cases.

Rébora also discussed the implications of an Argentine law that allowed divorce if the couple remained separated ten years without showing any desire to reunite. He saw no difference between that option and divorce by mutual consent, which the law rejected. Why, he argued, could not an innocent party be granted the right to separate from a spouse by her or his own will? The legal definition of divorce was illogical and contributed to the erosion of the sense of duty intrinsic in the marriage contract. He wished to see a restitution of the moral elements of family law, and though the essence of his juridical thought was conservative, he pronounced himself in favor of absolute divorce. To him this was a more honest solution than allowing the rigidity of indissolubility to undermine the rights of either partner.

In 1932 there was a rare broad political and ideological unity behind a draft under consideration in the Argentine Congress. Members of several parties (Socialists, Democrats, Progressives, Radicals, and National Democrats) agreed to support it. The bitter anticlericalism of the turn of the century was absent from the discussions, and feminist advocates had created an atmosphere more amenable to the recognition of women's rights. A bill to grant Argentine women political rights was under consideration that same year. The feeling that Argentina and democracy were at a crossroads demanding moderate progress and change to avert the expansion of right-wing elements may well have been behind the deputies' support for the suffrage and divorce bills. Recognition of some of the issues for which feminists had struggled for more than a decade seemed to be reaching high tide and became a popular stance for congressmen.

Staunch supporters of divorce such as socialist Enrique Dickmann argued that separation of church and state over forty-five years before remained incomplete as long as total dissolution of marital ties was not achieved. In 1932 roughly 50 to 60 percent of marriages were confirmed by the church, and the rest were recorded in the civil register. Those who chose a religious marriage, argued Dickmann, did not have the right to impose the indissolubility they chose on those who did not.[49] Catholic influence on politics and daily life was subtle but strong. There was open concordance between church and state, with the latter holding the important right of nominating the church hierarchy and keeping an ambassador in the Vatican. Although not controlling education, the church had been very active in organizing male and female workers, especially under the leadership of Monsignor Miguel de Andrea, whose career spanned the mid-1920s to the mid-1950s. Catholic publications and Catholic writers favored a separate sphere for women, preferably at home as mothers, and opposed any move to liberalize marriage.[50]

Socialist Silvio Ruggieri's 1932 divorce bill restored adultery in both sexes as a legal cause for divorce but reiterated previous drafts by other deputies. In a list of fourteen potential causes, mutual consent was the last.[51] Throughout the years, successive bills had changed positions on the causes for divorce, and Ruggieri's bill was no exception. Shifting suggests insecurity about what could be an acceptable mainstream position. Any bill appearing to give divorce an easy time might fare badly, and deputies appeared to be seeking a compromise formula that could carry public opinion.

The debate of two critical bills in Congress moved female and feminist associations to campaign for both causes. Leading this effort were socialist associations in Buenos Aires and Rosario.[52] Socialist La Vanguardia followed the debates and anticipated a conservative church-led counterattack, but it claimed that the legislation was conceived with no antireligious purpose. It was simply the final consequence of the civil marriage law.[53] Divorce was approved by the Chamber of Deputies with ninety-two votes in favor and twenty-six against, but its fate was similar to the suffrage legislation debated the same year. It never received Senate approval and was shelved for the rest of the decade. Twenty-two years passed before absolute divorce was legalized by General Juan D. Perón in 1954.

Argentina was one step ahead of Chile: absolute divorce passed in the Chamber of Deputies. Yet in both countries the powerful conservative and traditionalist viewpoint of the upper economic and social classes and the Catholic Church won the day. The growing influence of extreme right-wing groups is another intellectual and political trend difficult to pinpoint but unwise to dismiss. Neither Argentina nor Chile was impressed that Uruguay had a standing divorce record that could be used to show a change in the status quo. Did divorce have an important impact on the family in the only country where it was legal? Data from Uruguay sustain the claim that relatively few people resorted to divorce and that it posed no threat to the stability of the Uruguayan family. Furthermore, Argentines seeking divorce in Uruguay inflated divorce figures. In 1907, the year divorce legislation was approved, only one divorce took place. Between 1907 and 1943, 13,041 divorces had taken effect. The overall ratio of divorces to marriages was 18.5/1,000. In 1920, for example, the ratio of divorce was 30/1,000. In 1931 the ratio was the highest between 1907 and 1943 — 64/1,000. By 1943 the ratio 50.6/1,000. The divorce rate reached a plateau between 1941 and 1943 (fig. 6).[54]

The arguments used to initiate divorce suits demonstrate how people used the law. Between 1935 and 1939, 50 to 60 percent of the divorces were "by the sole will of the woman." Those by mutual consent were in a decided minority — between 10 and 20 percent — while those contested varied between 20 and 25 percent. In 1939 the relative rate of divorce by mutual consent increased significantly from 16 to 22 percent, with a corresponding decline in divorces by the sole will of the woman from 62 to 51 percent. Although the chronological stretch of the statistics does not allow a final generalization about the acceptance of divorce, the seed planted by Deputies Arena and Areco in 1912 had yielded the desired fruit. Women were using the available avenue to end unwanted marriages with a minimum of personal embarrassment. Divorces took place most frequently between the seventh and the eleventh years, as the statistical trend between 1935 and 1939 suggested, but the span extended from the fifth year to the twentieth. The less vulnerable years were the first four and the period between twenty and thirty years.[55]

"Divorce" data from Argentina in 1927 showed 841 cases in the federal capital and the provinces of Catamarca, Córdoba, Entre Ríos, Jujuy,

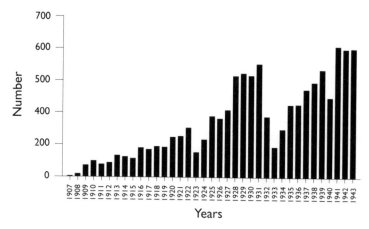

FIGURE 6.   Divorces in Uruguay, 1922–1943.
Uruguay, *El movimiento civil y la mortalidad en la República Oriental del Uruguay*
(Montevideo: Imp. National, 1890–1943).

La Rioja, Tucumán, and San Luis. Of these 536 (64.2 percent) had been initiated by women. A relatively small number of suits, 111 or 13.8 percent, were suspended by mutual agreement. Similarly, 144 cases were resolved judicially. Tucumán, Córdoba, and the federal capital had the highest incidence of divorces, with 302, 258, and 139 cases respectively. Of 57 divorce awards quoted by one source around 1927, 72 percent found the husband guilty of bad treatment and abandonment.[56] Although men continued to retain the power to block any reform of the law, women carried the burden of defining the limits of their tolerance. Lacking judicial or historical studies on divorce in any of the three countries, further analysis of divorce's social effects is impossible, but it is safe to conclude that its impact was more emotional than real and that no wave of family breakdowns ever materialized. Argentina only briefly legalized divorce in the 1950s, and Chile remained adamant against it. Only fifty years after the last significant debates in the period under review, marriage finally became a true civil contract in both countries.

Women and Divorce

In the early years of the century feminists' energies focused on education and Civil Code reform. Few activist women were contemplating divorce as a practical option when the uproar over civil marriage had not completely settled down. The popularity of divorce is highly questionable. In October 1905, during the early stages of the discussion of divorce in Uruguay, Deputy Vicente Ponce de León used a letter he claimed was signed by 93,000 persons and handed to him by "several ladies of our society" to protest the bill. The document denounced divorce as an attempt against the Christian family and the rights and decorum of women. No argument would force Uruguayan women to betray their religion, for which they were willing to renounce any pleasure to be derived from the freedom to dissolve an unhappy marriage. These women also feared the humiliation of being abandoned by their husbands.[57]

Opposition to divorce was kindled by fear of economic and personal abandonment. Most middle-class women, unprepared for any work outside the home, could not ignore this reality. Those who signed the statement believed that immigration affected marriage negatively: Uruguayan women marrying immigrants were more vulnerable to abandonment than women in countries without much immigration, they claimed. The presumed shiftlessness of immigrants accounted for this biased perception of their marital unfaithfulness. The xenophobic inference could be neither proved nor disproved but was directly connected to a final call to Uruguayan patriotic pride. Any offense against Uruguayan women was an offense against the motherland. The reaffirmation of women's role in the family as bastions of faith and self-sacrifice called on them to exchange freedom for a patriotic mission. They should not be deprived of the very security they had helped to construct for themselves and their children.[58]

Women in favor of divorce added little new to the arguments men used. The few who wrote on this subject during the first decade of the century viewed divorce as a form of liberation for both genders and a welcome exit from unhappy marriages. Uruguayan María Abella de Ramírez opened the columns of her magazine *Nosotras* to the discussion of divorce in 1902, when the Olivera draft was under study. Abella regarded divorce as a means to end the "barbaric" concept of indissoluble marriage, a form of slavery in which women were the victims and men the overseers.

Answering her call for opinions on divorce, socialist Justa Burgos Meyer fulminated against the defeat of the Olivera bill by so-called Christians who denied help to those who had to bear unhappy marriages. An anonymous female anarchist contributor sang the praises of "free unions." She astutely denounced the fact that even those who favored divorce manipulated the concept of honor to the detriment of women. Undoubtedly, the anonymous writer stated, the law of the strongest predominated in Argentine legislation:

men always had the upper hand. Abella de Ramírez praised Olivera's second attempt to win support for his divorce draft. She squarely denounced the church as an enemy of women and of all freedom. She condemned the hypocrisy behind those couples who preserved their social standing by maintaining a public facade of marriage that covered a private life of hatred, ill treatment, and deception. Only love should cement all unions. Olivera would eventually receive the grateful thanks "of all the slaves he wished to redeem." [59]

Abella equated the success of feminist ideas with the success of divorce. Women would advance little by merely knowing about their rights unless they had the means to break their chains. Adulterous women were the exception, not the rule, and those who fell into that trap were often murdered by husbands who opted for that swift resolution to their anger. Divorce liberated women from physical and mental abuse, and Argentine women had to understand its true meaning and discard the fears sowed by the church. She also urged the members of Congress to vote in favor of "a just and humanitarian reform." Abella's was the most vigorous female voice raised against divorce for several decades. The restrained yet passionate anger of her writings makes her stand above any other Southern Cone woman writing on this topic.

Another important statement on divorce early in the century came from socialist Carolina Muzilli, who spoke as "a modern woman" at the 1910 First International Feminine Congress in Buenos Aires. She represented socialist thought on the subject, and though she never called herself a feminist, her reasoning followed feminist and nineteenth-century liberal arguments. She reminded her audience of the implications of indissolubility, such as a life without love for both spouses, masculine escapades in the form of consensual unions—a form of adultery—and the birth of illegitimate children. The galling hypocrisy of a double moral standard fostered by such situations would end with the adoption of divorce. She also foresaw many social benefits, such as a decline in prostitution, a boost to the social status of all women, and another moral step toward their liberation.

Muzilli's paper was endorsed by the Socialist Feminine Center and the National Union of Freethinking Women, led by María Abella de Ramírez. During its discussion Elvira Rawson de Dellepiane, already a well-known feminist, showed what might have been a general apprehension about the legal form a divorce law could take. She wanted to see divorce tightly regulated by the law to prevent its abuse by ill-intentioned husbands and to protect children as much as possible. Her concern was disputed by more determined supporters, such as socialists Sara Justo and María Abella de Ramírez, who were keen on upholding the freedom implied in the option to choose divorce. Both women took the Uruguayan divorce law as a model, stating that the sole will of either spouse was sufficient to warrant divorce. With one stated vote of opposition, the congress made an official declaration of support for divorce, with a proviso for careful regulation of its process, and declared it a "law of moral cleansing within marriage."[60]

Resolute feminists, socialists, and freethinkers were ready for divorce in 1910. The Argentine Centro Socialista Femenino reiterated a reform program at the congress in which divorce figured second only to suffrage and came ahead of legislation regulating the labor of women. This was probably a tactical move designed by the socialist women attending the congress to gain adherents to their cause. In the ensuing years *La Vanguardia* occasionally published articles on behalf of divorce, especially when divorce drafts were introduced in congress by Socialist deputies or senators.[61] During the rest of the period under review female divorce supporters had very limited access to the press and published mostly in women's and socialist magazines.

By 1910 early working-class Chilean feminists, who had first challenged the patriarchal family and capitalism in their own newspapers, had moved to the back of the stage. Middle-class feminism was in its formative stage and had still not fully matured as an intellectual and social force. This explains the scarcity of statements on divorce in that country. In 1915 Delie Rouge, who later became a feminist advocate, criticized existing "divorce" legislation in her country as granting men de facto freedom while leaving women morally bankrupt. If men had the choice of finding happiness outside an unhappy marriage, she stated, why not women? Like Uruguayan deputy Domingo Arena, Rouge believed divorce would bring women more respect from men and, in fact, could help cement some marriages.[62] Rouge, and other women after her, did not discuss divorce on exclusively female terms, as Abella de Ramírez had done. She was careful to present it as an option for both sexes.

In 1922 *Acción Femenina,* the organ of the Chilean Partido Cívico Femenino, made a cautious statement on divorce through its male editor, César A. Sangüeza. In principle he found divorce acceptable, but before it was introduced in Chile women should be prepared to earn a living. In his opinion divorce in Chile would mean that many women and their families would become destitute.[63] An informal poll among the readers reflected indecision and unpreparedness.[64] This was not the case for Zulema Arenas Lavín, who published an article supporting divorce in the first anniversary issue of *Ac-*

ción Femenina. She made veiled allusions to women's sexual needs and their right to a new marriage. There was more to divorce than "civilization" and moral progress.[65]

The 1924 congressional debate on divorce raised some female response. Delia Rouge again addressed the issue in *Revista Femenina,* the reorganized *Acción Femenina.* A more conservative Rouge followed the magazine's new editorial restraint and now defined divorce as a negative influence on the family.[66] In 1924 she was willing to accept divorce, but only for admissible reasons. It was imperative to protect children and women without economic means, but she had little tolerance for the frivolity of women who had obtained a separation without being prepared to work and remained financially dependent on their "ex-husbands." To protect women after a divorce, as well as ensure the welfare of the children born from clandestine relationships, she would restrict divorce to childless couples, those suffering incurable or transmissible diseases, those abandoned for many years (mostly women), and those whose spouses were incarcerated for life. Her shift from strong support to ambivalence on divorce may have been prompted by the current concern for child welfare, but it also reflected a personal retrenchment into conservatism. As alternatives to divorce, she proposed moral advice to married couples, a mixture of older stereotypes such as maternal suffering and paternal pride, feminism expressed as gender equality within marriage, and moral reform stated as education in ethical values. Her proposals divested divorce of its character of "liberation," stressing instead the need for protective mechanisms to guarantee the welfare of the weak within the family—that is, the child and the mother.

Partido Cívico Femenino did not have a clearly defined attitude toward the 1924 divorce bill, but if the selection of a response to a readers' poll is indicative, it seemed to incline toward the protection of women. The opinion of the president of the Club de Señoras of the city of Talca, selected for publication by the group's magazine, echoed the fears of abandonment, for which most women were unprepared.[67] It also expressed deep respect for the "sacred and immutable bond of marriage" and suggested that instead of divorce the deputies should support legislation for social hygiene, milk canteens, the education of women, and social welfare. The defense of home, childhood, and morality shows how tentative Chilean feminism was in the 1920s and how strong was the conservative foundation of that society compared with the Uruguayan. The priority given to social welfare programs also suggests the greater need for them in a nation that had just begun to organize such services.

Chilean women commenting on the 1933 divorce bill remained divided in their opinion. Some were concerned about the fate of children; others, such as the influential upper-class conservative Adela Edwards de Salas, preferred to see women gaining political and civil rights first and discussing divorce afterward. Yet others thought the project was untimely because the nation had more pressing issues to solve.[68] Some feminists, excited by the "success" of the suffrage campaign—municipal voting having been adopted in 1932—hoped for a similarly favorable outcome with the divorce bill. Pushing for divorce immediately after the acceptance of female municipal voting, however, was simply not advisable. Conservatives argued that the bill was a political gambit of the Radical Party to regain popular support, although it is unclear how "popular" divorce was and what gain any political party could accrue from supporting legislation of questionable acceptance in a traditional country like Chile. But given the tilt toward the Left and social consciousness in this period's politics, an airing of ideas such as divorce and female suffrage suggests nothing more than willingness to consider reforms. Politically, it would do no harm to any party to test the wind.[69]

Amid arguments and counterarguments, the opinion of Amanda Labarca, a founder of feminism in Chile, was particularly important. In 1933 this respected feminist and educator spoke out against the social hypocrisy that permitted members of the upper class to pay for a religious annulment under false pretenses—such as having been married in the wrong jurisdiction— but did not allow legalization of divorce that would give the same benefit to people of lesser economic means. She claimed there were more annulments in Chile than outright divorces in France and that magistrates had accepted a de facto divorce jurisprudence by annulling a marriage whenever the couple agreed on it. Like other feminists, she resented that women living legally separated from their husbands could not form a new family, whereas men who chose to do so illegally were forgiven by society. She reiterated the argument that the pain caused within a home by the tyranny and indifference of a husband would be finished when women could end an unhappy marriage. As an educator, she was also concerned with the suffering of children in a decade when childhood began to gain a firm place as a target of social reform. But though she argued for the internal "hygiene of the family," her main objective was to obtain redress for women and balance in gender relations.[70]

Labarca's arguments were rebutted a year later by the Catholic *Voz Femenina* through the writings and lectures of Carmela Correa de Garcés, who injected an interesting interpretive twist by arguing that men were attempting to draft a divorce law for their own benefit, thus dispossessing women of their right to have a voice in its making. Men did not have the right to appropriate the law, and Chilean women should reject such attempts.[71] Chilean women, argued the newspaper in successive issues, did not marry for adventure. Men were the most common cause of ruined marriages. *Voz Femenina* echoed fears that divorce would lift all restraint against their taking first action in divorce cases.[72] This was a true call for gender solidarity, pitting women against men in an effort to galvanize female public opinion. In the mid-1930s some leading Chilean conservative women adopted a philosophy of gender separatism as a source of moral and political strength. Their opposition to divorce could be enhanced if they could persuade other women that men's priorities were not as lofty as women's. This made sense in a period when Southern Cone women of various political persuasions equated womanhood with moral superiority.

Gender Issues in the Divorce Debate

The analysis of the arguments over divorce is illuminating. Nowhere are the mores of society more clearly revealed than in the debate over the foundation of the family and the bonds that keep its members together. Equality of the sexes, hierarchical power, control of sexuality, issues of honor and fidelity, rejection of a double standard of moral behavior, and freedom to love pitted against the duty to keep the family together were key topics discussed throughout four decades of argument. The quick enactment of divorce legislation in Uruguay set the stage for a prolonged and unresolved contest of wills in Argentina. Though less spirited, the Chilean discussion invoked the same values and elicited similar responses.

Among opponents of divorce, no argument was more pervasive than the natural differences of the sexes, the physiological fate that destined women for some roles and men for others. Nature had intended complementarity and symmetry, and no human law would change that reality. Their orthodoxy gave patriarchal values the respect of tradition. Women and men, argued Uruguayan Amaro Carve in 1905, were not physically equal. On the side of women were grace, weakness, passivity, and sweetness, on that of men, vigor and energy.[73] Conservative jurists and traditional intellectuals saw in marriage not only a balance for these antithetical qualities but above all a protective shelter for women. Some of the defenders of the indissolubility of marriage hinted that they really did not believe in the juridical equality of the sexes. Although refraining from accepting women's intellectual inferiority, Argentine conservative jurist Alfredo Colmo believed there was no "biological, psychological, or social equality between man and woman," and therefore juridical equality "was inconceivable."[74] To address such gender inequality, traditional jurists used the concept of protection for the weaker of the two—the woman—to maintain the key legal formula of marriage without divorce. Indeed, the protective shield of marriage was perhaps the reason most often cited by divorce detractors. The questions of whom and how marriage protected were critical. In their complex answers lies the key to understanding the conservative mentality.

Divorce, it was argued, would break the restraints that held back undesirable personal passions and shielded both men and women from their own natural sexual weaknesses. The most obvious protection that indissolubility gave women was from abandonment after time destroyed their beauty and their husbands lost interest in them. That was the opinion of Uruguayan Catholic jurist Vicente Ponce de León in 1905 and, thirty years later, of Chilean Catholic newspapers *El Imparcial* and *Voz Femenina* of Santiago. Furthermore, women had a "certain age" for marrying (up to twenty-five), claimed Ponce de León. After that age their marriage opportunities declined considerably. Opponents and supporters of divorce alike addressed women's aging on similar grounds. It made women more vulnerable to abandonment.[75] If a woman added divorce to age, she ended with far fewer chances to remarry than a man. The assault on women's most intimate sources of insecurity—the loss of marriage and the loss of beauty—was a clever psychological strategy.

Ponce de León and others resorted to European statistics to prove that divorced women remarried less often than divorced men. Although the debate over remarriage statistics bore no fruit amid argument and counterargument, the cultural perception that women lost more in a divorce than men was unassailable in the minds of many men and women. Uruguayan conservative Colorado José Espalter aptly defined this attitude in 1912 when he stated that "what men and women contribute to marriage is very different. If a marriage breaks down, the husband . . . takes out all or almost all that he put into it. Women, on the contrary, leave everything or almost everything behind: their first love . . . their youth . . . their beauty."[76] It was only just to establish safeguards to protect them; this was the essence of true equality. Justice as protection of the weaker was one of the bases of Uruguayan feminism, although compensatory feminists and traditionalists reached different conclusions on divorce from its premises.

Male and female sexuality played an important role in the arguments against divorce. For a generation raised in the ambiguities of late nineteenth-century sexual restraints and at the same time facing what Uruguayan historians José P. Barrán and Benjamín Nahum have described as the discovery of a new eroticism at the turn of the century, the explicit discussion of the problems of male sexual proclivities was indeed a remarkable novelty. The thrust of this argument was for the protection of women from men who could not and would not inhibit their unbridled sexuality. Marriage contained men's natural polygamy claimed Ponce de León. If men could, they would seek one woman after the other. Divorce would uncover the human beast, giving men license to indulge in lust.[77] Thirty years later the Chilean *El Imparcial* reiterated the threat of aggressive male sexuality and the unrestrained satisfaction of men's lower passions as one result of the freedom divorce would grant them. Argentine Juan Bautista Terán envisioned men having a new wife every season.[78] Surprisingly, the idea of a woman's marrying a new man every season never occurred to him. Female sexuality was not discussed, but throughout the many debates on divorce men did not hesitate to uncover and expose their own reprehensible sexual practices, to "educate" women on the risks they incurred by accepting divorce and to remind other men of the moral traits they hid under a conniving patriarchy.

Sexuality was tackled differently by anarchists, who, at the other extreme, rejected marriage on principle and carried out a long-term propaganda campaign against that institution, disrupting some Catholic lectures against divorce. For anarchists, sexuality could not be bound by any juridical social tie. Free love meant forming sexual relationships based on love. Marriage, especially socially arranged marriage, was nothing more than prostitution for the woman. In rebutting the anarchists' arguments against marriage and their advocacy of free love, Uruguayan conservative Amadeo Almada accused them of irresponsibility about caring for their offspring, whom the state would have to support. Marriage "made" the family, where moral values resided and were transmitted to the new generation. Only underdeveloped countries preserved promiscuity and "defective" forms of family organization.[79] Anarchist opposition to marriage became a paradigm to be recalled by those opposing divorce in the 1930s. In Argentina Juan Bautista Terán labeled the proposed divorce legislation "socialist" and "anarchist" in an effort to politicize the issue and weaken support for divorce in the chambers.[80]

Although less aggressive in their arguments than the anarchists, other ideological supporters of divorce were just as firm in their belief that it would help liberate many women from sexual subservience. María Abella de Ramírez showed no inhibition in reminding a journalist of *La Prensa* (Buenos Aires) that "divorced" women who took a consensual husband were not just seeking financial support; they also had physiological needs.[81] Deputy Carlos Olivera, defending his 1901 divorce bill, wished to see women's behavior in sexual matters guided by their own free will rather than preserved by social and personal punishments.[82] That same year, Socialist deputy Enrique del Valle Iberlucea, then beginning his political career, highlighted the importance of sexual liberation through divorce, explaining that his support was based on two beliefs: it would help free women from the worst of servitudes, sexual servitude, and it would contribute to women's legal emancipation. Divorce was not an economic issue, he argued, or the proletariat would not be affected by it. Divorce was a bourgeois reform, but not a question of morals or religion. It concerned reform of the family system and the personal liberation of the female sex.[83] Del Valle Iberlucea's emphasis on personal rather than economic factors was not his alone. Socialists and freethinkers of the early period showed a strong sensitivity to women as individuals, perhaps influenced by anarchism and liberalism. They were able to make room for personal factors within the class framework of their analysis. In 1907 Palacios emphatically stated that his divorce bill had the "sexual redemption of woman" as an objective. Six years later he argued that industrial development had created a new foundation for the family, which from then on would operate "on a greater sexual freedom tempering the supremacy of men."[84]

Sexual relations between an estranged couple were the subject of Colorado senator Domingo Arena's comments during the discussion of the 1912 divorce reforms in Uruguay. He claimed to have forced himself to discuss such a "crude" concept because it was in many people's minds. He made a strong case for upholding the rights of a woman who, lacking any emotional attachment to her husband, had to suffer "the matrimonial yoke and suffer, against her best instincts, her husband's contact."[85] Using an anarchist argument (he had held anarchist sympathies in his early career), he defined such a situation as a form of prostitution imposed by the law, and he attacked the Catholic Church for placing the stigma of sin on sexual matters. In his support Ricardo Areco, author of the 1912 reforms, stated that no law should force the payment of the matrimonial debt. José Espalter, who opposed the divorce reform bill, was equally against a wife's sexual subservience, calling the matrimonial debt without love a "monstrosity." He argued, however, that though the law could not enforce certain obligations, emotionally estranged couples should not forget that they had many other commitments to stay together.[86]

Implicit in the discussion of male sexuality was whether love was necessary to the stability of marriage. Divorce opponents argued that moral duty was the key element in marriage, and the two most important moral duties were fidelity and preserving the welfare of the family.[87] They demanded sacrifice and the submission of the individual to the benefit of the social group. But who would bear the greatest sacrifice for the benefit of the family? Fidelity and sacrifice were notions that male legal experts and politicians handled with practiced artfulness. Whenever discussed, they applied more to women than to men, despite uneasy acknowledgment that men were not exempt. A double standard of morality was defended with arguments that traced it back to biblical roots, reinforced by positivist notions of women's role in the family and society. Fidelity dignified women, stated Uruguayan Amaro Carve in 1905. Divorce would lead women away from their duties and the holy mission God had awarded them: care of the home and children's education.[88] Chilean Ramón Briones Luco, a strong supporter of civil marriage, favored divorce only when female infidelity led to loss of male honor. In a two-volume work on marriage and divorce, he argued twice for marriage dissolution in cases involving male honor. He quoted lengthy passages from Alexander Dumas's (son) arguments for murdering a treacherous and unrepentant adulterous wife. Briones Luco claimed not to subscribe to such violence, but he tacitly endorsed that line of argument by stating that divorce offered the only alternative to a man haunted by his wife's infidelity.[89] He acknowledged that fidelity was an obligation of *both* spouses but supported "without trepidation" the canonical concept that the wife's infidelity was more grievous than the husband's. Although male adultery pained the wife, it did not leave "traces" in the marriage. In contrast, a wife's adultery introduced a stranger's child into the family, interrupting and adulterating the "physiological and psychic heritage of the husband."[90] In explaining his position, he ventured several eugenics-based notions about the transmission of "bad genetic traits" from a potential lover. Why a lover's genetic traits should be inferior to the husband's was not explained. The key presumption was that the husband should have the assurance that his genes and his genealogical pedigree were safeguarded by his wife's fidelity. Thus the cloak of "science" lent new life to the old concept of male honor and male right to sexual monopoly over a chosen female. In 1918 Briones Luco sponsored a divorce bill that allowed a dissolution of marriage after five years' "separation of bodies." Among the valid reasons for divorce, he and the rest of the cosponsors of the bill stated that adultery in a woman should be treated more severely "for reasons of social order, and even physiological reasons."[91]

Ambiguity regarding ethical responsibility within marriage colored even

the arguments of those who challenged the values dominating gender relations. Setembrino Pereda's divorce bill, submitted to Uruguayan representatives in April 1902, retained female adultery as acceptable grounds. Defending its criminalization, Pereda stated that it was more than an issue of "public
order." Female adultery "affected the honor of the husband so deeply and
irrevocably that it did not admit any decorous reconciliation. This offense
has no possible exoneration. It is only extinguished with death."[92] During
the debate men were adamant about maintaining their code of honor. Men's
transgressions were also of public order, but they were not as offensive as
those of married women.

Not all supporters of divorce shared such ideas. In 1905 Uruguayan Guzmán Papini y Zas proposed liberating *both* sexes from current social and
sexual mores: "no more enslaved men and servile women."[93] As defined by
some Uruguayan and Argentine reformers, divorce was not a challenge to accepted ethical values. Alfredo Palacios maintained that only mutual consent
to remain together gave marriage its moral base. For Víctor Pesenti keeping two people bound against their will was the worst kind of immorality.[94]
Over and beyond ethical nuances of forced or voluntary togetherness, the
moral scale was still tipped against women. Balestra's and Olivera's bills in
Argentina accepted equal legal accountability for both sexes, but traditional
cultural values challenged the novelty of this approach. Oneto y Viana's 1905
divorce bill confirmed women's adultery in all instances, but only scandalous adultery for men.[95] The 1907 Uruguayan divorce law preserved a double
standard, reflecting the ambiguity that most male legislators — even those
friendly to women — maintained about the wife's infidelity. In essence, men
retained their right to define the degree of crime and apportion the punishment and reaffirmed their belief that women were more accountable than
men in matters of infidelity.[96]

These sets of values were not challenged by the 1913 Uruguayan divorce
reform. It favored women by seeking an easier way out of marriage, but the
concept of honor remained mostly a female burden. Ironically, the proponents and supporters of that reform believed they were upholding a *feminist*
cause that would liberate women within marriage.[97] Palacios and Conforti
returned to equal legal and moral accountability, and Mario Bravo in 1918
denounced a double standard of guilt as "an embarrassing cynicism" of the
law. He took pains to establish equality and reciprocity in his draft, allocating the same bases for divorce for men and women. This position was
adopted by subsequent socialist bills.[98] Leopoldo Bard's bill turned the clock

back by accepting female adultery without mitigation while attaching several conditions to the man's adultery. Ultimately the only accepted divorce bill — that of Uruguay — condoned men's sexual transgressions.

Divorce and the Family

Opponents and supporters of divorce had very different views on how it would affect the family. The ties linking feminism, divorce, and reforms in gender relations within the patriarchal family were obvious to supporters and detractors alike, but they derived different conclusions from the interconnectedness. Conservative opponents placed great weight on the family as the place where the solid values of the past were perpetuated under the vigilance of both parents, with the father leading the way for his spouse and his children. In this context duty and responsibility were above selfish desires for personal happiness or rights. Feminism disrupted the foundations of the family by changing gender roles and altering the value assigned to them. In an outright rejection of feminism, Ponce de León proudly stated that women in his country declined to join "the course of modern feminism" and showed a blessed ignorance of the ideology that purported to redeem them from slavery. He claimed that Uruguayan women preferred the role of queens of their homes, while men preferred to maintain it as a place of solace and rest.[99] Others stressed the social objectives of marriage and women's specific physical role in procreation. Since marriage had the purpose of procreation, women were supposed to give up their personal rights by the very act of becoming mothers and should not use self-gratifying formulas such as divorce to forgo the fulfillment of their social duties.[100]

Argentine socialist Enrique Dickmann bolstered the father's role in the family in an effort to show the symmetry of both genders in sustaining it. Fathers brought the daily sustenance for the nursing mother and the infant child. This mutual dependency of male and female within the family did not, in his opinion, demand subordination of the rights of one spouse. Dickmann was one of the few writers of the period to present fatherhood in a positive and creative manner. Underlining the complementarity of gender roles, he argued for spouses' mutual respect and for freedom to maintain or reject those roles. He also tackled the argument that divorce contributed to a decline in births, a contention used by some opponents. Dickmann was quick to point out that the practice of birth control by the upper classes and child mortality among the working poor — not divorce — were the most logical explanations for the trend.[101]

Supporters of divorce were as concerned about the family as their opponents but differed in their understanding of the ideal home. They claimed to protect women and children from the constant and much cited abuses—physical and moral—of many husbands. Harmony and happiness in the home were the only forces binding men and women and capable of generating a sound atmosphere for the care of children. Suffering, sacrifice, and duty were not elements in their personal and social vocabulary. They agreed with divorce detractors that home was a place for setting moral examples, but the antagonism created between spouses by forced cohabitation and the pain created by abandonment were the worst possible education for children.[102] The church had no moral right to impose indissolubility in the name of false family stability. If ecclesiastical authorities could control neither physical and emotional abuses nor adultery, civil authorities had no alternative but to support absolute divorce.[103]

Defenders of divorce pressed love, personal freedom, and happiness as the bases of marriage. Although the concept of legal freedom to end a contract was an important argument throughout the debates, the need to find emotional satisfaction in marriage was equally important. To the fears used by conservative opponents, liberal divorce defenders opposed the utopia of happy self-fulfillment in marriages held together by a common will. A different attitude guided those who wished to make the marriage bonds voluntary. "Marriage is the legitimate association of two persons of different sex, based on mutual esteem and love," defined Uruguayan Pérez Olave in 1905.[104] Anything else was a form of bondage comparable to personal slavery. The right to happiness that belonged to all human beings and the right to express love through wedlock were two of the concepts Leopoldo Bard used in his divorce draft. If love, the only basis of marriage, was missing, marriage must be annulled.[105] Alfredo Palacios fused the theme of motherhood with that of love to argue that if women had the right to be mothers, that right had to be based on love. Thus love was applied not only to gender relations, but to the maternal function of the woman within the family. A mother not surrounded by love should not remain tied to her marriage. This emphasis on love, happiness, and voluntary companionship reveals a change in sensibilities already under way at the beginning of the century. Although these concepts had an uphill struggle to be accepted as legally meaningful in Argentina and Chile, they were the basis for reform elsewhere. Duty, social order, and morality as reasons to remain married were slowly replaced in most people's understanding by love, happiness, and personal and sexual satisfaction.

Divorce was one of the several answers feminists and social reformers provided to the broader question of how gender relations had to change to suit women's new roles in society. The quest for gender equality followed many paths, and the right to break the marital bonds was one of them. Argentine Mario Bravo best formulated how the freedom to maintain or break their personal union allowed *both* genders to establish a new conjugal morality.

> The consecration of new rights for women will inhibit men from abusing their present legal dominion and maintaining women as mere reproductive agents, or dominated under the honorable title of wife. This law will also make women conscious of their new role, appreciative of men as their partners in the fundamental task of forming a family, and not simply as the temporary prisoners of their flattery, or as mere transients whose company they must abandon at the first dark challenge from life.[106]

Feminists and social reformers in the Southern Cone struggled to translate this new formula of mutual responsibility and appreciation into law, but legislation alone could not accelerate the desired change in values and personal attitudes. In two nations the legislated formulation failed to expedite a process that needed more time to erode the influence of the church and many centuries of a patriarchal cultural heritage.[107]

CHAPTER 8

Women's Politics and Suffrage
in Argentina

In 1900 Argentina was the South American meeting ground for contemporary Western thinking on the changing role of women. But the meeting was only one of minds. The social reality was far from reflecting the arguments already being made by male and female intellectuals and labor leaders. Having distinguished itself in promoting female education, Argentina counted a select number of educated women who by 1900 were prepared to go beyond defending women's rights in women's magazines.[1] Before the open advocacy of suffrage, Argentina passed through a formative period rich in ideas, sparked by enthusiastic and well-informed women who supported each other while maintaining their autonomy.

The discussion of women's political rights had its foundations in mid-nineteenth-century legal studies. Carlos Pellegrini's study of electoral rights and Florentino González's lessons on constitutional rights—both published in 1869—concluded that women were capable of exercising the vote but did not support immediate suffrage.[2] For Pellegrini suffrage was inherent in citizenship, but he demanded literacy for participation in political life. Dismissing specious arguments of female "moral and intellectual" inferiority, he saw no reason to deny suffrage on such grounds. However, he believed that women required more education to put them at the same level of preparation as men. Once women's intellect was exercised and strengthened, they could join men in the body politic. He did advise caution in adopting suffrage. He favored suffrage for single or widowed women, to avoid political conflicts within the home. Argentines could wait to see the results of female suffrage in other countries before acting.

Also denying natural limitations and extolling the positive sides of women's participation in civic life were Luis A. Mohr, José Miguel Olmedo,

Octavio Iturbe, and Pedro E. Aguilar, young lawyers initiating their careers between 1873 and 1895. Olmedo joined those who deplored how women had not been properly educated to assume their natural rights. Iturbe, writing in 1895, favored the egalitarian objectives of European feminism and socialism. Aguilar also supported the principle of female suffrage, but like Pellegrini and González he was an evolutionist, preferring to wait before applying it to Argentina. Mohr was the most openly supportive of women's participation in public life, and the most critical of his narrow-minded contemporaries.[3] A more typical position was that of José Manuel Estrada, a constitutional law professor who in 1902 was willing to sacrifice women's rights for the sake of domestic harmony. Suffrage was a universal, unconditional, and absolute right for men, but political functions were incompatible with woman's role in the family. "Electoral rights cannot not be conferred to women, who do not have it as a natural right, without risk to democracy, liberty, and the order imposed by God on human societies."[4] Estrada was not alone. For the next four decades many argued along similar lines, although toning down the apocalyptic visions of social disaster should women be allowed to vote. Subversion of gender roles within family and society was an intimidating thought. Even female advocates of women's emancipation were more interested in equality of education and legal equality for married women than in suffrage.[5]

The foundation of the Argentine National Council of Women in 1900 appeared to usher in a new era in women's history. Affiliated with the European National Councils of Women, it had behind it one of the most active innovators of her times, Dra. Cecilia Grierson.[6] The National Council's first president, Alvina Van Praet de Sala, was a member of the highest Buenos Aires social circles, and under her the Council began to steer away from controversial issues. In less than a decade the National Council of Women had alienated Grierson, and in 1910 they split.[7] Having dissociated itself from feminism, the Council continued to act as a center for technical and home education for women of limited means and to host literary and artistic events. To counter the 1910 First International Feminine Congress, the Council organized its own meeting in May 1910. Participants spoke on topics such as welfare institutions, technical education for women, moral education for children, and regulation of female home industrial labor and child labor. Several of the speakers judged political rights for women "inopportune." Celia La Palma de Emery, a leading Catholic conservative, posited that "exaggerated or misunderstood feminism" was "pernicious." Carolina Jaime de Freyres had kinder words for feminism, which she found "based on an ideal of nobility and goodwill that embraces all good doctrines and aspirations," although she did not accept all its premises.[8]

Freyres's sympathies were her own. The National Council remained a conservative association with no interest in feminism. In the early 1920s it offered classes in languages, accounting, literature, shorthand, writing, and such and maintained a library for students and members. Since public libraries were scarce in Buenos Aires, this service was welcome. In 1919 the National Council joined the Patriotic League, a conservative nationalist Catholic association. In praise of its activities, an Argentine diplomat described the Council as "promoting the elevation of feminine culture . . . as well as preparing the weaker sex for the struggle of life. It does not pursue the noisy and aggressive emancipation envisioned by some feminist propaganda, as extreme as it is absurd."[9]

Early disappointment with the National Council prompted a group of university graduates to leave the organization in 1904 to found the Centro de Universitarias Argentinas and Centro Feminista in 1905. Although their activities are not well known, the Universitarias acted as a lobbying group. In 1909 they protested the breach of child labor laws and offered their free service as inspectors.[10] The Centro Feminista, founded by Dra. Elvira Rawson de Dellepiane, supported legal reforms to improve women's status and promoted women's education and welfare for unwed mothers and military conscripts.[11] The Centro changed its name to Centro Juana María Gorriti, named after a revered educator, to avoid alienating potential supporters.[12] Education remained the solid base upon which women built their choices and defined themselves in the public arena. Unquestionably, the leading women of this generation had public involvement in mind. The issue was whether it would evolve into the pursuit of political rights or whether other economic and social objectives were more relevant. Elvira V. López, an educator and a member of the university women's groups, considered political rights premature but expected women to achieve them. Another early university graduate, Dra. Cecilia Grierson, founder of the first Argentine nursing school in 1885, was too busy to engage in theoretical debates on suffrage. Public recognition for her long career in teaching child and health care, as well as musical and physical education, substantiated her idea that there was a political dimension to public health.[13]

In 1910 María Abella de Ramírez founded the Liga Feminista Nacional in her home in La Plata; it was affiliated with the International Alliance for Women's Suffrage (Berlin).[14] The Liga Feminista proposed a four-point statement of principles endorsing the civil rights of married women, political rights for women, divorce, and protection to childhood.[15] Dra. Julieta Lanteri, whose flamboyant style, directness, and daring challenges to the establishment gave her national notoriety, founded the Liga para los Derechos de la Mujer y el Niño, operating in Buenos Aires in 1911. As its name implied, this group promoted women's and children's well-being through protective legislation. Lanteri proposed educator Francisca Jacques for a post on the National Education Council, a challenge for the male-dominated bureaucracy that nominated and appointed its members without consultation and, according to her, disregarding the best candidates.[16] Her suggestion was ignored. The League was the main organizer of the 1913 National Congress on Childhood, and continued a vigorous life for a few years more. As one of its main pillars, Julieta Lanteri undertook to break all rules of "propriety" and femininity to promote women's suffrage.

Another important women's organization was Unión y Labor, a group founded in 1909 to help Argentine women establish kinship through civic work and protecting children. To support their organization and help finance a children's home, the founders began publishing a magazine by the same name in October 1909.[17] The organization underscored women's role as educators and promoted their participation in those public areas for which they had a special talent, such as labor organizing and inspecting women's prisons. Unión y Labor was a highly intellectual, socially engaged, and well-informed group that kept abreast of international women's rights. The magazine published articles on suffrage, although they believed it was a right that could be postponed. This was their position in late 1910, reiterated in October 1911, when they pledged not to foster the ambition for suffrage among Argentine women. First women had to moralize society and educate their children in the strictest civic ethics.[18]

Freethinkers [librepensadores] were another element in the women's organization picture in this first decade. Freethinkers' origins were Masonic, but membership in a lodge was not required. Since 1906 María Abella and Julieta Lanteri had been associated with the librepensadores international league. A 1908 National Congress of Freethinkers in the provincial city of Córdoba attracted 267 delegates. The congress endorsed female suffrage.[19] In 1909 Abella and Lanteri went a step further with the foundation of the Liga Nacional de Mujeres Librepensadoras in Buenos Aires, and in 1910 they began publishing La Nueva Mujer for feminists and freethinkers.[20] Freethinker activists retained the anticlerical bent of their Masonic roots and supported "radical" ideas that often shocked other women. There is no indication of how many women joined Lanteri and Abella de Ramírez in the League, but Lanteri was more than capable of maintaining the association by her own wits. The feminist freethinkers attended the 1910 First International Feminine Congress, but they left few traces thereafter.

The Left Organizes Women

Since the mid-1890s socialists and anarchists had been organizing and mobilizing the growing number of blue-collar workers in Argentina. Socialism and anarchism were introduced by the thousands of immigrants who arrived there in regular waves after the 1870s. In response to the growing number of women working for wages between 1890 and 1910, socialists and anarchists developed women's cadres to secure women's support for their organizations.

Although the Socialist Party had in principle accepted the equality of men and women since its formative days, it neither formulated any specific policy nor took any steps to pursue that goal until April 1902 to April 1903, when it supported the foundation of two associations for women, the Centro Socialista Femenino and the Unión Gremial Femenina. Both institutions were the brainchildren of Fenia (Sonia) Chertcoff, her sisters Mariana and Adela, and a few other budding socialist women.[21] Educating women in socialism was regarded as a worthwhile effort and certainly as necessary within the broader goals of the party, which then engaged in a political struggle with anarchists over control of the labor force.

The Centro Feminista organized special programs for children and mothers, but its tasks went beyond social work. Its leaders were politically aware women, and some of them emerged as natural leaders in the promotion and lobbying of legislation. Gabriela Laperrière de Coni was the intellectual author of the first law regulating women's and children's work, better known as Ley Alfredo Palacios for the Socialist deputy who presented it to the Chamber of Deputies.[22] After the enactment of the Palacios law, socialist women organized a committee to survey its enforcement. Later they organized support for striking workers and lobbied against the importation of alcoholic beverages and against direct taxation. The leaders of the Centro Socialista Femenino regarded themselves as feminists, a definition they had already accepted in 1903 and that in the 1910s would be fully developed by women like Alicia Moreau.[23]

The Unión Gremial and the Centro Socialista began their activities with the full support of the Socialist Party. In its Fifth Congress (May 1903) Fenia Chertcoff was seated as the only woman participant, and in August she was quickly appointed as a delegate to the National Party Council.[24] Another important sign of the new policy on women's issues was the inclusion of female speakers in the monthly lectures the party sponsored in its several centers. In 1903 Maria Ponti, Thomasa H. Cupayolo, and Sixta Montero emerged as able speakers. Ponti and Cupayolo shared the podium with men such as Alfredo Palacios, Antonio Zaccagni, and Enrique Dickmann. In May *La Vanguardia* remarked that Cupayolo's lecture at Belgrano on the principles of socialism was a happy promise of her future as a propagandist.[25] Women's attendance at these meetings was also taken as a sign that socialism was beginning to gain a foothold in the home. Judging by the detailed reporting of Sixta Montero's address in La Boca on 15 August—with four hundred persons of both sexes in attendance—some of the women scored a resounding success, much to the surprise of male commentators.

The female speakers used a message mixing women's liberation and socialist propaganda. Montero, for example, deplored women's subordination to men, especially the tyranny of the father at home and the education in submission women received in school and home alike. She blamed capitalism, urging women workers to unite and to join the Socialist Party, the best defender of working women's rights.[26] During its first year of existence (1904), Unión Gremial's activities were reported both in *La Vanguardia* and in the anarchist newspaper *La Protesta*.[27] Unión Gremial attempted to organize several groups of working women in resistance associations and targeted the employees of the garment industries, who had begun to show signs of willingness to strike. It seems that the anarchist competition significantly restricted the socialist propaganda, however. The anarchists were already on their guard against Unión Gremial by late 1904, reporting the socialists' "failure" among the female workers, who wanted to adhere strictly to the anarchist agenda.[28]

The split between anarchists and socialists increased with time and affected male and female workers alike. Although Unión Gremial was still alive in 1907, its activities remain obscure. Between 1904 and 1905 it was apparently the center of a power struggle between the two groups. A blurred report of this incident in *La Protesta* suggests that at the end of 1904 each group went its own way.[29] *La Vanguardia* privileged the activities of the Centro Socialista in its pages, and it remained the dominant socialist feminine association, continuing to sponsor activities on behalf of women and children workers and to support the party throughout the first three decades of the century. The party delegated women and children's issues to a small number of brilliant and committed women who rendered constant service to the socialist cause. After its tenth party congress in 1912, the socialists agreed to promote their ideology among working women through pamphlets and lectures, to make them aware of the rights and duties they had "agreed to by giving their energies, life, [and] the future of the race to benefit labor and industry." [30]

The Socialist Party used various means to strengthen its connections with some women workers' associations, such as the shoe textile workers, and tobacco workers.[31] In some instances party speakers addressed women's groups; in others *La Vanguardia* published articles denouncing working conditions in some plants. In 1913 Centro Socialista sponsored child-care services for working mothers—*recreos infantiles*—an idea credited to Fenia Chertcoff.[32] After 1915 she devoted much of her time to these and to children's education. Child care was very popular and in great demand, expanding throughout the years and receiving municipal subsidies from 1920 onward.[33] These were pragmatic answers to the needs of working women that socialists offered their followers as rewards.

The Socialist Party's position on women's rights took final shape by 1915 and did not change much thereafter. Men and women such as Palacios, Coni, Camaña, and Muzilli exalted the working woman and demanded special treatment and concessions because women were considered physically more vulnerable than men and their maternal role should not be endangered. This dichotomy was never resolved by either socialists or feminists. They regarded equal rights and protection as complementary and a fair solution to the demands made on women by industrialization and economic pressures, on the one hand, and home and the family on the other.[34]

After the passage of the 1912 male suffrage legislation, the possibility of greater political participation by the working class posed a new challenge for the socialists and became one of the party's high priorities. Several feminist women groups began arguing for an open discussion of female legal equality. Expanding the women's agenda could mean cutting back on topics of specific interest to working women. Alicia Moreau's was the voice of a new outlook on women's issues within the Left. Writing for *Revista Socialista Internacional* in 1911 as a young activist, Moreau saw suffrage as a right women had to struggle for. Skeptical of lawyers and of men in general, she was of the opinion that legislators were not initiators in reform movements: they supported reform when they had no other choice. Reform ideas had to take root in society before they received legal sanction. Women had to organize and work for suffrage.[35] Although socialist support for Centro Socialista Femenino was not undermined, socialist female leaders saw fit to join hands with nonsocialist feminist groups to pursue legal and political equality throughout the 1920s and 1930s. The internal split of the party after 1915, and the foundation of a Partido Socialista and a Partido Socialista Independiente, did not affect the individual socialist ideological commitment to women's causes. On that issue both wings of socialism followed paths already defined in the early years of the decade.

The Anarchist Approach

Between 1895 and 1920 anarchists had a healthy lead in the intense rivalry that developed between anarchists and socialists over organizing labor in Argentina.[36] Anarchists stood against the family as a bastion of bourgeois social control. Men and women were above all individuals, not members of a family. A strong anticlericalism added an extra dimension to anarchist struggle against the state and capitalism, making their approach to women workers politically explosive and liable to internal contradictions.

Anarchists first targeted women with their propaganda in the mid-1890s. *La Voz de la Mujer,* a newspaper directed by women, began publication in 1895, but hostility from male anarchists to the independent stance adopted by its women editors forced them to tone down their rhetoric. *La Voz de la Mujer* discussed personal and social sexual emancipation, family relations, and clerical domination. There was little discussion of the specific problems faced by working women, wages, female working conditions in Argentina, or politics beyond the ranks of labor.[37] The women anarchists of the period— Virginia Bolton, Teresa Marchisio, Irma Ciminaghi, and others—began to organize small groups of women anarchists, and it is probable that they wrote much of *La Voz de la Mujer.*[38]

By 1905 the anarchists had captured a sizable share of the budding labor movement in Argentina and had organized several female resistance societies. Domestic servants struck in 1888, and by 1900 female employees of the textile and garment industries began to use the political leverage provided by resistance and strikes. In 1901 the women of La Argentina, a shoe factory, struck for twenty days and planned to start a resistance society. Similar strikes were organized by washerwomen, telephone operators, shoe-factory employees, ironers, garment workers, and others, who used them to gain small raises in salaries and shorter working hours.[39]

The women who voiced the anarchist agenda in 1895 through *La Voz de la Mujer* tried to take advantage of this situation and establish alliances with female workers. Maxine Molyneux indicates that though anarchists welcomed women, they were not keen on complete female independence.[40]

After the demise of *La Voz de la Mujer,* writings on women found a place in *La Protesta Humana,* the main anarchist newspaper in Buenos Aires. Writings in *La Protesta* before 1901 used the image of the working woman in the factory as a springboard to discuss other issues.[41] Between 1900 and 1902 Pietro Gori supported prohibiting women's night work, and anarchists of the Argentine Workers' Federation voted to support equal pay for women and the organization of women workers.[42]

The attention *La Protesta* paid to women's activities reflected a realization of their new role in society and helped create a favorable climate for the discussion of issues related to their welfare. In 1903 anarchist-dominated Federación Obrera Argentina (FOA) had one woman among the eighty delegates and included the regulation of women's and children's labor on its agenda. At its fourth congress (1904) FOA received delegations from male and female ironers. This congress discussed the "moralization and emancipation" of women, mostly the problem of prostitution. The organization stood by the concept of restricting night work for women and children.[43]

Federación Obrera Regional Argentina (FORA), successor to FOA, counted a woman representative, Juana Rouco Buela, a Spanish immigrant and staunch anarchist. In 1907 the Primer Centro Femenino Anarquista was founded in Buenos Aires with nineteen members.[44] Anarchists made important gains among angry but as yet politically untrained women. *La Protesta* printed information on their meetings and published numerous articles denouncing their working conditions, long working hours, and meager wages. When the shirtmakers of several factories went on strike in November 1904, *La Protesta* praised "the spontaneous rebellion that is so beautiful in women whose rights have been trampled upon."[45]

News of female workers' participation in the 1904 strikes organized by tailors, ironers, and telephone operators moved to the front page of *La Protesta,* and on 8 December their role was discussed at length by an anonymous writer — possibly editor Alberto Guiraldo. He welcomed their endeavors as a sign of growing mental and social liberation and a prerequisite for the advent of social revolution. However, he thought that their participation had not been completely effective. He considered that the women had shown poor organization and lack of decisiveness and attributed this problem to their lack of experience.[46] Criticized on the following day for his apparently derisive comments, the writer quickly disclaimed any desire to dismiss their efforts, which he described as a "true feminist advent," deserving direction and support.[47]

After 1910 anarchist women repudiated feminism and socialism and refused to discuss women's suffrage or any bill proposing to regulate child and women's labor. In the early 1920s the presence of other than working-class women in the labor market posed important questions to anarchists, who answered in an ideological manner. An anarchist writer accused feminism of having created a serious problem for which society was not yet ready: how to combine a career outside the home with the traditional responsibilities of motherhood. Engaged in the dismissal of bourgeois or "reformist" ideas, anarchists continued to rely on the formula of individual freedom over socialist reform. In 1918 María Rotella, a hard-core anarchist, angrily rejected the idea of founding an anarchist feminine center, arguing that the idea was "ridiculous" and "counterproductive." Anarchism did not foster any special female niches.[48]

The founding in 1922 in Necochea of an anarchist newspaper directed by Juana Rouco Buela ran against anarchist ideology and was criticized by the Buenos Aires core. She defended the newspaper, stating that women would become more deeply committed and personally engaged in social reform if they had a publication of their own. Her critics considered the publication contrary to the anarchist principle of nonseparation of genders in all social activities.[49] Anarchists never found a formula to adapt themselves to women's changing social and economic roles. They repeated strategies and slogans more suitable to the conditions of labor at the beginning of the century than in the mid-1920s. Their denial of the need to identify and define issues specific to the female sex in a period of growing sensitivity to women's problems suggests a politically unwise rigidity. Their approach to the liberation of both sexes from the ties of sexual, religious, and state repression involved an uncomfortable juxtaposition of the concepts of individual freedom with the complementary of the sexes that led them into an ideological cul-de-sac.[50]

The High Years of the Suffragist Campaign, 1919–1932

The adoption of universal male suffrage in 1912 signaled the beginning of a period of political democratization in Argentina that lasted another eighteen years. During this period feminism and the civil and political emancipation of women were thoroughly debated by both men and women. Unlike Uruguay, where two main parties dominated the political arena, in Argentina political life was fragmented and tempestuous. No major party excepting the Socialists declared for female suffrage immediately after 1912. Some remembered that in 1862 San Juan, capital city of the western province of the same name, had a municipal organic law that made no gender distinctions in

defining voters. Voters were taxpayers with property and professional qualifications. To be elected, a person had to be over twenty-two years of age,
literate, and a property owner or a professional with a minimum income.
The vote had been used in a very discreet manner by a few women, and San
Juan had no imitators elsewhere.[51]

Municipal and national suffrage were the options in Argentina, and both
formulas were tried in numerous bills for nearly three decades after 1916,
when universal male suffrage was first exercised. In that year Francisco
Correa, a member of the Demócrata Progresista Party, introduced a bill
for female municipal enfranchisement. It restricted the vote to native-born
women who controlled their own property. Given that the Civil Code put
married women under their husbands' tutelage for the administration of
their possessions, the result would have been suffrage for a limited number
of single or widowed women. The bill denied women the right to be elected
and openly aimed at minimizing the participation of naturalized women to
maintain the advantage of male Argentines. The inclusion of women in the
electoral process was regarded as a political rehearsal. Expecting few risks
under the prescribed premises, the bill was a gentleman's gesture toward
women but reserved the political plums for men. When the municipal election law for Buenos Aires was approved in August 1917, the national Chamber of Deputies entertained the idea of enfranchising women, but the lack
of a quorum defeated this attempt.[52]

The end of World War I heralded a new period of political restless-
ness among urban Argentines. The climate was propitious for testing new
ground. The feasibility of female suffrage was reinforced by the news of
women's activities in World War I and by the ongoing debate in the United
States, England, and France. Opinions varied from unconditional support
to tenacious opposition, but the precondition of education and preparation
for suffrage lingered in the minds of many who paid lip service to the concept but preferred to see it tested elsewhere.[53] To the conservatives women's
suffrage was unnecessary. Sustained by fervent nationalism and elitism, they
continued to regard women as mothers and wives at home and regretted the
weakening of Argentine society by alien influences.[54]

Before women could become voters, however, a key technical problem
had to be resolved. Citizenship was defined by eligibility for suffrage, and in
Argentina citizens were obliged to register for military service. Since women
did not qualify for military service, how could they be citizens?[55] Most suffragists decided to ignore the issue and went ahead campaigning and organizing their own groups, but one woman decided to test the waters. It was

Dra. Julieta Lanteri's mission to shake the legal restrictions on citizenship, the first step to challenging suffrage restriction itself. Born in Italy in 1873, she had lived most of her life in Buenos Aires and was married to an Argentine. As such she was entitled to request naturalization. Up to the early 1900s a few foreign women had been naturalized, but her case caused a flurry among jurists and feminists. Appointed a lecturer in the Faculty of Medicine, Lanteri had to be a citizen to accept the post, and since a citizen was a person entitled to vote, she requested that right. Her case was reviewed by a federal judge, whose decision was emblematic of the period, a mixture of straight interpretation of the law and traditional social mores. The judicial decision, confirmed by the federal capital deputies, challenged the assumption that female citizens were not entitled to vote. The constitution made no distinction between the sexes in the definition of rights and liberty guaranteed to all human beings. Those rights derived from the sovereignty of the people and the republican form of government. Women had become the equals of men and were just as vital to the future of Argentina. Therefore their cooperation could not be ignored, and their capacity to become active in the management of public interests could not be denied. He had the duty to declare that "their right to citizenship is consecrated in the constitution and therefore women have, in principle, the same political rights of male citizens."

Having gone this far, the judge qualified his boldness. In practice such rights were subordinated to cultural factors, though the latter were also subject to change. The denial of political rights to Argentine women was based on old legal doctrines adopted by the writers of the Civil Code as an expression of their times, but the feeling of nationality and love for the motherland was a "natural and subjective phenomenon" that women shared with men. In fact he thought that, as mothers and as teachers, women already exercised the highest political rights when they taught children to love the motherland and discharge their rights and duties as citizens. This judicial decision was corroborated in 1921 by federal attorney Horacio Rodríguez Larreta, who cited article 20 of the Constitution and an 1869 law prescribing the requirements for citizenship. There was no limitation by sex in either one, and Julieta Lanteri was simply exercising a right guaranteed by the Constitution. Nationality and citizenship were indistinctly used there, but it was assumed that citizenship implied a number of rights and duties legislated a posteriori.[56] After this crucial clarification supporters of female suffrage knew its enactment depended entirely on the will of Congress to change the electoral laws. It was also the benchmark on which male and female feminists were to base their arguments in favor of suffrage for the next quarter of a century.

Julieta Lanteri, as an indefatigable activist, had no intention of stopping her campaign for suffrage. After receiving her citizenship she requested military induction so as to become fully enfranchised. It was denied then and again in 1927, when she requested it before the federal justice in the city of La Plata. Her lawyers argued that male citizens exempted from military service for a variety of reasons did not lose their right to vote but could not make the judge see that point. Lanteri took her case all the way to the Supreme Court, which refused to give an opinion, arguing that such matters were not within its realm.[57] While Julieta Lanteri pursued a legal resolution of her case, suffragists and activists of both sexes founded women's groups for suffrage and other social causes, mostly under the feminist banner, and mostly understood as having a "political" meaning. The Socialist Party took the initiative by founding the Unión Feminista Nacional, headed by Dra. Alicia Moreau, in October 1918. Since no organization could effectively reach the public without its own journal, Unión Feminista Nacional began publishing *Nuestra Causa* in May 1919. It ran for over two years, rapidly becoming the privileged forum for all feminists supporting suffrage.[58] In 1919 Elvira Rawson de Dellepiane founded the Asociación Pro-Derechos de la Mujer to promote changes in the legal system and address the issue of women's civil and political rights. One of its members was Radical Party deputy Rogelio Araya, who put his influence in Congress at the service of the association's goals. The Radical Party was then in power, but President Hipólito Yrigoyen showed no interest in women's suffrage.[59] On a different front, Blanca C. de Hume organized the Comité Femenino de Higiene Social to spread the principles of the International Abolitionist Federation, which sought to deregulate prostitution and end the double standard of morality. As Argentina and Uruguay began to cooperate in a public campaign against prostitution, Dra. Petrona Eyle became president of the Argentine branch, the Asociación Argentina contra la Trata de Blancas, a position she held through 1928.[60] She was *Nuestra Causa*'s director for a short time. In this political scenario Julieta Lanteri founded her Partido Feminista Nacional, and journalist Adelia de Carlo founded the Partido Humanista, with a sixteen-point program of legal and political reform.[61] All these organizations were the pillars of socially oriented feminism in Buenos Aires.

Partido Humanista's program contained all the essentials of feminism: social, economic, and political emancipation to guarantee women autonomy in administering their property, equality in control over their children, equal responsibility in adultery cases, and other points considered prerequisites to achieve full stature as citizens.[62] Julieta Lanteri's Partido Feminista Nacional was organized to challenge the political system and to participate in the election trial to be carried out by women on 7 March 1920, as described below. The first objective was carried out by repeating Lanteri's request for military registration for herself and several of the party members on 2 August 1919. They were rejected by the registry's employees because they lacked authorization from their superiors. Lanteri had an interview with the war minister, who turned her petition down.[63] Despite the official rejection, Lanteri's party received support from some quarters. *La Razón* of Buenos Aires gave it a warm welcome.[64]

The party platform, published by *La Prensa* in October 1920 when Lanteri was running for a council seat, advocated suppressing all municipal taxes and establishing a single progressive land tax. It also proposed public and welfare services such as cheap and safe housing, price regulation of consumer products, equal pay for both sexes, expansion of educational and recreational services, creation of municipal health services for infectious diseases, child care, communal kitchens for the poor, homes for old people, and the abolition of regulated prostitution. It was the kind of program that embraced all needs and dispensed solutions for all urban problems.[65]

The first generation of feminists—those born in the last twenty years of the nineteenth century—led this incursion into the public arena, interacting among themselves, sharing activities, exchanging idea, and thus helping to shape a new cohort of women activists while defining the parameters of feminist social reform. There was considerable cooperation and cross-fertilization of ideas. Comité Femenino de Higiene Social inaugurated its activities with a lecture on standards of morality delivered on 24 April 1920 by Elvira Rawson de Dellepiane. Article 5 of the Asociación Pro-Derechos de la Mujer endorsed the end of regulated prostitution, the special concern of Hume's organization. Blanca C. de Hume was given space in *Nuestra Causa*, which also published the platform and activities of Lanteri's Partido Feminista Nacional. Poet Adela García Salaberry was secretary of the party, and in March 1920 she replaced Petrona Eyle as director of *Nuestra Causa*.[66] This magazine recorded a generous camaraderie and sharing of interests throughout its two years of publication that spoke well of the cohesion of women in these early years of activism.[67]

Although suffrage was not the feminist organizations' only concern, they were willing to use all means to press politicians and political parties on real universal suffrage. Alicia Moreau took the initiative. In October 1919 she attended the International Workers' Congress in Washington, D.C., and an International Congress of Women Physicians in New York.[68] There she became acquainted with Carrie Chapman Catt and the National Suffrage Association. Moreau, already a firm believer in social and personal equality before her trip to the United States, returned convinced that a campaign to promote suffrage in Argentina was worthwhile and founded the Comité Pro-Sufragio Femenino. The committee would carry out a mock election for women with the cooperation of the Partido Feminista Nacional. To bolster the women's effort and the concept of female candidates, the Socialist Party included a woman candidate on its official list, Alcira Riglos de Berón de Astrada.

Blanca C. de Hume, Petrona Eyle, Emma Day, Elvira Rawson de Dellepiane, Adela García Salaberry, and others acted as presidents of several voting sections and as vote counters. Comité Pro-Sufragio Femenino urged women of all social classes to vote, stating that "all women have interests to defend and rights to affirm." According to *La Prensa* and *La Vanguardia*, 161,144 men voted in the 1920 municipal elections, 72.6 percent of the 222,230 registered to vote. Over 4,000 women voted in the mock election. The Socialist Party carried the day. Although the final count was confusing, the socialists had 1,912 votes as of 10 March, while Julieta Lanteri won 1,300 — or 1,730 — according to a contemporary source, and the Radical Party polled nearly 700. For three weeks before the election Lanteri campaigned vigorously; she was confident she would obtain at least 4,500 votes, and four times that number as time passed and women became accustomed to voting. Although the results of the vote did not come close to her expectations, she received almost as many votes as some male candidates.[69]

Radical Party deputy Rogelio Araya, true to his commitment to women's suffrage, submitted a bill on 25 July 1919. He proposed to modify the article on political rights—which referred specifically to male Argentines eighteen years old and over—to add "women twenty-two years and over." Article 1 of the electoral law would be similarly rewritten. Araya argued that women's suffrage was no longer a "utopian" reform but a recognized right in several countries. He underlined the qualities he believed made women not just as apt for suffrage as men, but better qualified. Women had greater social responsibility and ethical integrity, demonstrated by their considerably lower crime rate. Adding to that their role as pillars of the family, one could expect nothing short of a marked improvement of moral values in politics with their enfranchisement.[70] The difference in voting age was not explained, but it followed common belief that women needed preparation for voting. Feminists groups raised no objection at the time.

Feminists lobbied men at several levels, always peacefully and courteously, through signed documents in which they carefully explained their demands and their solutions to existing problems. Their endeavors in the early 1920s suggest a strong drive to disseminate their viewpoint and earn recognition and approval from men and women alike. Unión Feminista Nacional, for example, organized well-attended artistic and literary evenings in which women such as Alfonsina Storni and Socialist senator Enrique del Valle Iberlucea spoke on women's inequalities before the law.[71] Another form of lobbying was to submit to deputies petitions signed by thousands of women. In April 1920 Unión Feminista Nacional gathered 7,000 signatures to support Del Valle Iberlucea's bill to reform the Civil Code.[72] Also in that year Unión Feminista Nacional wrote to the president of the Buenos Aires municipal council in support of a proposed municipal suffrage bill. The letter asked that all women be included, without any privileges. A commission headed by Alicia Moreau paid a visit to several councilors, who promised their cooperation.[73] The bill was not approved, but women lost neither interest nor zeal.

In June 1920 Unión Feminista Nacional and Comité Pro-Sufragio Femenino reelected Alicia Moreau and Adela García Salaberry and decided to repeat the March suffrage exercise by voting for the municipal candidates of the established political parties. The second voting exercise was set for 20 November 1920, and in the ensuing months speakers and writers addressed the issues of women's political and civil rights in preparation for the event.[74] The two organizations supported the Partido Feminista Nacional and its candidate Julieta Lanteri, who was again running as an unofficial candidate. In preparation for the November municipal election, Lanteri developed a platform that received space in the best-known national daily news media.[75] She was again denied official recognition of her candidacy, because she was not registered in any electoral list and was not an "elector."[76] The elections took place on 20 November, the same day as elections for municipal councils. The voting tables for women were staffed from 8 A.M. to 6 P.M. Women of all ages and nationalities were encouraged to vote. La Vanguardia asked the voters to sign two petitions after voting. One was addressed to the Chamber of Deputies, urging approval of the reform of the Civil Code. The other was addressed to the Senate and requested municipal suffrage for women. The feminists were willing to settle for that.[77]

The mock voting was explained by Julia G. Games as "education and moral preparation" for voting.[78] Political engagement was a consequence of suffrage, not vice versa. Voting to learn how to vote was a twist in the logic of suffrage. Alicia Moreau explained that the mock vote would oblige women to think about suffrage.[79] Unión Feminista made ample use of posters spelling out its demands: suffrage to struggle against sexism, bad taxes, vice, gambling, alcoholism, and infectious diseases.[80] A suffrage exercise also demanded a defense of its compatibility with the home and femininity. A *lady,* wrote A. Capocci in *Nuestra Causa,* can be a suffragist and a leader as well. She used Elvira Rawson de Dellepiane as an example of a "woman with talent, with admirable feminist capabilities, a mother and an austere matron in an honorable home." A feminist could be chic; feminism did not make any woman ugly. "In Argentina feminism is on the right track of seriousness, exquisite tact, and culture." Despite this compliance with femininity, the commitment to the cause was reaffirmed: "Suffrage is not feminism, but without the vote feminism dies."[81]

The results of the women's election were not published in the main city newspapers, but one source quoted 5,914 voters. The journalistic nature of the suffrage debate encouraged the expression of opinions in a capital that prided itself on high literacy rates and an energetic press. Santa Fé Province was going ahead with a constitutional reform (approved in 1921) to confirm female suffrage that kindled the hopes of feminists in Buenos Aires.[82] An informal poll in the form of interviews with notable male and female intellectuals was published in 1921. It confirmed the expected dissent and support, as well as nuances in personal interpretation. There was a fascinating diversity of opinions, many revealing lingering masculine reservations about female suffrage. A. Orzábal de la Quintana, for example, argued that "true respect" for women could not be achieved without legal equality. The respect and honor suffrage conferred on women would trigger their self-confidence. Only in such circumstances could they exercise their fullest influence on society.[83] This "friendly" opinion dismissed the self-confidence women had demonstrated up to that point and assumed that women's inferiority feelings were rooted in the legal denial of their ability so that a change in social structure would inevitably lead to intellectual and emotional change. In this picture women were passive receivers of actions beyond their power who would react positively to favorable incentives.

Another interesting opinion was that of Rodolfo Senet, who attempted to balance end of the century deterministic psychological and somatic theories with the potential political virtues they could allow. Assuming an elitist interpretation, Senet derided ignorant people who believed in the psychological equality of men and women. Surely no sane person could believe such aberration. Male and female had complementary but different capabilities; gender comparisons made no sense. Some women, unfortunately, had become infected with the idea of equality and were unwilling to accept that men had "a creative imagination of greater scope." Even if women were fully educated they would never catch up with men in some fields unless men remained stationary. How could gender differences be turned into an asset? Senet's believed the answer lay in the affirmative use of women's richly emotional and affective nature. "A female electorate would triumph in all cultivated communities because there was a need to introduce [women's] moral factor as an . . . inhibiting factor, to regulate the impulses of masculine intellectuality."[84] Mothers were necessary in the government of the family, and communities ruled exclusively by men were "orphan" societies. Senet was unsure what the future would bring when the female electorate began to exercise its rights, but he would not stop the process. He only hoped that the maternal functioning of women in society would not deprive their own families.

Senet represented the response of men who would surrender their primacy in society, but not without making it clear that men remained intellectually superior and that women's contribution was largely to make society less virile, saving men from themselves. Close to Senet's reasoning was that of José Bianco, a journalist and suffrage supporter who published several articles on feminism between 1916 and 1927, portraying the sexes as different but complementary. As long as women did not betray their "biological physiognomy" and claimed moral and juridical — not physical — equality, he would support their cause. He was an advocate of female economic independence but believed that feminism masculinized women.[85] Other men backed the idea of separate spheres of activity based on the genders' different aptitudes.[86] Since these same arguments could easily be used to oppose women's suffrage, their ambiguous message reflects the reluctance with which influential Argentines contemplated suffrage in the 1920s and the 1930s. Traditionalism and conservatism were making an ideological return in the mid-1920s and remained an important obstacle.[87]

With great perspicacity, Alicia Moreau defined the reluctant male in 1921. She used a literary work, *Divertidas aventuras de un nieto de Juan Moreyra* by Carlos Payrós, to analyze male response to feminism in Argentina. The descendants of Juan Moreyra, she claimed, were successful politicians who retained a hatred for culture and expected women to be submissive. They could not accept independent and cultivated women and preferred to patronize women rather than allowing them to become free through just legislation. She remembered her own experience as a member of female committees, visiting deputies to seek their support for reform of the Civil Code. As soon as the women spoke of the law, she said, men's smiles disappeared. Women could expect nothing from such traditionalists: they should "sweep them away."[88]

Throughout 1920 and 1921, Unión Feminista Nacional held meetings en-livened by films and lectures on the meaning of feminism and planned an antialcohol campaign. This was not a large organization. By April 1921 it had forty members, but this small membership worked hard to establish and maintain contacts with international associations for women's suffrage.[89] In July 1922 a conservative bill by Juan José Frugoni proposed the vote for women over twenty years of age holding a diploma from a secondary school or higher. Frugoni considered it "iniquity" to deny the vote to educated women while alcoholic, illiterate, and homeless males "converted elections in political bacchanals in which democracy played the role of a "vulgar pros-titute."[90] His bill was not acted on.

Such was the situation of suffragists and suffrage in the early 1920s. The 1923 Fifth Pan-American Conference had recommended a study of the fea-sibility of women's civil and political equality, and Radical Party deputy Leopoldo Bard assumed the task of reviving of the issue of political rights.[91] His 1925 bill was very similar to Rogelio Araya's 1916 project in that men would gain political rights at age eighteen and women at age twenty-two, but Bard's bill included both native and naturalized men and women.[92] Bard maintained that approval of his bill would be a sign of Argentina's cultural and social capability and rebutted the argument that suffrage would de-stroy the family by using examples of countries where it had already been adopted. He also dismissed the fear of clerical influence over female voters as irrelevant. On the other hand, he did not believe in inflated expectations that better legislation would result from women's political activities. Simply put, social evolution led to an intellectual leveling of the sexes and a new reality. Many Argentine males, he added wistfully, ignored the ability of their own women while making ample display of their own lack. Bard quoted in full Enrique del Valle Iberlucea's 1919 defense of women's suffrage and cited the arguments of Uruguayan statesman Baltasar Brum and the opinions ex-pressed in Miguel Font's published poll of notable Argentines. His bill was shelved and disregarded as others had been.

In 1926 the much awaited and discussed reform of the Civil Code was ac-complished. The recognition of new civil rights for women was a concession many deputies agreed to as the lesser of two evils. Suffrage was not neces-sarily more palatable or more feasible after the broadening of civil rights. The Radical Party, which had controlled the administration since 1918, was bitterly divided over its leadership and was in no condition to rally behind women's suffrage. Party members interested in social change put their efforts behind welfare legislation, an acceptable and desirable political asset less threatening than suffrage. Conservatives and nationalists viewed suffrage as a corroding influence on womanhood and the home. Even among those who favored it there were differences of opinion on how extensive it should be.[93] Women's suffrage fought an uphill battle, given the rising expectations of feminists and the increasing resistance of traditionalists of both sexes.[94]

In November 1928 the Third International Feminine Congress took place in Buenos Aires, with Elvira Rawson de Dellepiane as president and Paulina Luisi in attendance. They gave the keynote addresses and set the tone of the meeting, which focused on women's multiple social roles and the main social problems they could help solve. The participants spoke on child care, alcoholism, prenuptial certificates, eugenic sterilization, schools of social service, movies for children, women's prison reform, peace, literature, and North American imperialism. The feminist agenda was full of current social concerns, but in their opening statements Rawson de Dellepiane and Luisi reminded the audience of the past years of struggle and of the rooted prejudice "against any feminist statement." They were realistic about how much further they still had to go before their demands were met. Rawson de Dellepiane and Peruvian delegate María Ramírez de Vidal read papers on suffrage on 4 December and obtained the public endorsement of women's vote by the congress.[95] This was a feminist congress, not a suffragist one, and the reaffirmation of its ideological stand was the only action it could take. In the meantime, in the province of San Juan, under a new constitution women voted in the provincial elections of 28 April 1928.

Suffrage continued to be feminism's acid test in the ensuing years. Jurist Juan Carlos Rébora, in a study of the effects of removing women's civil disabilities from the Civil Code, concluded that by assuming occupations that legally required citizenship, women had already become "legal" citizens and thus were entitled to vote.[96] In Uruguay, a country closely watched by Argentines, the Alliance for Feminine Suffrage renewed its campaign for suffrage in 1929. New Argentine suffrage bills were not long in materializing. On 11 September 1929, Deputy José María Bustillo introduced one that required voters to be literate. The bill defined who could vote and left it up to women whether to register.[97] This compromise would have pleased many who sat on the fence of women's political rights, but it was not satisfactory for militant feminists, who regarded any qualification as a surrender to traditionality.

Socialist senator Mario Bravo presented yet another bill only a few days after Bustillo's. He proposed enfranchising all women and dismissing the literacy qualification. Bravo regarded suffrage as a natural right already proved to be beneficial to society, as the experience of European countries demonstrated. As voters women would be the protectors of home and family life, of children and the aged, and upholders of public morality.[98] Bravo's bill was not acted on. In 1929 Argentina was on the eve of a political crisis that would unleash the forces of conservatism and militarism during the following decade. Feminists and socialists, as supporters of world peace since the early 1920s, understood that the vote could enable them to protest growing worldwide militarism.[99] The second Yrigoyen administration was coming to a political standstill worsened by declining foreign trade and worldwide economic depression. On 6 September 1930 a military coup led by the conservative general José F. Uriburu put an abrupt end to elected government. Between September 1930 and November 1931, when elections were held to restore the nation to political order, there was an intense power struggle between traditional civilian and army nationalist leaders, conservative liberals, and the deposed Radical Party. This situation was resolved with the election of a "liberal" general, Agustín P. Justo in 1931, and the early death of General Uriburu. However, the ensuing years were dominated by conservative politics, worsened by the absence of the Radical Party from the polls. Politics was sustained by a coalition of several small parties and the conservative leadership.

Against that uninspiring and sometimes depressing backdrop, feminists continued to call for suffrage, which they hoped would be the crowning act of many years of preparation and propaganda. The tantalizing appeal of a victory against traditional forces seemed to incite the feminist groups. In 1930 two organizations were founded to promote suffrage, the Comité Socialista Pro-Sufragio Femenino, and the Comité Pro-Voto de la Mujer. The socialist group leaned strongly on staunch feminists such as Alicia Moreau de Justo, who broadcast some of her essays. Speaking in October 1930, just after the deposing of President Yrigoyen, she bemoaned the misuse of male universal suffrage, pinning her hopes on a better use of the vote by women.[100] The second organization, Comité Pro-Voto de la Mujer, was organized by Carmela Horne de Burmeister on 1 July 1930, two months before the military coup. It had as its motto *Patria y Caridad* [Motherland and Charity], which read like a throwback to the spirit of the early 1900s but clearly implied an alignment with traditionalist forces. Acknowledging the work of past feminists, the founder expressed her disappointment at the slow progress toward suffrage and explained her decision to organize a campaign to "prepare Argentine women to form a great feminist party to defend the interests of the nation and to struggle for the protection of women and children, independent of any political party."[101] Sometime in 1932 the committee changed its name to Asociación Argentina del Sufragio Femenino and reiterated its purpose to promote suffrage, prepare women to understand the meaning of equality, carry out a "discreet and convincing campaign" to put an end to ignorance and indifference, and convince all people that equality before the law did not affect women's femininity. The association also proposed to promote welfare institutions, monitor women's and children's workplaces, and establish ties with other women's groups. Once women's suffrage was achieved the association would support candidates who worked for the consolidation of democracy. The association defined itself as moderate, not a "hotheaded, disturbing, ignorant, or impulsive feminist" group. It would always bear the seal of "the highest culture and the most sublime goodness."[102]

The original committee claimed to be inclusive of all women, but its leadership was obviously middle class and conservative. In 1932 Monsignor Gustavo J. Franceschi and Deputy José María Bustillo lent the association their support. Horne de Burmeister was an adroit organizer, and within a year she had established provincial committees in Mendoza, Buenos Aires, Corrientes, and Catamarca, recruited socialist speakers Alicia Moreau, Juana María Beguino, and Victoria Gucovsky, and introduced feminist activism to women such as Silvia Saavedra Lamas, an upper-class Catholic. This was a traditionalist and at times patronizing feminist association. Women, it maintained, were capable and responsible and would be a moderating force in society, working to relieve the "difficulties and misery of our people."

Despite a split in the Socialist Party, socialism was strong enough in the early 1930s to sustain smaller socialist women's groups (Agrupaciones Femeninas Socialistas and Centro Socialista Femenino). It is unclear which of the socialist factions these female organizations belonged to. In June 1931 *Mujer!* appeared, a short-lived socialist magazine "at the service of women's cause."[103] In November 1931, on the eve of elections to restore political normality, *Mujer!* published a socialist organizations' statement urging men not to waste their votes and criticizing the Radical Party for its split into two factions—one supporting and one rejecting deposed president Yrigoyen. People should stop relying on "providential men." *Mujer!* urged men to return the government to civilians; Argentina needed fewer arms and more books.[104] Argentina did not return to civilian rule until 1936, but after the election of General Juan B. Justo neither socialists nor feminists had any objection to participating in politics. The campaign for suffrage sailed at full speed alongside bills for absolute divorce.

The Suffrage Legislation: Disappointment and Long Hopes

The stabilization of politics allowed women's suffrage to regain its momentum. In 1932 two socialist factions submitted suffrage bills. One was under the care of Fernando de Andreis, the other under Silvio L. Ruggieri. In May the socialist women's suffrage committee stepped up its campaign, although it could not match Carmela Horne's organization. Radio, used for talks on suffrage and other issues, was capable of reaching thousands of women. Perhaps this explains the thousands of signatures in support of suffrage that Asociación Argentina del Sufragio was able to present to the Deputies. By September 1932 Horne claimed 166,532 signatures.

The parliamentary sessions began in May 1932, and women's vote was placed on the calendar. At the parliamentary opening ceremony, Horne's organization distributed 30,000 fliers, and on 3 May the Asociación Argentina del Sufragio Femenino presented the Deputies a request for suffrage with over 10,000 signatures. At this point the association endorsed suffrage for native-born literate Argentine women twenty-two years of age. Naturalized women with long residence in Argentina and their children born in Argentina would also qualify. The association argued that the desire to vote would stimulate illiterate women to learn to read. Those who did not learn showed they had no interest in politics. The association also chose to favor suffrage over divorce, then under discussion. The endorsement of suffrage restrictions and the opposition to divorce betrayed the conservatism and nationalism of this group.[105]

While the parliamentary debate on national suffrage was taking place, a new bill for municipal suffrage was introduced on 8 June 1932, reviving the terms of the 1922 proposal.[106] Procedural considerations limped along in the municipality, while the significant debate took place in Congress. There women's suffrage swept through the rank and file with unexpected force. On 4 August 1932 the parliamentary commission studying the project recommended full debate of a bill granting suffrage to all Argentine women at age eighteen regardless of literacy and eliminating military conscription. Suffrage was defined as a compulsory duty. The bill proposed to begin registering women between March and April 1933. This truly liberal and sweeping bill took note of previous proposed restrictions and carefully eliminated them.[107] In preparation for the discussion of the bill women supporters gave press conferences and political parties took official positions.[108]

The bill was debated on 15 and 16 September. Deputies in favor of suffrage delivered enthusiastic paeans to women, some of them recanting past doubts. Women would be the crux of an ascending movement for Argentina, claimed Socialist deputy Fernando de Andreis, but conservative deputy José Bustillo persisted in wanting to see suffrage as a qualified exercise until its success could be verified. Deputy J. I. Aráoz sided with him in not supporting compulsory suffrage, arguing that nothing could be gained by forcing those who did not want to vote. Furthermore, he expressed his own distaste about seeing his own wife and daughters forming part of a political committee in the future. In making his case for voluntary suffrage Bustillo stated that the legislation under consideration "was not the fruit of any active movement, but spontaneous act of the legislators wishing to improve democracy." Deputy Uriburu resurrected the threat to the home and male authority and followed Bustillo in believing there was no collective desire for suffrage in Argentina. He expressed the traditional view that there was no need to import an alien law without considering the nation's "moral and social climate." Bustillo and Uriburu ignored the years of discussion, organization of groups, and propaganda carried out by organizations and individuals. Their remarks show that some men either were not listening or chose to ignore a feminist sentiment evident since the early years of the century, as well as the more recent surge. The denial of their existence was a bitter comment for feminists, but other deputies mended fences by acknowledging the feminist movement in Argentina.

Socialist Ruggieri praised his party for advocating women's political rights and noted that the legislation had been accomplished without social violence. At the end of his speech women following the debate approved noisily and were threatened with eviction by the president of the Chamber of Deputies. Their voices refuted Bustillo's statements about their "nonexistence." Socialist Enrique Dickmann also made a spirited defense of suffrage, recognizing the maturity of Argentine women and their aptitude for participating in politics. He expected an improvement in the quality of politics because of female intervention. Nonetheless, his expectations focused on traditional tasks such as municipal administration, legislation for children, education, hospitals, and labor. Other deputies shared these ideas. After two days of debates the legislation was approved on 17 September 1932, earning a round of applause from the deputies and the spectators.

The discussion of female suffrage received extensive press coverage. After its passage, conservative La Prensa commented that "suffrage did not answer the . . . general and unequivocal opinions and sentiments of Argentine women, strangers up to now to the excitement of politics." The ideological influence of foreign examples was blamed for the decision. Like the conservatives in the chambers, the newspaper gave no recognition to Argentine feminists and suffragists, stating that "one or another isolated movement without repercussions cannot be judged an appreciable manifestation of feminism among us." The editorialist opined that suffrage would cause perplexity and confusion among women "lacking information or interest concerning public affairs." A "secular tradition" made the political practice of illiterate men less dangerous because men were accustomed to listening and thinking about politics.[109] These disparaging comments reflected the unspoken feelings of many opponents and the undercurrent of resentment that help to explain the bill's neglect in the Senate.

The suffrage bill required Senate approval, and supporters knew that the moral victory achieved in the Chamber of Deputies did not guarantee success among its more intractable conservative members. The senatorial committee in charge of moving the debate on the bill demurred; the majority preferred to study the project before making a decision. On 20 September fourteen senators voted against a debate and eight voted in favor. The bill was shelved until the next session to study costs of implementation and was never recalled for debate.[110] On 25 September disappointed women answered the call of Alianza Femenina del Sufragio Universal and Asociación Pro-Derechos de la Mujer and gathered in front of the Congress building. After one speaker recalled the tenacity of Dra. Julieta Lanteri, already dead, Elvira Rawson de Dellepiane reaffirmed the principles of Argentine feminism and suffragism in an emotional statement:

> The desire to reclaim rights that should have never been denied was not the only reason drawing us into this crusade. The incentives behind our unequivocal and persistent struggle were many, to wit: the almost complete obliviousness to social problems of vital importance of legislators and the government; the sad fate of abandoned mothers and fatherless children; the precarious and inferior economic situation of women who work for a living; social attitudes that denigrate [women's] actions and values; the vexatious and inhuman dependency imposed on them under hybrid and maliciously conceived laws; the gag applied to all their expressions and enthusiasm as citizens; the always growing spectacle of a brand of politics dangerous for the organization and stability of the country; the increasing neglect of citizen's virtues and duties by a great number of men who placed their personal ambitions and bastard party interests before the interest of the nation.[111]

The compelling drive for serving the nation through suffrage was frustrated, but it spurred the formation of new women's groups committed to that goal. Agrupación Nacional Femenina pledged to help create a strong civic atmosphere and support the best politicians. It planned to take a greater interest in agricultural and rural problems, work for the reduction of several vexing taxes, and carry on a campaign for the propagation of cooperativism.[112] The inclusion of goals not directly related to welfare and motherhood — such as taxation and development of resources — indicates a desire to inject themes of national interest and demonstrate their capacity to discuss them. The Asociación Argentina del Sufragio Femenino became the Partido Argentino Feminista at the end of 1935. By that time it had a branch in La Plata and had organized a series of conferences on women and female suffrage. Its objective was to enable women to elect their own representatives, as "a purely feminine renovating and regulating force."[113]

Between 1933 and 1935 women's organizations pursued a variety of feminist and women's goals. Asociación Cultural Clorinda Matto de Turner, founded by journalist Adelia de Carlo, and Alianza Femenina Pro-Paz were intellectual and pacifist associations respectively. Other names recorded during 1933 were Agrupación Nacional Femenina, Círculo Argentino Pro-Paz, Liga Femenina Pro-Paz del Chaco, and Confederación Femenina Argentina.[114] *Mujeres de América*, a monthly magazine, began publication in 1933 and welcomed writings of women from several countries on women's rights, suffrage, Pan-Americanism, peace, literature, and social prophylaxis. It made no bones about siding with Bolivia during the Chaco war between Bolivia and Paraguay in 1933–35.[115]

Time passed, and the Senate failed to act upon the bill approved by the Deputies. Senators never spoke about it; they simply ignored it. Feminists and supporters felt it as a stab in the back. Twenty years of effort had been wasted in the country where women's political awareness had first developed. Although ten of those years were spent on understanding the full meaning of feminism and strengthening its foundations, the rejection of suffrage in the 1930s was the result of increased antifeminism and a backlash of militarism and fascism in a country facing a serious economic crisis. Socialist senator Alfredo Palacios in 1933, and Palacios and Mario Bravo in 1935, attempted without success to move the bill through the Senate. Some women were running out of patience. *Mujeres de América* published an article by a Dominican woman in favor of taking the vote from "whoever it may come from," reflecting the feelings of the Argentine women who published this journal. The editorial of May–June 1935 accused right-wing politicians of being against women's causes and praised the Left's defense of women's rights.[116]

The dialogue on feminism and suffrage continued throughout the late 1930s, spurred by scurrilous schemes to subvert some of the reforms already achieved. A proposal to modify the Civil Code and abrogate the economic independence of women prompted the formation of the Unión Argentina de Mujeres in 1936. One of Argentina's leading women writers, Victoria Ocampo, joined the feminist camp for a short time to denounce this and other bills that would require demeaning permits for women who wished to work.[117] In a graceful literary style she reiterated the principles that feminists before her had established. Her intellectual prestige served to underline the chasm between conservatives and reformers, but her fleeting intervention in the feminist cause did not change the direction of events. The socialist feminists began publishing *Vida Femenina* in August 1933. It was a solid source of suffrage support, although it covered a wide gamut of topics. Behind it were established feminist and newcomers to the socialist and feminist arena. In February 1934, facing the election for national deputies and councilors for Buenos Aires, an editorial asked women to influence men's choices.[118] The editorial argued that women continued to be accused of being apathetic and ignorant. It was a duty to refute such accusations by taking a greater interest in politics. Socialists continued to rely on the formula of righteous moral struggle.

In the mid-1930s Alicia Moreau de Justo began to develop an acid but lucid critique of Argentine politics that she carried on relentlessly through the 1940s. She characterized congressional politics as a farce in which the interests of the nation counted for nothing. Faced with a female electorate they did not know how to manipulate, the senators prevaricated. They feared — she thought — that women would change the character of politics. Thus their only choice was to maintain the status quo and avoid any action on the suffrage bill.[119] In April 1935 socialist Adolfo Dickmann addressed the fears of those who, supporting women's suffrage, asked themselves whether women's votes would not enlarge the conservative ranks and support right-wing regimes. He advised putting aside such apprehensions, because change was inevitable and worth trying.[120] Back in the trenches in 1937, Moreau de Justo mocked the aristocratic men who mingled with the rough masses to earn the rewards of corrupt politics, and after recalling the bedlam of fourteen years, she patiently outlined again the many reasons for women's suffrage.[121] Gender condemned women even though they worked, paid taxes, and obeyed the same laws. Suffrage was just and would incorporate a new healthy element into the political process. There was little new in her message, but by the same token those who opposed suffrage were also repeating arguments five decades old.[122]

Efforts to revive the suffrage issue in 1938 by Santiago Fassi and Alfredo Palacios, and in 1942 by Silvio Ruggieri brought no results. Feminine suffrage was a mockery in the Senate, and attempts to revive prospects for municipal suffrage in Buenos Aires failed repeatedly between 1932 and 1939.[123] In 1938 Deputy Santiago Fassi brought up the feeling of impending crisis in the democratic world and called on the principle of democracy and the reaffirmation of faith in the representative republican system to support women's suffrage. He also reminded the legislators that female suffrage was a "solemn promise given by political parties" and a shared aspiration of the majority of deputies. Argentina officially endorsed women's suffrage in the 1938 Eighth Inter-American Conference in Lima, an empty stance that underlined the futility of some official declarations.[124] Ruggieri's 1942 bill was based on the 1932 law approved by the Deputies and officially still under scrutiny in the Senate. He argued that the financial viability of the bill should pose no problem for a government that paid for more expensive and less important projects.[125] Obviously there was no further room for reinterpreting or improving the 1932 bill. The only choice left to suffrage opponents was to continue to turn a deaf ear to the issue, but that tactic began to weaken that year. In September a senatorial commission approved the 1932 bill, freeing it for discussion in the Senate.[126] Hope was on the horizon.

Unfortunately, on 4 June 1943 a military coup deposed President Ramón Castillo, and the hopes for a debate on female suffrage evaporated: suffrage, as approved in 1932, was a thing of the past. Suffragists and feminists began to look into the future. World War II elicited feelings of hope, relevance, and urgency from several intellectuals interviewed by *Vida Femenina*. The war underlined the fact that women suffered its consequences as much as men without having a voice in national and international affairs. The president of the Inter-American Commission for Women, Ana Rosa S. de Martínez Guerrero, expected the war to cause the same sway toward democratization as World War I. The postwar period could not be based on any terms other than those of equality and democracy. She forecast the universal adoption of feminine suffrage in Latin America after the war. Other women also pinned their hopes on this.[127]

All suffrage arguments had been repeated ad nauseam, and democracy became a meaningful symbol in a nation dominated by a military, right-wing cadre with open disaffection for women, labor, socialists, Jews, and the nations fighting Nazi Germany and fascist Italy. Women like Alicia Moreau did not endear themselves to the administration by denouncing political fraud and corruption while urging all women to join Unión Democrática, a political opposition group.[128] Democracy, however, was the wrong symbol to use in those days. Some men were more interested in preparing women for war and asking them to produce more children as an act of patriotism in times of danger than in demanding female suffrage in the name of equality and democracy.[129] Suffrage was too closely associated with socialism, pacifism, and Pan-Americanism to appeal to the military mentality of those who ruled Argentina from 1942 to 1946. It had to wait for a populist revival under General Juan Domingo Perón and his wife Eva Duarte and the aegis of postwar populism.

CHAPTER 9

Women's Politics and Suffrage
in Chile

———— Unlike the earlier working women's associations, the female organizations established in Chile after 1915 were largely organized by educated women to promote other middle-class women's interest in feminine education, equality before the law, and self-expression. The genesis of middle-class feminism took place on 17 June 1915, when Amanda Labarca founded the Círculo de Lectura, an association of middle- and upper-class educated "married and single women . . . to read together, discuss intellectual affairs, and promote the culture of the Chilean woman by every means possible."[1] There were no avowed feminists in the original group, but some of the founders subsequently adopted feminism. Among the best-known were Delia Matte de Izquierdo, a sculptor, and writers Inés Echevarría de Larraín ("Iris") and Elvira Santa Cruz Ossa ("Roxane"). According to Labarca's biographer, the association had three hundred members in 1916.[2] The Círculo had no connection with any religious institution, which was unusual in Santiago, where women's organizations were expected to establish ties with the church. The Círculo had to defend its independent position hardly three months after its foundation because of criticism from religious quarters for its secular orientation.[3] A group of women from the Círculo founded "almost immediately," according to Labarca, the Club de Señoras. The latter was the brainchild of Delia Matte de Izquierdo, and its members were the social and intellectual elite.

The Club de Señoras was a female response to the traditional male club and attempted to fill the gap left by the slowly disappearing social gatherings [*tertulias*] traditionally held in late nineteenth-century Chilean elite homes.[4] Its members' persistence and social clout succeeded in dispelling the initial antagonism of some husbands, conservative newspapers, and even members of the clergy.[5] The Club de Señoras was still active in the late 1930s. In its initial stage it established several branches in provincial cities, and Delia Matte de Izquierdo arranged lectures, classes, films, concerts, and receptions for literary and political figures in the capital.[6] As the association expanded, it started classes in sewing and cooking, thus combining traditional upper-class women's activities with those oriented toward helping women of lesser means. Knowingly or not, the Club de Señoras was preparing middle- and lower-class women for services elite women required, while the enrichment of their own intellect deepened the social gap between them and those who attended the Club's technical classes. The Círculo and the Club were transitional institutions between the past and the future. They embodied a form of genteel feminism that promoted new roles for women but adhered to traditional female activities and pursued only limited changes. Within these boundaries, the two organizations had an important message of self-esteem for educated middle-class women: they sought to demonstrate that Chilean women were intellectually ready for social and political roles outside the home.[7]

The Círculo de Lectura and the Club de Señoras shared aspirations and membership, but because their objectives were slightly different they remained separate. We may speculate that women like Labarca, who felt that intellectual pursuits should be accompanied by greater involvement in social reform, would not be satisfied with activities that encouraged social glitter rather than intellectual development. In an article describing the activities of the Club de Señoras, member Sra. Jesús Palacios de Díaz praised both institutions for having demonstrated that women could administer their associations without male help. She differentiated between "quiet and respectful" women who knew the limits of their rights and "nervous" women who wished to break those limits in "obfuscation." The Club de Señoras was a "quiet and intelligent feminine movement," "engaged in a voyage of recreation, art, and learning."[8] In 1925, for example, the Club offered a cycle of sixteen conferences on a variety of subjects ranging from women in science and physicians and society to a discussion of Mme Curie and radium. Of sixteen speakers, only three were women.[9]

The Círculo de Lectura eventually divided into two institutions in 1919, the National Council of Women and the Centro Femenino de Estudios. The Council was founded by journalist Celinda Arregui de Rodicio for socially involved women who wanted to establish connections with similar groups abroad. The Council opened a boardinghouse for female students, offered classes in English, French, literature, and child care, and sponsored public lectures by some of its members on literary and historical themes.[10] It also established contact with other National Councils, and in 1923 it sent a representative to the Pan American Conference in Baltimore.[11] The Council served as a forum for members, such as Amanda Labarca, who wanted to encourage a faster pace in the social and mental growth of Chilean women.

Their activities did not prepare the members of the Círculo de Lectura and the Club de Señoras for the events that took place shortly after they organized. In 1917 Chileans were taken by surprise by two bills introduced in Congress. One, sponsored by young members of the Conservative Party, called for women's suffrage. The other, sponsored by the Radical Party, called for the complete dissolution of marriage. Luis A. Undurraga, representative for Curicó, sponsored a simple three-article bill to reform the suffrage law. Article 1 added "of both sexes" to the article entitling citizens to vote. In addition to citing the pioneering nineteenth-century Chilean advocate of women's rights Abdón Cifuentes, he cited the Seneca Falls Declaration of 1848 and the example of the state of Wyoming in the United States, which had granted political rights to its female citizens. He argued that the Chilean constitution of 1837 granted suffrage to literate Chilean citizens over twenty-one. No statement excluded women from citizenship, and women were as intelligent and well prepared to exercise that right as men.[12] Most people of that generation had forgotten that in 1875 several women in San Felipe and La Serena had asked to be registered as voters, having read the electoral law referring to "all Chileans" to define voters. As the Civil Code stated, the male pronoun comprised both sexes.[13] The Club de Señoras has been given credit for influencing the Young Conservatives' suffrage bill.[14] Undurraga lent his support to the cause for several years more, and his bill served as an inspirational text for the women who became involved in the discussion of their own political role in the 1920s.[15]

For Amanda Labarca 1917 was a memorable year, because these bills opened a debate on the condition of Chilean women. Even though she did not expect the bills to be approved, she felt their discussion showed that most women, regardless of class and faith, agreed on the need to change their legal status.[16] Labarca was optimistic in her generalization, but she had grounds to believe that a politically influential nucleus of women shared her ideas. Among them was Martina Barros de Orrego, one of the prestigious members of the upper-middle-class elite. Although considerably older than the newly emerging feminists, she fully supported suffrage and gave it her wholehearted endorsement.[17]

Neither suffrage nor the reform of the Civil Code was approved, but the discussion of women's rights among Santiago's high society broke the comfortable world of traditional roles in which both genders lived in those years.[18] How receptive were middle-class Chilean women to the concept of feminism and political activity in 1915? Labarca glosses over this subject in her recollections, but the objectives of women's organizations in the ensuing years, their activities, and their members' writings suggest that during this initial period many were flirting with the concept but were doubtful about its implications. Those who expressed their opinions in the mid-1910s were reluctant to accept more than a qualified version of feminism.

In 1916, soon after the Círculo de Señoras was founded, a short-lived women's newspaper, La Voz Femenina, was founded to cater to the "distinguished ladies of our society." In its opinion "violence" in feminism generated hatred and ridicule of women. The newspaper's director, Teresa Valderrama Larraín, declared herself and her readers feminine but not feminist. News of English and North American radical feminists arriving in Chile led this group to associate feminism with street tactics they repudiated. Contributors believed that for Chilean women political rights were in the future, and they praised the roles of wife and mother as the greatest female mission. Evolution was the answer, posited a contributor who declared she had no aspirations to suffrage. To her economic independence, recognition of the true worth of female labor, and education answered women's needs.[19]

Similar feelings were expressed in the conservative newspaper Zig-Zag in November 1917 by an anonymous male writing on the divorce and suffrage bills. He thought the bills were part of a political game between conservatives and liberals to outdo each other.[20] These ideas lingered into the early 1920s. The first prize of the Valparaíso Floral Games in 1923 went to Josefa Gili de Peláez for a study of women in society. As a preamble to her thoughts on women, she struck a nationalist chord by stating that Chileans should borrow from other people only what was beneficial to them. Any ideology advocating women's encroachment on male roles did not serve the nation well. She praised female participation in the professions but asked women never to abandon their homes. "Women are not yet very necessary in public life. . . . Let us, above all, be mothers to our children and mistresses of our homes." It was against such traditional opinions that women had to define the meaning of feminism to them and decide what objectives they would pursue for a change of female role in society.[21]

Despite a cautious start and nagging trepidation about radical feminists, the early 1920s offered an auspicious climate for the discussion of feminism. Labor unrest, concern with public health, the growing appeal of populism among the lower middle class and the workers, and a sense of noblesse oblige in politics among the ruling elite stimulated the discussion of welfare and social reform. Feminism, understood as a movement that would encourage able women to work for the benefit of society, could help achieve social improvement in Chile. The role women played in the nation's future became a key theme in the writings of jurists, politicians, educators, and women themselves.

In 1920 the Radical Party, supporting a program of social and political reform, saw its candidate Arturo Alessandri elected to the presidency, marking an important turning point in Chilean history. Alessandri was aware of women's changing social and economic role, and during his presidential campaign he spoke in favor of reform in women's legal status. He recognized their potential as future members of the electorate and did not hesitate to address women's organizations to support their cause and his own. After his inauguration he continued to cultivate his image among them. In the early 1920s the National Council of Women was ready to support female municipal suffrage as a preparation for national suffrage and the reform of the Civil Code. Its members approached Arturo Alessandri and Pedro Aguirre Cerda to advise them on women's rights, and the two men discussed the practical problems of obtaining the bill's approval in the Chamber of Deputies.[22]

Two bills to reform the Civil Code were introduced in Congress in 1922, sponsored by Senator Eleodoro Yáñez and Deputy José Maza.[23] In 1923 President Alessandri gave a public lecture on the rights of women before the Women's National Council and called the existing legislation affecting women a "legal barbarity," declaring himself in favor of equal political and civil rights for women. He criticized the legislators for tying his hands, as they had done on other matters, and reiterated his support for women's issues in the opening legislative session in June 1924.[24] No established male party placed women's rights at the top of its political agenda, and by publicly supporting them Alessandri had nothing to lose and much to gain. Like most other politicians, he showed some caution on women's enfranchisement because he thought the number qualified to vote was still very small. Alessandri did not achieve any reform affecting women during the stormy years of his first administration, but women's groups gave him their wholehearted support.

The National Council of Women's position on female suffrage reflected the changes taking place in Chile during the early 1920s. After their initial cautious approach, middle-class Chileans warmed to the idea of female suffrage, although public opinion was undecided. Those who favored female suffrage at this early point argued that women were capable of participating in public affairs and that their contribution would be useful to the nation. Some, such as Alejandro Valdés Riesco, endorsed the municipal vote as the first step toward full political rights to assuage some of his colleagues' fears of women's voting for the Left. He was enthusiastic about a future society guided by both genders and believed it would be "the most grandiose and solemn transformation since the fall of the Roman Empire." Senator Enrique Zañartu Prieto, a member of the conservative Liberal Party, supported a bill to grant middle-class women equal rights with men. Middle-class women were educated and accustomed to act independently. In his opinion 80 percent of Chilean women had earned their liberation. What he demanded from women was education and economic responsibility. If his "calculation" was correct, working women had to be included in his definition of middle class.[25] Valdés Riesco and Zañartu Prieto were simply agreeing that men had to stop idealizing women or "protecting" them in an absurd and humiliating manner. The political and civil rights of women were not an issue of politics but a "spontaneous movement of human justice." [26]

Even Catholic women's organizations began to probe the subject of women's rights. At the December 1922 Valparaíso meeting of Juventud Católica Femenina, Teresa Ossandón lectured on feminism, and Father Clovis Montero lent his support to women's suffrage.[27] Between 1921 and 1922 two female parties launched Chilean women into endeavors hardly envisioned only five years before. A Partido Femenino Progresista Nacional was founded by Sofía de Ferrari Rojas in February 1921, and in 1922 Ester La Rivera de Sangüeza founded the Partido Cívico Femenino.[28]

Defining a Political Objective: The Initial Years

The foundation of two women's parties in Santiago was noteworthy for a country with such fragile middle-class feminist foundations. These parties were not true political organizations, however, but associations oriented toward civic issues. Sofía de Ferrari Rojas was a determined woman, though not a social revolutionary. In March 1920 she founded a "national feminine newspaper" in Santiago called *Evolución,* which later served as the mouthpiece for her party. The title reflected the spirit behind it. Its stated objective was to encourage women to think about their rights, advising them to cultivate science, letters, the arts, education, and social work to achieve equality. *Evolución*'s position on suffrage reflected the change in times. Its first number carried an article by Carlos Silva Cruz supporting female suffrage as a right so far denied to women by men exercising their traditional power. In Cruz's opinion women who sought their enfranchisement were not simply seeking a right but were fulfilling their duty. This ethical component in the definition of women's rights was important in the development of the political ideology of Southern Cone women's associations. Despite his support, Silva Cruz's formula to enfranchise women was evolutionary. Women should get the vote after preparing by performing civic duties in the municipal arena.[29]

In subsequent numbers Sofía de Ferrari reprinted a defense of women's suffrage written by Abdón Cifuentes in 1865, published articles on feminism, and reported on women's clubs.[30] On March 1921 the newspaper published the political principles of the Partido Femenino Progresista Nacional, Ferrari's creation, and it changed its subtitle to "National Feminist Newspaper." The party was steered by a directorate of six council members, a treasurer, two secretaries, a vice president, and a president.[31] The party assumed that gender was no obstacle to performing one's duty to work for others and for national peace. Ferrari would not endorse any political party but would support all men working for the collective well-being. The program identified the Constitution, the Civil Code, and the Penal Code as reform targets and urged women to express their opinions on how to change them. It also invited "honorable women of goodwill" to join its ranks. *Evolución* changed its name to *Evolución Ascendente* and seems to have survived at least through May 1921. Partido Femenino Progresista Nacional was still alive in 1923, when Sofía Ferrari and Luisa Zanelle López traveled to Baltimore to participate in the Pan American Conference of Women. After this date there are no traces of its activities.

The second female party founded in Santiago had the same moderate approach to women's engagement in public life. Partido Cívico Femenino was founded in 1922, and its program comprised twelve points. Suffrage was number 9. Preceding it in rank were equal pay for equal work, child care in industries employing women, credit unions for workers, sex education, an end to the double standard of morality, and the encouragement, recognition, and protection of lower- and middle-class women's labor. The party founded a magazine, *Acción Femenina*, to publicize its goals, and its first number appeared in 1922. Partido Cívico Femenino disavowed any type of "anarchic feminism" that robbed women of their natural charms, converting them into neuter beings and undoing the balance of the sexes. It claimed, however, to support feminism as an ideology that would "ennoble" women, make them better citizens, and teach them to promote human progress. The newspaper's name spoke for itself and for the spirit of the party, claimed a writer for the journal: "Women should stop leaning on men for support." Women should take the initiative and work for reform. "Let us work . . . the hour of our liberation has come."[32]

The founders of Partido Cívico Femenino chose persuasion over aggression and capitalized on the socially acceptable role of women as mothers and social workers. During its first year party members interviewed politicians sympathetic to their goals and published their statements and speeches. Among them were President Arturo Alessandri, Ramón Briones Luco, senator for Tarapacá and author of a treatise on divorce, Luis A. Undurraga García Huidobro, the conservative deputy for Curicó who in 1917 introduced the bill to grant suffrage to women, and Eleodoro Yáñez, senator for Valdivia and author of a bill for female suffrage.[33] In December 1922 Partido Cívico Femenino claimed to have over 1,200 letters of support from women all over Chile. The leadership felt that the "feminist movement answered a deep need in the soul of Chilean women."[34] Its newspaper published articles explaining feminism, interviews with male and female supporters, news from other feminists in North and South America and Europe, literature, and even coverage of women's sports. The party directorate wrote to members of Congress asking them to endorse the reform of the Civil Code, female suffrage, labor contracts for nonunionized workers, and fringe benefits for workers. Although the initial issues had reflected a cautious approach, as time passed both the party and its journal seem to have become more comfortable with their objectives, as reflected in articles on politics and the home, education and coeducation, and women's achievements in Chile and abroad. Feminism was by far the most common word it used for the process of change it advocated—the nonviolent pursuit of women's civil and political rights to give them equality before the law. The party believed that the interests of the family had become social interests, and modern women asked for legal emancipation so as to collaborate in drafting legislation dealing with their interests and those of their children. Women were conscious that in claiming their rights they assumed duties, but they were eager to fulfill them as part of a moral social mission. The party understood that women had to take responsibility for their own social emancipation, casting away indifference, vanity, and self-deprecation to become their own advocates.[35] In defining its objectives it delineated what would become the mainstream of Chilean feminism for many years.

On the issue of political rights, the party was unambiguous. Writing for the organization, César A. Sangüeza, the founder's husband, argued against the apprehensions raised by its opponents, who suggested that women would abandon their homes and their duties as mothers. To the contrary, he saw a mother-citizen as the best source of civic education for her children. Sangüeza's ideological axis was the home and the maternal and didactic ability women possessed and could use in the civic arena. He also believed that women's nobility and ethical virtues could improve the quality of politics: "The inclusion of women in the legislative bodies is not only necessary but indispensable, because we believe it will save the national mores."[36] In mid-1923 the party created three commissions for handling recruitment, education, and propaganda, and a host of new names began to appear on its roster. October 1923 is the last available issue of *Acción Femenina*. It seems that between 1923 and mid-1924 there were important changes in the party's format. Ester La Rivera and her husband were not in Santiago in late 1923, and after that year they disappeared from the feminist scene for a decade.

Revista Femenina appeared in May 1924, claiming to carry out the program of the Partido Cívico Femenino, which at this point was under the leadership of a permanent commission. Among its members at that time were dentist and writer Graciela Mandujano and sociologist Elvira Rogat, who maintained a high feminist profile through the 1920s and 1930s.[37] The party restated its pursuit of the civil, economic, and political rights of women, with the support of numerous female associations.[38] Yet the publishers were ambivalent as to what route they should follow. On 5 October 1924 the magazine's editorial board confessed that its members feared being confused with "feminists" wearing glasses, short hair, and flat shoes. They were also afraid of prejudice and felt unready to help solve other women's problems with their vote, but their readers were urged to conquer any fear covering "moral cowardice." Those who felt unready to change should at least remove obstacles from the reformers' path. This mixed message suggests a conservative feminism that did not recant its position yet did not advance beyond safe boundaries. Sympathetic references to several Catholic organizations suggested a certain affinity between *Revista Femenina* and members of traditional women's organizations. *Revista Femenina* appears to have ceased publication in November 1924, perhaps because of the constitutional crisis in September. By then Catholic organizations such as Juventud Católica Femenina and Unión Patriótica de Mujeres de Chile had joined the campaigns for women's civil and political rights, although the former was not loudly vocal about political rights.[39]

Chilean women were obviously afraid of *garçonismo*, a trait identified with "liberated" women, inaccurately associated with European feminists as women provocatively dressed and enjoying complete personal and sexual freedom.[40] Leading women journalists such as Elvira Santa Cruz Ossa ("Roxane") were still unsure that politics was a field for women, who should first obtain equality before the law. Social welfare was a better goal for those interested in improving the motherland. Not all activist women shared her opinion, however, and the debate they engaged in showed their uneasiness about suffrage.[41]

Women's divided opinions were reflected in the constitutional assembly meeting in 1925 to draft a new constitution to replace the first constitutional charter adopted in 1833. Feminism had not made enough of an ideological dent in the mind of male jurists and politicians, who skirted the issue of female suffrage and ratified that right for men only. One Partido Demócrata Femenino or Partido Femenino Democrático seems to have been founded in the mid-1920s, and it is remembered for proposing a modification to the new constitution's electoral law to allow female suffrage.[42] Between 1925 and 1930, expressed interest in suffrage waned. Chilean democracy was put to the test after a constitutional crisis, the exile and return of President Alessandri, and a coup d'état that put the nation under the military regime of General Carlos Ibáñez del Campo. This was a period of regrouping for women's organizations. Partido Femenino Democrático dissolved in 1927; the vacuum was filled by Bando Femenino, an organization that combined the membership of Partido Femenino Democrático and members of the permanent committee of the International Feminine Congress that took place in Santiago in 1926. Bando Femenino was led by feminist Celinda Arregui de Rodicio. In 1929 and 1930 she traveled in Spain and Spanish America, establishing ties with other women's organizations and speaking on Chilean women. Bando Femenino supported the 1928 International Feminine Congress in Buenos Aires. It carried out a press campaign for cheap housing and women's suffrage and in 1930 helped found the Liga Internacional Femenina Pro-Sufragio y Paz, which maintained ties with the League of Nations and other European organizations. The theme of universal peace had already appeared in writings of Partido Cívico Femenino's members, and it would reappear in the programs of most female organizations in the 1930s as militarism rose in Europe.[43]

In 1927 Chilean women celebrated the fiftieth anniversary of the enactment of the 1877 Amunátegui law that had opened the doors of the university for them. Chilean middle-class women were proud of their achievements in education, social work, and literature, but that year they had to regret the unopposed election to the presidency of General Carlos Ibáñez in a special election after the resignation of President Emilio Figueroa. The illusion of an unshakable respect for the Constitution was gone.

A new association, Unión Femenina de Chile, was founded on 26 October 1927 by educator Aurora Argomedo. Graciela Mandujano has been given credit for the idea of this women's association.[44] On 28 October 102 persons gathered to elect the first directorate, and by 1932 Unión Femenina claimed the support of over one thousand women from all walks of life. The idea of a union of women of all classes for the task of national regeneration was to become an important element in the 1930s. Unión Femenina focused on reforming women's legal, social, and political condition.[45]

During its first years Unión Femenina de Chile carried out cultural and social welfare projects, offering free medical attention and self-improvement courses to members and nonmembers alike. It supported the publication of a book—*Charlas femeninas*—by Delia Ducoing, a journalist who began to develop her interpretation of feminism in its pages. In 1931 the organization began to subsidize *Nosotras*, a magazine directed by Ducoing. There was no urgency in this association's program. It chose the gentle path of "apolitical" activity aimed at creating a consciousness of needs among urban Chilean women.

Political Definitions and Mobilization in the Early Thirties

Chile's unstable situation was the catalyst for women's mobilization in the 1930s, as a response to a nation besieged by economic problems, a fragmented labor movement, and the lack of an articulate political response to the challenge posed by the armed forces and the conservative elements. The 1924–25 constitutional crisis had not resolved the polarization between the president and Congress, and the presence of a general "elected" without opposition irked the traditional elite as well as labor. After 1929 the Chilean economy fell into a deep depression that exacerbated the many unresolved problems of public health, housing, and social welfare.

Service and charity were assumed to be women's civic responsibilities, and the state counted on them to fill its many gaps in social welfare during the early years of the century, but by the early 1930s charity was replaced by social reform and social work. Feminist ideas intensified and politicized women's service mission. Educated professional women claimed the ability and the right to become public persons engaged in social work rather than private benefactors. A considerable number of organizations channeled women's effort into the body politic, even though the traditional disclaimer of "nonpolitical" remained a fixed feature of their self-definition.

In the 1930s women's organizations proliferated. Some had been founded years before, others were brand new. While several remained cultural, others became temporarily "political" to support suffrage and the reform to the Civil and Penal Codes. Yet others tried to mobilize women as a pressure group to obtain passage of social legislation but disclaimed affiliation with any party. Last, some established political parties saw fit to organize female wings and actively pursue the election of "their" women after the passage of a municipal suffrage law. Between 1930 and 1932, suffrage became the leading issue for most feminist groups in Chile. That male voters had seen their own right to vote challenged and manipulated by the military may have caused women deep concern about the loss of the constitutional framework of the nation.[46] The bumpy road to political and economic recovery gave their organizations a ready-made agenda, which they attempted to address with their limited experience in activism.

In 1931 Chile was rapidly heading toward a political crisis as its military president, General Carlos Ibáñez, lost support among key sectors of the population. The unrest favored a bolder approach by activist women, who felt that their sex could no longer ignore political issues. In July 1931 women protested the Ibáñez regime in two public marches. Women's participation in street demonstrations had never been popular, even in the early days of the century when female members of mutualist societies were actively organizing against factory owners. Mores were changing fast.

Carlos Ibáñez was forced out of the presidency in July 1931, and Chile passed through several months of political unrest and a short experiment with a socialist republic in 1932 before returning to political normality. In September 1932 a military coup brought to power a caretaker government that prepared the nation for a national election. Women saw a window of opportunity open and quickly gathered their forces in several organizations, ready to emerge as political contenders. Between 1931 and 1932 several associations developed or expanded a political agenda that, while focusing on suffrage, comprised a broad spectrum of social issues. Male support unfolded as time passed.[47]

Unión Femenina de Chile and Delia Ducoing

Unión Femenina de Chile was the most important and best organized women's group in 1931, when it began to expand geographically to form a truly national organization. In July 1931, shortly after Ibáñez's downfall, it called for a meeting with all women workers' organizations to send the interim government a petition for full political rights for women. In addition to inviting Micaela Cáceres de Gamboa, the dean of mutualist organizations, Unión Femenina asked over a dozen other personalities, including Catholic leaders, to join efforts with professional women's groups to pursue suffrage.[48] In December 1931 Unión Femenina de Chile had started a branch in the city of Magallanes that by 1933 had organized a musical group and opened a tearoom. It also offered lectures, special classes, and legal services for women.[49] One of the two women in the organization's directorate was president of a needleworkers' association, and the other was head of a female sports club. A third branch was founded in the northern port of Iquique in November 1932, and a fourth branch was established in Talca in mid-1933.[50]

Unión Femenina de Chile attempted to be an inclusive organization appealing to working-class and middle-class women. Throughout 1931 its magazine, Nosotras, published articles on working men and women and the Chilean economic and social crisis.[51] Among its contributors were Amanda Labarca, Gabriela Mistral, who sent occasional articles, Victoria Gucovsky, an Argentine socialist, and a host of lesser-known Chilean writers. The magazine also printed feminist news from other Latin American nations. In its first editorial it denied being "suffragist" in the English style: Chilean women should persuade society of the justice of their demands. Feminism, it sustained, adopted the national character of countries. In Chile women "could never surrender the sense of motherhood that surrounds and penetrates our understanding of life."[52]

Trying to broaden the organization's membership, Delia Ducoing was a speaker at the forty-fifth anniversary of the foundation of the Sociedad de Obreras no. 1, of Valparaíso in December 1932. Nosotras informed its readers on women's work and demanded equal pay for equal work.[53] Unión Femenina de Chile also displayed its social bent by stating its concern over the quality of life among the nitrate workers in the north and criticizing the performance of nitrate producer Compañía Salitrera de Chile and its "capitalist ambitions." It also reported on the illegal seizure of Mapuche land, on inflation, and on cooperatives.

Notwithstanding its "apolitical" standing, in 1932 Nosotras made political decisions, such as supporting some socialist goals and rejecting communism. In 1933 the editors were prepared to take the socialists to task for not having included any issues on women in their program.[54] Unión Femenina de Chile consistently advocated women's suffrage. Its leader understood that without the vote women lacked leverage to influence any change in the legis-lation restricting their rights. Neither femininity nor the home would suf-fer from female participation in politics, the writers in *Nosotras* reassured their readers. Chilean women were educated, capable, and willing to help the motherland, and their maternal sensitivity gave them a special feeling for some social problems. Suffrage "answered [women's] need to undertake an ample, apostolic task of peace and harmony among all social classes."[55] The vote, argued contributors to *Nosotras*, would be the key to other objec-tives such as the legal investigation of out-of-wedlock births, the inclusion of women in interparliamentary commissions and the appointment of women as counselors to the national ministries.[56] These women were aware of the full meaning of citizenship, and their writings show a well-rehearsed and well-understood set of political ideas. Those male political "technicians" who pondered how to classify women for suffrage, argued writer María Mon-vel (pen name for Tilda Brito) in January 1932, should note that "the only conditions they should take into consideration were those demanded from men." Was suffrage a privilege or a right? Who had given men the right to "concede" suffrage? Monvel asked rhetorically.[57]

Nosotras reflected to a significant degree the opinions of Delia Ducoing, who was its director through November 1933, and wrote under the pen name Isabel Morel. Her brand of feminism was explained in a book titled *Charlas femeninas,* published in 1930 and sponsored by Unión Femenina de Chile.[58] Defining what she regarded as feminism, Ducoing rejected the "London suf-fragettes'" feminism as outmoded. "At present, true feminism is gentle and admirable." "Feminism is a labor of conscientious rights, of maternal senti-ments, of admirable generosity."[59] Like others before her in the Southern Cone, Ducoing dressed feminism up in a soft, feminine garb and assigned it several gender-related and socially oriented tasks. She ranked them in the following order: the promotion of welfare, social hygiene, female education; the reform of the Civil Code to strengthen women's rights within marriage; protective legislation for working women and children; liberal arts careers for women; female enfranchisement; and international peace.

Although Ducoing defended women's right to work for wages, she still assigned them a special role of love, support for the male sex, altruism, and generosity toward others. Although she argued that suffrage was the right of citizens of both sexes, she proposed that it also gave women's ma-ternal feelings an outlet in promoting children's welfare. Chilean feminists, she claimed, did not wish to imitate "Saxon women in England and the United States," much as they were admired and respected. Latin character and culture determined for Chilean women an ideal of "conscious order."[60] Ducoing's views were restated in many ways by many other women in other organizations in the 1930s. She was well informed on the varieties of feminism outside Chile. She knew North American feminism firsthand, having visited the United States in the late 1920s, met Doris Stevens, and visited the headquarters of the National Women's Party.[61] She knew what she wanted for Chile. For several years Unión Femenina maintained ties with North American feminist personalities and the National Women's Party, and it also established ties with women's organizations in Argentina, Cuba, Peru, Colombia, and Mexico.[62]

Municipal Suffrage: Halfway to Full Citizenship

Early in 1932 another organization joined the suffrage campaign. Bando Femenino supported the foundation of Partido Femenino Nacional, led by journalist Celinda Arregui de Rodicio and Cleophas Torres, a writer and educator who acted as its second president. This new party was a lay organization with no religious ties that encouraged women of all social classes to participate in the campaign for suffrage and elect women to the municipalities.[63] It published a magazine, *Voz Femenina,* of which only one issue has survived.[64] *Voz Femenina* urged women to unite in a "white army" to defend women's rights and bring peace among men who, carried away by ambition and personal interests, had lost all love for the motherland. Partido Femenino Nacional supported equal rights for men and women and noted that some female workers' associations still lacked their own headquarters after more than forty years. Nobody could contain the tide of change arriving in Chile, stated *Voz Femenina.* To argue with those who struggled against feminism was a waste of time. Retrogrades who wished to stop the ascent of women were defeated and in retreat under the burden of their egotism.

In the 1933 reconstruction atmosphere, the concept of female suffrage had a compelling strength despite the opposition of conservative personalities. In February a Comité Pro-Derechos de la Mujer was organized in Santiago to pressure deputies to approve suffrage legislation. The committee established a branch in Valparaíso, where Marta Vergara, later an active leftist, was among the members. Congressional debates on female suffrage that year were attended by committee members, who listened intently and politely. After the deputies approved the suffrage bill, the women visited senators to urge final ratification.[65] The willingness of Chilean deputies to give women their rights as citizens was qualified. Suffrage, approved on 9 March 1934, was restricted to municipal elections and to literate women over twenty-one.[66] Literacy qualifications also applied to male voters and reduced the number of potential voters of both sexes to the educated. Women's exclusion from national elections was a more serious restriction because it kept men in control of national politics. Santiago's *El Mercurio* gave suffrage a polite reception. It welcomed a law that broadened the "great social mission already undertaken by women in the home" and hoped they proved themselves capable of offering a "useful, intelligent, and necessary" collaboration with men in a time of institutional reconstruction.[67] The ball was in the women's court, but they were not challenged to do more than support men with their traditional gender skills.

Chilean feminists were not disappointed with the restrictions imposed. Since the early 1920s municipal suffrage had been discussed as a desirable exercise in political rights and a moderate solution to the issue of women's voting. Once it was approved there was a surge in organizations seeking to embody and to channel women's awakening. Established and newly formed groups defined their objectives and carried out recruiting campaigns among different sectors of society, a strong testimonial of the vitality of this period. Chilean politics were volatile in the 1930s, and women's organizations evolved rapidly to adjust from the short suffrage campaign to elections in 1935. A rapid turnover in leadership changed the character of their political orientation and explains why some meandered between the center and the Right and others between the center and the Left, with some well entrenched at each end of the spectrum.

Political Issues and Organizations: The Right and the Center

In 1934 Amanda Labarca, one of the earliest feminists, was still slightly skeptical about women's political abilities, a strain of her conservatism that refused to fade. She feared women would make the same mistakes as men, engaging in personalism and snobbery and failing to sustain high ethical standards in politics. Her idealism about women's political influence made her hesitate. Elcira Rojas de Vergara, president of Partido Cívico Femenino, declared herself against militancy in men's parties but was enthusiastic about women's administrative capacities, which they would demonstrate as they were elected to municipal posts. Adela Edwards de Salas, a conservative member of the social elite, also saw a promising future for women in municipal affairs. She favored a strict gender line in the organization of women's efforts. "We are tired of suffering masculine governance and men's use of the capitalist failure as an excuse for their own ineptitude." To her, only male egotism could explain why men had never asked women to help resolve the economic and ethical problems of the contemporary world.[68]

After 1933 the organizations that had galvanized women's efforts to form national gender-based pressure groups began to compete, although their programs were very similar. Male political leaders regarded women's organizations as adjunct or allied groups, useful to raise issues and gather votes at the base of the political ladder, but without the necessary clout to get political prizes in the national elections. Before the second municipal election, however, politically astute women began to agitate in favor of "full" political rights for a greater share in shaping national policies. This would become their main objective throughout the 1940s.

To overcome the fragmentation, several leading women began to organize umbrella organizations with general programs amenable to all and stating opinions on national problems. The strength gained by numbers could give credibility to their voice. One such effort was the Comité Ejecutivo Nacional de Mujeres de Chile [National Executive Committee of Chilean Women], founded in May 1933. Adherence to political parties was not favored by this association, which preferred a specifically feminine show of patriotism and strength.[69] The National Executive Committee of Chilean Women comprised groups of diverse political complexions, such as the Unión Femenina de Chile, the needleworkers' union, the union of business employees, the conservative Liga de Damas Chilenas, and the child-welfare organization Patronato de la Infancia. Among its personalities were Adela Edwards de Salas, writer Elvira Santa Cruz Ossa, and Elcira Rojas de Vergara, president of Partido Cívico. The fate of this umbrella organization is uncertain, but it may have split without achieving its goals.

The Comité Pro-Derechos de la Mujer, a useful nucleation effort, attempted to maintain its legitimacy and presence on the Chilean scene, but its heterogeneous composition and the rise of other organizations conspired against it. In late March 1933 it apparently rebuked women who remained on the margins of feminism, raising some resentment among older leaders such as Adela Edwards de Salas and Elvira Santa Cruz Ossa, who made public statements reminding others of their long labor on behalf of working women and children. It is unclear how the Comité Pro-Derechos de la Mujer operated through the 1930s, but the drive for suffrage in the presidential elections and the implementation of social legislation gave it a second wind in the early 1940s. In 1941 the committee was associated with a Club Femenino America. Both signed a program for civil, political, social, and economic equality for Chilean women that included protection for pregnant women, voluntary motherhood with the use of "methods to limit birth," and the rehabilitation of prostitutes. Elcira Rojas de Vergara headed the committee. The adoption of the principle of voluntary motherhood was "radical" for the times, and shows the influence of left-wing female organizations as well as of eugenics.[70]

The concept of a national female "apolitical" organization to mobilize women was undermined when Delia Ducoing and Unión Femenina de Chile split in November 1933 owing to a clash of personalities and objectives. Accusations flared between the Unión Femenina de Chile and Ducoing, the party charging her with being overbearing and wanting to impose her views on the organization.[71] The socially oriented Unión Femenina de Chile was accused of being communist, a charge it denied in May 1934. Calling on Christian sisterhood, Unión Femenina de Chile gave its support to a new umbrella organization, Agrupación Nacional de Mujeres, which reiterated the union of femininity and feminism, supporting a program in which social legislation was paramount. It included the defense and protection of motherhood, fair remuneration for women's work, compulsory treatment of "social diseases," enforcement of the prenuptial certificate, repression of alcoholism and gambling, better housing, and a revision of the Civil and Penal Codes. Unión Femenina de Chile maintained its autonomy and its program for collective improvement and cooperation with working people. It planned to continue offering medical services to its members. It also maintained ties with the Inter-American Commission of Women and with North American feminists.[72]

Ducoing favored an internationally oriented program, although she remained concerned with the immediate realities of working Chileans. In November 1933, as she announced the dissolution of her ties with Unión Femenina de Chile, she gave her support to Legión Femenina de Educación Popular in Valparaíso, later renamed Legión Femenina de America.[73] In January 1933 Legión Femenina declared 150 members. By 1935 it had offices in Talca, Santiago, and Rancagua. The Talca branch had 215 members.[74] In its report for that year the Valparaíso office mentioned distributing clothes among children and elderly people. During the following year this office also offered classes in child care, domestic economy, fashions, sewing, piano, languages, and so on.[75]

Delia Ducoing retained the magazine *Nosotras* after her split with Unión Femenina de Chile. Through 1934 the editorials defined her organization's broadly utopian policies and goals. She declared her Legión Femenina de

America an organization for all the women of Latin America. Women should avoid political manipulation and defend justice and truth. She used the word América as a guide to the objectives of the group: The letter A suggested alliance; M stood for *mujeres,* women in action; E was for evidence that their children were their jewels; R stood for reaction to achieving the creation of a United States of Latin America; I, for the immediate beginning of their crusade; C for *contra* [against] women's apathy; and A for their arms: ideas, the pen, and action.[76] Ducoing established connections with other Latin American feminists and women's peace organizations, including the International Women's League in the United States.[77] In the name of pacifism and intercontinental confraternity, the organization protested the opening of the Chaco war between Bolivia and Brazil.

Legión Femenina de America remained oriented toward protection of the home and ennoblement of womanhood, in search of the solution to problems affecting the family, including divorce.[78] Its activities, as reported in 1936, were genteel projects such as visits to older people's homes and children's parties to distribute clothes and sweets.[79] Alienation from local or national politics limited its impact on national life, but such social and pacifist organizations allowed women to find a vehicle for fraternizing and injecting some ideological content, vague as it was, into their daily lives. Similar organizations in Argentina and Uruguay reflect common sentiments and objectives among women of the three countries.

Politics, however, remained an important signifier of women's organizations. The perception of women as a new political element worthy of consideration is corroborated by the founding of feminine wings in a number of parties throughout the mid-1930s. The Socialist Party established a women's section, Acción de Mujeres Socialistas, in 1933, and the Radical Party established its own in 1934.[80] The Radicals counted with Amanda Labarca and encouraged female activities through a women's Radical Assembly.[81] In 1931 the conservative Valparaíso's Liberal Democratic Youth began publishing a journal, *Política Feminista,* to encourage women to join the Liberal Party's ranks. The journal carried articles condemning the exploitation of women's labor and supported unrestricted female enfranchisement.[82] These organizations attempted to mobilize women on behalf of the parent organization, but without giving them an entry into the male domain of serious politics. A Partido Demócrata Femenino was being organized at the end of 1935; early in 1936 it elected a directorate and agreed to meet on Fridays.[83] Whether women should establish separate parties or join men's parties remained a source of contention.[84] In the mid-1930s some women favored a double militancy. Adela Edwards de Salas, a staunch advocate of women's associations, ran for office in the Conservative Party. Among women of the Left there was the same inclination to devise a female agenda within a female group but to put it to the test through an established party. Women of all ideological leanings had the opportunity to try their political wings throughout these years—test their own abilities and also test men's willingness to support them. They accepted the separation of their activities as a comfortable way of carrying out their business.

Conservative parties and traditionalist women had the least trouble in defining their relationship with their male counterparts, and they were among the first to have women elected to city councils and mayoral posts. One of the most distinguished was Adela Edwards de Salas, who in 1934 organized Acción Nacional de Mujeres de Chile. Edwards, who had been associated for many years with Cruz Blanca, a philanthropic Catholic women's organization, decided to enter politics when the municipal vote was discussed in 1932. She foresaw the use of suffrage to devise laws that would, in her opinion, close the opening that existing legislation left for abuses against the family, women, and children. Renouncing the presidency of Catholic Action to avoid a conflict of interests, she attempted to create a political organization among her peers. Her failure led her to seek other women with similar interests, but after an unsuccessful attempt to form a civic group with other conservative women, she continued to head Acción Nacional de Mujeres de Chile. Those who decided not to join Edwards de Salas organized themselves as Acción Patriótica de Mujeres de Chile.[85]

Edwards devised an inclusive, traditional Catholic program "of women of the Right" to celebrate and strengthen the motherland, womanhood, and childhood and followed the papal encyclicals *Rerum novarum* and *Quadragesimo Anno*. Acción Nacional de Mujeres had 18,000 women registered in 1935, a number that speaks for the ability of right-wing political groups to attract members. In 1935 the organization celebrated its second anniversary with a national meeting. Among the speakers were several working women, who demanded a raise in the minimum wage and the presence of women in government welfare agencies and in labor unions.[86] The association of working women with conservative clerical-oriented organizations is not surprising. Since the turn of the century the church had diligently recruited working women, and the marriage of Catholicism and feminism had been well articulated by men such as Bernardo Gentilini, who in 1929 wrote a lucid defense of an active and committed Christian feminism.[87] Another speaker at the Second National Assembly remarked on the need to have a feminine electorate "clean of any suspicion or surrender" and stated that women could no longer afford to be mere spectators in national politics. Edwards de Salas claimed that feminism called attention to the neglect of women's interests in the legislature and public affairs. She reiterated that Acción Nacional de Mujeres did not seek votes and was not any party's instrument. It was an association intent on fighting a moral battle on behalf of women and children.

The other Catholic association, Acción Patriótica de Mujeres de Chile, was a well-organized group that plunged into municipal politics in its first year, developed programs within Santiago, and published its own magazine, *Voz Femenina*, which first appeared in May 1935.[88] This association sought to gather women of all social classes to study and attempt to solve social problems in light of Catholicism. Its leaders were middle-class if not upper-class women. Although disclaiming any association with political parties, they did not renounce politics. Acción Patriótica signed a pact with the Conservative Party "as an act of prudence," claiming that this alignment did not affect its independence and freedom of action.[89] The "civic apostolate" they had in mind was to be pursued by actively promoting women's, students', industrialists', and workers' associations in what sounds like a semicorporatist approach to politics. Acción Patriótica was particularly interested in higher wages, public health care, and public housing. Before splitting from Acción Nacional de Mujeres it had identified over 10,000 women eligible for voter registration. This was the pool from which both organizations hoped to draw their members.

During 1935–36, *Voz Femenina* published articles on a variety of issues such as divorce, which it adamantly opposed, a public housing bill, improvement of national education, and a bill for a "family wage" that would allow wives to stay home and raise their children. Although it was desirable for women to stay at home, an article conceded that poor women had to work to help their husbands. Work as domestics was desirable in such cases because it was within another home, though the essay regretted the low pay domestics received. The organization had an employment office and ran advertisements for well-recommended cooks and maids for general housework.[90] Acción Patriótica received the support of another Catholic newspaper, *El Diario Ilustrado*, on the grounds that it went beyond the "merely political" in its goals to embrace social activities that benefited women.[91] In its class-conscious and patronizing approach, this organization did not differ much from earlier charitable organizations. It was far removed from feminism but very much a potential electorate for conservative parties.

Political Issues and Organizations: The Center and the Left

In the active arena of Chilean female mobilization three other organizations stand out: the Partido Cívico Femenino, the Partido Nacional de Mujeres, and the Movimiento Pro-Emancipación de la Mujer de Chile, known as MEMCH. The first two were centrist middle-class organizations that attempted to carry on the mainstream feminism of the 1920s. MEMCH was decidedly left of center.

Partido Cívico Femenino (founded in 1922) and its magazine *Acción Femenina* returned to active life in 1934. Its president was Elcira Rojas de Vergara, an experienced feminist from the preceding decade; the magazine's director was writer Gladys Thein. Having retraced its roots, the "new" party called for a full-blown program: solidarity among women interested in the advancement of their sex; reevaluation of female labor; adoption of a single standard of morality and deregulation of prostitution; welfare legislation for the working class; family prophylaxis (prenuptial health certificates); investigation of paternity; sex education; an end to political corruption, and full suffrage for women. Protection of mothers and children was a special objective requiring social and health measures such as the eradication of alcoholism, tuberculosis and venereal disease, gambling, and pornography.[92]

The rebirth of the party produced a more active and socially engaged organization. In the first issue of *Acción Femenina* Rojas de Vergara stated her preference for women's parties and welcomed writers of different ideological orientation such as Adela Edwards de Salas and Felisa Vergara. The magazine defined itself as an "eclectic journal" that put women's interests above political convictions or religious creeds.[93] The subjects discussed in *Acción Femenina* throughout several years of publication reflected mid-1930s feminism and included all the themes of interest to the party. News from women and feminists abroad kept the readers in touch with events such as the "sexual reform" in Russia and the new legislation applied to German women.

Like other organizations, the party founded a "club" to attract new members. It would serve nonalcoholic beverages, offer legal advice, preferably by a female lawyer, sell merchandise manufactured by the members, open an employment service for domestic and office work, and offer courses in languages, accounting, fashions, decorative arts, and so on.[94] The magazine echoed the national dialogue on political issues affecting women with a consistent feminist tone, favoring the relaxation of any legislation obstructing women's individual, social, and economic freedom. The party's eclectic attitude was evident in its position on the first municipal elections. A December

1934 editorial criticized the established political parties for opening "feminine sections" without taking time to explain their ideological standing to women.[95] Shortly thereafter Lucía Marticorena de Martín lamented that men's parties had taken advantage of municipal suffrage despite their lack of well-defined programs for municipal improvement. It was the task of the new voters, women and foreigners, to rid municipal government of political manipulation and to trace new paths in politics.[96]

In September 1935 "Página Obrera," a column devoted to labor issues, appeared in the journal for the first time, launching a period of ideological radicalizing. This reorientation in the content of articles suggests a struggle within the organization, but we lack other evidence. By the end of 1935 anarchist and socialist articles began to appear in *Acción Femenina* alongside more gender-oriented, traditional essays and news. The leftist essays denounced women's and children's working conditions and wages and blamed the bourgeois state and the capitalist system for trying to solve the world and national economic crises by squeezing the workers. The solution proposed for such ills was straightforward Marxism: the abolition of wages and the appropriation of the means of production by the workers, standard fare in the ideology of leftist unionism.[97] Peruvian *aprismo* and women in the Aprista Party, a profile of the International Women's League for Peace and Freedom, and reports on *conventillos* [multiple-dwelling tenements], the Spanish civil war, Puerto Rican nationalism, political prisoners in Peru, Paraguay, and Guatemala were also discussed in the journal.[98] This leftist cycle lasted over a year.

In October 1936 the magazine published a redefinition of the party's program. It was a mixture of older feminist principles and leftist ideas. The party would struggle for female solidarity, protection of maternity as a "social function," increased participation of women in municipal welfare institutions, universal suffrage, full civil rights, and sex education. Furthermore, it subscribed to a nationalist goal, the "great anti-imperialistic principles in defense of the economic and social Indoamerican national patrimony." It would fight for a "democracy free of racial hatred or privileges denigrating the human personality."[99] The frequent references to *aprismo* and "Indoamerican" ideals indicate strong connections with Peruvian dissent, perhaps through Magda Portal, whose writings found a place in Chilean and Argentine women's publications of the period. In March 1937 the party appointed Elcira Rojas de Vergara director of the journal. Amanda Labarca was in charge of the editorial council. The editorial for that month endorsed the concept of "Indoamerican feminism," upheld by all Latin women "united throughout the continent with the purpose of defending the wealth of our great Indoamerican nation against the advances of imperialism." This harangue was followed by a pacifist appeal to women, calling on them to struggle against the use of their children — the men of the future — as instruments of destruction. Women should unite against war and, hand-in-hand with men, struggle against inequality, servitude, and privileged minorities.

We may wonder whether such views reflected those of the director and editor or whether they expressed the feeling of more radicalized feminists of the Left. Neither Rojas de Vergara nor Labarca was previously associated with extreme political positions. If there was a struggle within the party and the journal, it was resolved in September 1937, when *Acción Femenina* announced in its editorial a "new life" as the forum of the thinking woman. The journal vowed to inspire confidence in the achievement of its cultural goals. Special attention would be given to the problems of Chile and the Americas.[100]

After September 1937 there was much less enthusiasm in the party's support of radical ideologies. In the January–February 1938 issue, *Acción Femenina* declared its goals to be "essentially feminine," that is, the ennoblement of women through the full achievements of their rights, not irresponsible rebellion. In August the editorial extolled women's political role as one of peace, love, fraternity, and concordance.[101] Thus it appears that the Partido Cívico Femenino stepped back from its temporary departure from mainstream feminism and returned to the political nonsectarian attitude it had originally set for itself.

An exclusively women's party with stated electoral goals was organized in 1935 and consolidated in 1936. It was the Partido Nacional de Mujeres, organized by Agrupación Nacional de Mujeres, which had emerged as a sister organization of the Unión Femenina de Chile. The party was based in Valparaíso and Viña del Mar, and Graciela Lacoste, a long-standing feminist, was elected as its first president. Romelia de Badilla, a member of the Unión Femenina de Chile since the early 1930s, was a notable party member, one of the first women elected to the municipality of Valparaíso.[102]

Partido Nacional de Mujeres claimed to cut across social class with a membership united to pursue improvement of women's legal status and the "correct and conscious" exercise of their rights.[103] In November 1936 the party celebrated its first assembly. The party's directorate believed the crisis in Chilean society was due to the lack of a civic conscience among its public servants and proposed to elect honest ones. The party disavowed violence in the task of social change; its work would be "serene, indefatigable, and ordered" and based on a spirit of Christian social solidarity. Specifically it called for the union of all women and broader political rights for them; protective legislation and equal pay for women workers; prenuptial health certificates and compulsory treatment of "social" diseases; better housing for workers; and lower prices for staple products. Peace and the disarmament of nations were also on the agenda.[104] It seems that this party was founded to elect women to the municipalities and to continue the task of educating women politically, but its electoral performance in the 1938 elections remains unknown.

A more radical challenge was the choice of another organization. It was not a party proper but an umbrella group composed of several organizations and seeking to formulate a program appealing to women of all social classes, although its core had an obvious leftist orientation. MEMCH was founded in May 1935 to strengthen women's voices to reach the higher levels of national politics. Not being a political party, it could only call attention to problems demanding a political solution and advise its members on political action.

The special attention MEMCH gave to working women was reflected in the list of speakers in its first public meeting on 19 December 1935. They were all union men and women. The theme of labor conditions and the right of workers remained central to MEMCH, and its directorate did not hesitate to challenge other women's organizations that did not properly address the situation of workers.[105] Yet its most prominent leaders were professional middle-class women, well traveled and well versed in international affairs. MEMCH had its own magazine, *La Mujer Nueva*, to convey its message to the public. No other feminine publication of its period in any of the countries of the Southern Cone extolled the labor and suffering of working women as intensely as *La Mujer Nueva*.[106] Elena Caffarena, a lawyer from an industrialist family, was MEMCH's main pillar. She remained loyal for several decades. Caffarena was married to a member of the Communist Party and had been one of the first official inspectors of women's manufacturing plants in the 1920s. Her dedication to the cause of women, especially working women, was unshakable.

Early in 1935 Caffarena wrote one of the first essays in the journal stating that the most important goal of MEMCH was women's economic liberation, understood as "having the minimum that all human beings need to subsist—that is, bread, shelter, and clothing." "The role of MEMCH," she wrote, "will be that of propaganda and orientation because only through the efforts of all working women we will transform our aspirations into reality."[107] Her strong personality and excellent oratory helped her steer MEMCH's course for five years. Marta Vergara, previously noted as a collaborator in *Acción Feme-nina*, was also an important member of the group, representing it abroad on several occasions and leaving behind some eloquent essays.[108]

MEMCH's feminist ideology was daring. It pursued "the integral emanci-pation of women, especially the economic, juridical, biological and political emancipation."[109] Contraceptives and planned motherhood were viewed as part of the effort to redeem the working mother from the burden of chil-dren who generally died in early infancy. On the other hand, its support of protective legislation for working mothers and children conformed to the aspirations of most women's groups and watered down the more aggressive leftist rhetoric of some of its members.

MEMCH had a substantial number of communists as members. Their pres-ence was a source of friction with other women's organizations and even within itself, yet for several years Caffarena succeeded in keeping the ideol-ogy of class struggle out of MEMCH. The organization's commitment to the rights of working women would later generate difficulties with the politi-cal interests and styles of middle-class women. Caffarena's attempt to pre-vent radicalization did not go without opposition, and eventually she was removed. In 1940 María Ramírez, a communist worker-leader and mem-ber criticized the official "apolitical" attitude adopted by MEMCH as in-compatible with some of its principles. Ramírez felt that it was slacking in its campaigns against economic problems. *La Mujer Nueva* should orient women workers in the provinces; the organization should encourage more participation from female unions, especially the Confederation of Chilean Workers. Caffarena responded that though the organization remained apo-litical, this did not mean that members renounced affiliation with the parties of their choice. "Each organization has its own functions. For class struggle we have unions; for political struggle we have political parties; for women's struggle we have feminine organizations such as MEMCH."[110]

MEMCH shared the broad 1930s feminist agenda by campaigning for com-plete equality before the law, protesting with other organizations a con-gressional attempt to reduce women's minimum wage and taking a strong stance before all political parties, including socialists and communists, for not considering women's interests.[111] In 1940 it urged that the same protec-tion sought for working women be extended to working men but did not exempt the state from providing welfare services to working mothers and small children.[112] Defining its support for universal suffrage in 1937, MEMCH followed the classic formulation of women as mothers, workers, educated minds, and members of a democracy, entitled to vote on the same footing as men. When MEMCH decided to throw its support behind a presidential candidate, as detailed below, it overcame its own leftist leanings. This success was due to Caffarena's apt leadership. She mastered the art of mixing feminism and class consciousness for political purposes.

MEMCH also had a very able leader in Marta Vergara, who maintained a dual commitment to the radical Left and to feminism. In 1940 she succeeded in articulating the difficult connection between feminism and class, arguing that workers should head the claim for any legitimate right, such as civil and political rights, without trying to carry bourgeois women into economic struggles alien to their own class interests. Any attempt to force such issues on the bourgeoisie would weaken the organization and lead to the triumph of the reactionaries. Women, however, must not forget that men, whether bourgeois or workers, still lacked an understanding of women's problems. "We must struggle indefatigably against the harm they cause us now, tomorrow, and always, until we uproot from future male generations any idea . . . of dominance of one sex over the other."[113]

Suffrage as Female Praxis

Behind Chile's women's organizations was a political purpose: to be heard by the men in the government and to gain the opportunity to implement their objectives. All the organizations active in the 1930s had a keen interest in broadening women's political rights. The 1920s skepticism about female suffrage rapidly dispelled during the Ibáñez administration, when a general rejection of his military government let women flex their political muscles. Having participated publicly in the unrest that preceded Ibáñez's demise, Dra. Ernestina Pérez, a pioneer feminist physician, and Adela Edwards de Salas organized a public gathering to support Radical Party candidate Juan Esteban Montero. The strong showing of women impressed many men who had not recognized the changes taking place in the preceding decade. Later that year, after Montero's election, a group of women visited him to cash in on some concessions, such as his support for feminine suffrage. Montero obliged with a recommendation to the Chamber of Deputies, which was not heeded.[114]

Municipal suffrage was approved in 1934. How did women, as individuals and through female organizations, react to that right? The existing women's "parties," such as Partido Cívico Femenino, realized that most women were unprepared for the challenge and began helping them assume their responsibilities and register to vote.[115] Few women raised any objections to the literacy restrictions.[116] In the rush to prepare candidates for the first municipal elections, the Conservative and Liberal Parties got ahead; their candidates received the endorsement of *El Diario Ilustrado*, a conservative mouthpiece.[117]

For the 7 April 1935 elections 76,049 women and foreigners registered to vote, largely from the provinces of Santiago and Aconcagua. Of these, 66,113 voted, roughly one-fourth the number of the men voting (264,598). Out of ninety-eight women candidates, twenty-five were elected. The largest number belonged to the Conservative Party, which elected sixteen women to different city councils, nine of them in Santiago. Adela Edwards de Salas and Elena Doll de Díaz, of Acción Nacional de Mujeres de Chile, were among them. The Liberal Party elected five women, two of them in Santiago. The Radicals obtained very few votes from women (7,912 votes), and they had two women elected; one apparently resigned. Two more women, an independent and a Democrat, were elected.[118]

Acción Patriótica de Mujeres de Chile, the conservative group that had antagonized Adela Edwards and her Acción Nacional de Mujeres de Chile, elected a working-class Santiago woman, Natalia Rubio Cuadra. They also elected a more aristocratic member, Elisabeth Subercaseaux Errázuriz. It also elected councilwomen in Copiapó, San Felipe, Yungay, Melipilla, and San Bernardo.[119] These women were elected with the support of the Conservative Party, but as members of Acción Patriótica. Rubio Cuadra's stated interests were workers' housing, transportation to workplaces, and low prices for food staples. After the elections, Acción Patriótica lobbied for the passage of a housing bill long neglected in the Senate, while Cuadra organized a project to study women's work, proposed tramways for the use of poor schoolchildren, and collaborated with Acción Patriótica in the political education of nurses and store employees.[120]

Postelection analyses showed different perceptions of women's future in politics. Conservative *Zig-Zag* acknowledged that it was fair for women to want liberation from their situation: "Man has always treated woman badly." Yet an anonymous writer, "Ajax," was skeptical about the mirage of women's independence. In trying to imitate men, women were committing a fundamental error and were heading into a disagreeable competition. "Ajax" pointed out that men were beginning to feel threatened by women because many of them were, indeed, as efficient as men or better. Although this essay did not suggest that a backlash was forthcoming, it attempted to persuade women to remain womanly, because "women's mysterious physiological texture" did not prepare them for a constant struggle with men.[121]

El Diario Ilustrado, proud of its conservative wisdom, gloated over women's proven capacity to assume the duties of suffrage. Women had rejected "pernicious" influences and put their votes at the service of order, peace, political honesty, and democracy.[122] Some women criticized the Radical Party and the Left for not having included a single female candidate.[123] Shortly after the elections, *Acción Femenina* interviewed Pedro Aguirre Cerda, then head of the Radical Party, asking about the results of the election, feminism, suffrage, and the future of women. Aguirre Cerda was not displeased with the results, despite the overwhelming victory of the Right. He would not oppose women's participation in national elections even if they voted for conservatives. The Radical Party was unready to support national female suffrage, but it would study the appropriate timing for that decision. Yet he saw the need to speed up the liberation of women — implying that conservatives had won because women were not yet politically prepared to vote against them. He favored women's political participation through established parties, but he praised the civic work carried out by Partido Cívico Femenino. As for the first term of the recently elected councilwomen, he did not expect they would change much because they lacked training for that office. Aguirre Cerda showed a slight skepticism about women's political ability but remained supportive of their long-term goals. He expected that time would give Chilean women significant political maturity and that the Radical Party would reap some of the fruit, but neither he nor the party was willing to hasten the process.[124]

Women's Organizations and Male Backlash

Between 1935 and 1938 women's organizations struggled to accelerate the political education of their sex and gain a piece of the electoral turf. These objectives were carried out through a variety of means. Intellectually, the most important were their publications, but other propaganda means were not overlooked. Yearly assemblies served to reinvigorate members and gain access to the press. Provincial committees or clubs were also important for gaining a foothold beyond the cities of Santiago and Valparaíso. Leaders went on speaking tours, received visitors from abroad, gave social teas, and opened facilities for working mothers or students. The discussion of legislation for divorce in 1935 and the debates occasioned by the recommendation of the 1936 medical convention in Valparaíso for the legalization of abortion gave some women the opportunity to speak on those topics. But the economic plight of working women, the unequal rate of payment for women, the high cost of living, the high rates of illegitimacy, and infant mortality remained the most important domestic themes. Women also discussed the rise of fascism and the limiting of women's roles in countries like Germany and Italy, the specter of another European war, the Chaco war, the Spanish civil war, and the status of women in other Latin American countries. Not all feminist organizations and personalities responded to these topics with the same enthusiasm. Controversial issues such as abortion were commented on only by the most radical publications, such as *La Mujer Nueva*. Sex education appeared discreetly in the pages of *Acción Femenina*.

Domestic political themes were the most relevant, but international events such as the Inter-American meeting in Montevideo and the 1936 International Conference on Peace in Buenos Aires gave Chilean feminists an opportunity to prove at home the universality of their aspirations. In 1936 women of diverse political orientations found some common causes on which to make a show of strength and unity. Arturo Alessandri's second term in the presidency was a disappointment for most feminists. His efforts to obtain economic stability at the cost of lowering most people's standard of living, especially the workers', irked activist women. A committee demanding lower prices for food staples united a diverse group of women who, on 8 October, gathered in the Politeama Theater to protest the high cost of living. Wearing mostly dark dresses and hats, women such as Cora Cid of the Liberal Party, Elena Caffarena of MEMCH, Cleophas Torres, president of the National Women's Party, Norma Calderón, a member of the union of railroad workers, and a department store employee spoke of their discontent with the country's economic situation and with Alessandri's policies. As they left the theater, some women were harassed by members of the army.[125]

Another issue that brought women together was a bill proposing quotas for women in government offices. Backed by the Ministry of Labor, the bill would have restricted women to no more than 20 percent of the labor force in municipal and national offices. Women were displacing men from the labor pool, and a male backlash seemed likely.[126] Another of Alessandri's bills proposed a minimum wage for workers and would have reduced the earnings of women working in jobs "appropriate of their sex" by 30 percent. This bill affected the wages of women working in many industries.[127] These were not the only attempts to restrict women's access to employment or their wages. In November 1936 the Valparaíso municipal supervisors agreed not to consider their female employees for raises, promotions, or bonuses. The number of women affected in this instance was small—twenty—but the practice was against the law of the country.[128] Not surprisingly, Gabriela Mistral, writing from Lisbon in December of that year, stated that her understanding of feminism was economic: equal wages for both sexes.[129]

The discrimination bills ran against the Labor Code enacted in 1923 during the first Alessandri administration and were too naked for the Chilean Congress to swallow, especially at a time when women's political mobilization was gaining momentum and the economic situation of the working classes was so strained. Deputy Francisco Walker was among those most strongly opposed to any restriction of women's labor or wages.[130] There were other deputies, such as Arturo Olavarría, who still argued that women used their earnings as pin money, displacing male heads of families. Congress turned down the bills. Throughout the discussions of these bills women made a significant show of unity. MEMCH, Partido Cívico Femenino, and the women's section of the Radical Party joined forces to lobby against the proposed laws. The Inter-American Commission on Women and the Unión Argentina de Mujeres, led by Victoria Ocampo, also protested.[131] MEMCH also denounced the facts that military service was required to gain access to some administrative departments and that the Dirección del Trabajo itself had a limit of 10 percent women as labor inspectors.[132]

Unfortunately, women's organizations associated with MEMCH risked being marked as radical and losing votes or moral support. This happened to Acción de Voluntades Femeninas, founded in 1937 to promote the welfare of mothers and children, equitable salaries for women, decent housing for workers and suffrage in the national elections. Its program was partly written by members of MEMCH, but Amanda Labarca wrote the articles on educational goals. Catholic Action denounced Voluntades Femeninas for being associated with the "international feminine movement that intended to introduce ruinous ideas among women." Without mentioning MEMCH, the Catholic hierarchy saw a communist trap for good Catholic women under cover of philanthropic ideas.[133] Despite this liability, MEMCH succeeded in maintaining the allegiance of several diverse women's organizations and became their mouthpiece during the presidential elections of 1938.

Women and the 1938 Elections

Both municipal and national elections took place in 1938. Women could vote only in the first, but their concern with the second surpassed any previous experience and reaffirmed the growing commitment of women's organizations to civic affairs. Over 60,000 women registered to vote in organized groups.

The so-called left-wing organizations claimed 18,072, and traditional parties had 42,062. The number of female candidates increased: forty women ran for office and a total of 74,759 women cast their votes, an increase of about 8,000 since 1935.[134] María Aguirre and Enriqueta Silva were the labor representatives of the far Left. Aguirre had also been strongly endorsed by *Acción Femenina*, the journal of Partido Cívico Femenino. MEMCH's inability to get its candidates elected suggests that, despite its active propaganda, women were yet not regarded as worth the risk by leftist voters. Another well-known woman defeated in the elections was writer Elvira Santa Cruz Ossa ("Roxane"); a pen name was not sufficient accreditation for public office. The conservative Asociación Nacional de Mujeres de Chile elected Elena Doll de Díaz and Amelia Díaz for Santiago. By 1941, two-thirds of the women registering for elections were conservative. That most women voted conservative was deplored by left-wing organizations, which had reason to be disappointed with the performance of their candidates.[135] The Liberal, Radical, and Independent Parties ranked well behind the Conservative Party in number of votes and in female candidates elected. Some parties never bothered to put forward or support female candidates.[136]

In the 1938 national elections, a coalition of center and left parties and the Chilean Labor Federation entered the campaign as a national Popular Front, supporting the Radical Party candidate, Pedro Aguirre Cerda.[137] Alessandri supported his former minister of finance, Gustavo Ross. The formation of the Popular Front did not fail to elicit a response from feminist organizations. Militants in the Partido Cívico Femenino and MEMCH threw their support behind Aguirre Cerda. MEMCH participated actively in the Popular Front, criticizing most parties for their lack of interest in women's issues and urging them to change their attitudes and support women's suffrage.

As the official candidate of the Popular Front in 1938, Aguirre Cerda showed that his "evolutionary" attitude about women's social and political role had not changed. In an interview for MEMCH's *La Mujer Nueva*, he stated his respect for women's work, as the son of a widow with seven children. He promised to continue to support women's education and protective legislation and women's participation in the administration of welfare institutions. Asked if he favored "family limitation," he said no. He favored, instead, aid for working mothers and welfare services for children.[138] After his election he reiterated his intention of offering Chilean women ample participation in the economic, educational, and administrative affairs of the community. Aguirre Cerda appointed Graciela Contreras de Schnake mayor of Santiago in 1939, and in March 1941 he appointed Olga Boetcher governor of the department of La Unión. Presidents could appoint mayors to cities with over 100,000 inhabitants, and this was a political gesture to win women over. Boetcher's appointment earned Aguirre Cerda protest from members of his own party.[139] During his brief presidency, he paid lip service to women's organizations, attending the meetings of the National Council of Women and even some of MEMCH's meetings. His most important contribution to women was a bill endorsing their participation in the national elections,[140] and his premature death in November 1941 left women without a friendly, if paternalistic, supporter at the highest political level. Although he claimed he saw in women's community participation "a great moral equilibrium," his statements suggest that he still viewed them largely as intellectual and emotional companions to men.[141]

For most women's organizations the 1930s were a decade of mobilization and hope, if not unity. Whether Congress would have granted women full political rights as requested by Aguirre Cerda is a moot point. Their political growth in ten years was remarkable, but an era came to an end with Aguirre Cerda's death and the dissolution of the Popular Front in 1941. For MEMCH, the most politically radical group of the 1930s, its second national congress was also a swan song. When MEMCH's delegates met in late October 1940 there were forty-four committees throughout the nation, with 110 delegates from diverse economic backgrounds, although mostly working women. Elena Caffarena was secretary-general.[142] The subjects causing most debate were the cost of living, international peace, and the group's own internal organization. The political committee recommended national suffrage and charged the national executive committee with drafting a bill addressing the issue. Among the recommendations on labor were protective laws for all workers and for pregnant women; improvement of child welfare services; and improvement of social services. Other topics receiving consideration were regulation of food prices and rents, restrictions on the export of staple foods, taxation of foreign businesses, loans to small farmers, and agrarian reform. Finally, the congress declared for peace and against fascism and imperialism. This was a mature political agenda in no way inferior to that of any male party. Unfortunately, MEMCH fell prey to internal dissension. The communist members moved to control the congress and thus alienated the intellectual middle-class groups. They ousted Caffarena from her post as secretary-general, replacing her with a long-standing liberal feminist, Graciela Mandujano, whom they also supported for the municipal council in the 1941 elections. She lost.[143]

After 1941 several women's organizations struggled to survive separately and to focus on enfranchisement. Wartime realities forced people to concentrate on the economy rather than social reform, especially since there was no commitment to those objectives in the program of newly elected president, Juan Antonio Ríos Morales. In 1941 Elena Doll de Díaz, a city councillor for Santiago, ran for the third time. One of her supporters offered her as an example of being in politics "without losing femininity." She was praised for supporting women's rights "without falling into the exaggerations and aggressiveness associated with feminism."[144] She had been elected through the Conservative Party, but it was claimed that she had become the party's best critic, and in 1941 she was running dissociated from any party and heading a list that included two other well-known activist women. Her program was heavy on welfare for workers of both sexes: equal wages, bonuses for married men, sanitation, and "popular restaurants." She also wanted to provide electric trolleys for workers living beyond the city's perimeter and to improve garbage disposal.[145] The 1941 municipal elections were disappointing. In Santiago eight nonconservative women candidates ran for election. Three were independent, two were socialists, and one each ran for the Popular Front, the Falange Nacional Party, and the Democratic Party. Three had no affiliation. None was elected.[146]

Even though women were elected mayors and city councillors, reuniting into a common front after 1941 was difficult and was not achieved until November 1944, when the Federación Chilena de Instituciones Femeninas (FECHIF) became a reality. FECHIF succeeded because it had the support of women who had carved a name for themselves in the 1920s and 1930s, such as Amanda Labarca, Graciela Mandujano, and María Aguirre. FECHIF introduced a new project for suffrage in 1945. Following a general post–World War II trend, Chilean deputies accepted the inevitable and recommended the approval of suffrage in 1946. The final thrust was made by a temporary alliance of women's organizations in 1947, known as the Comité Unido Pro-Voto Femenino, and the revival of MEMCH, which joined FECHIF. Congress took two more years to study, discuss, and recommend female enfranchisement, which, under presidential pressure, became law on 15 December 1948.[147]

During the critical period between 1915 and 1940, what began as a hesitant mainstream middle- and upper-class feminist desire for self-definition matured into a complex picture of female activism that, in the politically volatile atmosphere of the mid-1930s, gave Chilean women the opportunity to choose any stance between Catholic traditionalism and outright communism. The choice made was conservative and middle-class, as was the electorate. For all its political fireworks, the Left had to resort to national coalitions to win political leverage, and at the municipal level it could raise no support for the women's agenda. By 1940 Chilean women had learned the ropes of political organization, but they suffered from the same political fragmentation that afflicted men in politics. Although the multiple organizational efforts carried out by women qua women were critical in gaining a strong sense of self-reliance and knowledge of gender issues, these factors did not guarantee success in the larger political arena. There men retained their secure position of dominance.

CHAPTER 10

Women's Politics and Suffrage
in Uruguay

Uruguayan feminists emerged into national life in the middle years of the second decade of the twentieth century. Despite their late arrival, they were among the most outspoken feminists in the Southern Cone. The slow development of a female feminist core was partly due to the lack of a good educational base. No significant gains in primary and secondary education were made until the turn of the century, and few women reached the university level before 1905. Paulina Luisi became the first woman to receive a *bachillerato,* or preuniversity degree, in 1899 and the first woman doctor to graduate in Montevideo in 1909.[1] Traditional codes of social behavior precluded women assuming any leading role beyond the home. Uruguay was a country of ranchers and cattlemen involved in political feuds throughout much of the nineteenth century. The political arena was strongly masculine and not just male dominated. One of the last local caudillo revolts took place during the first administration of José Batlle y Ordóñez, under whose leadership the nation took a sharp turn toward stability. By the mid-1910s the country was engulfed in a process of social reform that affected women profoundly.

José Batlle y Ordóñez, president of Uruguay in 1903–7 and 1911–15, was a strong supporter of women's rights and feminist issues. He believed in the need to "liberate" Uruguayan women from old-fashioned ideas and clerical influence. The help he and his Colorado Party lent to feminists throughout the critical years in which they controlled the legislative and the executive branches of the government cannot be overestimated.[2] As president and as leader of his party his direct participation was limited, given the demands of his office, but his ideas were refined and developed mostly by his political disciples and the intellectual elite of the Colorado Party. Additional intellectual support to women and feminism came from the Socialist Party: although it had little political clout, its leaders gave feminists additional voices in congressional debates.

Early Feminists: Defining Positions

Before 1915 only one female feminist personality stands out — María Abella de Ramírez (1863–1926), a pathbreaking figure in the reform of gender relations and women's role in society.[3] Uruguayan by birth, she lived most of her life in the Argentine city of La Plata. She began publishing in local newspapers in 1898, and early in 1900 she attempted to found a club (Club de Señoras) for the physical, moral, and intellectual betterment of women. The club would have been a social center where women could gather to participate in activities such as calisthenics, housekeeping classes, games, and reading. The isolation of women in their daily routines, she explained, bred discontent at home. Giving them an opportunity to get out of the house and broaden their sphere would release personal and family tensions. Behind this goal, however, lay another, vastly more meaningful. Joining the club would bring women together to exchange ideas and prove to them and others that they were capable of doing more than taking care of home, husband, and children.[4]

Abella's commitment to women's causes led her to found *Nosotras* in July 1902. Described as "a feminist literary and social magazine," this publication launched the editor, then thirty-nine years of age, into a very active decade throughout which she developed a plan for female political and social engagement and built a body of feminist thought that was remarkably open for her period. In its two years of life *Nosotras* examined a variety of ideas on the emancipation of women and acted as a forum for the discussion of social issues affecting men, women, and the family.[5] By 1902 she had already crossed over from the idea of an educational and recreational association to outspoken feminism. In her quest for personal intellectual freedom, Abella de Ramírez joined the Society of Freethinkers, a group of men and women who wished to shed religious and social inhibitions. The freethinkers gave her what she demanded from others, freedom from prejudice.[6]

The International Congress of Freethinkers met in Buenos Aires in 1906 and Abella attended, contributing a plan for the liberation of women. This Minimum Plan of Female Demands addressed both sexes and listed reforms necessary to achieve gender equality. The plan called for equal education, equal employment opportunities and equal wages, a share in the administration of the family property, freedom of movement, and freedom for married women to choose an independent lifestyle. Sharing rights over the children [*patria potestad*] with their husbands was another key point in her plan. She also listed absolute divorce, equality of all children before the law, toleration but nonregulation of prostitution, and political rights for women.[7] It is unclear whether the list ranked the objectives in order of importance to its author, but they show her priorities. The plan showed an internal progressive widening of women's horizons, from freeing the mind and the self from economic dependence and marital subordination to the ultimate accomplishment of casting a political vote.

The next stage in her development as a feminist was the foundation of the National Feminist League [Liga Feminista Nacional] in her La Plata home on 29 May 1910.[8] The League pursued the foundation of feminist centers in Argentina following a "broad plan" and a "narrow plan" of reforms. The bases of the National Feminist League reflect the mixture of liberal and social feminism that she defined with the help of her friend Dra. Julieta Lanteri, with whom she began to collaborate by the end of the decade. In August 1910 one of her daughters and a small group of advanced law students helped her found a Feminist Center in La Plata. By December there was another in Santa Fe, a city north of Buenos Aires.[9]

On 10 May 1910 Abella de Ramírez launched another magazine in La Plata, *La Nueva Mujer*, to act as the mouthpiece of Liga Feminista. Her freethinker companion Julieta Lanteri was assistant director. *La Nueva Mujer* seems to have lasted through 1912.[10] The League and its magazine were her forum for establishing ties with women abroad and other women's organizations in Argentina. After 1910 the freethinkers founded a National League of Women Freethinkers that organized the Confederación Femenina Latino-Americana to support women's and children's rights.[11] Ties between some feminists and freethinkers were close at this point, although "freethinking" was not a feature of early feminism. Also in 1910, Abella de Ramírez attended the First International Feminine Conference in Buenos Aires and traveled to Montevideo to found a branch of the Federación Femenina Pan-Americana. The Federación was the idea of Chilean María E. de Muñoz and was founded after the First International Feminine Congress. Its nonpolitical program sought the uplift of women, the prosperity of the home, the moralization of customs, and universal peace.[12]

La Nueva Mujer raised eyebrows in some circles, including those representing women's interests. The editors of the Buenos Aires–based magazine

Unión y Labor criticized *La Nueva Mujer* in August 1910, hardly two months after welcoming its publication. *Unión y Labor* considered the articles aired in Abella's magazine "almost obscene" and lamented that women who had the duty to moralize and educate were giving such bad examples. To remain faithful to journalistic honesty, the editors published the principles of the Feminist League, although they condemned its sentiments.[13] What in *La Mujer Nueva* could have been deemed "almost obscene"? There was nothing in the Feminist League program or in its journal that departed from standard feminist standing on civil and political rights. However, the editors of the Buenos Aires publication were apparently offended by *La Mujer Nueva*'s condemnation of imprisonment for adultery, the recommendation that the church-controlled institution for "deviant" women, El Buen Pastor, be closed down, and the League's call for the abolition of municipally controlled houses of prostitution.[14] This display of prudery in cosmopolitan Buenos Aires suggests that women's groups were still unready to support socially risky causes and opinions. Abella's activities after 1912 are difficult to trace, although some of her essays were reprinted in other women's publications. She was in the avant garde of feminism, drawing the blueprint that a decade later would guide women in creating viable organizations to channel women's efforts toward their own liberation.

One year before the publication of Abella de Ramírez's *Nosotras*, Celestina Margain de León, a journalist and writer, had launched *La Defensa de la Mujer* in Montevideo. The anticlerical and pro-feminist Margain sustained the defense of "modern woman" from the pages of her short-lived newspaper. She upheld women's legal aspirations and their rights as wife, mother, sister, and friend.[15] In the second number she began to develop the theme of the unwarranted tyranny of men within the home. By the third number she was receiving support letters from several men.[16] The newborn newspaper was soon engaged in an ideological battle with the conservative *La Tribuna Popular*, which ridiculed its message and its director. Margain answered in kind and promised to engage her publication in the discussion of anarchism, the exploitation of women's labor, and the restrictions of the church.[17] Unfortunately, lacking any evidence of further issues, we know neither whether Margain kept her promise nor how long her newspaper survived.

Until the emergence of Paulina Luisi in the second decade of the century, men were the main standard-bearers of social and gender reform in Uruguay. The debate over divorce in the first years of the century proved that sustained by feminism, social reform could become an issue eminently suited for debate in the public arena. By the time the first divorce legislation was under revision in 1912, women's suffrage emerged as part of a broader movement to expand popular participation in the government. Although the main proponent of female suffrage was a Colorado Party member, socialists endorsed it from the start. Their participation in the debate added an ideological dimension that gave women's vote a few more adversaries, but a clearer definition of the ethical aspects of female citizenship.

In 1914, having obtained the passage of a controversial amendment to the divorce legislation, some Colorado Party members became interested in women's political rights. In July of that year Deputy Héctor Miranda introduced a bill to enfranchise women at the national level. He dismissed the alternative of a municipal vote as too narrow and ineffective, arguing that voting for a president did not require their special preparation. If, as some claimed, politics was a "dirty business," he was convinced that women, as the sex with higher moral sense, would elevate its character.[18] Miranda's arguments were shared by most advanced reformers and would become standard suffragist discourse in the 1920s and 1930s. The Partido Nacional or Blancos, the Colorado's ideological adversary, and the conservative and Catholic press opposed the bill, arguing that though women were no less intelligent than men, men had developed a leadership that women were unable to equal or challenge. Moreover, nature had also imposed on women the supreme task of maternity, which demanded most of their energy.[19]

Although Miranda's proposal failed to gain support in Congress, it raised the issue before the public. If most deputies were uninterested, some women were ready to endorse it. Apparently, female teachers were persuaded of the benefits of the vote and founded the Asociación Magisterial Pro-Sufragio Femenino, reported by El Día to be in existence in September 1915. Although very little is known about its activities, it was still operating in 1922, when it asked the government to appoint Paulina Luisi to the Council of Public Welfare [Consejo de Asistencia Pública], and made a public statement supporting the legitimacy of women's suffrage on grounds that the vote would allow women to promote social progress and to cooperate in the task of dignifying humanity.[20]

Unfortunately the cause of women's suffrage had powerful opponents. One of them was a respected jurist, Justino E. Jiménez de Aréchaga, who in 1915 published his interpretation of women's rights under the Constitution. Jiménez de Aréchaga spoke directly against Héctor Miranda's bill. Miranda had argued that the Constitution did not specifically deny women that right, and that its negation resulted from an arbitrary interpretation of its spirit. Jiménez, contrariwise, was persuaded that women's suffrage was not in the spirit of the Constitution, whose designers had specifically described that right as belonging to all "free men." He took the word men to mean a biological male, not the pattern for the species.[21]

These contradictory interpretations had a chance to be discussed in the 1916 Constitutional Convention, called to redefine the political structure of the nation. Batlle was no longer president of Uruguay, having been defeated in his bid to win office for the third time. The new political charter was supposed to give the nation the opportunity of confirming Batlle's idea of a constitutional system in which the presidency would rotate among members of a governing council. Another important issue was the extension of suffrage, which up to then was restricted by property qualifications. Supporters of the expansion of the suffrage base assumed it would apply to men only, but that stance had been eroded by Miranda's 1914 bill on female suffrage.

The debates in the Constitutional Convention were the first serious test of the political viability of female suffrage. Since the outset, supporters of women's rights counted on a number of committed *batllistas* and socialists Emilio Frugoni and Pablo Celestino Mibelli. On the other hand, they found plenty of opposition among several members of the National Party. Beginning in April 1917, conservatives Juan José Segundo, Amador Sánchez, and others engaged in a verbal battle against women's suffrage.[22] Sometimes an air of jocosity was created by the puns of suffrage opponents, who used quips to detract from the seriousness of the issue.

Pursuing the acceptance of political rights for women, Mibelli proposed that in defining suffrage "men" be replaced by "persons," a simple reform formulation used shortly thereafter by Baltasar Brum. He cited the increasing number of women workers who wanted citizenship and emancipation but could not effectively defend their rights as workers without the vote. Emilio Frugoni gave a long and articulate speech in women's defense using what were becoming the "archetypal" economic arguments for political empowerment. He stressed how changes in the economic structure of the family reflected change in society. Women's wages were essential to sustain their families, and their labor in factories and offices was of primary importance to the economy. Their economic responsibilities entitled them to a say in the nation's destiny and in shaping legislation that affected them. Suffrage would let them support those who promoted and protected their rights and would help prevent their exploitation as workers. Frugoni denied the validity of the argument that political rights would lead women away from the home. Women, like men, could take an active interest in politics without abandoning their family obligations; they were already politically engaged as members of interest groups. The convention, he forthrightly stated, should not deny suffrage to women who wanted it while granting the vote to many men who did not.[23]

For suffrage opponents such as Juan José Segundo the vote had subversive qualities that would "pervert" women and make them "dangerous." Why go ahead with a project for universal suffrage when other countries had just granted the municipal vote? Women, he posited, did not need *any* vote. They had no personality of their own, and they should remain satisfied with being good wives and mothers. He refused to acknowledge that some women had to go out to work, stating that such a situation should not exist. Men *ought to assume* all the responsibility to sustain the home. Conservatives and traditionalists adopted a moral imperative that was rapidly becoming obsolete but that served to coalesce the votes of those unsure about the benefits of change. Their position was that the Uruguayan reality did not call for any revision in women's rights. This attitude was not surprising; in 1912 conservative deputy Melián Lafinur stated that professional women were a danger to the stability of the family and incapable of fulfilling their maternal mission.[24]

Activist women thus accused were indeed learning the realities of national politics and the strings they had to pull to be heard. During the constitutional discussions the members of the newly founded National Council of Women submitted a petition in favor of women's enfranchisement to members of the convention. Sixty-six women signed another letter in support of the constitutional reform. Deputy Juan A. Cachón deemed the petition of the National Council unrepresentative of Uruguayan motherhood; he argued that the signatories were a group of intellectual women whose views were not shared by the rest of the population.[25]

The opposition of the conservative Partido Nacionalista and the lukewarm support of many Colorados were enough to stop approval of female suffrage. At the end of the Constitutional Convention it remained as a blueprint for the future. The constitutionalists left a door open to its approval by endorsing a compromise formula proposed by Juan Antonio Buero. It gave the legislature power to determine when to grant women the vote. To achieve that end, the bill had to receive a two-thirds majority of votes from the members of both chambers.[26] Defeat of the constitutional suffrage reform did not stall female political awakening. Colorados and socialists had a good idea of the potential uses of the feminine vote, and just as important, a budding female leadership was realizing that to become effective they had to organize. On 18 March 1917 a group of women published a political manifesto in *El Día* stating that "woman has, in addition to the mission proper of her sex, the right to intervene, and make herself heard, in the development of political events . . . that affect her in a direct manner."[27] They already had a forum — the National Council of Women.

The National Council of Women: Putting Feminism in Place

For Uruguayan women the most significant event of 1916 was the foundation of the Uruguayan National Council of Women, a member of the International Councils of Women, which would galvanize feminist activities for the critical formative years. Founded on 30 September, the National Council was the brainchild of Paulina Luisi, whose boundless energy, deeply felt feminism, European travels, and connections with other feminist organizations made her the leader of Uruguayan feminism for the next two decades. On 17 July the National Council began publishing its own magazine, *Acción Femenina*, to expound its ideas and report its activities to the membership.[28]

Following the guidelines of the International Council of Women, the Uruguayan branch welcomed all women to work on behalf of the moral, intellectual, material, economic, and legal improvement of their sex. These objectives followed elementary principles of equity and justice to define the equivalence of both sexes and the unity of the human couple. The Council wanted to avoid the estrangement of men from women, a concern they shared with other women's groups in the Southern Cone. To keep on course the Council declared itself nonreligious and apolitical. It would respect each member's faith while hoping that all political parties would share its objectives. It seems likely that this initial statement was written at least in part by Paulini Luisi. The Council had a roster of notable women who later distinguished themselves as feminists, such as Dra. Isabel Pinto Vidal, Clotilde Luisi, Fanny Carrió de Polleri, and Adela Rodríguez de Morató.

The National Council's first public statement sent a strong message of social consciousness to women of the middle and upper classes, its most likely members. It reminded them of the harsh conditions under which working women lived and raised their children and criticized the men who had participated in the Constitutional Convention for denying political rights to women in the name of homelife. They had ignored the thousands of women who worked at jobs from sunrise to sunset to sustain their homes. They could deny those women the right to vote, but as legislators and men they were unwilling to protect and respect them. The bitterness of the Council's comment was followed by an enumeration of its goals: promotion of health and social welfare, attainment of full legal rights and better working conditions for women, equal standards of moral behavior for men and women, and the promotion of education, civic awareness, and peace for all.[29] Unity of "heart and mind" should guide the Council members as thinking women concerned with social problems. As an umbrella organization, the Council comprised several associations, none of which, in the Uruguayan case, had other than charitable or intellectual purposes. To manage its affairs the Council had several internal committees that reflected its interests and activities: hygiene, housing, legal rights, suffrage, peace, and labor were the most important. Shortly after its foundation, the Council began a campaign against tuberculosis and alcoholism and promoted child care and child health as national priorities.[30]

The closing of the Constitutional Convention prompted the Council to initiate a suffrage campaign. The Council regarded approval of women's vote under the conditions delineated above as giving them a base that women in other nations lacked.[31] In December 1917 a group of Council women gathered at the university to begin drafting a strategy for the suffrage campaign.[32] Lobbying and engaging in political activism were new responsibilities that were soon to become the core of future actions. Despite the initial commitment to suffrage, most of the Council's efforts during its first year were on behalf of a Regional Congress against Alcoholism, which took place the third week of April 1918. Suffrage was linked to alcoholism. The Council pointed out that countries where women voted had the most effective legislation against alcohol and had reduced consumption. Participants in the congress were encouraged to show the strength of their conviction by supporting women's suffrage "not as an expression of political ambition," but as a way to help women achieve more egalitarian and humane laws.[33] Congress organizers declared it a "feminist event" insofar as it was the first conference organized by women in Uruguay.[34]

In June 1919 the Council's members, still believing that enfranchisement was around the corner, held a second "suffragist assembly" to explain the role of women in politics and define the objectives of female voting. The keynote speaker, Fanny Carrió de Polleri, defined the Uruguayan National Council of Women's feminism as humanitarian, nonpartisan in politics and religion, seeking the protection of children and women, and without hostility to men. She regretted that Uruguayan women, titled queens of the home, had to sit on a fragile throne next to those the law had denied the right to vote "for lacking intellectual aptitude." Neither their intellectual achievements nor their competence and capability for work raised women above the level of any inexperienced man over eighteen. She urged all Uruguayan women to join in a common effort to move forward with feminism and female emancipation, to prepare themselves to fulfill their political duties, and to let the political authorities learn that their goal was suffrage.[35] The work plan she had in mind for women in politics was geared toward solving urban problems, such as building satisfactory housing for workers, correcting underpayment of working women, protecting pregnant women and homeless children, and uprooting alcoholism and cigarette addiction. These themes followed the main pattern of feminist concerns in the Southern Cone.

The suffrage issue demanded a special organization that could act independently of the National Council of Women, leaving it free for other work. In 1919 Luisi organized the Alianza Uruguaya de Mujeres para el Sufragio Femenino, a separate association still under the umbrella of the National Council of Women. The Alianza affiliated itself with the North American Alliance for Feminine Suffrage, led by Carrie Chapman Catt, and established ties with the Asociación Argentina Pro-Derechos Femeninos, led by Elvira Rawson de Dellepiane. Once organized, the Alianza began its campaign by expressing support for a municipal vote bill submitted by deputy Alfeo Brum to the congressional Legislative Commission. The Alianza urged the members of Congress to enact a law to enable Uruguayan women to carry out the "legitimate social duty of rendering service to the different domains of public welfare,"[36] but the Constitutional Convention motion stood in the way. The Brum bill collapsed for lack of congressional interest.

In the meantime the Council pressed for other issues. Under Paulina Luisi's leadership this organization became involved in the campaign against the "white slave trade," the importing of prostitutes from Europe to Montevideo and Buenos Aires. The Alianza urged the newly elected president Baltasar Brum to ask Congress to ratify the articles of the 1910 Paris Convention against the trade. Brum complied promptly with the Council's request, in October 1919. His support was a moral victory for the Council, which continued a letter campaign urging members of Congress to support this measure. Uruguay ratified the convention in the mid-1920s.[37]

That the Alianza had been founded to sustain the suffrage campaign did not stop the National Council from pursuing that issue on its own. Early in 1920 the National Council floated the idea of a municipal suffrage bill, an attractive alternative to the national vote. This project would automatically enroll women as voters for the presidential and congressional elections two years after its enactment.[38] Unfortunately the Council's hope for congressional support was not forthcoming. *Automatic* enfranchisement of women was the last option most legislators would have taken, since it ran against the prescription of the Constitutional Convention.[39]

The problems suffrage was encountering in Congress obliged the Alianza to abandon its exclusive concern with it and redefine its agenda. In October 1922 the members agreed to expand the scope of their activities to include *any* cause of benefit to women and children. They reasoned that women should prove that while asking for their political rights they were not indifferent to social problems.[40] The Alianza sponsored a ten-point social program that included better housing, street cleaning, effective enforcement of primary education with the banning of private schools, and the abolition of secular and religious retreat institutions ("to end the propagation of sexual degeneration"). It also endorsed the creation of circulating libraries and a tax on tobacco.[41] This program was suggested by Paulina Luisi, and the Alianza decided to adopt and publicize it despite its controversial anticlerical bent. Through 1925 the Alianza supported legislation enabling women to act as notaries, attorneys, and auctioneers, and the recognition of their rights to act as witnesses and legal guardians for minors. Even though in the 1920s the Alianza never failed to support the suffragist cause, its program became indistinguishable from those of other feminist organizations.

The lack of confidence created by the congressional members' unreadiness to approve suffrage legislation was a strong factor in the diversification of activities. Another was the internal struggle within the National Council and its increasing alienation from the Alianza. Already in 1919 the National Council's internal committee on suffrage called its efforts "the most unrewarding and destined to receive the greatest resistance."[42] On the other hand, some women in the Council had the false feeling that the emphasis on women's issues was no longer so urgent. They were convinced of the validity of their cause and assumed they had a strong national support.[43]

Unfortunately, this confidence was misplaced. In 1922 Isabel Pinto Vidal, addressing the Council's fourth annual meeting, confessed that she was having great difficulty getting feminism accepted by uncommitted women. She acknowledged problems in gaining new members, even among working women who should have been willing to join them but who were neither thinking of associating themselves with the Council nor supporting it. Before she left the presidency at the end of the year she insisted on the urgency of carrying out more propaganda on the Council's behalf, suggesting visits to industries and offices to educate all women in the exercise of their rights. In her opinion no woman should be passed over for lack of education. All women of goodwill could and should join the National Council.[44]

If suffrage was a much tougher bone than feminists expected, it was not for lack of support from the top of the political hierarchy. In 1921 President Baltasar Brum wrote a sweeping bill removing all the gender impediments from the Civil Code and granting women suffrage in national elections. He believed that suffrage was a question of justice and should be adopted whether or not it benefited the Colorado Party. He dismissed fears that women would vote either for Catholic candidates or for those chosen by their male relatives. Women would become "enlightened" as they became interested in politics, overcoming their forced isolation. Brum stressed the dignity suffrage would confer without depriving women of their femininity or distracting them from their home and maternal duties. Brum never concealed his sympathies for feminism and used the term without any reservations.[45] His bill was introduced in Congress by several Colorado deputies, but it lingered in the chambers "for study," and no action was taken on it.

Assessing its future, the Council recognized the need to expand into the provinces where women were doubtful about the organization. In 1922 the nuclei in Rocha and Durazno were having a tough time staying above water, even though the latter had gathered 150 signatures in support of women's rights.[46] The Council did all it could to maintain a variety of activities, assert its own public profile, and regain the momentum it had enjoyed during its first trienium. It remained in touch with international feminist organizations; had a member—Angela Díaz—writing a weekly column in La Mañana; sponsored lectures and studies on social and feminist issues; and printed educational material in its magazine. Yet all these pursuits were carried out by a small circle of educated women and men and appealed only to equally educated potential members. The nucleus of many women's organizations seems to have been their middle-class base supplemented by wavering support from members who joined for a relatively short time and left when their interest declined.

The National Council's influence on working women was limited, although it sought to include them in its constituency. The most effective efforts to cater to the needs of female workers took place in 1918, when the Council lobbied several senators to vote for a bill to provide chairs so women employees could sit down in moments of rest. It was dubbed ley de la silla. They eventually took the lobbying to Baltasar Brum, a cabinet member at the time, who interceded on behalf of the workers and obtained the Senate's approval. In the same year the Council also put pressure on the Ministry of Industry to have the teaching of typesetting included in the Women's Industrial School [Escuela Industrial Femenina]. In the Council's opinion this profession was eminently suitable to women, but male typesetters were adamantly opposed to women as coworkers. The Council submitted a report to the Industrial School on the most desirable occupations for women. Prefaced by a statement that women were capable of most occupations, it suggested a list of fifteen trades in which they could be most successful. They were craft oriented and traditional in nature, such as leatherworking, jewelry making, metalworking, industrial drawing, sculpture, manufacturing ceramic products, and basketwork, among others. However, they included photography, industrial chemistry, and jobs operating industrial machinery. The Council was attempting to gain support for forms of employment denied to women in most industries, where men were assigned the better-paid jobs of running the heavier equipment. Women already ran machines in textile, shoe, and hat factories, but the Council proposed that they should be given the same opportunity in other industries. Minister Juan J. de Aréchaga endorsed the recommendation and passed it to the Council for Industrial Education. Over the protest of the typesetters, the school purchased equipment for teaching women.[47]

The Council's Commission on Labor successfully intervened on behalf of a group of telephone operators at the local company, La Uruguaya. A group of discontented operators got in touch with Paulina Luisi through Deputies Emilio Frugoni and Pablo Celestino Mibelli, then general secretary of the Socialist Party. The telephone operators complained of excessive working hours and unreasonably low wages. Luisi organized them into a union with the help of the Socialist Party in December 1918, and accompanied by several other members of the National Council, she visited the company's management with the workers' petitions. The company asked for a month to respond, but the workers decided to press their case before the deadline because of repeated abuses. At that point the Oficina Nacional del Trabajo [Labor Office] and Isabel Pinto Vidal intervened and reached an agreement with the management. The telephone operators stayed in touch with the Council, which served as a mediator between them and the company through 1922.[48] Despite this small victory, the Council was in no position to exercise more than moral pressure in specific cases. Its only other program for poor or working women was a series of lectures (fifty up to 1918) in night schools. In 1922 the National Council appealed to the Senate to resolve the fate of a bill regulating the working hours of women and children that had lingered in that body for over ten years.[49]

Although projects to devise better working conditions and improve the lot of working women were ethically and intellectually laudable, the Council fell short of being a vehicle for their mobilization. Such a role could not have been achieved by a group of mostly professional women with a great deal of goodwill but little knowledge of labor politics. Empathy and understanding were one thing, but organizational clout among working women was a different kettle of fish.

The Long Decade: Problems along the Path

Between 1922 and 1932 the feminist cause, the National Council of Women, and suffrage faced many challenges and achieved some success. Because the feminist movement in Uruguay was so strongly dominated by the National Council and its founder, Paulina Luisi, these years revolved around the relationship between the two. The political association between the reformist wing of the Colorado Party, the Socialist Party, and feminism was also a key factor in the development of events. The increasing internal problems within the Colorado Party, and the growing strength of the Nationalist Party opposition, made feminist causes vulnerable to political maneuvering. The ideological support of the small Socialist Party was of no significant political help except for reminding other parties of the unresolved problems affecting women and children. On the other hand, its support alienated antisocialists from feminism.

When Isabel Pinto Vidal remarked on the increasing difficulties facing suffrage and the need to diversify and broaden the Council's base, the institution was beginning to weaken under internal personality struggles. Luisi was very much in demand outside Uruguay to speak about her multiple initiatives.[50] Born in 1875, she was at the peak of her intellectual capabilities between 1916 and 1932, when she gave herself wholeheartedly to all feminist and public health causes. Her time with the National Council was necessarily shared with many other activities, and since she was surrounded by other capable women who were also strongly driven, it was to be expected that some friction would develop.

Early in April 1922 there was a break between Luisi and Pinto Vidal. Internal politics and irregularities in the administration of the organization were at the bottom of the split. Luisi submitted her resignation on 1 December 1921, alleging tampering with the minutes of the meetings, which were recorded irregularly and without approval of the membership.[51] She felt that this affair had not been properly addressed by Pinto Vidal, who was interim president of the Council during one of her absences. Pinto Vidal offered to give all the oral and written satisfaction necessary to make Luisi stay. Luisi accepted the note and remained within the Council, but the troubles did not end there.[52] Fanny Carrió de Polleri seems to have become irritated by one of Pinto Vidal's public speeches that the press assumed was representative of the Council. Carrió, like Luisi, decided to leave the organization but was persuaded to reconsider.[53] Carrió stayed in the Council, and in November she was working on establishing ties with the provinces. The Council's success in the capital and the provinces depended on overcoming these personality clashes.[54]

Although the Council faced internal tensions, the Alianza's image was bolstered throughout 1922 by positive exposure. Luisi represented it at the 1922 Pan American Women's Conference in Baltimore, presided over by Carrie Chapman Catt. She was elected honorary vice president.[55] The Alianza also received letters of adherence from a few women's organizations such as the Comité Magisterial Pro Sufragio Femenino, led by another feminist, Ana Matheu de Falco, and other charitable institutions willing to join the suffrage campaign, such as the Uruguayan League against Tuberculosis, the Copa de Leche, and the Departmental Women's Council of Durazno. La Bonne Garde, a charitable institution, the Beneficence and Asylum Society of Salto, and the Association for the Deaf and Dumb refused endorsement, arguing that they were nonpolitical. If they perceived the Alianza's lobbying activities as "political," they were very near the truth.

Luisi's growing disaffection for the National Council eventually determined the renaming of the Alianza para el Sufragio Femenino, which in 1922 turned into Alianza Uruguaya de Mujeres, in line with the program of the International Women's Suffrage Alliance.[56] Two years later the fire smoldering between Luisi and the National Council flared up. In a newspaper interview in July 1924, Luisi vented her discontent with the Council, which she claimed was no longer the organization she had founded, although she did not elaborate. She stated that the Council was not even keeping up with the already antiquated ideas of the International Council of Women. Her remarks were not flattering for the Uruguayan Council of Women, while her fondness for the Alianza, which she regarded as the "advanced" group of Uruguayan women, was obviously biased. The Council was further offended by Luisi's disclaimer that she had represented the organization at the 1924 Copenhagen meeting of the International Council of Women. In response, the Council printed a letter Luisi had written to them on February 1924, stating, among other matters, that she would attend the meeting as the Council's secretary of foreign relations.[57]

The ensuing break between the Council and Luisi brought to a standstill the publication of *Acción Femenina*, which did not reappear until December 1925. Luisi was the main feature of that issue, which reported what appears to have been a reconciliation, followed by a public event in her honor in

December 1924. Speeches by Rosa Mauthone Falco, Dr. Santín C. Rossi, the Spanish writer Mercedes Pinto, and others, along with newspaper notes on the event, were reprinted in the 1925 issue, its swan song. Ironically, the publication of this last issue of *Acción Femenina* coincided with another fiery exchange between Pinto Vidal, Catalina ("Cata") Castro de Quintero, the Council, and Luisi. In 1925 Luisi had spent three months in Europe, commissioned to learn about "professional orientation." She was angry with Pinto Vidal for having made some changes in the wording of the fly sheets issued by the Commission on Moral Unity without consulting her. Luisi also claimed that the Council had accused her of wanting to change the site of the organization to Paris. Despite entreaties from the members in late October 1925, Luisi accused some "elements" in the Council of being subversive and asked for the reorganization of the Council and the removal of such "perturbing elements."[58]

Although the chain of such disruptive squabbles remains unclear, Luisi resigned from the presidency in late December 1925. Before her resignation she had urged the Council to initiate a fly-sheet campaign to make the organization better known and stimulate a larger attendance at its meetings. Early in January 1926 the Council seems to have had second thoughts about Luisi's removal; Carolina Torres de Abellá wrote to Luisi, promising to invalidate the minutes of the Council to persuade her to return to the fold.[59] There are few clues on the resolution of this internal personality clash, but it shows that in politics women did not differ much from men.

Although Luisi distanced herself from the Council, she never lost her ascendancy over the Alianza Uruguaya de Mujeres. In 1926 she was named the Alianza's president for life. She remained a vigorous leader, attending a congress on syphilis in Buenos Aires and a feminist congress in Paris in 1926, taking charge of the organization of lectures on social hygiene for the normal school between 1925 and 1930, and participating in the 1928 Third International Feminine Congress in Buenos Aires as a representative of the Council and the Alianza.[60] In 1927, before a trip to Europe, she was reported to be in poor health and to have declined a public celebration in her honor sponsored by both institutions.[61]

Despite the internal problems faced by the National Council, its propaganda was influential enough to create the appropriate ambience for discussing feminist ideas and suffrage in Montevideo. The Council's tactics were mostly intellectual, consisting of petitions and letters sent to public figures and members of Congress. They were not always successful, but they were persistent.[62] Luisi never ceased to stir Uruguayans with her bold defense of sex education, her campaign to abolish regulated prostitution, and her un-relenting pursuit of women's rights. In 1921, when Baltasar Brum penned his bill to reform the Civil Code and to enfranchise women, the press paid at-tention to the proposal. Luisi gave an interview to the popular Argentine magazine *Caras y Caretas,* in which she linked educator José Pedro Varela, as well as presidents Batlle and Brum, to feminism. Throughout the inter-view Luisi worked on a piece of lace, a detail the journalist did not fail to note and report. Luisi was not a woman who had much time to crochet, but a feminist physician talking about suffrage with a hook in her hands was a well-planned exercise in personal theatrics, mixing feminism and femininity for the sake of the cause.[63]

Uruguayan feminist debate in the early 1920s was based on arguments common to the other two countries of the Southern Cone, but Luisi suc-ceeded in injecting themes of her own, such as pacifism. Having traveled to Europe shortly after the end of World War I and become acquainted with the goals of the League of Nations, she tied disarmament to the future of childhood and humanity. Cosigning with Rosa Mauthone, as president and secretary of the Alianza, she asked President Brum for a statement in favor of disarmament, reminding him that Uruguay had been the first nation to propose a league of nations at The Hague in 1906.[64] Under her influence, pacifism and opposition to fascism and militarist aggression were to remain strong points in Uruguayan feminism.

Like those in Buenos Aires and Santiago, Uruguayan newspapers engaged in a couple of informal "polls" on feminism, by asking well-known male intellectuals their opinions on the subject. In mid-1921 the conservative *El País* printed several of them. Notably, the conservative jurist José Irureta Goyena, who ten years later would rewrite the Penal Code and cause a legal stir, expressed his opposition to suffrage on the grounds that each sex had its biophysical genetic characteristics. Another opponent invented a new term, *machonismo,* for what he described as a desire to copy men and derail women from the path nature had placed them on. On the other hand, the notable national writer Juan Zorrilla San Martín declared himself a feminist. However, he thought that Uruguayan society had to adjust to the changes proposed; women were not ready to exercise the vote because "society" was not prepared for their active participation in politics.[65]

While *El País* was interviewing intellectuals, a "Colorado feminist," writ-ing in *El Día,* explained the political advantages the vote could bring to whichever party was ready to put it into motion. The proper channeling of women's votes could benefit the Colorados if the party was astute enough to open to the opportunity knocking at its doors. For example, Colorado soldiers, unable to cast a vote, could count on their wives to vote for the party. Equally, the wives of public employees, policemen, and retirees could vote for the party. The underlying assumption was that women could be manipulated by male family members. This was a demeaning argument, contrary to the female feminists' view that women were intellectually prepared to think for themselves and vote on their own interests.[66] The political potential of the female vote that the male "Colorado feminist" savored in advance would become a compelling argument ten years later, but the opportunistic use of women's vote suggested by El Día's contributor reflected an opinion that could have been expressed by many men.

Not all batllistas thought along naked lines of political expediency. Sebastián Morey, also writing in El Día, defined feminism as women's ability to "direct themselves." Morey was an enthusiastic feminist who supported the concept of women-only political centers endorsing female candidates and helping women to protect themselves from the corruption of established political parties.[67] In 1921 the legal adviser of the Alianza Uruguaya de Mujeres, jurist Joaquín Secco Illa, favored the pursuit of political rights over the reform of the Civil Code. Uruguayan legislation, he argued, placed limits on women's civil rights, but these limits were not as complete as those affecting their political rights.[68] Among women, opinion on suffrage was divided. The magazine Página Blanca carried out an inquiry among a group of sixteen women that included a worker and a poet. Four declared against and twelve in favor of Brum's reform project. The well-known poet Juana de Ibarbourou, one of those interviewed, gave an ambiguous answer, stating that "modern woman does not aspire to become masculine." She declared she was not a feminist, reflecting the persistent fear of losing femininity and the feeling that women were not ready for such freedoms. Ibarbourou illustrates the quandary of educated women facing a change that they longed for but were unable to accept, given the deep roots of their education and sensibility. In 1929 she published a poem in Mundo Uruguayo expressing her desire for the freedom enjoyed by men. In 1932, in the same publication she strongly opposed the passage of the female suffrage bill, arguing that it would destroy home and family and reiterating the need to retain femininity.[69]

The Communist Party attacked the Alianza Uruguaya de Mujeres and female suffrage as "class" tools that male bourgeois would use to get additional votes from middle-class women without redeeming the working woman. An irate "Zoraida" replied in a local newspaper, stating that people achieved rights first and then moved forward to buttress them through social change. The Alianza's intellectual middle-class membership, argued Zoraida, was not against justice for the proletariat.[70] The closing of the class gap was an important goal in the feminist agenda, but one that virulent communists of the period were unwilling to accept. In the midst of this intellectual exchange, Deputy José Salgado proposed a bill for voluntary municipal suffrage, arguing that denial of suffrage to women was the result of social prejudice and an act of injustice. The Legislative Commission of the Chamber of Deputies advised the approval of this formula, but nothing came of it.[71]

The Colorado Party restated its ideological program in 1925 in a *Carta orgánica* that reaffirmed the principles of civil and political equality of men and women along the lines suggested by former president Brum,[72] but the party still could not obtain a majority of votes within Congress to pass any reform bill. Five years went by before suffrage regained momentum and returned to the limelight. The impasse created by the demise of *Acción Femenina* and the animosities among the female feminist leaders took place at a time when the already troubled waters of Uruguayan politics were further muddled by the fragmentation of the Colorado Party and the growing political power of the conservative Nacionalistas. The 1925 elections gave the majority of seats in the Senate to the Blancos of the Nationalist Party and placed Luis Alberto Herrera in the presidency of the collegiate council that ruled along with the president (Consejo Nacional de Administración). The political supremacy of the Colorados was dissolving, while the strength of the Blancos was threatening to put a halt to the reformist spirit of their political enemies.[73]

Suffrage: "Women Have Legitimately Earned It"

In 1928 Uruguay celebrated its first hundred years of republican life. José Batlle Ordóñez died on 20 October of 1929, and with his demise an unusual period in national life came to a close. The Uruguayan economy was beginning to be affected by the depression of the world market and would worsen in the ensuing years. It is difficult to explain why the debate on women's suffrage and women's rights reignited that year, but the international pressure exerted by the Pan-American conferences and the increasing number of countries that were granting national suffrage to women—including Ecuador—may have had a positive influence. It is also possible that both Colorados and Blancos hoped to see their popularity enhanced by a "liberal" reform in the midst of financial insecurity. Female suffrage could deflect attention from the economic situation, gain votes for their parties, and earn them a patriotic badge on the celebration of their nation's centennial. Feminists were gathering strength to renew the suffrage campaign, perhaps under the influence of an International Feminine Congress that had taken place in Buenos Aires in 1928, which Paulina Luisi and members of the National Council of Women had attended.[74]

By the end of 1929 the Alianza had remounted a women's rights campaign that at this time seems to have had an irresistible attraction for a number of earlier enemies. The Alianza restated its goals by publishing a second edition of its early program.[75] Section 1 dealt with the civil rights of women within marriage and the family and the problems of determining paternity. Section 2 pressed for women's equal access to education and work, and equal pay for their work. Section 3 advocated a single moral standard for both sexes and the abolition of prostitution. Section 4 dealt with equal access for women to government employment. It argued that if women could become part of the administrative bureaucracy they would gain a beachhead from which to fight the social ills affecting the nation. Section 5 demanded universal suffrage, access to state employment based on merit, not gender, and equal rights for women while employed in such positions.

Placing political rights at the end of the list was consonant with the view, held by the Alianza and other feminine groups, that though the vote was the "axis of all vindications," it was also a tool to reform society, not an end in itself. Paulina Luisi had best expressed this concept when she wrote in 1919, "Feminism is one of the phases in the solution of the social problem. Within feminism, suffrage is one of the elements for solving the problem, but it is in itself insufficient to find all answers."[76] Insisting on a program that placed welfare and gender relations above the means of achieving them, women feminists could use to their advantage the rhetoric of justice that most male politicians seemed to favor. A welcome boost was a letter from the daughters of María Abella de Ramírez, calling the Alianza's program a statement of all the feminist aspirations of their beloved and unforgettable mother.

A mounting interest in female suffrage developed throughout 1929. The request of Elda Orona for a "citizen's certificate" so she could accept a public service post sparked an important legal discussion. The law, as stated in the National Civic Register, stated that nobody could occupy a post in the administration without proof of citizenship. In a spirited discussion of the meaning of the "citizenship" and the implications of this request, Andrés Lerena, a member of the Electoral Court, expressed his view that the 1917 constitution used "men" to mean the human species. Elda Orona, in his opinion, was requesting the qualification of citizenship, not the *exercise* of citizenship — the vote. Thus he supported her. It was granted in March 1929 but, being prefaced by a negation of the right to vote, this concession carried no consequences for most women.[77]

In October 1929 the Alianza again requested the commission in charge of the centenary celebrations and its president, Baltasar Brum, to grant women suffrage. The most acid reaction to this move came from La Tribuna Popular, a radically conservative newspaper. Flatly denying the existence of more than a dozen feminists in the nation, the newspaper described a bleak future for the nation if women intervened in politics. It remained intransigent through December, when after forecasting the impending chaos of the Uruguayan family, it concluded that to grant the vote to slaves was to misinterpret the spirit of suffrage and to erode the prestige of the parliament granting it. Women were subordinate to men and lived in a position of inferiority. Although the statement fell short of calling women "slaves," the comparison was close enough.[78]

Such a bitter and uncompromising position was exceptional. Most newspapers in Montevideo looked on female suffrage with sympathy and endorsed it. Baltasar Brum and staunch feminists such as Paulina Luisi and Rosa Mauthone Falco gave interviews to the press and made statements on the meaning of democracy and the potential social benefits of women's participation in politics. The time had arrived for political parties to prove why they supported female suffrage.[79] On 5 December the Alianza organized a public meeting at the university in support of the suffrage legislation. The official document was written by Paulina Luisi, and new feminists took part. Their speeches covered the main themes of the feminist agenda, such as the need to recognize the presence of women in history, their role in education, their economic evolution, and the inequalities of the legal system and its implications for professional women.[80] El Día eulogized this act as "having shown the intellectual superiority and exquisite femininity" of Uruguayan women.[81] At this crucial point it was important to reiterate the impeccable "feminine" credentials of the feminists who were so boldly appealing to enter a traditionally male domain. The traditionalists, such as Deputy Dardo Regules — later to be among those staunchly opposed to the new Penal Code and decriminalization of abortion — made sure to restate for public consumption his support to suffrage but his opposition to "feminists who masculinize."[82]

An intense press campaign was maintained for the following two years, and some earlier opponents began to mellow. Luis Alberto Herrera, head of the conservative Nationalist Party, had a change of heart. In 1929 he declared that Uruguayan legislation on women's suffrage was "obsolete" and in need of change. His opinion had changed, he stated, after seeing North American women vote, though he would not go so far as granting the vote to prostitutes and women associated with them.[83] In its 1930 convention the party adopted women's suffrage as part of its platform.[84] Laura Carrera de Bastos, representing the Catholic viewpoint, claimed that as early as 1906 she had spoken on behalf of feminism during the Uruguayan-Argentine Franciscan Congress and therefore had been the "first" woman to speak on behalf of the idea.[85] She obviously had never read the work of María Abella de Ramírez.

Suffrage found support in other Catholic quarters. An anonymous writer in *Juventud*, a journal of the Catholic students of Salto, saw no reason or right to deny the vote to women, who bore the same burden of taxes as men and had the same legal obligations. Socially, the writer asserted, women could bring into politics three very desirable elements: moderation, peace, and respect for the home. The absence of those three elements in public life explained narrow nationalism, democratic insanity, and the increasing disorganization of the family. Educating women in the problems of public life would assure Uruguayans of the triumph of their aspirations for social and family renovation. "We need women's collaboration to defend the home. . . . We must have faith in the Christian spirit of our women."[86] Thus young Catholics were willing to incorporate women in a process of social and political change, although they portrayed such change as a return to stability rather than further innovation or the disruption of social order. Like those in Chile, the Uruguayan traditionalists had already assessed the value of new potential allies in their policies and were hoping to win them over.

The opposition of "old" and "young" in matters related to women's suffrage was a theme picked up by *América Nueva*, a women's journal that began publication in Montevideo in October 1932. Directed by Zulma Núñez, it defined its political orientation as nationalist, suffragist, pacifist, and internationalist.[87] An anonymous contributor viewed opposition to women's suffrage as the antiquated ideological position of "old people." The Chamber of Deputies, as opposed to the Senate, represented youth, and youth accepted women's rights with confidence. Less inclined to polarization and favoring evolutionism was Alberto Lasplaces; also writing in *América Nueva*, he saw the breaking down of opposition to women's votes as a result of the "profound evolution of social life." Women had proved their intellectual capacity and their stamina for work outside the home. Nobody had the right to keep them from cooperating in the solution of social problems. Lasplaces did not fail to note, however, that all political parties hoped they "could benefit" from women's votes. Although he believed that women would easily exercise their political rights, he harbored no illusions that they would always vote "correctly." They would simply vote as well or as badly as men. His was a frank assessment of the utilitarian aspects of women's suffrage, lacking the romantic cloak supplied by other supporters.[88]

Throughout 1930 and 1931 the Alianza and feminists in general continued to buttress their position on suffrage with propaganda, letters to political figures, and the reorganization of cells in the provinces.[89] Opponents raised old arguments that seemed to convince only a few. Thus Carmen Piria argued in May 1930 that the passive Latin woman called for "passion, sweetness, and humility" and was unsuited for politics.[90] Others pointed out how the Civil Code maintained women in a state of subjection that demanded attention more urgently than did political rights.[91]

In late March 1932 the Alianza started an umbrella organization comprising all the groups favoring female enfranchisement, naming it Comité Pro-Derechos de la Mujer. By midyear, it was recruiting the members of other women's associations in the provinces as well as in the capital.[92] The leading force behind the propaganda campaign was a new figure, Sara Rey Alvarez, who personally visited all the members of Congress and the leaders of several parties, urging them to pass the suffrage legislation. Rey Alvarez had studied philosophy and psychology in Brussels and London in the mid-1920s. Her interest in feminism was inspired by the Swedish feminist Ellen Key. While in Belgium and England she had met Marcella Ranson, Louise Van Den Plas, and Emmeline Pankhurst. After her return to Uruguay in 1928 she became deeply involved in the women's movement.[93]

Since 1930 a congressional commission for the study of female suffrage had been in place, but delays plagued the discussions. The Nationalist Party members demanded that the expense of setting up the infrastructure for women's voting be investigated before the bill was discussed. They also wanted to hold up the final enactment of the bill until a minimum number of women registered to vote. This request, one of its members later claimed, was meant to allow the registration of women from distant areas of the nation; the party felt the one-year period suggested was not long enough to give them time. While all these issues were discussed among the deputies, the suffrage bill was approved by the senators under the auspices of Pablo Celestino Mibelli and Claudio Viera. The Senate bill was voted on without discussion at Mibelli's urging. His rationale was that all arguments against it had been dismissed during the twenty years it had been under scrutiny. The approved bill was entered into the Deputies' docket on 13 December 1932.[94]

The discussion of the suffrage project in the Chamber of Deputies had begun in October 1932. It proved to be a contest among political leaders to demonstrate to each other and to the nation their long-standing belief in women's votes.[95] Presented with the embarrassing situation of a bill approved by the less "popular" of the two legislative bodies, several deputies called for its approval without discussion, but political animosities moved deputies to engage in personal harangues against each other's parties. The communist deputy, after stating his support for the bill, took the opportunity to make a long tirade against capitalist exploitation of working women, exposing the poor working conditions and low wages of female teachers, telephone operators, and women working in the meatpacking plants and textile factories. He also denounced the bourgeois and *batllista* feminist women who served the interests of war and hunger. He urged working women to use their political rights intelligently in the struggle of the working people.

Deputy Alonso Montaño, representing the Blancos from the Nationalist Party, claimed that women's suffrage had been a part of their ideology for many years. He lamented that suffrage would not be accompanied by full civil rights, and addressing the communist deputy Gómez y Lazagarra, he stated that women's intervention in politics would become the strongest deterrent to the advance of communism. He hinted that the addition of 450,000 votes would be a challenge for all political parties but claimed that numbers alone were not the main reason to pass the bill. Another member of the Nationalist Party denounced the haste with which *batllistas* wished to approve the bill, pretending to erase their neglecting to approve suffrage when they had the opportunity many years before.

Such remarks prompted the *batllistas* to defend their party's position, which they dated back to 1914, and to accuse the Nationalists of being the real obstacle in the approval of women's suffrage since then. The Socialists could not pass up the occasion to remind *batllistas* that they had aligned themselves with others to establish the two-thirds majority required to approve female suffrage and had thus helped delay its adoption. In the midst of increasing accusations and rebuttals about whose party had the privilege of initiating and supporting women's suffrage, Nationalist Eduardo Víctor Haedo rose to recognize the work carried out by the women themselves, acknowledging Paulina Luisi as the precursor of suffrage. "Let me repeat that female suffrage is not a conquest of any political party or any public man: women have legitimately earned it in the workplace, in the factory, in the university." In one instant the applause of the public in the gallery obliterated the narrow political concerns of the deputies. Haedo struck a winning point, restoring to women the credit that most deputies were willing to forget in the pursuit of their own interests and the enhancement of their egos. Among the arguments recalled to support women's suffrage, the leading one was the basic justice owed to women, but this argument for equity was enhanced by the traditional appeal of the special sensitivity that motherhood gave women and the hope that they would put a measure of idealism, tolerance, and understanding in public life, which had for too long been dominated by crude materialism.[96] After two days of discussion the Chamber of Deputies approved female suffrage on 14 December 1932. The feminist leaders were ecstatic. Sofía Alvarez Vignoli, Clotilde C. de Pérez, Elola de Andreasen, Sara Alvarez Rey, Clotilde Luisi, and others made numerous statements to the press. Nothing short of a utopian future lay ahead for the thrilled feminists. People must have faith in women's work, stated Alvarez Vignoli. They have "intelligence, character and virtue," a trilogy of "eternal superiorities."[97] Progress and the well-being of women and children would result from women's access to politics. She itemized vagrancy, alcoholism, prostitution, and gambling as "torturing problems" that only women, with their "love and maternal tenderness, could face and resolve with dignity." The need to group together and elect women to Congress was expressed by Clotilde C. de Pérez, who expected female deputies to represent women's needs better than men.[98]

A Women's Party: Hopes Defined and Shattered

The possibility of women becoming candidates as well as voters was already taking shape in the mind of Sara Rey Alvarez during the suffrage discussion. She began sounding the idea of a feminist party immediately after passage of the law. Speaking to the press, she discussed the economic problems women confronted as producers within the economy and explained why they should work for a more equitable distribution of wealth. She also spoke of education and the protection of children as the highest social priorities for women.[99]

The gestation of Sara Rey Alvarez's party was short. On 15 January 1933 she launched the Partido Independiente Democrático Femenino (PIDF), in the belief that women should not dilute their energy within traditional male parties. The party's platform was written by a group of women meeting on 10 January. Internal disagreements over a proposal to redefine the existing divorce law immediately caused a split in its ranks. Two formulas were discussed. One recognized the equity of granting men rights equal to those of women, who sued for divorce "on their sole will." In the present circumstances, however, it would be inadvisable to adopt that formula, and they chose to support the existing law. The second formula contemplated renouncing divorce by the sole will of the woman to adhere to a strict equality of the sexes.

Both formulas attempted to address the absolute equality of the genders before the law. Although the discussion was theoretical, since no alteration of the divorce bill was at hand, it was important to some feminists as a matter of principle. The group supporting the status quo had a majority by two votes. Those who lent their support to the second formula believed it was a "superior" understanding of feminism: protecting women implied their inferiority. Since no conciliation was apparent, the group supporting the elimination of divorce "by the sole will of women," headed by Sofía Alvarez Vignoli de Demichelli, left the organization by 20 January.[100] Soon thereafter she was in the newspaper headlines, having proposed the recognition of women's rights to the Seventh Pan American Conference that took place in Montevideo in 1933.[101]

The group's defection did not affect PIDF's foundation. Its general program was delineated in ten points. Twenty-three additional points defined the program for social action. The general program reflected long-standing feminist principles such as equal civil rights, the suppression of regulated prostitution, and the protection of mothers and children. The social program was specifically geared toward the writing and enforcement of legislation implementing the general program and responded to the economic recession affecting the nation. For example, the party demanded legislation guaranteeing a minimum wage, unemployment insurance, and workers' health insurance. It also prohibited children's work, endorsed Penal Code reform, and proposed land reform, protection of the cattle industry, substitution of direct taxes for the graduated income tax, and development of agricultural cooperatives. PIDF chose to campaign for the plural executive — a return to the 1918 constitution, adoption of popular initiatives for municipal and national legislation, the right to appeal legislation enacted without proper consultation with the people, and conservation of the national patrimony under state protection.[102] Undoubtedly the party was "radical" for its time, and too close for comfort to the politics of the Left.

The women who founded this party were ready to discuss national political issues that transcended home and childhood, a situation Rey Alvarez reiterated to the skeptical men who could not conceive of women in politics.[103] The founders claimed that followers of worldwide feminism did not have to confine themselves to women's issues. They hoped to fulfill the aspirations "of all the productive elements of the nation, be they intellectual, industrial, commercial, administrative or manual," to achieve economic equilibrium and social harmony.[104] PIDF defined itself as a party *exclusively* for women, starting its life with a clean slate, totally dissociated from all that had theretofore been regarded as bad in the political system. It also capitalized on the concept that women could inject honesty and social consciousness into politics. Ideologically, it declared itself against communism and fascism, seeking to establish an understanding among all working people. A working person was anybody whose income derived from his or her own physical efforts, whether small merchant or industrial employee.[105] *Ideas y Acción,* the party's newspaper, began publication in June 1933.

Sara Rey Alvarez's intriguing personality is revealed mostly through her writings. She had definite political acumen, as is evident in her writings, but was under the spell of a messianic role for women. Uruguay's "rotten political situation," in her opinion, favored the formation of her party, which was bound to offer new blood to an "infected and degenerate" political atmosphere. Rey Alvarez believed that most male political parties had sweet words for women (*jarabe de pico*) but were interested only in collecting their votes. Regrettably, women were already beginning to register in traditional male parties that copied the same program for social change she had proposed two years before to the Alianza Femenina.[106]

Throughout nearly six years of life, *Ideas y Acción* and the party campaigned constantly for a broad spectrum of female and social causes, adopting a social reformist stance in which the state was to provide protection and welfare to its citizens. It favored the unfinished reform of the Civil Code and the abolition of state-controlled prostitution. On the other hand, when it took sides on abortion, it opposed legalization, encouraging instead a stronger support of aid to mothers and children.[107] On labor issues it supported workers' demands for higher salaries and deplored the dismissal of employees from meatpacking plants. The party disagreed with the exclusion of women from night work and stood against closing any occupation to women. Rey Alvarez also called on women workers to demand reform in a recently approved law for maternity insurance that required contributions from both employee and employer. She believed that employers would stop hiring women to avoid paying their share. The state was responsible for social welfare; no law should put the welfare burden on the workers' shoulders.[108] The foundation of the Partido Feminista did not entail the disappearance of the Comité Pro-Derechos de la Mujer. On 17 December 1933 the committee had a meeting attended by 300 persons.[109] Sara Rey Alvarez reported that the Alianza also remained as a separate institution, but confined to a membership of 25, later reported to have grown to 101.[110]

The "rotten" political atmosphere mentioned by Rey Alvarez and other women and men throughout 1932 finally burst at the end of March 1933. On 31 March President Gabriel Terra carried out a coup d'état to put an end to the sui generis Uruguayan system, the plural executive. The storm had been presaged since mid-1932, and all members of the legislature had been aware of it while they deliberated on female suffrage. A deliberative assembly was quickly organized with the cooperation of the Nationalist Party, and a new constitution abolishing the *colegiado* presidency approved in 1918 was adopted in April 1934, going into effect in May of the same year, and Terra was appointed president for the term 1934–38. The *batllistas* did not acknowledge the fait accompli and abstained from political life for several years. One of the most unfortunate outcomes of this coup was the suicide of Baltasar Brum. He refused to live under a regime that betrayed the 1917 constitution.[111] Uruguayan feminists lost a staunch supporter with his death.

The Terra regime was keenly interested in returning Uruguay to normality. Enabling women to vote in the elections planned for 1938 could add credibility to the new political order.[112] The registration of women began as early as May 1933. PIDF did not believe in political abstention even though it opposed the 1934 constitution, and it sought to recruit women to vote in whatever election the Terra regime would offer.[113] True to her ideas, Rey Alvarez used *Ideas y Acción* to argue her political program throughout the late 1930s. Numerous issues urged women to register to vote and criticized the government's meager efforts to recruit women into politics and to register members of minority parties. The magazine called for allocating more days for opposition parties to register and disputed the existing plan, which called for fixed days to register in the party of one's choice. Women's registration continued apace, and according to *Ideas y Acción*, 120,000 were registered by September 1937, even though the process had been slow and inefficient during the first several years.[114]

Elections took place, as scheduled, in 1938. The Colorado Party was internally fragmented, and none of its sections participated. PIDF hoped for the support of working women, but it did not get a single candidate elected. It received exactly 139 votes in an election in which only about 50 percent of those registered cast their votes. A survey of the parties participating in the 1938 elections does not break down the voters by sex, and it is difficult to determine how many women went to the polls and what influence they had in the election of any candidate.[115] *El Día* estimated that 30,000 women had voted; *Ideas y Acción*'s estimate of 130,000 women registered must have been incorrect. Anticlerical as usual, *El Día* assumed that many of the women voters had followed the lead of the Catholic Church, which worked hard to register women voters.[116]

PIDF's poor showing in the elections, after five years of propaganda, was a disaster it seemed the party could not recover from. After the elections it continued to publish its newspaper through 1939. In March of that year the party's executive committee dissolved because of the absence of several of its directing members, and an emergency committee was appointed to elect a new directing body.[117] By 1939 the party was running out of life; little is known about its fate after then. The greatest problem this party encountered and shared with other gender-based parties was women's own hesitation about participating in politics and their misgivings about an exclusively female party. PIDF met strong opposition from several quarters. The Argentine Socialist Party derided its foundation in an article titled "Feminismo mal entendido" (Misunderstood feminism), published in *La Vanguardia* in December 1932.[118] Two members of the Luisi family also made public comments against women-only parties. Clotilde Luisi de Podesta, Paulina's sister, was of the opinion that such parties would lead women to form interest groups that would inevitably degenerate into subordinate positions at the mercy of male groups. Female parties, in her opinion, had three flaws. They expressed a sentiment of antisocial egotism; they were too weak to be effective in confronting male parties; and their programs were too limited. To her women who could not socialize with men in men's parties suffered from "antisocial egotism." She saw gender separation in politics as a negative narcissistic indulgence, aggravated by shortness of intellectual sight. She urged women to join established parties and struggle from within to inject their special interests in social and moral themes into their programs.[119] Paulina Luisi also stated her skepticism about women's parties and claimed not to share many points in their platforms. Journalist Zulma Núñez, founder of *América Nueva,* was more conservative in her arguments than the Luisi sisters. She believed a woman's party simply mimicked the demands of other parties, creating an "absurd situation of battle between the sexes." Women should be the companions, not the enemies, of men and should join established parties with their male relatives.[120] This reluctance to isolate themselves in female parties was similar to that expressed by several notable Chilean women during the same period. At the close of the decade a number of women's organizations continued their diverse activities on behalf of several political causes while denying any "political" affiliation.[121]

End of an Era? Beyond Suffrage

Attaining suffrage did not signify the end of an era for Uruguayan women. The coup d'état rekindled civic pride among many veteran politicians who were torn between respect for the constitution and the pragmatic desire to return to normality with an honorable record. The lame political life Uruguayans experienced between 1933 and 1938 did not deter discussion of such key issues as the 1933 Penal Code and abortion, or the adoption of an extensive plan for protecting children and recruiting women as social workers.

Once suffrage was achieved, established parties saw fit to organize women's sections. By 1936 many political exiles were returning to the country, and the election announced for 1938 offered the Terra administration the means to validate the constitutional changes and restore confidence in the future of the nation. The Colorado Party had a women's committee, the Comité Nacional Femenino Batllista, organized in 1931.[122] Its purpose was to support the Colorado Party, although it is unclear which of its factions. A Club Femenino Batllista Dr. Baltasar Brum existed in 1936, as well as the Comité Femenino Nacional Independiente, Unión Femenina contra la Guerra, and Alianza Femenina por la Democracia.[123] The Colorados published their platform in February 1936, proving that they remained a vital and strong opposition entity. It endorsed female suffrage and female eligibility for all political posts. It also endorsed protective legislation for minors and children, pre- and postpartum compulsory leave for women, child care for working mothers, and a monthly bonus for one year to help defray the costs of maternity and nursing children.[124]

Uruguayan feminists and activists of several political complexions and interests organized a National Congress of Women in April 1936. The organizers attempted to include small independent women's groups and working women's organizations, a plan that elicited the compliments of *El Día* as "very fruitful for the feminist movement in general." [125] This congress was the project of a Comité Femenino contra la Guerra y el Fascismo, a pacifist organization of unknown provenance but leftist affiliation that acted as an umbrella organization for this national event.[126] The congress was a success. Delegates from Cuba and Argentina joined the Uruguayans. The speakers discussed women's participation in the pursuit of justice and the solution of national problems and the search for international peace. Paulina Luisi and Sara Rey Alvarez joined *batllista* women such as Juana Amestoy de Mocho, who made a rather unexpected statement on the state's duty to provide contraceptive information and to encourage scientific research on contraception. This was an answer to the raging controversy over abortion and the only recorded statement of a Colorado woman on the issue.

More predictably, Luisi spoke on her two main interests at the time: international peace and the rights of working women. Taking a more ideological attitude than on most occasions, she proposed that capital be returned to those who produced it, and that capitalism become socialism, be it Christian socialism, evolutionary socialism, or even totalitarian socialism, according to the level of evolution of each country. Such political statements were not usual from Luisi, who shunned political activism in the Socialist Party. The congress endorsed the milder of the two motions, disapproving the more radical call for the adoption of socialism. Her speech on working people's rights contained a rather advanced concept of equality for male and female workers. The regulation of working hours, apprenticeship, wages, and workers' insurance should be guided by the occupation, not by the sex of the worker. These principles ran against the deeply rooted concept of special protection for women and minors endorsed by the congress. Nonetheless, they were given a vote of support by the delegates.[127]

Suffrage achieved and peace reaffirmed, the decade ended with mixed results for women. The political party that had so affirmatively supported social change for women did not participate in the first election in which women voted. The administration had won a struggle to redefine the meaning of abortion and reaffirmed a double standard of morality. The reform of the Civil Code was still pending. On the other hand, a welfare system for the protection of mothers and children was in place, and Uruguayan women had been exposed to an invigorating discussion of gender roles unique in the Southern Cone—and elsewhere in Latin America—for the sympathetic role played by the leading party and the government itself. The payoff was to come in the following decade, when political life was fully restored and women were elected to Congress, where they spoke on their own behalf in the reform of the Civil Codes.

The *batllista* Colorado Party entered the 1942 electoral campaign. Several women ran as deputy candidates in the national election. The old alliance between women and Batlle's party had its final political reaffirmation as women broke into the most masculine of all domains. A National Feminine Batllista Committee agitated for several women candidates and for full female participation in the elections. The party presented twenty-one women candidates.[128] Integrated into several of the "lists" used to group candidates, and in the political podium, women did not look as foreign as conservatives and antisuffragists of the 1920s and early 1930s had anticipated.

Women were given special instructions on how to vote, taking care not to smear the ballot's envelope with lipstick so as to avoid its invalidation.[129] Batlle's party carried the election with 131,888 votes against 32,197 for the Nationalist Party.[130] Coloradas Isabel Pinto Vidal and Antonelli Moreno were elected as senator and deputy, respectively. By 1946, when the Civil Code was finally reformed, several women—including a member of the Communist Party—sat with men in the halls of Congress and took part in crafting legislation. With the election of women to Congress a cycle of political activism had reached its goal and closed a chapter that had begun forty years before. Uruguayan women had taken less time than Frenchwomen to achieve suffrage and, compared with Chileans and Argentines, had done much better.

That activism that leading Uruguayan women so relished was no accident. It was nurtured by a caring generation of feminists—male and female—who succeeded in reconciling the essence of femininity and motherhood to the essence of feminism, the defense of the human rights of women. They were led by one of the most outspoken women of her generation, Paulina Luisi, who did not hesitate to speak in public about the unspeakable, but whose unimpeachable character was respected by all. The state behind reformers and feminists was a powerful machine that for many years was sensitive to women's needs, even though its understanding of gender relations bore the patriarchal stamp of its period. In the critical 1940s the system lived up to the challenges posed by the early social reformers, and in 1946 it accepted with grace the last change envisioned by that generation, the reform of the Civil Code. Uruguayan women achieved all the benefits and rights dreamed of by Abella de Ramírez, Luisi, Rey Alvarez, and a score of other less-known but worthwhile leaders. The flaws remaining in the picture of gender achievements and gender relations were of a cultural nature, not to be wiped out by outright legislation. All that could have been accomplished by discussion and legal reform was realized. The question that could not be answered at that time was whether this complete cycle of achievements would become an enticement to conformity for women and complacency for men.

No historical work is ever definitive, and this one is no exception. Nonetheless, it hopes to place feminism within the history of social change in the Southern Cone nations and on the spectrum of intellectual and social ideologies of the first half of the twentieth century. Feminist aspirations to change gender relations, women's and children's working conditions, the role of the state as a welfare provider, and the perception of women's social role beyond home boundaries place feminism squarely in the center of the active movements for social and political reform. Feminism flourished parallel to socialism, anarchism, the labor struggle, populism, and university reform and shared with them the task of changing the nature of society and politics. In doing so it faced enormous cultural barriers and institutional obstacles that had to be chipped away inch by inch. Like the standard-bearers of other social movements, male and female feminists saw moments of victory and defeat, but most of the time they worked day by day, inspired by the strength of their own ideas and the inevitability of change, but without expecting "historical" recognition. Some is due now.

Feminism became a topic of intellectual and political debate beginning in the second decade of the century. A review of legislative proceedings, newspapers, and magazines reveals to the sensitive eye women's emergence into the discussion of national issues and strategies of policymaking. Recognizing these themes hinges on learning to detect gender-related issues, which were not always called "feminism." This caveat notwithstanding, the term came to be understood as a reevaluation of women's roles in society, encompassing a vast field of discussion: the nature of women as human beings, their mental and physical abilities, the limits of the family's and society's demands on them, and the meaning of change in their legal status for husbands and fathers, for women themselves, for the family as an institution, and for the nation as a political entity. Wrapped in less philosophical terms, these topics were the foundation of feminism, whether or not it went by that name. Some of the social problems that preoccupied feminists and their response to them have been introduced in the preceding chapters. Here I will review the meaning of some of the themes I have presented.

Within the complex Southern Cone social frame, the issue of representation arises. What women did feminists represent? Self-defined, self-declared, and even closet feminists of both sexes were decidedly a minority in all the countries. Yet as with many other historical situations, numbers alone did not reflect the short- and long-term influence these determined people had in redefining women's social role. Feminism was not exclusive to one sex or one social class; it purported to represent all women. The struggle to achieve universality in feeling and representation is evident in the exploratory debates between socialists and mainstream feminists and in the reasons working-class women writers gave for embracing all women in a general aspiration to equality. One historical lesson we may learn from this early experience is that feminists did not hesitate to manipulate the political moment by using the arguments most suitable for the period. The Argentine Comité Pro-Sufragio Femenino, founded in 1919, mixed socialist, maternalist, and individualist feminism. Aligned with the committee was Julieta Lanteri, whose National Feminist Party espoused a variety of social causes despite her strong individualist feminism. Umbrella organizations founded in the 1930s did not become polarized in their ideology and tried to accommodate diverse elements. Chilean MEMCH was definitely labor and left oriented, but its leaders opted to remain officially centrist. Ultimately we must see that the difficulty of categorizing feminism speaks for its being capable of evolution and of adapting to changing political realities rather than being a fixed set of ideas. The mosaic of attitudes within feminism was natural and mirrored the development of feminism elsewhere as well as the national political scene of these three countries, where contestatory politics signaled the passing of old oligarchies and the emergence of labor and an urban middle class. Above all, feminism was a strong binding element among men and women seeking a new role for women in society and a mantra for incorporating gender into all forms of social reform.

Class and ethnicity also need to be examined along with feminist representation. The meaning of the terms was as complex as the reality. For most of the period under review feminist organizations and leaders were mainly middle class. Class-conscious working women's associations like those organized early in the century slowly weakened or disappeared. Building a consensus on women's new role in society required refraining from any jarring class radicalism, to avoid alienating political support among mainstream parties such as the Chilean and the Argentine Radical Parties and the Colorado Party in Uruguay. When the Argentine Asociación Argentina del Sufragio Femenino, headed by Carmela Horne de Burmeister, endorsed a suffrage bill disqualifying young women, illiterate women, and recent immigrant women, it showed a mixture of age, class, and nationalist discrimination all the more ironic for an organization led by a woman with non-Spanish surnames. Such exclusionary projects and several similar Argentine suffrage bills did not represent all feminists. A review of the statements of most feminists (male and female) and most feminist groups since 1900 shows a commitment to unrestricted suffrage regardless of class, age, or education. In Chile, the country with the greatest class tensions, literacy qualifications were applied to the first essay in female suffrage, but this restriction applied to men as well. Aiming at forfeiting inner class strain and preserving gender interest as a common denominator, the most left-oriented of all Chilean women's groups, MEMCH, quashed the aspirations of the radical Left to build a class appeal within the organization. This attitude became more central as feminists sought support for female suffrage. Appeals to women's solidarity regardless of class suggest that feminist associations were conscious of cleavages but concentrated on unity for the sake of suffrage, discouraging open discussion of class problems.

This reality does not belittle working-class participation in the shaping of feminism early in the century and in the 1930s. Socialist ideological influence in the three nations reinforced the driving theme of social change that underlies all feminist groups and feminist thought. This is easier to see in socialist-based groups than in others, but a close examination of the programs and activities of other organizations of the 1920s and 1930s, whether women's parties, ad hoc suffrage groups, or women's organizations, shows a distinctive awareness of social ills. Nonetheless, sympathy with the plight of the working class did not translate into radical politics. Feminists did not harbor politically revolutionary ideas. The complacency implied in their acceptance of a patriarchal state reformism alienated their social reform formula from revolutionary movements in the second half of the century.

Ideologically, feminism in the Southern Cone was not troubled by ethnicity. The migratory waves that enlarged the population of Buenos Aires and Montevideo had a common thread of European roots and their predominant masculinity. Italians, Jews, Spaniards, and the native born who mingled in the workplace were essentially people dispossessed of wealth, citizenship, and social status. These conditions they shared with most women, regardless of ethnic background or class. This common lack of rights established ties between feminists and social reformers, most of whom were migrants or first-generation citizens. Ethnic concern was less pronounced in Chile, which received much less immigration. The indigenous elements in Chile and Argentina were removed to remote provinces, and the small population of African extraction in Montevideo had no political clout. Feminist writing, even in the earliest periods, focused on the integration and improvement of the nation rather than on analysis of its diverse ethnic groups. Nationalism was one of the most important feminist subtexts.

As social reformers and nation builders, feminists were driven by the idea of constructing a new and better future for all. In the 1930s el bien público and the construction of a stronger base for a more prosperous and peaceful national life were uppermost in the program of Agrupación Nacional de Mujeres de Chile, for example, and Acción Femenina challenged those who could not imagine women being interested in the destiny of the motherland.[1] In 1932 Amanda Labarca made public her support for a political organization because its purpose was to study and solve national problems: "Today we should not discuss doctrines or partisan programs; something bigger is on the agenda: the very life of the nation."[2] A few years later, Alicia Moreau de Justo stated that political participation was the only choice for women interested in saving Argentina from its inexorable decline.[3] Nationalism, among feminists, meant working for social reform, not patriotic declarations. Whenever they looked outside for models, they did so in hope of finding viable methods to solve national problems. Yet feminism was regarded xenophobically by cultural traditionalists.[4] Traditionalists and conservatives, who interpreted nationalism as the preservation of time-honored customs within an Iberian and Catholic culture, antagonized liberal reformers, socialists, and feminists as imitators of foreign ideas that threatened national criollo roots. This hostility has to be seen in the context of a constant tension between nationalism, fear of immigration, and a desire to achieve cosmopolitanism that began to develop in the 1880s. The close association of many feminists with socialism, and with peace movements after the First World War and through the 1930s, cast a negative light on them among right-wing nationalists, especially in the 1930s, when conservatism kindled corporatism and fascism. Feminists felt the subtle but real pressure of this critique and insisted on their cultural ties with national culture rather than foreign models.[5]

Southern Cone feminism strongly advocated state intervention and state support to ensure a fairer allocation of the national resources and temper the excesses of capitalism. It was essential to provide for those in need and without voice or access to politics: workers, women, and children. Failure to look after women's and children's interests, feminists claimed, could only lead to national failure and a weaker state. This perception pushed the understanding of citizenship beyond politics and into a service frame. People were the nation, and serving their needs was the ultimate duty of responsible citizens. Serving the people implied several forms of social reform, without which much of the feminist agenda would collapse. State control over social issues was uneven and was not completed or enforced for several decades, but its debate was an essential component and definer of feminist political culture, as well as an important goal in twentieth-century Latin American politics.

Although not necessarily feminist, labor politics was the first arena for women's own politicization and for the recognition of their presence by male workers as well as by politicians. Although mutualist organizations and confessional unions, not dealt with in this book, were the favored form of association by most women, mainstream and socialist feminists were intellectually preoccupied by labor politics even though they never had much leverage over that or over unions. They missed some important issues, such as domestic work, the main occupational source of female employment, regulated only in Uruguay, and women's lack of representation in labor unions. Their urban roots also precluded much attention to rural workers, but these were weaknesses of the labor movement, not just of feminists.

Feminist labor politics was torn between economic motivations and gender awareness. Members of the female labor force in the Southern Cone and the rest of Latin America in the first half of the century were predominantly single. For such workers, equal pay may have been more meaningful than compensation for motherhood or protective legislation restricting women's work. Yet the compensatory nature of the maternalist feminism espoused by socialists and feminists compelled them to ask the state for protection as well as for equal wages. The fusion of feminism and maternalism in labor matters did much to enhance the economic value of women's labor and to obtain welfare legislation to correct the intolerable abuses of unharnessed capitalism and industrial development. But unquestionably it contained contradictory messages. Maternalist feminism reinforced the state's authority over women while strengthening the image of women as mothers. When the state failed (as it did) in providing women with equal wages and in enforcing some welfare measures, women were left with an earnings gap very difficult to overcome and a set of protective laws that demanded further struggle for complete implementation. In labor politics and labor ideology, feminists fought their first and longest war on a battleground mined by contradictions. The cause was never resolved to anybody's satisfaction, but it entitled them to argue most other points in the agenda for social change.

Motherhood was a flexible concept that served a multiplicity of purposes, and it remained an overarching theme in Southern Cone feminism. Other historians have already pointed out its significance as a moral and political force and a tool of women's empowerment in Latin America in the first half of the century.[6] Yet it is important to underline that this power was not to be taken for granted. It was sculpted out of a raw cultural tradition of worshiping an abstract notion belied by legal realities. At the turn of the century legal motherhood was meticulously confined within the family and subjected to male jurisdiction. Feminists argued for endowing motherhood with real power and eliminating the contradictions between mother worship and lack of real rights within the family. They endorsed the state's duty to protect all mothers and children. Motherhood was transformed from an inert force into a dynamic one — a function that was essential to the social body, demanded care and sustenance, and had the capacity, in feminists' view, to generate much good for the motherland.

Women's collective activity, whether educational, social, or political, was regarded as an extension of maternity. This explains the success of the congresses on childhood and the political consensus on the construction of a state apparatus for protecting mothers and children throughout the 1920s and the 1930s. Although maternalist politics is essential to understanding Southern Cone feminism, it should not be conflated with feminism. Feminism, understood as a drive for legal equality and based on the assumption of civil rights by women, was a key component of mainstream and socialist feminism, as is shown by a review of the arguments in support of Civil Code reform and divorce. Women's demonstrated intellectual capacity and their ability to perform effectively in industrial and administrative jobs entitled them to all the rights men enjoyed. To Southern Cone feminists, civil rights were of a different nature than motherhood, which conferred knowledge and sensitivity. Without the former, women could not fully exercise the latter.

If womanhood and motherhood were to be given their complete due, fatherhood had to be reexamined, which necessitated the reevaluation of sexuality and gender relations, addressing illegitimacy as a social problem and an issue of personal ethics. Human sexuality and its social consequences entered public discussion early in the century tied to public health, but the discourse was never fully mastered by feminists of either sex during the period under review. They were comfortable only with an abstract challenge to a patriarchal society's double standard of morality and what it meant for the human realities of illegitimacy, child mortality, and men's avoidance of full paternal responsibility. Acceptance of the "protection" argument and the state's services as a father by default deprived feminists and women in general of a true challenge to patriarchal values in gender relations. Men dominated the dialogue on sexuality and its implications despite the contribution of outstanding women such as Paulina Luisi. A different outcome would have been very difficult in societies stressing femininity and shaped by Roman Catholic views of human sexuality.

Because women were reluctant to shed their role as mothers in the 1930s, and because feminists were women of their time and culture, their challenge to male-dominated sexual ethics was limited to attempts to make men accept their moral responsibility for procreation. Their challenge to the double standard of morality was flawed. Opening fire on irresponsible male sexuality, but accepting its consequences, did little to change gender relations at their sexual level. For their part, men expressed a medical sensibility rather than a deeper challenge to the predominance of male values in gender relations. Acceptance of "honor abortions" by opponents as well as supporters of freer women's sexuality indicated the contortions that advocates and opponents of reproductive rights were forced into by the ambiguity of compensatory feminism and the patriarchal stance of its opponents.

Traditionalists and conservatives assuming the defense of patriarchal values could turn motherhood and femininity against feminists, as they did during the discussion of divorce, sexual mores, and abortion. They attempted to transform motherhood as a social function, which feminists had used to empower women, into a warped form of nationalism in which femininity was reduced to motherhood and motherhood became a reproductive duty to the state. Fortunately, the ideas of extremists such as Argentine Carlos Bernaldo de Quirós did not gain universal acceptance. However, the reaffirmation of the biological destiny of the sexes, which feminists truly never disavowed and actually endorsed on most occasions, gave the state the power to define what models of motherhood and childhood were desirable. The paradigm of exemplary motherhood retained most of the traditional features of unconditional devotion to the child and sublimation of homelife to balance other deficiencies in women's social and economic standing. It was not until the 1980s that Southern Cone feminists assumed a more individualist stance and began to speak out against official patriarchal notions and institutions inherited from the 1930s *puericultura* model.

Contemporary feminist groups in Southern Cone nations have questioned the validity of legislation that gives women no choice about motherhood, but there has been no change in official position since the 1930s. Traditional attitudes toward gender relations and motherhood by both genders are resilient, and the state takes a central role in preserving such roles. The yeast that activated women's mobilization in the 1920s and 1930s was gender consciousness, but gender functions lessened the weight of individual rights and this consciousness was lost in the 1950s, after suffrage, a concession to individual rights, became a national reality and class became a dominant factor in the political philosophy of post–World War II Latin America. Demographic growth obliged many nations to change their stance on family planning, regarded by some nations as a desirable alternative to uncontrolled population growth. The economics of poverty and development, not gender issues, determined that change. None of the Southern Cone nations led in the discussion of such issues: on the contrary, they remained unwilling followers. Slow demographic growth reinforcing their maternalist policies and their relapse into periods of military leadership explain the endurance of 1930s visions of gender roles and gender relations.[7]

The emergence of women as actors and objects in politics at the turn of the century is beyond question if one understands politics as the quest for public voice and power. By the time all men began to vote, feminists were already voicing their desire to become full citizens. Gender-typed issues such as divorce, health, and child care became "political" by the second decade of the century, when they were discussed as options in national policy. Stepping into a field previously dominated by men and where they were mostly unwelcome demanded a definition of political behavior and a choice of objectives irrespective of political orientation. Although the definition of a standard political affiliation had to wait until suffrage was a reality, when it came female political culture was already framed by gender.

Women's political definition in the 1930s left several resilient features in the area's politics: the transfer of motherhood to a political level beyond the home but not divorced from it; a gender-typed political activity that used female symbols to generate political power; and a yearning for participatory politics — democratic if possible — buttressed by social justice. In arguing their case, feminists also expanded an understanding of democracy based on the participation of both sexes in the civic arena that remains little appreciated by general analyses of the struggle for democracy in the Southern Cone — as well as the rest of Latin America. The mobilization of political forces on behalf of women's national suffrage in Chile and Argentina in the 1940s had enough drama to stir gender and class issues, and it also speaks of a key step toward democratizing society. In 1945 Alicia Moreau de Justo assessed her past feminist experience and expressed what she expected the world to be as a result of the changes since her own youthful political engagement. As one of the few women who had participated in feminist activities since the first decade of the century, her opinion merits review, for she was witnessing the end of the first cycle of feminism in the Southern Cone. She believed that democratic progress could take place only when both genders were "emancipated" from old prejudices. She saw clear connections between the public and private spheres when she stated that "in a democracy, freedom (and all its implicit risks) begin at home."[8] Furthermore, only in a democracy, which is the expression of collective will, could women as mothers understand the value and true meaning of the connection between home and the rest of society. The higher their understanding of maternal responsibility, the greater their desire to have the means to influence collective actions. Only such participation gave women respect for themselves and for their role in the nation.[9] Today's understanding of the power of a well-orchestrated mothers' movement, the use of domestic concerns in questioning economic and social policies, and the insistence on having women considered as a special interest group can be traced to the suffragists' validation of domestic metaphors to buttress female participation in the public arena. On Moreau's definition rests the understanding that sustained women's participation as mothers, sisters, and daughters in the resistance to militarism in the three nations between 1975 and 1985. On the other hand, present-day feminists in the Southern Cone might contend that the emancipation of both sexes and true gender equality has yet to take place.[10]

The understanding of citizenship as cosubstantial with the experience of nurturing and mothering was the most important heritage left by the first two generations of feminists and social reformers in the Southern Cone. The commonality of their vision is nowhere better illustrated than in passages from the writing of two very different women, Chilean mainstream feminist Amanda Labarca and Argentine anarchist Antonia de Carras. Writing for their respective and dissimilar constituencies, both expressed faith in the ability of their sex to solve the problems of their generation and their nations. They saw through different lenses but found common grounds to believe that social change not only was within the power of women but depended on their actions. Carras believed that "in time, woman will possibly be the one to interest herself with double intensity in the betterment (moral as well as material) of the race. Doubtless she feels humanity deeper in her entrails. No one better than woman, therefore, to set the guidelines to present and future generations. May she be the light of the day and the true genesis of a new world."[11] Amanda Labarca stated: "It seems to me that we women understand these problems [individuality and understanding of family needs] not only with cold reasoning, but with all our blood palpitating with human warmth. Perhaps because we are weaker we suffer deeper within us these deathly antinomies. She who suffers the most is like a bent bow: she has greater energy to leap into the fight. This is why I believe that if the reaction [solution] does not come from women, it will come from nowhere."[12]

This self-confidence may be judged utopian and flawed, but it nurtured a profound mental transformation in two generations of women who moved from a polite expression of their discontent to the creation of their own social and political philosophy.

Illegitimate Births and Legitimation: Uruguay, 1890–1943

Year	Legitimations[a]	Illegitimates	Total Live Births
1890	537	5,362	27,889
1891	362	5,696	28,696
1899	670	7,857	30,719
1900	782	8,021	30,589
1901	787	8,517	31,703
1902	672	8,232	31,526
1903	767	9,017	32,600
1904	416	6,396	26,984
1905	969	9,580	33,709
1906	1,038	8,953	32,578
1907	1,014	8,971	33,657
1908	902	9,075	35,520
1909	975	9,271	35,663
1910	942	9,587	35,927
1911	1,259	9,873	37,530
1912	1,142	10,204	39,171
1913	1,304	9,330	40,315
1914	1,395	8,093	38,571
1915	1,648	8,704	38,046
1916	1,650	8,097	36,893
1917		9,103	36,752
1920	2,245	11,426	39,335
1921	1,907	11,246	39,611
1922	1,824	11,458	40,261
1923	1,907	11,608	44,632

Year	Legitimations[a]	Illegitimates	Total Live Births
1929	4,031	12,457	44,236
1930	3,661	12,775	45,718
1931	3,370	12,221	44,854
1932	3,011	12,586	44,036
1933	3,182	11,898	41,650
1934	4,092	11,987	41,337
1935	5,315	12,253	41,426
1936	7,055	11,852	40,755
1937	7,928	12,833	41,337
1938	8,608	11,261	41,701
1939	8,555	11,737	42,862
1940	8,882	11,359	42,893
1941	9,387	11,800	44,287
1942	9,032	11,012	42,670
1943	7,613	10,539	43,500

Source: Uruguay, El movimiento del estado civil y la mortalidad (Montevideo: Imp. Nacional, 1929-43), p. 54 of each yearly volume.

[a]In the 1890s the census differentiated between "recognitions" and "legitimations." To legitimize a child marriage was necessary. I have put the two categories together. In the 1930s data for births occurring in previous years but registered later were added to each year's natural births. I have not included those additions, since they did not disaggregate legitimates from illegitimates and my main purpose was to show the correlation between them. See also Uruguay, Síntesis estadística de la República O. del Uruguay (1940) (Montevideo: Dirección Nacional de Estadística, 1940), and Anuario estadístico de la República Oriental del Uruguay (1943) (Montevideo: Imp. Nacional, 1944).

Acknowledgment of Out-of-Wedlock Parenthood by Gender: Uruguay, 1903–43

Year	KF-UM	KM-UF	UP	Total Illegitimate
1903	111	131	4	246
1904				
1905	3,875	5,148	601	9,580
1907	1,952	4,904	443	8,971
1908	3,690	4,976	462	9,075
1909	3,968	4,767	553	9,271
1910	3,914	5,054	604	9,587
1911	4,281	5,228	477	9,873
1912	5,113	4,935	313	10,204
1913	5,008	4,211	300	9,330
1914	4,391	3,734	245	8,093
1915	4,733	4,100	287	8,704
1916	4,199	4,180	203	8,097
1917	4,906	4,441	155	
1920	5,225	6,490	211	11,426
1921				11,246
1922	5,423	6,349	318	11,458
1923	5,536	5,819	322	11,608
1929	5,978	6,338	141	12,457
1930	6,062	6,580	133	12,775
1931	5,679	6,401	141	12,221
1932	5,490	6,735	141	12,586
1933	5,189	6,376	126	11,898
1934	5,002	6,548	163	11,987
1935	5,101	6,588	210	12,253

Year	KF-UM	KM-UF	UP	Total Illegitimate
1936	4,796	6,592	254	11,852
1937	4,844	6,583	454	12,833
1938	4,392	6,199	367	11,261
1939				11,737
1940	4,287	6,697	375	11,359
1941	4,621	6,727	452	11,800
1942	3,942	6,605	465	11,012
1943	3,265	6,761	513	10,539

Source: Uruguay, El movimiento del estado civil y la mortalidad en la República Oriental del Uruguay (Montevideo: Imp. Nacional, 1890–43), p. 6 of each yearly volume.

Note: KF-UM: known father–unknown mother; KM-UF: known mother–unknown father; UP: unknown parents. This source has additional figures for children born before each year but registered in a subsequent year, during the 1930s. Since these additional numbers do not furnish information on the gender of the parent registering the child, I did not use them. The total number of illegitimate births is not necessarily the total of the three preceding columns. The census does not explain the method of compiling the total number of illegitimates. Years missing were unavailable.

NOTES

Introduction

1. See Anna Macías, *Against All Odds: The Feminist Movement in Mexico to 1940* (Westport CT: Greenwood, 1982); K. Lynn Stoner. *From the House to the Streets: The Cuban Woman's Movement for Legal Reform, 1898–1940* (Durham NC: Duke Univ. Press, 1991); June Hahner, *Emancipating the Female Sex: The Struggle for Women's Rights in Brazil, 1850–1940* (Durham NC: Duke Univ. Press, 1990); Francesca Miller, *Latin American Women and the Search for Social Justice* (Hanover NH: Univ. Press of New England, 1991).

2. Nestor Tomás Auza, *Periodismo y feminismo en la Argentina: 1830–1930* (Buenos Aires: Emecé, 1988).

3. Darío Cantón, *Universal Suffrage as an Agent of Mobilization* (Evian, France, 1964).

4. Elsa Chaney, *Supermadre: Women in Politics in Latin America* (Austin: Univ. of Texas Press, 1979); Evelyn P. Steven, "The Prospects for a Women's Liberation Movement in Latin America," *Journal of Marriage and the Family* 35, 2 (1973): 313–21; Jane Jaquette, "Female Political Participation in Latin America," in June Nash and Helen Safa, eds., *Sex and Class in Latin America* (New York: Praeger, 1976).

Chapter 1 : Feminism in the Southern Cone

1. There was no "woman movement," as described by Nancy F. Cott, in the Southern Cone. Women and men writing on the possibility of education, the utilizing of women's abilities, and women's rights in the 1850s and 1860s often used the term *emancipación* [emancipation]. This term continued to be used alongside *feminismo* through the late 1920s. Between 1898 and 1910, however, *feminismo* was the word most frequently used to express a variety of legal and social changes affecting women in the family and in the workplace. The following works have been useful to me for comparative purposes. Nancy F. Cott, *The Grounding of Modern Feminism* (New Haven: Yale Univ. Press, 1987); Charles Sowerwine, *Sisters or Citizens? Women and Socialism in France since 1876* (Cambridge: Cambridge Univ. Press, 1982); Steven C. Hause and Anne R. Kenney, *Women's Suffrage and Social Politics in the French Third Republic* (Princeton: Princeton Univ. Press, 1984); Karen Offen, "Defining Feminism: A Comparative His-

torical Approach," *Signs* 14 (autumn 1988): 119–57; Nancy Cott, "Comment on Karen Offen's 'Defining Feminism: A Comparative Historical Approach,'" *Signs* 15 (autumn 1989): 203–5; Sally M. Miller, ed., *Flawed Liberation: Socialism and Feminism* (Westport CT: Greenwood, 1981); Mari Jo Buhle, *Women and American Socialism, 1870–1920* (Urbana: Univ. of Illinois Press, 1981); William Leach, *True Love and Perfect Union. The Feminist Reform of Sex and Society* (New York: Basic Books, 1980); Aileen S. Kraditor, *The Ideas of the Woman Suffrage Movement: 1890–1920* (New York: Norton, 1981); Susan Kinsley Kent, *Sex and Suffrage in Britain, 1860–1914* (Princeton: Princeton Univ. Press, 1987); Seth Koven and Sonya Michel, eds., *Mothers of a New World: Maternalist Politics and the Origins of Welfare States* (New York: Routledge, 1993); Sonya Michel and Seth Koven, "Womanly Duties: Maternalist Politics and the Origins of Welfare States in France, Germany, Great Britain, and the United States, 1880–1920," *American Historical Review* 95, 4 (1990): 1076–198.

2. For the development of feminism in other areas, see Anna Macías, *Against All Odds: Feminism in Mexico to 1940* (Westport CT: Greenwood, 1982); Yamila Asize, *La mujer en la lucha* (Río Piedras PR: Editorial Cultural, 1985); Marifran Carlson, *¡Feminismo! The Woman's Movement in Argentina from Its Beginnings to Eva Perón* (Chicago: Academy Chicago, 1988); K. Lynn Stoner, *From the House to the Streets: The Cuban Woman's Movement for Legal Reform, 1898–1940* (Durham NC: Duke Univ. Press, 1991); June Hahner, *Emancipating the Female Sex: The Struggle for Women's Rights in Brazil, 1850–1940* (Durham NC: Duke Univ. Press, 1990); Mayra Rosa Urrutia and Maria de Fátima Barceló Miller, "Temperancia y sufragismo en el Puerto Rico del siglo XX (Santurce PR: Centro de Investigaciones Académicas Univ. del Sagrado Corazón, 1990); Francesca Miller, *Latin American Women and the Search for Social Justice* (Hanover NH: Univ. Press of New England, 1991); Edda Gaviola A. et al., *Queremos votar en las próximas elecciones: Historia del movimiento femenino chileno, 1913–1952* (Santiago: Centro de Análisis y Difusión de la Condición de la Mujer, 1986).

3. The most influential liberal feminist work was John Stuart Mill, *On the Subjection of Women* (1869), first translated into Spanish by Chilean Martina Barros Borgoño in 1873. See "La esclavitud de la mujer," *Revista de Santiago* 2 (1872–73). Among socialists, August Bebel's *Woman under Socialism* (1879) was very influential.

4. Silvia Rodríguez Villamil and Graciela Sapriza, *La inmigración europea en el Uruguay: Los Italianos* (Montevideo: Banda Oriental, 1982), 52–54. Over half of the immigrants were Spaniards and one-third were Italians. In the 1880s this ratio was inverted; David Rock, *Argentina, 1516–1987: From Spanish Colonization to Alfonsín* (Berkeley: Univ. of California Press, 1987), 163–64; Carl Solberg, *Immigration and Nationalism: Argentina and Chile, 1890–1914* (Texas: Univ. of Texas Press, 1970), 38; Peter De Shazo, *Urban Workers and Labor Unions in Chile, 1902–1927* (Madison: Univ. of Wisconsin Press, 1983), 5.

5. See chapters 2 and 7 for further information on these women's activities. For Alicia Moreau, see Mirta Henault, *Alicia Moreau de Justo* (Buenos Aires: Centro Editor de América Latina, 1983); Blas Alberti, *Conversaciones con Alicia Moreau de Justo y Jorge Luis Borges* (Buenos Aires: Mar Dulce, 1985).

6. Consejo Nacional de Mujeres del Uruguay, *Estatutos y reglamentos* (Montevideo:

El Siglo Ilustrado, 1917); *Acción Femenina*, vols. 1–4 (1917–20), passim. See also chapter 10.

7. See chapter 9 for further information on women's activities. See also *Actividades femeninas en Chile* (Santiago: La Ilustración, 1928).

8. *Unión Femenina de Chile* 1, 1 (1934): 3; *Nosotras* 2, 43 (1933): 5.

9. See *Actividades femeninas en Chile*, 103–385; Jennie Howard, *In Distant Climes and Other Years* (Buenos Aires: America Press, 1931); Georgette M. Dorn, "Sarmiento, the United States, and Public Education," in Joseph T. Criscenti, ed., *Sarmiento and His Argentina* (Boulder CO: Lynne Rienner, 1993), 77–91.

10. As examples, see, Alfred G. Meyer, *The Feminism and Socialism of Lily Braun* (Bloomington: Indiana Univ. Press, 1985); Jean H. Quataert, *Reluctant Feminists in German Social Democracy, 1885–1917* (Princeton: Princeton Univ. Press, 1979).

11. "La mujer médica," *La Vanguardia* (Buenos Aires), 25 June 1904, 2.

12. Fenia Chertcoff de Repetto, "Carta Abierta," *Nosotras* 1, 36 (1903): 359–63; "El movimiento socialista femenino," *Almanaque del Trabajo* 1 (1918): 141–45.

13. *La Vanguardia*, 31 Dec.–1 Jan. 1907 (joint issue), 1.

14. See *Nosotras* 2, 31 (1903): 394–95; 2, 41 (1903): 426–29; 2, 47 (1903): 483–85.

15. Justa Burgos Meyer, "Feminismo socialista," *Nosotras* 2, 48 (1903): 513–15. For Fenia Chertcoff's response, see 2, 40 (1903): 402–4.

16. *La Vanguardia*, 8 Sept. 1907, 1.

17. Argentina, Cámara de Diputados, *Diario de Sesiones* 1 (1907): 1066.

18. *La Vanguardia*, 11 Apr. 1912, 2.

19. On Uruguayan feminist politics see chapter 10.

20. *La Aurora Feminista* (Santiago) 1, 1 (15 Jan. 1904): 1–8.

21. *La Alborada* (Santiago), 6 Apr. 1907, 1; 11 Nov. 1906, 1. See also Asunción Lavrin, "Women, Labor and the Left: Argentina and Chile, 1900–1925," *Journal of Women's Studies* 1–2 (fall 1998): 89–113. Elizabeth Hutchinson, "El feminismo en el movimiento obrero chileno: La emancipación de la mujer en la prensa obrera feminista, 1905–1908," Working paper, Series Contribuciones, no. 80, Santiago: FLACSO, 1992.

22. *La Palanca* (Santiago) 1, 3 (1908), 35.

23. *La Reforma* published several articles on women from June through November 1906. See also *El Despertar de los Trabajadores*, 18 Apr. 1916, 2; 30 Nov. 1921, 1.

24. Juan Varras M., "Feminism," *La Reforma*, 4 Oct. 1906.

25. See *El Despertar de los Trabajadores*, 1 Oct. 1912, 1; 12 Mar. 1914; 21 Apr. 1914; 23 Jan. 1915, 1; 13 Feb. 1916, 1; 4–15 Mar. 1913, detailing the visit of Belén de Zárraga, all on p. 2; 16 Jan. 1915, 4; 21 Feb. 1915; 15 June–4 July 1915, p. 1 of each issue for Zárraga's second visits; 6 Oct. 1916; 31 Oct. 1916. Her name is also spelled Sárraga.

26. *El Despertar de los Trabajadores*, 15 Feb. 1913, 3; 25 Feb. 1913, 2; 14 June 1913.

27. As examples, see issues of 9 Jan. 1921, 5; 28 Jan., 1; 2 and 19 Feb., 3; 6 Mar. 1921, 3; 16 Apr., 3; 9 and 29 Sept., 1; 7 and 29 Oct., 1; 30 Nov., 1; 9 Jan. 1923, 4; 14 June 1923, 4. Volumes for 1919 and 1920 of *El Despertar de los Trabajadores* were missing.

28. *La Alborada* 1, 12 (1906): 2. Also in *La Alborada*, see Ricardo Guerrero, "Como tratamos a la mujer," 2, 20 (1906): 3; A. Calderón, "La mujer," 1, 14 (1906): 3; Carmela Jeria G., "Como emanciparnos," 2, 29 (6, 1906): 1; Ariadna, "Nuestra Condición," 2,

22 (1906): 1 and 2, 26 (1906): 1. Also *El Despertar de los Trabajadores,* 29 Mar. 1923, 1; 17 Sept. 1916, 1.

29. Maxine Molyneux, "No God, No Boss, No Husband: Anarchist Feminism in Nineteenth-Century Argentina," *Latin American Perspectives* 13, 1 (1986): 119–45; *Nuestra Tribuna* 1, 2 (1922): 4; 1, 3 (1922): 1.

30. Juan Vargas M., "Feminismo: La mujer obrera," *La Reforma,* 4 Oct. 1906; *El Despertar de los Trabajadores,* 21 Apr. 1914, 2–3; "Mujeres, despertad," *El Despertar de los Trabajadores,* 28 Oct. 1913, 2; 31 Oct. 1916, 1.

31. *Historia del Consejo Nacional de Mujeres* (Buenos Aires: Oceana, 1936); Luis R. Longhi, *Sufragio femenino* (Buenos Aires: A. Baiocco, 1932), 133–34.

32. Elvira Rawson de Dellepiane, "Emancipación social y económica de la mujer argentina," *La Universidad Popular* 1, 2 (1905): 19–26.

33. Elvira Rawson de Dellepiane, "La campaña feminista," in Miguel J. Font, *La mujer: Encuesta feminista* (Buenos Aires, 1921). Also reproduced in Longhi, *Sufragio femenino,* 138–39.

34. Abella's writings are found in *Nosotras* (July 1902–Aug. 1904). She also edited *La Nueva Mujer* as a mouthpiece for the National Feminist League that she founded in 1910. See also her *Ensayos feministas,* 2d ed. (Montevideo: Siglo Ilustrado, 1965).

35. *Nosotras* 2, 48 (1903): 511–12.

36. *Nosotras* 2, 47 (1903): 483–85.

37. See *Nosotras* 2, 39 (1903): 394–95; 2, 41 (1903): 426–29; Abella de Ramírez, *Ensayos feministas,* 66, 94–95.

38. Abella de Ramírez, *Ensayos feministas,* 53.

39. María Abella de Ramírez, "¡Ser madre!" *Nosotras* 3, 63–64 (1904): 742–43. In 1910 Argentine feminist Elvira Rawson de Dellepiane founded the Sociedad Juana María Gorriti (the name of another Argentine educator), a shelter for unwed mothers. See *La Nueva Mujer* 1, 4 (1910), editorial; 2, 17 (1911): 7–9.

40. Abella de Ramírez, *Ensayos feministas,* 13–15.

41. *La Nueva Mujer* 1, 1 (1910): 10. María Abella de Ramírez encouraged the use of the term "feminist."

42. *Primer Congreso Femenino Internacional de la Republica Argentina: Historia, actas y trabajos* (Buenos Aires: A. Ceppi, 1910), 37–38.

43. *Primer Congreso Femenino,* 33–48.

44. "La libertad no supone poder hacer todo cuanto se quiere, sino saber querer todo cuanto se debe." See *Primer Congreso Femenino,* 42.

45. Elements of liberal feminism remained as a source of inspiration for later feminists. In 1946 Uruguayan female deputy Magdalena Antonelli Moreno claimed she had always been guided by feminist principles, defining them as "the legitimate equality [of men and women] in fundamental rights," "the complete female liberation from ignorance . . . [and the] deliverance from the unconditional submission that kills the sense of responsibility and moral and intellectual liberation." See Uruguay, Cámara de Diputados, *Diario de Sesiones* 465 (1945–46): 501.

46. See Asunción Lavrin, "Female, Feminine and Feminist: Key Concepts in Understanding Women's History in Twentieth Century Latin America," University of Bristol

Occasional Lecture Series no. 4 (Nov. 1988). In Spanish the word for "feminine" refers to that which pertains to women.

47. *Primer Congreso Femenino,* 238–65.

48. María de Jesús Alvarado, "Femenismo" [*sic*], in *Primer Congreso Femenino,* 265–74. See also Centro de Documentación sobre la Mujer, *Boletín* 3, 1-2 (1988): 10–11; Elsa M. Chaney, "Significado de la Obra de María Jesús Alvarado Rivera" (lecture) (Lima: CENDOC-MUJER, 1988).

49. Uruguayan Paulina Luisi traveled extensively in Europe beginning in 1913. Alicia Moreau and Amanda Labarca traveled in the United States in the 1920s, Carrie Chapman Catt toured South America in 1923, and Doris Stevens gathered a substantial number of votes among Latin Americans for her married women's citizenship proposals at The Hague. For further data see Francesca Miller, "The International Relations of Women of the Americas, 1890–1928," *The Americas* 43, 2 (1986): 171–82, and her *Latin American Women and the Search for Social Justice* (Hanover NH: Univ. Press of New England, 1991), 82–84, 94–96.

50. On women's social role, see Alfredo Lombardi, "La mujer y su función social," *El Monitor de la Educación Común* (Buenos Aires) 39 (Apr. 1910): 544–50. He stated, "Do not obstruct women's path to science and progress . . . but for the goodness of all, let us not forget what is our [respective] place in society. Women [belong] in the family and for the family for the sake of society and humanity." While discussing the creation of secondary schools for women in 1912, conservative Uruguayan deputy Melián Lafinur deprecated education because "the question of feminism begins with such [educational] stimulants." See María Julia Ardao, *La creación de la Sección de Enseñanza Secundaria y Preparatoria para Mujeres en 1912* (Montevideo: Florensa y Lafón, 1962), 34–35. Female education is discussed by Eugenio M. Hostos, *La educación de la mujer* (Santiago: Imp. Sud-América, 1873); Carlos Octavio Bunge, *El espíritu de la educación* (Buenos Aires: Penitenciaría Nacional, 1901). Chile was the only nation that appointed a woman, Amanda Labarca, to the Ministry of Education in the mid-1920s.

51. María Isabel Salthou, "El problema feminista," doctoral thesis in Philosophy and Letters, Univ. of Buenos Aires, 1920. For supporters of a feminism inclusive of maternal roles, see Francisco Gicca, *La mujer: Su pasado, su presente y sus reivindicaciones en el porvenir* (Buenos Aires: Mercantil, 1915); Mercedes G. Humano Ortiz, *Emancipación de la mujer* (Buenos Aires: José Traganti, 1918); W. Tello, "El feminismo argentino," *Revista de Derecho, Historia y Letras* 63 (Aug. 1919): 456–59; Ernesto Nelson, "Feminismo de ayer, de hoy y de mañana," *Nosotros* 15, 36 (1920): 441–59; José Bianco, *Mi feminismo* (Buenos Aires: L. J. Rosso, 1927); Amanda Labarca. *¿A dónde va la mujer?* (Santiago: Extra, 1934).

52. Ernesto Quesada, *La cuestión femenina* (Buenos Aires: Pablo E. Coni, 1899), 12–20, 32–35.

53. María Abella y Ramírez, "La mujer moderna o feminista," *Nuestra Causa: Revista Mensual del Movimiento Feminista* (Buenos Aires) 1, 5 (1919): 99.

54. Keynote speech by Dra. Ernestina López, *Primer Congreso Femenino Internacional,* 35–36.

55. "Women should have—just like men—the freedom to develop their abilities."

Our association [the Uruguayan National Council of Women] seeks for half of the human species all the rights . . . to fulfill their duties. . . . . That in full possession of their freedom and will, strong in their rights, and proud of their destiny, they may fulfill . . . the sublime duties of maternity. . . . For middle-class women and men the term 're-demption' may look like an exaggeration. But they have no notion of the suffering of working women. Men discussing the Constitution know nothing about the homes of servants or factory workers. They cannot deny political rights to women in the name of motherhood." *Acción Femenina* (Uruguay) 1, 1 (1917): 1–2.

56. Alicia Moreau, "El feminismo en la evolución social," *Humanidad Nueva* 3, 4 (1911): 356–75.

57. Interview with Herminia C. Brumana in Miguel Font, *La mujer: Encuesta feminista* (Buenos Aires, 1921). Brumana was a well-known Argentine journalist.

58. J. Fernando Carbonell, *Feminismo y marimachismo* (Montevideo: Centro Natura, 1909), passim.

59. Laura Correa de Bustos, *Feminismo cristiano* (Montevideo: Buena Prensa, 1907), passim. The "terrible feminists" who put off María Teresa León de Sebastián were the "London street suffragists." María Teresa León de Sebastián, *La mujer en el hogar y la vida* (Buenos Aires: Tailhade, 1928), 10–11.

60. Isabel G. de la Solana, *La mujer, la caridad y la doctrina del feminismo* (Buenos Aires: E. Molina, 1911).

61. *La Protesta*, 9 Sept. 1923; article signed by Praxedes Guerrero.

62. Interview with Luis Reyna in Miguel Font, *La mujer*, 136–41.

63. *Acción Femenina* (Santiago) 1, 1 (1922): 17–18. See also speech by Angela Costa on feminism, as reported in *Nuestra Causa* (Buenos Aires) 2, 14 (1920): 43.

64. Lucía Marticorena de Martín, "Miscelánea política," *Acción Femenina* (Santiago) 6, 4 (1935): 3.

65. Vera Zouroff [Esmeralda Zenteno], *Feminismo obrero*, Cuadernos de Cultura Obrera (Santiago: El Esfuerzo, 1933), 9–10.

66. *Mujeres de América* 1, 2 (1933): 13–15.

67. Rosa Scheiner, "Lo real en la emancipación de la mujer," *Vida Femenina* 2, 14 (1934): 20–22; Josefina Marpons. "¡Ciudadanas!" *Vida Femenina* 1, 5 (1933): 19, 35.

68. Darwin Peluffo Beisso, *Femineidad y política: Sobre el voto de la mujer* (Monte-video, 1931), passim. Argentine Rodolfo Senet also believed there was an unbridgable biological and psychological difference between men and women, but he supported female suffrage based on assets in women's character. See Font, *La mujer,* 55–57. See also Felipe S. Velázquez, *El proyecto de ley instituyendo el voto cívico femenino* (San Luis: Celorrio, 1933), passim.

69. See *Nosotras* (La Plata) 2, 63–64 (1904): 742–43; *Nosotras* (Valparaíso) 1, 15 (1931): 3; *Ideas y Acción* (Montevideo) 1, 4 (1933): 2.

70. Labarca, *¿A dónde va la mujer?* 170.

71. Carlos Vaz Ferreira, *Sobre feminismo* (Buenos Aires: Sociedad Amigos del Libro Rioplatense, 1933), passim. Vaz Ferreira (1872–1959) was a very influential Uruguayan philosopher whose ideas on feminism have been overlooked. This lecture was printed eighteen years after it was delivered at the University of Uruguay in Montevideo. See

also Emilio Frugoni, *La mujer ante el derecho* (Montevideo: Indo-Americana, 1940), passim.

72. See chapter 3 for the discussion of these topics.

73. Font, *La mujer,* passim. Argentina, Cámara de Diputados, *Diario de Sesiones* 6 (1926): 61. Speech by Deputy Leopoldo Bard; Baltasar Brum, *Los derechos de la mujer: Reforma civil y política del Uruguay* (Montevideo: Serrano, 1923), passim.

74. Alberto H. Ebensperger, *De la capacidad legal de la mujer* (Santiago: Imp. Chile, 1910).

75. *La Nueva Mujer* 1, 7 (1910): 3–4; 1, 13 (1911), editorial. For Lanteri's case, see chapter 8.

76. Rock, *Argentina, 1516–1987;* Julio Heise G., *Historia de Chile: El período parlamentario, 1861–1925,* 2 vols. (Santiago: Andrés Bello, 1974; Editorial Universitaria, 1982); Federico Gil, *The Political System of Chile* (Boston: Houghton Mifflin, 1966), 35–92; José Pedro Barrán and Benjamín Nahum, *Batlle, los estancieros y el imperio británico,* 7 vols. (Montevideo: Banda Oriental, 1979–86).

77. José Manuel Estrada, *Curso de derecho constitucional,* 3 vols. (Buenos Aires: Cabaut, 1901-2), 2:336; Florentino González, *Lecciones de derecho constitucional* (Buenos Aires: J.A. Bernheim, 1869), 125–28.

78. Quotation from Argentine deputy Guasch Leguizamon in 1910. See *La Vanguardia,* 2 Sept. 1910, 1. "Feminist demands encouraged mixing women's legitimate and noble aspirations with pointless hopes for a life radically opposed to their nature." For antecedents of this attitude in the nineteenth century, see Carlos Pellegrini, *Estudio sobre el derecho electoral* (Buenos Aires: Imp. del Plata, 1869), 10–26; Pedro E. Aguilar, *Derecho electoral* (Buenos Aires: Argos, 1893), 95–110.

79. *La Mujer: Periódico Quincenal* 2 ([Apr.?] 1898): 27.

80. See the opinion of Argentine Ernesto Colombres, as quoted by Clorinda Matto de Turner in her magazine *El Búcaro Americano* 2, 19–20 (1898): 318–20. Octavio Iturbe, *El sufragio de la mujer* (Buenos Aires: Montes, 1895), passim. He cited Pierre Leroux, August Bebel, J. J. Rousseau, Charles Fourier, and John Stuart Mill.

81. See Clorinda Matto de Turner, "La mujer y la ciencia," *El Búcaro Americano* 2, 19–20 (1898): 318–20. See also her "El camino luminoso de la mujer," *El Búcaro Americano* 2, 15 (1897): 254–55, and Eva Angelina, "La emancipación de la mujer," *El Búcaro Americano* 1, 7 (1896): 127–30.

82. *Unión y Labor* 1, 12 (1910): 22–23; 2, 17 (1910); 3, 25 (1911), editorial. Educator Sara Justo, sister of the ideological leader of the Socialist Party in Argentina, decried women who aped men's political practices. She envisaged them as voters but not as *members* of the government. See Sara Justo, "La mujer y la política," *Unión y Labor* 1, 4 (1910): 24–26.

83. *Primer Congreso Femenino Internacional,* 368–78, 400–413.

84. Moreau, "El feminismo y la evolución social," 356–75; Juana Beguino, *La mujer y el socialismo* (Buenos Aires: Marinoni, n.d.). This book must have been written after 1918 because the author refers to World War I as a past event.

85. Alicia Moreau, "Por que pedimos el derecho al sufragio," *Nuestra Causa* 3, 24 (1921): 272. In Uruguay, socialist Emilio Frugoni used the economic argument of

women's labor to support his proposal to include female suffrage in the new constitution drafted in 1917. See Emilio Frugoni, *Los nuevos fundamentos* (Montevideo: Maximino García, 1919), 57.

86. In Argentina the province of Santa Fe discussed a reform to its constitution to give literate women over twenty-one full political rights. This suffrage was not totally democratic, but feminists were willing to accept it as the lesser of two evils. The same idea was proposed in 1929 by Carmela Horne de Burmeister, a conservative feminist. The Santa Fe constitutional reform also boosted the feminists' claim that feminism was not restricted to the capital of the nation. See *Nuestra Causa* 3, 24 (1921): 273–74, 275.

87. Salthou, "El problema feminista en la República Argentina," passim.

88. Velázquez, *El proyecto de ley instituyendo el voto cívico femenino.*

89. Further details about their activities are in chapters 8, 9, and 10.

90. *La Prensa* (Buenos Aires), 31 Oct. 1919, 11; *Nuestra Causa* 1, 4 (1919): 83; 2, 13 (1920): 10.

91. Adelia di Carlo in *Nuestra Causa* 2, 8 (1920): 126. The enthusiasm some women experienced for the feminist and suffragist ideas expressed itself in suffragist and feminist "hymns" written for their social gatherings. I have found three for Chile.

92. See chapter 10 for further details on this party.

93. Minelli was quoted in *Mujeres de América* (Buenos Aires) 1, 1 (1933): 8.

94. *La Vanguardia*, 31 Dec. 1932, 1.

95. *América Nueva* (Montevideo) 1, 8 (1933), editorial; 1, 9 (1933), editorial; National Archives of the Nation, Montevideo, Paulina Luisi's papers, box 257, folder 8, no. 25.

96. "Nuestra ideología," *Nosotras* 1, 15 (1931): 3.

97. Adela Edwards de Salas, "Respondiendo a un manifiesto," in *Nosotras* 2, 40 (1933): 3. A similar feeling was expressed by yet another Chilean, Elena Caffarena, who organized the largest umbrella organization in Chile in 1935, the Movimiento Pro-Emancipación de la Mujer en Chile (MEMCH). See *La Mujer Nueva* (Santiago) 3, 27 (1941): 2.

98. Mario Bravo, *Derechos políticos de la mujer* (Buenos Aires: La Vanguardia, 1930), passim. See also Rogelio Araya's opinion, as quoted by Leopoldo Bard in his own support of a bill for women's suffrage, in Argentina, Cámara de Diputados, *Diario de Sesiones* 2 (1925): 30; Uruguay, Asamblea General, Cámara de Representantes, *Diario de Sesiones* 381 (1932–33): 125–40; *El Mercurio* (Santiago), 10 Mar. 1933, 3.

99. *El Día*, 24 Jan. 1924, 6.

100. Alicia Moreau de Justo, "Carrera hacia el abismo," *Vida Femenina* 5, 55 (1938): 4–5; "Nazismo y fascismo en la Argentina," 5, 57 (1938): 4–5; "El escenario y las bambalinas," 6, 67 (1939): 4–5, 33; "¡Fuera el judío! El grito de la Edad Media," 5, 62 (1938): 4–5; "El trágico destino de los niños del mundo," 6, 70 (1939): 4–5, 31.

101. *Mujeres de América* 1, 1 (1933): 15.

Chapter 2 : Labor and Feminism

1. Working conditions in the cigarette-manufacturing plants El Sport and La Italia and the garment factories La Criolla and La Victoria, Montevideo, are described in

labor newspapers and served as a base for this vignette. Women were forbidden to talk among themselves in most factories, and time spent in the toilet was measured. Infractions of internal discipline were penalized with cash fines, and they had to pay for anything they broke. *El Trabajo* (Montevideo), 10 and 17 Sept. 1901, 1; 5 Oct. 1901, 1; *Justicia* (Montevideo), 20 Feb. 1922, 2; 24 Feb. 1922, 2. In 1910 textile factories employing mostly women had a nine- to ten-hour schedule. See Argentina, Departmento Nacional del Trabajo, *Boletín* 12 (31 Mar. 1910): 8-9. See also 4 (Mar. 1908): 454-56.

2. Argentina, Departamento Nacional del Trabajo, *Boletín* 42 (1917): 173-76. In 1917 a family of four required a minimum of 4.23 pesos daily to cover the most elementary needs. See also José Pedro Barrán and Benjamín Nahún, "Las clases populares en el Montevideo del novecientos," in José Pedro Barrán, Benjamín Nahún, et al., *Sectores populares y vida urbana* (Buenos Aires: CLACSO, 1984), 11-36.

3. Charles Bergquist, *Labor in Latin America: Comparative Essays on Chile, Argentina, Venezuela, and Colombia* (Stanford: Stanford Univ. Press, 1986); Peter De Shazo, *Urban Workers and Labor Unions in Chile, 1902-1927* (Madison: Univ. of Wisconsin Press, 1983); Hernán Ramírez Necochea, *Historia del movimiento obrero en Chile* (Santiago, 1956); Moisés Poblete Troncoso, *La organización sindical en Chile y otros estudios sociales* (Santiago: R. Brias, 1926); Virginia Krzeminski F., "Alessandri y la cuestión social," in Claudio Orrego V., et al. *Siete ensayos sobre Arturo Alessandri Palma* (Santiago: Instituto Chileno de Estudios Humanísticos, 1979), 165-258; Catalina H. Wainerman and Marysa Navarro, *El trabajo de la mujer en la Argentina: Un análisis preliminar de las ideas dominantes en las primeras décadas del siglo* XX (Buenos Aires: Centro de Estudios de Población, 1979); Catalina H. Wainerman, *La mujer y el trabajo en la Argentina desde la perspectiva de la Iglesia Católica* (Buenos Aires: Centro de Estudios de Población, 1980); Donna Guy, "Women, Peonage and Industrialization: Argentina, 1810-1914," *Latin American Research Review* 16, 3, (1981): 65-89; Sandra McGee Deutsch, "The Visible and Invisible Liga Patriótica Argentina: Gender Roles and the Right Wing," *Hispanic American Historical Review* 64, 2 (1984): 233-58, and idem, "The Catholic Church, Work, and Womanhood in Argentina, 1890-1930," *Gender and History* 3, 3 (1991): 304-25; Maxine Molyneux, "No God, No Boss, No Husband: Anarchist Feminism in Nineteenth-Century Argentina," *Latin American Perspectives* 13, 1 (1986): 119-45; Mirta Zaida Lobato, "Trabajo y mujer: Participación femenina en la industria de la carne, el caso de las obreras del Frigorífico Armour, 1915-69," paper presented at the Sixth Yale Conference on Latin American Labor History, 22-23 Apr. 1989; Jorge Balbis, "La situación de las trabajadoras durante el primer batllismo," in Jorge Balbis et al., *El primer batllismo: Cinco enfoques polémicos* (Montevideo: Centro Latinoamericano de Economía Humana and Banda Oriental, 1985); Silvia Rodríguez Villamil, "La participación femenina en el mercado de trabajo uruguayo: 1880-1914," in *La Mujer en el Uruguay* (Servicio de Documentación Social) 4 (1982): 211-18.

4. Juan S. Lois, "De la conveniencia del profesorado de la mujer," *El Atacameño* (Atacama, Chile), 20 Mar. 1883; Tancredo Pinochet Le Brun, *La educación de la mujer* (Santiago: Francia, 1908); Eduvige Casanova de Polanco, *Educación de la mujer* (Valparaíso, Imp. de la Patria, 1871); Ernesto Turenne, "Profesiones científicas para la mujer," *Revista Chilena* 7 (1877): 352-427; Carlos Octavio Bunge, *La educación,* in *Obras com-*

pletas de Carlos Octavio Bunge, 3 vols. (Madrid: Espasa-Calpe, 1928); Cecilia Grierson, *Educación técnica de la mujer* (Buenos Aires: Penitenciaría Nacional, 1902); José Pedro Varela, *Obras pedagógicas,* 2 vols. (Montevideo: Ministerio de Instrucción Pública y Previsión Social, 1964), 2:209–22.

5. Graciela Sapriza, "La imagen de la mujer y sus variantes, 1880–1910," in Servicio de Documentación Social, *La mujer en el Uruguay,* 4, 1982, 219–23; "Slave of Labor," published in *La Antorcha* (Santiago), Mar. 1921, 2.

6. Eduardo Acevedo, *Anales históricos del Uruguay,* 6 vols. (Montevideo: Berreiro y Ramos, 1934), 5:206. In February 1899 *La Voz del Obrero* reported the "awful lack of work we are experiencing in Uruguay." See 3, 1, (1899): 43, 1.

7. Turn-of-the-century Uruguayans and Argentines carefully distinguished between natives and foreigners in all statistical data.

8. See Donna Guy, *Sex and Danger in Buenos Aires: Prostitution, Family, and Nation in Argentina* (Lincoln: Univ. of Nebraska Press, 1991). Guy argues that immigrant women had a slight edge over native women in the labor market in Argentina up to the middle of the 1910s. See also Guy, "Women, Peonage, and Industrialization," 77–78.

9. De Shazo, *Urban Workers and Labor Unions in Chile,* 20, 30, 71–72, 86, 99–101, 107, 115, 150, 172–73.

10. The Argentine third national census was taken in 1914 and the fourth in 1946. In Uruguay there was no national census between 1908 and 1963. In Chile there were national population censuses in 1908, 1920, 1930, and 1940.

11. See Adolfo Dorfman, *Historia de la industria argentina* (Buenos Aires: Solar/ Hachette, 1970), 66–173.

12. Julio Mafud, *La vida obrera en la Argentina* (Buenos Aires: Proyección, 1976), 130; Elena Gil, *La mujer en el mundo del trabajo* (Buenos Aires: Libera, 1970), 38–39.

13. Mafud, *La vida obrera,* 143–47.

14. Argentina, Provincia de Buenos Aires, *Censo general de población, edificación, comercio e industria,* 3 vols. (Buenos Aires: Compañia Sud-Americana de Billetes de Banco, 1910), 1:52, 54.

15. The 1909 municipal census included working minors. There were 13,380 minors of both sexes working in factories, more than the number of women alone and one-fifth the total number of workers. A 1908 survey of thirty-four textile plants in Buenos Aires showed 4,028 women workers and 1,054 minors of both sexes against 2,006 men. See Láutaro Durañona, "Informe del Departamento Nacional de Higiene sobre el trabajo en las casas de confecciones," Argentina, Departamento Nacional del Trabajo, *Boletín* 7 (31 Dec. 1908): 605–9.

16. Argentina, Provincia de Buenos Aires, *Censo general de la ciudad de La Plata* (La Plata: La Popular, 1910), 39. See also Argentina, Rosario de Santa Fe, *Tercer censo municipal* (Rosario, 1910), 102. In Santa Fe the main occupational categories were industries and commerce, 2,161; domestic service, 2,025; garments, sewing, and embroidery, 1,595; washing and ironing, 1,091; teaching, 585; prostitution, 587. See also data cited by Guy, "Women, Peonage, and Industrialization," 78–79.

17. Argentina, *Tercer censo nacional,* 8: 6–8. Industrial classification and data on industrial employment were questionable because of an industrial crisis that had closed

down many factories. Many provinces failed to send data on their textile industries. The compiled data represented only "half of the personnel effectively employed in industry."

18. Argentina, Departamento Nacional del Trabajo, *Boletín* 42 (1919): 103. Of a total of 4,076 minors, nearly one-quarter (1,162) were employed in the garment industry.

19. Argentina, Departamento Nacional del Trabajo, *Boletín Informativo*, ser. 6, 17, 186–88 (1935): 4325.

20. Juan Rial and J. Klaczo, *Uruguay: El país urbano* (Montevideo: Banda Oriental, 1981), 49–58, 109–10.

21. Rial and Klaczo, *Uruguay,* 62–65; José Pedro Barrán and Benjamín Nahum, *Batlle, los estancieros y el imperio británico,* 7 vols., vol. 1, *El Uruguay del novecientos* (Montevideo: Banda Oriental, 1979), 159–211.

22. Uruguay, *Censo municipal del departamento y de la ciudad de Montevideo* (Montevideo: Dirección General de Censos y Estados, 1892); Balbis, "La situación de las trabajadoras durante el primer batllismo," 106.

23. Rodríguez Villamil, "La participación femenina en el mercado de trabajo uruguayo: 1880-1914," 211–18; Silvia Rodríguez Villamil and Graciela Sapriza, *Mujer, estado y política en el Uruguay del siglo* xx (Montevideo: Banda Oriental, 1984), 30–32.

24. Uruguay, Oficina del Trabajo, *Salarios de obreros* (Montevideo: Ministerio de Industrias, Trabajo e Instrucción Pública, 1908), passim; José Pedro Barrán and Benjamín Nahum, "Las clases populares en el Montevideo del novecientos," in José Pedro Barrán, Benjamín Nahum, et al., *Sectores populares y vida urbana* (Buenos Aires: CLACSO, 1984), 11–36; Balbis, "La situación de las trabajadoras," 115–16.

25. Uruguay, *Anuario estadístico* (1919) (Montevideo: Imp. Nacional, 1920), 103–5. Half of the female workforce (2,894 women) earned less than 1 peso daily. Nearly half of the male minors (5,440 out of 11,218) earned the same as women.

26. Jorge Sosa F. and Victoria Beloso L., *El trabajo de la mujer* (Montevideo: Oficina Nacional del Trabajo, 1923).

27. Chile, *Censo levantado el 28 de noviembre de 1907* (Santiago: Universo, 1908).

28. Chile, Oficina del Trabajo, *Boletín* 4 (1914): 143. Immigrant labor was negligible in the blue-collar jobs. On the other hand, 18.4 percent of white-collar workers were immigrants.

29. Chile, *Anuario estadístico,* 9, Industria Manufacturera, 1916 (Santiago: Universo, 1917), 24–229. In 1916 there were 2,202 women working for garment shops as tailors.

30. Chile, *Anuario estadístico,* 9, Industria Manufacturera, 1921 (Santiago: Universo, 1922), 24–25.

31. Chile, Oficina del Trabajo, *Boletín* 16 (1926): 141. Early in 1926 there were 8,466 women and 1,680 minors working in 248 out of 672 manufacturing plants in Santiago. Although the total number of male workers was not given the pattern follows the official figures released by the Labor Office for 1925. See Chile, Oficinas del Trabajo, *Boletín* 11 (1926–27): 201–6. "Informe de las Inspectoras del Trabajo, Srtas. Santa Cruz y Caffarena, al Ministro del Trabajo y de la Previsión Social."

32. Chile, Comisión Central del Censo, *Resultados del X censo de la población efectuado el 27 de noviembre de 1930,* 3 vols. (Santiago: Universo, 1931–35). See vol. 3.

33. Between 1920 and 1930 the proportion of industrial workers declined from 30.2 to 23.8 percent, but this is probably due to a different classification pattern. For other sources see María Gertosio Rodríguez, *La actividad económica de la mujer* (Santiago: La Simiente, 1944), 44; *Geografía económica de Chile*, 4 vols. (Santiago: Corporación de Fomento de la Producción, 1950), vol. 2.

34. Mafud, *La vida obrera*, 165–76.

35. Juan Bialet Massé, *El estado de las clases obreras argentinas a comienzos del siglo*, 2d ed., prologue and notes by Louis A. Despontín (Córdoba: Univ. Nacional de Córdoba, 1968), 154, 246–47, 566–67, 595, 605, 611; Juan Alsina, *El obrero en la República Argentina*, 2 vols. (Buenos Aires: Imp. Calle de Mexico no. 1422, 1905), passim.

36. Alsina, *El obrero*, 1:47, 49, 51, 52, 344, 346; 2:44, 46, 47, 278.

37. Richard J. Walter, *The Socialist Party of Argentina, 1890–1930* (Austin: Univ. of Texas Press, 1977), 77–87; José Ingenieros, *La legislation du travail* (Paris: Edouard Cornely, 1906), passim.

38. Francisco Hunneus Gana, *Por el orden social* (Santiago: Soc. Imp. Lit. Barcelona, 1917); Krzeminski F., "Alessandri y la cuestión social," 165–257.

39. José P. Barrán and Benjamín Nahum, *Batlle, los estancieros y el imperio británico*, vol. 2, *Un diálogo difícil, 1903–1910* (Montevideo: Banda Oriental, 1981); Domingo Arena, *Batllismo y sociedad: La "cuestión obrera" en el Uruguay* (Montevideo: Librosur, 1986), and idem, *Batlle y los problemas sociales en el Uruguay* (Montevideo: Claudio García, 1939).

40. *La Vanguardia*, 9 Jan. 1907, 1. Her research on Buenos Aires labor conditions served as the intellectual base for a bill sponsored by Alfredo Palacios to regulate the number of working hours and restrict the labor of women and children in the city.

41. Argentina, Departamento Nacional del Trabajo, *Boletín* 7 (31 Dec. 1908): 579–87. She visited forty-eight establishments manufacturing a variety of products: cigarettes, silver articles, garments, matches, book binding, card boxes, textiles, etc. to review "the safety, health, instruction and morality of the women and children of the factories."

42. Durañona, "Informe del Departamento Nacional de Higiene sobre el trabajo en las casas de confecciones," 606–9. Women comprised 75 percent of all workers.

43. Nicolás Cuello, *Ejemplo noble de una mujer* (Buenos Aires, 1936), 42–51; *La Vanguardia*, 22 Jan. 1910, 1; 18 Aug. 1910, 2. The Socialist Party sponsored frequent visits to factories to document and denounce violations of the existing legislation. See issues of 8, 9, 19, 20 Sept.; 8 Oct. 1910; and 11 and 12 Jan. 1915.

44. Argentina, Departamento Nacional del Trabajo, *Boletín* 12 (Mar. 1910): 8–22; 17 (June 1911): 262–63.

45. Argentina, Departamento Nacional del Trabajo, *Boletín* 16 (Mar. 1911): 24–31.

46. Barrán and Nahum, *El Uruguay del novecientos*, 174–90.

47. Bunge, *La educación*, 127–31. Bunge took a social Darwinist stance in his early works.

48. Argentina, Departamento Nacional del Trabajo, *Boletín* 3 (Dec. 1907): 356–59.

49. Carolina Muzilli, "El trabajo femenino," *Boletín Mensual del Museo Social Argentino* 2, 15–16 (1913): 65–90.

50. Argentina, Departamento Nacional del Trabajo, *Boletín* (Nov. 1912): 305–25.

51. David Rock, *Argentina, 1516–1987: From Spanish Colonization to Alfonsín* (Berkeley: Univ. of California Press, 1987), 191–95; Alejandro Ernesto Bunge, *Los problemas económicos del presente* (Buenos Aires, 1920), passim.

52. Argentina, Departamento Nacional del Trabajo, *Boletín* 42 (1919): 9–11. For a detailed report on wages, see 13–61.

53. Chile, Oficina del Trabajo, *Boletín* 5 (1915): 127–35; 8 (1922): 62–97.

54. Grace Thorni, "Depreciación del trabajo femenino," *Acción Femenina* 4, 1 (1934): 31; 4, 3 (1934): 13.

55. Uruguay, Oficina del Trabajo, *Salarios de obreros;* Balbis, "La situación de las trabajadoras," 108–11.

56. Balbis, "La situación de las trabajadoras," 109–11.

57. Sosa and Beloso L., *El trabajo de la mujer*, passim.

58. Uruguay, Ministerio de Industrias, *El salario real, 1914–26* (Montevideo, 1927), 62–67. Money devaluation and inflation erased up to 22 percent of the nominal value of wages.

59. "Protective legislation for minors is equally protection for working women. Argentine law, following the lead of foreign laws, believes that the weakest elements in industry, women and minors, deserve equal protective measures. Our law, however, protects minors better than women." Argentina, Departamento Nacional del Trabajo, *Boletín* 38 (Aug. 1918): 45.

60. Bialet Massé, *El estado,* 151–52, and passim through 158. For information on Rosario, see 346, 248, 544, 565–66, 594. Further comments on tuberculosis are on 350–51.

61. Argentina, Departamento Nacional del Trabajo, *Boletín* 33 (1914–16): 176 ff., 179. Very few male members of the family were engaged in the putting-out system. See also *Boletín* 25 (1913): 878–79.

62. Argentina, Departamento Nacional del Trabajo, *Boletín* 25 (1913): 909–17.

63. Argentina, Departamento Nacional del Trabajo, *Boletín* 42 (1917): 107–15. See also *Boletín* 25 (1913): 900–903. No detailed reports on home work are available for the 1920s and 1930s.

64. Enrique del Valle Iberlucea, "Proyecto de ley reglamentando el trabajo a domicilio," Argentina, Departamento Nacional del Trabajo, *Boletín* 25 (1913): 918–48.

65. Elena Caffarena M., "El trabajo a domicilio," Chile, Oficina del Trabajo, *Boletín* 10, 7 (1924–25): 97–135.

66. Amanda Hermosilla Aedo, *La mujer en la vida económica* (Santiago: Universo, 1936), 66–79.

67. Mafud, *La vida obrera,* 147; Asunción Lavrin, "Women, Labor and the Left: Argentina and Chile, 1900–1925," in Cheryl Johnson-Odim and Margaret Strobel, eds., *Expanding the Boundaries of Women's History* (Bloomington: Univ. of Indiana Press, 1992), 89–113; Hobart A. Spalding Jr., *La clase trabajadora argentina (Documentos para su historia, 1890–1912)* (Buenos Aires: Galerna, 1970), passim.

68. Minors (under eighteen) made up 21.6 percent of the total number of industrial workers in Montevideo. See Barrán and Nahum, "Las clases populares en el Montevideo del novecientos," 11–31.

69. "Reglamentación del trabajo de las mujeres y de los niños," *Almanaque del Tra-*

bajo 8 (1925): 153–56; Dorfman, *Historia de la industria,* 254. In 1913 national holidays were included as rest periods. In 1932 and 1934 closing on Saturday afternoon and closing after 8 P.M. were legislated. See also Argentina, Departamento Nacional del Trabajo, *Boletín* 45 (Feb. 1920): 138; Guy, "Women, Peonage, and Industrialization," 83–84. The province of Mendoza did not have its own full labor legislation until 1919. See *Compendio de las Leyes no. 9688, 731 y 732 y su reglamentación* (Mendoza: Escuela Alberdi, 1920).

70. Enrique Díaz de Guijarro, *La ley de trabajo de mujeres y menores ante la jurisprudencia* (Buenos Aires: Antología Jurídica, 1932), 1–19. Unsafe or unhealthful industries were the distillation of alcohol; the making of toxic dyes and varnishes containing copper or arsenic; and the manufacture of explosives, glass, polished metals, and any other materials producing airborne irritants. Children and women were also forbidden work as stevedores, in foundries, or operating machinery with fast-moving parts or requiring fire, and they were banned from businesses selling alcoholic beverages. Argentina, Departamento Nacional del Trabajo, *Boletín* 48 (Nov. 1921): 28. Special regulations applicable to the federal capital would apply. Nursing could take place every two hours, and chairs should be provided to female employees in all commercial businesses. Indemnization for delivery would be administered by the National Labor Department and would be paid for by the industries and their managers. There were thirty-eight categories of labor forbidden to women.

71. Balbis, "La condición de la mujer trabajadoras," 123–27.

72. Acevedo, *Anales históricos del Uruguay,* 6:62–65, 208–10, 525. Uruguay, Instituto Nacional del Trabajo, *Publicaciones* (Montevideo: Imp. Nacional, 1935); Uruguay, Oficina Nacional del Trabajo, *Boletín* 4 (Sept.–Dec. 1919): 36–37; Uruguay, Instituto Nacional del Trabajo, *Descanso semanal del servicio doméstico* (Montevideo: Imp. Nacional, 1935).

73. *La Mujer Nueva* 3, 25 (1940): 2.

74. Ector Escribar Mandiola, *Tratado de derecho del trabajo* (Santiago: Zig-Zag, 1944), 239.

75. Del Valle Iberlucea, "Proyecto de ley reglamentando el trabajo a domicilio," 935.

76. José A. Ruiz Moreno, *Legislación social argentina: Colección de leyes obreras y de previsión social* (Buenos Aires: El Ateneo, 1925), 190–201.

77. Alejandro Ruzo, *Política social* (Buenos Aires: L. J. Rosso, 1918), passim. Ruzo favored regulating the hygienic conditions of home work.

78. Alberto Sanguinetti Freire, *Legislación social del Uruguay,* 2 vols. (Montevideo: Barreiro y Ramos, 1947), 1:303–17.

79. Chile, *Proyecto del Código del Trabajo y de la previsión social* (Santiago: Imp. Nacional, 1921); Escribar Mandiola, *Tratado de derecho del trabajo.* See also Graciela Vivanco Guerra, *Bosquejo del problema social en Chile* (Santiago: Dirección General de Prisiones, 1951), for changes through the 1940s.

80. Agustín Ortázar E., comp., "Las leyes del trabajo y de previsión social de Chile," and idem, "Decreto-ley sobre protección a la maternidad obrera y salas cunas," Chile, Oficina del Trabajo, *Boletín* 10 (1924–25): 288–98.

81. Balbis, "La situación de las trabajadoras," 120, 123–25.

82. Alfredo Palacios, *La defensa del valor humano* (Buenos Aires: Claridad, 1939), 14–23. Anarchists stood against any regulation of women's work because they argued that working women could hardly afford the leisure of resting without pay.

83. Argentina, Departamento Nacional del Trabajo, *Boletín* 45 (Feb. 1920): 119.

84. Díaz de Guijarro, *La ley de trabajo de mujeres y menores ante la jurisprudencia*, 10–11.

85. Florencio Escardó, "La protección del niño y la acción política de la mujer," *Vida Femenina* 1, 5 (1933): 16–17; "Madres obreras," *Vida Femenina* 1, 12 (1934): 22, 27.

86. Argentina, Departamento Nacional del Trabajo, *Boletín Informativo* ser. 6, 16, 177–78 (1934): 4,201. The law included female workers in the mining, manufacturing, and transport sectors. Article 20 allowed the construction of maternity homes — up to 30 percent of the maternity fund could be used for that purpose. The first five articles of Law 11.934, approved in 1934, were the same proposed by Bard ten years before. In September 1933 Argentina ratified the 1919 Washington convention on female work.

87. Argentina, Departamento Nacional del Trabajo, *Boletín Informativo*, ser. 6, 17, 186–88 (1935): 44,329.

88. Francisco Walker Linares quoted by Hermosilla Aedo, *La mujer en la vida económica*, 115.

89. Hermosilla Aedo, *La mujer en la vida económica*, 51n.

90. "Una ley que interesa a todas las mujeres: Dirección de maternidad e infancia," *Vida Femenina* 4, 42 (1937): 6–7, 14.

91. Uruguay, Cámara de Representantes, *Diario de Sesiones* 455 (1943): 16, for the lack of observance of the regulations on women and minors' work, see Alejandro Lopetegui, *Como se vive en la pampa salitrera* (Antofagasta: Skarnic, 1933), 17; Peter Winn, *Weavers of Revolution: The Yarur Workers and Chile's Road to Socialism* (New York: Oxford Univ. Press, 1986), 34, 40, 44, 83.

92. Alicia Moreau de Justo, *¿Que es el socialismo en la Argentina?* (Buenos Aires: Sudamericana, 1983), 112.

93. *La Prensa*, 28 Mar. 1920, 4; 1, 2, 3 Dec. 1928, 9.

94. Olga Maturana Santelices, "Las bondades del seguro de lactancia," *Nosotras* 3, 51 (1933): 8; "Las mujeres que trabajan en las empresas concesionarias de servicios públicos," in Palacios, *La defensa del valor humano*, 101–42. Monsignor Gustavo Franceschi, a pillar of the Catholic Church, joined Palacios in denouncing the practice, which they argued weakened the family and encouraged illegal unions. See also Josefina Marpons, "Protección a la maternidad," *Vida Femenina* 2, 20 (1935): 8, 10; "Como vive la obrera chilena," *La Mujer Nueva* 1, 8 (1936): 4–5.

95. Augusto Turenne, "Organización del trabajo de la madres protegidas," *Boletín de Salud Pública* 2, 9 (1933): 692–708.

96. Uruguay, Cámara de Representantes, *Diario de Sesiones* 444 (Apr. 1941): 63; 455 (Sept.–Dec. 1943): 16.

97. Luciano Morgado, "Anotaciones de un obrero sobre la mujer proletaria," *Acción Femenina* 4:12 (Dec. 1935): 50–52.

98. *La Mujer Nueva* 2, 17 (1937): 7; 2, 22 (1938): 3; 3, 25 (1940): 3.

99. Argentina, Departamento del Trabajo, *Boletín Informativo*, ser. 6, 18, 195–97

(1935): 4,560–73. The garment union, founded in 1935, had 5,000 members by 1936. Members' gender is not stated, but they were probably largely female, because it comprised the seamstresses employed by the industry. On the 1935 strike of Argentine garment employees, see Alicia Moreau de Justo, "Un rincón de pesadilla," *Vida Femenina* 3, 26 (1935): 12–13. For an analysis of women's reluctance to act within the labor movement, see *La Mujer Nueva* 1, 3 (1936): 4.

100. Alicia Moreau de Justo, "La ley de protección de la maternidad," *Vida Femenina* 9, 101–2 (1942): 4–9.

101. "El trabajo de las mujeres," *El Trabajo* 1, 5 (1901): 1; *La Nueva Senda*, 18 Sept. 1909, as quoted by Graciela Sapriza, *Memorias de rebeldía: Siete historias de vida* (Montevideo: Puntosur, 1988), 40.

102. Juana María Beguino, "A las mujeres," *La Voz del Obrero* (Montevideo), ser. 2a. first Sunday in May 1902, 3.

103. *Primer Congreso Femenino Internacional de la República Argentina: Historia, Actas y Trabajos* (Buenos Aires: Ceppi, 1910), 233; Patricia Hilden, "Re-writing the History of Socialism: Working Women and the Parti Ouvrier Français," *European History Quarterly* 17, 3 (1987): 285–306. See also Fenia Chertcoff, "Las obreritas," *La Vanguardia*, 8 Sept. 1910, 1.

104. Esther Valdés de Díaz, "Despertar," *La Alborada*, 18 Nov. 1906; "Reglamentación de las horas de trabajo para la mujer obrera," 17 Mar. 1907, 1; 24 Mar. 1907, 1; 14 Apr. 1907, 1; 21 Apr. 1907, 1; 19 May 1907, 1–2.

105. Mutualist societies like those organized in Chile attempted to build welfare protection in the absence of any state policy. Resistance societies were the embryo of the more complex labor organizations emerging during the early 1910s. See Sara Cádiz B., "Sobre organización femenina," *La Reforma* (Santiago), 28 June 1906; *El Trabajo* (Montevideo), 18 Sept. 1901, 1; 23 Sept. 1901, 1.

106. Hernán Ramírez Necochea, *Historia del movimiento obrero en Chile*, 235–36, 247. See also the writings of Luis Eduardo Díaz, Esther Valdés de Díaz, and Sara Cádiz in *La Reforma*. *La Vanguardia* of Buenos Aires also consistently supported socialist women's activities and the organization of women workers.

107. *La Aurora* 1, 3 (1899): 2–3; *Despertar* 3, 19 (1907): 163–64; 4, 1–2 (1908): 13, 14; 4, 11 (1908): 75; *El trabajo* 1, 1 (1901) and subsequent issues throughout 1, 52 (1901) chronicled strikes by women workers. *El Anárquico*, 18 Mar. 1900, praised labor as a means of female emancipation, as quoted in Sapriza, *Memorias de rebeldía*, 40.

108. In his 1905 labor report, Argentine Juan Alsina mentioned the Círculo de obreros católicos. It was then fifteen years old and had 20,000 members. This association was "in opposition to the terrible propaganda of communism and impiety." See Alsina, *El obrero*, 129. See also Deutsch, "The Catholic Church, Work, and Womanhood in Argentina, 1890–1930," 304–25, and Wainerman and Navarro, *El trabajo de la mujer en la Argentina: Un análisis preliminar de las ideas dominantes en las primeras décadas del siglo XX*, passim.

109. Alejandro E. Bunge, *Riqueza y renta de la Argentina* (Buenos Aires: Agencia General de Librería y Publicaciones, 1917), 130, 281–90. Bunge stuck to the assumption that 1.5 million adult women had no occupation. His list of occupations and median

salaries includes only men. By 1950 Chileans officially began to recognize female labor and to admit its growing importance. See *Geografía económica de Chile,* 2:163–66. Several late nineteenth-century economic planners in Uruguay debated the potential economic value of women's work. See Balbis, "La situación de las trabajadoras," 119.

110. See, for example, *Vida Femenina* 1, 3 (1933): 17; 1, 11 (1934): 30; 2, 20 (1935): 8, 10; 3, 20 (1935): 12–13; 5, 65 (1938): 24–25, 44; 10, 105–6 (1942): 18–19, 44–45.

111. *La Mujer Nueva,* 1, 9 (1936): 5; 2, 17 (1937): 7. For further information on MEMCH, see ch. 9.

112. *La Mujer Nueva* 3, 27 (1941): 4.

113. Thorni, "Depreciación del trabajo femenino."

114. See *Vida Femenina* 3, 29 (1935): 12, 20; 4, 45 (1937): 12; 5, 51 (1937): 6. Of special interest are Rosa Scheiner, "El despertar de la mujer obrera," *Vida Femenina* 3, 29 (1935): 13, 20, and Paulina de Ortello, "La mujer en la huelga de los obreros de la construcción," 3, 29 (1935): 42–43; María L. Berrondo, "La mujer en la fábrica," *Vida Femenina* 7, 79 (1940): 28–30; Jorge A. Chinetti, "La mujer en la industria y el gremialismo," *Vida Femenina* 10, 105–6 (1942): 18–19, 44–45.

115. Guy, *Sex and Danger in Buenos Aires,* 77–104; Uruguay, Consejo Nacional de Higiene, *Recopilación de leyes de carácter sanitario* (Montevideo: Siglo Ilustrado, 1918), 431, 463–73; Uruguay, Consejo Nacional de Higiene, *Reglamento de la prostitución* (Montevideo: Barreiro y Ramos, 1905).

116. "Estatutos de la Federación Obrera de 1894," in Spalding, *La clase trabajadora argentina: Documentos para su historia, 1890–1912,* 116, 144, 266–67.

117. Gabriela L. Coni, *A las obreras: Consideraciones sobre nuestra labor.* Biblioteca de Propaganda 9 (Buenos Aires: Gallarini, 1903).

118. For Coni's writings in *La Vanguardia,* see 11 June 1904, 1, 3; 25 June 1904, 2; 25 Feb. 1905. See also Donna Guy, "Emilio and Gabriela Coni: Reformers, Public Health and Working Women," in Judith Ewell and William Beezley, *The Human Tradition in Latin America: The Nineteenth Century* (Wilmington DE: Scholarly Resources, 1989), 223–48.

119. Angel Giménez, *Consideraciones de higiene sobre el obrero en Buenos Aires,* dissertation (Buenos Aires: Gallarini, 1901), passim.

120. Gertosio Rodríguez, *La actividad económica de la mujer,* 28, 35–36.

121. Spalding, *La clase trabajadora,* 266, 267, 270, 271, 273, 279.

122. *La Vanguardia,* 28 Jan. 1905, 1.

123. María Muñoz, "A las mujeres," *La Aurora* 1, 3 (1899): 2–3.

124. See *La Alborada,* 21 Apr. 1907, 1; 19 May 1907, 1–2; Blas Alberti, *Conversaciones con Alicia Moreau de Justo y Jorge Luis Borges* (Buenos Aires: Mar Dulce, 1985), 41–45, 50, 65, 108–10. "In those days [ca. 1900–1905] a young woman who went out alone, especially at night, was labeled [a bad woman]." Women attending socialist centers met between 5:00 and 7:00 P.M. in order to return home before nightfall.

125. *La Alborada,* 16 Dec. 1906, editorial "Las mujeres en las cantinas," 1.

126. José Nakens, "Prostitución," *La Protesta Humana,* 3 Sept. 1899, 2.

127. Argentina, Departamento Nacional del Trabajo, *Anuario Estadístico* 42 (1917): 168.

128. Chile, *Proyecto del Código del Trabajo*, 13, 14.

129. Argentina, Departamento Nacional del Trabajo, *Boletín* 48 (Nov. 1921): 28.

130. Hermosilla Aedo, *La mujer*, 38, 107–8.

131. José Virginio Díaz, *Problemas sociales del Uruguay* (Montevideo: Siglo Ilustrado, 1916), 144. For early praise of the industriousness of poor working women, see Agustín Bravo Cisternas, *La mujer a través de los siglos* (Valparaíso: El Progreso, 1903), 77–78.

132. Vera Zouroff [Esmeralda Zenteno], *Feminismo obrero* (Santiago: El Esfuerzo, 1933), passim.

133. María Teresa León de Sebastián, *La mujer en el hogar y la vida* (Buenos Aires: Tailhade, 1928), 12.

134. Juan Carlos Rébora, *La emancipación de la mujer* (Buenos Aires: La Facultad, 1929), 21–23, 65–69.

135. Roxane [Elvira Santa Cruz Ossa], "El feminismo y la política chilena," *El Mercurio* (Santiago), 8 June 1924, 3. Santa Cruz Ossa was appointed inspector of female labor by a temporary government in 1925. In that capacity she recommended the regulation of female labor.

136. *La Alborada*, 19 May 1907, 1–2. In 1907 labor demand was at a peak because Chile was experiencing a great rise in exports.

137. Uruguayan Emilio Frugoni occasionally expressed shared pessimistic views on women's labor. See Balbis, "La situación de las trabajadoras," 116–17.

138. *Nuestra Tribuna*, 15 Sept. 1922.

139. *Vida Femenina* 1, 12 (1934): 22, 27.

140. José Luis López Ureta, *El abandono de familia* (Santiago: Nascimento, 1933), 30–31.

141. Ajax, "La mujer cívica," *Zig-Zag*, 26 Apr. 1935.

142. Perla Marino, "Que se respete el trabajo honrado de la mujer," *Nosotras* 1, 21 (1932): 8; Hermosilla Aedo, *La mujer*, 155 ff.

143. Ibid., 133, 155 ff.

144. Chile, Cámara de Diputados, *Sesiones Ordinarias* 2 (1936): 601, 1824, 2028; *Estadística Chilena* 7, 12 (1935): 518–31.

145. *La Mujer Nueva* 1, 7 (1936): 1, 4; 1, 12 (1936): 1; 1, 13 (1937): 6.

146. *La Mujer Nueva* 1, 7 (1936): 4. There are no data on male wages. In 1934 Chilean Grace Thorni stated that women employees and professionals earned half of men's pay. See "Depreciación del trabajo femenino," 30–31. In 1948 women earned 57 percent of men's wages. See *Geografía económica de Chile*, 2:222.

147. Carlos Bernaldo de Quirós, *Eugenesia jurídica y social*, 2 vols. (Buenos Aires: Ideas, 1943), 2:145–81. This work expanded ideas already stated in his *Problemas demográficos argentinos* (Buenos Aires, 1942), 121–29.

148. Bernaldo de Quirós, *Problemas demográficos*, 69–71.

149. Santiago Labarca, in a lecture on women's emancipation. Rebuttal by María Aracel in *La Mujer Nueva* 2, 16 (1937): 3.

150. *La Mujer Nueva* 2, 22 (1938): 2. This is a unique sociological inquiry with no match in Uruguay or Argentina.

151. Berrondo, "La mujer en la fábrica," 30.

Chapter 3 : *Puericultura,* Public Health, and Motherhood

1. On living and working conditions in the urban centers of the Southern Cone at the turn of the century, see, José Pedro Barrán and Benjamín Nahum, *Batlle, los estancieros y el imperio británico,* 7 vols., vol. 1, *El Uruguay del novecientos* (Montevideo: Banda Oriental, 1979); James R. Scobie, *Buenos Aires: Plaza to Suburb, 1870–1910* (New York: Oxford University Press, 1974); Leandro Gutiérrez, "Condiciones de la vida material de los sectores populares en Buenos Aires (1880-1914)," *Revista de Indias* 41 (Jan.–June 1981): 167–202; Virginia Krzeminski F., "Alessandri y la cuestión social," in Claudio Orrego V. et al, *Siéte ensayos sobre Arturo Alessandri Palma* (Santiago: Instituto Chileno de Estudios Humanísticos, 1979), 165–257.

2. Javier Gomensoro, "La evolución de la asistencia y el nuevo concepto de salud pública," *Boletín de Salud Pública* (Montevideo) 2, 9 (1933): 713. Solidarity in this instance means duty.

3. See Emilio Coni, *Higiene social* (Buenos Aires: Coni, 1918), and idem, *Memorias de un médico higienista* (Buenos Aires: Flaiban, 1918); Angel Giménez, *Consideraciones de higiene sobre el obrero en Buenos Aires* (Buenos Aires: Carlos Gallarini, 1901).

4. *Revista Chilena de Hijiene* 20 (1914): 15. For a report of the state of public health and its institutional care in Chile in 1911, see Pedro Láutaro Ferrer R., *Higiene y asistencia pública en Chile* (Santiago, 1911).

5. Luis G. Middleton C., *Apuntes sobre legislación sanitaria* (Santiago: Lourdes, 1911); Ernesto Medina Lois et al., *Medicina social en Chile* (Santiago: Aconcagua, 1977), 41–59. The 1918 Sanitary Code stipulated the foundation of the Dirección General de Sanidad.

6. Before 1925 Chile had a welfare service (Beneficencia y Asistencia Pública), created in 1832 and revised in 1886 and 1920. See Marta Niedbalski, *La asistencia social* (Santiago: Nascimento, 1934), 238–76.

7. Pan American Union (PAU), *Bulletin* 59 (1925): 732.

8. PAU, *Bulletin* 66 (1932): 145–49. *Boletín Sanitario* began publication in January 1927.

9. *Actas y trabajos de la Tercera Jornada Sanitaria de Chile, 1940* (Santiago: Servicio Nacional de Salubridad de Chile, 1941), passim.

10. Luis D. Brusco, *Contribución al estudio de la ley de creación del Consejo Nacional de Higiene* (Montevideo: El Siglo Ilustrado, n.d.); *Libro del centenario del Uruguay,* 2 vols. (Montevideo: Capurro, 1925), 2:623.

11. Uruguay, Consejo Nacional de Higiene, *Recopilación de leyes, decretos, reglamentos, ordenanzas y resoluciones de carácter sanitario* (Montevideo: El Siglo Ilustrado, 1918).

12. *Revista Uruguaya de Dermatología y Sifilografía* 1–2 (1936–37): 74.

13. PAU, *Bulletin* 66 (Feb. 1932): 149–50.

14. Uruguay, Ministerio de Salud Pública, *Memoria, 1936–38* (Montevideo, 1938); Uruguay, Ministerio de Salud Pública, *Boletín de Salud Pública,* ser. 2, 1, 1 (1941).

15. Juan Carlos Veronelli, *Medicina, gobierno y sociedad* (Buenos Aires: El Coloquio, 1975), 43–63.

16. Guillermo Rawson, *Estadística vital de la ciudad de Buenos Aires* (Buenos Aires:

Imp. de la Nación, 1877), 14–15. For further medical data on infant death, see Enrique L. Day, *La mortalidad entre los recién nacidos* (Buenos Aires: La Mendocina, 1895). Infant mortality is death occurring before one year of age; child mortality, between one and five years. Most statistical sources do not include stillbirths.

17. Coni, *Higiene social*, 81–85. Statistics were imprecise for these years. Dr. Alberto Peralta Ramos cited death rates for babies under one year as fluctuating between 90 and 100/1,000 in 1901–11, noting a decline to 80/1,000 by 1921. See Alberto Peralta Ramos, *Puericultura postnatal* (Buenos Aires: Spinelli, 1922).

18. Argentina, Provincia de Buenos Aires, *Anuario estadístico de la provincia de Buenos Aires* 1924, 141.

19. Argentina, Provincia de Buenos Aires, *Anuario estadístico de la provincia de Buenos Aires* 1940 (La Plata, 1943), 114.

20. Alfredo Commentz, "Estadísticas de mortalidad, natalidad y morbilidad en diversos países europeos y en Chile," in Congreso Nacional de Protección a la Infancia, *Trabajos y actas* (Santiago: Imp. Barcelona, 1913), 315–33; Salvador Allende G., *La realidad médico-social chilena* (Santiago, 1939), 79–80. A 1900 measles epidemic causing thousands of children's deaths prompted the foundation of the first children's hospital in January 1901. See Ferrer R., *Higiene y asistencia pública en Chile*, 283.

21. *Boletín de Hijiene i Demografía* 7, 12 (1905); 9, 12 (1907). In 1905 the total number of deaths reported was 13,241, of which 6,532 were of children under five.

22. Chile, *Anuario estadístico* (1930) (1932), 4.

23. Chile, Dirección General de Estadística, *Estadística Chilena* 8, 8 (1935): 533.

24. Allende G., *La realidad medico-social chilena*, 80–81. Malta, second in rank, had 190/1,000 deaths. Next in line were Egypt and Hungary.

25. *El Mercurio* (Santiago), 12 June 1928.

26. Chile, Dirección General de Estadística, *Estadística Chilena* 8, 12 (1935): 532.

27. Julio A. Bauzá, *La mortalidad infantil en el Uruguay* (Montevideo: Peña, 1920), passim. In 1901 the rate was 28 percent; in 1911–15 it was 40 percent (p. 36).

28. PAU, *Bulletin* 60 (1926): 1269.

29. Eduardo Acevedo, *Anales históricos del Uruguay*, 6 vols. (Montevideo: Barreira y Ramos, 1936), 2:303. See also Luis Morquió, *El problema de la mortalidad infantil* (Montevideo: Rosgal, 1931), passim. Checking the various figures against each other, the mortality rate for children under one year varied between 11 and 13 percent. This tallies roughly with the figures provided by the 1926 First Pan American Conference of National Directors of Public Health.

30. Uruguay, Dirección General de Estadística, *Síntesis estadística de la República O. del Uruguay* (Montevideo, 1940), 23; Uruguay, *Anuario estadístico* (Montevideo: Imp. Nacional, 1943), 1:36.

31. Data for comparison taken from Uruguay, Dirección General de Estadística, *Sintesis estadística de la república O. del Uruguay*, 25. In 1930 Czechoslovakia had an infant death rate of 147/1,000 and Lithuania's was 155/1,000. In 1937 Sweden and Switzerland had rates of 47 and 46/1,000, respectively. See also Allende G., *La realidad médico-social chilena*.

32. Amanda Grossi Aninat, *Eugenesia y su legislación* (Santiago: Nascimento, 1941), 174. Comparative statistics tend to vary according to the source, and the researcher must exercise much caution in using them. Numbers cited here derive from secondary sources and are used as indexes to the medical problem.

33. For information on abortion see chapter 5.

34. Little historical attention has been paid to women's health, especially during and after pregnancy. See Ferrer G., *Higiene y asistencia pública en Chile,* 278–79; Romero Aguirre, "El cuidado del embarazo y la asistencia del parto como factores de protección a la infancia," in Congreso Nacional de Protección a la Infancia, *Trabajos y actas,* 210–18, and Dr. Alcibíades Vicencio, "Organización del Instituto de Puericultura," in the same source, 227–31.

35. Allende G., *La realidad médico-social chilena,* 144. Alicia Moreau de Justo, "La protección de la madre y el niño no es un problema aislado," *Vida Femenina* 4, 42 (1937): 11–13. Moreau de Justo used a report issued by a deputy from Catamarca.

36. Grossi Aninat, *Eugenesia y su legislación,* 189.

37. Juan Emilio Corvalán A., *Importancia de la educación científica de la mujer,* 2d ed. (Valparaíso: Excelsior, 1887), passim; Eduvigis Casanova de Polanco, *Educación de la mujer* (Valparaíso: Imp. de la Patria, 1871), and idem, "Reflexiones sobre la educación publica de la mujer en Chile," *Revista de Instrucción Primaria* (Valparaíso), 1, 1 (1876); 1, 2, 4–5, (1876), 16–18; 1, 8 (1876), 89–91; Tancredo Pinochet Le Brun, *La educación de la mujer* (Santiago: Francia, 1908); Carlos Octavio Bunge, *La educación,* in *Obras completas de Carlos Octavio Bunge* 3 vols. (Madrid: Espasa-Calpe, 1928), 3:43–52.

38. R. Florencio Moreyra, "Lijeras observaciones al proyecto de educar científicamente a la mujer," *Revista Chilena* 7 (1877): 603–15; Nancy Leys Stepan, *The Hour of Eugenics: Race, Gender and Nation in Latin America* (Ithaca: Cornell Univ. Press, 1991), 93.

39. Ferrer R., *Higiene y asistencia pública,* 306–12; Chile, *Anuario estadístico,* 2 (1912), 70; A. Vicencio, "Organización del Instituto de Puericultura," in Congreso Nacional de Protección a la Infancia, *Trabajos y actas,* 225–31.

40. Coni, *Higiene social,* 81 ff.

41. Teresa Prats de Sarratea, *Educación doméstica de las jóvenes* (Santiago: A. Eyzaguirre, 1909), 304–50; *El Mercurio,* 13 Nov. 1929, 3; María Rosa Baró de Engo, *Tratado de economía doméstica, corte y confección, y labores* (Buenos Aires: Gráfico Ferraro, n.d.).

42. Enrique A. Feinmann, "Una nueva ciencia de la mujer: La puericultura," *Revista de Derecho, Historia y Letras* 54 (1916): 562–76.

43. Gregorio Aráoz Alfaro, *El libro de las madres* (Buenos Aires: Agustín Etchepareborda, 1899), passim; Alicia Moreau, "Consejos a las madres," *Almanaque del Trabajo* 2 (1919): 129–33; Estanislao S. Zeballos, "Mortalidad infantil: Una obra digna de la piedad de mujeres serias," *Revista de Derecho, Historia y Letras* 50 (Apr. 1915): 597–600.

44. "El Club de Madres," *Boletín Mensual del Museo Social Argentino* 1 (Sept. 1912): 345–47.

45. *Unión y Labor* 1, 1 (1909). Those writing for *Unión y Labor* under the directorship of Matilde T. Flairoto were Sara Justo (sister of Socialist leader Juan B. Justo), Andrea Moch, Ernestina López, María Teresa de Basaldúa, and Alicia Moreau. Feminist men

such as Ernesto Nelson and Carlos N. Vergara wrote occasional articles. See also Néstor Tomás Auza, *Periodismo y feminismo en la Argentina, 1830–1930* (Buenos Aires: Emecé, 1988), 102–3.

46. "Conclusiones presentadas por el grupo femenino Unión y Labor al Congreso Femenino Internacional," *Unión y Labor* 1, 9 (1910): 13–15; editorial, 2, 16 (1911): 2. *Unión y Labor* was also interested in the cause of street children, especially newsboys, and in professional schools for boys. There were six professional schools for girls but none for boys.

47. María C. de Spada, "Alimentar a la madre para salvar al hijo," *Unión y Labor* 1, 11 (1910): 15–17. The female association Juana Manuela Gorriti and a delegate from the National Department of Hygiene coadministered the first *hogar maternal* in Buenos Aires. See *Unión y Labor* 1, 1 (1909); 1, 5 (1910): 25; 1, 9 (1910): 27; 2, 21 (1911): 27, 31, 32.

48. *Unión y Labor* 2, 15 (1910): 3, 25 (1911): 26.

49. *Unión y Labor* 4, 45–46 (1913): 2.

50. Elvira Rawson de Dellepiane, "Los niños débiles ante la educación," in *Primer Congreso Femenino Internacional de la República Argentina* (Buenos Aires: Ceppi, 1910), 102–11.

51. *Primer Congreso Femenino,* 364–66. See Peruvian Dora Meyer's remarks on the importance of prenatal and postnatal care, 250.

52. Congreso Nacional de Protección a la Infancia, *Trabajos y actas,* "Protección de las madres durante el embarazo, el parto y el puerperio: Su influencia sobre la mortalidad infantil," 137–44, 536; and comments by Sofía Rojas de Aliste on 556. See also Rafael Edwards, "Apuntes, observaciones y propuestas sobre el tema legislación del trabajo de los niños, de las madres y de las mujeres encinta," 417–54. For summaries and conclusion, see 531–67. See Chile, *Censo levantado el 28 de noviembre de 1907* (Santiago: Universo, 1908); Chile, *Anuario estadístico* (Santiago: Universo, 1916), 1:90, 96.

53. All the information on the congress is based on detailed reports in *La Nación,* 13–19 Oct.; *Unión y Labor* 2, 18 (1911): 28–29.

54. *La Nación,* 17 Oct. 1913, 14.

55. *Primer Congreso Americano del Niño* (Buenos Aires: Escoffier, Caracciolo, 1916), passim.

56. On wet nurses, see Estela Pagani and María Victoria Alcaraz, *Las nodrizas en Buenos Aires: Un estudio histórico (1880–1940)* (Buenos Aires: Centro Editor de América Latina, 1989), 9.

57. Summary based on reports published in *La Prensa* of Buenos Aires, 17–25 May 1919.

58. Feinmann, "Una nueva ciencia en la educación de la mujer: La puericultura," 562–76; *Unión y Labor* 4, 45–46 (1913). The journal applauded the teaching of child care in what it regarded as a successful campaign against "old prejudices" that did not see the use of teaching such "natural and inherently" womanly subjects in the schools.

59. In Chile instruction comprised "notions of eugenics" and the effects of syphilis on heredity. Between 200 and 250 normal school teachers took the course yearly. Much had yet to be done in terms of teaching child care. A source noted that of the nearly

600,000 girls in public and private schools, only 15 percent received instruction on the subject. See *Acción Femenina* (Santiago) 5, 16 (1936).

60. Alicia Moreau (signing as A.M.), in *La Vanguardia* (Buenos Aires), 9 and 27 Feb. 1917. For several years *La Vanguardia* had a column for mothers titled "Rincón de las Madres," dispensing advice on child care.

61. *La Vanguardia*, 2 Dec. 1932, 1.

62. Martín L. Becerra, "Debe enseñarse la puericultura a los alumnos varones?" *Vida Femenina* 3, 25 (1935): 30–31, 34.

63. Coni, *Higiene social*, 127–28. The National Council of Education cut the program short in 1917 and reduced it to providing milk and bread.

64. *Acción Femenina* 4, 28–29 (1920): 48–55, 98–105. Report by Haydee B. de Brignole; 4, 30–31 (1920); 4, 32–33, (1920); and 4, 34–35 (1920): 184–96.

65. *El Mercurio* (Santiago) covered this event. See October issues.

66. *El Mercurio* (Santiago), 26 October 1924, 23.

67. See Cora Mayers, "Educación sanitaria," Chile, Dirección General de Sanidad, *Boletín Sanitario* 1, 7 (1927): 402–6. A translation into English appeared in Pan America Union (PAU) *Bulletin* 62 (Nov. 1928): 111–15. Also by Cora Mayers, *La mujer defensora de la raza* (Santiago: Imp. Santiago, 1925), passim, and "El examen físico de los escolares y la educación sanitaria," Chile, Dirección General de Sanidad, *Boletín Sanitario* 1, 3 (1927): 118–21.

68. Emilio R. Coni, *Puericultura práctica argentina* (Buenos Aires: Coni, 1920), 24–25.

69. Carlos Illanes Beytia, "Influencia de la mujer en la higiene social de la infancia," Chile, Dirección General de Sanidad, *Boletín Sanitario* 1, 10 (1927): 668–81. In 1929 a league was founded in the Escuela Superior de Niñas 26 in Santiago. See *El Mercurio* (Santiago), 23 Nov. 1929, 3.

70. PAU, *Bulletin* 58 (1924): 316.

71. PAU, *Bulletin* 58 (1924): 657, 1061; 59 (1925): 20; 60 (1926): 730. For the organization of children's kitchens, see 56 (1924): 676–82.

72. PAU, *Bulletin* 60 (1926): 202.

73. PAU, *Bulletin* 56 (1923): 95.

74. PAU, *Bulletin* 58 (1924): 207.

75. PAU, *Bulletin* 59 (1925): 1142.

76. PAU, *Bulletin* 59 (1925): 740; Mayers, "El examen físico de los escolares y la educación sanitaria." For the *Ley de protección a la maternidad obrera*, see *El Mercurio*, 22 Mar. 1925, 5.

77. PAU, *Bulletin* 60 (1926): 733.

78. *El Mercurio*, 9 Jan. 1928, 3. Information on the Society for the Protection of Children (Sociedad Protectora de la Infancia) is available on issues of 3 and 5 June 1928. The assumption that working-class mothers were ignorant was very strong among the Chilean doctors who participated in the First Congress for the Protection of Childhood (1912).

79. Lucas Sierra, *Bases de la higiene moderna: Papel que en la difusión de sus princi-*

pios debe desempeñar la mujer (Santiago: Universitaria, 1916). See comments by Margarita Escobedo during the First Congress for the Protection of Childhood (1912) in *Trabajos y actas,* 552, and comments by Delia Rouge in *Acción Femenina* 4, 4 (1935): 13.

80. Enrique Deformes, "Los concursos de lactantes en Valparaíso," in Congreso Nacional de Protección a la Infancia, *Trabajos y actas,* 297–304. The society distributed 30,000 pamphlets with information for nursing mothers. For the 1910–11 competition, 305 mothers registered and 175 finished. For the 1911–12 competition, 285 mothers registered.

81. Coni, *Higiene social,* 251.

82. *La Nación,* 1 July 1916, 3; *El Mercurio* (Santiago), 8 Nov. 1929, 14. On the decline of demand for wet nurses, see Pagani and Alcaraz, *Las nodrizas en Buenos Aires,* 18–19, 21, 26.

83. Uruguay, Consejo Nacional de Higiene, *Recopilación de leyes,* 94; PAU, *Bulletin* 56 (1923): 417.

84. *El Mercurio* (Santiago), 19 Jan. 1922.

85. PAU, *Bulletin* 58 (1924): 1063. This meant 143,954 bottles of milk each month. The Asilo Maternal, part of the Patronato, sheltered 37 mothers and 76 babies, providing lunches, clothing, and layettes for needy mothers and children. See Ferrer R., *Higiene y asistencia pública,* 299–301. Protectora de la Infancia was an orphanage run by nuns, funded partly by the government and partly by private patronage. In 1928 it sheltered 934 children of various ages. See *El Mercurio* (Santiago), 2, 3, and 5 June 1928 for news on this institution.

86. Chile, Dirección General de Estadística, *Estadística anual de demografía y asistencia social* (1930) (Santiago, 1930), 99.

87. Argentina, City of Buenos Aires, *General Census of the Population, Building, Trades and Industries of the City of Buenos Aires* (Buenos Aires: Compañía Sudamericana de Billetes de Banco, 1910), 3:431–32. The inspection of the quality and safety of wet nurses' milk had been initiated in 1902, suppressed for economic reasons in 1904, and reinstalled in 1906. Wet nurses could not get employment without a health certificate as stipulated in a decree of 22 Mar. 1905. Protección a la Infancia had a dairy close to Buenos Aires to provide the milk it distributed.

88. Coni, *Higiene social,* 81–86.

89. Ibid., 76.

90. *El Mercurio* (Santiago), 8–16 Nov. 1929. We must note at this point the existence of a Museo del Niño, opened in 1924, endowed by the German embassy and by philanthropist Elisa Parada de Miguel.

91. PAU, *Bulletin* 58 (1924): 849. In 1924 Montevideo became the site of the International Bureau of Child Welfare, supported by the Pan American Union. See PAU, *Bulletin* 58 (1924): 1286.

92. PAU, *Bulletin* 59 (1925): 601–3.

93. PAU, *Bulletin* 60 (1926): 101, 839.

94. PAU, *Bulletin* 56 (1923): 676–81.

95. Coni, *Higiene social,* 247–54. In 1918 Coni described these institutions as a combination of clinics, hostels, and meal centers. See also PAU, *Bulletin* 56 (1924): 676–82.

96. PAU, *Bulletin* 59 (1925): 20.

97. PAU, *Bulletin* 60 (1926): 730.

98. PAU, *Bulletin* 58 (1924): 316.

99. PAU, *Bulletin* 59 (1925): 45.

100. PAU, *Bulletin* 60 (1926): 202.

101. Peralta Ramos, *Puericultura postnatal,* passim.

102. Roxane, "Entrevista a la directora de la Escuela de Servicio Social, Srta. Leo Cordemans," *El Mercurio* (Santiago), 16 June 1929, 11. Since the early 1920s women educators had been calling for female education in "social work." See *El Mercurio* (Santiago), 28 Feb. 1922, 3. Statement by Rosa Prats de Ortúzar.

103. Marta Niedbalsky, writing in 1934, cites the *visitadoras* as the latest advance in the activities of public welfare. See *La asistencia social* (Santiago: Nascimento, 1934), 234.

104. Uruguay, Consejo del Niño, *Memoria del primer ejercicio, 1934–1940* (Montevideo: Institutos Penales, 1940), 163 ff.

105. Javier Gomensoro, "Propaganda y educación higiénicas," *Boletín de Salud Pública,* ser. 2a, 1 (Jan.–Mar. 1941): 92–95.

106. Uruguay, Consejo del Niño, *Reglamento de la División de la Segunda Infancia* (Montevideo: Mosca, [1941]), 38–41. For Aráoz's ideas see, Peralta Ramos, *Puericultura postnatal,* 22.

107. Uruguay, Consejo del Niño, *Memoria del primer ejercicio,* 269; Uruguay, Consejo del Niño, *Reglamento de la Division de la Segunda Infancia,* 39.

108. Ibid.

109. Grossi Aninat, *La eugenesia y su legislación,* 180–81, 185.

110. Uruguay, *Código del Niño* (Uruguay: Fundación de Cultura Universitaria, 1980). At the outset the council was under the jurisdiction of the Ministry of Public Health. In 1935 it was switched to the jurisdiction of Public Instruction.

111. See chapter 5 for views on abortion and the definition of fetal rights.

112. Uraguay, *Código del Niño,* arts. 48–54, 12–13; Uruguay, Consejo del Niño, *Memoria del primer ejercicio,* 51, 53, 129.

113. Chile, Cámara de Diputados, *Diario de Sesiones* 2 (1935): 2,065.

114. *El Mercurio* (Santiago), 18 Mar. 1925, 19; 19 Mar. 1925, 21; 22 Mar. 1925, 5.

115. *El Mercurio* (Santiago), 9 June 1929, 32: "La maternidad no debe ser una carga imposible para la mujer." At that point the project embraced *centros maternales* kindergartens and the investigation of illegitimate paternity. See also Grossi Aninat, *Eugenesia y su legislación,* 189.

116. Grossi Aninat, *Eugenesia y su legislación,* 194–96.

117. Argentina, Cámara de Diputados, *Diario de Debates* 2 (1932): 120. The thesis was that it was necessary to take care of the mother to ensure the health of her children. It cited the North American Children's Bureau as its model.

118. Ernesto Nelson, *Asociación por los Derechos del Niño: Nuestros propósitos* (Buenos Aires, 1935).

119. Asociación por los Derechos del Niño, *Declaración de principios. Tabla de los derechos del niño. Concepto del servicio social. Estatutos* (Buenos Aires, 1937), passim.

These and other plans for the care of children followed the Charter for the Rights of Children, issued in Geneva in 1932.

120. Argentina, Departamento Nacional del Trabajo, *Boletín* 38 (Aug. 1918): 11–50; Argentina, Departamento Nacional del Trabajo, *Boletín Informativo*, ser. 6, 16, 177–78 (1934): 4324. For the Leopoldo Bard project, see Argentina, Cámara de Diputados, *Diario de Sesiones* 2, 67 (1925). The congressional commission in charge of studying both projects recommended them favorably in September 1926. See Argentina, Cámara de Diputados, *Diario de Sesiones* 5 (1926): 71–72.

121. Alfredo L. Palacios, *La defensa del valor humano* (Buenos Aires: Claridad, 1939), 10–83. The law was published in *Vida Femenina* 4, 42 (1932): 6–7, 14, 39. A bill banning the employment of children in domestic service was proposed by Socialist deputy Bruno Pietranera in 1934. See *Vida Femenina* 1, 8 (1934): 29; Alicia Moreau, "El niño: Esperanza de la humanidad," *Vida Femenina* 3, 30 (1936): 4–5; Josefina Marpons, "Protección a la maternidad," *Vida Femenina* 2, 21 (1935): 8, 10, and another article with the same title in 3, 34 (1936): 30–31.

122. Argentina, Cámara de Diputados, *Diario de Sesiones* 6, 42 (1926).

123. Alicia Moreau de Justo, "La ley de protección de la maternidad," *Vida Femenina* 9, 101–2 (1942): 4–9.

124. Juan Francisco Espino, "Desnatalidad: Sus causas y remedios," *Vida Femenina* 6, 71 (1939): 29–31; Adolfo Rubinstein, "Protección a la infancia," in "Opinan los candidatos socialistas," *Vida Femenina* 7, 77 (1940): 29, 46.

125. Grossi Aninat, *Eugenesia*, 188.

Chapter 4 : Feminism and Sexuality

1. Donna Guy, *Sex and Danger in Buenos Aires: Prostitution, Family, and Nation in Argentina* (Lincoln: Univ. of Nebraska Press, 1991). See also Juan Antonio Rodríguez, *Profilaxis de la sífilis* (Montevideo: El Siglo Ilustrado, 1917); Rafael Sienra, *Llagas sociales: La calle Santa Teresa* (Montevideo: Oriental, 1896); Miguel Becerro de Bengoa, *Prostitución clandestina y policía* (Montevideo: El Siglo Ilustrado, 1924); Luis M. Otero, *El problema de la prostitución* (Montevideo: La Industrial, 1925); Alfredo Vidal y Fuentes, *Sobre reglamentación y abolicionismo de la prostitución* (Montevideo: El Siglo Ilustrado, 1925); Enrique Feinmann, "La mujer esclava: Historia social de la moralidad," *Atlántida* 11 (1913): 161–87; Liga Chilena de Higiene Social, *Contribución al estudio de las enfermedades sociales* (Santiago, 1925). Institutions in charge of public health in the three nations (such as the Ministerios de Salud Pública or Consejos de Salud Pública) issued numerous reports on syphilis and prostitution beginning in the early 1900s.

2. For an analysis of ecclesiastical attitudes on sex, see José Pedro Barrán, *Historia de la sensibilidad en el Uruguay*, vol. 2, *El disciplinamiento (1860–1920)* (Montevideo: Banda Oriental and Facultad de Humanidades y Ciencias, 1990).

3. Blas Alberti, *Conversaciones con Alicia Moreau de Justo y Jorge Luis Borges* (Buenos Aires: Mar Dulce, 1985), 41–45, 65, 108–10.

4. Elvira Rawson de Dellepiane, "Apuntes sobre higiene en la mujer," tesis inaugural, Facultad de Ciencias Médicas, Universidad de la Capital, Buenos Aires, 1892.

5. Rawson de Dellepiane, "Apuntes," 41.

6. *La Protesta Humana,* 13 June 1897, 1; *La Protesta,* 19 Dec. 1904, 3–4; 5 Aug. 1905; 5 Aug. 1913, 3–4.

7. *La Protesta Humana,* 13 June 1897, 1–2.

8. A stringent anarchist strain advocated complete individualism, especially in matters of sexual union. See *La Protesta,* 19 Feb. 1910, 1.

9. *La Protesta,* 18 Jan. 1905, 2–3.

10. *La Protesta,* 5 Aug. 1905, 2. Anarchists often used the terms male and female (*macho, hembra*), which underlined the frankness of their message. Such terms were usually applied to animals, not people.

11. *La Protesta,* 2 Aug. 1902, 2–3; 17 Sept. 1918, 1.

12. *La Protesta,* 2 Aug. 1902, 2–3.

13. *La Protesta,* 26 Jan. 1919, 3. José Scalise, whose book on women, society, and children was partially reprinted in *Nuestra Tribuna,* 1 July 1924, 4, stressed the pleasure of sexual relations.

14. Proletarians should never forget that their offspring would also become proletarians and the future subjects of capitalist exploitation, stated Argentine *La Protesta,* 5 Aug. 1913, 3–4.

15. *La Palanca,* Aug. 1908, 19. Infanticide, mentioned by *La Palanca,* is difficult to gauge in Chile or elsewhere. The discovery of dead fetuses was reported occasionally in national newspapers. See *El Mercurio* (Santiago) 8 June 1928, 11; *El Día* (Montevideo), 26 May 1916, 16. In 1909 Uruguayan socialist Emilio Frugoni explored abortion and infanticide, stressing class and gender factors. See "Infanticidas," in Emilio Frugoni, *La mujer ante el derecho* (Montevideo: Indo-Americana, 1940), 204–7; José Nakens, "Infanticidio," *La Protesta Humana* (Buenos Aires), 15 Oct. 1898, 2. See also Kristin Ruggiero, "Honor, Maternity, and the Disciplining of Women: Infanticide in Late Nineteenth-Century Buenos Aires," *Hispanic American Historical Review* 72, 3 (1992): 353–73.

16. Clara de la Luz, *La mujer y la especie* (Santiago: Imp. Lee, 1913).

17. Victor Soto Román, "La familia," *El Despertar de los Trabajadores,* 22 Feb. 1913, 2.

18. G. Hardy, "Familia y limitación de los nacimientos," *El Sembrador,* 20 Nov. 1926, 2; idem, "Amor libre, maternidad libre," 15 Jan. 1927, 2.

19. "El folleto generación consciente y el presidente de la Junta de Sanidad," *El Sembrador,* 20 Nov. 1926, 2.

20. *Nuestra Tribuna,* 1 Apr. 1925, 2. The books were Luis Bulffi, *The Womb's Strike,* Franck Sutor, *Responsible Generation,* and Jean Morestan, *Sexual Education.* The advertisement urged men to be guided by reason, not by "gross instincts."

21. *Nuestra Tribuna,* 15 June 1924, 4. Puerto Rican Luisa Capetillo commented on the predicament of women who bore children almost by force under sexual enslavement.

22. *Nosotras* 1, 1 (1902): 6–7.

23. Maria Abella de Ramirez, *Ensayos feministas* (Montevideo: El Siglo Ilustrado, 1965), 29–33.

24. Lucia [pseud.], "Feminismo," *La Nueva Mujer,* 1, 14 (1911): 7–8.

25. See Angela A. Pérez, "A la conciencia de las maestras," *Acción Femenina* (Montevideo), 4, 50 (1924): 14–16.

26. Aurora Estrada y Ayala de Ramírez Pérez, "Una sola moral para los dos sexos," *Nosotras* (Valparaíso) 2, 46 (1933): 1.

27. Blanca C. de Hume, "La mujer ante los problemas morales," *Acción Femenina* (Uruguay) 3, 23–24 (1919): 148–51; idem, "Unidad de la moral," *Nuestra Causa* 1, 5 (1919): 193–205; Consejo Nacional de Mujeres del Uruguay, *Informe correspondiente al primer trienio, 1916–1919* (Montevideo: El Siglo Ilustrado, 1920).

28. "El matrimonio," *La Nueva Mujer* (La Plata), 2, 31 (1912): 7–8.

29. *Unión y Labor* 1, 11 (1910): 32.

30. Dora Mayer (*sic*) "La moral femenina," *Primer Congreso Femenino Internacional de la República Argentina* (Buenos Aires: A. Ceppi, 1910), 241–58.

31. Raquel Camaña, *Pedagogía social* (Buenos Aires: La Cultura Argentina, 1916), passim. This volume, published posthumously, reprinted articles published in several journals.

32. *La Nación*, 15 Oct. 1913, 14.

33. *La Nación*, 8 July 1916, 12; *Primer Congreso Americano del Niño* (Buenos Aires: Escoffier, Caracciolo, 1916); Paulina Luisi, *Pedagogía y conducta sexual* (Monevideo: El Siglo Ilustrado, 1950), 222, 227.

34. "Enfermedades venéres y sifilíticas," in *Reglamento de la prostitución* (Montevideo: Consejo Nacional de Higiene, 1924), 43–54.

35. Alfredo Fernández Verano, *Para una patria grande y un pueblo sano* (Buenos Aires: Fabril Financiera, 1938), 108.

36. Francisco Gicci, *Educación sexual: Consejos a los padres* (Buenos Aires: Mercatili, 1914), passim.

37. Luisi, *Pedagogía*, 282–83.

38. See Vidal y Fuentes, *Sobre reglamentación y abolicionismo de la prostitución*, passim; *Reglamento de la prostitución*; Uruguay, *Ley orgánica de Salud Pública* (Montevideo: Imp. Administración de la Lotería, 1936); Uruguay, *Boletín del Consejo de Salud Pública* 2, 7 (1933), 207–9; Paulina Luisi, *Otra voz clamando en el desierto: Proxenetismo y reglamentación*, 2 vols. (Montevideo, 1948); J. J. Beretervide and S. Rosenblatt, *Glándulas endocrinas y prostitución* (Buenos Aires: Ateneo, 1934); Roque Roses Lacoigne, *Informe sobre el problema antivenéreo y la prostitución en Buenos Aires: Proyecto de ordenanza* (Buenos Aires: Gráfica, 1931); Donna Guy, "White Slavery, Public Health and the Socialist Position on Legalized Prostitution in Argentina, 1913–1936," *Latin American Research Review* 23, 3 (1988): 60–80.

39. Rodríguez, *Profilaxis*, passim.

40. Fernández Verano, *Para una patria grande*, 108 ff; *Acción Femenina* 4, 32–33 (1920): 226.

41. Fernández Verano, *Para una patria grande*, 44. He saw feminism as a strictly economic issue and suspected any ideology that would "masculinize" women.

42. Chile, Cámara de Diputados, *Boletín*, 1917, 131. The first Chilean Sanitary Code was approved in 1918.

43. Chile, Cámara de Diputados, *Boletín*, 1918–19, 882.

44. Liga Argentina de Profilaxis Social, *Memoria y balance correspondientes al ejercicio de 1926* (Buenos Aires: P. Ventriglia, n.d.). See also *Liga Argentina de Profilaxis*

Social, volante 5, 6, and 10. The League was a private institution maintained by private funds. In 1926 several industries had donated about half its budget of 7,142 pesos.

45. Liga Argentina de Profilaxis Social, *Memoria y balance correspondientes al ejercicio de 1934* (Buenos Aires, 1934).

46. Pan American Union (PAU), *Bulletin* 58 (1924): 1169.

47. PAU, *Bulletin* 59 (1925): 415. The League issued doses of neosalvarsan, a drug believed to help cure venereal disease. It claimed to have administered 11,000 prophylactic "treatments."

48. *El Mercurio* (Santiago), 10 Mar. 1925, 19. *Cruz Roja Obrera,* a labor newspaper in the town of Parral, inaugurated its prophylaxis section to teach about "diseases of social transcendence." A labor newspaper, *El Nuevo Régimen,* praised the work of the Liga Chilena de Higine Social in "Salvando la raza," 23 Nov. 1921, 1.

49. *El Mercurio* (Santiago), 19 Mar. 1925, 18.

50. Chile, Ministerio de Bienestar Social, *Boletín* 2, 21 (1930): 24. See also Chile, Ministerio de Higiene, Asistencia, Previsión Social y Trabajo, *Boletín* 1, 5 (1927): 2; Chile, Servicio Nacional de Salubridad de Chile, *Actas y trabajos de la Tercera Jornada Sanitaria de Chile, 1940* (Santiago, 1941), 196–207.

51. *El Mercurio* (Santiago), 21 and 27 Mar. 1924, 17, 20 for lectures to workers' associations by Dr. Ernestina Pérez. See also *Actividades femeninas en Chile* (Santiago: La Ilustración, 1928), 416–19; Cora Mayers, *La mujer defensora de la raza* (Santiago: Imp. Santiago, 1925).

52. See articles by Legnani in *El Día,* 13, 19, 21, 23, and 24 Jan. all printed on p. 4 of the daily editions.

53. Alicia Moreau de Justo, "Educación sexual y educación moral," in *Hacia la extinción de un flagelo social* (Buenos Aires: Fabril Financiera, 1937); "La lucha contra el mal venéreo," in *Por la salud de la raza* (Buenos Aires: Estab. Gráfico Argentino, 1936). These publications were paid for by the Liga Argentina de Profilaxis Social.

54. Luisi, *Pedagogía,* 131.

55. *Primer Congreso Americano del Niño.* Luisi was a delegate of the Uruguayan committee in the First Argentine National Congress on the Child, which took place in Buenos Aires in 1913, and was president of the Uruguayan delegation to the 1916 American congress. See Luisi, *Pedagogía,* 227.

56. See Luisi, *Pedagogía,* 58–59, 131–52, 284, 286–87; *Acción Femenina* (Uruguay), 3, 1 (1919): 22, and 3, 25–26 (1919): 191.

57. Luisi, *Pedagogía,* 131–52, 286–87, 293–96, 304–9; Mateo Legnani, *Discurso contra la ley de represión al proxenetismo: El abolicionismo y el reglamentarismo* (San José: Empresa Caputi, 1924), 5.

58. Luisi, *Pedagogía,* 103.

59. Ibid., 27–28, 60–61.

60. Ibid., 55, 71, 82–84, 141, 146, 149. For Luisi sex education embraced several disciplines: pedagogy helped people educate their will; moral education helped subdue the instinct to the will; science imparted sound instruction on anatomy, physiology, hygiene, and prophylaxis; eugenics made people aware of the health of future generations.

61. Luisi, *Pedagogía,* 27.

62. Ibid., 43, 93, 161–67. Erotic behavior in films and looser canons of gender relationships disturbed some feminists such as Luisi, who favored censoring films to curb their influence on the young.

63. Luisi, *Pedagogía*, 126.

64. Ibid., 45, 66, 108.

65. Ibid., 74, 85–86.

66. Ibid., 116, 135, 381.

67. Mara Licyh, "Educación sexual," *Vida Femenina* 1, 3 (1933): 20–21; idem, "Educación sexual," *Vida Femenina* 1, 5 (1933): 10–11; Thelma Reca, "La educación sexual en las jornadas pedagógicas," *Vida Femenina* 3, 31 (1936): 10, 13; idem, "Educación sexual," *Vida Femenina* 3, 32 (1936): 12–13; Mercedes Pinto, "Sobre educación sexual," *Acción Femenina* 4, 10 (1935): 13–15; Unsigned article in *Nosotras* 4, 60 (1934): 5.

68. Chile, Servicio Nacional de Salubridad, *Actas y trabajos de la Tercera Jornada Sanitaria, 1940*, 196–207.

69. Carlos Bernaldo de Quirós, *Eugenesia jurídica y social*, 2 vols. (Buenos Aires: Ideas, 1943), 2:88–93. See also his *Problemas demográficos argentinos* (Buenos Aires, 1942), 111.

70. Primer Congreso Nacional de Protección a la Infancia, *Trabajos y actas* (Santiago: Imp. Barcelona, 1912). See papers by Eduardo Moore, 201–9, and Dr. Alfredo Commentz, 315–33. Children of unwed mothers, they thought, were more likely to be neglected and more vulnerable to disease and sickness, producing a high index of child mortality. Matching illegitimacy to mortality rates became a standard argument among feminists from the mid-1910s onward.

71. José Espalter, *Discursos parlamentarios*, 8 vols. (Montevideo: Florensa, 1912), 5:329.

72. Argentina, Provincia de Tucumán, *Anuario estadístico, 1920* (Tucumán, 1920), 69. See also Luis Morquió, *El problema de la mortalidad infantil* (Montevideo: Rosgal, 1931). Morquió correlated figures but did not establish a causal relation. Dr. Julio A. Bauzá also thought that illegitimacy enhanced the risk of child mortality, although he cited no statistical information. See Julio A. Bauzá, *La mortalidad infantil en el Uruguay* (Montevideo: Peña Hnos, 1920), 27; idem, "The Infant Mortality Rate of Uruguay," PAU, *Bulletin* 60 (1926): 1269.

73. For children's mortality rates, see chapter 3. The only statistics on the mortality of illegitimate children are for "stillborn" children, not those who died after birth. Between 1931 and 1935 the Chilean percentage of stillbirths among illegitimate births climbed from 41 to 51 percent. Stillbirths were related to poor maternal health, fetal defects, venereal disease, and several other medical problems. See Chile, Dirección General de Estadística, *Estadística Chilena* 8, 8 (1935): 532.

74. José Luis López Ureta, *El abandono de familia* (Santiago: Nascimento, 1933). This legal study cited data on child abandonment in Santiago provided by the children's court. From 1929 to 1931 4,138 children were abandoned. Out of these 3,200 were legitimate and 868 illegitimate. These numbers do not sustain the feminist connection between illegitimacy and abandonment.

75. The few studies available for the colonial period suggest that out-of-wedlock

births were very high. There are no studies for any of the Southern Cone nations. See Thomas Calvo, "The Warmth of the Hearth," in Asunción Lavrin, ed., *Sexuality and Marriage in Colonial Latin America* (Lincoln: Univ. of Nebraska University Press, 1989), 287–312.

76. Arturo M. Bas, *El cáncer de la sociedad* (Buenos Aires: Sebastián de Amorrortu, 1932), 235.

77. Cleophas Torres, "Responsabilizar la maternidad," *Acción Femenina* 6, 20 (1937): 3; Robert McCaa, *Marriage and Fertility in Chile: Demographic Turning Points in the Petorca Valley, 1840–1976* (Boulder CO: Westview, 1983).

78. Chile, *Anuario estadístico* (Santiago: Dirección de Estadística, 1930): 4; Chile, Dirección General de Estadística, *Estadística Chilena* 8, 8 (1935): 532; Markos J. Mamalakis, *Historical Statistics of Chile: Demography and Labor Force* (Westport CT: Greenwood, 1978), 25.

79. Uruguay, *Anuario estadístico* (1920) (Montevideo: Moderna, 1922), 16; *Anuario estadístico* (1930) (Montevideo: Dirección General de Estadística, 1930), 6; Uruguay, *Anuario estadístico de la República Oriental del Uruguay* (Montevideo: Imp. Nacional, 1940); Uruguay, Dirección General de Estadística, *Síntesis estadística* (Montevideo, 1940); Uruguay, Dirección General del Registro del Estado Civil, *El movimiento del estado civil y la mortalidad* (annual reports throughout this period); Uruguay, Dirección General de Estadística General de la República, *Apuntes estadísticos para la Exposición Universal de Paris* (Montevideo: Vapor La Tribuna, 1878).

80. Uruguay, Dirección General de Estadística, *Síntesis estadística*, 13.

81. Argentina, Mendoza Province, *Anuario de la Dirección General de Estadística de la Provincia de Mendoza* (1914) (Mendoza: Tarde, 1916), 21; Argentina, Provincia de Córdoba, Dirección General de Estadística, *Anuario correspondiente al año de 1925* (Córdoba: Imp. de la Penitenciaría, 1927), 28; Argentina, Provincia de Tucumán, *Anuario Estadístico, 1920*, 69; Argentina, Dirección General de Estadística de la Nación, *Anuario estadístico* (Buenos Aires, 1936), 24.

82. *La Prensa*, 18 May 1919, 5.

83. See also Alejandro E. Bunge, *Una nueva Argentina* (Buenos Aires: Kraft, 1940), 167–84. Bunge defined illegitimacy as a "social stain." He proposed subsidies for the parents of legitimate children as an incentive to marriage.

84. Ann Twinam, "Honor, Sexuality, and Illegitimacy in Colonial Spanish America," in Lavrin, *Sexuality and Marriage in Colonial Latin America*, 118–55.

85. Uruguay, *Código Civil de la República Oriental del Uruguay,* vol. 2 of *Códigos de Uruguay anotados,* Colección Abadie-Santos (Montevideo: Moderna, 1942), 42. Title 6, "Of Paternity and Filiation." In the colonial period a "natural child" was that born to an unmarried couple. If the child was born to a single woman from a married man, then the baby was registered as "illegitmate." To escape pejorative nomenclature children were commonly recorded as "of unknown father" or even as "of unknown mother." They could also be recorded as *hijo de iglesia,* or ward of the church. Census takers in the Southern Cone simply recorded legitimate and illegitimate. See also Uruguay, *Ley del Consejo de Protección de Menores: Decreto reglamentario* (Montevideo: Escuela Nacional de Artes y Oficios, 1911), passim.

86. A legitimated child was one born in special circumstances to married parents. For example, if the parents were separated—or after 1907 divorced—but the child was born within the period allowed to assume *conception* within marriage, the child was legitimate.

87. Uruguay, *Código Civil*, 39–47.

88. Uruguay, Cámara de Representantes, *Diario de Sesiones* 234 (July–Sept. 1914): 226–27.

89. Uruguay, Cámara de Representantes, *Diario de Sesiones* 234 (July–Sept. 1914): 223, 252; 468 (Sept.–Jan. 1946–47): 124. In September 1946 further modifications were suggested to liberalize the process of legitimation.

90. Argentina, *Código Civil*, in *Códigos de la República Argentina* (Buenos Aires: Compañía Sudamericana de Billetes de Banco, 1901), 57 ff.

91. *Códigos de la República Argentina*, 57, 63–72. Mothers of children born out of wedlock had *patria potestad* over their children once they recognized them as such, but judges could restrict or suspend such parental rights if they deemed it to be in the interest of the children. They could also determine the trusteeship of children recognized only by their mothers, who in no case could exercise guardianship. For children interned in institutions of public welfare, the institution exercised the right of *tutela* or trusteeship. The guardianship of *expósitos* or abandoned children would be determined by a judge. See Juan Carlos Rébora, *La emancipación de la mujer: El aporte de la jurisprudencia* (Buenos Aires: Facultad, 1929), 36–37. Rébora reasserts that the 1870 Civil Code granted *patria potestad* to the mother of children born out of wedlock.

92. Arturo Fernández Pradel, "Prevención de la criminalidad infantil," in Primer Congreso Nacional de Protección a la Infancia, *Trabajos y Actas*, 472–73.

93. López Ureta, *El abandono de familia*, 47. He favored more protection for abandoned wives and their children but made no proposal on behalf of unwed mothers.

94. Uruguay, Dirección General de Estadística, *El movimiento civil y la mortalidad en la República Oriental del Uruguay* (Montevideo) yearly volumes, 1890–1940.

95. Uruguay, Dirección General de Estadística, *El movimiento civil*, 1890–1940.

96. Argentina, Provincia de Tucumán, *Anuario de estadística*, 69–70.

97. Uruguay, *Código Civil*, 55. title 7, on *patria potestad*. In Uruguay female offspring were under a modified form of *patria potestad* until age thirty; single women required parental permission to leave home before that age though if their parents had remarried they were free to leave without permission. See *Código Civil*, 56. This proviso was in place in the early 1940s, as an example of the asymmetry of rights between male and female in family law.

98. Rébora, *La emancipación*, 37.

99. Carlos Perujo, *Filiación natural*, (Montevideo: La Idea, 1879). He favored changes in the Civil Code. On the opposite side were Florencio Vidal, *Paternidad y filiación*. (Montevideo: Imp. del Plata, 1893); Domingo Arena, *La presunción de legitimidad* (Montevideo: Lagomarsino y Vilardebó, 1910). Arena admitted no assumption of paternity unless there was an established sexual relationship; Enrique del Valle Iberlucea, *El divorcio y la emancipación civil de la mujer* (Buenos Aires: Cultura y Civismo, 1919). On p. 100 he quoted the opinion of Argentine law professor Esteban Lamadrid against

the legal equality of natural children and the investigation of paternity. Del Valle Iberlucea's divorce project contained a clause on natural children's equality.

100. Uruguay, Cámara de Representantes, *Diario de Sesiones* 234 (20 Aug. 1916): 252–
90.

101. Luisa Daco D., *Eugenesia y su legislación en varios países* (Santiago: Lourdes,
1934), 26.

102. López Ureta, *El abandono de familia*, 14.

103. Juan E. Corbella, "Las madres solteras tendrán refugio," *Vida Femenina* 5, 55
(1938): 13–14, 46.

104. Juan P. Pressaco, "Hijos legítimos," *Vida Femenina* 2, 13 (1934): 6–7.

105. Eusebio F. Giménez, "Capacidad jurídica de la mujer," *Acción Femenina* (Uruguay) 3, 21 (1919): 95–100; Aurora Estrada y Ayala de Ramírez Pérez, "Una sola moral
para los 2 sexos," *Nosotras* (Valparaíso) 2, 46 (1933): 1.

106. Amanda Labarca H., "Mortalidad infantil y natalidad ilegítima," *Acción Femenina*, 4, 10 (1935): 22–24.

107. Uruguay, Dirección General de Estadística, *El movimiento civil y la mortalidad
en la República Oriental del Uruguay*, yearly volumes.

108. Manuel Gortari, "La asistencia obstétrica en campaña," *Boletín de Salud Pública*, Jan.–Mar. 1941, 96–102.

109. Uruguay, Cámara de Representantes, *Diario de Sesiones* 456 (1943): 151.

110. Ibid., 152.

111. Cleophas Torres O., "Responsabilizar la maternidad," *Acción Femenina*, Mar.
1937, 3; Lucas Buenaire, "Madres solteras," *Vida Femenina* 5, 63 (1938): 20–21. I suspect
the writer was Alicia Moreau.

112. "Programa del Partido Independiente Demócrata Femenino" *Ideas y Acción* 1, 1
(1933): 1. She also supported a broad social welfare plan to protect all children.

Chapter 5 : The Control of Reproduction

1. Sir Francis Galton, *Essays on Eugenics* (London: Eugenics Education Society, 1909);
Havelock Ellis, *The Task of Social Hygiene* (New York: Houghton Mifflin, 1912); Eduardo
Pradel Hanicewicz, *Matrimonio civil y eugenesia* (Valparaíso: Imp. América, 1926);
Luisa Daco D., *Eugenesia y su legislación en varios países* (Santiago: Lourdes, 1934);
Julio León Palma *La eugenesia* (Concepción: El Aguila, 1937); Amanda Grossi Aninant,
Eugenesia y su legislación (Santiago: Nascimento, 1941); Luis Jiménez de Asúa, *Libertad
de amar y derecho a morir*, rev. ed. (Buenos Aires: Losada, 1942); Carlos Bernaldo de
Quirós, *Eugenesia jurídica y social*, 2 vols. (Buenos Aires: Ideas, 1943); Luis López Ara-
vena, *Los impedimentos dirimentes del matrimonio y la eugenesia.* (Santiago: Dirección
General de Prisiones, 1946); Nancy Leys Stepan, *"The Hour of Eugenics": Race, Gender,
and Nation in Latin America* (Ithaca: Cornell Univ. Press, 1991).

2. Stepan, "Hour of Eugenics," 62–101.

3. "Lucha contra las enfermedades sociales: Informe del Dr. Alberto Brignoli al Consejo de Salud Pública," Uruguay, Ministerio de Salud Pública, *Boletín de Salud Pública*
2, 7 (1933): 15–25.

4. Alfredo Fernández Verano, *Reforma sanitaria del matrimonio* (Buenos Aires: La Semana Médica, Spinelli, 1931), passim. Early in his career (1921) Fernández Verano had been sympathetic to the sterilization of individuals with genetic defects. He accepted the idea that certain human types had degenerative propensities. Thus, he asserted, Argentine *criollos,* mestizos, mulattoes, and blacks were predisposed to tuberculosis. Assuming there were some superior races, he was optimistic about Argentina's future if the nation continued to encourage European immigration. See his *Para una patria grande y un pueblo sano* (Buenos Aires: Fabril Financiera, 1938), 36, 47. Although published in 1938, this work was written in 1921.

5. Chile, Ministerio de Higiene, Asistencia, Previsión Social y Trabajo, *Boletín* 1, 6 (1927): 5 ff.

6. Lucas Sierra, *Bases de la higiene moderna: Papel que en la difusión de sus principios debe desempeñar la mujer* (Santiago: Universitaria, 1914).

7. Raquel Camaña, *Pedagogía social* (Buenos Aires: La Cultura Argentina, 1915), passim.

8. Carolina Muzilli, "El mejor factor eugenético," *La Vanguardia,* 16 Feb. 1917, 1; "El mejor factor eugénico: La tuberculosis," 17 Feb. 1917, 1; "El mejor factor eugénico: El alcoholismo," 18 Feb. 1917, 1; "El mejor factor eugénico: Las más acertadas medidas eugénicas," 19 Feb. 1917, 1. These articles expounded a thesis and did not propose specific measures for adopting eugenics policies. Only one contains suggestions on the control of alcoholic beverages, on the assumption that alcohol had negative genetic consequences. For a biographical sketch of Muzilli, see José Armagno Cosentino, *Carolina Muzilli* (Buenos Aires: Centro Editor de América Latina, 1984). See also, Carolina Muzilli, "Para que la patria sea grande," *Colección Pensamiento Argentino* 3, 1 (1918): 3.

9. She specifically condemned the theories of Napoleon Colyasnni, author of *Superior and Inferior Races.* The artificial insemination devices proposed by Laponge to perpetuate the qualities of "superior stud men" were characterized as *descabellada* [absurd] by Muzilli in her 19 February article.

10. Another Argentine socialist supporting eugenics in those early years was Alicia Moreau, who as a physician underlined the connection between heredity and transmissible diseases. See A. M. [Alicia Moreau], "La herencia patológica," *La Vanguardia,* 9 Feb. 1917, 5.

11. Paulina Luisi, *Algunas ideas sobre la eugenia* (Montevideo: El Siglo Ilustrado, 1916); "Eugenismo," *Acción Femenina* 3, 23–24 (1919): 143–44.

12. PAU, *Bulletin* 60 (1926): 466–70.

13. Moisés Poblete Troncoso, "Hacia la despoblación," *El Mercurio* (Santiago), 1 June 1924, 3.

14. This organization was mentioned by Poblete in his "Hacia la despoblación," and its activities were recorded in *El Mercurio* in March 1924. See issues of 25 and 27 Mar., announcing a lecture series on syphilis.

15. *El Nuevo Regimen* (Santiago) 1, 19 (1921): 1.

16. *La Vanguardia,* 24 Dec. 1932, 5.

17. Grossi Aninat, *Eugenesia,* 226.

18. Ibid., 104.

19. Ibid., 154–55.

20. "La eugenesia en pro del racismo," *Unión Femenina de Chile* (Valparaíso) 1, 4 (1934): 2.

21. Bernaldo de Quirós, *Eugenesia jurídica y social*, 1:57–58. See also Stepan, *"Hour of Eugenics,"* 116–28.

22. Pradel Hanicewicz, *Matrimonio civil y eugénico;* Daco, *Eugenesia y su legislación en varios países*, passim; Jiménez de Azúa, *Libertad de amar y derecho a morir*, passim; Luis López Aravena, *Los impedimentos dirimentes*, passim; Bernaldo de Quirós, *Eugenesia jurídica y social*, passim; Enrique Díaz de Guijarro, "Matrimonio y eugenesia," *Jurisprudencia Argentina* 2 (1942), sec. *Doctrina*, 23.

23. Pradel Hanicewicz, *Matrimonio civil y eugénico*, 5.

24. Ibid., 94–95; Díaz de Guijarro, "Matrimonio y eugenesia," passim.

25. See Pedro Foix, *Problemas sociales de derecho penal* (Mexico: Sociedad Mexicana de Eugenesia, 1942); Fernando Amores y Herrera, *Fundamentos sociológicos de la eugenesia matrimonial* (Caracas: Gutenberg, 1928); Eduardo Vasco, *Temas de higiene mental, educación y eugenesia* (Medellín: Bedout, 1948); Roberto Estenos MacLean, *La eugenesia en América* (Mexico City: Instituto de Investigaciones Sociales, Univ. Nacional, 1952); Stepan, *"Hour of Eugenics,"* 76–84.

26. Segunda Conferencia Panamericana de Eugenesia y Homicultura. *Actas* (Buenos Aires: Frascoli y Bindi, 1934), 126 ff.

27. Díaz de Guijarro, "Matrimonio y eugenesia," passim.

28. Carlos Bernaldo de Quirós, *Eugenesia jurídica y social,* passim, and idem, *Problemas demográficos argentinos* (Buenos Aires, 1942), passim.

29. Fernández Verano, *Para una patria grande*, 162; Daco D., *Eugenesia y su legislación*, 32–34.

30. Juan Astorquiza Sazzo, "Eugenesia y certificado médico pre-nupcial," in Chile, Servicio Nacional de Salubridad de Chile, *Actas y trabajos de la Tercera Jornada Sanitaria, 1940* (Santiago, 1941), 399.

31. Liga Argentina de Profilaxis Social, *Memoria y balance correspondiente al ejercicio de 1926* (Buenos Aires: Ventriglia, n.d.), passim.

32. Argentina, Cámara de Diputados, *Diario de Sesiones* 2 (24 June 1925): 255. He proposed a budget for sanitary clinics and encouraged sex education in secondary and normal schools.

33. *El Mercurio* (Santiago), 19 Mar. 1925, 18. In March 1924 Salas toured southern Chile with railroad cars fitted with exhibits and clinics, giving lectures on social diseases in small-town theaters. He later told *El Mercurio* that in town such as Lota, seven men out of ten had syphilis. *El Mercurio* (Santiago), 26 Mar. 1924, 3.

34. Grossi Aninat, *Eugenesia,* 105; Chile, Ministerio de Bienestar Social, *Boletín* 2, 21 (1930): 24.

35. Chile, Ministerio de Higiene, Asistencia, Previsión Social y Trabajo, *Boletín* 1, 5 (1927): 2 ff.; 1, 6 (1927): 5–7.

36. Chile, Ministerio de Bienestar Social, *Boletín* 2, 17–19 (1929): 31, 2, 21 (1930): 24.

37. Argentina, Cámara de Diputados, *Diario de Sesiones* 1 (1927): 570–81.

38. Ibid. 1:622–25.

39. Astorquiza Sazzo, "Eugenesia y certificado médico prenupcial," 363.

40. Astorquiza Sazzo, "Eugenesia y certificado médico," 374.

41. López Aravena, *Los impedimentos dirimentes del matrimonio y la eugenesia*, 43.

42. Astorquiza Sazzo, "Eugenesia y certificado medico," 401.

43. Liga Argentina de Profilaxis Social, *Memoria y balance correspondientes al ejercicio de 1934* (Buenos Aires, 1934). A separate pamphlet with the same title but without information on publisher and date states the data are for 1931.

44. Segunda Conferencia Panamericana de Eugenesia y Homicultura, *Actas*, 126 ff.

45. Ibid.

46. Emilio Frugoni, *La mujer ante el derecho* (Montevideo: Indo-Americana, 1940), 227–28.

47. See the opinion of Uruguayan doctor Miguel Becerro de Bengoa in *América Nueva* 1, 7 (1933): 5.

48. Fernández Verano, *Para una patria grande*, passim. In 1938 he regarded the certificate as preventive medicine.

49. Segunda Conferencia Panamericana de Eugenesia y Homicultura, *Actas*, 126 ff. Emphasis is mine.

50. Dr. Nicolás V. Greco, "Perfeccionamiento de la ley nacional no. 12.331 de profilaxia de las enfermedades venéreas," in *América contra el peligro venéreo* (Buenos Aires: Imp. Argentina, 1941), 9–20; *Estado actual de la lucha antivenérea en el país* (Buenos Aires: Spinelli, 1936), 13; Bernaldo de Quirós, *Eugenesia jurídica y social*, 2:12–21; Donna J. Guy, *Sex and Danger in Buenos Aires: Prostitution, Family, and Nation in Argentina* (Lincoln: Univ. of Nebraska Press, 1991), 187–89.

51. Bernaldo de Quirós, *Problemas demográficos argentinos*, 1:109.

52. *El Mercurio* (Santiago), 21 Dec. 1934, 21; Chile, Cámara de Diputados, *Boletín* 1 (1935): 650. For an earlier discussion, see Cámara de Diputados, *Boletín* 1 (1930): 2499.

53. *Unión Femenina de Chile* 1, 5 (1934): 4.

54. Grossi Aninat, *Eugenesia*, 107.

55. Enrique Fernández Bobadilla, *Defensa de la raza y aprovechamiento de las horas libres* (Santiago: Cóndor, 1943).

56. *Acción Femenina* 1, 12 (1923): 11–14.

57. *Acción Femenina* 6, 21 (1937): 3.

58. *Acción Femenina* 1, 8 (1923): 20.

59. *Vida Femenina* 1, 2 (1933): 10–11.

60. *Acción Femenina* 4, 4 (1935): 40.

61. Marta L. Licyh, "Educación sexual," *Vida Femenina* 1, 5 (1933): 10–11.

62. Grossi Aninat, *Eugenesia*, 156. The term of incarceration was not specified in Chilean legislation, only the degree of punishment.

63. Felícitas Klimpel Alvarado, *La mujer, el delito y la sociedad* (Buenos Aires: Ateneo, 1945), 231–34. Provincial governments had the right to establish their own codes. For instance, in 1933 the province of Córdoba was contemplating a bill establishing thera-

peutic abortion. See Juan B. González, *El aborto terapeútico* (Córdoba, 1933). The Sixth Latin American Medical Congress that took place in Santiago in 1928 established that the final decision on therapeutic abortions rested with the physician.

64. Antonio Camaño Rosa, *Código Penal de la República Oriental del Uruguay* (Montevideo: Ediciones Jurídicas Amalio M. Fernández, 1980), 176–78, and idem, *El delito de aborto* (Montevideo: Bibliográfica Uruguaya, 1958); Miguel Becerro de Bengoa, *Gotas amargas: El aborto criminal y la ley* (Montevideo: El Siglo Ilustrado, 1922), 48. For an outline of legislation on abortion in Latin America, see Klimpel Alvarado, *La mujer, el delito y la sociedad,* 260–66.

65. *La Vanguardia,* 5 Jan. 1917, 5.

66. Paulina Luisi, "Maternidad," *Acción Femenina* 3, 25–26 (1919), 179–83; idem, "Natalidad," *Acción Femenina* 4, 32–33 (1920): 228–30.

67. Paulina Luisi, *Pedagogía y conducta sexual* (Montevideo: El Siglo Ilustrado, 1950), 108. In 1919 Luisi stressed that both sexes should be responsible for their sexual acts. See "Informe," *Acción Femenina* 1, 6 (1917): 109–10.

68. Becerro de Bengoa, *Gotas amargas,* 44.

69. Augusto Turenne, *La maternidad consciente: Procreación voluntaria en la mujer. Un problema de obstetricia social* (Montevideo: La Industrial, 1929).

70. Turenne criticized the legal abortions then practiced in Russia as harmful for the female body, but he supported sterilization of "deficient" beings as a eugenics measure. He favored either temporary or permanent ligation of the fallopian tubes as the safest method.

71. Turenne's reports and public lectures are quoted in Frugoni, *La mujer ante el derecho,* 209–10.

72. Camaño Rosa, *El delito de aborto,* 9–11, 88–89. Argentine jurisprudence did not consider honor a mitigating circumstance in the judgment on abortion.

73. José Irureta Goyena, *Delitos del aborto, bigamia y abandono de niños y otras personas incapaces* (Montevideo: Barreiro y Ramos, 1932). As cited by Klimpel Alvarado, *La mujer,* 250.

74. Uruguay, *Código Penal* (Montevideo: Ministerio de Instrucción, 1934).

75. "No es punible la lesión causada con el consentimiento del paciente, salvo que ella tuviera por objeto sustraerlo al cumplimiento de un ley, o inferir un daño a otros."

76. Antonio Camaño Rosa, *El delito de aborto,* 27; idem, *Código Penal anotado* (Montevideo: Barreiro y Ramos, 1944), 45.

77. The new code had to be approved by the legislature. See Uruguay, Cámara de Representantes, *Diario de Sesiones* 382 (1933): 35–36, 68–75.

78. Uruguay, Cámara de Representantes, *Diario de Sesiones* 385 (1934): 8, 134–47, 157–67.

79. Ibid., 157–67.

80. Uruguay, *Registro nacional de leyes de la República Oriental del Uruguay* (Montevideo: Imp. Nacional, 1936, 35. For abortion elsewhere in Latin America, see also Klimpel Alvarado, *La mujer,* 250–53, 260–66.

81. *El Día,* 14 Feb. 1935.

82. Uruguay, Cámara de Representantes, *Diario de Sesiones* 390 (1935): 6.

83. Uruguay, Cámara de Representantes, *Diario de Debates* 393 (1935): 115–16; 394 (1935): 9.

84. Uruguay, Cámara de Representantes, 32d Legislature, *Dictamen de la Comisión Especial en la Parte del Proyecto Relativo al Aborto: Aborto voluntario y homicidio piadoso* (Montevideo: José Florensa, 1935).

85. Salvador García Pintos, *El nuevo derecho del aborto libre* (Montevideo: Editorial Juan Zorrilla San Martín, 1934); J. Pou Orfila, *Los problemas del aborto contra natura y la lucha antiabortiva* (Montevideo: El Siglo Ilustrado, 1936).

86. Augusto Turenne, *La protección pre-natal del niño* (Montevideo: García, y Cía., Editores, 1935).

87. *El Día,* 13 Jan. 1935, 8.

88. Turenne, quoted in Frugoni, *La mujer ante el derecho,* 211–12.

89. Quoted in ibid., 215–16. See also Camaño Rosa, *El delito de aborto,* 27.

90. Juan César Mussio Fournier, *Hombres e ideas* (Montevideo: Imp. Uruguaya, 1939), passim.

91. Uruguay, Ministerio de Salud Pública, *Memoria, 1936–38* (Montevideo, 1938), "Proyecto que modifica el Código Penal en lo que se refiere a la penalidad del aborto," "Proyecto de Ley," and "Texto de la Ley," 1–30; Mussio Fournier, *Hombres e ideas,* 135.

92. Mussio Fournier, *Hombres e ideas,* 135.

93. Ibid., 140–42; Emilio Frugoni, "El aborto voluntario," in *La mujer ante el derecho,* 208–22.

94. *Ideas y Acción* 3 (Aug. 1935): 52, 53, editorial page.

95. *Ideas y Acción* 5 (Aug. 1937): 1.

96. *El Día,* 24 Apr. 1936, 8.

97. Frugoni, *La mujer ante el derecho,* passim.

98. Camaño Rosa, *El delito de aborto,* 29–30.

99. Uruguay, Cámara de Representates, *Diario de Sesiones* 411 (1937): 27, 62–63; Camaño Rosa, *El delito de aborto,* 31–32, 86–99. See also Camaño Rosa, *Código Penal anotado,* 42–43.

100. Salvador Allende G., *La realidad médico-social Chilena,* (Santiago, 1939) 85.

101. Grossi Aninat, *Eugenesia y su legislación,* 189. It is unclear whether these were self-induced operations in need of medical attention or legitimate interventions.

102. Salvador Allende G., *La realidad médico-social,* 85–86.

103. Chilean authorities registered the number of women treated in the hospitals of Santiago after induced abortions through 1973. There was a steady rise in the number through 1966, especially between 1955 and 1966. Family planning measures begun in 1963 helped reduce induced abortions as registered in those institutions. For further information, see Tegualda Monreal, "Determining Factors Affecting Illegal Abortion Trends in Chile," in *New Developments in Fertility Regulations: A Conference for Latin American Physicians* (Chantilly VA: Pathfinder Fund, 1976), 123–32; Benjamín Viel, "Patterns of Induced Abortion in Chile and Selected Other Latin American Countries," in *Epidemiology of Abortion and Practices of Fertility Regulation in Latin America: Selected Reports* (Washington DC: Pan American Health Organization, 1975), 1–8.

104. *El Mercurio* (Santiago), 13 Jan. 1936, 17. According to official statistics, in 1935 twelve of every hundred infants under one month old died. Chile, Dirección General de Estadística, *Estadística Chilena* 8, 8 (1935): 533. See also *Actas y trabajos de la Tercera Jornada Sanitaria de Chile* (Santiago: Servicio Nacional de Salubridad de Chile, 1941), 169.

105. *El Mercurio* (Santiago), 19 Jan. 1936, 27.

106. "El aborto," *El Siglo* (Mulchen), 25 Jan. 1936, 6.

107. Monckeberg was well known as a practicing Roman Catholic. *El Mercurio* of Santiago and Valparaíso published news on this debate. See their respective issues for 23, 25, 26, and 27 Jan. 1936. *El Mercurio* (Valparaíso), Carlos Monckeberg, "En defensa de la vida," 25 Jan. 3, and Mauricio Weistein, "Natalidad y Judaísmo," 27 Jan., 3 Klimpel Alvarado, *La mujer, el delito y la sociedad*, 253–58.

108. Chile, Cámara de Diputados, *Boletín*, October 1917, 131. Letter dated 8 Sept. 1917.

109. *La Mujer Nueva* 1, 1 (1935), 3; 1, 4 (Feb. 1936), 1, 3; 1, 6 (1936): 1. In November 1935 María Antonieta Garafulic, in "Proyecciones del movimiento emancipacionista femenino," stated: "In regard to the limitation of births . . . we must repeat ad nauseam that this is not a problem of ethics, but one of economics. Therefore it should not be dealt with in a sectarian or emotional manner, but with scientific and economic criteria. It is a duty to encourage responsible motherhood."

110. Astorquiza Sazzo, "Eugenesia y certificado medico pre-nupcial," 382. Astorquiza Sazzo was a member of the editorial board of the feminist magazine *Acción Femenina* in late 1938. See also Mauricio Weistein in *El porvenir del matrimonio* (Santiago: Kegan y Cía, 1933). Weistein doubted the benefits of eugenics, supported contraceptives, and rejected abortion.

111. Osvaldo L. Bottari, *Profilaxis del aborto criminal* (Buenos Aires: La Semana Médica, 1916). I am indebted to Donna Guy for a copy of this work. Bottari favored strict rules for the control of abortions.

112. Fernández Verano, *Por una patria grande*, 41–42.

113. Alfredo Palacios, *La defensa del valor humano* (Buenos Aires: Claridad, 1939), 10–35, 58–83.

114. Ibid., 72–77.

115. Bernaldo de Quirós, *Problemas demográficos argentinos*, 1:74.

116. Bernaldo de Quiros, *Eugenesia jurídica y social*, 2:128 ff.

117. Bernaldo de Quirós, *Problemas demográficos argentinos*, 1:73–74.

118. Gonzalez, *El aborto terapéutico*, passim.

119. Grossi Aninat, *Eugenesia*, 159.

120. Luis Jiménez de Asúa, *Cuestiones penales de eugenesia, filosofía y política* (Potosí: Universitaria, 1943), 47–64.

121. Jiménez de Asúa, *Cuestiones penales de eugenesia*, 47–64. "¿Puede la mujer, en el ejercicio de su derecho a ser madre conscientemente, hacerse abortar cuando no desee la maternidad o quiera poner término al número de sus hijos?" "Confieso que no me atrevo a ir tan lejos."

Chapter 6 : Reform of the Civil Codes

1. The Chilean Civil Code was written by Andrés Bello and adopted in 1858. The Uruguayan Civil Code written by Tristán Narvaja, was approved in 1868. In Argentina the code, approved in 1871, was written by Dalmacio Vélez Sarsfield.

2. Argentina, *Código civil argentino*, in *Códigos de la República Argentina* (Buenos Aires: Compañía Sudamericana de Billetes de Banco, 1901); Uruguay, *Código Civil de la República Oriental del Uruguay* (Paris: Rosa Bouret, 1871); Aníbal Echeverría y Reyes, *Colección de códigos de la República de Chile* (Santiago: Roberto Miranda, 1895). The Penal Codes defined the punishment meted out for some actions held to be criminal, such as uxoricide, rape, and forced prostitution. Commercial Codes regulated activities performed by women in commercial transactions. Many were pragmatic corollaries of principles established in the Civil Code.

3. See Mariano V. Loza in his 1876 medical thesis, quoted in Ricardo Molas, *Divorcio y familia tradicional* (Buenos Aires: Centro Editor América Latina, 1984), 59, 153.

4. For a discussion of the struggle between church and state in Chile, Argentina, and Uruguay, see J. Lloyd Mecham, *Church and State in Latin America* (Chapel Hill: Univ. of North Carolina Press, 1966), 201–60. See also Ricardo Krebs et al., *Catolicismo y laicismo: Seis estudios* (Santiago: Pontificia Univ. Católica de Chile, 1981), passim; José Pedro Barrán, *Historia de la sensibilidad en el Uruguay,* vol. 2, *El disciplinamiento (1860–1920)* (Montevideo: Banda Oriental and Facultad de Humanidades y Ciencias, 1990).

5. Echeverría y Reyes, *Colección de Códigos,* Civil Code article 102.

6. James A. Brundage, *Law, Sex, and Christian Society in Medieval Europe* (Chicago: Univ. of Chicago Press, 1987), 510–14, 562–75.

7. Argentina, *Códigos de la República Argentina,* Civil Code articles 1261, 1280.

8. Baldomero Llerena, *Concordancias y comentarios del Código Civil argentino* (Buenos Aires: Jacobo Peuser, 1899), 447.

9. Argentina, *Códigos de la República Argentina,* Civil Code articles 207–20, 221–37. Unauthorized acts and contracts by a woman entailed only her property. Women suing their own husbands did not need permission to do so. Uruguay, *Código Civil de la República Oriental del Uruguay,* articles 127–44, 162–70; Echeverría y Reyes, *Colección de Códigos,* Civil Code articles 131–78, 1715–92.

10. Llerena, *Concordancias y comentarios,* 1:444, 450.

11. Part of a legal decision quoted by Leopoldo Bard on 12 August 1926. See Argentina, Cámara de Diputados, *Diario de Sesiones* 6 (1926): 75.

12. Alvaro Guillot, *Comentarios del Código Civil,* 2 vols., 2d ed. (Montevideo: Jerónimo Sureda, 1928). First printed in 1893. See 1:435–39.

13. Uruguay, *Código Civil de la República Oriental del Uruguay,* articles 232–65; Echeverría y Reyes, *Colección de Códigos de la República de Chile,* Civil Code articles 240–63; Argentina, *Códigos de la República Argentina,* Civil Code articles 298–344.

14. Echeverría y Reyes, *Colección de Códigos,* Civil Code articles 219–63.

15. Juan Carlos Rébora, *La emancipación de la mujer: El aporte de la jurisprudencia* (Buenos Aires: La Facultad, 1929), 38.

16. In 1856 Bishop Hipólito Salas issued a decree in support of the Civil Code. See Juan Carlos Rébora, *La familia chilena y la familia argentina*, 2 vols. (La Plata: Tomás Palumbo, 1938), 1:37; Pedro Felipe de Azúa e Iturgoyen, *Sínodo de Concepción [Chile], 1744* (Madrid and Salamanca: Consejo Superior de Investigaciones Científicas and Univ. Pontificia de Salamanca, 1984), 203–7. Parents' right to dissent to the marriage of their underage children was legally established by a royal *pragmática* extended to the Spanish possessions in 1778. See Daisy Rípodas Ardanaz, *El matrimonio en Indias: Realidad social y regulación jurídica* (Buenos Aires: Conicet, 1977).

17. Julio Zegers, "Los derechos civiles de la mujer en la legislación Chilena," *Revista Chilena* 2 (1917): 449–56. He also proposed striking down all the legal impediments established by the Commercial Code and allowing remarried widows to retain *patria potestad* over the children of their first marriage.

18. Alejandro Valdés Riesco, *La mujer ante las leyes chilenas: Injusticias. Reformas que se proponen* (Santiago: La Ilustración, 1922), 21.

19. José Luis Romero, *El desarrollo de las ideas en la sociedad argentina del siglo* xx (Mexico City: Fondo de Cultura Económica, 1965), 47–81; José Pedro Barrán and Benjamín Nahum. *Batlle, los estancieros y el imperio británico*, vol. 1, *El Uruguay del novecientos* (Montevideo: Banda Oriental, 1979).

20. Nicolás Minelli, *La condición legal de la mujer* (Montevideo: Rius y Becchi, 1883). Luis Mohr, quoted below, also referred to Montesquieu in his own writings on behalf of women.

21. Luis A. Mohr, *La mujer y la política* (Buenos Aires: G. Kraft, 1890), passim.

22. Santiago Vaca Guzmán, *La mujer ante la lei civil, la política i el matrimonio*, 2 vols. (Buenos Aires: Pablo E. Coni, 1882).

23. Mohr, *La mujer y la política*, passim. Mohr reprinted the principles of the Sociedad de Igualitarios de la República Argentina, a political group formed as a result of the 1890 coup, calling for full civil rights for women and legal equality of all children.

24. Julio Heise G., *Historia de Chile: El período parlamentario, 1861–1925* (Santiago: Andrés Bello, 1974), 128–30.

25. Mario Bravo, *Derechos civiles de la mujer* (Buenos Aires: El Ateneo, 1927), 72–78.

26. Justa Burgos Meyer, "Separación de bienes matrimoniales," *Nosotras* 1, 38 (1903): 377–80.

27. Bravo, *Derechos civiles*, 78–79.

28. Argentina, Cámara de Diputados, *Diario de Sesiones* 1 (1907): 1066–68; Bravo, *Derechos civiles*, 78–79.

29. Argentina, Cámara de Diputados, *Diario de Sesiones* 1 (1907): 1066. Article 2 enabled women to be members of cooperative or mutualist societies and to open bank accounts without their husbands' authorization. Article 5 enabled divorced women to dispose of their property at their own will. Article 6 enabled women to practice any "licit" profession and administer their earnings themselves.

30. Argentina, Cámara de Diputados, *Diario de Sesiones* 6 (1926): 39, 61.

31. Yezud Urquieta O., *La desigualdad sexual en nuestro derecho* (Santiago: Imp. Chile, 1910); Alberto Ebensperger H., *De la capacidad legal de la mujer* (Santiago:

Imp. Chile, 1911); Luis A. Constela J., *Condición jurídica de la mujer en Chile*, (Santiago de Chile: R. Zorrilla, 1910); Guillermo Echeverría Montes, *Derechos civiles de la mujer* (Santiago: Cervantes, 1893).

32. Valdés Riesco, *La mujer ante las leyes chilenas*, 16–21.

33. Uruguay, Cámara de Representantes, *Diario de Sesiones*, 14 July 1914. Copy available in the Archivo Paulina Luisi, Montevideo, Archivo General de la Nación, box 257, folder 3, no. 13. Hereafter referred as AGN, PL. See vol. 233 of the congressional debates.

34. Elvira V. López, *El movimiento feminista* (Buenos Aires: Mariano Moreno, 1901), 97–150.

35. "Separación de los bienes matrimoniales," *Nosotras* 2, 38 (1903): 377–79.

36. María Abella y Ramírez, *Ensayos feministas*, 2d ed. (Montevideo: Siglo Ilustrado, 1965), 106–7; *Nosotras* 1, 3 (1902): 6.

37. Elvira Rawson de Dellepiane, "La campaña feminista en la Argentina," in Miguel L. Font, ed. *La mujer: Encuesta feminista* (Buenos Aires, 1921), 75. Her draft gave married women control over their earnings and the right to open their own bank accounts. Women could be witnesses, and in case of divorce they could keep their children unless they had a tarnished reputation.

38. *Primer Congreso Femenino Internacional de la República Argentina: Historia, actas y trabajos* (Buenos Aires: A. Ceppi, 1910), 33–48.

39. *Primer Congreso Femenino Internacional*, 379, 388–99; 409–13.

40. *La Vanguardia*, 13 May 1910, 1.

41. See chapters 8, 9, and 10.

42. See Leopoldo Bard's supportive stand in Argentina, Cámara de Diputados, *Diario de Sesiones* 6 (1926): 76, 78.

43. Rébora, *La emancipación de la mujer*, 21–23, 67–69. Rébora collaborated with Palacios on a reform draft that was aired at a University congress in La Plata in 1923. As a punctilious jurist, he had objections to the legal implications of bills proposed in Congress, but he never opposed the principles of family law reform. See Argentina, Cámara de Diputados, *Diario de Sesiones* 4 (1926): 73–74. Also Rébora, *Los regímenes matrimoniales en la legislación argentina* (Buenos Aires: Editora Coni, 1922).

44. Argentina, Cámara de Diputados, *Diario de Sesiones* 6 (1926): 78.

45. See Ebensperger H., *De la capacidad legal de la mujer*, passim.

46. *Actas de las sesiones plenarias de la Quinta Conferencia Internacional Americana*, vol. 1 (Santiago: Imp. Universitaria, 1923), 287–95; *Pan American Conference of Women* (Baltimore, 1922); *Pan American Bulletin* 62 (Sept. 1928): 339–44, 875–79; *Proceedings and Report of the Columbus Day Conferences Held in Twelve American Countries* (New York: Inter-American Press, 1926); Alicia Moreau de Justo, *La mujer en la democracia* (Buenos Aires: El Ateneo, 1945), 68–75; Francesca Miller, "Latin American Feminists and the Transnational Arena," in Emilie Bergman et al., *Women, Culture, and Politics in Latin America* (Berkeley: Univ. of California Press, 1990), 10–26.

47. Bravo, *Derechos civiles de la mujer*, 81–94.

48. Rébora, *La emancipación de la mujer*, 23–25; Bravo, *Derechos civiles de la mujer*, 99–131.

49. Argentina, Cámara de Diputados, *Diario de Sesiones* 3 and 4, (1926), passim. Ré-

bora discusses the law point by point in *La emancipación de la mujer*. See also Alberto Escudero, *De la mujer casada y el nuevo régimen matrimonial* (Buenos Aires: Lajouane y Cía, 1928). 51.

50. Rébora, *La emancipación de la mujer*, 26–37.

51. Ibid., 263–69; Escudero, *De la mujer casada*, 47–60.

52. Rébora, *La emancipación de la mujer*, 46. He argued that women had had civil rights as citizens since the outset of the independence. The reforms enacted by the 1926 legislation simply removed obstacles to performing several functions.

53. Valdés Riesco, *La mujer ante las leyes chilenas*, 25.

54. Carlos Calderón Cousiño, *El feminismo i el Código Civil* (Santiago: Balcells y Cía. 1919), passim.

55. Felícitas Klimpel, *La mujer chilena: El aporte femenino al progreso de Chile, 1910–1960* (Santiago: Andrés Bello, 1962), 56–57.

56. Valdés Riesco, *La mujer ante las leyes*, 9–14.

57. *Acción Femenina* 1, 3 (1922): 4.

58. *El Mercurio* (Santiago), 5 Feb. 1922, 3; 8 Feb. 1922, 3.

59. *Acción Femenina* 1, 1 (1922): 6.

60. Mariano Bustos Lagos, *Emancipación de la mujer: Consideraciones sobre su acción, sus derechos, y su instrucción* (Santiago: Excelsior, 1923).

61. Clarisa Retamal Castro, *La condición jurídica de la mujer en la legislación chilena* (Concepción: El Sur, 1924).

62. See editorial, "La emancipación de la mujer," *Acción Femenina* 1, 11 (1923); "Los derechos de la mujer: Intoxicaciones de realidad," 1, *Acción Femenina* 7 (1923): 7.

63. *Revista Femenina* 1, 5 (1924): 3.

64. Roxane, "El feminismo y la política chilena," *El Mercurio*, 8 June 1924, 3, 8 Mar. 1925, 3, and 22 Mar. 1925, 3. Roxane was appointed inspector of female labor by the temporary government (Junta de Gobierno) in 1925, and she praised labor regulation and other social legislation enacted at the beginning of that year.

65. *El Mercurio*, 11 Oct. 1924, 14.

66. "Words from a Catholic on Feminism," *Revista Femenina* 1, 4 (1924): 24 (a translation of a French source).

67. *El Mercurio* (Santiago), 13 Mar. 1925, 11. *El Mercurio* endorsed the reform in its editorial of 19 March. See also Amanda Labarca, *¿A donde vá la mujer?* (Santiago: Ediciones Extra, 1934), 174, 167–72. On the same day Dr. Maza also signed a bill establishing equal salaries for male and female teachers.

68. *Historia de la Ley no. 5521 de 19 de Diciembre de 1934 que reformó los Códigos Civil y de Comercio en lo concerniente a la capacidad de la mujer* (Santiago: Prensas de la Univ. de Chile, 1935). Among the members of the commission were jurist Arturo Alessandri Rodríguez and future president Juan Esteban Montero.

69. Chile, Cámara de Diputados, *Boletín de Sesiones Extraordinarias* 1 (1933): 934, 1116; Esteban Mena R., *La mujer y sus derechos* (Valparaíso: Imp. Royal, 1931), passim.

70. See the full text in *Acción Femenina* 6, 4 (1935): 33 ff.

71. Arturo Alessandri Rodríguez, *Tratado práctico de la capacidad de la mujer casada, de la mujer divorciada perpetuamente y de la mujer separada de bienes* (Santiago: Imp.

Universitaria, 1940), passim. See comments on this law by Emilio Frugoni in *La mujer ante el derecho*, 59–60.

72. *Acción Femenina* 1, 1 (1917): 8, 27–29, 33–35; L. de Bonaccorsi, "Reflexiones sobre la mujer casada," *Acción Femenina* 2, 5–6 (1918): 81–86; Consejo Nacional de Mujeres, *Informe correspondiente al trienio 1916–19 y Memoria correspondiente al ejercicio 8–9* (Montevideo: El Siglo Ilustrado, 1920).

73. Uruguay, *Diario de Sesiones de la H. Convención N. Constituyente de la República Oriental del Uruguay* (1917), 4 vols. (Montevideo: Imp. Nacional, 1918), 3:55–56, 85–89, 494–95. Also recorded in Uruguay, *Diario Oficial*, 7 May 1917, vol. 47, no. 3392. The main discussion took place on 23, 27, and 30 April 1917.

74. Efraín González Conci and Roberto B. Giudice, *Batlle y el batllismo* 2d ed. (Montevideo: Medina, 1959), 354; Magdalena Antonelli Moreno, in Uruguay, Cámara de Representantes, *Diario de Sesiones* 465 (1945–46): 498–99.

75. Speech delivered on 27 December 1918 and recorded in Baltasar Brum, *Los derechos de la mujer: Reforma civil y política del Uruguay* (Montevideo: José María Serrano, 1923), 28–29.

76. Brum, *Los derechos de la mujer*, 5–6; Alfredo Traversini and Lilian Lastra, *El Uruguay en las primeras décadas del siglo* xx (Montevideo: Kapelusz, 1977), 24.

77. Brum, *Los derechos de la mujer*, 65–204. This discussion is a summary of the key arguments of this bill.

78. Ibid., 179–80. This reform had been already proposed by Deputy Juan Antonio Buero in 1915, when it was approved by the Chamber of Deputies. The Senate had failed to discuss it.

79. Ibid., 123–24. The existing Civil Code considered both parents as having rights but undermined those of mothers by stating their subordination in the execution of such rights. Brum acknowledged that in most marriages there was a de facto coadministration of rights. Should a breakdown occur in the marital relationship, it was desirable to legalize that situation.

80. Ibid., 48.

81. *Feminismo Internacional* 1, 6 (1923): 3. The mouthpiece of an organization by the same name, with branches in several Latin American nations and Spain, it praised Brum's sincerity, generosity and idealism in dealing with women's rights. Brum's project was quoted by Leopoldo Bard in 1925 as a model for Argentina. See Argentina, Cámara de Diputados, *Diario de Sesiones* 2 (1925): 15.

82. *Acción Femenina* 6, 9 (1923): 53–54; 7, 50 (1924): 1–12.

83. Alianza Uruguaya y Consejo Nacional de Mujeres, *La mujer uruguaya reclama sus derechos políticos* (Montevideo, 1919), 105–11, 127–32.

84. María Nélida Madoz Gascue de Bartesaghi, *En defensa de la mujer* (Montevideo: El Demócrata, 1931), passim. Apathy among Catholic women about joining the new reformist currents could only lead to the approval of legislation without their input, which in the long run could be more detrimental to society and to the family.

85. Frugoni, *La mujer ante el derecho*, 36–37.

86. Ibid., 65; Uruguay, Cámara de Representantes, *Diario de Sesiones* 465 (1945–46): 500.

87. Séptima Conferencia Internacional Americana, *Actas y antecedentes* (Montevideo, 1933); Sofía Alvarez Vignoli de Demichelli, *Derechos civiles y políticos de la mujer* (Montevideo, 1934). Her husband supported Gabriel Terra's coup d'état.

88. Moreau de Justo, *La mujer en la democracia*, 72–73.

89. For suggestions to the constitutional assembly on women's rights, see Juan Ambrosoni, *Horas de meditación: Los derechos políticos y los derechos civiles de la mujer* (Montevideo, 1934), passim.

90. *El Día*, 12 Feb. 1936, 8.

91. Uruguay, AGN, PL, box 258, folder 1, no. 40. The party withdrew from the conference after an argument between Paulina Luisi and Sara Rey Alvarez over procedural matters.

92. *El Día*, 20 Apr. 1936, 6.

93. Martín R. de Echegoyen, *Informe de la Comisión de Constitución y Legislación del Senado* (Montevideo, 1938).

94. Gregorio Marañón, *Tres ensayos sobre la vida sexual* (Madrid: Biblioteca Nueva, 1929), passim.

95. See *Ideas y Acción*, Mar. 1939, special issue. Also quoted in Frugoni, *La mujer ante el derecho*, 54.

96. Frugoni, *La mujer ante el derecho*, 13–102; Carlos Vaz Ferreira, *Sobre feminismo* (Buenos Aires: Sociedad Amigos del Libro Rioplatense, 1933), passim.

97. For a succinct biography of Julia Arévalo, see Graciela Sapriza, *Memorias de rebeldía: Siete historias de vida* (Montevideo: Puntosur, 1988), 11–129. For the discussion of the Antonelli bill see Uruguay, Cámara de Representantes, *Diario de Sesiones* 453 (1943): 51, 183–91; 458 (1944): 7, 216; 465 (1945–46): 358, 492–504.

98. Uruguay, Cámara de Diputados, *Diario de Sesiones* 465 (1945–46): 501.

99. Labarca, *¿A donde va la mujer?* 169.

100. Among them was Paulina Luisi, who in 1936 favored complete gender equality in the legislation regulating women's right to work and working conditions. See *El Día*, 20 Apr. 1936, 6. She believed that all national legislation and international accords should drop any mention of civil status, that women's rights should be the same as men's, and that women should have the same freedom of choice and protection owed to male workers. See also a Chilean viewpoint in "La igualdad de derechos para la mujer," *Acción Femenina* 6, 25 (1937): 8. She rejected the concept of protection for women in labor legislation but conceded that certain stages in life (old age) or conditions (maternity) deserved special consideration.

Chapter 7 : Divorce

1. Ricardo Krebs et al., *Catolicismo y laicismo: Seis estudios* (Santiago: Pontificia Univ. Católica de Chile, 1981). Of special interest is Sol Serrano, "Fundamentos liberales de la separación del estado y la iglesia, 1881–1884," 153–82; José Luis Romero, *El desarrollo de las ideas en la sociedad argentina del siglo* xx (Mexico City: Fondo de Cultura Económica, 1965); José Pedro Barrán, *Batlle, los estancieros y el imperio británico*, vol. 5, *La reacción imperial-conservadora, 1911–1913* (Montevideo: Banda Oriental, 1984).

2. Uruguay, *Código Civil de la República Oriental del Uruguay* (Paris: Rosa Bouret, 1871); Aníbal Echeverría Reyes, *Colección de códigos de la República de Chile*, (Santiago: Roberto Miranda, 1895), 55; Juan Carlos Rébora, *La familia chilena y la familia argentina*, 2 vols. (La Plata: Tomás Palumbo, 1938), 1:49–63, 91–115. For Chile, see Ramón Briones Luco, *Origen y desarrollo del matrimonio y el divorcio en la familia humana*, 2 vols. (Santiago: Ilustración, 1909), 89–118; Uruguay, *Debates parlamentarios: Discusión de la Ley de Matrimonio Civil Obligatorio* (Montevideo, 1885); Uruguay, Cámara de Senadores, *Primera y segunda discusión sobre el proyecto de matrimonio civil obligatorio* (Montevideo: Laurak-Bat, 1885).

3. Ricardo Rodríguez Molas, *Divorcio y familia tradicional* (Buenos Aires: Centro Editor América Latina, 1984), 77.

4. For the ecclesiastical position see Ricardo Krebs, "El pensamiento de la iglesia frente a la laicización del estado en Chile, 1875–1885," in Krebs et al., *Catolicismo y laicismo*, 27–33; Sofía Correa Sutil, "El partido conservador ante las leyes laicas, 1881–1884," in Krebs et al., *Catolicismo y laicismo*, 97–99.

5. James A. Brundage, *Law, Sex, and Christian Society in Medieval Europe* (Chicago: Univ. of Chicago Press, 1987), 94–98, 114–17, 199–203, 225, 242–45, 288–96, 370–78, 453–58. Divorce legislation was not changed by the Council of Trent (1545–63), which revised the canonical statements defining marriage. Tridentine law was still valid in the late nineteenth century; Daisy Rípodas Ardanaz, *El matrimonio en Indias: Realidad social y regulación jurídica* (Buenos Aires: Conicet, 1977).

6. *La Protesta Humana* (Buenos Aires), 13 June 1892. "There is nothing more absurd than marriage indissolubility; nothing more fictitious or contrary to human nature." See also issues of 13 June 1897; 2 Aug. 1902; 29 Dec. 1904. *El amigo del pueblo* (Montevideo), 1, 6 (1900); *La Aurora* (Montevideo) 1, 3 (1899).

7. Manuel T. Narvaja, *El divorcio: Consideraciones generales y proyecto de una ley para la república* (Montevideo: El Siglo Ilustrado, 1892), passim; José Pedro Barrán, *Historia de la sensibilidad en el Uruguay*, vol. 2, *El disciplinamiento (1860–1920)* (Montevideo: Banda Oriental and Facultad de Humanidades y Ciencias, 1990), 72–74.

8. Setembrino E. Pereda, *El divorcio* (Montevideo: El Siglo Ilustrado, 1902).

9. Mariano Soler, *Pastoral de Excmo. Sr. Arzobispo sobre el divorcio* (Montevideo: Marcos Martínez, 1902).

10. Barrán, *Batlle, los estancieros y el imperio británico*, 5:155.

11. Carlos Oneto y Viana, *Ley de divorcio: Proyecto sancionado por la Honorable Asamblea General de la República Oriental del Uruguay el 24 de octubre de 1907* (Montevideo, 1907); Uruguay, Cámara de Representantes, *Diario de sesiones* 184 (1906): 134.

12. In favor of divorce were Setembrino Pereda, already mentioned, and Guzmán Papini y Zas, *El divorcio ante la ciencia y el arte* (Montevideo: Tipografía Moderna, 1905). Against divorce were Amadeo Almada, *El divorcio ante la razón, el derecho y la moral* (Montevideo: A. Barreiro y Ramos, 1905); Amaro Carve, *Contra el divorcio* (Montevideo: A. Barreiro y Ramos, 1905); Vicente Ponce de León, *El divorcio* (Montevideo, 1905); José Espalter, *Discursos parlamentarios*, 8 vols. (Montevideo: Florensa, 1912), vols. 4 and 5.

13. Uruguay, Cámara de Representantes, *Diario de Sesiones* 184 (1905): 158. Pereda

delivered his defense of divorce in the Ateneo in April 1902 without any public demonstrations.

14. Uruguay, Cámara de Representantes, *Diario de Sesiones* 183 (1905): 290-301.

15. Ibid., 290-306, 399-412, 431-46, 560-72, for discussions between September and October 1905. This law was modified in 1910 to refine the meaning of several articles, such as the prohibition of marriage for two years after a divorce by mutual consent. See ibid., 203 (1910): 390, 414-15, 533-49.

16. Eduardo J. Couture, *El divorcio por voluntad de la mujer: Su régimen procesal* (Montevideo: A. Barreiro y Ramos, 1931), passim. The Swiss 1907 divorce law allowed dissolution on grounds of irreconcilable differences, but the grounds for divorce had to be stated and decided on by a judge.

17. José P. Barrán and Benjamín Nahum, *Batlle, los estancieros y el imperio británico*, vol. 3, *El nacimiento del batllismo* (Montevideo: Banda Oriental, 1982), 146-47. Batlle knew of Alfred Naquet's *Vers l'union libre* from his travels throughout Europe between 1904 and 1908.

18. Domingo Arena, *Divorcio y matrimonio* (Montevideo: O. M. Bertani, 1912), 107 and passim.

19. Briones Luco, *Origen y desarrollo del matrimonio,* 2:89 ff.

20. Novoa argued for a change in the name of the existing process of "divorce," saying that it should be called separation because it did not dissolve the bond completely. Rébora, *La familia chilena y la familia argentina,* 138-39; Briones Luco, *Origen y desarrollo del matrimonio,* vol. 2 passim.

21. Julio Heise G., *Historia de Chile: El período parlamentario, 1861-1925,* 2 vols. (Santiago: Andrés Bello, 1974; Universitaria, 1982), 1:216-68; J. Lloyd Mecham, *Church and State in Latin America* (Chapel Hill: Univ. of North Carolina Press, 1966), 214-24; Brian H. Smith, *The Church and Politics in Chile: Challenges to Modern Catholicism* (Princeton: Princeton Univ. Press, 1982), 86-105.

22. *El Mercurio* (Santiago), 11 June 1924, 3.

23. Smith, *Church and Politics in Chile,* 98-100, for the results of two studies on the nature of Chilean religious observance.

24. Mariano Bustos Lagos, *Emancipación de la mujer: Consideraciones sobre su acción, sus derechos, y su instrucción* (Santiago: Excelsior, 1923).

25. Luis María Acuña, *El divorcio ante la razón, la historia y la estadística* (Valparaíso: Chas, Editor, 1934), 198.

26. *Nosotras* 2, 44 (1933): 6; 2, 45 (1933): 5-7.

27. *Nosotras* 5, 65 (1935): 16.

28. *El Imparcial* (Santiago), 1 July 5; 12 July 4; 16 July 4; 23 July 4; 4 Aug. 1935, 4.

29. *Voz Femenina* 4, 1 (1935): 1, 2; 1, 6 (1935): 1.

30. Amanda Grossi Aninat, *Eugenesia y su legislación* (Santiago: Nascimento, 1941), 103.

31. Argentina, Cámara de Diputados. *Diario de Sesiones* 2 (1932): 563-69.

32. Argentina, *Divorcio: Debates en la Cámara de Diputados* (Buenos Aires: El Comercio, 1902), 1-11.

33. Rodríguez Molas, *Divorcio y familia tradicional,* 96 ff.; Argentina, *Divorcio,* 39-45,

95–98; Argentina, Cámara de Diputados, *Diario de Sesiones* 1 (1922): 286–97. Two members of the commission opposed it; a third, Luis M. Drago, offered his own version.

34. *La Vanguardia*, 11 July 1903, 2; 1 Aug. 1903, 1.

35. Argentina, Cámara de Diputados, *Diario de Sesiones* 1 (1907): 539–46.

36. Argentina, Cámara de Diputados, *Diario de Sesiones* 1 (1913): 40, 44–46. This bill accepted the traditional separation of bed and table for practicing Catholics but allowed dissolution for those who chose it. It retained the double standard of adultery for men and women and allowed divorce by mutual consent after two years of marriage. To ensure children's welfare Conforti would oblige the father to award them 50 percent of his assets before a second marriage.

37. Argentina, Cámara de Diputados, *Diario de Sesiones* 2 (1913): 467, 470, 478–83, 939; 1 (1914): 556, 559. The 1913 Palacios draft was cosigned by Socialists Juan B. Justo, Mario Bravo, and Nicolás Repetto.

38. José A. Mouchet, "El divorcio," *Humanidad Nueva* 6 (1913): 305–15.

39. Argentina, Cámara de Diputados, *Diario de Sesiones* 2 (1917): 95–107; 4 (1918): 653.

40. The 1918 Bravo bill was based on another presented by Deputy De Tomaso in 1917 and was signed by three Radicals, three Socialists, and one member each of the Democratic Party and Conservative Party.

41. *La Vanguardia*, 3 June 1918, 1; Mario Bravo, *Familia, religión y patria* (Buenos Aires: La Vanguardia, 1932). This is the second printing of a lecture originally delivered in 1919. In 1929 Bravo, by then a senator, introduced yet another divorce bill. See *La Vanguardia*, 15 Sept. 1929, 1.

42. Enrique del Valle Iberlucea, *El divorcio y la emancipación civil de la mujer* (Buenos Aires: Cultura y Civismo, 1919). Antonio de Tomaso introduced two bills in 1922 and 1924. Juan B. Justo was a cosponsor of the 1913, 1917, and 1927 bills. Silvio Ruggieri introduced a bill in 1932. That same year Bravo and Palacios submitted a second bill. See Argentina, Cámara de Diputados, *Diario de Sesiones* 2 (1932): 563–69.

43. Argentina, Cámara de Diputados, *Diario de Sesiones* 1 (1922): 286–97, 1 (1928): 479–87; 2 (1932): 563–69.

44. Argentina, Cámara de Diputados, *Diario de Sesiones* 1 (1928): 479–87.

45. Enrique Dickmann, *Emancipación civil, política y social de la mujer* (Buenos Aires, 1935), 40.

46. The discussion of Rébora's ideas is based on his *La emancipación de la mujer: El aporte de la jurisprudencia* (Buenos Aires: La Facultad, 1929). See especially 112–13, 115–16, 130–33, 258–59, 268–69.

47. Rébora was annoyed by opposite interpretations by two judges of whether women had to live with their husbands after a "divorce" if they wished to be provided for by him. Rébora could not accept as "justice" the decision that a man could oblige a woman to live where he did.

48. *Jurisprudencia criminal*, Biblioteca Policial 72 (Buenos Aires: Policía de la Capital, 1941), 129–32.

49. Dickmann, *Emancipación civil*, 41.

50. Mecham, *Church and State in Latin America*, 225–51; Sandra McGee Deutsch,

"The Catholic Church, Work, and Womanhood in Argentina, 1890–1930, *Gender and History* 3, 3 (1991): 304–25.

51. Silvio L. Ruggieri, *Divorcio* (Buenos Aires: La Vanguardia, 1932), 45. This bill included adultery or any other "carnal act" with persons of either sex as a legitimate cause for divorce. The wording in Spanish is ambiguous, and it seems to include homosexuality. See also *La Prensa*, 22 Sept. 1932, 11; 24 Sept. 1932, 12.

52. The female society Labor y Constancia, and socialist women in Rosario supported the bill. See *La Vanguardia*, 18 Aug. 1932, 7; 20 Aug. 1932, 1; 17 Sept. 1932, 7. Some women's socialist groups supported divorce on the grounds that it would bring order and peace to many homes.

53. *La Vanguardia*, 21 Aug. 1932, 1; 23 Aug. 1932, 1; 20 Sept. 1932, 1; 22 Sept. 1932, 2–3; 23 Sept. 1932, 1.

54. Uruguay, *El movimiento del estado civil y la mortalidad de la República Oriental del Uruguay en el año 1917* (Montevideo: Imp. Nacional, 1918), 7; Uruguay, *Anuario estadístico de la República Oriental del Uruguay* (Montevideo: Moderna, 1922); 14; Uruguay, Dirección General de Estadística, *Síntesis estadística de la Republica O. del Uruguay* (Montevideo, 1940), 25–27; Uruguay, *El movimiento del estado civil y la mortalidad de la República Oriental del Uruguay en el año de 1941* (Montevideo: Imp. Nacional, 1941), 5, 15; Uruguay, Dirección General de Estadística, *Anuario estadístico* (Montevideo, 1943), 18. There were 250 divorces in 1920, 712 in 1930, 500 in 1940, and 806 in 1943. The number of divorces declined sharply between 1931 and 1934, years of instability and depression, but began to climb after 1935.

55. Uruguay, *El movimiento del estado civil y la mortalidad, 1941;* Uruguay, *Anuario estadístico* (1943).

56. Julio Zícari, *Evolución social: Acotaciones al divorcio* (Buenos Aires: Jesús Menéndez, 1932), 42–48.

57. Uruguay, Cámara de Representantes, *Diario de Sesiones* 183 (1905): 404–5.

58. Ponce de León, *El divorcio,* 19–22.

59. Abella's ideas are in *Nosotras* 1, 2 (1902): 1, 4 (1902): 63; 1, 6 (1902): 85; 1, 26 (1903): 233; 1, 33 (1903): 309; 1, 35 (1903): 330; 2, 57–58 (1904): 660–63.

60. *Primer Congreso Femenino Internacional de la República Argentina: Historia, Actas y Trabajos* (Buenos Aires: Ceppi, 1910), 416–28.

61. See, for example, *La Vanguardia,* 8 Apr. 1915.

62. Delie Rouge [Delia Rojo], *Mis observaciones* (Santiago: Imp. New York, 1915), passim.

63. *Acción Femenina* 1, 3 (1922): 22–23.

64. *Acción Femenina* 1, 7 (1923): 20–21.

65. *Acción Femenina* 1, 12 (1923): 11–14.

66. Delia Rouge, "Algo sobre el divorcio," *Revista Femenina* 1, 3 (1924): 21–22; 1, 24 (1924): 15–16.

67. Elisa Rivera de Hederra, "La mujer chilena ante el divorcio," *Revista Femenina* 1, 3 (1924): 19–20.

68. For Adela Edwards's opinion, see *Nosotras* 2, 44 (1933): 6. See also Lola L. de Lassalle, "El divorcio y el sufragio femenino," *Vida Femenina* 1, 3 (1933): 30.

69. Paul W. Drake, *Socialism and Populism in Chile, 1932–52*, (Urbana: Univ. of Illinois Press, 1978), 99–132.

70. Amanda Labarca, "En defensa del divorcio," in *¿A donde va la mujer?* (Santiago: Extra, 1934), 203–15.

71. *Voz Femenina* 1, 4 (1935): 2. Correa de Garcés rejected divorce. See *Voz Femenina* 1, 8 (1935): 5.

72. *Voz Femenina* 1, 7 (1935): 2.

73. Carve, *Contra el divorcio*, 13; Ponce de León, *El divorcio*, passim.

74. Quoted at length in Del Valle Iberlucea, *El divorcio y la emancipación de la mujer*, 110–15; Juan A. Figueroa claimed that juridical equality of men and women within marriage was an idea far too advanced for Argentina. See pp. 139–41 of Del Valle Iberlucea's *El divorcio*.

75. See opinions of Deputies Ernesto Padilla and E. S. Pérez in Argentina, *Divorcio*, 420, 534. See also *Voz Femenina* (Chile) 1, 7 (1935): 2, 4.

76. Espalter, *Discursos*, 5:353.

77. Ponce de León, *El divorcio*, 80, 96–97. Men and women would be debased by loosening the sexual restrictions marriage imposed. "In that form of decadence inaugurated by divorce, marriage will have to be defined as the fortuitous encounter of male and female to reproduce the human species, the bestial race that I do not know we could still call the human race. See also Barrán, *Historia de la sensibilidad en el Uruguay*, 2:125–52.

78. *El Imparcial* (Santiago), 1, 12, 16, 23 July 1935; Juan B. Terán, *El divorcio* (Buenos Aires: Colegio, 1932), 3.

79. Almada cited India and Turkey as undesirable examples. See Almada, *El divorcio*, 15–18.

80. Terán, *El divorcio*, passim.

81. *Nosotras* 1, 35 (1903): 333.

82. Rodríguez Molas, *Divorcio y familia tradicional*, 133–34.

83. Del Valle Iberlucea, *El divorcio*, 155–207.

84. Argentina, Cámara de Diputados, *Diario de Sesiones* 1 (1907): 542–46; 2 (1913): 470.

85. Arena, *Divorcio y matrimonio*, 95 and passim.

86. Espalter, *Discursos*, 5:294–97, 315–16, 320, 338.

87. Ponce de León, *El divorcio*, 31; Espalter, *Discursos*, 5:326, 338–39, 344, 391. See Argentine Esteban Lamadrid's opinion, as transcribed in Del Valle Iberlucea, *El divorcio*, 86–87.

88. Carve, *Contra el divorcio*, 39, 55. "Marriage has educated and accustomed women to prefer fidelity and with it him who dignifies her." "Divorce makes woman deviate from the path of her duties, makes her abandon the sacred mission God has assigned her in this world: to mold family and home and educate her children."

89. Briones Luco, *Origen y desarrollo*, 2:223–25.

90. Ibid., 248.

91. Chile, Cámara de Diputados, *Boletín*, sesiones extraordinarias (1918), 103.

92. Pereda, *El divorcio*, 57. "This type of offense deserves no mercy; such offense can only be paid with death."

93. Papini y Zas, *El divorcio ante la ciencia y el arte,* 16.

94. Argentina, Cámara de Diputados, *Diario de Sesiones* 1 (1907), 539; 2 (1913): 478–83.

95. Oneto y Viana, *Ley de divorcio,* passim.

96. For the 1907 Uruguayan law, see Luco, *Origen y desarrollo,* 2:272 ff.

97. Barrán and Nahum, *El Uruguay del novecientos,* 82–84; Eduardo Couture, *El divorcio por voluntad de la mujer: Su régimen procesal* (Montevideo: Barreiro y Ramos, 1931).

98. Argentina, Cámara de Representantes, *Diario de Sesiones* 4 (1918): 662.

99. Ponce de León, *El divorcio,* 24.

100. Arturo M. Bas, *El cáncer de la sociedad* (Buenos Aires: Amorrortu, 1932), passim.

101. Dickmann, *Emancipación civil,* 47, 52–55.

102. Benítez Ceballos (from Catamarca), "El Divorcio," *Nosotras* 2, 57–58 (1904): 660–63.

103. Francisco L. Sasso, *El divorcio* (Buenos Aires, 1902), passim.

104. Uruguay, Cámara de Representantes, *Diario de Sesiones* 183 (1905): 294.

105. Argentina, Cámara de Diputados, *Diario de Sesiones* 1 (1928): 479–87.

106. Argentina, Cámara de Representantes, *Diario de Sesiones* 4 (1918): 662.

107. See Barrán, *Historia de la sensibilidad en el Uruguay,* vol. 2, passim.

Chapter 8 : Women's Politics and Suffrage in Argentina

1. Nestor Tomás Auza, *Periodismo y feminismo en la Argentina, 1830–1930* (Buenos Aires: Emecé, 1988); Jim Levy, *Juana Manso, Argentine Feminist,* La Trobe Univ. Institute of Latin American Studies, Occasional Paper no. 1 (Boondora, Australia: La Trobe Univ. Press, 1977); Francine Masiello, *Between Civilization and Barbarism: Women, Nation and Literary Culture in Modern Argentina* (Lincoln: Univ. of Nebraska Press, 1992); Samuel Guy Inman, "Paraná, Exponent of North American Education," PAU, *Bulletin* 53 (July–Dec. 1921): 463–74.

2. Carlos Pellegrini, *Estudio sobre el derecho electoral* (Buenos Aires: Imp. del Plata, 1869); Florentino González, *Lecciones de derecho constitucional* (Buenos Aires: J. A. Bernheim, 1869).

3. Luis A. Mohr, *La mujer y la política: Revolucionarios y reaccionarios* (Buenos Aires: G. Kraft, 1890); José Miguel Olmedo, *La mujer ciudadana* (Córdoba: Imp. del Estado, 1873); Octavio Iturbe, *El sufragio de la mujer* (Buenos Aires: A. Monkes, 1895); Pedro E. Aguilar, *Derecho electoral* (Buenos Aires: Argos, 1893).

4. José Manuel Estrada, *Curso de derecho constitucional,* 3 vols. (Buenos Aires: Cabaut y Compañia, 1901–2), 2:322–38.

5. Trinidad M. Enríquez and María Eugenia Echenique in *La Ondina del Plata* as examples. *La Ondina del Plata* was published in Buenos Aires between 1875 and 1879. See 1, 43 (1875): 505–7; 1, 43 (1875): 543–45; 2, 3 (1876): 25–27; 2, 5 (1876): 54–56; 2, 6 (1876): 61–63; and 2, 33 (1876): 385–87.

6. Marifran Carlson, *¡Feminismo! The Woman's Movement in Argentina from Its Beginnings to Eva Perón* (Chicago: Academy Chicago, 1988), 87–104. For Cecilia Grierson, see Cecilia Grierson, *Homenaje póstumo: Discursos* (Buenos Aires: López, 1937). Her

role as an educator is highlighted in idem, *Educación técnica de la mujer: Informe presentado al Sr. Ministro de Instrucción Pública de la República Argentina* (Buenos Aires: Penitenciaría Nacional, 1902; idem, *Instituciones de enfermera y masagistas en Europa y la Argentina* (Buenos Aires: J. Penser, 1901); Clorinda Matto de Turner [La Dirección], "Cecilia Grierson," *El Búcaro Americano* 1, 6 (1896): 114.

7. Cecilia Grierson, *Decadencia del Consejo Nacional de Mujeres de la República Argentina* (Buenos Aires, 1910), passim. Grierson accused the Council of becoming more interested in elitist literary and musical soirées than in social issues. The Council's directorate disapproved of Grierson's participation in the 1910 First International Feminine Congress, labeled "liberal and feminist."

8. *La Prensa* (Buenos Aires), 14 May 1910, 11; 15 May 1910, 11.

9. Consejo Nacional de Mujeres de la Republica Argentina, *Memoria presentada por la Señora Presidenta de la Biblioteca del Consejo Nacional de Mujeres, Doña Carolina Jeria de Argerich: Correspondiente al año 1920–21* (Buenos Aires, 1921); Sandra McGee Deutsch, *Counterrevolution in Argentina, 1900–1932: The Argentine Patriotic League* (Lincoln: Univ. of Nebraska Press, 1986), 89; *Guía de la Oficina de Informaciones del Consejo Nacional de Mujeres* (Buenos Aires: Alfa y Omega, 1912).

10. *Unión y Labor* 1, 1 (1909). Their offer was rejected because the law did not provide for such services. Heading the Universitarias was Dra. Petrona Eyle, with Matilde T. Flairoto, a journalist, as secretary and Sara Justo, dentist and sister of socialist leader Juan B. Justo, as treasurer.

11. *La Nueva Mujer* 1, 4 (1910), editorial; Gina Lombroso Ferrero, "La mujer en la República Argentina," *Revista de Derecho, Historia y Letras* 31 (Dec. 1908): 518–27. Lombroso was struck by the lack of communication between the sexes and the general ignorance of the female workers. She supported the educational work carried out by feminists, for whom she had nothing but praise.

12. Carlson, *¡Feminismo!* 103.

13. She was never invited to teach in the school of medicine. As she commented on this, she revealed the undercurrents of her feminism: "The reasons and arguments given [for the denial] would fill a chapter against the intellectual and economic feminism that I have always defended." Quoted in Grierson, *Homenaje póstumo*, 66–67.

14. Luis R. Longhi, *Sufragio femenino* (Buenos Aires: Baiocco, 1932), 138–39; Elvira Rawson de Dellepiane, "La campaña feminista en la Argentina," in Miguel J. Font, *La mujer: Encuesta feminista* (Buenos Aires, 1921), 73–80.

15. Longhi, *Sufragio femenino*, 139; *La Nueva Mujer* 1, 2 (1910): 8.

16. *Unión y Labor* 2, 18 (1911): 28–29; 2, 24 (1911): 1–30; 3, 26 (1911): 30; 3, 30 (1912): 30.

17. *Unión y Labor* 1, 1 (1909).

18. *Unión y Labor* 1, 12 (1910): 22; 2, 20 (1911): 3; 2, 22 (1911): 13–16; 3, 25 (1911), editorial and 16.

19. *Revista Socialista Internacional* 1, 1 (1908): 94–95.

20. Another feminist center was reported in Santa Fe. See *La Nueva Mujer* 1, 7 (1910): 5; 1, 12 (1910).

21. Nicolás Cuello, *Ejemplo noble de una mujer* (Buenos Aires, 1936); Fenia Chertcoff de Repetto, "El movimiento socialista femenino en la República Argentina," *Alma-*

naque del Trabajo 1 (1918): 141-45. Fenia Chertcoff (1869-1928), a Russian Jewish emigré and schoolteacher, was among the first women to join the Socialist Party. She married Dr. Nicolás Repetto in 1901 and devoted the rest of her life to organizing services for women and children within the party. *La Vanguardia* carried news of her activities for many years.

22. Carolina Muzilli, "El trabajo femenino," *Boletín Mensual del Museo Social Argentino* 2, 15-16 (1913): 65-90; Donna Guy, "Emilio and Gabriela Coni, Reformers: Public Health and Working Women," in Judith Ewell and William Beezley, eds., *The Human Tradition in Latin America: The Nineteenth Century* (Wilmington DE: Scholarly Resources, 1989); 223-48; Hobart A. Spalding Jr., *La clase trabajadora argentina: Documentos para su historia, 1890-1912* (Buenos Aires: Galerna, 1970).

23. Chertcoff de Repetto, "El movimiento socialista femenino en la República Argentina." Other Centro leaders were Carolina Muzilli, Fenia Chertcoff, Raquel Messina, Juana María Beguino, and Alicia Moreau.

24. *La Vanguardia*, 16 May 1903, 1.

25. *La Vanguardia*, 30 May 1903, 1.

26. *La Vanguardia*, 22 Aug. 1903.

27. *La Protesta*, 11 Nov. 1904, 11; 8 Dec. 1-2.

28. *La Protesta*, 8 Dec. 1904, 1-2.

29. *La Protesta*, 11 Nov. 16, 1904.

30. Spalding, *La clase trabajadora*, 87-88.

31. *La Vanguardia*, 13 Apr. 1907. Party's support for women's activities, in *La Vanguardia*, 28 Jan. 24-25 Sept. 1905; 26 Mar. 1907, 10 Mar. 22 Oct. 1915.

32. Cuello, *Ejemplo*, 99.

33. The city's municipal council or Concejo Deliberante required the *recreos* to move from the socialist centers to secure their subsidies (23,000 pesos in 1923). In the mid-1930s there were ten of these centers. The municipality began funding its own *recreos* in 1933, using the socialist institutions as a model. See Cuello, *Ejemplo*, 102-28.

34. That such restrictions could deprive some women of work was not an acceptable argument to socialists. See *La Vanguardia* 11, 12, 13 Jan. 1915.

35. Alicia Moreau, "El sufragio femenino," *Revista Socialista Internacional* 3, 4 (1911): 93-94.

36. Argentine anarchists followed the ideological guidelines developed by Enrique Malatesta, E. Z. Arana, Juan Creaghe, and Gustave Lafarge. See Iaacov Oved, *El anarquismo y el movimiento obrero en Argentina* (Buenos Aires: Siglo XXI, 1978); Diego Abad de Santillán, *El movimiento anarquista en la Argentina desde sus comienzos hasta el año 1910* (Buenos Aires: Argonauta, 1930), and idem, *La F.O.R.A.: Ideología y trayectoria* (Buenos Aires: Proyección, 1971); Enrique Dhorr, *Lo que quieren los anarquistas* (Buenos Aires, 1900), 12-14.

37. Maxine Molyneux, "No God, No Boss, No Husband: Anarchist Feminism in Nineteenth-Century Argentina," *Latin American Perspectives* 13, 1 (1986): 119-45. A similar lack of concrete suggestions for working women's activities is found in writings published elsewhere. See "A las jóvenes proletarias," *La Protesta Humana*, 1 Aug. 1897, 2.

38. Molyneux, "No God," 130.

39. *La Protesta Humana*, 17 Aug. 1901, 3; Mirta Henault, "La incorporación de la mujer al trabajo asalariado," *Todo es Historia* 183 (Aug. 1983): 42–53. Strikes are duly recorded in *La Protesta*. *La Vanguardia* is less helpful on this matter.

40. Molyneux, "No God," 128–29.

41. See *La Protesta Humana*, 13 June 1897, "La mujer y la familia"; 1 Aug. 1897, "A las jóvenes proletarias"; 7 Jan. 1900, "El amor en el matrimonio"; 28 Oct. 1900, "Contra el amor por el amor"; 2 Aug. 1902, "La mujer considerada como factor social"; 30 Aug. 1902, "Amor con amor se paga." *La Protesta Humana* and its sequel *La Protesta* served as the most important arena of debate for anarchists. The short-lived *La Batalla* (1910) hardly discussed any women's issues.

42. Molyneux, "No God," 129.

43. Oved, *Anarquismo*, 356–60.

44. Juana Rouco Buela, *Historia*, 15. Other names mentioned by Rouco Buela are those of Elisa Leitar and María Reyes. For Juana Rouco Buela, see *Historia de un ideal vivido por una mujer* (Buenos Aires: Reconstruir, 1964). See also "Juana Buela," in Graciela Sapriza, *Memorias de Rebeldía: Siete historias de vida* (Montevideo: Puntosur, 1988), 58–76. Her name was Buela, but she adopted "Rouco" as a subterfuge to avoid detention in Argentina when she returned to that country illegally in 1909.

45. *La Protesta*, 5, 16 Nov. 1904.

46. *La Protesta*, 8 Dec. 1904.

47. *La Protesta*, 10 Dec. 1904.

48. "Reflexiones de una mujer," *La Protesta*, 6 Feb. 1918.

49. See *Nuestra Tribuna* 1, 2 (1922): 4; 3, 36, (1924): 4.

50. The ideal situation for a woman would be self-sufficiency, which would break her dependence on man. "A woman will be able to be alone, and whereas that autonomy and freedom do not consist in being alone, it is also true that the ability to be alone as one of the preconditions of freedom. When one cannot be alone it means that one is tied to somebody. This is what has happened to women up to now; she has been tied to the family and to man." J. M., "El problema feminista," *La Protesta*, 9 Sept. 1923. See also F. S. Merlino, "La familia," in Dhorr, *Lo que quieren los anarquistas*, 12–14.

51. *Unión y Labor* 1, 12 (1910): 22–23. San Juan was the birthplace of Domingo F. Sarmiento, statesman, educator, and firm believer in women's rights. See also Aldo A. Cocca, *Ley de sufragio femenino* (Buenos Aires: El Ateneo, 1948), 14–17.

52. Cocca, *Ley de sufragio femenino*, 14–17.

53. Mariano Abril, "El sufragio femenino," *Revista de Derecho, Historia y Letras* 45 (May 1913): 95–99.

54. Clodomiro Cordero, *La sociedad argentina y la mujer* (Buenos Aires, 1916); on Argentine nationalism, see Carl Solberg, *Immigration and Nationalism: Argentina and Chile, 1890–1914* (Austin: Univ. of Texas Press, 1970), 132–57.

55. On 13 May 1910, the same day the National Council of Women's congress began, the attorney general of the province of Buenos Aires denied two women accountants the right to exercise their profession on the basis that they lacked "citizenship," that is, the right to vote. Citizenship tied to suffrage was hurting women in other than political ways.

56. Mario Bravo, *Derechos políticos de la mujer* (Buenos Aires: Vanguardia, 1930), 34–57; Juan Carlos Rébora, *La emancipación de la mujer: El aporte de la jurisprudencia* (Buenos Aires: Facultad, 1929), 39–40; Longhi, *Sufragio femenino,* 151; Katherine S. Dreier, *Five Months in the Argentine from a Woman's Point of View* (New York: Sherman, 1920), 221–23.

57. Longhi, *Sufragio femenino,* 151; Bravo, *Derechos políticos de la mujer,* 40–41; Argentina, Cámara de Diputados, *Diario de Sesiones* 6 (1932): 31.

58. *Nuestra Causa* 2, 14 (1920): 80–82. According to Katherine Dreier, Unión Feminista Nacional had 120 members in December 1919. See Dreier, *Five Months,* 237.

59. *Nuestra Causa,* 2, 13 (1920): 10.

60. On prostitution see Donna J. Guy, *Sex and Danger in Buenos Aires: Prostitution, Family, and Nation in Argentina* (Lincoln: Univ. of Nebraska Press, 1991), passim.

61. *Nuestra Causa* 1, 5 (1919): 111, 114; 2, 13 (1920): 22; 1, 12 (1920): 280.

62. *Nuestra Causa* 1, 12 (1920): 280; 2, 13 (1920): 125–27. For information on Di Carlo, see *Mujeres de America* 3, 16 (1935): 32–33, and Lily Sosa de Newton, *Diccionario biográfico de mujeres argentinas* (Buenos Aires: Plus Ultra, 1986), 191–92.

63. *Nuestra Causa* 1, 5 (1919): 114.

64. *La Razón,* 2 Aug. 1919, 2.

65. *La Prensa,* 31 Oct. 1920, 11; Dreir, *Five Months,* 227–28.

66. *Nuestra Causa* 1, 12 (1920): 273.

67. For feminist network activities in Argentina, Uruguay, and Peru, see *Nuestra Causa* 1, 8 (1919), passim; 1, 12 (1920), passim; 2, 13 (1920), passim; 2, 14 (1920), passim.

68. Mirta Henault, *Alicia Moreau de Justo* (Buenos Aires: Centro Editor de América Latina, 1983), 66–69.

69. *Nuestra Causa* 2, 13 (1920): 10; *La Prensa,* 4 Mar. 1920, 11; 7 Mar. 1920, 10; 8 Mar. 1920, 9; *La Vanguardia,* 2 Mar. 1920, 5, 8; 6 Mar. 1920, 5, 9; 7 Mar. 1920, 9; 8 Mar. 1920, 1; 9 Mar. 1920, 1; 11 Mar. 1920, 1; 12 Mar. 1920, 1; 13 Mar. 1920, 1; 14 Mar. 1920, 1; Dreier, *Five Months,* 233; *La Prensa,* 8 Mar. 1920.

70. Argentina, Cámara de Diputados, *Diario de Sesiones* 2 (1925): 30–31; *Nuestra Causa,* 2, 14 (1920): 80–82; Cocca, *Ley de sufragio femenino,* 32–34.

71. *Nuestra Causa* 1, 5 (1919): 114–15.

72. *Nuestra Causa* 2, 13 (1920): 10; 2, 14 (1920): 83.

73. *Nuestra Causa* 2, 13 (1920): 20.

74. *Nuestra Causa* 2, 14 (1920): 42; *La Vanguardia,* 2 Nov. 1920, 4.

75. *Nuestra Causa* 2, 19 (1920): 154, 157–58.

76. *La Vanguardia,* 20 Nov. 1920, 2. The municipal electoral junta took the decision.

77. *La Vanguardia,* 20 Nov. 1920, 9.

78. *Nuestra Causa* 2, 19 (1920): 148.

79. *Nuestra Causa* 3, 24 (1921): 272.

80. *Nuestra Causa* 2, 19 (1920): 152–53, 154.

81. *Nuestra Causa* 2, 19 (1920): 163–65 (italics added).

82. Victor O. Garcia Costa, "*Los primeros años del movimiento* feminista y la primera sufragista sudamericana," *Boletin del Instituto Histórico de la Ciudad de Buenos Aires* 4, 6 (1982): 65–75. Cocca, *La ley del sufragio,* 9. Female suffrage in Santa Fe was adopted

in principle but not enacted until 1932. The right relapsed for a short period and was revived in May 1938, when qualified municipal vote was readopted. See *Nuestra Causa* 3, 24 (1921): 272.

83. Font, *La mujer,* 54.

84. Font, *La mujer,* 55–57.

85. José Bianco, *Mi feminismo* (Buenos Aires: L. J. Rosso, 1927), passim.

86. See opinion of Victorio Delfino of La Plata, reproduced by Deputy Leopoldo Bard in his bill for women's suffrage. Argentina, Cámara de Diputados, *Diario de Sesiones* (1925): 28.

87. David Rock, "Intellectual Precursors of Conservative Nationalism in Argentina, 1900–1927," *Hispanic American Historical Review* 67, 2 (1987): 271–300.

88. Alicia Moreau, "Los nietos de Juan Moreyra," *Nuestra Causa* 2, 22 (1921): 219–22.

89. *Nuestra Causa* 2, 22 (1921): 233. Early in 1921 this organization took over the administration and publication of *Nuestra Causa* under a commission formed by Alicia Moreau, B. W. de Gerchunoff, and E. B. Bachofen; 2, 16 (1920): 76–80. Asociación Pro-Derechos de la Mujer was interested in underprivileged boys living in precarious health conditions in several sectors of the city of Buenos Aires. See *Nuestra Causa* 2, 14 (1920): 43.

90. Argentina, Cámara de Diputados, *Diario de Sesiones* 2 (1925): 32.

91. Francesca Miller, "Latin American Feminism and the Transnational Arena," Emilie Bergman et al., *Women, Culture, and Politics in Latin America* (Berkeley: Univ. of California Press, 1990), 10–26.

92. Argentina, Cámara de Diputados, *Diario de Sesiones* 2 (1925): 8–38.

93. Deutsch, *Counterrevolution in Argentina,* 87–91, 201; Gino Germani, "Hacia una democracia de masas," in Torcuato S. Di Tella et al., *Argentina: Sociedad de masas* (Buenos Aires: Editorial Universitaria, 1965), 206–27.

94. Julia Casal de Espeche, *Misión social de la mujer argentina* (La Plata: Olivieri y Domínguez, 1922). Casal accused Argentine women of neglecting their duties at home. A foreword to this book written by Estanislao Zeballos called suffrage a "detestable slavery and a humiliation for women."

95. *La Vanguardia,* 5 Dec. 1928, 5; 8 Dec. 1928, 2, 6; See *La Prensa* (Buenos Aires), issues of 30 Nov.–16 Dec. 1928. Socialist *La Vanguardia* did not show much interest in this congress.

96. Rébora, *La emancipación de la mujer,* 39–55.

97. Cocca, *Ley de sufragio,* 63–71.

98. Bravo, *Derechos políticos de la mujer,* passim.

99. On 4 May 1924 Unión Feminista Nacional stated its support of the Women's International League for Peace and Freedom, meeting in Washington DC. See PAU, *Bulletin* 58 (Aug. 1924): 848; Francesca Miller, "Latin American Feminism," 16. On pacifism see "Third International Feminine Congress," *La Prensa,* 12 Dec. 1928, 23.

100. *La Vanguardia,* 5 Oct. 1930, 1.

101. Carmela Horne de Burmeister, *Como se organizó en la Argentina el movimiento femenino en favor de los derechos políticos de la mujer por el Comité Argentino Pro-Voto de la Mujer, hoy Asociación Argentina del Sufragio Femenino* (Buenos Aires: Riera y Cía,

1933), passim; Asociación Argentina del Sufragio Femenino, *Fines y propósitos de los estatutos* (Buenos Aires, 1932).

102. Asociación Argentina del Sufragio Femenino, *Fines y propósitos,* 7–8.

103. Only three numbers remain: 1, 2 (1931); 1, 3 (1931); 1, 4 (1932).

104. *Mujer!* 1, 3 (1932): 25.

105. Horne de Burmeister, *Como se organizó,* 27–28. Longhi cites 12,000 signatures; see Longhi, *Sufragio,* 157.

106. Cocca, *Ley de sufragio femenino,* 22–24.

107. Argentina, Cámara de Diputados, *Diario de Sesiones* 6 (1932): 22–111; Cocca, *Ley de sufragio femenino,* 100–123.

108. *La Prensa,* 1 Sept. 1932, 12; 3 Sept. 1932, 11; 11 Sept. 1932, 13. See also *La Vanguardia,* 18 Aug. 1932, 7; 22 Sept. 1932, 1.

109. *La Prensa,* 18 Sept. 1932, 10, editorial.

110. *La Vanguardia,* 21 Sept. 1932, 1.

111. *La Prensa,* 25 Sept. 1932, 10.

112. *La Vanguardia,* 21 Sept. 1932, 5.

113. *Mujeres de América* 1, 1 (1933): 48; 2, 10 (1934): 51; 2, 9 (1934): 61; 3, 17 (1935).

114. *Mujeres de América* 1, 1 (1933): 48–49; 1, 3 (1933): 41, 59; 1, 5 (1933): 53; 1, 6 (1933): 49; 2, 10 (1934): 53; 3, 16 (1935): 32–33.

115. This magazine was published between January 1933 and September–December 1935. Director Nelly Merino's sickness in late 1935 may have caused its demise.

116. *Mujeres de América* 3, 13 (1935): 22; 3, 15 (1925): 9–10.

117. *¿Merecemos las mujeres argentinas este agravio?* Broadsheet, Buenos Aires, n.d.; Victoria Ocampo, *La mujer y su expresión* (Buenos Aires: Sur, 1936); Carlson, *¡Feminismo!* 177–78.

118. *Vida Femenina* 1, 7 (1934), editorial.

119. *Vida Femenina,* 3, 27 (1935): 12–13, 16; 33, 28 (1936): 14–15; 3, 26 (1935), editorial. See article by Dr. Dora Miranda in 3, 26 (1935): 5.

120. Adolfo Dickmann, "¿Es oportuno renovar la campaña por el sufragio femenino?" *Vida Femenina* 2, 21 (1935): 16.

121. Alicia Moreau de Justo, "El momento político," *Vida Femenina* 5, 49 (1937): 4–6; idem, "Diez razones en favor del sufragio femenino," *Vida Femenina* 5, 61 (1938): 4–5.

122. Rebuttals of women's rights in this period still used a mixture of elitist attitudes about the low capacity of the nonelite for political rights. See Felipe S. Velázquez, *El proyecto de ley instituyendo el voto cívico femenino* (San Luis: Celorrio, 1933).

123. Cocca, *Ley de sufragio,* 24–29.

124. Argentina, Cámara de Diputados, *Diario de Sesiones* 2 (1938): 580–82; *Diario de Sesiones* 3 (1939): 713; Cocca, *Ley de sufragio,* 122–51. The 1938 Palacios is reproduced in *Vida Femenina* 5, 59 (1938): 13–14, 33–34.

125. Silvio L. Ruggieri, "El voto femenino," *Vida Femenina* 10, 103–4 (1942): 4–5, 21.

126. *Vida Femenina* 10, 103–4 (1942): 27.

127. "Contestan las presidentas de instituciones femeninas," *Vida Femenina* 10, 103–4 (1942): 6–9, 24–27; Lucila Virasoro de Pucci, "La mujer y la post-guerra," *Vida Femenina* 10, 109–10 (1943): 18–20; Carlson, *¡Feminismo!* 183–84.

128. Alicia Moreau de Justo, "Hay que terminar con el fraude," *Vida Femenina* 10, 107–8 (1943): 20–21. Women's groups continued their activities throughout the 1940s. The April–May 1943 issue of *Vida Femenina* reported a *Jornada Femenina* that took place on 17 April 1943; Berta Kaplanski, "En torno a los derechos femeninos," *Vida Femenina* 10, 109–10 (1943): 32–33.

129. Ernesto Fantini Pertiné, *La mujer, factor de la victoria* (Buenos Aires: Biblioteca del Oficial del Círculo Militar, 1942). Women were essential for the defense of the nation. Although he defended democracy and women's new role in society, he regarded "having many children" as an act of patriotism (p. 336). He believed that women could strengthen their character in times of war.

Chapter 9 : Women's Politics and Suffrage in Chile

1. As quoted in Catharine M. Paul, "Amanda Labarca H.: Educator to the Women of Chile" (Ph.D. diss., School of Education, New York Univ., 1967), 23–24; Paz Covarrubias, "El movimiento feminista chileno," in Paz Covarrubias and Rolando Franco, comps., *Chile: Mujer y sociedad* (Santiago: Alfabeta for UNICEF, 1978), 615–48; Edda Gaviola A. et al., *Queremos votar en las próximas elecciones: Historia del movimiento femenina chileno, 1913–1952* (Santiago: Centro de Análisis y Difusión de la Condición de la Mujer, 1986).

2. Paul, "Amanda Labarca," 24.

3. Gaviola A., *Queremos votar*, 35. On women's clubs of the period, see, Felícitas Klimpel, *La mujer chilena (El aporte femenino al progreso de Chile), 1910–1960* (Santiago: Andrés Bello, 1962), 235–40.

4. See Martina Barros de Orrego, *Recuerdos de mi vida* (Santiago: Orbe, 1942), 60–67, 92, 102–3.

5. Barros de Orrego, *Recuerdos de mi vida* 290, 342–47. Late nineteenth-century evening *tertulias* in the homes of the social and political elite were the means of socialization for politicians and men of letters. Married women with recognized social rank opened their homes for a weekly meeting to discuss art, politics, and literature. The gatherings gave them an opportunity to hear the men and to become acquainted with ideas and personalities. It remains unclear to what extent women themselves participated in the exchange. See *Recuerdos*, 169–82, 246–50, 285. See also Amanda Labarca H., *¿A donde va la mujer?* (Santiago: Extra, 1934), 141, 144–47; Roxane [Elvira Santa Cruz de Ossa], "La dignificación del trabajo de la mujer," *Revista Femenina* (Santiago) 1, 1 (1924). In opposition was *El Diario Ilustrado* and *La Unión*. See Gaviola A., *Queremos votar*, 35.

6. For the opening of a branch in Talca on 17 September 1918, see *Evolución* (Santiago) 2, 18 (26, 1921): 3.

7. Labarca H., *¿A donde va la mujer?* 129–31, 136, 141–47.

8. Sra. Jesús Palacios de Díaz, "El Club de Señoras en Santiago de Chile," *Revista de Derecho, Historia y Letras* 69 (May 1921): 70–72. In 1931 the Club made a public statement that its members would get rid of unnecessary belongings to help alleviate the economic crisis. See *Nosotras* 1, 3 (1931): 2.

9. *Primera Serie de Conferencias Dadas en el Club de Señoras,* 1925 (Santiago: Zamoraso y Caperán, 1926).

10. Labarca, *¿A donde va la mujer?* 135, 161–65. Labarca's information is unclear on whether the Círculo annexed itself or merged into the Council.

11. *Pan American Conference of Women* (Baltimore: National League of Women Voters, 1922), 80. The official representatives were Graciela Mandujano and Sra. Beltram Mathieu, wife of the Chilean ambassador to Washington. Two university students and the representatives of the National Progressive Party also joined.

12. Chile, Cámara de Diputados, *Boletín de Sesiones Extraordinarias,* October 1917, 57–61, 75. Undurraga also supported reforms in the Civil Code.

13. *El Ferrocarril* (Santiago), 16 Nov. 1875, 1; 21 Nov. 1875, 2.

14. Gaviola A., *Queremos votar,* 34–35.

15. See *Acción Femenina* 1, 1 (1922): 23; 1, 2 (1922): 19–21; 1, 3 (1922): 18–22; 1, 10 (1923): 14.

16. "Nosotras, 1917," in *¿A dónde vá la mujer?* 125–32.

17. Gaviola A., *Queremos votar,* 19. Barros de Orrego was a conservative feminist. She believed in female intellectual ability but granted men physical and mental superiority. Women "have moral forces never equaled by man." See Barros de Orrego, *Recuerdos de mi vida,* 266. See also editorial, "¿Avanza el movimiento feminista?" *Revista Femenina* 1, 2 (July 1924): 3.

18. For a discussion of the outcome of this and subsequent bills, see chapter 6.

19. *La Voz Femenina* (Santiago) 1, 1 (1916): 1; 1, 2 (1916): 2; 1, 3 (1916): 2. Only three numbers have survived in the National Library of Chile.

20. Sombra [pseud.], "Feminismo, feminidad y hominismo," *Zig-Zag,* 17 Nov. 1917.

21. Josefa Gili de Peláez [pseud. Teresa de Aragón], *Orientaciones de la mujer ante el porvenir de la raza* (Valparaíso: Roma, 1923). Gili, wife of the director of *El Mercurio* of Valparaíso, believed Chilean women were unprepared to exercise their civic duties and that education and protection of working women were more desirable goals for social activists.

22. Gaviola A., *Queremos votar,* 36. According to Labarca, the Council formally proposed eliminating all legal obstacles to women's activities and called for female suffrage. Amanda Labarca, "Evolución femenina," in *Desarrollo de Chile en la primera mitad del siglo* xx, 2 vols. (Santiago: Editorial Universitaria, 1953), 1:119.

23. Labarca, "Evolución femenina," passim; Gaviola A., *Queremos votar,* 35.

24. *Acción Femenina* 1, 11 (1923): 3–5.

25. *Acción Femenina* 1, 3 (1922): 4; 1, 7 (1923): 4.

26. Juan Ignacio León Noguera, *Situación jurídica de la mujer* (Santiago: La Ilustración, 1921), 18–19, 20–36; Oscar Alvarez A., "Al margen del feminismo," *Acción Femenina* 1, 1 (1922): 18–20; Alejandro Valdés Riesco, *La mujer ante las leyes chilenas: Injusticias y reformas que se imponen* (Santiago: La Ilustración, 1922), 59–66.

27. Gaviola A., *Queremos votar,* 36. Clergyman Clovis Montero was an enthusiastic supporter of female suffrage. In 1922 and 1923 he gave speeches to Catholic audiences in support of women's suffrage. See *Acción Femenina* 1, 4 (1922): 21; 1, 11 (1923): 11.

28. See Labarca, *¿A dónde va la mujer?* 135; *Evolución Ascendente* 2, 18 (1921). Women's

religious associations were better organized by this time. In 1924 the Asociación de la Juventud Femenina Católica claimed to have 105 centers in the nation, and the Asociación Cristiana Femenina had just opened a new club center. See *Revista Femenina*, 1, 2 (1924): 3.

29. *Evolución* 1, 1 (1920). A second article was published in *Evolución Ascendente* 1, 13 (1920).

30. *Evolución Ascendente*, 1, 14 (1920): 5; 1, 15 (1920): 1; 2, 16 (1921): 1. The article ended in 2, 20 (1921): 1.

31. *Evolución Ascendente* 2, 18 (1921): 4.

32. *Acción Femenina* 1, 5 (1923): 2–3.

33. *Acción Femenina* 1, 5 (1922): 8–10; 1, 2 (1922): 19–21; 1, 11 (1923): 3–5.

34. *Acción Femenina* 1, 4 (1922): 3–4. By February 1923 the journal had correspondents in twelve cities, including La Serena, Valparíso, and Viña del Mar. The party was strongest in Concepción. See 1, 9 (1923): 1–2.

35. "¿Que clase de feminismo defendemos y por que?" *Acción Femenina* 1, 1 (1922): 17.

36. C. S. La R. [César A. Sangüeza La Rivera], "La mujer en la política," *Acción Femenina* 1, 8 (1923): 8–9; idem, "La mujer en la política y el hogar," *Acción Femenina* 1, 7 (1923): 16. He believed that "a unanimity of the highest and most prestigious personalities of the country supported female suffrage."

37. *Revista Femenina* 1, 1 (1924).

38. *Revista Femenina* 1, 1 (1924): 21. During this second period *Revista Femenina* published articles supporting women's economic independence, equal pay for equal work, and the new role of women in professional activities such as nursing, child care, and foreign affairs.

39. "Aspiraciones femeninas a la plenitud de los derechos," *El Mercurio* (Santiago), 11 Oct. 1924; Jesús Mena de Ruiz Tagle, "Unión Patriótica de Mujeres de Chile," *El Mercurio*, 17 Oct. 1924. See also 4 Oct. 1923; 18 Oct. 1924. Jesús was a name used by Chilean women.

40. The model for *garçonismo* was the novel *La garçonne* by French feminist writer Victor Margueritte. See review of the book and comments on women following this fashion in *El Mercurio*, 4 Mar. 1923, 5; 14 Oct. 1924, 20.

41. Roxane, "La mujer chilena y la política," *El Mercurio* (Santiago), 2 Mar. 1924; "El feminismo y la política chilena," *El Mercurio* (Santiago), 8 June 1924; María Eugenia Martínez, "La política y las mujeres," *El Mercurio* (Santiago), 4 Mar. 1923; Graciela Mandujano, "Sobre feminismo y politiquerías," *El Mercurio* (Santiago), 10 June 1924.

42. Gaviola A., *Queremos votar*, 37. Other women's associations founded during the early 1920s were either charitable and Catholic or else cultural in character. See Klimpel, *La mujer*, 239. There is some discrepancy in the sources on the name of the Partido Femenino Democrático. *Voz Femenina* used this name, not Partido Demócrata Femenino.

43. *Voz Femenina* 1, 1 (1932): 3. Subsequent information on Bando Femenino's activities are found in this issue.

44. *Unión Femenina de Chile* 1, 1 (1934): 2.

45. "Unión Femenina de Chile: Sus finalidades, su organización," in Delia Ducoing de Arrate [Isabel Morel], *Charlas femeninas* (Viña del Mar: Stock, 1930).

46. Until the 1920 election male votes were restricted. The nation was governed by an elite called *fronda aristocrática* [aristocratic frond]. See Federico G. Gil, *The Political System of Chile* (Boston: Houghton Mifflin, 1966); Julio Heise G., *Historia de Chile: El período parlamentario, 1861–1925* (Santiago: Andrés Bello, 1974), vol. 2 of this work was published as *El período parlamentario, 1861–1925: Democracia y gobierno representativo en el período parlamentario* (Santiago: Universitaria, 1982); Paul W. Drake, *Socialism and Populism in Chile, 1932–1952* (Urbana: Univ. of Illinois Press, 1978); Brian Loveman, *Chile: The Legacy of Hispanic Capitalism* (New York: Oxford Univ. Press, 1979); Ben G. Burnett, *Political Groups in Chile: The Dialogue between Order and Change* (Austin: Univ. of Texas Press, 1970). A good survey of Chile's "social question" is Virginia Krezminski F., "Alessandri y 'la cuestión social,'" in Claudio Orrego V. et al., *Siete ensayos sobre Arturo Alessandri Palma* (Santiago: Instituto Chileno de Estudios Humanísticos, 1977), 165–258. For Alessandri, see Ricardo Donoso, *Alessandri: Agitador y demoledor,* 2 vols. (Mexico City: Fondo de Cultura Económica, 1952); Robert J. Alexander, *Arturo Alessandri: A Biography,* 2 vols. (New Brunswick: Rutgers Univ. Latin American Institute, 1977).

47. Esteban Mena R., *La mujer y sus derechos* (Valparaíso: Imp. Royal, 1931), passim.

48. *Nosotras* 1, 1 (1931): 3–5.

49. *Nosotras* 2, 35 (1933): 8; 2, 36 (1933): 6. Unión Femenina de Chile sponsored lectures and training courses for women, provided legal and medical services for members of limited means, and participated in several charitable drives.

50. See *Nosotras* issues of 2, 32 (1932): 21; 2, 46 (1933): 4; *Unión Femenina de Chile* 1, 1 (1934): 3.

51. *Nosotras* 1, 4 (1931): 1, 3; 1, 6 (1931): 3; 1, 10 (1931): 3; 1, 12 (1931): 7; 1, 13 (1931): 3, 8. Among the topics discussed were employment, centralization and municipal self-administration, the value of Chilean currency, Araucanians (Mapuches) and their land problem, and needleworkers' salaries. See 1, 16 (1932): 8, 1, 18 (1932): 10.

52. *Nosotras* 1, 1 (1931): 3. These may have been the ideas of Delia Ducoing, who was the magazine's editor.

53. *Nosotras* 2, 33 (1933): 7. See protest for the unjust judicial decision against a female labor leader in Magallanes in 1, 18 (1932): 10; 1, 20 (1932): 8.

54. *Nosotras* 1, 23 (1932): 1, 3. Graciela Lacoste, a successful feminist leader in the mid-1930s, wrote on behalf of the socialist regime, asking her readers not to confuse socialism and communism. The editorial regretted that socialists "had not included women . . . as a new factor in the social order." See also 1, 24 (1932): 3.

55. *Nosotras* 1, 5 (1931): 4.

56. *Nosotras* 2, 33 (1933): 3.

57. *Nosotras* 1, 1 (1931): 5; 1, 2 (1931): 4; 1, 5 (1931): 3; 1, 14 (1931): 3; 1, 16 (1932): 1; 1, 18 (1932): 8; 1, 25 (1932): 1, 5; 2, 36 (1933): 6.

58. Ducoing, *Charlas femeninas.*

59. "Feminismo," in Ducoing, *Charlas femeninas,* 181–84.

60. "El derecho al sufragio" and "Extensión cultural," in Ducoing, *Charlas femeninas,* 56–59, 65–68.

61. *Nosotras* 1, 8 (1931): 4.

62. See, for example, *Nosotras* 1, 20 (1932): 3; 1, 21 (1932): 4; 2, 28 (1932): 4; 2, 34

(1933): 1; 1, 22 (1932): 4; 2, 28 (1932): 4; 2, 47 (1933): 1; 3, 53 (1933): 3, 6–7; 3, 55 (1934): 3.
In May 1932 (1, 22): 4, she wrote an open letter to Muna Lee Muñoz Marín, correcting
misconceptions on Chilean suffrage printed in *Equal Rights*, a feminist journal published in Washington DC.

63. *Nosotras* 1, 17 (1932): 8; 2, 46 (1933): 3.

64. *Voz Femenina: Organo de Defensa de los Derechos de la Mujer Chilena* 1, 1 (1932).
The director was Elvira Rogat. In 1933 *Nosotras* mentioned the magazine, stating "it
had a short life." See *Nosotras* 2, 46 (1933): 3. The party had its own headquarters and
a library.

65. *Nosotras* 2, 36 (1933): 7; 2, 37 (1933): 7; 2, 38 (1933): 6; *Unión Femenina de Chile* 1,
1 (1934): 3.

66. *Nosotras* 2, 37 (1933): 3; 2, 38 (1933): 5, 6. This represented a compromise among
differing opinions.

67. *El Mercurio* (Santiago), 11 Mar. 1933, editorial.

68. *El Mercurio* (Santiago), 10 Mar. 1933, 3; *Nosotras* 2, 40 (1933): 3.

69. *Nosotras* 2, 43 (1933): 5.

70. Comité pro-Derechos de la Mujer, *Programa de igualdad civil, política, social y
económica de la mujer chilena* (Santiago: Cultura, 1941), passim. *La Mujer Nueva* 2, 21
(1938); 3, 27 (1941). Among the committee's honorary presidents were Amanda Labarca
and Josefina Dey de Castillo.

71. *Unión Femenina de Chile* 1, 5 (1934): 4–5; *Nosotras* 2, 39 (1933): 7; *Unión Femenina de Chile* 1, 1 (1934): 1; *Nosotras* 3, 54 (1933): 1.

72. *Unión Femenina de Chile* 1, 6 (1934): 1, 5, 7.

73. *Nosotras* 3, 55 (1934): 6; *El Mercurio* (Valparaíso), 19 Nov. 1935, 9. Legión Femenina de América was founded by Ecuadorean sociologist and educator Rosa Borjas de
Icaza and introduced in Chile by Ducoing. On 20 November *El Mercurio* reported "a
hundred or so" members. See p. 9.

74. *Nosotras* 3, 55 (1933): 11; 5, 65 (1935): 14.

75. *Nosotras* 4, 60 (1934): 6–7; 4, 64 (1935): 7.

76. *Nosotras* 4, 61 (1935): 11. See also *El Mercurio* (Valparaíso), 3 Nov. 1936. This association was described as a purely feminine organization reflecting the subtle character
of women. Its activities denoted "a maternal fiber," and its cause was that of all ailing
humanity.

77. See also *Nosotras* 3, 56 (1934); 4, 58 (1934): 5; 4, 59 (1934).

78. *Nosotras* 4, 64 (1935): 9; 5, 65 (1935): 16.

79. *El Mercurio* (Valparaíso), 19 and 20 Nov. 1936. At this time, Legión Femenina
had nuclei in Talca, Concepción, Chillán, and Penco.

80. *El Mercurio* (Valparaíso), 4 Dec. 1935, 15. The rules of the association were drawn
this day in an assembly presided over by the president of the Radical Assembly of Santiago, Víctor Salas Romo; *La Mujer Nueva* 1, 7 (1936): 8.

81. Klimpel, *La mujer chilena*, 121.

82. *Política Feminista* (Valparaíso) 1, 1 (1931) to 1, 5 (1932). It was described as the
"official organ of the Liberal Democratic Feminine Youth of Valparaíso."

83. *El Mercurio* (Santiago), 2 Jan. 1936.

84. *Acción Femenina* 4, 1 (1934): 10–12.

85. This process is well explained in an undated three-page leaflet printed by Acción Nacional de Mujeres de Chile. See "Acción Nacional de Mujeres de Chile."

86. *El Mercurio* (Santiago), 15 June 1935, 15; 21 June 1; 22 June 15; 23 June 5 and 29.

87. Bernardo Gentilini, *Acerca del feminismo* (Santiago: Apostolado de la Prensa, 1929).

88. *Voz Femenina* 1, 1 (1935). Fifteen numbers are available, running through January 1936.

89. *Voz Femenina* 1, 7 (1935): 1.

90. *Voz Femenina* 1, 4 (1935): 4; 1, 11 (1935): 2.

91. *Voz Femenina* 1, 5 (1935): 2.

92. *Acción Femenina* 4, 1 (1934): 3.

93. *Acción Femenina* 4, 6 (1935): 10–11; 4, 7 (1935): 1; 4, 8 (1935): 3, 7, 9; 4, 9 (1935): 13. This journal welcomed writers and themes as diverse as María Lacerda de Moura, a Brazilian feminist writing on Mussolini and his policy on women; Argentine communist Juan Lazarte, writing on the economic independence of women; interviews with the president of the female branch of the Liberal Party; and excerpts from a book on gender relations by French sociologist André Lorulat. Gabriela Mistral, Carlos Vaz Ferreira, and Alfonsina Storni also published there.

94. *Acción Femenina* 4, 1 (1934): 26.

95. "Mal remediable . . . ?" *Acción Femenina* 4, 3 (1934): 1. The journal became very politicized in the ensuing two years.

96. *Acción Femenina* 4, 5 (1935): 3–4.

97. *Acción Femenina* 4, 9 (1935): 24; 4, 12 (1935): 48, 50, 54.

98. *Acción Femenina* 6, 20 (1937): 4, 18–19, 33–34; issue of March 1937, lacking volume number, pp. 4–5; 6, 21 (1937): 9, 23; 6, 22 (1937): 11–12; 6, 23 (1937): 18; 7, 28 (1938): 4; 7, 29 (1938): 14–15.

99. *Acción Femenina* 5, 17 (1936); 5, 28 (1937); 7, 24 (1937).

100. *Acción Femenina* 6, 24 (1937), editorial.

101. *Acción Femenina* 7, 38 (1938); 6, 28 (1939), editorial.

102. *El Mercurio* (Santiago), 19 June 1935, 3; *La Mujer Nueva* 1, 11 (1936): 8. It was not organized until October 1936.

103. *El Mercurio* (Valparaíso), 18, 26 Nov. 1935. One Partido Demócrata Femenino was reported by *El Mercurio* of Valparaíso on 9 Dec. 1935.

104. *El Mercurio* (Valparaíso), 30 Oct. 1936, 8; 11 and 15 Nov. 1936, 8.

105. *La Mujer Nueva* 1, 3 (1936); 3. See also 1, 5 (1936): 2, 4; 1, 7 (1936), editorial, 4; 1, 12 (1936): 1; 2, 15 (1937): 7; 3, 35 (1940): 2. MEMCH took Unión Femenina de Chile to task not only because the latter had not invited MEMCH to an exhibition of women's work, but because Unión showed that women worked but did not underline how little they earned. See 1, 9 (1936): 5.

106. See *La Mujer Nueva* 1, 8 (1936): 4–7.

107. Elena Caffarena de Jiles, "Emancipación económica," *La Mujer Nueva* 1, 2 (1935): 2. See also MEMCH: *Antología para una historia del movimiento femenino en Chile* (Santiago: Minga, n.d.), 34.

108. Marta Vergara, *Memorias de una mujer irreverente* (Santiago: Zig-Zag, 1961). She became a communist admirer and eventually joined the Party. After she traveled to the United States in the early 1940s, however, she had a change of heart and left the Party.

109. *Estatutos del Movimiento Pro-Emancipación de las Mujeres de Chile* (Santiago: Valparaíso, n.d.).

110. *La Mujer Nueva* 3, 27 (1941): 2.

111. *La Mujer Nueva* 1, 12 (1936): 1; 1, 13 (1937): 3; 2, 16 (1937): 8; 2, 18 (1937): 2, 6, 7; 2, 23 (1939): 4.

112. *La Mujer Nueva* 3, 27 (1941). This issue was devoted to the debates and principles adopted in the second national congress.

113. *La Mujer Nueva* 3, 26 (1940): 3.

114. *Nosotras* 1, 4 (1931): 1. See also Gaviola A., *Queremos votar,* 48–49.

115. *Acción Femenina* 4, 3 (1934), editorial; 6, 5 (1935): 3–4; 4, 35 (1935): 9. For women who advocated participation in the national elections, see *Acción Femenina* 4, 2 (1934): 6.

116. In 1931 a *balmacedista* women's group (admirers of the ideology of former president Manuel Balmaceda) was organized in Valparaíso. It published an ephemeral newspaper, *Política Feminista.* In March 1932 the group protested the literacy requirement as a "crack of the oligarchy's whip" that disqualified working women. See *Política Feminista* 1, 4 (1932): 1.

117. *El Diario Ilustrado* 2 Mar. 1935, 10; 3 Apr. 1935, 9; 5 Apr. 1935, 3; 6 Apr. 1935, 15.

118. Chile, Dirección General de Estadística, *Estadística Chilena* 8, 8 (1935): 320–23. Among men, 39 percent of potential voters cast their votes. See Gaviola A., *Queremos votar,* 61–62. For political cartoons of this issue, see *Topaze* 3, 141 (1935); 3, 142 (1935); 3, 143 (1935); *El Mercurio* (Santiago), 7 Apr. 1935.

119. *Voz Femenina* 1, 1 (1935): 2.

120. *Voz Femenina* 1, 5 (1935): 3; 1, 7 (1935): 1; 1, 15 (1936): 1.

121. Ajax, "La mujer cívica," *Zig-Zag,* 20 Apr. 1935.

122. *El Diario Ilustrado,* 9 Apr. 1935, 3.

123. *Acción Femenina* 4, 6 (1935): 3–4. See also Vergara, *Memorias,* 111.

124. *Acción Femenina* 4, 6 (1935): 19–21.

125. *Acción Femenina* 5, 14 (1936): 19–22; *La Mujer Nueva* 1, 11 (1936): 4; Gaviola A., *Queremos votar,* 51–52.

126. *La Mujer Nueva* 1, 7 (1936): 1.

127. Chile, Cámara de Diputados, *Boletín* 2 (1936): 601.

128. Lucy, "Siempre las mujeres," *El Mercurio* (Valparaíso), 18 Nov. 1936, 3.

129. Interview with Gabriela Mistral, *El Mercurio* (Valparaíso), 2 Dec. 1936.

130. Francisco Walker Linares, "Igualdad para la mujer empleada," *El Mercurio* (Valparaíso), 4 Dec. 1936, 3.

131. Chile, Cámara de Diputados, *Boletín* 2 (1936): 1824; *La Mujer Nueva* 1, 12 (1936): 1; 1, 13 (1937): 6.

132. Vergara, *Memorias,* 160–61.

133. *Defensa de la Acción de Voluntades Femeninas* (Santiago, n.d.), passim.

134. Gaviola A., *Queremos votar,* 62–63; Klimpel, *La mujer chilena,* 116.

135. *Acción Femenina* 12, 36 (1938); 13, 38 (1939); *La Mujer Nueva,* June 1941 [no vol. no.], 3.

136. Chile, Dirección General de Estadística, *Estadística Chilena* 8 (1935): 320–23; *La Mujer Nueva* 3, 25 (1940): 8; *La Mujer Nueva,* June 1941, 3.

137. John Reese Stevenson, *The Chilean Popular Front* (Philadelphia: Univ. of Pennsylvania Press, 1942).

138. *La Mujer Nueva* 2, 21 (1938): 2.

139. Arturo Olavarría Bravo, *Chile entre dos Alessandri* (Santiago: Nascimento, 1962), 474–76; Klimpel, *La mujer chilena,* 114–16. The intendent [*intendente*] was the real governing power in a province. The intendent had to be a registered voter, and no woman was able to occupy that post before 1949.

140. *La Mujer Nueva* 3, 27 (1941): 7; Paz Covarrubias, "El movimiento feminista chileno," in Covarrubias and Franco, *Chile: Mujer y sociedad,* 633.

141. *Acción Femenina* 12, 36 (1938): 6; 12, 38 (1939): 35.

142. *La Mujer Nueva* 3, 27 (1941): 1 ff.

143. Vergara, *Memorias,* 169–71.

144. Chile, Biblioteca Nacional Sección Referencias Críticas, Archivo Joaquín Edwards Bello, box 96. Her campaign motto was "Elena Doll de Díaz does not promise anything. Her past guarantees her performance."

145. Ibid.

146. *La Mujer Nueva,* June 1941 [no vol. no.], 3.

147. Personal interview with Elena Caffarena and Blanca Poblete, Santiago, 1985; Klimpel, *La mujer chilena,* 92–100.

Chapter 10 : Women's Politics and Suffrage in Uruguay

1. José P. Barrán and Benjamín Nahum, *El Uruguay del novecientos,* vol. 1 of *Batlle, los estancieros y el imperio británico* (Montevideo: Banda Oriental, 1979), 126–34; Silvia Rodríguez Villamil, *Las mentalidades dominantes en Montevideo (1850–1900),* 2 vols. (Montevideo: Banda Oriental, 1968).

2. José Pedro Barrán and Benjamín Nahum, *Batlle, los estancieros y el imperio británico,* 7 vols. (Montevideo: Banda Oriental, 1979–86); Justino Zavala Muñiz, *Batlle: Héroe civil* (Mexico City: Fondo de Cultura Económica, 1945); Milton I. Vanger, *José Batlle y Ordóñez of Uruguay: The Creator of His Times, 1902–1907* (Cambridge: Harvard Univ. Press, 1963); Efraín González Conzi and Roberto B. Giudice, *Batlle y el batllismo,* 2d ed. (Montevideo: Medina, 1959); Domingo Arena, *Batlle y los problemas sociales en el Uruguay* (Montevideo: Claudio García, 1939); Isabel Pinto Vidal, *El batllismo, precursor de los derechos civiles de la mujer* (Montevideo: Talleres Gráficos BM, 1951). Pinto Vidal was among the active feminists of the 1920s and 1930s. On women's history and feminism, see Alba G. Cassina de Nogara, *Las feministas* (Montevideo: Instituto Nacional del Libro, 1989); Silvia Rodríguez Villamil and Graciela Sapriza, *Mujer, estado y política en el Uruguay del siglo* xx (Montevideo: Banda Oriental, 1984).

3. Abella de Ramírez has been placed in this chapter on grounds of her birth, education, intellectual formation, and strong family ties in Uruguay.

4. "Club de Señoras" and "La unión," in *Ensayos feministas* (Montevideo: El Siglo Ilustrado, 1965), 76–82. These essays were first published in La Plata in 1908, under the title *En pos de la justicia.*

5. *Nosotras,* a biweekly, began publication in La Plata in June 1902. It apparently survived through August or September 1904.

6. The freethinkers had a strong anticlerical bent and were regarded as experts on theosophy. See *Unión y Labor* 1, 6 (1910): 30.

7. María Abella de Ramírez, "Programa mínimo de reivindicaciones femeninas," in *Ensayos feministas,* 13–15.

8. *La Nueva Mujer* 1, 2 (1910): 4.

9. See *La Nueva Mujer* 1, 7 (1910), 5; 1, 2 (1910): 6, 13; 1, 13 (1911): 13. The membership of both centers is unknown.

10. The last issue available is no. 32, 15 May 1912.

11. *La Nueva Mujer* 1, 1 (1910): 4. One Argentine branch was founded in Tolosa. Abella established correspondence with the directors of Buenos Aires *Unión y Labor* in March 1910.

12. *La Nueva Mujer* 1, 7 (1910); 1, 8 (1910): 8; 1, 11 (1910); 1, 14 (1911): 7–8; 2, 16 (10): 3; *Unión y Labor* 1, 9 (1910): 26. Dra. Cecilia Grierson was the honorary president of Federación Femenina Pan-Americana in 1910. It is unclear if this is the same organization as the Confederación Femenina Latino-Americana.

13. *Unión y Labor* 1, 11 (1910): 32; 2, 15 (1910): 2.

14. See Kristin Ruggiero, "Wives on 'Deposit': Internment and the Preservation of Husbands' Honor in Late Nineteenth-Century Buenos Aires," *Journal of Family History* 17, 3 (1992): 253–70.

15. *La Defensa de la Mujer* 1, 1 (1901): 1–7. Only three numbers (May–June 1901) survive at the National Library in Montevideo.

16. Letter from Hugo Castaño, founder of the newspaper *El Adelanto,* written and directed by women, Buenos Aires, 19 May 1901.

17. *La Defensa de la Mujer* 1, 3 (1901), passim.

18. Archivo General de la Nación, Montevideo, Archivo Paulina Luisi, box 257, folder 2, Uruguay, *Diario Oficial de Sesiones de la Cámara de Representates* 35, 2582, (1918): 285–95, hereafter cited as AGNM, PL.

19. Quotations from the editorials from *La Democracia,* the National Party journal, *El Bien,* a Catholic newspaper, and *El Siglo,* a conservative newspaper, during July 1914; Barrán and Nahum, *El Uruguay del novecientos,* 87–89.

20. AGNM, PL, box 257, folder 2, and box 250, folder 6. This group supported the activities of the Alianza Pro-Sufragio Femenino.

21. Justino E. Jiménez de Aréchaga, *El voto de la mujer: Su inconstitucionalidad* (Montevideo: Peña Hermanos, 1915), passim.

22. AGNM, PL, box 257, folder 2. The *Diario Oficial* ran all the constitutional debates. See also *Diario de Sesiones de la H. Convención N. Constituyente de la República Oriental del Uruguay* (1917), 4 vols. (Montevideo: Imp. Nacional, 1918). See 3:87–88 for the final discussion of the possibility of female suffrage.

23. Emilio Frugoni, "Los derechos políticos de la mujer," in *Los nuevos fundamentos* (Montevideo: Maximino García, 1919), 43–90.

24. Reported in *Unión y Labor* 3, 51 (1912): 17–18; emphasis added. Uruguayan deputy Daniel Muñoz also vilified women's rights.

25. Emilio Frugoni, "Los derechos políticos de la mujer," 66; AGNM, PL, box 257, folder 2.

26. Baltasar Brum, *Los derechos de la mujer: Reforma civil y política del Uruguay* (Montevideo: José María Serrano, 1923), 24–28. Nationalists were also opposed to the municipal vote. See AGNM, PL, box 257, folder 2.

27. AGNM, PL, box 257, folder 5; *El Día*, 18 Mar. 1917, 3.

28. Consejo Nacional de Mujeres del Uruguay, *Estatutos y reglamentos* (Montevideo: El Siglo Ilustrado, 1917).

29. *Acción Femenina* 1, 1 (1917): 1–5.

30. See *Acción Femenina* 1, 3 (1917), passim; 1, 4 (1917): 113–15; 1, 5 (1917): 158–60.

31. *Acción Femenina* 1, 6 (1917): 83.

32. *Acción Femenina* 2, 1 (1918): 13.

33. *Acción Femenina* 2, 3–4 (1918): 48–51.

34. Ibid., 80. For the first time in Uruguay, the orchestra providing music for the event was directed by a woman, Elizabeth S. de Michaelson Pacheco, a composer and a member of the National Council.

35. Fanny Carrió de Polleri, "Movimiento sufragista," speech reprinted in *Acción Femenina* 3, 18–19 (1919): 64–69.

36. AGNM, PL, box 257, folder 2; Alianza Uruguaya para el Sufragio Femenino, books 1 and 2 (4 Aug. 1919 through December 1921 and 9 May 1932 through 27 June 1934.

37. *Acción Femenina* 4, 27 (1920): 2–3; 4, 28–29 (1920): 58, 4, 30–31 (1920): 76.

38. *Acción Femenina* 4, 28–29 (1920): 61–63; 4, 30–31 (1920): 110–13.

39. *Acción Femenina* 6, 49 (1923): 50. A 1923 municipal vote bill met no success.

40. AGNM, PL, box 257, folder 2.

41. AGNM, PL, box 275, folder 2, no. 35; Alianza Uruguaya para el Sufragio Femenino. Alianza Uruguaya de Mujeres, 34–35.

42. Consejo Nacional de Mujeres, *Informe*, 86.

43. *Acción Femenina* 4, 37–39 (1922): 16; 5, 43–46 (1922): 68.

44. *Acción Femenina* 5, 43–46 (1922): 66–68; 5, 49 (1923): 35–37.

45. Brum, *Los derechos de la mujer*, 9–54 and passim.

46. *Acción Femenina* 5, 40–42 (1922): 36, 38–43; 5, 43–46 (1922): 65–68, 89–91.

47. *Acción Femenina* 2, 5–6 (1918): 114–16; Consejo Nacional de Mujeres del Uruguay, *Informe correspondiente al primer trienio, 1916–19 y Memoria correspondiente al ejercicio 1918–1919* (Montevideo: El Siglo Ilustrado, 1920), 29–33.

48. Consejo Nacional de Mujeres del Uruguay, *Informe*, 33–35, 52, 104; *Acción Femenina* 2, 5–6 (1918): 114–16; 4, 37–39 (1922): 5.

49. *Acción Femenina* 5, 43–46 (1922): 104.

50. Luisi was a socialist but rarely acted in concert with the Socialist Party. The Uruguayan government was happy to maintain cordial relations with such a well-known and prestigious figure and appointed her official representative of the nation to several international conferences, although she received little financial support. See Josefina Marpons, *Paulina Luisi: Una personalidad brillante y singular* (Buenos Aires: Torfano, 1950); Arturo Scarone, *Dra. Paulina Luisi: Datos biográficos hasta 1937* (Montevideo:

CISA, 1948); Asunción Lavrin, "Paulina Luisi: Pensamiento y escritura feminista," in Lou-Charnon-Deutsch, ed., *Estudios sobre escritoras hispánicas en honor de Georgina Sabat-Rivers* (Madrid: Castalia, 1992), 156–72.

51. AGNM, PL, box 252, folder 1, no. 3. Letter from Fanny Carrió de Polleri to Paulina Luisi.

52. AGNM, PL, box 250, private correspondence of Paulina Luisi, nos. 53 and 57. Letter to Paulina Luisi from Isabel Pinto Vidal, 7 Apr. 1922; Letter from Luisi to Isabel Pinto Vidal, 14 April 1922. See Pinto Vidal, *El batllismo.*

53. AGNM, PL, box 250, folder 6, nos. 6–10. Undated letters, one of them from Catalina Castro de Quintela to Fanny C. de Polleri.

54. AGNM, PL, box 350, folder 6, nos. 66, 72, 81, 88, 91, 100, 101.

55. AGNM, PL, box 257, folder 4, nos. 30, 37, 45, 46.

56. AGNM, PL, box 252, folder 1, no. 8, *La Mañana,* 16 Dec. 1923; no. 15, *El Día,* 12 Dec. 1923; Silvia Rodríguez Villamil and Graciela Sapriza, "Feminismo y política," *Hoy es Historia* 1, 4 (1984): 16–31.

57. *Acción Femenina* 7, 50 (1924): 18–19.

58. AGNM, PL, box 250, folder 6, nos. 69, 72, statement by Luisi, Nov. 1925; no. 82, 84, letters to Paulina Luisi from Carolina Torres de Abellá, 22 Dec. 1925 and 2 Jan. 1926; no. 64, letter to Paulina Luisi from Catalina ("Cata") Castro de Quintela, 25 Oct. 1925; nos. 40, 51, letter from Catalina Castro de Quintela to Paulina Luisi, 20 May 1924. Josefina Marpons, who knew Luisi well as a friend, underlines that Luisi had a "rough character" [*temperamento áspero*], talked loudly, loved polemics, and could make people feel uncomfortable. On the other hand, she had a gift for organizing women and a penchant for justice.

59. AGNM, PL, box 250, folder 6, nos. 82 and 84, letters of 22 Dec. 1925 and 2 Jan. 1926 to Paulina Luisi from Carolina Torres de Abellá; Alianza Uruguaya para el Sufragio Femenino, Libros de Actas, 59–61, meeting of 17 Dec. 1925.

60. AGNM, PL, box 251, folder 1, no. 29, papers of the Alianza Uruguaya de Mujeres, December 1926; box 252, folder 1, nos. 35 and 36, *El Día* and *La Mañana,* issues of 23 Jan. 1929.

61. AGNM, PL, box 252, folder 1, no. 30, clipping from *El Imparcial,* 23 Oct. 1927.

62. The Council unsuccessfully requested that a woman be considered for a position on the national welfare committees, such as the Consejo de Asistencia Pública or the Patronato de Delincuentes, both of which were steered by men. It also acted on behalf of Ofelia Machado Bonet, who had been denied the right to act as a notary.

63. AGNM, PL, box 257, folder 4, no. 13, *Caras y Caretas,* 20 Aug. 1921.

64. AGNM, PL, box 257, folder 4, no. 14. Letter published in *El Día, La Mañana,* and several other papers.

65. AGNM, PL, box 257, folder 5, no. 7, *El País,* 5 July 1921. For Irureta Goyena's reforms to the Penal Code, see chapter 5.

66. AGNM, PL, box 257, folder 5, no. 11, *El Día,* 21 July.

67. AGNM, PL, box 257, folder 5, no. 13, *El Día,* 17 July 1921; *Acción Femenina* 4, 34 (1920): 173–74.

68. AGNM, PL, box 250, folder 6, no. 24.

69. AGNM, PL, box 257, folder 5, no. 15, *Página Blanca* 6, 62 (1921). See quotations in Rodríguez Villamil and Sapriza, "Feminismo y política," 16–31.

70. AGNM, PL, box 252, folder 1, nos. 18 and 19, *Justicia* 14 Jan. 1924; *El Siglo*, 16 Jan. 1924.

71. AGNM, PL, box 257, folder 5, no. 21, *El Día*, 13 July 1924; no. 22, *La Razón*, 17 July 1924.

72. Brum was satisfied with his party's feminist accomplishments. See *El Día*, 24 Jan. 1924, 6.

73. Rodríguez Villamil and Sapriza, "Feminismo y política," 27.

74. AGNM, PL, box 252, folder 1, no. 35. Reports in *El Día*, 23 Jan. 1929, *La Mañana*, 23 Jan. 1929, and *La Prensa* (Buenos Aires) 30 Nov. 1928, 28. See chapters 8 and 9 for the Argentine and Chilean situations.

75. Alianza Uruguaya y Consejo Nacional de Mujeres, *La mujer uruguaya reclama sus derechos políticos* (Montevideo, [1930?]). Since April 1929 the Alianza had approached all female organizations in Uruguay — as well as those of mixed gender membership — calling for their support. See AGNM, PL, box 258, folder 1, no. 19, *La Mañana* 29 Apr. 1929.

76. *Acción Femenina* 3, 2 (1919): 27–58.

77. AGNM, PL, box 257, folder 5, nos. 26, 28, 29, reported in *El Ideal* (Montevideo), 6 Feb. 1929; *El Día* (Montevideo) 10 Feb. and 16 Mar. 1929. This case is similar to that of Dra. Julieta Lanteri in 1911 Argentina. See chapter 8.

78. AGNM, PL, box 257, folder 6, nos. 40, 41, *El Imparcial* 3 and 13 Oct. 1929; folder 7, nos. 28, 35, 6 and 7 Dec. 1929.

79. AGNM, PL, box 257, folder 5, nos. 39, 41, 43, 44, 45, 46, 48, 49, 50, 51; folder 7, nos. 1, 3, 4, 5, 7, 13, 22. These items review statements in *El Imparcial, El Oribista, El Ideal, La Prensa* (Buenos Aires), *El Día, La Opinion*, and *La Tarde* of Salto, throughout November 1929. *El Ideal* was a dissident *batllista* newspaper founded by José Batlle y Ordóñez.

80. AGNM, PL, box 257, folder 7, nos. 42 and 44, *El Imparcial*, 13 and 14 Dec. 1929; folder 6, no. 44, *El Imparcial*, 6 Dec. 1929; box 257, folder 5, no. 35, *El Día*, 6 Nov. 1929; box 252, folder 1, no. 46, 47.

81. AGNM, PL, box 257, folder 5, nos. 35, 36, 38, *El Día*, 6 Nov. 1929. Also reported in *La Mañana*, 8 Nov. 1929 and commented on in *El Día* in its editorial of 8 Nov. 1929.

82. AGNM, PL, box 257, folder 7, no. 10, statement in *La Tarde* of Salto, 23 Nov. 1929.

83. AGNM, PL, box 257, folder 5, nos. 30, 31.

84. Uruguay, Cámara de Representantes, *Diario de Sesiones* 381 (Dec. 1932–Mar. 1933): 132.

85. AGNM, PL, box 257, folder 5. In 1919 Herrera published a series of articles in a traditional women's publication, *Vida Femenina*, eulogizing North American women and the advance of the female sex in that country, but said nothing about change for Uruguayan women. See *Vida Femenina* (Montevideo) 2, 6 (1919).

86. J. M., "El voto femenino," in *Juventud* (Organo de la Asociación de Estudiantes Católicos de Salto, Uruguay) 1, 6 (1932): 2.

87. *América Nueva* 1, 1 (1932), editorial, 4; 1, 4 (1932), editorial; 1, 7 (1933): 7. Several issues are available at the National Library of Montevideo.

88. "¿Votarán o no? *América Nueva* 1, 1 (1932): 4; Alberto Lasplaces, "El voto femenino," *América Nueva* (1933): 4.

89. We are informed that the Salto cell had forty-eight members in June 1930. See AGNM, PL, box 250, folder 6, no. 98, letter of 10 Oct. 1929; no. 100; box 250, folder 8, nos. 8, 13, 36, 40. For a letter to the Legislative Commission and two thousand supportive signatures, see no. 46, 4 May 1931, box 252, folder 3, no. 31.

90. AGNM, PL, box 257, folder 8, published in *El Imparcial*, 18 May 1930.

91. AGNM, PL, box 257, folder 8, no. 5, *La Razón* (Paysandú), 5 July 1930.

92. AGNM, PL, box 250, folder 8, no. 107, letter draft, 5 July 1932, addressed to the president of a feminist chapter in La Rocha. This source states that seventeen organizations had petitioned Congress for women's suffrage.

93. AGNM, PL, box 252, folder 1, no. 87, news in *El Imparcial*, 31 Mar. 1932.

94. Uruguay, Cámara de Representantes, *Diario de Sesiones* 381 (Dec. 1932–Mar. 1933): 97, 124–43.

95. Uruguay, Cámara de Representantes, *Diario de Sesiones* 380 (October 1932): 10–11. Speech by Sebastián Bouquet of the Colorado Party.

96. Uruguay, Cámara de Representantes, *Diario de Sesiones,* 381 (Dec. 1932–Mar. 1933): 125–40.

97. AGNM, PL, box 257, folder 8, no. 27, statements for *El Pueblo*, 22 Dec. 1932.

98. AGNM, PL, box 257, folder 8, nos. 22, 23, statements for *Crítica;* box 260, folder 1; AGNM, PL, box 257, folder 8; box 258, folder 1.

99. AGNM, PL, box 257, folder 8, no. 23, statements for *El Pueblo,* 21 Dec. 1932.

100. AGNM, PL, box 258, folder 1, no. 20, *El Pueblo,* 20 Jan. 1933.

101. AGNM, PL, box 258, folder 1, no. 36, *El Pueblo,* 15 Mar. 1934. Alvarez Vignoli de Demichelli wrote several works on women's rights, alcoholism, and *patria potestad* and collaborated in drafting the Código del Niño, especially the chapters on investigation of paternity and adoption.

102. *Ideas y Acción* 1, 1 (1933): 1–2.

103. See 5, 80 (1937), letter to Hector Payses Reyes.

104. AGNM, PL, box 257, folder 8, no. 28, statement published by *El Imparcial*, 15 Jan. 1933.

105. *Ideas y Acción* 1, 11 (1933): 2; 1, 12 (1933), editorial, and 4–5; 2, 28 (1934), editorial; 5, 75 (1937): 1, 2.

106. AGNM, PL, box 250, folder 8, nos. 45, 46. Correspondence between Sara Rey Alvarez and Paulina Luisi, who was in Madrid at the time, dated 23 Jan. 1933 and 6 Mar. 1933; *Ideas y Acción* 5, 79 (1937): 1.

107. See a defense of the reform of the Civil Code in *Ideas y Acción* 3, 64 (1936), and 6, 77 (1937): 2; March 1939, special issue. For other issues, see 1, 21 (1934); 5, 75 (1937). Alvarez Rey supported voluntary maternity but opposed abortion. See *Ideas y Acción* 3, 52 (1935); 3, 53 (1935); 5, 78 (1937).

108. *Ideas y Acción* 3, 52 (1935); 5, 76 (1937); 5, 78 (1937); 5, 76 (1937); 5, 83 (1937); 1, 15 (1934); 5, 76 (1937); 5, 79 (1937): 2, 11. *Ideas y Acción* always stood for the right to strike and emphasized the lower wages paid to women. See 4, 67 (1936); March 1939, special issue. Other topics discussed were the limitation of the extension of landownership, 1,

12 (1933), and the right of private educational institutions to exist and to teach subjects not available in official schools. This ideological position resulted from the administration's opposition to "popular universities" on the grounds that they taught Marxist doctrines. See 6, 77 (1937). Support of the rights of children and pacifism were also important ideological points. See 3, 64 (1936); and 3, 57 (1935): 1.

109. See AGNM, PL, box 257, folder 8, no. 32, report in *El Ideal.*

110. The report of twenty-five members of the Alianza is in AGNM, PL, box 250, folder 8, nos. 45–46 (1932, 1933); box 252, folder 1, nos. 185–88. This membership list is undated, but it is filed with materials dating no later than 1935.

111. On Baltasar Brum, see Juan Carlos Welker, *Baltasar Brum: Verbo y acción* (Montevideo: Imp. Letras, 1945).

112. AGNM, PL, box 257, folder 8, no. 30, report in *El Imparcial,* 2 May 1933.

113. *Ideas y Acción* 1, 23 (1934); 2, 28 (1934).

114. *Ideas y Acción* 1, 6 (1933): 1; 1, 8 (1933): 1; 1, 10 (1933); 1, 11 (1933); 5, 80 (1937). See also 3, 66 (1936).

115. See Uruguay, Dirección General de Estadística, *Síntesis estadística* (Montevideo, 1938), 26–27; *El Día,* 28 Mar. 1932, 7–8.

116. *El Día,* 29 Mar. 1938, 8.

117. Special issue, March 1939.

118. *La Vanguardia,* 31 Dec. 1932, 1. It compared the founders to the "grotesque types of Mistress Pankhurst."

119. AGNM, PL, box 257, folder 8, no. 25, *El Sol,* 22 Dec. 1932. "Timonil," writing for *El Sol,* believed that a female political organization [*agrupación política*] would only perpetuate the current "chaotic situation." See also AGNM, PL, box 260, folder 1, no. 96.

120. *América Nueva* (Montevideo) 1, 8 (1933), editorial; 1, 9 (1933), editorial.

121. Among the organizations active at the end of the 1930s were a Comité Nacional Femenino Batllista, founded in 1931 to support the party, and Comité de Reafirmación Democrática, an antifascist organization sending aid to republican Spain. Among the cultural clubs was Asociación Cultural Femenina. *El Día,* 5 Apr. 1938, 8; 6 Dec., 9; 17 Dec., 8. There was also a committee to support the International Feminine League for Peace and Freedom. See AGNM, PL, box 252, folder 5; box 253, folder 1. Professional women had founded the Acción Feminista de Mujeres Universitarias in 1935. See AGNM, PL, box 252, folder 7. Although I have not dealt with cultural organizations, a significant number of these women's clubs were founded in the 1930s in the three countries.

122. *El Día,* 2 Jan. 1936, 6. Dates for the foundation of this organization are given as 1933 and 1938. See *El Día,* 17 Dec. 1938, 8.

123. *El Día,* 3 Mar. 1938, 8; 8 Apr. 1936, 7; 3 May 1936, 8.

124. *El Día,* 12 Feb. 1936, 8.

125. *El Día,* 3 Apr. 1936, 9. A Feminine Conciliation Committee organized proletarian women, whose activities remain unknown. Needleworkers were also involved in the organization of the congress. See issue of 12 Apr., 7.

126. *El Día,* 8 Jan. 1936, 8; 12 Jan. 1936, 8.

127. *El Día,* 19 Apr. 1936, 8; 20 Apr., 6; 21 Apr., 8; 22 Apr., 8; 23 Apr., 8; 24 Apr., 8.

128. *El Día,* 9 Nov., 6. See issues for October, November, and December 1942. There

is news on female electoral activity in practically every issue. See, for example, 2 Oct. 6; 19 Oct., 6; 5 Nov., 7; 18 Nov., 7.

129. *El Día*, 29 Nov., 6.

130. *El Día*, 30 Nov., 5.

Epilogue

1. "La mujer en la política," *Acción Femenina* 1, 8 (1923): 18; "Declaración de principios: Agrupación Nacional de Mujeres de Chile," *Unión Femenina de Chile* 1, 5 (1934): 4-5.

2. "La mujer y la política," in Amanda Labarca, *¿A donde vá la mujer?* (Santiago: Extra, 1934), 226. Conservative groups in the 1930s also expressed their concern for the national destinies. See, for example, the 1937 statement of Chilean Acción de Voluntades Femeninas that their goal was "to remain in the service of any initiative related to the welfare of the nation, regardless of its source." *Defensa de Acción de Voluntades Femeninas* ([Santiago]: Comité Central, 1937), 16.

3. Alicia Moreau de Justo, "Nuestra política: Juicios de una espectadora," *Vida Femenina* 3, 27 (1935): 12-13, 16.

4. On immigration and nationalism, see James R. Scobie, *Buenos Aires: Plaza to Suburb, 1870-1910* (New York: Oxford Univ. Press, 1974), 237-44; Carl Solberg, *Immigration and Nationalism: Argentina and Chile, 1890-1914* (Austin: Univ. of Texas Press, 1970); José P. Barrán and Benjamín Nahun, *Un diálogo difícil: 1903-1910*, vol. 2 of *Batlle, los estancieros y el imperio británico* (Montevideo: Banda Oriental, 1981), 164-73. For a strong attack on feminism and an alien influence and a defense of traditional national culture, see Clodomiro Cordero, *Las sociedad argentina y la mujer* (Buenos Aires, 1916).

5. See, for example, Amanda Labarca describing Chilean feminism as "molded to our idiosyncrasy," "in accordance with our temperament," "different from those forged by women of the Saxon race." *¿A donde vá la mujer?* 138, 147.

6. K. Lynn Stoner, *From the House to the Streets: The Cuban Women's Movement for Legal Reform, 1898-1940* (Durham NC: Duke Univ. Press, 1991), 127-45; Francesca Miller, *Latin American Women and the Search for Social Justice* (Hanover NH: Univ. Press of New England, 1991), 68-109.

7. Jane S. Jaquette, ed., *The Women's Movement in Latin America: Feminism and the Transition to Democracy* (Boston: Unwyn Hyman, 1989); Jane S. Jaquette, "Women, Feminism and the Transition to Democracy in Latin America," *Latin America and the Caribbean Contemporary Record* 5 (1985-86): 843-62; Suzana Prates and Silvia Rodríguez Villamil, "Los movimientos sociales de mujeres en la transición a la democracia," in Carlos Filgueira et al., eds., *Movimientos sociales en el Uruguay de hoy* (Montevideo: CLACSO, CIESU, Banda Oriental, 1985), 158-95; Myrna Silva, Judith Astelarra, and Alicia Herrera, *Mujer, partidos políticos y feminismo* (Santiago: Documenta, 1985); María Elena Valenzuela, *Todas íbamos a ser reinas: La mujer en el Chile militar* (Santiago: Ediciones Chile y América, CESOC, 1987).

8. Alicia Moreau, *La mujer en la democracia* (Buenos Aires: El Ateneo, 1945), 198-99, 217.

9. Moreau, *La mujer,* 95–98.

10. See *Participación política de la mujer en el Cono Sur,* 2 vols. (Buenos Aires: Fundacion Federico Naumann, 1987); Adriana Muñoz Dálbora, *Fuerza feminista y democracia: Utopía a realizar* (Santiago: Documentas, 1987); Asunción Lavrin, "Unfolding Feminism: Spanish-American Women's Writings, 1970–1990," in Abigail J. Stewart and Domna Stanton, eds., *Feminist Scholarship: Thinking through the Disciplines* (Ann Arbor: Univ. of Michigan Press, 1995).

11. *Nuestra Tribuna* 1, 3 (1922): 2. "Posiblemente ha de ser la mujer la que andando el tiempo se interesará doblemente y con ahinco por el perfeccionamiento (tanto moral como material) de la raza; pues es ella, indiscutiblemente, la que siente más en sus entrañas a la humanidad, nadie mejor que la mujer, por lo tanto, para marcar orientaciones a la presente y futura generaciones." "Sea ella la luz del día, el verdadero génesis de un nuevo mundo."

12. "¿A donde va la mujer?" in *¿A donde va la mujer?* 65. "Me parece que las mujeres comprendemos estos problemas no sólo con la frialdad de la razón, sino con toda nuestra sangre palpitante de calor humano. Acaso porque somos más débiles, sufrimos más entrañablemente las mortales antinomias de este tipo de cultura [mayor respeto a la individualidad . . . comprensión de las necesidades familiares]. Y quien sufre más, es como un arco tenso: tiene mayores energías para dispararse a la lucha. He aquí por qué creo que la reacción, si no viene del lado de la mujer, no surgirá de parte alguna."

BIBLIOGRAPHY

For reasons of space, this bibliography will not include the long list of articles published in newspapers or magazines that constitutes one of the richest sources of information on gender relations, feminist issues, motherhood, and childhood. Although this omission is regrettably necessary, readers should be aware that journalism was the key forum for women's writings and for the debate on social reform and are advised to seek further materials in the newspapers and magazines listed below. References to specific articles are found in the notes, which contain materials not listed here. Throughout the text and notes, translations are my own.

The main libraries and archives consulted were

Argentina. Biblioteca Juan B. Justo; Biblioteca Nacional; Biblioteca Socialista; Biblioteca de la Academia de Ciencias Históricas; Biblioteca de la Universidad de La Plata; Biblioteca de la Facultad de Ciencias Económicas; Biblioteca de la Facultad de Filosofía y Letras; Archivo General de la Nación.

Chile. Biblioteca Nacional; Biblioteca del Congreso.

The Netherlands. International Institute of Social History, Amsterdam.

United States. Library of Congress, Washington DC; Columbus Library, OAS, Washington DC.

Uruguay. Archivo General de la Nación, Montevideo, and its special collection, Archivo Paulina Luisi; Biblioteca Nacional.

Newspapers

La Alborada, Santiago; *El Amigo del Pueblo,* Montevideo; *La Aurora,* Santiago; *La Aurora Feminista,* Santiago; *El Derecho a la Vida,* Montevideo; *El Despertar de los Trabajadores,* Iquique, Chile; *El Día,* Montevideo; *El Diario Ilustrado,* Santiago; *El Imparcial,* Santiago; *Humanidad Nueva,* Buenos Aires; *Ideas y Acción,* Montevideo; *Justicia,* Montevideo; *Juventud,* Salto, Uruguay; *El Mercurio,* Santiago and Valparaíso; *La Nación,* Buenos Aires; *Nuestra Tribuna,* Necochea, Argentina; *La Prensa,* Buenos Aires; *La Protesta,* Buenos Aires; *La Protesta Humana,* Buenos Aires; *La Reforma,* Santiago; *La Tierra: Semanario Anarquista,* Salto, Uruguay; *La Tribuna Popular,* Montevideo; *La Vanguardia,* Buenos Aires; *La Vanguardia,* Valparaíso; *La Voz del Obrero,* Montevideo; *Zig-Zag,* Santiago. Other newspapers are cited in the notes.

Magazines

Acción Femenina, Santiago; *Acción Femenina: Revista Mensual Ilustrada. Organo Oficial del Partido Cívico Femenino,* Santiago; *Acción Femenina,* Montevideo; *Almanaque del Trabajo,* Buenos Aires; *América Nueva,* Montevideo; *Boletín de la Asociación del Trabajo de Chile,* Santiago; *Boletín Mensual de Museo Social Argentino,* Buenos Aires; *El Búcaro Americano,* Buenos Aires; *La Camelia,* Buenos Aires; *La Defensa de la Mujer,* Montevideo; *Mujer!* Buenos Aires; *Mujeres de América,* Buenos Aires; *La Mujer Nueva,* Santiago; *Nosotras,* La Plata; *Nosotras,* Valparaíso; *Nuestra Causa,* Buenos Airs; *La Nueva Mujer,* La Plata; *La Ondina del Plata,* Buenos Aires; Pan American Union, *Bulletin,* Washington DC; *Revista Chilena,* Santiago; *Revista Chilena de Hijiene,* Santiago; *Revista de Derecho, Historia y Letras,* Buenos Aires; *Revista de Instrucción Primaria,* Valparaíso; *Revista Femenina,* Santiago; *Revista Socialista Internacional,* Buenos Aires; *Topaze,* Santiago; *Unión Femenina,* Valparaíso; *Unión Femenina de Chile,* Santiago; *Unión y Labor,* Buenos Aires; *La Vanguardia,* Buenos Aires; *Vida Femenina,* Buenos Aires; *Voz Femenina,* Santiago.

Official Sources

Actas de las sesiones plenarias de la Quinta Conferencia Internacional Americana. Santiago: Imprenta Universitaria, 1923.
Argentina. *Código civil argentino.* In *Códigos de la República Argentina.* Buenos Aires: Compañía Sudamericana de Billetes de Banco, 1901.
Argentina. *Divorcio: Debates en la Cámara de Diputados.* Buenos Aires: El Comercio, 1902.
———. *Tercer censo nacional de la República Argentina.* 10 vols. Buenos Aires: Rosso y Cía., 1916.
Argentina. Cámara de Diputados. *Diario de Sesiones.*
Argentina. City of Buenos Aires. *Year-Book of the City of Buenos Aires, 1910–11.*
Argentina. Departmento Nacional del Trabajo. *Anuario Estadístico* 42 (1917).
———. *Boletín.*
———. *Boletín Informativo,* 1934, 1935.
Argentina. Dirección General de Estadística de la Nación. *Boletín.* 1936.
Argentina. Provincia de Buenos Aires. *Anuario estadístico de la provincia de Buenos Aires.* Buenos Aires: Baiocco, 1926.
———. *Anuario estadístico de la provincia de Buenos Aires.* La Plata, 1943.
———. *Censo general de la ciudad de La Plata.* La Plata: La Popular, 1910.
———. Dirección General de Estadística. *Boletín,* 1924, 1936, 1943.
———. *Legislación del trabajo de la provincia de Buenos Aires.* La Plata: Impr. Oficiales, 1937.
Argentina. Provincia de Córdoba. Dirección General de Estadística. *Anuario correspondiente al año de 1925,* Córdoba: Penitenciaría, 1927.
Argentina. Provincia de Tucumán. *Anuario Estadístico, 1920.* Tucumán, 1920.
Argentina. Rosario de Santa Fé. *Anuario Estadístico de la ciudad de Santa Fé, 1929.*

————. *Tercer censo municipal.* Rosario, 1910.

Chile. *Anuario estadístico.* Santiago: Universo, 1916.

————. *Proyecto del Código del Trabajo y de la previsión social.* Santiago: Imp. Nacional, 1921.

————. *Sinopsis* Estadística i Jeográfica, 1902, 1905.

Chile. Cámara de Diputados. *Boletín.*

Chile. *Censo levantado el 28 de noviembre de 1907.* Santiago: Universo, 1908.

Chile. Comisión Central del Censo. *Resultados del X censo de la población efectuado el 27 de noviembre de 1930.* 3 vols. Santiago: Universo, 1931–35.

Chile. Dirección General de Estadística. *Estadística Chilena.*

Chile. Dirección General de Sanidad de Chile. *Boletín Sanitario.*

Chile. Liga Chilena de Higiene Social. *Contribución al estudio de las enfermedades sociales.* Santiago, 1925.

Chile. Ministerio de Bienestar Social. *Boletín.*

Chile. Ministerio de Higiene Asistencia, Prevision Social y Trabajo, *Boletín.*

Chile. Ministerio de Industrias y Obras Públicas. *Boletín de la Oficina de Trabajo.*

Pan American Conference of Women. Baltimore, 1922.

Proceedings and Report of the Columbus Day Conferences Held in Twelve American Countries. New York: Inter-American Press, 1926.

Uruguay. *Anuario estadístico.* Montevideo: Imp. Nacional, 1901–43.

————. *Censo municipal del departamento y de la ciudad de Montevideo.* Montevideo: Dirección General de Censos y Estados, 1892.

————. *Código Civil de la República Oriental del Uruguay.* Paris: Rosa Bouret, 1871.

————. *Código Civil de la República Oriental del Uruguay.* Vol. 2. of *Códigos de Uruguay anotados.* Colección Abadie-Santos. Montevideo: Imp. Moderna, 1942.

————. *Diario de sesiones de la H. Cámara de Representantes.*

————. *Diario de sesiones de la H. Convención N. Constituyente de la República Oriental del Uruguay* (1917), 4 vols. Montevideo: Imp. Nacional, 1918.

————. *Ley del Consejo de Protección de Menores: Decreto reglamentario.* Montevideo: Escuela Nacional de Artes y Oficios, 1911.

————. *Libro del Centenario del Uruguay.* 2 vols. Montevideo: Capurro y Cía., 1925.

————. *Registro nacional de leyes de la República Oriental del Uruguay.* Montevideo: Imp. Nacional, 1936.

Uruguay. Cámara de Representantes. *Diario de Sesiones.*

————. 32d Legislature. *Dictamen de la Comisión Especial en la Parte del Proyecto Relativo al Aborto: Aborto voluntario y homicidio piadoso.* Montevideo: José Florensa, 1935.

Uruguay. Consejo Nacional de Higiene. *Recopilación de leyes, decretos, reglamentos, ordenanzas y resoluciones de carácter sanitario.* Montevideo: El Siglo Ilustrado, 1918.

Uruguay. Departamento Nacional del Trabajo. *Boletín.*

Uruguay. Dirección General de Estadística. *Síntesis estadística de la República O. del Uruguay.* Montevideo, 1940.

Uruguay. Dirección General del Registro del Estado Civil. *Movimiento del estado civil.* Montevideo, 1890–1943.

Uruguay. Instituto Nacional del Trabajo. *Descanso semanal del servicio doméstico.* Montevideo: Imp. Nacional, 1935.

————. *Publicaciones.* Montevideo: Imp. Nacional, 1935, 1936.

Uruguay. Ministerio de Industrias. *El salario real, 1914–26.* Montevideo, 1927.

Uruguay. Ministerio de Salud Pública, *Boletín de Salud Pública.*

————. *Memoria, 1936–38.* Montevideo, 1938.

Uruguay. Oficina del Trabajo. *Salarios de obreros.* Montevideo: Ministerio de Industrias, Trabajo e Instrucción Pública, 1908.

General Histories

Acevedo, Eduardo. *Anales históricos del Uruguay.* 6 vols. Montevideo: Berreiro y Ramos, 1934.

Alexander, Robert J. *Arturo Alessandri: A Biography.* 2 vols. New Brunswick: Rutgers Univ. Latin American Institute, 1977.

Allende G., Salvador. *La realidad médico-social chilena.* Santiago, 1939.

Arena, Domingo. *Batlle y los problemas sociales en el Uruguay.* Montevideo: García, 1939.

————. *Batllismo y sociedad: La "cuestión obrera" en el Uruguay.* Montevideo: Librosur, 1986.

Barrán, José Pedro. *Historia de la sensibilidad en el Uruguay.* Vol. 2, *El disciplinamiento (1860–1920).* Montevideo: Banda Oriental and Facultad de Humanidades y Ciencias, 1990.

Barrán, José Pedro, and Benjamín Nahum. *Batlle, los estancieros y el imperio británico.* 7 vols. Montevideo: Banda Oriental, 1979–86.

Barría Serón, Jorge. *Los movimientos sociales de Chile: 1910 hasta 1926.* Santiago: Editorial Universitaria, 1960.

Bunge, Alejandro E. *Riqueza y renta de la Argentina.* Buenos Aires: Agencia General de Librería y Publicaciones, 1917.

Díaz, José Virginio. *Problemas sociales del Uruguay.* Montevideo: El Siglo Ilustrado, 1916.

Di Tella, Torcuato S., Gino Germani, et al. *Argentina: Sociedad de masas.* Buenos Aires: Editorial Universitaria, 1965.

Drake, Paul. *Socialism and Populism in Chile, 1932–1952.* Urbana: Univ. of Illinois Press, 1978.

Donoso, Ricardo. *Alessandri: Agitador y demoledor.* 2 vols. Mexico City: Fondo de Cultura Económica, 1952.

Dorfman, Adolfo. *Historia de la industria argentina.* Buenos Aires: Solar/Hachette, 1970.

Eyzaguirre, Jaime. *Chile durante el gobierno de Errázuris Echaurren, 1896–1901.* 2d ed. Santiago: Zig-Zag, 1957.

Feliú Cruz, Guillermo. *Alessandri: Personaje de la historia.* Santiago: Nascimento, 1950.

Geografía económica de Chile. 4 vols. Santiago: Corporación de Fomento de la Producción, 1950.

Germani, Gino. "Hacia una democracia de masas." In Torcuato S. Di Tella et al., *Argentina: Sociedad de masas*, 206–27. Buenos Aires: Editorial Universitaria, 1965.

Gil, Federico. *The Political System of Chile*. Boston: Houghton Mifflin, 1966.

González Conzi, Efraín, and Roberto B. Giudice. *Batlle y el batllismo*. 2d ed. Montevideo: Editorial Medina, 1959.

Gutiérrez, Leandro. "Condiciones de la vida material de los sectores populares en Buenos Aires (1880–1914)." *Revista de Indias* 41 (Jan.–June 1981): 167–202.

Heise G., Julio. *Historia de Chile: El período parlamentario, 1861–1925*. 2 vols. Santiago: Andrés Bello, 1974; Editorial Universitaria, 1982.

Hunneus Gana, Francisco. *Por el orden social*. Santiago: Soc. Imp.-Lit. Barcelona, 1917.

Krebs, Ricardo, et al. *Catolicismo y laicismo: Seis estudios*. Santiago: Pontificia Univ. Católica de Chile, 1981.

Mecham, J. Lloyd. *Church and State in Latin America*. Chapel Hill: Univ. of North Carolina Press, 1966.

Mouchet, Enrique. *Juan B. Justo: Ensayo preliminar sobre su vida, su pensamiento y su obra*. Buenos Aires: La Vanguardia, 1932.

Olavarria Bravo, Arturo. *La cuestión social en Chile*. Santiago: Imp. de la Penitenciaría, 1927.

Orrego V., Claudio, et al. *Siete ensayos sobre Arturo Alessandri Palma*. Santiago: Instituto Chileno de Estudios Humanísticos, 1979.

Pinto Vidal, Isabel. *El batllismo, precursor de los derechos civiles de la mujer*. Montevideo: Talleres Gráficos BM, 1951.

Rock, David. *Argentina, 1516–1987: From Spanish Colonization to Alfonsín*. Berkeley: Univ. of California Press, 1987.

———. "Intellectual Precursors of Conservative Nationalism in Argentina, 1900–1927." *Hispanic American Historical Review* 67, 2 (1987): 271–300.

Romero, José Luis. *El desarrollo de las ideas en la sociedad argentina del siglo xx*. Mexico City: Fondo de Cultura Económica, 1965.

Ruzo, Alejandro. *Política social*. Buenos Aires: Rosso y Cía., 1918.

Sanguinetti Freire, Alberto. *Legislación social del Uruguay*. 2 vols. Montevideo: Barreiro y Ramos, 1947.

Scobie, James R. *Buenos Aires: Plaza to Suburb, 1870–1910*. New York: Oxford Univ. Press, 1974.

Solberg, Carl. *Immigration and Nationalism: Argentina and Chile, 1890–1914*. Austin: Univ. of Texas Press, 1970.

Stepan, Nancy Leys. *"The Hour of Eugenics": Race, Gender and Nation in Latin America*. Ithaca: Cornell Univ. Press, 1991.

Traversini, Alfredo, and Lilian Lastra. *El Uruguay en las primeras décadas del siglo xx*. Montevideo: Kapeluz, 1977.

Vanger, Milton I. *José Batlle y Ordóñez of Uruguay: The Creator of His Times, 1902–1907*. Cambridge: Harvard Univ. Press, 1963.

Vivanco Guerra, Graciela. *Bosquejo del problema social en Chile*. Santiago: Dirección General de Prisiones, 1951.

Walter, Richard J. *The Socialist Party of Argentina, 1890–1930*. Austin: Univ. of Texas Press, 1977.

Welker, Juan Carlos. *Baltasar Brum: Verbo y acción.* Montevideo: Imp. Letras, 1945.

Zavala Muñiz, Justino. *Batlle: Héroe civil.* Mexico City: Fondo de Cultura Económica, 1945.

Gender Issues, Feminism, and Women's History: General

Bernaldo de Quirós, Carlos. *Eugenesia jurídica y social.* 2 vols. Buenos Aires: Ideas, 1943.

Bonaparte, Luis. *Nuevas orientaciones en el carácter educacional de la mujer: Críticas feministas.* Buenos Aires: N. Tommasi, 1909.

Bondivenne, Luis. *La mujer: Su educación y destino social.* Buenos Aires: Courier de La Plata, 1875.

Brandau G., Matilde. *Educación de la mujer.* Santiago: Imp. y Enc. del Comercio, 1902.

Bunge, Carlos Octavio. *La educación.* In *Obras completas de Carlos Octavio Bunge,* 3 vols. Madrid: Espasa-Calpe, 1928.

———. *El espíritu de la educación.* Buenos Aires: Penitenciaría Nacional, 1901.

Casanova de Polanco, Eduvige. *Educación de la mujer.* Valparaíso: Imp. de la Patria, 1871.

Corvalán A., Juan Emilio. *Importancia de la educación científica de la mujer.* 2d ed. Valparaíso: Excelsior, 1887.

Daco D., Luisa. *Eugenesia y su legislación en varios países.* Memoria de prueba para el título de Licenciado en Leyes. Santiago de Chile: "Lourdes," 1934.

Ellis, Havelock. *The Task of Social Hygiene.* New York: Houghton Mifflin, 1912.

Fernández Verano, Alfredo. *Reforma sanitaria del matrimonio.* Buenos Aires: La Semana Médica, E. Spinelli, 1931.

Galton, Sir Francis. *Essays on Eugenics.* London: Eugenics Education Society, 1909.

García Pintos, Salvador. *El nuevo derecho del aborto libre.* Montevideo: Juan Zorrilla San Martín, 1934.

Gaviola A., Edda, et al. *Queremos votar en las próximas elecciones: Historia del movimiento femenino chileno, 1913–1952.* Santiago: Centro de Análisis y Difusión de la Condición de la Mujer, 1986.

Grossi Aninant, Amanda. *Eugenesia y su legislación.* Santiago: Nascimento, 1941.

Hostos, Eugenio María. *La educación de la mujer.* Santiago: Sud-América, 1873.

Jiménez de Asúa, Luis. *Libertad de amar y derecho a morir.* Rev. ed. Buenos Aires: Losada, 1942.

Lavrin, Asunción. "Female, Feminine, Feminist: Women's Historical Process in Twentieth Century Latin America." Occasional Paper, University of Bristol, School of Modern Languages and Department of Hispanic, Portuguese, and Latin American Studies, fall 1989.

———. "Women, Labor, and the Left: Argentina and Chile, 1900–1925." In Cheryl Johnson-Odim and Margaret Strobel, eds., *Expanding the Boundaries of Women's History,* 249–77. Bloomington: Univ. of Indiana Press, 1992.

León Palma, Julio. *La eugenesia.* Memoria de prueba para el grado de Licenciado en la Facultad de Ciencias Jurídicas de la Universidad de Chile. Concepción: El Aguila, 1937.

Marañón, Gregorio. *Tres ensayos sobre la vida sexual.* Madrid: Biblioteca Nueva, 1929.

Miller, Francesca. "Latin American Feminism and the Transnational Arena." In Emilie Bergman et al., *Women, Culture, and Politics in Latin America,* 10–26. Berkeley: Univ. of California Press, 1990.

———. *Latin American Women and the Search for Social Justice.* Hanover NH: Univ. Press of New England, 1991.

Pinochet Le Brun, Tancredo. *La educación de la mujer.* Santiago: Imp. Lit. Francia, 1908.

Pou Orfila, J. *Los problemas del aborto contra natura y la lucha antiabortiva.* Montevideo: El Siglo Ilustrado, 1936.

Prats de Sarratea, Teresa. *Educación doméstica de las jóvenes.* Santiago: A. Eyzaguirre i Ca., 1909.

Recabarren, Luis Emilio. *La mujer y su educación.* Punta Arenas: El Socialista, 1916.

Séptima Conferencia Internacional Americana. *Actas y antecedentes.* Montevideo, 1933.

Turenne, Ernesto. "Profesiones científicas para la mujer." *Revista Chilena* 7 (1877): 352–427.

Varela, José Pedro. *Obras pedagógicas.* 2 vols. Montevideo: Ministerio de Instrucción Pública y Previsión Social, 1964.

Women's Auxiliary Conference. *Report: Second Pan American Scientific Congress.* Washington DC: Government Printing Office, 1916.

Feminism and Women's History
Argentina

Aguilar, Pedro E. *Derecho electoral.* Buenos Aires: Argos, 1893.

A las muchachas que estudian. Buenos Aires: La Question Social, 1895.

Alberti, Blas. *Conversaciones con Alicia Moreau de Justo y Jorge Luis Borges.* Buenos Aires: Mar Dulce, 1985.

Armagno Cosentino, José. *Carolina Muzilli.* Buenos Aires: Centro Editor de América Latina, 1984.

Asociación Argentina del Sufragio Femenino. *Fines y propósitos de los estatutos.* Buenos Aires, 1932.

Asociación Femenina Antiguerra de Mendoza. *La Argentina en el panorama americano.* Mendoza: Imp. Diferido-Interno, 1936.

Auza, Nestor Tomás. *Periodismo y feminismo en la Argentina, 1830–1930.* Buenos Aires: Emecé, 1988.

Balbastro, Arturo E. *La mujer argentina: Estudio médico-social.* Buenos Aires: Sud-América, 1892.

Beguino, Juana María. *La mujer y el socialismo.* Buenos Aires: Marinoni, n.d.

Bernaldo de Quirós, Carlos. *Eugenesia jurídica y social.* 2 vols. Buenos Aires: Ideas, 1943.

———. *Problemas demográficos argentinos.* Buenos Aires, 1942.

Bianco, José. *Mi feminismo.* Buenos Aires: L.J. Rosso, 1927.

Biblioteca del Consejo Nacional de Mujeres, Doña Carolina Jeria de Argerich: Memoria correspondiente al año 1920–21. Buenos Aires, 1921.

Bravo, Mario. *Derechos civiles de la mujer.* Buenos Aires: El Ateneo, 1927.

————. *Derechos políticos de la mujer.* Buenos Aires: La Vanguardia, 1930.

————. *Familia, religión y patria.* Buenos Aires: La Vanguardia, 1932.

Camaña, Raquel. *Pedagogía social.* Buenos Aires: La Cultura Argentina, 1916.

Carlson, Marifran. *¡Feminismo! The Woman's Movement in Argentina from Its Beginnings to Eva Perón.* Chicago: Academy Chicago, 1988.

Casal de Espeche, Julia. *Misión social de la mujer argentina.* La Plata: Olivieri y Domínguez, 1922.

Cassagne Serres, Blanca A. *¿Debe votar la mujer?* Buenos Aires: Licurgo, 1945.

Comité Argentino de Moralidad Pública. *Memoria correspondiente al ejercicio del año 1913.* Buenos Aires: J. Girodano, 1914.

Consejo Nacional de Mujeres de la República Argentina. *Congreso y Exposición del Centenario.* Buenos Aires: Alfa y Omega, 1910.

————. *Memoria presentada por la Señora Presidenta de la Guía de la Oficina de Informaciones del Consejo Nacional de Mujeres.* Buenos Aires: Alfa y Omega, 1912.

Cordero, Clodomiro. *La sociedad argentina y la mujer.* Buenos Aires, 1916.

Cuello, Nicolás. *Ejemplo noble de una mujer.* Buenos Aires: n.p., 1936.

Del Valle Iberlucea, Enrique. *El divorcio y la emancipación civil de la mujer.* Buenos Aires: Cultura y Civismo, 1919.

Deutsch, Sandra McGee. *Counterrevolution in Argentina, 1900–1932: The Argentine Patriotic League.* Lincoln: Univ. of Nebraska Press, 1986.

Dickmann, Enrique. *Emancipación civil, política y social de la mujer.* Buenos Aires, 1935.

Dreier, Katherine S. *Five Months in the Argentine from a Woman's Point of View.* New York: Sherman, 1920.

Fantini Pertiné, Ernesto. *La mujer, factor de la victoria.* Buenos Aires: Biblioteca del Oficial del Círculo Militar, 1942.

Feijóo, María del Carmen. "Las luchas feministas." *Todo es Historia,* Jan. 1978, 7–23.

Font, Miguel J. *La mujer: Encuesta feminista.* Buenos Aires, 1921.

Gicca, Francisco. *La mujer: Su pasado, su presente y sus reivindicaciones en el porvenir.* Buenos Aires: Mercantil, 1915.

González, Juan B. *El aborto terapéutico.* Córdoba, 1933.

Grassi, Estela. *La mujer y la profesión de asistente social.* Buenos Aires: Humanitas, 1989.

Grierson, Cecilia. *Decadencia del Consejo Nacional de Mujeres de la República Argentina.* Buenos Aires, 1910.

————. *Educación técnica de la mujer: Informe presentado al Sr. Ministro de Instrucción Publica de la Republica Argentina.* Buenos Aires: Penitenciaría Nacional, 1902.

————. *Homenaje póstumo: Discursos.* Buenos Aires: Imp. López, 1937.

————. *Instituciones de enfermera y masagistas en Europa y la Argentina.* Buenos Aires: J. Penser, 1901.

Guía de la Oficina de Informaciones del Consejo Nacional de Mujeres. Buenos Aires: Alfa y Omega, 1912.

Guy, Donna J. *Sex and Danger in Buenos Aires: Prostitution, Family, and Nation in Argentina.* Lincoln: Univ. of Nebraska Press, 1991.

Henault, Mirta. *Alicia Moreau de Justo.* Buenos Aires: Centro Editor de América Latina, 1983.

Horne de Burmeister, Carmela. *Como se organizó en la Argentina el movimiento feme-nino en favor de los derechos políticos de la mujer por el Comité Argentino Pro-Voto de la Mujer, hoy Asociación Argentina del Sufragio Femenino.* Buenos Aires: Imp. Riera, 1933.

Humano Ortiz, Mercedes G. *Emancipación de la mujer.* Buenos Aires: José Traganti, 1918.

Iturbe, Octavio. *El sufragio de la mujer.* Buenos Aires: Montes, 1895.

León de Sebastián, María Teresa. *La mujer en el hogar y la vida.* Buenos Aires: Tail-hade, 1928.

Levy, Jim. "Juana Manso: Argentine Feminist." La Trobe Univ., Institute of Latin Ameri-can Studies, Occasional Paper no. 1. Boondora, Australia: La Trobe Univ. Press, 1977.

Longhi, Luis R. *Sufragio femenino.* Buenos Aires: A. Baiocco, 1932.

López, Elvira V. *El movimiento feminista.* Buenos Aires: Mariano Moreno, 1901.

¿Merecemos las mujeres argentinas este agravio? Broadsheet, Buenos Aires, n.d.

Moreau, Alicia. "Feminismo y evolución social." *Humanidad Nueva* 3, 4 (1911): 356–75.

———. "El sufragio femenino." *Humanidad Nueva* 3, 4 (1911): 93–94.

Moreau de Justo, Alicia. *La mujer en la democracia.* Buenos Aires: El Ateneo, 1945.

———. *¿Que es el socialismo en la Argentina?* Buenos Aires: Sudamericana, 1983.

Mohr, Luis A. *La mujer y la política: Revolucionarios y reaccionarios.* Buenos Aires: G. Kraft, 1890.

Ocampo, Victoria. *La mujer y su expresión.* Buenos Aires: Sur, 1936.

Olmedo, José Miguel. *La mujer ciudadana.* Córdoba: Imp. del Estado, 1873.

Primer Congreso Femenino Internacional de la República Argentina: Historia, Actas y Trabajos. Buenos Aires: A. Ceppi, 1910.

Quesada, Ernesto. *La cuestión femenina.* Buenos Aires: Pablo E. Coni, 1899.

Rawson de Dellepiane, Elvira. "La campaña feminista en la Argentina." In Miguel L. Font, ed., *La mujer: Encuesta feminista,* 73–80. Buenos Aires, 1921.

Rébora, Juan Carlos. *La emancipación de la mujer: El aporte de la jurisprudencia.* Buenos Aires: La Facultad, 1929.

Ruggiero, Kristin. "Honor, Maternity, and the Disciplining of Women: Infanticide in Late Nineteenth-Century Buenos Aires." *Hispanic American Historical Review* 72, 3 (1992): 353–73.

Solana, Isabel G. de la. *La mujer, la caridad y la doctrina del feminismo.* Buenos Aires: E. Molina, 1911.

Sosa de Newton, Lily. *Diccionario biográfico de mujeres argentinas.* Buenos Aires: Plus Ultra, 1986.

Velázquez, Felipe S. *El proyecto de ley instituyendo el voto cívico femenino.* San Luis: Celorrio, 1933.

Chile

Acción Nacional de mujeres de Chile: Reportaje a la Señora Presidenta de la Acción Nacio-nal de Chile, Doña Adela Edwards de Salas. Santiago: Universo, 1934.

Actividades femeninas en Chile. Santiago: La Ilustración, 1928.

Barros de Orrego, Martina. *Recuerdos de mi vida*. Santiago: Orbe, 1942.

Bravo Cisternas, Agustín. *La mujer a través de los siglos*. Valparaíso: El Progreso, 1903.

Bravo-Elizondo, Pedro. "Belén de Sárraga y su influencia en la mujer del Norte Grande." *Literatura Chilena* 13, 47–50 (1989): 31–39.

Bustos Lagos, Mariano. *Emancipación de la mujer: Consideraciones sobre su acción, sus derechos y su instrucción*. Santiago: Excelsior, 1923.

Chaugui, René. *La mujer esclava*. Santiago: Marión, 1934.

Comité pro Derecho de la Mujer. *Programa de igualdad civil, política, social y económica de la mujer chilena*. Santiago: Cultura, 1941.

Covarrubias, Paz, and Rolando Franco, comps. *Chile: Mujer y sociedad*. Santiago: Alfabeta for UNICEF, 1978.

Ducoing de Arrate, Delia [Isabel Morel]. *Charlas femeninas*. Viña del Mar: Stock, 1930.

Edwards Bello, Oscar. *La superioridad en la mujer*. Santiago: Zig-Zag, 1937.

Estatutos de la Acción Unida de las mujeres de Chile. Santiago: S. Vicente, 1936.

Estatutos de la Asociación de Mujeres Universitarias de Chile. Santiago: Prensas de la Univ. de Chile, 1939.

Estatutos de la Legión Protectora de la Mujer. Santiago: Imp. Artística, 1929.

Estatutos de la Sociedad Acción Social Femenina. Arica: El Ferrocarril, 1933.

Estatutos de la Sociedad Femenina "Carmela de Prat." Santiago: Artes Gráficas, 1936.

Estatutos del Consejo Nacional de Mujeres de Chile. Santiago: La Nación, 1938.

Gaviola A., Edda, et al. *Queremos votar en las próximas elecciones: Historia del movimiento femenino chileno, 1913–1952*. Santiago: Centro de Análisis y Difusión de la Condición de la Mujer, 1986.

Hermosillo Aedo, Amanda. *La mujer en la vida económica*. Santiago: Universo, 1936.

Una hija del país. *Poderosa acción de la mujer chilena en la salvación nacional*. Santiago: Imp. Aurora, 1906.

Historia de la ley no. 5521 de 19 de diciembre de 1934 que reformó los Códigos Civil y de Comercio en lo concerniente a la capacidad de la mujer. Santiago: Prensas de la Univ. de Chile, 1935.

Hutchison, Elizabeth. "El feminismo en el movimiento obrero chileno: La emancipación de la mujer en la prensa obrera feminista, 1905–1908." Working paper, Series Contribuciones, no. 80. Santiago: FLACSO, 1992.

Jambrina, Ariel. *La mujer ante Dios y ante los hombres*. Santiago: Nascimento, 1931.

Klimpel Alvarado, Felícitas. *La mujer, el delito y la sociedad*. Buenos Aires; El Ateneo, 1945.

Labarca, Amanda. *¿A dónde va la mujer?* Santiago: Extra, 1934.

———. "Evolución femenina." In *Desarrollo de Chile en la primera mitad del siglo* XX. Santiago: Editorial Universitaria, 1953.

Labra Carvajal, Armando. *La educación de la mujer ante el programa del Partido Radical*. Santiago: Imp. Franklin, 1912.

Liga de Damas Chilenas. *Memoria correspondiente al año 1929*. Santiago: Arturo Prat, 1929.

López Ureta, José Luis. *El abandono de familia*. Santiago: Nascimento, 1933.

Luz, Clara de la. *La mujer y la especie*. Santiago: Imp. Lee, 1913.

Mena R., Esteban. *La mujer y sus derechos.* Valparaíso: Imp. Royal, 1931.

Miranda, Marta Elba. *Mujeres chilenas.* Santiago: Nascimento, 1940.

Paul, Catharine M. "Amanda Labarca H.: Educator to the Women of Chile." Ph.D. diss., School of Education, New York Univ., 1967.

Rébora, Juan Carlos. *La familia chilena y la familia argentina.* 2 vols. La Plata: Tomás Palumbo, 1938.

Santa Cruz, Lucía, Teresa Pereira, Isabel Zegers, and Valeria Maino. *Tres ensayos sobre la mujer chilena.* Santiago: Editorial Universitaria, 1978.

Vergara, Marta. *Memorias de una mujer irreverente.* Santiago: Zig-Zag, 1961.

Vidal, Virginia. *La emancipación de la mujer.* Santiago: Quimantú, 1972.

Una voz de orden para las mujeres chilenas: La Liga de Damas Chilenas da a conocer sus anhelos en orden a la solución de la crisis económica. Santiago: Claret, 1931.

Zouroff, Vera. [Esmeralda Zenteno]. *Feminismo obrero.* Santiago: El Esfuerzo, 1933.

Uruguay

Abella y Ramírez, María. *Ensayos feministas.* 2d ed. Montevideo: El Siglo Ilustrado, 1965.

Alianza Uruguaya y Consejo Nacional de Mujeres. *La mujer uruguaya reclama sus derechos políticos.* Montevideo, [1930?].

Alvarez Vignoli de Demichelli, Sofía. *Derechos civiles y políticos de la mujer.* Montevideo, 1934.

Ambrosoni, Juan. *Horas de meditación: Los derechos políticos y los derechos civiles de la mujer.* Montevideo, 1934.

Ardao, María Julia. *La creación de la Sección de Enseñanza Secundaria y Preparatoria para Mujeres en 1912.* Montevideo: Florensa y Lafón, 1962.

Becerro de Bengoa, Miguel. *Gotas amargas: El aborto criminal y la ley.* Montevideo: El Siglo Ilustrado, 1922.

Brum, Baltasar. *Los derechos de la mujer: Reforma civil y política del Uruguay.* Montevideo: José María Serrano, 1923.

Carbonell, J. Fernando. *Feminismo y marimachismo.* Montevideo: Centro Natura, 1909.

Cassina de Nogara, Alba G. *Las feministas.* Montevideo: Instituto Nacional del Libro, 1989.

Consejo Nacional de Mujeres del Uruguay. *Estatutos y reglamentos.* Montevideo: El Siglo Ilustrado, 1917.

——— . *Informe correspondiente al primer trienio 1916–19 y Memoria correspondiente al ejercicio 1918–1919.* Montevideo: El Siglo Ilustrado, 1920.

Correa de Bustos, Laura. *Feminismo cristiano.* Montevideo: Buena Prensa, 1907.

Echegoyen, Martín R. de. *Informe de la Comisión de Constitución y Legislación del Senado.* Montevideo, 1938.

Espalter, José. *Discursos parlamentarios.* 8 vols. Montevideo: Florensa, 1912.

Frugoni, Emilio. *La mujer ante el derecho.* Montevideo: Indo-Americana, 1940.

——— . *Los nuevos fundamentos.* Montevideo: Maximino García, 1919.

Lavrin, Asunción. "Paulina Luisi: Pensamiento y escritura feminista." In Lou Charnon-

Deutsch, ed., *Estudios sobre escritoras hispánicas en honor de Georgina Sabat Rivers*. Madrid: Castalia, 1992.

Luisi, Paulina. "Movimiento sufragista." *Acción Femenina* 3, 2 (1919): 27–58.

———. *Otra voz clamando en el desierto: Proxenetismo y reglamentación*. 2 vols. Montevideo, 1948.

———. *Pedagogía y conducta sexual*. Montevideo: El Siglo Ilustrado, 1950.

Madoz Gascue de Bartesaghi, María Nélida. *En defensa de la mujer*. Montevideo: El Demócrata, 1931.

Marpons, Josefina. *Paulina Luisi: Una personalidad brillante y singular*. Buenos Aires: Torfano, 1950.

Moratori, Arsinoe. *Mujeres del Uruguay*. Montevideo: Independencia, 1946.

Otero, Luis M. *El problema de la prostitución*. Montevideo: La Industrial, 1925.

Peluffo Beisso, Darwin. *Femineidad y política: Sobre el voto de la mujer*. Montevideo, 1931.

Pinto de Vidal, Isabel. *El batllismo, precursor de los derechos civiles de la mujer*. Montevideo: Talleres Gráficos BM, 1951.

Reglamento de la Federación Femenina Pan Americana: Sección Uruguaya. Montevideo: Gutenberg, 1911.

Rodríguez Villamil, Silvia, and Graciela Sapriza. "Feminismo y política." *Hoy es Historia* 1, 4 (1984): 16–31.

———. *Mujer, estado y política en el Uruguay del siglo* xx. Montevideo: Banda Oriental, 1984.

Sapriza, Graciela. "La imagen de la mujer y sus variantes, 1880–1910." Servicio de Documentación Social, *La mujer en el Uruguay*, 4th trimestre 1982, 219–23.

———. *Memorias de rebeldía: Siete historias de vida*. Montevideo: Puntosur, 1988.

Scarone, Arturo. *Dra. Paulina Luisi: Datos biográficos hasta 1937*. Montevideo: CISA, 1948.

Vaz Ferreira, Carlos. *Sobre feminismo*. Buenos Aires: Sociedad Amigos del Libro Rioplatense, 1933.

Labor Issues

Abad de Santillán, Diego. *La F.O.R.A.: Ideología y trayectoria*. Buenos Aires: Proyección, 1971.

———. *El movimiento anarquista en la Argentina desde sus comienzos hasta el año 1910*. Buenos Aires: Argonauta, 1930.

Alsina, Juan. *El obrero en la República Argentina*. 2 vols. Buenos Aires: Imp. Calle de Mexico no. 1422, 1905.

Asociación de Damas del Taller La Providencia. *Estatutos*. Buenos Aires: Penitenciaría Nacional, 1915.

Asociación de Obreras. *Memoria presentada a la Primera Asamblea Ordinaria*. Corrientes: Heineche, 1906.

———. *Memoria presentada a la Segunda Asamblea Ordinaria*. Corrientes: Heineche, 1907.

Balbis, Jorge. "La situación de las trabajadoras durante el primer batllismo." In Jorge Balbis et al., *El primer batllismo: Cinco enfoques polémicos*. Montevideo: Centro Latinoamericano de Economía Humana and Banda Oriental, 1985.

Barrán, José Pedro, and Benjamín Nahún. "Las clases populares en el Montevideo del Novecientos." In José Pedro Barrán, Benjamín Nahún et al., *Sectores populares y vida urbana*. Buenos Aires: CLACSO, 1984.

Berquist, Charles. *Labor in Latin America: Comparative Essays on Chile, Argentina, Venezuela, and Colombia*. Stanford: Stanford Univ. Press, 1986.

Bialet Massé, Juan. *El estado de las clases obreras argentinas a comienzos del siglo*. 2d ed. Córdoba: Univ. Nacional de Córdoba, 1968.

Bunge, Alejandro Ernesto. *Los problemas económicos del presente*. Buenos Aires, 1920.

Caffarena M., Elena. "El trabajo a domicilio." Chile, Oficina del Trabajo, *Boletín* 10, no. 7 (1924-25): 97-135.

Compendio de las leyes no. 9688, 731 y 732 y su reglamentación. Mendoza: Escuela Alberdi, 1920.

Coni, Gabriela. *A las obreras: Consideraciones sobre nuestra labor*. Biblioteca de Propaganda 9. Buenos Aires: Gallarini, 1903.

De Shazo, Peter. *Urban Workers and Labor Unions in Chile, 1902-1927*. Madison: Univ. of Wisconsin Press, 1983.

Deutsch, Sandra McGee. "The Catholic Church, Work, and Womanhood in Argentina, 1890-1930." *Gender and History* 3, 3 (1991): 304-25.

Dhorr, Enrique. *Lo que quieren los anarquistas*. Buenos Aires, 1900.

Díaz de Guijarro, Enrique. *La ley de trabajo de mujeres y menores ante la jurisprudencia*. Buenos Aires: 1932.

Dorfman, Adolfo. *Historia de la industria argentina*. Buenos Aires: Solar/Hachette, 1970.

Durañona, Láutaro. "Informe del Departamento Nacional de Higiene sobre el trabajo en las casas de confecciones." Argentina, Departamento Nacional del Trabajo, *Boletín* 7 (31 Dec. 1908): 605-9.

Escribar Mandiola, Ector. *Tratado de derecho del trabajo*. Santiago: Zig-Zag, 1944.

Gertosio Rodríguez, María. *La actividad económica de la mujer*. Santiago: La Simiente, 1944.

Gil, Elena. *La mujer en el mundo del trabajo*. Buenos Aires: Libera, 1970.

Giménez, Angel. *Consideraciones de higiene sobre el obrero en Buenos Aires*. Dissertation. Buenos Aires: Carlos Gallarini, 1901.

Guy, Donna. "Women, Peonage and Industrialization: Argentina, 1810-1914." *Latin American Research Review* 16, 3 (1981): 65-89.

Henault, Mirta. "La incorporación de la mujer al trabajo asalariado." *Todo es Historia* 183 (Aug. 1983): 42-53.

Hermosilla Aedo, Amanda. *La mujer en la vida económica*. Santiago: Universo, 1936.

Ingenieros, José. *La legislation du travail*. Paris: Edouard Cornely, 1906.

Mafud, Julio. *La vida obrera en la Argentina*. Buenos Aires: Proyección, 1976.

Molyneux, Maxine. "No God, No Boss, No Husband: Anarchist Feminism in Nineteenth-Century Argentina." *Latin American Perspectives* 13, 1 (1986): 119-45.

Muzilli, Carolina. "El trabajo femenino." *Boletín Mensual del Museo Social Argentino* 2, 15–16 (1913): 65–90.

Ortázar E., Agustín, comp. "Las leyes del trabajo y de previsión social de Chile," and "Decreto-ley sobre protección a la maternidad obrera y salas cuna." Chile, Oficina Nacional del Trabajo, *Boletín* 10 (1924–25): 288–98.

Oved, Iaacov. *El anarquismo y el movimiento obrero en Argentina*. Buenos Aires: Siglo XXI, 1978.

Palacios, Alfredo L. *La defensa del valor humano*. Buenos Aires: Claridad, 1939.

Paso, Leonardo. *La clase obrera y el nacimiento del marxismo en la Argentina*. Buenos Aires: Anteo, 1974.

Poblete Troncoso, Moisés. *La organización sindical en Chile y otros estudios sociales*. Santiago: R. Brias, 1926.

Ramírez Necochea, Hernán. *Historia del movimiento obrero en Chile*. Santiago, 1956.

"Reglamentación del trabajo de las mujeres y de los niños." *Almanaque del Trabajo* 8 (1925): 153–56.

Rodríguez Villamil, Silvia. "La participación femenina en el mercado de trabajo uruguayo: 1880–1914." Servicio de Documentación Social, *La Mujer en el Uruguay* 4 (1982): 211–18.

Rouco Buela, Juana. *Historia de un ideal vivido por una mujer*. Buenos Aires: Ed. Reconstruir, 1964.

Ruiz Moreno, José A. *Legislación social argentina: Colección de leyes obreras y de previsión social*. Buenos Aires: El Ateneo, 1925.

Santa Cruz de Ossa, Silvia, and Elena Caffarena. "Informe de las Inspectoras del Trabajo, Srtas. Santa Cruz y Caffarena, al Ministro del Trabajo y de la Previsión Social." Chile, Oficinas del Trabajo, *Boletín* 11 (1926–27): 201–6.

Sosa F., Jorge, and Victoria Beloso L. *El trabajo de la mujer*. Montevideo: Oficina Nacional del Trabajo, 1923.

Spalding, Hobart A., Jr. *La clase trabajadora argentina: Documentos para su historia, 1890–1912*. Buenos Aires: Galerna, 1970.

Valle Iberlucea, Enrique del. "Proyecto de ley reglamentando el trabajo a domicilio." Argentina, Departamento Nacional del Trabajo, *Boletín* 25 (1913): 918–48.

Wainerman, Catalina H. *La mujer y el trabajo en la Argentina desde la perspectiva de la Iglesia Católica*. Buenos Aires: Centro de Estudios de Población, 1980.

Wainerman, Catalina H., and Maryss Navarro. *El trabajo de la mujer en la Argentina: Un análisis preliminar de las ideas dominantes en las primeras décadas del siglo XX*. Buenos Aires: Centro de Estudios de Población, 1979.

Law and Legislation

Acuña, Luis María. *El divorcio ante la razón, la historia y la estadística*. Valparaíso: Chas, 1934.

Aguilar, Pedro E. *Derecho electoral*. Buenos Aires: Argos, 1893.

Almada, Amadeo. *El divorcio ante la razón, el derecho y la moral*. Montevideo: A. Barreiro y Ramos, 1905.

Alessandri, Rodríguez, Arturo. *Tratado práctico de la capacidad de la mujer casada, de la mujer divorciada perpetuamente y de la mujer separada de bienes.* Santiago: Universitaria, 1940.

——— . *Tratado práctico de las capitulaciones matrimoniales, de la sociedad conyugal y de los bienes reservados de la mujer casada.* Santiago: Universitaria, 1935.

Alvarez Vignoli de Demicheli, Sofía. *Derechos civiles y políticos de la mujer.* Montevideo, 1934.

——— . *Igualdad jurídica de la mujer: Alberdi, su precursor en América.* Buenos Aires: Depalma, 1973.

Ambrosoni, Juan. *Horas de meditación: Los derechos políticos y los derechos civiles de la mujer.* Montevideo, 1934.

Arechaga, Justino J. de. *Código Civil de la República Oriental del Uruguay.* Montevideo: A. Barreiro y Ramos, 1925.

Arena, Domingo. *Divorcio y matrimonio.* Montevideo: O. M. Bertani, 1912.

——— . *La presunción de legitimidad.* Montevideo: Lagomarsino y Vilardebó, 1910.

Arengo, Juan B. *Proyecto de ley electoral presentada al Exmo. Gobierno de la provincia.* Rosario de Santa Fé: Librería Clásica, 1894.

Bas, Arturo M. *El cáncer de la sociedad.* Buenos Aires: Amorrortu, 1932.

Bonaparte, Luis. *El divorcio y sus alrededores.* Santa Fé: Exito, 1917.

Briones Luco, Ramón. *Origen y desarrollo del matrimonio y el divorcio en la familia humana.* 2 vols. Santiago: La Ilustración, 1909.

Brusco, Luis D. *Contribución al estudio de la ley de creación del Consejo Nacional de Higiene.* Montevideo: El Siglo Ilustrado, n.d.

Calderón Cousiño, Carlos. *El feminismo i el Código Civil.* Santiago: Balcells, 1919.

Camaño Rosa, Antonio. *Código Penal anotado.* Montevideo: A. Barreiro y Ramos, 1944.

——— . *Código Penal de la República Oriental del Uruguay.* Montevideo: Amalio M. Fernández, 1980.

——— . *El delito de aborto.* Montevideo: Bibliográfica Uruguaya, 1958.

Canel, Eva. *El divorcio ante la familia y la sociedad.* Buenos Aires: El Correo Español, 1903.

Carve, Amaro. *Contra el divorcio.* Montevideo: A. Barreiro y Ramos, 1905.

Cocca, Aldo A. *Ley de sufragio femenino.* Buenos Aires: El Ateneo, 1948.

Constela J., Luis A. *Condición jurídica de la mujer en Chile.* Santiago: R. Zorrilla, 1910.

Couture, Eduardo J. *El divorcio por voluntad de la mujer: Su régimen procesal.* Montevideo: A. Barreiro y Ramos, 1931.

Daco D., Luisa, *Eugenesia y su legislación en varios países.* Santiago: Lourdes, 1934.

Del Valle Iberlucea, Enrique. *El divorcio y la emancipación de la mujer.* Buenos Aires: Cultura y Civismo, 1919.

Díaz de Guijarro, Enrique. *La ley de trabajo de mujeres y menores ante la jurispridencia.* Buenos Aires: Antología Jurídica, 1932.

Durá, Francisco. *El divorcio en la Argentina.* Buenos Aires: Esccuela Tip. Salesiana del Colegio de Artes y Oficios, 1902.

Ebensperger H., Alberto. *De la capacidad legal de la mujer.* Santiago: Imp. Chile, 1910.

Echeverría Montes, Guillermo. *Derechos civiles de la mujer.* Santiago: Cervantes, 1893.

Echeverría y Reyes, Aníbal. *Colección de códigos de la República de Chile.* Santiago: Roberto Miranda, 1895.

Escobar Mandiola, Hector. *Tratado de derecho del trabajo.* 2 vols. Santiago: Zig-Zag, 1944.

Escudero, Alberto. *De la mujer casada y el nuevo régimen matrimonial.* Buenos Aires: Lajouane, 1928.

Estrada, José Manuel. *Curso de derecho constitucional.* 3 vols. Buenos Aires: Cabaut, 1901–2.

Foix, Pedro. *Problemas sociales de derecho penal.* Mexico: Sociedad Mexicana de Eugenesia, 1942.

Gentilini, Bernardo. *El divorcio.* Santiago: Apostolado de la Prensa, 1924.

González, Florentino. *Lecciones de derecho constitucional.* Buenos Aires: J. A. Bernheim, 1869.

Guillot, Alvaro. *Comentarios del Código Civil.* 2 vols., 2d ed. Montevideo: Jerónimo Sureda, 1928.

Jiménez de Aréchaga, Justino E. *El voto de la mujer: Su inconstitucionalidad.* Montevideo: Peña Hermanos, 1915.

Jiménez de Asúa, Luis. *Cuestiones penales de eugenesia, filosofía y política.* Potosí: Universitaria, 1943.

León Noguera, Juan Ignacio. *Situación jurídica de la mujer.* Santiago: La Ilustración, 1921.

Llerena, Baldomero. *Concordancias y comentarios del Código Civil argentino.* Buenos Aires: Jacobo Peuser, 1899.

López Aravena, Luis. *Los impedimentos dirimentes del matrimonio y la eugenesia.* Santiago: Dirección General de Prisiones, 1946.

López Ureta, José Luis. *El abandono de familia: Estudio jurídico-social.* Santiago: Nascimento, 1933.

Martínez Vigil, Carlos. *El derecho de las madres.* Montevideo: El Demócrata, 1934.

Mina R., Esteban. *La mujer y sus derechos.* Valparaíso: Imp. Royal, 1931.

Minelli, Nicolás. *La condición legal de la mujer.* Montevideo: Rius y Becchi, 1883.

Mohr, Luis A. *La mujer y la política: Revolucionarios y reaccionarios.* Buenos Aires: G. Kraft, 1890.

Mussio Fournier, Juan César. *Hombres e ideas.* Montevideo: Imp. Uruguaya, 1939.

Narvaja, Manuel T. *El divorcio: Consideraciones generales y proyecto de una ley para la república.* Montevideo: El Siglo Ilustrado, 1892.

Oneto y Viana, Carlos. *Ley de divorcio: Proyecto sancionado por la Honorable Asamblea General de la República Oriental del Uruguay el 24 de octubre de 1907.* Montevideo, 1907.

Papini y Zas, Guzmán. *El divorcio ante la ciencia y el arte.* Montevideo: Moderna, 1905.

Pellegrini, Carlos. *Estudio sobre el derecho electoral.* Buenos Aires: Imp. del Plata, 1869.

Pereda, Setembrino E. *El divorcio.* Montevideo: El Siglo Ilustrado, 1902.

Perujo, Carlos. *Filiación natural.* Montevideo: La Idea, 1879.

Ponce de León, Vicente. *El divorcio.* Montevideo, 1905.

Pradel Hanicewicz, Eduardo. *Matrimonio civil y eugenesia.* Valparaíso: Imp. América, 1926.

Rébora, Juan Carlos. *La emancipación de la mujer: El aporte de la jurisprudencia.* Buenos Aires: La Facultad, 1929.

———. "Perniciosos matices de antagonismos en la reivindicación de los derechos de la mujer." Conference read at the Faculty of Law, Río de Janeiro, 28 July 1936. Pamphlet.

———. *Los regímenes matrimoniales en la legislación argentina.* Buenos Aires: Coni, 1922.

Retamal Castro, Clarisa. *La condición jurídica de la mujer en la legislación chilena.* Concepción: El Sur, 1924.

Rípodas Ardanaz, Daisy. *El matrimonio en Indias: Realidad social y regulación jurídica.* Buenos Aires: Conicet, 1977.

Rodríguez Molas, Ricardo. *Divorcio y familia tradicional.* Buenos Aires: Centro Editor América Latina, 1984.

Rouge, Delie [Delia Rojo]. *Mis observaciones.* Santiago: Imp. New York, 1915.

Ruggieri, Silvio L. *Divorcio.* Buenos Aires: La Vanguardia, 1932.

Ruiz Moreno, José A. *Legislación social argentina: Colección de leyes obreras y de previsión social.* Buenos Aires: El Ateneo, 1925.

Sanguinetti Freire, Alberto. *Legislación social del Uruguay.* 2 vols. Montevideo: A. Barreiro y Ramos, 1947.

Sasso, Francisco L. *El divorcio.* Buenos Aires: Imp. Los Buenos Aires, 1902.

Soler, Mariano. *Pastoral de Excmo. Sr. Arzobispo sobre el divorcio.* Montevideo: Marcos Martínez, 1902.

Urquieta O., Yezud. *La desigualdad sexual en nuestro derecho.* Santiago: Imp. Chile, 1910.

Uruguay. *Código Penal.* Montevideo: Ministerio de Instrucción, 1934.

———. *Código Civil de la República Oriental del Uruguay.* Paris: Rosa Bouret, 1871.

———. *Debates parlamentarios: Discusión de la Ley de Matrimonio Civil Obligatorio.* Montevideo, 1885.

Uruguay. Cámara de Senadores. *Primera y segunda discusión sobre el proyecto de matrimonio civil obligatorio.* Montevideo: El Laurak-Bat, 1885.

Valdés Riesco, Alejandro. *La mujer ante las leyes chilenas: Injusticias y reformas que se proponen.* Santiago: La Ilustración, 1922.

Vargas V., Víctor. *La mujer ante nuestra legislación civil.* Concepción: Soulodre, 1920.

Zañartú Larraín, Mario. *La mujer casada comerciante.* Santiago: La Ilustración, 1922.

Zícari, Julio, *Evolución social: Acotaciones al divorcio.* Buenos Aires: Jesús Menéndez, 1932.

Women, Childhood, and Public Health

Allende G., Salvador. *La realidad médico-social chilena.* Santiago, 1939.

Amores y Herrera, Fernando. *Fundamentos sociológicos de la eugenesia matrimonial.* Caracas: Gutenberg, 1928.

Aráoz Alfaro, Gregorio. *El libro de las madres.* Buenos Aires: Agustín Etchepareborda, 1899.

Argentina. Liga Argentina de Profilaxis Social. *Memoria y balance correspondientes al ejercicio de 1934.* Buenos Aires, 1934.

Bibliography

Asociación por los Derechos del Niño. *Declaración de principios. Tabla de los derechos del niño. Concepto del servicio social. Estatutos.* Buenos Aires, 1937.

———. *Memoria anual. Balance general. Cuenta de gastos y recursos.* Buenos Aires, 1941.

Bauzá, Julio A. *La mortalidad infantil en el Uruguay.* Montevideo: Peña, 1920.

Chile. Servicio Nacional de Salubridad de Chile. *Actas y trabajos de la Tercera Jornada Sanitaria de Chile, 1940.* Santiago, 1941.

Coni, Emilio R. *Higiene social.* Buenos Aires: Imp. Emilio Coni, 1918.

———. *Memorias de un médico higienista.* Buenos Aires: Flaiban, 1918.

———. *Puericultura práctica argentina.* Buenos Aires: Imp. Coni, 1920.

Consejo Nacional de Higiene. *El problema de la mortalidad infantil.* Montevideo: Rosgal, 1931.

Consejo Nacional de Mujeres de la República Argentina. *Primer Congreso Nacional de Servicio Social de la Infancia.* Buenos Aires, 1932.

Day, Enrique L. *La mortalidad entre los recién nacidos.* Buenos Aires: La Mendocina, 1895.

Díaz de Guijarro, Enrique. "Matrimonio y eugenesia." *Jurisprudencia Argentina,* 1942, 2, sec. *Doctrina,* 23.

Fernández Bobadilla, Enrique. *Defensa de la raza y aprovechamiento de las horas libres.* Santiago: Cóndor, 1943.

Fernández Verano, Alfredo. *Para una patria grande y un pueblo sano.* Buenos Aires: Fabril Financiera, 1938.

Ferrer R., Pedro Lautaro. *Higiene y asistencia pública en Chile.* Santiago, 1911.

García Pintos, Salvador. *El derecho a nacer y el niño concebido como persona jurídica.* Montevideo: Juan Zorrilla San Martín, 1936.

———. *El nuevo derecho al aborto libre.* Montevideo: Juan Zorrilla San Martín, 1934.

Gicci, Francisco. *Educación sexual: Consejos a los padres.* Buenos Aires: Mercatili, 1914.

Giménez, Angel. *Consideraciones de higiene sobre el obrero en Buenos Aires.* Buenos Aires: Carlos Gallarini, 1901.

Greco, Nicolás V. "Perfeccionamiento de la ley nacional no. 12.331 de profilaxia de las enfermedades venéreas." In *América contra el peligro venéreo.* Buenos Aires: Imp. Argentina, 1941.

Grossi Aninat, Amanda. *Eugenesia y su legislación.* Santiago: Nascimento, 1941.

Guy, Donna. "Emilio and Gabriela Coni, Reformers: Public Health and Working Women." In Judith Ewell and William Beezley, *The Human Tradition in Latin America: The Nineteenth Century,* 223–48. Wilmington DE: Scholarly Resources, 1989.

Irureta Goyena, José. *Delitos del aborto, bigamia y abandono de niños y otras personas incapaces.* Montevideo: Barreiro y Ramos, 1932.

León Palma, Julio. *La eugenesia.* Univ. de Chile. Concepción: El Aguila, 1937.

Liga Argentina de Profilaxis Social. *Memoria y balance correspondiente al ejercicio de 1926.* Buenos Aires: P. Ventriglia, n.d.

Liga Argentina de Profilaxis Social. Volantes 5, 6, and 10. Broadsheets.

Luisi, Paulina. *Algunas ideas sobre la eugenia.* Montevideo: El Siglo Ilustrado, 1916.

Mayers, Cora. *La mujer defensora de la raza.* Santiago: Imp. Santiago, 1925.

Medina Lois, Ernesto, et al. *Medicina social en Chile.* Santiago: Aconcagua, 1977.

Middleton C., Luis G. *Apuntes sobre legislación sanitaria.* Santiago: Lourdes, 1911.

Monreal, Tegualda. "Determining Factors Affecting Illegal Abortion Trends in Chile." In *New Developments in Fertility Regulations: A Conference for Latin American Physicians.* Airlie, Va.: Pathfinder Fund, 1976.

Moreau de Justo, Alicia. "Educación sexual y educación moral." In *Hacia la extinción de un flagelo social.* Buenos Aires: Fabril Financiera, 1937.

————. *La mujer en la democracia.* Buenos Aires: El Ateneo, 1945.

Morquió, Luis. *El problema de la mortalidad infantil.* Montevideo: Rosgal, 1931.

Nelson, Ernesto. *Asociación por los Derechos del Niño: Nuestros propósitos.* Buenos Aires, 1935.

Niedbalski, Marta. *La asistencia social.* Santiago: Nascimento, 1934.

Pagani, Estela, and María Victoria Alcaraz. *Las nodrizas en Buenos Aires: Un estudio histórico (1880–1940).* Buenos Aires: Centro Editor de América Latina, 1989.

Peralta Ramos, Alberto. *Puericultura postnatal.* Buenos Aires: E. Spinelli, 1922.

Pou Orfila, J. *Los problemas del aborto contra natura y la lucha antiabortiva.* Montevideo: El Siglo Ilustrado, 1936.

Primer Congreso Americano del Niño. Buenos Aires: Escoffier, Caracciolo, 1916.

Primer Congreso Nacional de Protección a la Infancia. *Trabajos y actas.* Santiago: Imp. Barcelona, 1912.

Protección a la infancia. Santiago: Imp. Barcelona, 1912.

Rawson, Guillermo. *Estadística vital de la ciudad de Buenos Aires.* Buenos Aires: Imp. de la Nación, 1877.

Segunda Conferencia Panamericana de Eugenesia y Homicultura. *Actas.* Buenos Aires: Frascoli y Bindi, 1934.

Serono, César. *Feminismo y maternidad.* Buenos Aires, 1920.

Sierra, Lucas. *Bases de la higiene moderna: Papel que en la difusión de sus principios debe desempeñar la mujer.* Santiago: Universitaria, 1914.

Turenne, Augusto. *La maternidad consciente: Procreación voluntaria en la mujer. Un problema de obstetricia social.* Montevideo: La Industrial, 1929.

————. *La protección pre-natal del niño.* Montevideo: Claudio García, 1935.

Uruguay. Consejo Nacional de Higiene. *Morbosidad y mortalidad infecto-contagiosa en la República del Uruguay, 1922–1925.* Montevideo: El Siglo Ilustrado, 1927.

Vasco, Eduardo. *Temas de higiene mental, educación y eugenesia.* Medellín: Bedout, 1948.

Veronelli, Juan Carlos. *Medicina, gobierno y sociedad.* Buenos Aires: El Coloquio, 1975.

Vidal, Florencio. *Paternidad y filiación.* Montevideo: Imp. del Plata, 1893.

Viel, Benjamín. "Patterns of Induced Abortion in Chile and Selected Other Latin American Countries." In *Epidemiology of Abortion and Practices of Fertility Regulation in Latin America: Selected Reports.* Washington DC: Pan American Health Organization, 1975.

Westein Westein, Mauricio. *El porvenir del matrimonio.* Santiago: Kegan, 1933.

INDEX

Italic numbers refer to plate numbers.

In the *Engendering Latin America* series